Peterloo:
The Case Reopened

William Hulton, *c.* 1828

Peterloo:
The Case Reopened

by

ROBERT WALMSLEY

Augustus M. Kelley . Publishers
New York . 1969

063938

71404

© 1969, Robert Walmsley

All rights reserved
MANCHESTER UNIVERSITY PRESS
MANCHESTER 13, ENGLAND

First published
in the United States
1969
by AUGUSTUS M. KELLEY
24 East 22nd Street, New York, N.Y. 10010

Library of Congress Catalog Card Number: 73–81146

PRINTED IN GREAT BRITAIN
BY W & J MACKAY & CO LTD, CHATHAM

To the Memory of
MAURICE PHILIP PARISER
Knight, Master of Arts
(1906–1968)

A Great Mancunian
Bookman and Friend

Contents

71404

Illustrations

Preface

The research, of which this study of Peterloo is the result, began many years ago from an interest in local history, and more particularly in the family of the Hultons in the parish of Deane in Lancashire. The Hultons had been prominent in the affairs of Deane parish for five hundred years and more. The volume of data gathered on one member of the family—William Hulton (1787–1864)—grew inordinately, mainly because his activities as a Justice of the Peace and a local magnate were reported more fully than those of his forbears, owing to the multiplying of local newspapers from the second decade of the 19th century onwards. One striking fact stood out in these papers. William Hulton's reputation in his own parish did not agree with the reputation the historians have given him as chairman of the Manchester magistrates at Peterloo. This was the clue which led me to a re-examination of that event known as the 'Manchester Massacre'.

When Dr Donald Read's *Peterloo—the 'Massacre' and its Background* appeared in 1958, I felt some disappointment that that work seemed to be no more than a glance at the part which I believed that William Hulton had played. As I re-examined some of my own notes I began to question some of Dr Read's conclusions, and I began, too, to add to those notes very extensively. Mr E. P. Thompson's monumental work, *The Making of the English Working Class* (1963), in which he took issue with Dr Read for somewhat playing down the Massacre, impelled me further to the task I had already taken up, that of trying to put the record straight of the long and complicated tangle which up to then had been Peterloo's fate as an event in history. Although disagreeing with Dr Read on major points, I freely admit that it was owing to his work in putting this occurrence into its national and local setting that this further study was made possible.

I would primarily pay tribute to the patience and tolerance of my wife, who for over two years has borne the brunt of my lucubrations, and to my dear friend, the late Alderman Sir Maurice Pariser, some time Chairman of the Manchester Libraries Committee and former leader of the Labour Party on the City Council, who for two years as well was a helpful, incisive, yet encouraging critic. During the last few days of his life he gave to this work his blessing as a citizen of Manchester and a lawyer. To Dr W. H. Chaloner, of Manchester University, for patient guidance and encouragement; to Mr T. L. Jones of the University Press for valuable help in preparing the manuscript for the press. To Mr R. Sharpe France, of the Lancashire County Record Office for assistance over many years; and to Mr V. I. Tomlinson and Mr E. Frow for their enduring interest and for the loan of invaluable material from their own collections.

The vast resources of the three great Manchester libraries have been indispensable. To Mr D. I. Colley (City Librarian), Mr K. D. King, and Mr M. A. Smith, of the Manchester Central Library, I owe more than I can say. To Miss Hilda Lofthouse (Chetham's Library), and Mr R. Hall (John Rylands Library) for the unique material those libraries possess placed at my disposal; and to Mr T. Ashworth (Bolton Borough Librarian) for ready assistance always.

One final note of gratitude is reserved to the now unknown countless owners of books whose precious volumes passed to their present abodes through my hands as an antiquarian bookseller. For the privilege of temporarily possessing their treasures I shall be eternally grateful.

Acknowledgements

I am indebted to the following for permission to quote from the books listed:

Collins Publishers, *Addington*, by Philip Ziegler; Pantheon Books, New York, *The Making of the English Working Class*, by E. P. Thompson; and Donald Read and Manchester University Press, *Peterloo. The 'massacre' and its background.*

Dramatis Personae

ANDREW, JONATHAN who held the civil office of Constable of Manchester in 1819; present on 16 August, and a witness in the Redford *v.* Birley trial, 1822.

BAMFORD, SAMUEL (1788–1872) the best known (after Henry Hunt) of the radicals, although he was not amongst the leaders on the hustings on 16 August; he was head of the Middleton contingent. As a weaver-poet and narrator of what occurred on St Peter's Field he has had undying fame.

BIRLEY, Capt. HUGH HORNBY (d. 1845) who, with Major Trafford, commanded the Manchester and Salford Yeomanry Cavalry on 16 August. Despite the vilification heaped upon him by the radicals, Birley continued to act in the public life of Manchester after Peterloo; was first president of the Manchester Chamber of Commerce.

BUXTON, MR. The legendary figure in whose house the Manchester magistrates met on 16 August. He had no other part in Peterloo, but 'Mr Buxton's house in Mount Street' has almost had as much currency as Peterloo itself.

BYNG, General SIR JOHN. Commander of the Northern District in 1819, involved in the military preparations for the Peterloo period. He was in later years Whig M.P. for Poole, and his speech in the House of Commons in 1832 on 'The Affray at Manchester' has some importance.

CARLILE, RICHARD (1790–1843). Radical, freethinker and publisher. Was on the hustings on 16 August supporting the leaders, but escaped arrest; imprisoned shortly afterwards for his alleged blasphemous publications. Wrote an eye-witness account of Peterloo and issued much radical propaganda on the event afterwards. Hunt in his evidence at his own trial disowned Carlile's part at Peterloo.

CLAYTON, EDWARD, Boroughreeve of Manchester, acting in his official capacity of St Peter's Field.

DERBY, EARL OF. Father of Lord Stanley (q.v.) was Lord-Lieutenant of Lancashire in 1819. As a Whig, he had some sympathy (as his letters shew) for the radicals' cause after Peterloo. He was subjected to radical caustic comment nevertheless.

ENTWISTLE, JOHN (see Sylvester, J.).

ETHELSTON, REV. CHARLES WICKSTEED (1767–1830). Manchester magistrate much maligned by the radicals for his part at Peterloo. He was not a member of the Lancashire and Cheshire magistrates' special committee, but was in Mr Buxton's house, signed the warrant for the arrests, and read the Riot Act. As a magistrate he had forwarded reports to the Home Office before 16 August.

FITTON, WILLIAM, the Royton radical leader, particularly prominent in the pre-Peterloo radical scene and arrested before the 16 August. Fitton was a most effective speaker and writer.

FLETCHER, COLONEL RALPH (d. 1832). Magistrate in the Bolton Division of the county. As early as 1812 Fletcher had earned for himself an uneniviable reputation in radical circles owing to his activities on the bench. In 1819–20 Col Fletcher's role was a minor one.

GIFFORD, SIR ROBERT (1779–1826) Attorney-General in 1819 who directed proceedings leading to the arrest and trial of Hunt. He was an important figure in the Parliamentary debates of 1819 and 1821.

HARMER, JAMES. Radical lawyer acting at Lancaster in September, 1819 and at the immediately-following Oldham Inquest on behalf of the Metropolitan Relief Committee for the Sufferers at Peterloo. Uusually regarded as having scored a triumph at the Oldham Inquest on the radicals' behalf, but whose efforts at both places were denigrated by Hunt.

HARRISON, REV. JOSEPH (b. 1780). Stockport Nonconformist radical preacher. Most active in the pre-Peterloo period as an orator, and in April, 1820, he was sent to prison for seditious public utterances at Stockport in July, 1819. His arrest took place on the hustings at the great Smithfield (London) meeting in July, 1819. but released on bail; he appeared to have no part in the proceedings of 16 August.

HAY, REV. WILLIAM ROBERT (1761–1839). Clerical magistrate, and up to 1823 Stipendiary Chairman of the Salford Quarter Sessions; appointed vicar of Rochdale, January, 1820. The most maligned of the magistrates in the immediate post-Peterloo period.

HEALEY, 'Doctor' JOSEPH. Oldham radical leader in the pre-Peterloo scene; imprisoned with Hunt and Bamford.

HULTON, WILLIAM (1787–1864) whose appointment as chairman of the special Committee of the Lancashire and Cheshire Magistrates formed in July 1819, thrust him into national notoriety at the early age of 31. He was the inveterate target of radical abuse.

HUNT, HENRY (1773–1835). Radical orator and demagogue, nationally well-known before 1819—stood unsuccessfully for Parliament for Bristol, 1812, and Westminister, 1816. Although the hero of the crowds he was distrusted by his colleagues. Imprisoned after Peterloo, he turned the tragedy of 16 August into a personal triumph. Elected M.P. for Preston 1830.

JOHNSON, JOSEPH (1791–1872). Hunt's Manchester lieutenant before 16 August, but disowned by Hunt afterwards because of his alleged breach of faith, the merits of which are assessable by comparing Hunt's charge with Johnson's reply. Imprisoned for one year for his part in Peterloo.

JOLLIFFE, LIEUT WILLIAM, nineteen-year-old officer with the Hussars on St Peter's Field, whose eyewitness account published in Pellew's Life of Sidmouth was resurrected and printed by Bruton in 1821.

L'ESTRANGE, LIEUT-COL GEORGE. The military commander in Manchester in 1819 acting under Major-General Sir John Byng, commander of the Northern District. Col L'Estrange's report to his superior written on the night of 16 August is of some importance.

MARSH, RICHARD (see Sylvester, J.).

MOORE, JOHN, who held the civil office of Constable of Manchester in 1819; present on 16 August, and a witness in the Redford v. Birley trial in 1822.

NADIN, DEPUTY-CONSTABLE JOSEPH (1765–1848). The paid police official in Manchester during and after Peterloo. Intensely disliked by radicals in Manchester on account of his office.

NORRIS, JAMES (d. 1838) the Manchester stipendiary magistrate, before 16 August the correspondent with the Home Office, but in the post-Peterloo period less active.

PEARSON, CHARLES. Radical lawyer active on Hunt's behalf in post-Peterloo days and loyal supporter of Hunt in later years. Pearson unsuccessfully defended Sir Charles Wolseley in March, 1820. Hunt maintained that Pearson's efforts on his behalf at Lancaster in September, 1819 and on the radicals' behalf at the Oldham Inquest later were 'crabbed' by the intervention of James Harmer, the 'Metropolitan "Rump" Committee's nominee'.

PHILIPS, FRANCIS, the apologist in print for the magistrates' and Yeomanry's case in his book Exposure of the Calumnies published November, 1819. It had but little effect on the torrent of criticism which had gathered by the time it appeared. John Edward Taylor's reply (Observations) annihilated it.

PRENTICE, ARCHIBALD (1792–1857) the Manchester reporter not present on St Peter's Field, but who claimed that his report of what occurred there was more authentic than those of the eye-witnesses. He was later editor and owner of the Manchester Times and his reports and comments therein together with his book Personal Recollections . . . of Manchester (1851) make him the greatest propagandist of the radical version of Peterloo.

PRESCOT, REV. CHARLES (d. 1820) rector of Stockport and magistrate, prominent in the pre-Peterloo Stockport scene, yet looked upon with some respect by the radicals.

REDFORD, THOMAS, the radical plaintiff in Redford *v.* Birley, April, 1822. Bamford portrayed Redford as an innocent victim at Peterloo, which no doubt he was. Hunt poured scorn on Redford's feeble case, alleging that if the Government had been allowed to choose one of the wounded victims to suit their case they could not have found a better one for their purpose than Thomas Redford.

SAXTON, JOHN THACKER, assistant editor of the *Manchester Observer* and radical orator, perhaps the most important radical chronicler in the pre-Peterloo period. Arrested on the hustings on 16 August but acquitted on his trial.

SCARLETT, JAMES (1769–1844) Whig M.P. 1819–34 taking part in all Parliamentary debates covering Peterloo and its aftermath in determined opposition to the Government. Counsel for the Crown in Hunt's trial, and for the defence in the radical Sir Francis Burdett's later court appearances. Portrayed by Hunt and other radical writers (quite unjustly) as the radicals' implacable opponent.

STANLEY, REV. EDWARD (1779–1849), later Bishop of Norwich, whose eyewitness account of the scene on St Peter's Field, and his evidence in Redford *v.* Birley, have been regarded as strongly supporting the radical view.

STANLEY, LORD (1775–1851) Whig M.P. and heir to the Earl of Derby. Active in the Parliamentary debates in November, 1819, pressing for inquiry. Because he appeared to be seeking out the truth from both sides he was ever afterwards dubbed as an opponent of the radicals, particularly by Hunt.

SWIFT, GEORGE. Young radical present on the hustings with Hunt on 16 August, who left an eye-witness account known only to historians since 1957. Was placed on trial with Hunt, but was acquitted.

SYLVESTER, J.; TATTON, THOMAS W.; ENTWISTLE, JOHN; MARSH, RICHARD; members of the magistrates' committee all of whom escaped the more devastating criticism levelled at some of their magisterial colleagues.

TATTON, THOMAS W. (See Sylvester, J.).

TAYLOR, JOHN EDWARD (1791–1844) cotton merchant and journalist in 1819, later the founder of the *Manchester Guardian* (in 1821). Although Taylor was lampooned by the radical press before the 16 August, he became their most intrepid defender afterwards in print. His *Observations* (1820), was the most serious indictment of the authorities to be issued.

TRAFFORD, THOMAS JOSEPH (Major). Senior officer of the Manchester and Salford Yeomanry Cavalry, but who escaped the virulent comment directed at his junior officer, Capt. Hugh Hornby Birley.

TRAFFORD, TRAFFORD, the magistrate who was with Lt-Col L'Estrange as the magistrates' representative on St Peter's Field. Escaped most of the malignant criticism in post-Peterloo days.

TYAS, JOHN. The London reporter for *The Times* newspaper, whose description of the events of 16 August is historic. He appeared as a witness in both Peterloo trials on the radical side. Accepted by all as an honest chronicler.

WOLSELEY, SIR CHARLES (1769–1846). Rich radical baronet of Staffordshire. Came to Manchester for the abandoned 9 August meeting, but not present on the 16. Provided bail for the indicted radicals. Imprisoned for his speech delivered on June 28, 1819, at Sandy Brow, Stockport; sentenced April, 1820.

Prologue: Re-examining 'The Examiner'

'We can be happy in re-examining *The Examiner*,' says Mr Robert Gittings, in an article on 'Leigh Hunt's *Examiner*'[1] 'for its humanity and its still topical political inspiration.'

After 1816, [Mr Gittings continues], Leigh Hunt's real nature as political writer re-asserts itself. The Spa Fields riots, the suspension of Habeas Corpus, the prosecutions of Hone and Carlile, the activities of Oliver the Spy in Nottingham and Derby, the election of 1818, and, above all, the Massacre of Peterloo in 1819, muster his full attention down to the smallest detail, and even invade his artistic columns. He records that in autumn, 1819, Kean played to northern audiences to the accompaniment of shouts of 'Peterloo' . . .

Leigh Hunt's August 1819, articles on Peterloo inspired Shelley, far away in Italy, to write in hot indignation his *Mask of Anarchy*:

> Let the horsemen's scimitars
> Wheel and flash, like sphereless stars
> Thirsting to eclipse their burning
> In a sea of death and mourning . . .

Leigh Hunt's burning indignation was not feigned (or temporary) as an exercise in 're-examining *The Examiner*' of 10th March, 1833, proves. The paper was then commenting on a newspaper report of a scene in the House of Commons, which stated that Sir Robert Peel's 'narrative of the murder of the Dillons affected the House with pity and horror to an indescribable degree'. Robert Peel after Peterloo had defended the Manchester magistrates in that same House. *The Examiner's* old 1819 indignation flared up again:

We hope some Member will give Sir Robert an early opportunity of displaying the same power of pathos in the description of the Manchester Massacre. He will describe the Magistrates, with the Parson among them, lolling from the window, when suddenly down came the Yeomanry in a thundering charge upon the immense, unoffending multitude—the shrieks of the women then rise up, the screams of the children, the cries, the expostulations, the execrations of the men—all is now one cloud of dust, and one din of rage and agony. Here and there is seen the flashing of a sabre as it goes grinding into a defenceless breast—here and there may be seen the convulsive heavings and the struggle of a body under the hoofs of a charger—here and there, the figures of flying men and women streaming with their own blood, with looks

---

[1] *Times Literary Supplement*, 23 November, 1967.

of amazement and agony;—but the worst is where vent is not for escape—where the throng is too dense for dispersion—and the soldiery ride and strike at a solid block of life, writhing and struggling in vain for flight—one hideous human agony.

To do justice to the horrors of this scene will require the highest powers of the Baronet, and then how he will pass from the terrible to the execrable, from moving our pity to firing our indignation, when he adds, that for this barbarous butchery the actors had his then Majesty's thanks! How will the House, so effably touched by the case of the Dillons, be moved by this tale of far greater horror?—Why, we must not be too sure that there not be a *laugh*. A Reverend Magistrate, who was promoted for his services on this occasion to one of the best livings in the country, was an eye-witness of the scene, and doubtless took the aristocratic view of it, in which there is no pity for un-washed; and having in his evidence deposed that he saw a wounded woman sitting by the road-side, he was asked what her condition was, or whether he could recognize her? His reply was that he 'did not take any particular notice, for (laughing as he spoke) *she was not very attractive'*.

That 10th March, 1833, issue of *The Examiner* doubtless had its impact on the 'lolling from the window' Manchester magistrates, most of whom were still alive to read it—including 'The Parson' the Rev. William Robert Hay, then Vicar of Rochdale. They may have recalled another London paper's comment, reprinted in the *Manchester Observer* of 9th October, 1819:

. . . The abominable conduct of the Magistracy of Manchester will accelerate (Reform) in no small degree, and fix a stigma upon their characters which none of them will have years enough remaining to wipe away '. . .

The 1819 prophecy (or curse) was coming true.

In the early afternoon of that fateful 16th of August, fugitives from St Peter's Field were fleeing out of Manchester. On the ancient high-way through Salford to Lancaster, Archibald Prentice gave a glimpse of some of them:

. . . I had not been at home more than a quarter of an hour, when a wailing sound was heard from the main street, and, rushing out, I saw people running in the direction of Pendleton, their faces pale as death, and some with blood trickling down their cheeks. It was with difficulty I could get anyone to stop and tell me what had happened. The unarmed multitude, men, women, and children, had been attacked with murderous results by the military . . .

Along that same road—which one writer has called 'the *Via Dolorosa* of the Lancashire reformers'—some days later Henry Hunt, Samuel Bamford, and others arrested on St Peter's Field were taken, accom-panied by a troop of Dragoons to face their judges at Lancaster Castle.

I

The Hulton Patrimony

On the road from Manchester to Lancaster and within the conurbation
of Greater Manchester lies an area which was formerly known as the
Three Hultons, three small townships once within the ancient parish of
Deane: Little Hulton, Middle Hulton and Over Hulton. The first-
named is still readily identifiable, the name being commonly used and
now forming part of the urban district of Worsley. At that point where
the 'built-up area' ends there is a boundary sign, Bolton. This sign hides
the boundary of Little Hulton and Middle Hulton. Bolton town lies
hidden, over the brow of the rising ground to the right, where there is
a cluster of cottages known as Edge Fold. The 'Edge' was in ancient
times 'Hulton Edge', but the first part of the name has long been lost,
and even the name Middle Hulton is seldom heard nowadays, so much
so that people living round about scarcely know it exists. Bolton's
sprawl has not yet caught up with this, its southern side, mainly because
the land is riddled with old colliery workings. Not content with honey-
combing underneath the ground, some ten or so years ago its surface
was convulsed and raked over by giant machines for open-cast coal. A
few years however have grassed it over and one might think that, after
the seemingly-endless eleven mile stretch of Manchester's built-up area,
one has reached open country. It is an illusion. There is only a mile or so
of fields, then comes Hulton Lane Ends and another boundary sign,
that of the urban district of Westhoughton. Again, here is another hidden township boundary; Middle Hulton ends and Over Hulton begins.
Modern usage has almost wiped out the name of Hulton, but it still
betrays itself in the swinging-sign of a public house on which is painted
the name, Hulton Arms. Over Hulton seems a typical suburb. A large
part, however, of the township's 1,360 acres consists of a wide tract of
enclosed park-land, in the heart of which, embowered in fine old trees,
stood Hulton Hall, the seat of an old Lancashire family whose origins go
back to the reign of King John.

From Hulton Lane Ends, Hulton Park stretches in one direction
almost to the boundary of Atherton, where cotton mills and the remains

of collieries bring Nature to an abrupt finish, and in another to the one-time colliery village of Chequerbent. Hulton Park, there since time immemorial, remains an oasis amidst the bricks and mortar and scarred landscape of south Lancashire, and although the name Hulton Park has a modern ring, the family were known as Hultons of the Park in the fourteenth century.[1]

Hulton Hall has gone, demolished ruthlessly by the present baronet, Sir Geoffrey Hulton, some five or six years ago. The word 'ruthlessly' is used advisedly. Sir Geoffrey only completed quickly what modern vandalism was accomplishing slowly but surely, for the depredations began after the contents of the Hall were sold by auction by Sir Geoffrey's father in 1947. Before that, it was habited, if habited could include a close-on-thirty-years' period when an ageing, erstwhile butler and his wife lived with dust-sheeted furniture and moth-balls, alone with the ghosts of long-dead Hultons for company. Then came the auction sale, and Sir Roger Braddyll Hulton began that which his son had to complete, the razing of a stately home to the ground. There were no cries of protest from preservers of ancient buildings, when the demolition-men moved in. The Hall was an undistinguished specimen of a stucco-covered country house, built no one quite knew when. Doubtless there were parts dating back to William Hulton (1625–94), but mostly it appeared to be of mid-eighteenth century date. The second baronet, Sir William Rothwell Hulton (1868–1943) was the last of his line to live in it, up to about the end of the first world war. His son, Sir Roger, immediately after his father's death began the real 'depredations' by selling-off the library; the empty library shelves and the dummy book-spines pasted on an inner door were to mock expectant book-buyers at the auction sale in 1947. The massive library table survived until the sale and was purchased by an enthusiastic buyer. Doubtless it is in use today, its present owner quite oblivious of its former occasional use as a 'catafalque' on which numerous dead squires of Hulton were wont to lie in state[2] prior to their removal to the family vaults at Deane Church.

Where Hulton Park ends at Chequerbent, a railway bounds the western limits of the Park. It was 'Beechinged' even before Beeching, for good Beeching reasons: it seemed to run from nowhere to nowhere, but, in actual fact it ran from a terminus at Bolton to Kenyon Junction some ten miles away. It was mainly a William Hulton-plus-George

---

[1] There are good accounts of the family history in *V.C.H. Lancashire*, V, p. 26, Baines, *History of Lancashire* (ed. Croston), III, 138.

[2] *Bolton Chronicle*, 24 May 1879.

Stephenson project dating back to 1828, the first railway in Lancashire, and for generations a little station nearby bore the sign, 'Chequerbent for Hulton Park'. The Kenyon Junction end of the line, on the Manchester–Liverpool Railway, was its link with the outside world. Only a modern railway history enthusiast would be able to work out how William Wilbraham Blethyn Hulton and his bride, in 1866, could travel from the Continent and alight at Chequerbent for Hulton Park station to be welcomed by hundreds of their tenants and workpeople, or how the melancholy piece of freight containing all that was mortal of another William Hulton could be brought from Leamington and unloaded at Chequerbent station amongst a similar though mourning crowd in 1864.

The railway however had other uses. Its original and prime object was to carry Hulton coals from the Squire's collieries to a wider market, and the name 'Hulton Collieries' on railway trucks was a familiar sight all over the north and north-west of England from the middle of the nineteenth century until the second world war.

The name was familiar too, because it recalled one of the worst mining disasters in history, the Hulton Colliery explosion of Christmas, 1910, when 344 men and boys lost their lives. Generations of Hulton squires were required to augment their public-school and Oxbridge upbringing by learning how to run coal pits. The family had early discovered the potential wealth that lay under their soil; they were mining it at least as early as 1550, but not for a long time afterwards were the deep-levels tapped. There were interruptions: when, for instance, the Scots army in 1715 commandeered their gin-horse[1]—the horse which worked the mechanism for winding-up the coal, and the Chartist rioters stopped the pits in 1839.[2] Large-scale mining in the 1880s took the active control of collieries out of the squires of Hulton's hands, but there were still coal royalties to take care of and lessees to watch. They were wise enough not to tap the pillar of coal which lay under their own hall, not even when the lower coal measures were being worked. The 2nd baronet was still arguing with his lessees for its retention when they wanted to nibble into it in the 1920s. He hardly foresaw then that in less than two decades the pillar of coal supporting the hall would be supporting only another stretch of the park.

The eighteenth-century Hulton Cottage, often in former times used as the family's 'dower-house', is now the 'seat' of the Hultons. The 4th baronet of Hulton is not the first squire to live there. It was sometimes

[1] DDHu/42/2, Lancashire County Record Office.
[2] *Bolton Chronicle,* 23 August 1839.

pressed into service as their residence by his apparently more opulent forbears when financial stringency forced them to cut down the expense of high living at the hall.[1]

Some squires lived away: at Leamington, at Southport, at Cheltenham, at Preston, all during the past century, but they were never 'absentee' landlords; they all kept up their local connections, as justices of the peace, guardians of the poor, local Conservative association presidents, and, until 1908, pillars of their parish church at Deane. An almost endless line of squires have lived and died on their estate at Hulton since the year 1167, and even if they died elsewhere, as some of them inconveniently did, two of them in the South of France, their relicts and survivors brought them all home to Hulton and to Deane Church.

The modest domestic accommodation at Hulton Cottage is hardly conducive to the hoarding of Hulton family relics. There are portraits, some belonging to the seventeenth century, and the wall of a short passage leading to the dining-room serves as a miniature 'long gallery' where hang the portraits of all the squires of Hulton dating back to the eighteenth century. True, they are suitably cut down to size by the process of photography, and the originals are in store somewhere; but what can a modern descendant do with a lineage like his! Some of the family treasures were sold even before the sale of 1947; an alleged Leonardo da Vinci[2] has gone, a J. M. Wright (1625–1700)[3] portrait has gone also; but there is still there (or in a bank strong-room) a silver gilt cup or porringer given to William Hulton by Charles II.

With Hulton Hall gone, the place to look for memorials of the Hultons is at Deane Church, two miles away, a fifteenth-century parish church in an area now almost swallowed up by a Bolton suburb. Almost, but not quite, for its north and west sides still retain the rural appearance of an isolated village church. It is Bolton's most ancient ecclesiastical monument. Just outside the churchyard stands Deane's old school (1820) built largely by the exertions of William Hulton (1787–1864), onetime trustee. Heads of his family were trustees from 1660 until 1908. Inside the churchyard wall is a tapering stone cross which covers the vault where the modern Hultons have been laid since about 1860. William Hulton (1844–1907) used to boast that his forbears cut down their oaks and lent their teams and labour to rebuild the ancient church in the fifteenth century.[4] Probably they did, for they were

[1] *Bolton Chronicle,* 8 May 1881 and v.d.
[2] *Bolton Chronicle,* 14 May 1881.
[3] *Bolton Journal,* 2 July 1881.
[4] *Bolton Chronicle,* 28 November 1885.

building not only a place of worship but a family mausoleum, which lasted until the 1857 Act of Parliament put a stop to burying them inside the church.

Deane Church, although ancient, is as undistinguished architecturally as was their family mansion. Inside the south wall is an old doorway, the Hulton Door, which today is a door only on the outside; it used to lead to the Hulton pew, but it was bricked up on the inside, as legend has it, by an irate nineteenth-century vicar to vex Squire Hulton. That however is a legend; it was bricked up in order to make the Hulton pew and that side of the church less draughty.

Inside the church Hulton evidences are everywhere. There are two Hulton chapels, one on the south side, the Hulton of the Park Chapel, the other on the north, the Hulton of Farnworth Chapel. The lectern is a Hulton lectern, the organ basically a Hulton organ; there are metal name-plates on many of the old pews covering at one time 280 sittings, each bearing the name William Hulton, once reserved for Hulton tenants. The church was restored in 1884, largely by Hulton initiative at which restoration the enthusiastic vicar had the idea of excavating underneath the chancel to construct a crypt. If the living Hultons co-operated in the restoration scheme the dead ones did not, and they were the Hultons who effectively foiled the crypt scheme; for under the chancel the Hulton mould and dust lies thickest. On the inside south wall of the church near the Hulton bricked-up doorway a little ornamental recess bears the inscription:

Juxta hoc sepulchrale Marmor, pietatis ergo et memoriæ positum, Reliquias suas condi voluerunt, Plurimi de stirpe Hultoniana.

'Near this sepulchral tablet, erected as an affectionate memorial, a great number of the Hulton family have caused their remains to be interred.' 'A great number' is an understatement, for century after century since the middle ages Hultons have been put away under the flagstones of Deane Church, and although one of the memorials states that those named thereon are buried in the vault beneath, there is no other evidence of vaults in the usually accepted sense, or if there was, all traces are now obliterated. For a family so ancient they have never been extravagant in the provision of memorials, for with the exception of three painted funeral hatchments with armorial bearings of William Hulton 1743, William Hulton 1773, and William Hulton 1800, there is none anterior to the early part of the last century; they have made up for it since with small but undistinguished specimens of the stonemason's art. The earlier Hultons have no memorials nor are there records of any at

Deane outside the pages of the church registers, and inscriptions on silver plate, although one William (1625-94) had his arms, alongside those of his wife, inserted in painted glass in the Hulton Chapel window.

William Hultons have been legion, for in every generation from 1645 to 1940, with one exception, the head of the family has borne the name William; the exception was Henry (1665-1737) whose contribution towards the family tree was a singular one; he remained a bachelor until he was seventy and then married a bride less than half his age. Luckily Henry's brother had a son William to follow on. Even this 'exception' must be qualified, for Henry had had an elder brother William who died young. Many of the Hultons did die young, but one William (1540-1624) put such a strain on his heirs that they, his son and grandson, died before him, and his great-grandson Adam Hulton succeeded him. Adam lived in troublous times; his great-grandfather had been a recusant, unable to stomach the religious changes of his day. Other members of his family had accepted the Elizabethan Settlement and brought up his heir as a conformer, by which means he was able to inherit the family patrimony without encumbrances. The Civil War found him an ardent Royalist anxious to serve his king. Some of his tenants were required by their master to fulfil their feudal military obligations, but Over Hulton standing where it did within the orbit of Parliamentary Manchester, Bolton and Deane had conditioned them otherwise. More than one refused to go for the king, and although one of them did serve with the besieged Lady Derby at Lathom House, he returned back to Hulton and, throwing his arms down before the irate Adam, declared he was going for Parliament.[1] Adam died before the 'troubles' were over, though not before he had suffered harassing experiences by minor sequestration by the Commonwealth overlords in his native Hulton, Deane and the town of Bolton.

Adam Hulton's heir, William Hulton, perhaps profiting by his father's experiences, sought a father-in-law who was a Commonwealth official at Whitehall. If William was a Royalist at heart, and he got himself elected a member of the Convention Parliament (for the borough of Clitheroe) which invited Charles II back into his own again, he did not neglect to avail himself of the opportunities his father-in-law's influence in the Cromwell Government afforded. From this stemmed an estate of 'adventure lands' in Ireland which the family held for about a century.

All the eighteenth-century William Hultons in contrast were as undistinguished as the architecture of their mansion, indeed it was probably with most of them in mind that James Croston in 1887, writing a

[1] DDHu/53/41, L.C.R.O.

volume entitled *The County Families of Lancashire and Cheshire,* was seemingly hard put (although he ought not to have been) to make his material spin out to form an interesting narrative. He described them, rather curiously, in these terms:

. . . For seven hundred years the Hultons have been gentlemen of character in blood and social position. They have done few striking things, performed no remarkable feats of prowess (in the Wars of the Roses or the Civil War), achieved no great distinction either at Court or in the Cabinet . . . yet were steady, clear-headed, singularly efficient men who never shirked responsibilities; men of good judgment and capacity, they have been useful rather than great . . .

Overlooking the rather left-handed compliment of 'useful rather than great', Croston's verdict that they had 'done few striking things' could very well be challenged. One William Hulton (1787–1864) had done a very striking thing indeed, and he had only been dead a mere twenty-three years when Croston wrote his account of the family's history. To leave unmentioned the William Hulton whose name had reverberated throughout the English-speaking world as chairman of the Manchester magistrates at Peterloo, and which has been reverberating ever since in every published history of the period, was an act of suppression probably intended to stifle controversy on an incident many thought best forgotten. Forgotten, that is, by those who found it increasingly hard to explain his conduct, but never to be forgotten by those who accepted the Radical Interpretation of Peterloo.

Lauded by some, but execrated by many, William Hulton had lived out a long life of seventy-six years. One forceful utterance had escaped his lips on 16 August 1819: 'Good God! Sir, don't you see they are attacking the Yeomanry. Disperse the meeting!' The sequel was what history has called The Manchester Massacre. As one very recent writer[1] has said:

The events at Peterloo have entered into British folklore. The name itself like Amritsar or Buchenwald, has acquired a rich and emotive significance, so that merely to mention it can be to declare loyalty to an ideology and to denounce a form of government. It has become the symbol of the struggle of the British working-classes for parliamentary reform and the savage repression of that movement by a reactionary oligarchy. The image it invokes is one of charging dragoons and butchered babes, a spectacular hecatomb in which the flower of progressive England was ruthlessly put to the sword.

The charge that Croston was guilty of an act of suppression in his

[1] Philip Ziegler, *Addington* (Lord Sidmouth), 1965, p. 371 et seq.

account of the Hultons is supported by the opinion of yet another recent historian, E. P. Thompson, in *The Making of the English Working Class*[1]:

. . . The enduring influence of Peterloo lay in the sheer horror of the day's events. In 1819 the action of the loyalists found many defenders in their own class. Ten years later it was an event to be remembered, even among the gentry, with guilt. As a *massacre* and as 'Peterloo' it went down to the next generation . . .

And, it must be added, to the next generation after that, and to this! Thirty feet down on the second tier of twenty-seven niches (in rows of three) in the Hulton vault, lies William Hulton, Peterloo Magistrate, awaiting Judgement Day, no doubt expecting then a fairer judgement than he has yet been given either by many of his contemporaries or by the verdict of history.

[1] Gollancz (1963), p. 683 et seq.

II

The Making of a Peterloo Magistrate 1787-1817

William Hulton was born on 23 October 1787, the second son of William Hulton of Hulton Park, and Jane, third daughter of Peter Brooke, of Mere, county Chester. Bad drains at Hulton Hall, or another of those one-hundred-and-one eighteenth-century hazards to infants had carried off his elder brother (also William) in January of that year, and destined the second son as the future Squire of Hulton, to a position in life which, but for accidents, would have rendered him as unremarkable (in the Croston sense) as all the other Hultons had been. Home influences of the young child can only be guessed at. His father was High Sheriff of Lancashire in 1789. He was also a 'sporting' squire, and there are memories of hunting over such unpromising hunting country as Worsley and Tyldesley,[1] a large part of the former now almost completely built over with council houses. There was also a string of race-horses at Manchester (Kersal Moor) Races, with winners in 1790 (Nicknark), 1791 (Hermit), and Mrs Hulton's horse (Church and King) in 1794.[2] Perhaps the latter is the best clue to the influences at work on the young boy. His father may have been using *his* influence, overtly or covertly, in Parliamentary affairs, for there is a letter from London (1793) concerning objections to a turnpike road bill. Government had apparently a novel way of dealing with objectors to legislation, for Hulton was informed quite bluntly that, 'It is decided by the Post Master that unless this Act passes, the Mail Coach ceases to go any longer further than Manchester'.[3] As Hulton Hall was twelve miles out, it is supposed that the Act passed.

Possibly the greatest influence on young Hulton's mind was an object-lesson on the changes and chances of this mortal life. He lost a younger brother in 1791, another in 1799, and his father (at the early age of 38) in 1800. Thus, at the age of twelve years eight months, in June 1800, William Hulton was thrust into his ancient patrimony,

---

[1] *Palatine Note Book* (1881), pp. 162-3; *Bolton Journal*, 25 June 1884.
[2] *Manchester Mercury* v.d.
[3] DDHu/31/1-2, L.C.R.O.

which, until he came of age, was administered by trustees; it was, no doubt, too, an object-lesson in taking his responsibilities seriously. After his brothers died, one sister, Frances Anne, remained; a portrait of the children, by Hoppner, used to hang at Hulton Hall.[1] In 1804 William Hulton matriculated, and proceeded M.A. at Brasenose College, Oxford, in 1807. It can only be guessed at the influences working on him, but in the family papers there is a glimpse of matters antiquarian: family pedigrees to revise, communications with the College of Arms, delving into the Hulton deeds, and in a local library[2] there is a little MS. notebook containing transcriptions of these with the sobering quotation on the title-page, 'For we are strangers before Thee and sojourners, as all our fathers were'. (Chron. I 24, 15.)

Oxford in 1804 was still the Church and King Oxford, the Protestant Ascendancy Oxford, and Evangelical Piety Oxford, all influencing the young Hulton. This period included one incident which seared into his mind, when with a tutor near Nottingham he had been horrified to see the Bible burnt in a public market square.[3] The British and Foreign Bible Society was later to find in William Hulton one of its most earnest supporters.[4] In 1804, whilst he was still at Oxford, his mother remarried. His step-father was a Lieutenant in the 16th Queen's Light Dragoons.

In 1808, at twenty-one, he came into his inheritance and married Maria Ford, his cousin, second daughter of Randle Ford of Wexham, Bucks., who was to share his changeful lot for over half a century. He took over the management of his estates, which then included considerably more land than his descendants inherited, some of which lay on the east side of Manchester—in Harpurhey and Denton. His 'management' included the selling of the Harpurhey estate,[5] then open country on the fringes of Manchester, but which was very soon to become a thriving suburban area. At the same time he purchased, perhaps through sentiment, as it belonged to a forbear of his—it really must have been sentiment because the bargain didn't include the mines and minerals—a small estate almost adjoining Hulton Park.[6] Whatever the reason, for this and other land transactions, he has come down in his own family as the 'spendthrift', the Hulton who expended the Hulton land inheritance.

[1] Exhibition of Fine Arts at the opening of Bolton Infirmary, Sept. 1881, No. 826.
[2] Bolton Central Library, MSS.
[3] *Bolton Chronicle*, 7 June 1845.
[4] *Bolton Chronicle*, 9 November 1878.
[5] *V.C.H. Lancashire*, IV, p. 270.
[6] DDHu/42/19, L.C.R.O.

1. William Hulton, *c.* 1807

Strictly local affairs, however, absorbed the young Squire. He was elected a member of the Manchester Agricultural Society in 1810, and in their awards for that year there was one of five guineas to Betty Seddon of Rumworth 'for thirty years servitude as a farm servant'. 'Servitude' seems a harsh word, but long servitude with the Hultons was common and was spoken of with pride in later days.

Expectancy of life among the Hultons was still an uncertain thing. His first-born, William Ford Hulton, died after a few months. Was the pattern of his father's family going to be repeated? He himself was the third William Hulton to succeed during minority. As it turned out, he had no great cause for anxiety, for his beloved Maria was to prove the most fruitful Hulton vine for over a century. She bore him 13 children. In 1833 there were still ten *surviving*, including a second William Ford Hulton. It might have been said that he was precocious. His great hero was the Younger Pitt, and if William Pitt could become Prime Minister in his twenty-fifth year, William Hulton could become High Sheriff of his native county in his twenty-fourth.

Twenty-four javelins, each engraved with the crests of William and his wife, used to be preserved at Hulton Hall; they are now housed in Lancaster Castle. They were carried by Hulton retainers in the cavalcade that led him into his high office in 1810. It was a touch of Hulton pageantry repeated, for the shafts had been used for the spear-heads which had escorted his father into the same office in 1789. The office was as picturesque as some of its duties were archaic. He duly appointed his deputy for 'granting replevins for the several Hundreds of Salford, West Derby, and Blackburn' on 27 February 1810.[1]

Hulton coal-mining interests became intensified after his marriage, and this, and later his rail-road building, probably accounted for the sale of land far away from his native Hulton. There were mining rights owned by his family for over a century in neighbouring Westhoughton still unexploited, and the new steam-engines in the growing town of Bolton were hungry for coals. He had manorial (and mining) rights too, on land no longer owned by his family on hard-by Deane Moor. William Hulton was looking ahead to the coming coal boom, but in the years 1811–12 there was thrust upon him a new (almost full-time) occupation as Justice of the Peace.

He had, of course, entered the Commission of the Peace at his coming-of-age in 1808, and probably it was a duty which he thought he could take in his stride as all his forbears did. He could not foresee that events were shaping then which, in twenty years' time, would

[1] *Cowdroy's Manchester Gazette*, 10 March 1810.

mean breakdown and chaos in a large area of a Justice of the Peace's duties—the administration of the poor laws—especially in South Lancashire, depressed and poverty-stricken in the aftermath of the Napoleonic wars. Nor could he foresee its concomitant, the great wave of industrial unrest, disaffection, incendiarism and riot which was to sweep almost to the threshold of Hulton Hall.

The Hammonds' *Skilled Labourer* (1919) has familiarized a wide circle of readers with the Luddite disturbances of 1812, the activities of black-faced spies, and even perhaps the march at midnight of the disaffected to Four Lane Ends, at Hulton; but more particularly perhaps with the alleged notorious Colonel Fletcher, Justice of the Peace in the Bolton Division. In this Bolton Division of county justices William Hulton's lot was cast, and scarce two miles from Hulton Hall was Westhoughton Factory, the hated symbol of the power-loom which deprived the handloom weavers of their livelihood, and which they burned down, in April 1812.

Even before this malign culmination of 1812 there were premature congratulations to local Justices from 'a numerous and respectable meeting in Bolton, expressing gratitude to the magistrates of the district for their prompt and judicious actions during the late disturbances'. Col. Fletcher received a vase, Mr Hulton a gold snuff-box.[1] It was a recital which was to become all too familiar to the young Justice pitched into the middle of it all.

It is beyond the scope of this work to do much more than glance at this watershed in William Hulton's life. But the early months of 1812 meant secret dark-night meetings of conspirators on Deane Moor, 'twistings-in' and swearing of unlawful oaths, midnight depositions taken at Hulton Hall, comings and goings of the Scots Greys, a man-hunt through fields and woods for the fugitives after the fire, and the rounding-up of prisoners for the Grand Assize at Lancaster in May 1812. The evidence at the trial makes grim reading. Job Fletcher clapped an Atherton farmer on the shoulder and observed: 'Tak' notice if yonder devil is not a-fire before three hours are over'. 'What devil?' he was asked. 'Yonder weaving factory at Westhoughton.'[2] Job Fletcher was hanged. The 'Calendar of State Prisoners confined in H.M. Gaol at the Castle of Lancaster of 25 May 1812' lists fourteen names 'committed by the Rev. Wm Hampson and William Hulton Esq., 29 April 1812 charged with having wilfully and maliciously set on fire and burnt a

---

[1] DDPR. 25/18, L.C.R.O.

[2] *The Trials of all the Prisoners at the Special Assizes . . . May 23, 1812 at the Castle of Lancaster.* Lancaster: 1812, p. 4.

weaving mill, warehouse and loomshop in possession of Thomas Rowe and Thomas Duncough, at Westhoughton'.

Four of the accused were executed: Job Fletcher (34), Thomas Kerfoot (26), James Smith (31), and Abraham Charlson (16). Three others of the accused were 'teen-agers'; William Hulton testified that one of them, John Bromilow (15), was 'a quiet, honest, industrious boy'.[1] He was acquitted. Not so the other youngster, Abraham Charlson (16). Several witnesses testified against him 'He had a scythe on a pole,[2] getting straw from a barn and taking it inside the mill . . .' Popular accounts of the tragedy in later years put him down as only twelve years of age and say that on the scaffold he cried out for his mother.

One prisoner was tried and found guilty of 'administering an unlawful oath to Holland Bowden'; he was transported for seven years. William Hulton testified:[3] 'I recollect coming home between one o'clock and two o'clock on Monday morning from Westhoughton Factory, and Bowden declared to me that he had been forced to swear an improper oath; he was in great fear at the time, and durst not go home till I had sent an armed man out to see if any people were in the road. He went away himself between two and three o'clock.' Bowden said he was a weaver by trade, but in April was in the service of an innkeeper at Hulton Lane Ends; he was met in the dark and forced to be 'twisted' and being much alarmed asked another man to go with him to tell Mr Hulton at midnight.

The disturbances of 1812 have been recounted by the Hammonds and others, and Colonel Fletcher's name was to go down to later generations as the radicals' arch-fiend. Arch-fiend or not, his name and memory were held in esteem by many, and an annual Col. Fletcher commemoration was held in Bolton until well on into the nineteenth century. William Hulton's part in the 1812 affair was quite likely a minor one; that it was not discreditable was the testimony of one of his later radical opponents in 1820:

At the commencement of your magisterial career hopes were cherished of your future usefulness and greatness . . . it was your unhappy fate to be associated with a practised, cool, and designing colleague [Col. Fletcher], who scrupled not to take advantage of your open disposition. When I refer to your public conduct in 1812, as it relates to all the circumstances connected with the burning of Westhoughton Factory, and contrast it with that of the arch-fiend who was the prime instigator of that horrid event, I have much to

---

1 *The trials . . . at Lancaster* p. 11.
2 Ibid., p. 6.
3 Ibid., p. 14.

offer in your favour. I well remember the interest you manifested for the un-happy sufferers at Lancaster, particularly the child [Abraham Charlson] that was executed; and I have also a perfect recollection of the strong indignation you evinced towards an abandoned informer at Chowbent, who wickedly encouraged the incendiaries, by promising to reward the most active among them with the greater share of bread and cheese, in order that he might be-tray them to the Magistrates . . .[1]

William Hulton's own thoughts and observations on this grim intro-duction, soon after his twenty-fourth birthday, into the keeping of the King's Peace are not on record. He could hardly have refrained from feeling that a Justiceship in these times was harder to fill than 'in good King George's glorious days', even though George III's long reign had still a few more years to run.

Hulton's traducer of 1820, who offered him this sop of a testimonial to his former excellences feared that he had fallen into bad company in his association with Col. Fletcher, and had thereby been corrupted. But his reputation was not to suffer again until the dark clouds rolled over him in1819.

In the middle of that second decade of the nineteenth century there is a glimpse of an unfamiliar William, in the shape of a 'buck', a 'glass of fashion and a mould of form'. This may have been because he retained a boyish appearance long after his majority; indeed, the Judge at Hunt's trial in 1820 (Hulton was then 32), observing privately that he seemed but a youth, could not believe that he had been in the Commission of the Peace for so many years. His traducers even at that time had called him 'The Dandy' and 'Polly Hulton'; Henry Hunt, as long as he lived, used the latter nickname tauntingly against him.

Hulton's father's modest racing stable had been kept up during his minority, but after one winning horse in 1816 at the Kersal Moor Races, which meetings lasted until 1837, there were no more Hulton horses. There is however one glimpse of high life in 1816, in *Cowdroy's Man-chester Gazette*, 7 December:

A curious circumstance happened on Thursday week—during the Mas-querade at Hulton Park, at which a brilliant assemblage of Nobility and Gentry were present, about 11 o'clock the company were astonished by the appearance of a gentleman in the character of a Jew; but on his displaying a few tricks and deceptions, it was instantly exclamed: 'It must be that Paragon and Emperor of Conjurors, Ingleby Senior,' and he was desired to put off his mask. He afterwards entertained the party for upwards of an hour, and returned with this additional title, with which he was unanimously saluted—

[1] *Manchester Observer*, 13 May 1820.

of the *only conjuror*. It will be seen by our paper that the above gentleman intends to exhibit here next week . . . he will leave this town with a joyful heart and a full purse.

From Ingleby's advertisement, he informed 'the Inhabitants of Bolton and its vicinity' that he was appearing at the Commercial Inn, but announced to the 'Nobility and Gentry of Manchester and Neighbourhood' that he would travel there in the course of the following week. The Manchester press however graciously allowed that Nobility and Gentry could also appear in Bolton, at Hulton Park.

Dr Read,[1] in noticing William Hulton as one of the committee of Lancashire and Cheshire magistrates appointed in July 1819, to take charge during the Manchester disorders, found it a little difficult to understand why he was chosen as chairman. 'His name', he says, 'does not appear in the Manchester Directory for 1819 as one of the magistrates "who usually attend the New Bailey courthouse"; nor even as one of the "Magistrates who reside in the neighbourhood". His interests thus seem to have been centred on county administration rather than that of Manchester.' Of Hulton as a magistrate this was true, but the Hultons had had a Manchester connection for centuries, dating back even before Ranulph Hulton's days as sub-deacon at Manchester Collegiate Church under Warden Huntingdon in 1465, for they were lords of Ordsall and had property in Deansgate and Long Millgate a century before this. But even if this link had worn a little thin they still had their Hulton pew in the Collegiate Church (now Cathedral), the ownership of which even in the seventeenth century could be traced as far back as there were records.

The family had links with the Free Grammar School. William Hultons had been Feoffees of Chetham's Hospital and Library in every generation since Humphrey Chetham's day and, in a less serious sphere, the last two William Hultons were leaders in Manchester's sporting life (cock-fighting[2] until it was stopped, and racing). It was however William Hulton, the 'Pittite', who broke into leadership in Manchester's loyalist circles in 1817.

The Manchester *Aston's Exchange Herald* (quoting the *Wheeler's Manchester Chronicle*) of 20 May 1817, takes up the tale:

Splendid Fete at Hulton Park. The worthy and esteemed owner of the soil, William Hulton, Esq., gave, on the 1st inst., a splendid entertainment to the Bolton Pitt Club. His hospitable mansion never contained guests who could be rendered more happy: the politest attention was displayed towards every

1 Read, *Peterloo: the Massacre and its Background*, p. 77.
2 *Manchester Mercury*, 4 July 1768.

individual, and although the party was numerous, well-effected arrangements yielded all the comfort and ease that could have been enjoyed by a smaller circle. Our correspondent says he cannot close his communication without a tribute of respect to the speeches of the worthy host, uttered on this occasion. The venerable principles of that illustrious Statesman, whose name the club bears, could not be set forth more correctly, with greater energy, or in more appropriate and elegant language. We trust therefore, that we may be permitted to offer our congratulations to the Manchester Pitt Club, in having to boast of such a chairman at the approaching Anniversary.

'Greats' at Oxford, a study of rhetoric, and a well-stocked library at Hulton Hall, are some indications of William Hulton's cast of mind. The only extant speech of his earlier years gives a clue to the man who was emerging. The 5th anniversary dinner of the Manchester Pitt Club was held on 27 May 1817, in the large room in the Exchange Building, a building used for purposes other than its name implies, and which is to figure several times in this narrative. There were two hundred members present, under the chairmanship of William Hulton, Esq. 'a gentleman possessing every requisite for this office; all the toasts he prefaced in elegant or appropriate exordia, in doing which he unfolded the various qualifications of a capacious mind, with the elevated energies of captivating eloquence which elicited continued bursts of applause from his admiring auditors'.[1]

It could have been that the bucolic squires of the Manchester and Cheshire area, who were amongst his hearers, were less gifted than this young scion of an ancient Lancashire house, or if not less gifted, less anxious to be pushed forward into leadership; and certainly most of the more prosperous Manchester manufacturers and tradesmen were less articulate and cultured than some to be found in Whig circles. John Edward Taylor, founder of the *Manchester Guardian*, was later publicly to rebuke Hulton for his doubtful taste in quoting Greek to an assembly of the Manchester Pitt Club, but there was nothing in bad taste in this early speech: perhaps an overweening admiration of De Lolme, borrowings from Edmund Burke, or a slavish modelling on Augustan figures. Young Hulton was proposing the toast, 'The Pride of Britain and the Admiration of the World—Our Glorious Constitution'.

It has been remarked by a renowned statesman, that 'if the prudence of reserve and decorum dictates silence in some circumstances, in others prudence of a higher order may justify us in speaking our thoughts'. And indeed it requires the sanction of some great authority to satisfy my own mind that I am not exposing myself to the charge of presumption, in venturing to

[1] *Aston's Exchange Herald*, 3 June 1817.

address you on a subject on which panegyric has exhausted the treasures of her urn, and admiration is dazzled by her eager gaze. To introduce to you that sacred and beloved object, the British Constitution, is to rouse in the hearts of a British assembly every sentiment of manly honour and patriotic devotion. However feeble the hand that strikes the chord, these notes of loyal harmony will vibrate. If professional skill and execution were required, how inadequate must be my best exertions! I will not weary you by common-place assertions of my own inability; but in expressing my cordial concur-rence in your opinion, that it was desirable, from the peculiar circumstances of this association, you must allow me to say, that you would have given greater effect to your wishes by the appointment of a more able President. My whole heart and soul, however, embraces the good cause which this meeting is calculated to support; and I would rather incur the risk of being charged with an excess of zeal, than the certainty of sinking by indifference into insignificance and contempt. Thus influenced, I present myself to pay my homage to our glorious Constitution, the pride of Britons and the admiration of the world.

Under this vast aegis repose our liberties, encircled with wisely-ordained laws, and blessed with the sanction of a pure religion. In the minds of the majority of the people of England (and at this early stage I beg to be under-stood, that by the people I do not mean the preponderating weight of flesh and blood, but the associated qualities of intellect and education) Church and State are inseparable ideas; and long may our countrymen enjoy this happy and glorious connexion! If we wish to become acquainted with the spirit of the Constitution, we must look for information in our histories and records. All the reformations which have hitherto taken place have had reference to antiquity; and I fervently hope, that if any alteration shall be made hereafter, it will be carefully formed upon authority and example. Yet, with all my reverence for antiquity, I do not wish that the precedents should be taken from those primitive periods, so much the theme of modern eulogium. In truth, my knowledge of the Constitution does not extend to the aera of 'about twelve hundred years ago': but, in 1817, I am told to revise the lessons of my youth; and if I would have the Constitution, the whole Constitution, and nothing but the Constitution, I must look for the pure definition of the laws in the pocket-book of Alfred, or hear them expounded at Arthur's round table. I had conceived, Gentlemen, that you will, I think, support me in the opinion, that our liberties were as well defended, and our interests as well understood in Westminster Hall, under the presidency of an Abbot, as at a conclave at Stonehenge, under the regulations of a Druid.

With the encampment at Runnemede began the plain declaration of British rights, and there the third order in the State assumed an importance and acquired securities which were before unknown to them. Where is the Briton who does not glory in the enfranchisements of Magna Carta? forced not so much from regal as from feudal tyranny. But it was reserved for Henry the Third to build the proud palladium of English liberty, the House of Commons—that 'whole representative Majesty of the whole English nation'. I will not detain you by a journey during this twilight of the Constitution but bring you by forced marches to the moment when, as modern interpreters tell us, it shone in meridian splendour, during the merry days of good Queen Bess. Really, Gentlemen, from the lavish praises bestowed upon these halcyon times by our modern reformers, one would imagine that Queen Elizabeth had clung with amorous embrace to liberty and carried with her this inestimable companion to the same grave. But what shall we say, when we find amongst the State apartments of this gracious Princess, a Star Chamber, and a Court of High Commission: and that she executed her Royal commands on bishops and on judges by the aid of martial law? I mean no disparagement of this illustrious reign; but when we, who are here assembled, are urged to believe that Freedom was uncontrolled by Queen Elizabeth, but has been bound in fetters by George the Third, the fallacy must be exposed.[1]

Still, the political architecture of this date claims our veneration; and I give you the credit for too much taste to imagine, that you, who possess Queen Elizabeth mansions, would enlighten your halls by means of *French windows*; or because a few canker-worms appear in the *wainscot* of *British Oak*, you would substitute *Spanish Chestnut* or *American Pine*. We have seen enough of modern artificers in their erection of Temples of Liberty; and we are unwilling to submit our houses to the decision of their new academy. Would it not be the height of impertinence in private life, for every visitant at a well-proportioned mansion to suggest its total destruction, that on its ruins might be erected a more commodious building, on an undefined plan, at an undefined expense?

Let us advance to the glorious Reformation, an event on which we dwell with proud enthusiasm. But, were your rights better secured when King William assented to a bill for triennial parliaments, with a clause that a new parliament should be assembled within three years after the dissolution of the old one, than they are under the septennial act? You will, I trust, agree with me, that at no period of history has society enjoyed a greater share of well-ordered freedom than during the reign of George the Third.

Tell me, enlightened members of a free constitution, is it the want of liberty that brings one moment's pangs to your bosoms? Does the retrospect of your ancestors' freedom dart one arrow of envy into your hearts? 'It has been' (says Mr. Burke) 'the uniform policy of our Constitution to claim and assert our liberties, as an *entailed inheritance*. We have an *inheritable* Crown, and *inheritable* Peerage, and a House of Commons, and a people *inheriting* privileges, franchises and liberties from a long line of ancestors. This inestimable fund has become a chartered partnership between those who are living, those who are dead, and those who are yet to be born.'

[1] Habeas Corpus had been suspended in February 1817, and Acts passed to prevent public meetings, etc.—Read, p. 98.

Shall we then, sell the black-letter volumes of our great charters for any spurious editions printed with type of the National Convention, for Cochrane, Burdett and Company? The mind of the English people, I am persuaded, is not so perverted; but in reading the Constitution as explained by existing laws, they are convinced they require no reforming translators. These laws, emanating from our Constitution, are the best elucidation of the divine code. 'We know that religion is the basis of civil society, and the source of all good and all comfort!'

Dr Samuel Johnson, commenting on Bishop (Thomas) Newton's *Dissertations on the Prophecies*, said, 'This is Tom's Great Work. But how much of it is Tom's, and how much of it is great, are other questions'. Perhaps the same could be observed about William Hulton's maiden effort in Manchester loyalist circles. That it went down well with his auditors there is no doubt; that its sentiments were a faithful reflection of his political philosophy there is no doubt also; he never had, as was later proved, any intentions of 'revising the lessons of his youth', and the novelty of exchanging his black-letter volumes for newly-printed editions by Cochrane, Burdett & Co. had no appeal for him. How original, in 1817, was the theme of a destruction of a perfectly good building for a new one on 'an undefined plan, at an undefined expense' is not known, but there have been countless variations on that very same theme since that date. One pertinent fact, however, does emerge, and it is that Hulton had no hankering for the revival of a period in which martial law found a place. He did not realize that the time was near when he would be roundly accused of wanting to introduce it.

In the subsequent toast, 'To the Immortal Memory of the Rt. Hon. William Pitt', he expressed himself thus:

To you who have already expressed, with glowing animation, your love for your country, (for I look upon your country and constitution as synonymous terms) it must be gratifying to reflect, by whose means your national greatness has been upheld. How often has public calamity been averted by the seasonable energy of a single man! Have *we* had no such individual amongst us? I propose this question for your own solution, confident that, if the torrent of gratitude which rushes over your hearts does not sweep away all power of utterance, you will unanimously pronounce the revered, the hallowed name of Pitt.

'Statesman, yet friend to truth: of soul sincere,
In action faithful and in honour clear;
Who broke no promise; served no private end;
Who gained no title, and who lost no friend:
Ennobled by himself; by all approved;
Prais'd, wept, and honour'd, by the land he loved.'

If William Hulton had not been speaking from a prepared script, it might have been imagined that the adulation which he received after his previous peroration had gone to his head, with his 'Have we had no such individual amongst us?' Or, on the other hand, there might have been no idea in his mind in posing such a rhetorical question that his hearers might give it an answer two years later. A toast however (during his 'momentary absence from the chair') was proposed by Sir H. Mainwaring, Bart. to 'The President' and it was received with acclamation and drunk 'three times three'. Mr Hulton was touched; he said:

He should ever remember his exaltation to the head of that meeting with gratitude; and as to Manchester, its patriotism, zeal and example, had rendered it a monitor to all other towns. He trusted its commerce would rise again shortly from the pressure of a temporary cloud . . .

And to a toast to the magistrates (it was two months after the memorable 'Blanket Meeting'):

That what they (the magistrates) had during the recent circumstances so firmly dared to do, he thought they, the present company, might dare to justify.

There can be no doubt that from this moment William Hulton was, if not an actual, a potential leader in Manchester loyalist circles. It was, for him, a fateful and portentous meeting! Peterloo was only two years away.

III

Peterloo and the Historians

How haughtily he cocks his nose,
To tell what every schoolboy knows.

SWIFT

Perhaps not every schoolboy, but certainly a good many Manchester
and Salford schoolboys, could readily tell about Peterloo. They might
not tell a uniform story, nor would each embellish his narrative with
the same details; but however much their stories varied they could
hardly vary as much as historians have varied. If only Lord Liverpool's
Government in 1819 had done what almost the whole country was
clamouring for, and had promoted a full-scale inquiry into the transactions at Manchester on 16 August and issued a report. Nearly everybody said they ought to; but they didn't.

'Facts are stubborn things'; they get into the wrong order, some are
left out, some push their way in, but are overshadowed by other facts
. . . There is no lack of facts about Peterloo. They are a gigantic boxful
of jigsaw pieces, and no one yet has managed to fit them together
satisfactorily to form a complete picture. Every writer on the early
period of the nineteenth century in English history has dipped into this
boxful of pieces, with the exception perhaps of Sir Winston Churchill,
who, in his *History of the English Speaking Peoples* did not use them at all.

By and large most writers are agreed that a repressive Government, and
equally repressive magistrates, brutally put down a peaceable meeting
with tragic results. There have been gradations of emphasis: at one
extreme accusations of cold-blooded murder made by Hunt, Bamford,
and Carlile; more moderate, Hammonds' assertion that the Manchester
magistrates and Yeomanry acted 'with a levity that revolted every on-
looker',[1] which is similar to Trevelyan's[2] indictment of an action which
'disgusted the rising generation of Englishmen with anti-Jacobin
Toryism'. At the other extreme the milder view that the magistrates
were incompetent and panicked; or mildest of all, the view of a

[1] Hammond, *Town Labourer*. p. 92.
[2] Trevelyan, *Social History*, p. 477.

Manchester Guardian writer of 1938 who termed the incident a 'mis-judgement by local magistrates and police authorities'.

No writer since 1820 has ever offered a word in extenuation of the Yeomanry's conduct, although a few have found excuses for the Government of the day. Those few may perhaps preen themselves on their judgement, for Dr Donald Read, in his far-reaching study of Peterloo (1958), had practically exonerated the Government, and suggested that if the magistrates had strictly followed the Government's instructions, issued prior to the fateful day, there would have been no massacre. This implies that the magistrates and the Yeomanry were solely responsible. Mr Philip Ziegler, biographer of Lord Sidmouth (1965),[1] receives this 'let-off' for his subject with some relief, and expostulates with Mr E. P. Thompson (1963),[2] who quite frankly does not believe that the Government bore no responsibility for Peterloo. Mr Thompson's thesis is a violent reaction to the opinion that perhaps there is something to be said in extenuation of Peterloo. He reiterates with all the original vehemence of Hunt, Bamford, and Carlile that Peterloo 'really was a *massacre*'; it was 'class war':

There are two points about Peterloo which have, somehow, become lost in recent accounts. The first is the actual bloody violence of the day. It really was a *massacre* . . . The presence of so many women and children was overwhelming testimony to the pacific character of the meeting which (the reformers knew) all England was watching. The attack was made on this multitude with the venom of panic.

But the panic was not (as has been suggested) the panic of bad horsemen hemmed in by a crowd. It was the panic of class hatred. It was the *Yeomanry*—the Manchester manufacturers, merchants, publicans, and shopkeepers on horseback—which did more damage than the regulars (Hussars) . . . There is no term for this but class war. But it was a pitifully one-sided war. The people, closely packed and trampling upon each other in the effort to escape, made no attempt at retaliation until the very edges of the field, where a few trapped remnants—finding themselves pursued into the streets and yards—threw brick-bats at their pursuers . . .[3]

There are doubts lurking in the minds of some writers. 'We shall probably never be able', writes Mr Thompson, 'to determine with certainty whether or not Liverpool or Sidmouth were parties to the decision to disperse the meeting with force.' The operative words in that sentence are 'parties to the decision'. Dr Read may have shaken some of the certainties, which had been expressed before his book appeared,

[1] Ziegler, p. 371 et seq.
[2] Thompson, p. 683 et seq.
[3] Thompson, pp. 685–8.

that the Government undoubtedly were 'parties' to the repression; but there is a *certainty* implied in the word 'decision' as regards the magistrates. But even Dr Read,[1] in spite of all his investigation, ends his study: 'The final comment in any study of Peterloo must be one of caution . . . something must still be admitted as unknown.' Such an admission might be thought remarkable. There are masses of material, both primary and secondary: eyewitnesses' accounts, thick closely printed reports of the trials. The Home Office papers have been sifted, and many have appeared in print; there are files of newspaper reports; indeed, the historic issue of *The Times* of 19 August 1819, has recently been reprinted[2] and achieved wide circulation; and there is an extensive row of volumes of printed Parliamentary debates covering the period 1819–32 in which the transactions at Manchester are exhaustively reported. Many of the biographies of the period refer to it, and there is a minor classic of English literature (Bamford)[3] which has Peterloo as its central theme. Can it be that something has been overlooked?

Mr Thompson, conscious of the mass of material, and realizing that Peterloo was only the theme of a small part, though an important one, of his massive and impressively-documented study, observed: 'We need not give the hour-by-hour account (of Peterloo) once again.' Tedious though it may seem, a great deal of ground has to be gone over again, some which has never been gone over at all.

Dr Read's work (1958) is now the standard authority for any study of the happenings of 16 August 1819. It is more exhaustive than any which had appeared previously. In the centenary year, 1919, F. A. Bruton of Manchester Grammar School had issued his first study *The Story of Peterloo* and followed it in 1921 with his *Three Accounts of Peterloo*. Both works are quoted as standard modern authorities, and have been linked with Bamford's and Hunt's accounts as equally important. Dr Read's work is a much more detailed study of the background to Peterloo, and in this he owes little or nothing to Bruton, but on the events of the day admits his indebtedness to him. In 1924 Bruton issued his *Short History of Manchester and Salford*[4] and in this he condensed his *Story of Peterloo* into a few pages; and although it might be thought that he sketches his background-story rather naïvely, yet his account of the happenings of the day project faithfully what he believed had happened.

[1] Read, p. 208.
[2] 'Jackdaw' series, No. 17 (Jonathan Cape).
[3] Bamford, *Passages in the Life of a Radical*, 1844, 1893, 1967.
[4] Manchester: 1924, p. 172 et seq.

The Story of Peterloo. The facts seem to be these: a meeting was called for 12 o'clock on August 9th, 1819, in the area near St. Peter's Church, then unoccupied 'to take into consideration the most speedy and effective mode of obtaining Parliamentary Reform in the Commons House of Parliament; and to consider the propriety of the unrepresented inhabitants of Manchester electing a person to represent them in Parliament'. Henry Hunt was to preside, and the Boroughreeve, Constables, and Magistrates were invited to be present. The Magistrates some days later proclaimed the meeting to be illegal. The Reformers then sent a representative to Liverpool to take counsel's opinion, which supported the magistrates' decision. The meeting was therefore abandoned.

The Reformers now approached the Boroughreeve and Constables with a requisition signed by over a thousand, asking them to convene a meeting 'to consider the propriety of adopting the most legal and effectual means of obtaining a Reform in the House of Commons'. As the authorities appear to have made no reply to this, it was announced that a meeting would be held on the 16th. This the magistrates met by issuing a Royal proclamation enjoining people to abstain from drilling and so forth.

Meanwhile Mr. Hunt, who had heard nothing of the delay, had arrived via Stockport, and was warmly welcomed as he made his way to Smedley, where he was to stay. He issued a manifesto on August 11th which was couched in too violent language. Preparations were afoot, and the fatal day arrived.

The authorities were busy early. They posted a notice urging the peaceable inhabitants to remain indoors with their children and servants. At eleven o'clock the Magistrates took up their station at Mr. Buxton's house in Mount Street; 300 special constables were drawn up between this house and the hustings, and the military were posted out of sight. Several contemporary plans of the site are extant, and it is not difficult to reconstruct the scene. [Bruton here equates St. Peter's Field with the position of buildings in modern Manchester, with the hustings on or near the site of the Free Trade Hall.] From Mr. Buxton's house to the hustings a double cordon of between two and three hundred special constables, carrying their batons, formed a lane reaching right to the improvised platform, and the troops numbering between one and two thousand were disposed as follows: One troop of the Manchester Yeomanry (a raw corps recently formed mainly to assist the civil power) was concealed in Pickford's Yard, off Portland Street; a second troop of the same Yeomanry, with four troops of the 15th Hussars and eight troops of the Cheshire Yeomanry were waiting, dismounted, in Byrom Street and St. John Street, on the other side of Deansgate; another troop of Hussars was acting as escort to a detachment of Royal Horse Artillery posted in Lower Mosley Street with two long six-pounders; nearly the whole of the 31st Infantry were hidden in Brasenose Street; and some companies of the 88th, brought in the town for the occasion were 'in ambush' in the neighbourhood of Dickinson Street.

71404

Into the open space, thus surrounded, the Reformers—some of whom had marched from as far afield as Bury and Rochdale—poured unwittingly in excellent order, the result of previous drills to that end, with bands playing, silk banners held aloft, and girls in white dancing and singing; some approached by way of Mosley Street, others along Deansgate. Four or five abreast they marched, their banners, some of them were beautifully worked in coloured silk, proclaiming the Rochdale Union, the Lees and Saddleworth Union, the Royton Union, the Oldham Union, and so on; 'Universal Suffrage,' 'Annual Parliaments,' 'Vote by Ballot,' 'No Corn Laws,' et cetera. The design that provoked the most criticism afterwards and was used as 'evidence' at the trial, was a black one inscribed 'Equal Representation or Death.' The National Anthem was sung at twelve-thirty, and soon after one a procession headed by a barouche drawn by the people swept round the corner of Deansgate into Peter Street and made for the platform. Standing up in the carriage was Mr. Hunt; on the box-seat sat the president of the Manchester Female Reformers. Arrived at the hustings, Hunt was at once voted to the chair, and taking off his white hat, which had become the symbol of Radicalism, he began his speech, facing an impressive crowd of some sixty-thousand, consisting of men, women, and children.

The Magistrates, however, who had hitherto remained apparently in a state of indecision bordering on panic, and had sat up till midnight without being able to decide upon any definite plan of action, having reminded the Home Secretary that they had no power, as the law stood, to interfere with the meeting, had at length made up their minds. If a few of the inhabitants of Manchester could be prevailed upon to put their names to a paper stating that they considered the meeting a danger to the town, that would justify the authorities in arresting the leaders. Thirty names were at once forthcoming, and a warrant for the arrest of the speakers was handed to Deputy-Constable Nadin, a fierce-looking man, the paid official of the Court Leet. He declared that the three hundred special constables at his disposal were not a sufficient force to enable him to execute it. The Magistrates therefore despatched mounted messengers to Portland Street for the Manchester Yeomanry and to St. John Street for the Hussars and the Cheshires. A few minutes later, the Manchester Yeomanry came trotting round what is now the Mount Street corner of the Midland Hotel, and halting for a moment in great disorder, for they had no command of their horses, made a dash for the hustings, striking with their swords as they entered the crowd. Raw and untrained as they were, they were soon hopelessly entangled and dispersed that the chairman of the Magistrates afterwards described them as 'completely defeated.'

At this moment Lieut.-Col. L'Estrange cantered up Lower Mosley Street with the 15th Hussars and Cheshire Yeomanry, the latter riding along Wind-mill Street to the hustings, and halting there; 'What am I to do?' asked Lieut-Col. L'Estrange, looking up at the window where Mr. Hulton, the chairman was standing. 'Good God! Sir,' ejaculated that dignitary, without even waiting to consult his brother Magistrates, 'don't you see they are attacking the Yeomanry? Disperse the meeting!' It was a fateful decision. The sequel sent a thrill of horror throughout the whole country. The poet Shelley, who was in Italy, felt the thrill, and his *Mask of Anarchy* was the result. The Hussars had not even time to halt when the trumpeter sounded the charge, and beating back the crowd with the flats of their swords, and sometimes (as one of their own officers frankly acknowledged) with the edges also, they swept the square from Mount Street to Deansgate so rapidly and effectively that in ten minutes those who were watching from upper windows (and we have reliable accounts from several of such) looked down upon an empty space, empty save for human beings lying in heaps, sabred, crushed and trampled, and a group of perspiring horsemen dismounting to loosen their saddle-girths. The multitude that had assembled to consider the reform of the Commons were now fleeing, many of them bleeding, along the roads they had traversed a few hours before with bands playing and banners, their hearts full of an exultant hope that at last something was to be done for their suffering humanity. A careful investigation later by the Relief Committee put the casualties at eleven killed and nearly six-hundred wounded. One of the special constables was killed on the spot; others who had no sympathy with the Reformers were seriously injured.

All now was confusion. The streets were patrolled by the military; the shops were closed and silent; some rioting took place in the evening in the neighbourhood of New Cross, and the military were called out again with fatal results. Rumours of a large body of Reformers marching on the town armed with pikes, though quite baseless, produced considerable apprehension.

The immediate sequel: Much indignation was expressed in the country at the summary treatment of an assembly called together in an orderly manner to discuss Parliamentary reform; but the thanks of the Prince Regent were, nevertheless, conveyed by Lord Sidmouth to the authorities for their efforts to preserve the public peace; and Hunt and others were committed for trial on a charge of conspiracy. In the following year Hunt was sentenced to $2\frac{1}{2}$ years' imprisonment, and Samuel Bamford and three others to confinement for twelve months. Bamford has left a graphic and, apparently for the most part, fair account of the whole episode in his 'Passages in the Life of a Radical'. Hunt's autobiography and letters are less readable. Besides these, we have descriptions of the event by Bishop Stanley, Lord Hylton, and Mr. J. B. Smith, all of whom were present.

Bruton's shortened account seems a reasonable and an impartial narrative; to return however, to his detailed *The Story of Peterloo*,[1] here it is clear that there are omissions and misconceptions. He does not notice

---

[1] 'Bruton's general account of Peterloo seems particularly clear, concise, and well-informed, but even he cannot reconcile all the conflicting accounts.' (Redford, Prof. A.) *History of Local Government in Manchester* (1939) I, p. 252.

discrepancies in the evidence which he first brought into print (Stanley's Account) in two important instances; and he fosters, if he does not begin, the legend that the founder-to-be of the *Manchester Guardian*, John Edward Taylor, was an eyewitness to the massacre, when Taylor plainly says that he was not. This 'fact' has since been used in a brief account of Peterloo by one of Taylor's own descendants.[1] But the historian of the *Manchester Guardian*, Haslam Mills,[2] avoided the error, presumably by simply reading what Taylor himself had said. Many lesser authorities have leaned heavily on Bruton since that date.

A recent edition of the *Encyclopedia Britannica* quotes Bamford, Hunt and Bruton as the prime authorities for its article on Peterloo. Earlier editions had relied on a much older version written by W. E. A. Axon which is similar to a longer account of Axon's written in his *Annals of Manchester*[3] (1886). Axon died several years before Bruton's version appeared, so that his account is largely Bamford-Hunt inspired.

Samuel Bamford's version of Peterloo, in the several editions of his *Passages in the Life of a Radical*,[4] is the one that has had, almost certainly, the widest circulation. It did not appear in print until a full twenty years after Peterloo: his account of the day, or of the vital moments of it, is given below. The graphic and moving piece of writing, in which he describes the 'field' after the dispersion, has had a far wider currency than the work itself, for it has appeared in anthologies and has been quoted in part or in full by many historians:[5]

. . . Mr. Hunt, stepping towards the front of the stage, took off his hat, and addressed the people.

Whilst he was doing so, I proposed to an acquaintance, that, as the speeches and resolutions were not likely to contain anything new to us, and as we could see them in the papers, we should get some refreshment, of which I stood in need, being in not very robust health. He assented, and we had got to nearly the outside of the crowd, when a noise and a strange murmur arose towards the church. Some persons said it was the Blackburn people coming; and I stood on tip-toe, and looked in the direction whence the noise proceeded, and saw a party of cavalry in blue and white uniform, come trotting sword in hand round the corner of the garden wall, and to the front of a row of new houses, where they reined up in a line.

'The soldiers are here,' I said, 'we must go back and see what this means.'

[1] Ryan, R. *A Biography of Manchester* (1937), p. 25.
[2] Haslam Mills *The Manchester Guardian—A Century of History* (1921), p. 21 et seq.
[3] Axon, pp. 156–7.
[4] 1844, 1893, and 1967 (Introd. by [Dr] W. H. Chaloner) Frank Cass; and preface by Tim Hilton (Macgibbon—Fitzroy edn.).
[5] Bamford, I, p. 206 (1844).

'Oh,' some one made reply, 'they are only come to be ready if there should be any disturbance in the meeting.' 'Well, let us go back,' I said, and we forced our way towards the colours (arranged around the hustings).

On the cavalry drawing up they were received with a shout, of good will, as I understood it. They shouted again, waving their sabres over their heads; and then, slackening rein, and striking spur into their steeds, they dashed forward, and began cutting the people.

'Stand fast,' I said, 'they are riding upon us, stand fast.' And there was a general cry in our quarter of 'Stand fast.' The cavalry were in confusion; they evidently could not, with all the weight of man and horse, penetrate that compact mass of human beings; and their sabres were plied to hew a way through naked held up hands, and defenceless heads; and then chopped limbs, and wound-gaping skulls were seen; and groans and cries were mingled with the din of that horrid confusion. 'Ah! ah!' 'for shame! for shame!' was shouted. Then, 'Break! break! they are killing them in front, and they cannot get away'; and there was a general cry of 'break! break!' For a moment the crowd held back as in a pause; then there was a rush, heavy and resistless as a headlong sea; and a sound like low thunder, with screams, prayers, and imprecations from the crowd-moiled, and sabre-doomed who could not escape.

By this time Hunt and his companions had disappeared from the hustings, and some of the Yeomanry, perhaps less sanguinarily disposed than others, were busied in cutting down the flags-staves, and demolishing the flags at the hustings.

In the breaking of the crowd, the yeomanry wheeled; and dashing wherever there was an opening, they followed, pressing and wounding. Many females appeared as the crowd opened; and striplings or mere youths were also found. Their cries were piteous and heart-rending; and would, one might have supposed, have disarmed any human resentment; but here, their appeals were in vain. Women,—white-vested maids, and tender youths, were indiscriminately sabred or trampled; and we have reason for believing, that few were the instances in which that forbearance was vouchsafed, which they so earnestly implored.

In ten minutes from the commencement of the havok, the field was an open and almost deserted space. The sun looked down from a sultry and motionless air. The curtains and blinds of the windows in view were all closed. A gentleman or two might occasionally be seen looking out from one of the new houses before-mentioned, near the door of which, a group of persons (special constables) were collected, and apparently in conversation; others were assisting the wounded or carrying off the dead. The hustings remained, with a few broken and hewed flag-staves erect, and a torn and gashed banner or two dropping; whilst over the whole field, were strewed caps, bonnets, hats, shawls, and shoes, and other parts of male and female dress; trampled, torn, and bloody. The yeomanry had dismounted,—some

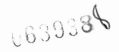

were easing their horses' girths, others adjusting their accoutrements; and some were wiping their sabres, Several mounds of human beings still remained where they had fallen, crushed down and smothered. Some of these still groaning,—others with staring eyes, were gasping for breath, and others would never breathe more. All was silent save those low sounds, and the occasional snorting and pawing of steeds. Persons might some times be noticed peeping from attics and over the tall ridgings of houses, but they quickly withdrew, as if fearful of being observed, or unable to sustain the full gaze of a scene so hideous and abhorrent.

Bamford includes another short additional account of that tragic ten minutes, as he saw it, in his next chapter:

Besides the Manchester Yeomanry, who as I have already shewn, did 'the duty of the day' there came upon the ground soon after the attack, the 15th Hussars and the Cheshire Yeomanry; and the latter, as if emulous of the Manchester corps, intercepted the flying masses, and inflicted some severe sabre wounds. The hussars, we have reason for supposing, gave but few wounds, and I am not aware that it has been shewn that one of those brave soldiers dishonoured his sword by using the edge of it. In addition to the cavalry a strong body of the 88th foot, was stationed at the lower corner of Dickinson-street: with their bayonets at the charge, they wounded several persons, and greatly impeded the escape of the fugitives by that out-let. Almost simultaneously with the hussars, four pieces of horse-artillery, appeared from Deansgate, and about two hundred special constables were also in attendance; so that, force for a thorough massacre was ready, had it been wanted.

Henry Hunt's versions are many, but in 1832 he was once more making attempts to bring up the Manchester affair in the House of Commons, and it was then that he gave his most carefully considered account.[1] On 15 March 1832, in a debate staged on 'The Affray at Manchester'[2] Hunt said:

. . . He had accepted the invitation to attend [the 9 August meeting, which was declared illegal] but with the proviso that he would take no part in electing a legislatorial attorney . . . he was induced to attend this meeting on the 16th of August, although with great reluctance on his part, as he apprehended that some pretence would be sought for on the part of the magistrates to create a disturbance, and in this he was correct, for the delay of a week which intervened between the two meetings allowed spies to be sent through the country by whose agency the people's passions were excited.

---

[1] *Parl. Debates*, 3rd series, Vol. X, 1211. In 1831, on attempting to introduce the subject of the 'Manchester Massacre' into the Reform Bill debate, the House attempted to shout Hunt down.

[2] *Parl. Debates*, 3rd series, Vol. XI, p. 251.

He had received some intimation of the proceedings of those persons employed as spies . . . and he was determined, in consequence, to be very wary and prudent in all he said and did, that no imputations should lie against him, particularly as he had heard that those spies were recommending the people to go armed to the meeting . . . He addressed a public letter to the people, cautioning them to give no ground for complaint on that head, particularly as the meeting was expected to be a large one, but to take every opportunity of showing that they had no unlawful intentions.

This letter, he was happy to say, had the desired effect; but a day or two before the meeting, he received information that it was the intention of the magistrates to arrest the chairman of the meeting . . . he immediately proceeded to the magistrates and offered to give himself up if there was a charge against him, but was assured there was none, nor was there any intention to interfere with the meeting . . . [the meeting a fine sight] . . . proceedings had but just commenced, when, without the least previous notice, the Manchester Yeomanry were let loose on the assembled multitude,[1] . . . with sabres newly sharpened for the occasion, they galloped over the people, cutting down all within their reach. No resistance was offered or intended. They made their way to the hustings where their captain [Birley] claimed him (Mr. Hunt) as his prisoner. He objected to being arrested by a military officer, when the constable of Manchester . . . &c. [Hunt] yielded; still the Yeomanry continued their execution upon the unresisting people; hundreds of whom were wounded, thrown down, trampled upon, or otherwise injured. The groans of the wounded, the horrid shrieks of the women, and the despair of the maddened wretches formed the most dreadful scene that could be imagined. He did understand, however, that, when the people found that they could not escape, they resisted in some few instances by throwing stones [Hunt then narrated the brutality of the Yeomanry] . . . 14 killed, 424 wounded, of whom 108 were females.

It was true, that it might be said, that some of these did not suffer from the sabres of the Yeomanry, but a very large proportion . . . were wounded in that manner; and at all events it was quite certain that no accidents whatever would have occurred but for the outrageous attack that had been made upon a peaceable multitude [his own injuries and slight wounds] . . . he believed he could prove, in opposition to the assertions of interested parties, that the Yeomanry had predetermined on slaughtering the people.

A modern editorial comment on Richard Carlile's 'eyewitness' account, first printed in *Sherwin's Weekly Political Register* for 18 August 1819, is given by Cole and Filson[2] (1965). Carlile had accompanied Hunt in his triumphal procession through Manchester to the field of Peterloo,

---

[1] In his earlier speech when he was shouted down, he had called them 'a drunken and infuriated Yeomanry'.

[2] *Select Documents—British Working Class Movements* (Macmillan 1965), p. 163.

but had escaped arrest when the rest were taken on the hustings. Cole and Filson say:

The Manchester election (of legislatorial attorney) meeting was cancelled, and instead a mass demonstration was arranged for August 16th. Reformers marched on into St. Peter's Field, coming from all the small villages of the neighbourhood. Their entirely peaceful meeting was broken up by deliberate massacre. Neither the anger and indignation that followed, nor the meetings, petitions and pamphlets, could turn the Government from its set determination to kill the working-class reform movement at any cost.

Carlile's version then follows:

. . . Mr. Hunt began his discourse by thanking them for the favour conferred on him, and made some ironical observations on the conduct of the magistrates, when a cart, which evidently took its direction from that part of the field where the police and magistrates were assembled in a house, was moved through the middle of the field to the great annoyance and danger of the assembled people, who quietly endeavoured to make way for its procedure. The cart had no sooner made its way through, when the Yeomanry Cavalry made their appearance from the same quarter as the cart had gone out. They galloped furiously round the field, going over every person who could not get out of their way, [Carlile had previously estimated the crowd at 300,000] to the spot where the police were fixed, and after a moment's pause, they received the cheers of the police as a signal for attack. The meeting at the entrance of the cavalry, and from the commencement of the business was one of the most calm and orderly that I have ever witnessed—hilarity was seen on the countenances of all—whilst the Female Reformers crowned the assemblage with a grace, and excited a feeling particularly interesting.

The Yeomanry Cavalry made their charge with a most infuriate frenzy; they cut down men, women and children, indiscriminately, and appeared to have commenced a pre-meditated attack with the most insatiable thirst for blood and destruction. They merit a medallion, on one side of which should be inscribed 'The Slaughter-men of Manchester', and a reverse bearing a description of their slaughter of defenceless men, women and children, unprovoked and unnecessary. As a proof of meditated murder on the part of the magistrates, every stone was gathered from the ground on the Friday and Saturday previous to the meeting, by scavengers sent there by the express command of the magistrates, that the populance might be rendered more defenceless.

Some of the details in this account, particularly the reference to the cart, and the Yeomanry galloping round the field, find no mention in any other account whatsoever.

The 'Annual Register' for 1819 reported thus:

[After Hunt had commenced to 'harangue' the crowd] He had not proceeded far, when the appearance of the yeomanry cavalry advancing towards the area in a brisk trot, excited a panic on the outskirts of the meeting. They entered the enclosure, and after pausing a moment to recover their disordered ranks, and breathe their horses, they drew their swords and brandished them fiercely into the air. The multitude, by the direction of their leaders, gave three cheers, to show that they were undaunted by this intrusion, and the orator had just resumed his speech to assure the people that this was only a trick to disturb the meeting, and to exhort them to stand firm, when the cavalry dashed into the crowd, making for the cart on which the speakers were placed. The multitude offered no resistance, they fell back on all sides. The commanding officer then approached Mr. Hunt, and brandishing his sword, told him that he was his prisoner. Mr. Hunt, after enjoining the people to tranquility, said, that he would readily surrender to any civil officer on showing his warrant, and Mr. Nadin, the principal police officer, received him in charge. Another person named Johnson was likewise apprehended, and a few of the mob; some others against whom there were warrants, escaped in the crowd. A cry now arose among the military of 'Have at their flags,' and they dashed down not only those in the cart, but the others dispersed in the field; cutting to the right and left to get at them.

The people were running in all directions; and from this moment the yeomanry lost all command of temper; numbers were trampled under the feet of men and horses; many, both men and women, were cut down by sabres; several, and a police officer and a female in the number, slain on the spot. The whole number of persons injured amounted to beween three and four hundred. The populace threw a few stones and brickbats in their retreat; but in less than ten minutes the ground was entirely cleared of its former occupants, and filled by various bodies of military, both horse and foot.

Mr. Hunt was led to prison, not without incuring considerable danger and some injury on his way from the swords of the yeomanry and the bludgeons of the police officers; and broken staves of two of his banners were carried in mock procession before him. The magistrates directed him to be locked up in a solitary cell, and the other prisoners were confined with the same precaution.

The town was brought into a tolerably quiet state before night, military patrols being stationed at the end of almost every street.[1]

The 'Annual Register's' account owes almost everything to the report given by Tyas, *The Times* reporter, who was an eyewitness on the

[1] The lack of knowledge of what actually occurred on St Peter's Field has not precluded historians from giving the impression that they were accurately informed. Colby, *Sources of English History* (Longmans 1899) adds his editorial note to the 'Annual Register' account: '. . . trouble arose between the crowd and the Lancashire Yeomanry who were present on the plea of preserving order. The troops charged and killed several persons, to the intense indignation of radical sympathisers in every part of the island. The "Annual Register" contains an impartial story of the affair.'

hustings with Hunt and who was placed under arrest with him. It is noticeable that there is no reference to the charge of the Hussars, but Tyas, of course, did not see this. The historic 19 August issue of *The Times*, in which Tyas's report appeared, is certainly the sole authority for this account.

J. H. Hudson,[1] writing at the time of the Peterloo centenary writes:

What seems to have happened, that the magistrates having ordered the arrest of Hunt, Nadin, who, finding his avenue of constables cut off near the platform by the crowd which densely surrounded it, reported that he could not effect the arrest. The Yeomen were called in to support the baffled Nadin and, intoxicated by hatred, and probably by liquor too, they commenced to hew their way through the audience. Whether the Riot Act was ever read or not hardly affects the issue. Reliable witnesses immediately above and below the windows of the magistrates' room swore they never heard it read. The magistrates swore they did read it. But this, if it was ever done, was probably accomplished in the same spirit as the gathering together of biased witnesses to state, that the town was in danger because of the meeting. The magistrates were more determined to cover themselves for the course they had decided upon than to carry out the spirit and letter of the law. Certainly the crowd could not have heard the Act read, and had therefore no warning of what was to happen. The chairman of the magistrates, taking fright for the safety of the Yeomen cried out to the Colonel of the Hussars . . . ['Save them' and follows on with a description of the carnage which followed.]

A mid-century (1868) review is given in a Manchester Liberal party account:[2]

The name of Peterloo is a landmark in the history of Reform. The contest between Toryism and Liberalism [today] is tame in comparison to the severe and undaunted struggles for political freedom and better government which took place in the earlier part of this century . . . degradation and misery became intolerable. Throughout the country, a spirit of deep and earnest indignation was aroused, and culminated in the memorable meeting of Reformers on 16 August . . . [processions and bands of music] The meeting was perfectly legal; and had its promoters and the people been left to themselves [it] would in all probability have dispersed in quietness and peace. But it was not to be. For many days previous to the meeting, the authorities, who were filled with distrust and hatred of the people, had made preparations on the most extensive scale to suppress the assembly. Although this intention on the part of the authorities was known throughout the country, it did not deter the people from pouring in from all quarters. When the vast multitude had got into something like order, and ready to commence

---

[1] Nat. Labour Press pamphlet 1919, pp. 19, 20.
[2] *A Short Historical Account of Peterloo,* Manchester n.d. [1868], p. 8.

proceedings, and before any violation of the law had been committed, orders were issued by Capt. Hornby Birley to the Yeomanry to disperse the meeting. The Yeomanry, under the sanction of the civic authorities, commenced a most ruthless attack on the people, irrespective of age or sex. The event sent a thrill of indignation throughout the country.

Dr Read[1] gives this pamphlet (although he misdates it by a few years) as an example of the force Peterloo was to have in Manchester politics later in the nineteenth century; he quotes the political propaganda the local Liberal party were squeezing out of it:

[Peterloo] will ever remain an indelible disgrace on that party who have done all they could to resist the legitimate power of the people, and who now as *Tories*—and here in Manchester too—have the temerity to solicit the suffrages of the working classes in the present contest, in order to use their power against the very men whose ancestors perished for freedom at Peterloo.

The pamphlet's impact on the Manchester electorate in 1868 may be assessed by the result of the poll:

Hugh Birley (Cons)[2]	15,482
Thos. Bazley (Cons)..	14,210
Jacob Bright	13,497
Joseph Hoare	12,688
Ernest Jones	10,746
Mitchell Henry	5,234

The names of all those killed at Peterloo, the names of the magistrates, the names of all the members of the Manchester Yeomanry in 1819, and a list of persons imprisoned with Mr Hunt, were all printed in this election pamphlet, with that of Captain (mis-titled as Commander) Hugh Hornby Birley alone printed in capital letters.[3] Capt. Birley of Peterloo had been dead more than twenty years, but his namesake was the Conservative candidate of 1868. It is not so curious after all that, in 1878, the Manchester Town Hall Committee, when deciding what incidents in Manchester's history were to be depicted by Ford Madox Brown for the Town Hall murals, and Peterloo was suggested, it did 'not seem to meet with favour.'[4] The subject was still charged with an explosive party-political bias. It was to remain so for a great deal longer.

[1] Read, pp. 206–7.
[2] The first Conservative M.P. to be returned for Manchester after the Reform Bill of 1832.
[3] The list was copied from Henry Hunt's Letter 'To the Radical Reformers . . .' dated 29 October 1822. pp. 13–16 (London: T. Dolby).
[4] Town Hall Committee (18 December 1878) Report on Murals (MS. in possession of writer).

In 1938, Dr E. Bosdin Leech of Manchester discovered a letter written to Samuel Argent Bardsley (1764–1851, a Manchester doctor and physician to the infirmary) by Earl Fitzwilliam, up to 1819 Lord-Lieutenant of the West Riding of Yorkshire, who, it will be remembered was removed from his lord-lieutenancy for his stand at the great York meeting held in protest after the Manchester affair of 16 August. Bardsley had written to him informing him that he had been misinformed as to the details of the transaction, but Earl Fitzwilliam was still maintaining that the inquiry proposed by the York Meeting should be held. The then *Manchester Guardian*[1] prefaced the letter thus:

Tomorrow is the 119th anniversary [of Peterloo] . . . the embers still smoulder if we may judge by the curious hesitancy of the promoters of the recent Manchester pageant to touch them. Peterloo has now been appropriated by the Left as a purely working-class affair. Yet it was a great deal more, and we are rather inclined to forget that most of the effect of Peterloo on history came from the way in which men of other classes reacted to it. One may speculate indeed whether, if a similar misjudgement by local magistrates and police authorities were to take place to-day, we should find anything like the same movement of protest among men of property. We have become more liberal and yet in other ways less liberal. It is hard now to conceive of a large section of the landed aristocracy putting itself in opposition to the Government because a few working men and women were killed or hurt in a supposed seditious assembly and because the Government backed the local magistrates in the use of the military.

The *Guardian* writer, not having Dr Bardsley's letter, surmised, 'since he [Bardsley] was a strong Tory and a member of the Manchester Pitt Club and much concerned with the growth of "seditious" opinions, its tenor can be imagined'. He then drew on the Hammonds for knowledge of Fitzwilliam as an 'honourable English gentleman'. He was a Whig, and

his horror of the French Revolution had carried him over to Pitt's side in 1793. But whereas perpetual panic and class feeling had brought most magistrates, as they had brought most statesmen, to regard the mass of their fellow-countrymen as enemies to be kept down by any methods, including force and fraud, Fitzwilliam preserved the scruples and traditions and larger outlook of liberalism in which he had been bred. If there had been a man of character in his position in Lancashire, the civil war of which Peterloo is the most striking example, would never have been carried to such brutal lengths.

There would appear to be some substance in Mr E. P. Thompson's

[1] *Manchester Guardian*, 15 August 1938.

comment that 'in 1819 the action of the loyalists found many defenders in their own class'. That party-political bias still exists in Manchester cannot be doubted. It was expressed in the proposal some years ago in the Manchester City Council that the ward, now St Peter's Ward, in which the site of Peterloo is absorbed, should be named Peterloo Ward. The proposal was rejected.

Historians, prior to Dr Read, have pronounced that a repressive government, and an equally repressive magistracy, brutally put down a peaceable meeting, with tragic results. One historian, however, Mr Keith Feiling, has put the transaction differently from most:[1]

But though they [the Government] were bound to keep order, the older men among them seemed to think repression was a cure, nor had they the vision or vitality to see that parliamentary reform had captured the artisan class. The Combinations Act had broken down, trade union action was incessant, but government did not discern that the sting could be taken out of industrial action by meeting democracy on its political side. That was illustrated by the events of 1819, when the unrepresented city of Birmingham elected an unofficial 'representative', and when political unions spread over Lancashire. It came to a head in August, at 'Peterloo,' the famous meeting in St. Peter's Field, Manchester, when something like 80,000 persons marched in to hear Orator Hunt, where the magistrates most culpably used the local yeomanry to arrest him after the crowd had assembled, and when the yeomanry were resisted and surrounded, employed the regular cavalry. Government then stood on the worst possible ground; eleven persons had been killed and many scores injured, but the magistrates pleaded self-defence; that the crowd had been drilled and bore threatening banners, and that the yeomanry were first attacked. The Cabinet, Canning included, felt their action had been wrong, but if they condemned them, no stand for law and order would be possible again; publicly therefore, they commended them, and introduced the Six Acts.

Mr Feiling does not appear to believe, like Mr Thompson, that the Government 'were parties to the decision to disperse the meeting by force', but Dr Read has since come to that conclusion. He differs however from Dr Read[2] (and from Bruton) in that he says that 'the

[1] *History of England* (Macmillan, 1959).
[2] The Manchester Yeomanry, however, unskilled as they were, soon got into difficulties in the crowd and began striking out. (Read, p. 133).
'. . . This agitation culminated in the disastrous Peterloo meeting in Manchester on 16 August 1819. The Manchester and Salford Yeomanry, sent into a crowd of some sixty thousand operatives to arrest 'Orator' Hunt and other radical speakers, became disorganized and began to attack the people. Hussars had to be sent in to help the yeomanry, and within a few minutes eleven people had been killed or fatally injured and about four hundred seriously hurt.'
(Donald Read *Press and People 1790–1850*, 1961) p. 47.

yeomanry were resisted and surrounded', and that the magistrates 'pleaded self defence' in that '. . . the yeomanry were first attacked.'

There are far-reaching implications in such assertions. Gone is Bruton's interpretation that the Yeomanry 'made a dash for the hustings, striking with their swords as they entered the crowd'; or Bamford's 'their sabres were plied to hew a way through naked held-up hands, and defenceless heads'; or Carlile's: the charge of the Yeomanry made 'with a most infuriate frenzy; they cut down . . . indiscriminately'. The well-informed student of the various narratives of Peterloo would exclaim that Bamford's *Passages in the Life of a Radical*[1] long ago exploded such theories that 'the Yeomanry were first attacked' in a devastating manner, nor could one read the printed reports of Hunt's trial and doubt that it was exploded. Or to leave original sources aside, Bruton's summing-up of all such evidence effectively disposed of such a claim. Mr Feiling posed more questions than probably he would have cared to answer, but he has apparently dug out of original sources points that were made at the time, but hardly ever raised since.

He has shown, too, that there were people (as Mr Thompson admits there were) who could defend the action of the local magistrates, people like Dr Bardsley, for instance, who maintained that Earl Fitzwilliam was misinformed. But on what grounds *could* they defend such actions when, as History has proved, they were utterly indefensible? 'Ten years after 1819', quoting Mr Thompson, 'it was an event to be remembered, even among the gentry, with guilt.' But was it? Would not Dr Read's admonition 'caution . . . something must still be admitted as unknown' have found more echoes then? That it was not a guilt complex that resisted the suggested Peterloo murals in Manchester Town Hall in 1878; or the pageant in 1938; or even the 'Peterloo Ward' proposals of later date; but resistance because the generally accepted, indeed, the almost wholly accepted version of Peterloo, had something of a questionable nature about it.?'

No one has ever seriously tried to refute the radical interpretation of Peterloo, since the case for it appeared to be so well documented. The only crack in the solid structure of it appeared when Dr Read found, from indisputable evidence, that the Government were not 'parties to the decision to disperse the meeting by force'. Mr Thompson argues, whether convincingly or not his readers must judge, that if there was evidence of this collusion it would not be permitted to survive in Home Office records, that it would have been destroyed. Mr Ziegler, in his

[1] It was Chapter XX.

biography of Sidmouth, expostulates with him; his comment is of interest:

Any theory propounded by so considerable an authority as Thompson deserves careful study but, as he himself admits, no direct evidence to support it exists in the Home Office papers. It could be, as he suggests, that such incriminating documents have been destroyed, but it is surely easier to believe that they were never written? The Home Office can fairly be criticised for the looseness with which they habitually supervised local magistrates. Lack of detailed directions was a constant complaint. It seems unreasonable to suppose that, in this one instance, their control was strict enough to dictate the whole pattern of blunders which led to the disaster.

In a short time, defending the magistrates, or even offering anything in the shape of an *apologia*, became utterly futile. This was soon equated with condoning (what it was soon dubbed to be) the massacre of innocents, the defence of the indefensible. That the Government should defend it seems to have surprised no one. Ziegler comments on this, after showing that modern evidence exonerates Sidmouth (and the Government) from complicity with the 'brutality':

It is more in line with Sidmouth's aversion to violence and his determination, wherever possible, to take the heat out of every conflict. His own assertion, that the news of the bloodshed at Manchester came as a complete surprise, can be accepted. The reasonable ground of criticism remains: the surprise, when it came, should have seemed a great deal more unpleasant than it did.

The rest of the Government, including even such a comparative liberal as Canning, and others were wholeheartedly behind him . . . but there were anyhow few observers ready to copy Canning's calm and faintly cynical detachment. The riding down by dragoons of decorous and defenceless citizens, even without the embellishments of drawn sabres and fatal casualties among women and children was admirably designed to disquiet the public conscience. The Whigs and Radicals had no intention of letting it rest again . . .

Mr Ziegler pursues this point:

The debate on Peterloo and on the Six Acts should have given the Whigs a matchless opportunity to destroy the Government's reputation and establish themselves as an honourable alternative, intent on justice and equity yet, in the long run, more able to protect the interests of property than those who relied solely on ferocious reaction to achieve their ends. The fact that they failed was partly due to the weakness of Tierney, the parliamentary leader, but even more to the deep lack of conviction of many of the Whig leaders in the doctrines to which they paid lip service . . .

That the 'matchless opportunity' given to the Whigs of destroying the Government's reputation was not pressed home, may or may not have been due to the weakness of Tierney and a 'deep lack of conviction' on the part of many of the Whig leaders. But the 'lack of conviction' may have had another cause; that they could not, and as time went on, *would* not, press their seeming advantage too hard, knowing then, as some did later, and as others 'feel' now, that there was something 'unknown', or inexplicable about the affair. Men like Lord Stanley, a Whig in the House of Commons, a man tarred with the same brush as the magistrates, was indeed something of an enigma to a Whig writer in *The Elector's Remembrancer* . . . 1822 who said:

LORD STANLEY. Voted for Catholic Emancipation; for repeal of taxes on reduction of establishment for the Queen. Votes well always, except when Lancashire magistrates, Lancashire yeomanry, or Lancashire gaolers are concerned. It is melancholy to see a man of his principles degrading himself into the defender of such conduct.

Lord Stanley's speeches in the House, James Scarlett's speeches, were a restraining influence on many; the latter arguing intensely on the one hand for public inquiry with the Whig Opposition, to which he belonged, yet who was to be briefed (surprisingly it may be thought) by the Crown as the prosecuting counsel against Hunt and the other Peterloo leaders on the other. These voices were finally, however, to be stilled, for the radicals had no intention of letting the matter rest, they pressed it as hard as they could, so hard indeed that the radical interpretation of Peterloo has been established as standard.

Peterloo, even after Ziegler, even after Read,[1] is still Peterloo Massacre, with the responsibility resting squarely on the shoulders of the magistrates. Mr Ziegler quotes Sidmouth's letter: 'even if they should utter sedition or proceed to the election (of a legislatorial attorney), Lord Sidmouth is of opinion that it will be the wisest course to abstain from any endeavour to disperse the mob, unless they should proceed to acts of felony or riot.' Mr Ziegler comments:

The magistrates, therefore, had acted in defiance of Sidmouth's instructions. He could at least have hinted publicly that this was so. He could have made some concession to the genuine sense of outrage felt by many who otherwise had nothing good to say for the activities of the radicals and the reformers.

[1] And even after Mr Feiling, for he says: that the magistrates 'most culpably used the local yeomanry to arrest [Hunt] . . . The Cabinet, Canning included, felt their action had been wrong, but if they condemned them, no stand for law and order would be possible again; publicly therefore, they commended them, and introduced the Six Acts.'

The fact that he did not shows insensitivity, lack of political acumen and an under-developed social conscience.

Even William Hulton's own grandson succumbed, at least in part, to the radical interpretation. He had probably read his grandfather's own copy of Bamford's *Passages in the Life of a Radical* which bears the signature 'William Hulton' on the fly leaves (now in the writer's possession).

The grandson, William Wilbraham Blethyn Hulton (1844–1907), was conducting a Conservative election compaign in the Westhoughton constituency in 1883,[1] when, at a meeting, a voice piped out from the back of the room: 'What about Peterloo?' He was perfectly prepared, he said, to answer. 'Perfectly prepared' it might be thought, because he had come with 'evidence' to the meeting which suggested that the questioner had been primed. W. W. B. Hulton then went carefully over the 'background' material, obviously culled from Philips *Exposure of the Calumnies* (1819), the only known authority setting out any sort of a case for the magistrates; but the gist of the 'explanation' was 'that the meeting of 16 August, an illegal meeting, came into collision with the Government forces, who were ordered by the Government to suppress the meeting, and sad as the facts may be . . .' etc.

[1] *Bolton Chronicle*, 10 February 1883.

IV

Manchester, January 1819

No one prior to Dr Read had attempted to fill in the background to those first months of 1819, the prelude to Peterloo. Are there further portents in that period of the tragedy which was to come?

It would be possible to put together from the loyalist press in Manchester a somewhat biased account of this period, but it would not give an answer to the question posed by Dr Read[1]—a question to which he never seemed to give himself a satisfactory answer. He says, regarding the loyalists of Manchester:

Their institutions were various, their offices were many, they had power and experience behind them. What was it that caused them, despite all their power and experience, to panic as they did at Peterloo?

The answers he gave were of intense radical activity, the evil influences of the radical press, the drilling; which led him to the conclusion that all this, combined with the 'impressive manner in which the meeting assembled in the morning of 16 August, was sufficient to convince them even before Hunt had begun to speak that the meeting was seditious and must be *dispersed*[2] at any cost'. And if one accepts Dr Read's premise of 'panic', Mr Thompson's conclusion appears to be not unreasonable:

The attack was made on this multitude with the venom of panic. But the panic was not (as has been suggested) the panic of bad horsemen hemmed in by a crowd. It was the panic of class hatred. It was the *Yeomanry*—the Manchester manufacturers, merchants, publicans, and shopkeepers on horseback—which did more damage than the regulars (Hussars) . . . There is no term for this but class war. But it was a pitifully one-sided war. The people, closely packed and trampling upon each other in the effort to escape, made no effort at retaliation until the very edges of the field, where a few trapped remnants—finding themselves pursued into the streets and yards—threw brick-bats at their pursuers . . .[3]

---

[1] Read, p. 83.
[2] Not Dr Read's italics.
[3] Thompson, p. 686–7.

'There is no reason to doubt', goes on Dr Read, 'the genuineness of all this loyalist alarm, excessive though it may appear in the light of after knowledge.' He then quotes an example of the panic in a loyalist household, adding: 'imaginary though the grounds for the panic may have been it was certainly sincere'. It is not, however, from panic-stricken loyalist sources that evidence must be sought nor from the effects on loyalist minds as expressed by them, but from the sources which caused it. Was it excessive? Was it imaginary?

A closer examination of what the loyalists saw and read, not in their own 'alarmist' press, but in the events of those months as mirrored in the radicals' own press, may help to give answers to those questions.

On January 18th, 1819, [Dr. Read says][1] Henry Hunt presided over a meeting of some 8000 operatives held on St. Peter's Field, Manchester. With this meeting, at the same place and with the same chief speakers as the Peterloo meeting of seven months later, the political course of the year 1819 opened in Manchester. A hint of things to come was given by the way the meeting was assembled. Just as on a larger scale in August, the Reformers displayed flags and banners, and some of them marched in regular order with music. Hunt's speech was confident, almost threatening . . .

It was one of the plaints of the loyalists in Manchester that their local reformers did not need Henry Hunt to tell them what in fact they told their Manchester followers the week before Hunt arrived. The *Manchester Observer* of the week previously had written thus (January 16):

Your right to petition, is here, however, *undoubted*. You may petition, indeed *you may*; but you will get *no answer*, nor *any consideration* of the prayer of your petition. Why then petition? Why not REMONSTRATE BOLDLY AND FIRMLY? Could you gain anything by an *abject submission* to *usurpation*, we should still say, do not degrade 'the human form erect' by such submission. But when nothing can be gained by servility, what slave would crouch beneath the stripe, and kneel to ask the insult of his master? Our REMONSTRANCES cannot share a worse fate than our PETITIONS; our indignation cannot be worse treated than our submission. Let us respect ourselves, and we shall soon be enabled to teach others to RESPECT US. *Despise us*, they cannot, however they may injure us if we stand upon the rock of our inherent rights, and have sufficient courage to defend them. On to the contest then, of *reason* against *power*, of argument against oppression. The watchwords of freemen are 'Annual Parliaments and Universal Suffrage'.

Hunt, in his speech, played on his audience as on an instrument (telling them much that the *Observer* had already said): 'If you say petition—

[1] Read, p. 106.

2. Hunting at Manchester or Jacobins turn'd out accompanied by Hussars & Hisses

there will be a petition; if you say remonstrate there will be a remonstrance. The question for me to submit to you will be whether
you will ever again submit to such infamous conduct; whether again you
will petition those who ought to be your servants, or whether you will
boldly remonstrate to the throne on your manifold grievances' (loud
applause; cries of no petition—remonstrate, remonstrate). Hunt went
on:

If our opponents will come here . . . We are now assembled on the very
ground where the brave Blanketeers were peaceably assembled, and where
they themselves were the rioters; and where they introduced the soldiers to
insult, assault and shoot, an injured and peaceable people. They dare not, my
friends; they are grown wiser from their fears; they dare not this day attempt
the same measures with us. They have, I understand, sent for a regiment of
horse; they know that we are always peaceable, hence their display of military force. But, wherever I appear in public, they honour me with the
attendance of soldiers—they are become my bodyguard. They are our
fellow-sufferers, and if the day should arrive when we are called upon to act
as our ancestors have done before us, to fight for our liberties, I have no doubt
we shall act together as brothers, for one common cause . . .[1]

Dr Read prints in detail the Remonstrance and the Declaration (of
policy) which emanated from this meeting, calling them 'important
statements of radical policy in the year of Peterloo:' 'between them they
outlined virtually every aspect of the radical reform programme. The
background of Peterloo was already being filled in.' Whatever effect
these statements of policy might have had in a different context of
events, they were completely over-shadowed by what actually happened.
It might be imagined, from Hunt's speech, that he was speaking with a
body of troops behind the crowd. There were no troops out. Dr Read
reports:

After enthusiastically passing these two manifestos, the meeting dispersed
peaceably. No arrests were made by the magistrates, and the troops, though at
the ready, remained in their barracks.

'Dispersing peaceably' and 'assembling peaceably' were to become relative terms in the months to come. In this instance, the *Observer*[1]
reports:

[After the meeting a procession moved off] At the end of Mosley Street, a
call was made to go up Oldham Street, but the people exclaimed 'Past the
Exchange! Past the Exchange!' and immediately turned the flags and music
down Market Street, and opposite that beautiful fabric [the Exchange] from

[1] *Manchester Observer*, 23 January 1819.

whence seemed to proceed some of the viper's embodied breath, the people made a complete stand and gave nine distinct shouts of applause, which re-echoed in the air like nine vollies of artillery. These distinct shouts were followed by one continual huzzaing making the welkin ring till [Hunt's] coach arrived at the inn.

Although the *Observer's* report of the day's proceedings are remarkably long they do not include some details reported by *Aston's Exchange Herald* (19 January) which comments on Hunt's effrontery in coming to Manchester; how he brought with him his own flag inscribed 'Hunt and Liberty', and 'Universal Suffrage', mounted on a red staff which was surmounted by a red Cap of Liberty. Hunt stopped his carriage at the front of the Exchange on the way to St Peter's Field, and tried to harangue the subscribers of the Newsroom who were 'looking at the most impudent man living' from the windows and doors. 'At the moment he opened his mouth he was saluted with every mark of indignant contempt and he was obliged to give up his intention.' All reports tell of the unfortunate collapse of the 'scaffolding or hustings' on which the orator and his supporters faced the crowd, when all were precipitated to the ground, happily without hurt; and of Hunt's attempt to address the crowd again from the upper window of the Windmill Inn. The *Observer* says:

Mr. Hunt, retired into the Windmill Public House, accompanied by his friends, with the intention of proceeding with the business of the day, and delivering their respective addresses through the window; when the landlord, with trembling limbs and quivering lips, announced to Mr. Hunt, that the indulgence could not be allowed. The gentlemen instantly retired; and a temporary hustings being immediately erected, the business was regularly proceeded in. Mr. Hunt then observed that such was the degraded state of the Manchester publicans, that the landlord did not dare to suffer him to address them through his window, lest he should lose his licence. He was afraid, it seems, to disoblige the boroughreeve—let the boroughreeve support him then, but let the people whom he has offended keep their money in their pockets.

The same evening, at a public dinner, Henry Hunt told his again enthusiastic auditors:

When the people of England generally follow the example of the people of Manchester, then will the Boroughmongering faction exclaim, that treason and rebellion are abroad. But, Gentlemen, their notions of treason and rebellion are not always to be found correct, and your conduct will prove that you dare to set them at defiance; and though what is laid down in the declaration [passed that day] may not be grateful to them or to the Prince Regent, yet it is highly honourable to the people of this town.

Not all the people of Manchester were to agree with Mr Hunt as to what was honourable to the town. The committee of Lancashire and Cheshire magistrates (of which William Hulton was appointed chairman) had not then been formed; until July 1819, magisterial functions for keeping the peace and sending reports to the Home Office were in the hands of James Norris, the Manchester stipendiary, in consultation with other magistrates meeting at the New Bayley courthouse. Norris had shown some apprehension when apprised of Hunt's visit, as his letters to Lord Sidmouth show, although this was written on the day of the meeting:

Norris to Sidmouth: 'The military and civil power were all in readiness on the shortest notice, so that if anything violent had happened we were prepared to put it down almost on the instant, though perhaps not without loss of some lives.'[1]

to which Hobhouse (Lord Sidmouth's secretary) had replied conveying his lordship's satisfaction at their state of preparation, and their forbearance in not calling out the military while the peace remained unbroken.

Norris did, in fact, report the military 'preparedness' for any eventualities arising from this meeting, in a letter to Lord Sidmouth of 25 January:

The military were ready in barracks if wanted, and a sergeant and two orderlys placed at an inn nearest the police, but none upon or near the ground.[2]

Dr Read comments on this:[3] 'Right up to and during the Peterloo crisis the Home Office continued to hope that the magistrates would display such forbearance. Unfortunately, by the middle of the year Norris and his colleagues, under the influence of continuous and ever-growing radical agitation, had lost all their calm of the previous January.' He also reports the Theatre Royal incident, when a disturbance occurred during a performance at which Hunt was present, and after which Hunt was 'forcibly removed' from the theatre. The following evening the theatre was closed when Hunt announced his intention of attending again with a bodyguard armed with sticks. 'On discovering' (that the theatre was to remain closed), Dr Read goes on, 'Hunt addressed the crowd outside the theatre and then returned to his inn. There, later in the evening, about a dozen "loyalist" roughs "in the garb of gentlemen" forced their way into his private room and challenged

1 *Reports of State Trials*, New Series, Vol. I (1888), App. B, p. 1371.
2 Ibid., p. 1371.
3 Read, pp. 106–8.

him and the three or four friends with him to a fight.' Read's account
ends thus:

So ended Hunt's visit to Manchester. The dangerous tendencies on both sides
had been amply displayed. The reformers' language had grown wild, wilder
probably than they meant. Remonstrance had replaced petition: 'resistance
to earthly tyranny' had become the call [a quotation from the 'Manchester
Declaration' printed in Dr. Read's appendix]. Much of this was certainly
only intended for effect and had no connection with any intended Radical
revolution; but the appearance was there to alarm 'loyal' minds. These
'loyalists' too had shown an unfortunate tendency, a distressing readiness to
use physical violence against the reformers. Violence on the Peterloo scale
was probably far from their minds, but an unhappy beginning had been made.
As yet, however, the magistrates remained calm.

All of which is fair comment so far as it goes; but the tendency to use
violence was not all on one side. After all, the radicals had thrown (or
dropped) one loyalist out of a theatre-box into the pit; there were
allegations of Hunt calling Hussar officers the 'bloody butchers of
Waterloo'; and he had arrived on the second evening with a bodyguard armed with sticks. The whole affair was nothing more than a
blown-up street brawl which ended with Hunt bringing one of the
'assailants' before the local magistrates, where the case was, rightly or
wrongly, dismissed. The whole miserable affair was reported at great
length in the local press, and out of it it is possible to re-create the impressions made on at least some of Manchester's citizens by Hunt's
visit: the visit of the crowd to demonstrate outside the Exchange which
Hunt was alleged to have called a 'den of corruption'; the terms of the
'horrid remonstrance' which was thought would disgrace the 'loyal
town of Manchester', probably because it reminded the Prince Regent
of the fate of other Royal personages, who hearkened not to the people's
complaints, namely Charles I and James II; and Hunt's alleged effrontery
in putting himself forward to speak for this 'loyal town' etc.

Hunt played up this incident for all he was worth, even to the extent
of writing a high-sounding letter of protest to the Duke of York, the
Army Commander-in-Chief, complaining of the 'most wanton,
cowardly assaults and violent outrages, that ever disgraced the annals of
a free country' committed by some Officers belonging to the 7th
Regiment of Hussars. The 'Reign of Anarchy', he wrote, 'had arrived in
this country' if these offences were not punished. He had, Hunt concluded, put the machinery of the Law into motion. He received the
carefully-worded and courteous reply, that His Royal Highness was
content to let the Law take its course.

That faithful radical chronicler, Samuel Bamford, records this incident in his simple unaffected prose in *Passages in the Life of a Radical*.[1] He deals with Hunt's visit to Manchester in January 1819, but devotes his *Passages* almost exclusively to the theatre incident. The *Passages* were published in 1844, but he had contemporaneously written some inspiring verses on the incident. In his *Passages* with becoming modesty he does not refer to them, but he does observe that the 'gentlemen' who had offered to fight Hunt and his companions 'were a set of "lucky dogs" '. 'Had they', he continues, 'been taken by us in the fact, there would have been a sore and pitiable account of them in the morning. But fate ordained otherwise,' Bamford continues, 'they escaped and we

> Whilst echoes were ringing
> Went laughing and singing
> To the merry green woods again.

Apart from the inaptness of the reference to the 'merry green woods' in Middleton in January, Bamford had a better verse to finish his account of the theatre incident:

> Oh! it had been well worth one's while
> To travel many a weary mile,
>   'Midst cold and wind and rain . . .'

That verse, however, ended with the threat to make them 'either play or pay when Hunt returns again', which, in 1844, would not have strengthened Bamford's insistence on the utterly peaceable nature of the meeting of 16 August 1819. Bamford's faithful chroniclings are not always found where chronologically they ought to be; they are, however, to be found, if with some difficulty. His 'Touch Him! Or, Verses occasioned by the Outrage committed upon Mr Hunt, and His Friends, at the Theatre, Manchester, on the evening of Friday, January 22nd, 1819, by Lord Uxbridge, Capt. Fraser, George Torr, and twenty or thirty other "Gemmen" of the same stamp,' are to be found in *Miscellaneous Poetry by Samuel Bamford, weaver, of Middleton in Lancashire, lately imprisoned in the Castle of Lincoln*. 8vo London (1821):

> Touch him, aye! touch him, if you dare;
> Pluck from his head one single hair—
>   Ye sneaking, coward crew:
> Touch him—and blasted be the hand
> That graspeth not a vengeful brand,
> To rid our long oppressed land
>   Of reptiles such as you.

[1] Bamford, Vol. I, p. 169.

Touch him—and by the eternal pow'r,
That very day, that very hour,
  Is curst oppression's last:
Then vengeance shall no longer stay,
The mighty flood shall break away:
  Our purse-proud tyrants vanity
  Shall to the earth be cast.

You *whisker'd whelp*,★ of borough-breed,
Shall surely rue his dastard deed,
  And so shall *Sawney*,† too:
Their chicken hearts, in that dread day,
Shall melt before their enemy;
A tougher game they'll have to play
  Than that of *Waterloo*.

Lift but a finger for his harm
Thou bloated ban-dog‡ of the swarm,
  That crowd to yonder den.
Dare it, and thy black sin-clad soul
Shall, in an instant, hell-ward howl!
To join Cerberus' damned growl,
  Barr'd down from God and men.

Why did the sparks, on Monday night,
With fallen crests decline the fight,
  And silent sneak away?
Oh! there were country clogs, I ween,
And trusty cudgels, too, were seen;
And sturdy tykes, so gaunt and keen,
  All come to see the play.

The Dandies shins, like rotten sticks,
Had snapp'd before the bumpkins' kicks,
  Had they but dar'd the tug:
Their ulcer'd throats had felt a grasp,
Crush'd flat, as in a giant's clasp,
  Or wild-bear's fatal hug.

Whiskers, and stays, and periwigs,
Had been pluck'd off by Burke's rude pigs,
  And trampled in the mire;

★ Lord Uxbridge
† The Scotch Captain
‡ George Torr

False teeth and noses would have flown,
Which the scabb'd rascals call their own,
Before the clog of country clown,
    Or cudgel's bruise so dire.

But true to Dandy stile and trim,
They risked neither life nor limb;
    Oh! it had cheered me,
To see our gallant gang so stout,
At clog and cudgel have a bout;
    So fast, so firm, amid the rout,
For *Hunt and Liberty*.

Oh! it had been well worth one's while
To travel many a weary mile,
    'Midst cold, and wind, and rain;
But come, my lads, some other day
We'll pin them, e'er they sneak away,
And they shall either play or pay
    When *Hunt* returns again.

Samuel Bamford's verses were to be first quoted by his radical friend, Dr Healey, at the great Ashton-under-Lyne meeting in June 1819, to be lost to sight and memory, as anything relevant, until after Bamford's release from prison in 1821, when his poems were first published. He did not include them again in later editions, and in 1844 modestly forbore mentioning them at a time when radical tendency to violence was muted. He substituted the innocuous lines on the 'merry green woods' in their place. Bamford as a radical chronicler is safe only when he is used chronologically.

That this January 1819 series of incidents exacerbated local feeling, both loyalist and radical, there can be no doubt; that there was an 'unfortunate tendency' (to quote Dr Read) 'a distressing readiness to use physical violence' was likewise true. 'Violence on the Peterloo scale,' continues Dr Read, 'was probably far from *their* minds, but an unhappy beginning had been made.' Dr Read's pronoun *their* is not italicized; in his context it stands for loyalist minds. It should stand for both loyalist and radical.

V

Sandy Brow: an Inspiration and an Incitement

Dr Read rightly says:[1]

The next important event locally was the Stockport Radical meeting of
February 15th. Harrison was the chief speaker, and a remonstrance to the
Prince Regent was passed similar to that at Manchester. A Cap of Liberty was
displayed which some mounted constables unsuccessfully attempted to seize.
After the meeting there was considerable disturbance in the town and the
Riot Act had to be read three times. Norris, the Manchester Stipendiary
magistrate, regretted the attempt on the Cap of Liberty 'as it gave the multitude an apparent triumph'. His fears were beginning to rise now: 'if these
meetings are continued to be held with impunity,' he wrote, 'it is quite
impossible but that in a few months it must lead us to the same state in which
we were last year'. The weavers' wages, he added significantly, 'are at present
extremely low.'

Henry Hunt had written to the 'Gentlemen of Stockport' (27
January) congratulating them on the formation of their Union Society;
a G. L. Bolsover had replied:[2]

Our object being to obtain a great and positive good, viz. *equal rights, equal
laws*, and equal justice; and our weapons being reason, discussion and per-
suasion, it follows that we shall obtain our object without either anarchy or
confusion. If reason, discussion, &c., are suppressed by the illegalised misgovernment of the country, the exigencies of time will suggest such measures as an enlightened and independent nation shall think proper to adopt
. . . If they ever think at all, the idea must harrow their very souls: to know
that the day of retribution will come, in spite of all the means they may take
to avoid it.

The activities of the Stockport radical movement have a greater importance in pre-Peterloo affairs than they have yet been given credit for.
Dr Read writes, 'by the end of April the rules of the Stockport Union
Society had been published by Harrison, and Unions on the Stockport
model had begun to spring up all over the area.' But there was another

---

[1] Read, p. 108.
[2] *Manchester Observer*, 6 February 1819.

Stockport 'model' which had a far greater significance, the more aggressive attitude taken up by the radicals.

The 15 February Stockport meeting was again (as at Manchester) 'considering the propriety of remonstrating with the Prince Regent'.

The *Manchester Observer* gave the affair full coverage:

It had previously been contemplated by those enlightened patriots, who had undertaken the management of the respective documents that were to be proposed . . . and to inspire the noble souls of Britons with the remembrance of their ancient constitutional birthright, that the Cap of Liberty and two handsome banners . . . 'No Corn Laws' and 'Rights of Man' should be hoisted.

It is not surprising, that these emblems were beheld by the vassals of corruption, with marks of reprobation. The profligate engines of despotism were in motion for several days previous to the meeting—and it was confidently asserted, that a regiment of returned transports, under the command of the all-potent Nadin, were in actual array against the People.[1]

Mr Fitton, who presided, said:

the people of Stockport, like the universal inhabitants of England, were weary of the joke of petitioning the Commons. He wished he could anticipate more favourable results from the measures that were about to be proposed for adoption. It was impossible for him to say which was the best mode of proceeding—this was clear; that something must be done, and that speedily. He then exhorted the meeting to hold fast to the Law, and suffer no wretched incendiary of Sidmouth to counteract their firmness and peaceable demeanour.

Again, as at Manchester, the strong terms of the Remonstrance reminded the Prince Regent of the fate of Charles I and James II, and the crowd was introduced to John Thacker Saxton who, during the next few months, was to prove that his oratorical powers were not less than his literary ones as writer in the *Observer*. He was alternately to rouse flagging radical spirits and depress loyalist ones by reporting his own speeches and adding his comments to those of others, which was to make the *Observer* the pride of its friends and the bane of its opponents. Saxton was eventually to find himself the named target for Yeomanry sabres at the hustings on St Peter's Field, although he actually came to no harm save that he was arrested and placed on trial with Hunt, Bamford, etc., only to be acquitted. At the Stockport meeting he was proposing a resolution in aid of Bagguley, Drummond, and Johnston (the still-imprisoned Blanketeers). Their names, Saxton said:

had become endeared to him in proportion to the obloquy that had been so ostentatiously cast upon them by, what the brave Wooler terms the trimming

[1] *Manchester Observer*, 20 February 1819.

policy of the Whigs, and none more than that snaffling hypocrite John Edward Taylor,[1] in a speech that took him three days and three nights to prepare for its appearance in a public newspaper, for no other purpose than to stigmatize the characters of men, who had ever been ready to fill up the gap their dastardly accusers had neither the courage nor the intellect to occupy himself.

Away, then, said Mr. Saxton, with these trimming politicians, whose motives have been so ably exposed by [Wooler]. They hover on the shore and mark the labouring vessel on her way. Let the winds blow and the waves roar—what care they? They are not on board [and if the storm be weathered] should the tall mast still tower in the spray, and bear aloft the unconquerable banner—who so ready, as such poltroons as Taylor, to sing the praises of the conflict they have seen—to describe the conquest they stood still and witnessed—to partake the triumphs they did not anticipate!! Away then, with all such cowards: away with such temporizing slaves . . . &c.

[Mr Saxton] next pointed most significantly to the Cap of Liberty—their constitutional ensign—a ruffian banditti are at this moment contemplating to wrest from your grasp. For his part, should an illegal seizure be attempted, his mind was made up, to perish in its defence. (Here the burst of approbation was indescribable).

The Rev. Joseph Harrison, nonconformist minister of Stockport, next spoke of the 'three' languishing in gaol. 'Are they not as worthy of liberty as yourselves?' (Yes, yes from all parts of the meeting) . . . 'Ah, friends, how is their liberty to be obtained?' (cries of 'That's the question!') 'Shall I advise you to take up arms and fight for it?' ('Yes, yes,' cried the people.)

No, no, that I will not do, [went on the Reverend gentleman] I will not advise you in this case at present. You have heard much, and read much, and thought much, therefore act as your own prudence dictates, and as the urgency of the case requires. You have petitioned long to no effect, now you are *remonstrating*, and perhaps it will be with as little effect. Words are but wind. But I know your patience—you have borne long—I know your humanity,— it must be dire necessity that will compel you to harsh measures. It is not cowardice, but a tender feeling for your fellow-creatures which makes you forbear in the manner you do. You are the patientest people in the world . . .[2]

---

[1] John Edward Taylor, later founder of the *Manchester Guardian*. 'After having so much in common with the organizers of the Peterloo meeting, the designation "Radical" is no misnomer for the middle-class group.' (Read, p. 73). Taylor was the leader of this group.

[2] Scarlett, prosecuting counsel at Hunt's trial, *State Trials*, p. 423, was to compare Hunt's speech at Peterloo with that of Antony on Caesar: 'Good friends, sweet friends, let me not stir you up to mutiny'. The ingenuous reporting of John Thacker Saxton here provides a better example.

The *Observer* report goes on to comment on the next speech of Wm.
Ogden, 'every sentence being received with marked approbation', when:

The chairman, aware of the uproar that was about to be commenced by a
gang of hired ruffians, was at this moment exhorting the people to peace and
good order; at the same time, he observed that their firmness in the exercise
of their constitutional rights would speedily be put to the test—when a
number of men on horseback, headed by some of the lowest dregs of the
law, under the employ of the Sheriff—fellows, we understand, of the names
of Birch, Walker, Pass, and others, mounted on horseback, and followed by a
multitude of ragamuffins, entered the ground, striking the women and
children with their sticks as they passed along. The ghastly countenances of
their miserable rips of leaders, betrayed the impious commission which they
were about to execute.

It was indeed laughable to see one stout, fat fellow, who reminded us of
Sir John Falstaff, address the chairman in these words: 'I-I-I-de-de-demand
th'-th'-th'-at Cup-Cap of Li-Li-Li-berty—in th'-th'-the name of the the
K'-King!!!' At this instant, a countryman stepped forward, and exclaimed:
'Thou art not the first scoundrel that has told a lie in the name of the poor Old
King, and I should na wonder if thou's been stuffing thy guts at his expense
now, so tak' this toothpick'; at the same moment the countryman gave Sir
John a most unwelcome salute on the left ear with a stout ash-plant. 'Oh
dear! oh dear!' exclaimed Sir John; 'Dear enough!' said John Bull, 'it has
been to us that work, for mony a year—thou sees, we put up a little Saving
Bonks, and now have a mite to spare for thee.' Some of the hired men,
bumbailiffs we were told, now attempted to seize the Cap of Liberty, when
the row, that had been courted by some of these hellish miscreants commenced. 'Stand, firm,' was the order of the day, and the air in an instant was
darkened with nature's ammunition, brickbats, stones and mud. The *Gentry*
on horseback had by this time quitted their bridle reins, (some of which, it
is said, were cut), and the necks and manes of the horses were every vestige
they could contrive to lay hold of, to enable them to keep the saddle. The
horses, with ten-fold more sense than their riders, unwilling to face '*the
pelting storm*', galloped from the ground, and all the *foot-pad crew* that were
enlisted for the Sandy Brow Expedition, were driven before the majesty
of the people with the rapidity of lightning. Thus, Johnny Gilpin's troop,
with all the horses they could muster, spavin'd, farcy'd, wind-gall'd and pole-
evil—commanded by Noodle and Doodle, Tom Thumb, Jack the Giant
Killer and the GREAT TOM PUDDING, were defeated in an instant,
and order was perfectly restored.

The *Observer* goes on:

The business of the meeting which previous to the disturbance had been
nearly concluded, was then proceeded in; and after a short speech from Mr.

Saxton, who had taken the Cap of Liberty and placed it for moment on his head, and replaced it on its wonted station, which was received with exclamations from the populace, the sincere and grateful thanks of the Meeting were presented to the chairman, for his firmness on this trying occasion, with nine times nine cheers and loud huzzas. . . .

The meeting, having been earnestly requested to retire to their homes, resolved first to see the chairman and speakers safe to the place where a most excellent dinner was provided for the occasion. A company of military, the Rev. Mr. Prescot, rector of Stockport, and a number of constables, &c., followed soon after. The crowd that surrounded the Wind-Mill room was immense, cheering the speakers, &c., as they went to dinner. The Riot Act was read.

There is an odd hiatus in the *Observer's* report at this point, which further research in the loyalist press could no doubt fill, but it does not act to the prejudice of these pre-Peterloo details. The reading of the Riot Act was evidently intended to order the crowd to disperse, and in the absence of further evidence it could be construed as another instance of the excessive alarm of the authorities. The sequel, reported by the *Observer*, however, resolves all difficulties:

The Riot Act was read; people nevertheless remained stationary. It is but justice to say, that the demeanour of Mr. Prescot towards Speakers and the Gentlemen who had signed the Requisition to the Meeting, was such as to entitle him to the thanks of the friends of Liberty; for when he found that his power both as a Magistrate and an inhabitant was ineffectual, he very politely requested Mr. Harrison to have the goodness to use his influence in order to induce the people to retire, being well persuaded, he acknowledged, that a word from him would have the desired effect. He assured Mr. Harrison and Mr. Fitton, that it was by no means his intention to take any person into custody, and could not but lament what had happened to disturb the peace of the town. If there had been any sentiments used at the Meeting which were improper, it would hereafter be his painful duty to call upon the respective parties who had delivered those sentiments.

Dr Read dwells at length on the clerical magistrates who were active at the period of Peterloo. The Rev. Mr Prescot has not had much notice, although in the context of pre-Peterloo affairs, he was equally important. That he was not amongst the Lancashire and Cheshire magistrates who formed the special committee which began to act in July 1819, may be thought surprising in view of his experience, and recent experience at that. It is not so surprising, when his age is considered. He was then seventy-five years old, and he died in March 1820 after being Rector of Stockport for 40 years.

Mr. Harrison [the *Observer* report continues] then went and addressed the multitude out of doors, desiring them to retire peaceably. But the people said 'No!—they only want us to go, that they may *take* you!' The people were at length prevailed on to retire, after they were assured all was safe, and that the Wind-Mill Room would be closed in one hour. This simultaneous movement of the people only proved an adjournment to the Market-Place, where a number of their friends had been abused by the vanquished party; and, indeed, there again the fight commenced; when the Military and Magistrates attended, a second time, and read the Riot Act. The multitude again dispersing; but rallied the following hour, and, we understand, gave their opponents such a complete drubbing, as they will have cause to remember to the last moment of their disgraceful existence. The Riot Act was read a third time; and the people retired to their houses, and as they went on, the streets rung in full chorus, the popular song of 'Millions be Free!'

At the dinner-party before these later events took place, the leaders basked in the light of the inspiring happenings of the day. Mr Fitton presided, he was the hero of the hour. A toast to 'The brave Patriots who so nobly defended the Cap of Liberty, on Sandy Brow, from the dastardly and contemptible attacks of the cowardly police of Stockport.' was received with enthusiasm. In proposing Mr Fitton's health, the Rev. Mr Harrison observed:

His conduct, I am sure, you cannot but approve of, for his manly and judicious endeavours to impress upon the minds of the people, at the Meeting, the necessity of acting lawfully at the critical moment, when the *Police* of Stockport attacked us on the hustings, and endeavoured to wrest the colours and Cap of Liberty from us. If he should be indicted (it is not likely he will) [Here Mr Harrison no doubt had complete faith in the Rev. Mr Prescot, J.P.'s forbearance] as chairman of the Meeting, for the conduct of that Meeting, I sincerely hope, that he may come off more than victorious.

The dinner-party broke up about 10.30. 'During the greater part of the evening, they were protected by the Military, outside the building, with fixed bayonets; which had only the effect of giving life and interest to the occasion.' At the end of John Thacker Saxton's careful report (there were some omissions) of this great meeting, he adds one of his more-than-self-revealing paragraphs, intended to inspire, if not to incite, the radicals to greater achievements; and at the same time intimidate those who were reading every word, wondering to what it was all going to lead:

Here the Row, which was conceived and hatched under the auspices of the Government party, ended: the next time they attempt such an unlawful interference in the lawful exercise of the People's Rights, our wish is, that their sousing may be doubled.[1]

Dr Read's brief comment[2] on a Norris-to-Home-Office letter written just after this Stockport event is not without justification: 'Norris's fears were beginning to rise now'. There is evidence, important it might be thought, of the magisterial attitude both in the Rev. Mr Prescot's conduct at Stockport and Mr Norris's reaction at a point of higher authority at Manchester. The latter 'regretted', so he informed the Home Office, 'the attempt on the Cap of Liberty, "as it gave the multitude an apparent triumph".'[3] Not without reason were Norris's fears beginning to rise; the Stockport incident was momentous. Within days of the event, Sandy Brow inspired verses:

SANDY BROW FIGHT

All hail! the day what I do see,
It is the Cap of Liberty,
Placed on the Rights of Man:
No Corn Laws! Britons shall be Free!
It is our Heavenly King's decree
That man shall have his Liberty;
And hinder it who can.

True peace and concord did pervade,
And due attention too was paid,
To what each Speaker said;
Till Tawny Jack's infernal crew,
With Pudding's gang and B——ch's too,
On Cock-horse got with much a-do,
To take the Cap 'twas said.

A monstrous Pudding, six feet high,
A solemn vow had made to die,
Or bring the Cap away:
Then off he set like Hudibras,
With Syderophel close at his a——s,
And all the Dandys fore and aft,
Stood gaping for their prey.

These bloated vampires rode about,
Till one curs'd hand was stretched out,
For th' Cap of Liberty;

---

[1] *Manchester Observer,* 20 February 1819.
[2] Above, p. 50.
[3] Quoting Read's note on H.O. 42/184, Norris to Sidmouth, 20 February 1819.

Then vengeance tinged with bitter gall,
Burst from each heart both great and small,
And courage true was firm with all,
To drub the Cavalry.

Then helter skelter sticks and stones,
From every side flew at the drones,
And drove them all away;
Wigs, stays and wiskers, took their legs,
And Dandy stunk with rotten eggs,
Still Pudding's now hangs on the pegs,
For Britons rul'd the day.

G.A., Stockport, 24 February 1819[1]

There was a still more inspired muse than G. A.'s at work on the stirring events at Sandy Brow which found expression soon afterwards in the local idiom:

Ha! han they ta'en our cap and flag;
Wot! han the Dandies ta'en 'em?
And did Reformers' courage lag,
An' could they not regain 'em?
And did the Gentles ride so gay,
Wi' Birch and Loyd afore 'em?
To sweep the 'Gruntin' herd away,
Or bravely gallop o'er 'em?

O! wot could stan' afore the might
O' Yeomanry so loyal?
Who came to drive the 'herd' aright,
An' would ha' no denial;
Until the stones began to fly,
An' heads began o' crackin',
An' then our Gallant Yeomanry
Were fain to find a backin'.

But first, came Birch, the Deputy,
Our cap and flag demandin';
I' faith, afore he'd said his say,
The Lubber lost his standin'!
For, up there stepp'd a lusty lad,
And knock'd his shanks fro' under;
An' laid his shoon into his ribs,
Which made him gasp an' wonder.

[1] *Manchester Observer,* 6 March 1819.

An' then came one o' Nadin's cubs,
    An' he essayed to take it;
But, Mister Bangy got his dubs,
    Which made him soon forsake it;
For, Saxton blun'd his thievin' e'e,
    An' gan his jaw a welter,
Which made him 'right about' to flee,
    As fast as he could skelter.

Then amblin' up the 'Gemmen' came,
    Towards the front o' th' Hustin';
But soon their folly did they blame,
    The 'rabblement' for trustin';
For sticks were up, and stones they flew,
    Their gentle bodies bruisin',
An' in a hurry they withdrew
    Fro' such unmanner'd usin'.

Then proudly let our banner wave,
    Wi' freedom's emblem o'er it,
And toasted be the Stockport lads,
    The lads who bravely bore it,
An' let the 'war-torn' Yeomanry
    Go curse their sad disasters,
An' count in rueful agony,
    Their bruises and their plasters.

It was the muse of Samuel Bamford, and the verses were quoted with
some pride by Dr Healey, Bamford's reformer friend, at Ashton-
under-Lyne, in June 1819, when the Epic of Sandy Brow was in the
making.[1] The poem appeared in the 1821 edition of Bamford's poems,
but has come down to the present day in the alleged complete edition,
entitled, 'The Fray at Stockport, written in 1818'.[2] Sandy Brow Fight
related the 'triumph' of the weavers and radicals over authority in a not
too unexceptionable way. In any case, the constables of Stockport were
unwise, as their superiors admitted, in laying hands on this admired,
though harmless, symbol displayed at a peaceful meeting. What might
have become a legend, The Sandy Brow Fight, was overshadowed by
Peterloo. Radical folk-lore is all the poorer for its loss.

Dr Read[3] reports the refusal of Lord Sidmouth to present to the

[1] *Manchester Observer*, 19 June 1819.
[2] The words 'written in 1818' do not appear in Bamford's 1821 edition. The verses
are not included in *Passages in the Life of a Radical* although they could have been considered appropriate.
[3] Read, pp. 108–9.

Prince Regent the Manchester and Stockport Remonstrances of January and February, and Hunt's assertion in a letter sent to Sidmouth on 29 May that he would find 'some other means of making the prayers and complaints of the suffering people' known to the Prince Regent. The result, declared the Manchester magistrates, was the spate of radical meetings.

Dr Read[1] writes:

Before the appearance of Hunt's letter, Norris had still been comparatively calm. Although one of his spies had promised to produce a Radical pike, he was not too disturbed: 'It had more of a threat than anything real in it', he wrote on May 26th, 'and I consider at present that it is chiefly used to keep alive the spirit of their adherents—in other words that they are not by any means *ready for action*'. Within less than three weeks, however, under the influence of the spate of Radical meetings, his whole attitude had changed. By June 15th he was reporting that 'a very short period of two *months* at the longest is spoken of as the great Day of Trial . . . a few weeks may blow this wicked conspiracy into a Flame.' The number of meetings was indeed impressive . . .

It was not altogether 'imaginary alarm' which enabled Mr Norris to forecast the 'day' with such remarkable precision two months before the date. It is true, as Dr Read says, that his attitude changed 'under the influence of the spate of Radical meetings'. Some meetings have been under review which do throw light on this period; there were others.

The *Manchester Observer*[2] reported the great outdoor Ashton-under-Lyne meeting of Monday, 14 June when twelve to fifteen thousand people were present. The Rev. Joseph Harrison was in the chair; he quoted a letter from that old radical warrior, Major Cartwight:

That obedience is due to the laws, when founded on the constitution; but when they were subversive of the constitution, then disobedience instead of obedience is due, and resistance becomes the law of the land.

These sentiments were received with cheers. A deputation from Stockport was present with an address:

. . . We request that you will not propose or adopt anything unless you are determined to carry it into effect, for you had better remain at home to starve quietly, than be frustrated in the legal and constitutional means you may pursue to recover your Rights . . . Your brethren in opposing and annihilating oppression, the Committee of the Stockport Union, 14th June, 1819.

The Stockport resolutions (sixteen in number) were agreed, including

[1] Read, p. 108.
[2] *Manchester Observer*, 19 June 1819.

one to consider the propriety of immediately going into the election of representatives, and the resistance to taxation. They pointed out that the legislature will not heed the complaints of the people, it made them (at Stockport) 'despair of ever being attended to unless the united voice of a whole People, speaking in a voice of Thunder, can bring the Government to a sense of duty'. The Stockport delegate (a Mr Wright Smith) delivered a trenchant speech: 'The combat, he was sure, would not be hopeless—the victory he was convinced was certain. The people had at length come to a due sense of the power they possessed . . . the inhabitants of Stockport . . . wished for a Union of the whole People. The cry of "Liberty or Death" would go from one extremity of the land to the other . . . and announced another Stockport meeting in fourteen days.'

John Thacker Saxton, in his dual role of speaker and commentator, was again to make the task of the interpretation of events easier:

J. T. Saxton was convinced they had *talked* long enough; the tyrants thought they could do nothing else . . . [their] plan had not been yet suggested, but he [Saxton] now held a confidential situation in the office of the most independent newspaper in the kingdom—the original *Manchester Observer* . . . its columns were open [to the best friends of Liberty] . . . they must feel the pulse of the whole kingdom . . . If the Reformers of England can be induced to assemble in their respective districts in one day, the People then speak in a voice of thunder . . . He had been given to understand that preparations were in agitation to seize upon the Cap of Liberty by the Yeomanry cavalry, and wrest it from the hands of the People at the point of the sword. He could assure the meeting he was not dismayed either from the number or condition of the enemy; and if their aide-de-camp was in the field he would give him to understand that it should be defended, at least, with the life of one man, if such an attack was made [that life was John Thacker Saxton's] . . . he would defend the banner under which he stood even at the cannon's mouth. (Very loud Huzzas). After exhorting the people to firmness and good order, Mr. Saxton retired amidst rapturous applause.

Then came one of John Thacker Saxton's self-revealing comments on the reception of his own speech, a paragraph in square brackets:

[Upon this resolution being put from the chair, we witnessed such a display of powerful nobbed sticks as we never recollect to have seen before.[1]—these

---

[1] 'Saxton attended the meeting [of 16 August] as a newspaper reporter and was no conspirator.' (Defence counsel for Saxton at Hunt's Trial [*State Trials*, p. 282], and [ibid. p. 283] in Saxton's defence): 'They had indeed been told that the people were armed with sticks which were carried like muskets; but what proof had they that they were not ordinary walking-sticks? Why not produce even one of these deadly weapons?'

weapons of self-defence we are convinced were not for the purpose of breaking the peace, but to preserve it against those privileged violators of the Law,
who, under a fancied security of protection from the Borough-despots, are
ever ready to disturb the harmony of the people when assembled in the
exercise of the Rights of Englishmen.]

Dr Healey was also prepared, he said, to defend their Cap of Liberty
'that eyesore to the shallow-sighted aristocracy . . . he had heard that
a reward of £50 had been offered if one was seized; (information, he
said, he had got from one of the Yeomanry cavalry) . . . 'He would
be glad to see the man . . .' Dr Healey then invoked the people to
rouse themselves from their degraded lethargy; but not to act with
violence, as their combined efforts might be called into action before
they were aware, when a legal and constitutional struggle for independence must be crowned with ultimate success. Then followed
one of Mr Saxton's less effective square-bracketed paragraphs:

[Here Mr. Harrison, with great good humour, inquired 'if any gentleman
amongst the crowd had any intention of appearing against the Speakers at
Lancaster Assize next, they would be obliging as to hold up their hands'.
This produced a great burst of laughter.]

On the chairman submitting the seventh resolution to the meeting, he observed that from experience and observation, the people might be given
to understand that their former exertions had produced little or no good:

it was now necessary to wait a few weeks to take the sense of the whole
nation upon the best and most effectual means of obtaining a radical reform
in the Commons House of Parliaments. Manchester must consult with Liverpool—Stockport with Manchester—Oldham with Stockport; and so on till
the whole opinion of the country is deliberately ascertained; then, should the
borough-tyrants stand out against the whole national voice, they must be
made to know their doom. . . . [He then eulogised Mr Hunt] that respected
individual . . . perhaps the object of the solicitude and regard of the whole
nation, than any other subject in the British dominions—a gentleman, whose
private character had been assailed by both town and country newspapers,
emanating from the factions of both Whig and Tory. Not satisfied with this,
Mr. Hunt had been compelled to make great sacrifices even in his fortune—
in fact, he had suffered every way that the engines of despotism were capable
of devising—indeed the torrents of abuse had poured so unsparingly upon his
devoted head, that in some instances they had staggered some of the best
patriots of the age; and he himself was at one period, at a loss what to think
of him; but he thanked God, the veil had been taken off, and he appeared
amongst the friends of Liberty in Lancashire in all the semblance of un-
sophisticated purity. He was, he conceived, most deservedly entitled to their

warmest thanks. He commented in very warm terms upon the treatment
Mr. Hunt experienced at the Manchester theatre, by dandy officers, &c., and
concluded with the two last verses of Bamford's poem on [that] occasion:
[He had earlier quoted Bamford's 'Sandy Brow' poem]:

> But, true to Dandy stile and trim,
> They risked neither life nor limb;
>   Oh! it had cheered me,
> To see our gallant gang so stout,
> At clog and cudgel have a bout;
> So fast, so firm, amid the rout,
>   For HUNT AND LIBERTY.

> Oh! it had been well worth one's while
> To travel many a weary mile,
>   'Midst cold and wind and rain;
> But, come my lads, some other day
> We'll pin them, ere they sneak away,
> And they shall either play or pay
>   When HUNT RETURNS AGAIN.

Henry Hunt, although it was not then known, was due back in August!
Dr Read's valuable radical 'time-table' for those summer months of
1819 fills in details. He quotes Archibald Prentice[1] on the impressive
number of meetings. ' "Meetings took place about the same time",
wrote Prentice, "at Oldham, Bolton, Royton, Bury, Heywood,
Stockport, Ashton-under-Lyne, Failsworth, Gee Cross, Lees, Middleton, Rochdale, Todmorden, Barnsley, Holmfirth, Leeds, and other
towns, all unrepresented in parliament." The extent of the new
organization,' continues Dr Read, 'of which these meetings were the
public reflection was emphasized at the important delegate meeting
which the Radicals were able to call at Oldham on 7 June. Delegates
from twenty-eight towns attended, the most important part of their
work being to lend the support of the Lancashire Radicals to a proposal
for a national meeting of Radical delegates in London. The national
connections and aspirations of the local reform movement were once
more made clear.

'The new power of the Radicals', Dr Read continues, 'was strikingly
demonstrated by what happened at the meeting held on St Peter's
Field on 21 June. This meeting, called by the distressed weavers to
petition either for relief for their distresses or for assisted emigration to
North America, was won over by the Radicals Saxton and [W.C.]

[1] Prentice *Historical Sketches . . . of Manchester* (1851), pp. 150–1.

Walker to the cause of Radical Reform. Resolutions were passed urging the election of delegates in readiness for the national Radical delegate meeting in London and supporting the principle of abstention from the use of exciseable articles.'[1]

Whether the weavers' meeting was 'won over' or 'taken over' could be considered a nice point. In the first place a similar meeting had taken place at Glasgow on 16 June (noted by Mr R. J. White[2]) 'illustrating how a meeting, intended for no political purpose, might be invaded and turned to political ends.' 'At Glasgow,' he continues, 'when 40,000 poor weavers met on 16 June, in order to petition the Prince Regent for passage-money to Canada[3] for the hopelessly unemployed, an amendment was moved that no good was to be expected from anything but annual parliaments, universal suffrage, and reduction of taxation. It was carried after speeches denouncing emigration and petitioning—although it was said that its supporters knocked down the hands of those who opposed it.'

The *Observer*[4] reported the Manchester meeting called for an almost identical purpose on St Peter's Field, saying that an 'amazing concourse of people attended'; a person of the name of Moore read the petition. It related the deplorable condition of the weavers, and, couched in the language of piety appealed to 'the Christian instincts of those in Parliament . . . they plead with them for the last time.'

Many of your petitioners [they pleaded] have witnessed numbers of their fellow-workmen drop into an untimely and silent grave; and they that are living must soon share the same fate under their present circumstances; and since your petitioners must die, it is surely immaterial to them, whether they die by famine or by the sword, but they respectfully leave men of superior knowledge to judge which has the greatest torment . . .

'The reading of the petition being over,' reported the *Observer*, a Mr W. C. Walker rigged, as the sea phrase is, from stem to stern in the habiliments of a sailor, immediately jumped on the hustings and addressed the people.[5]

[1] Read, pp. 109 and 23.
[2] R. J. White *Waterloo to Peterloo* (Mercury Books 1963), p. 179.
[3] The *Manchester Gazette*, 5 June 1819, reports a similar meeting of weavers at Carlisle a few days before.
[4] *Manchester Observer*, 26 June 1819.
[5] [None were] 'more likely to bring out all the sympathies and latent Radicalism of the London crowd. British "tars" . . . were noted for their riotous dispositions; "they are always the first to *turn out* . . . whether to fight, to drink, or to dance, or to *kick up a row*." They were the popular heroes of countless ballads of the Wars.'— E. P. Thompson (p. 606) on the arrest of Cashman in London.

[Walker reminded them that 'you in rags would soon perish with cold in North America where the winter is severe'] I would sooner suffer my timbers to be shivered to atoms than descend to petition the infernal tyrants who have neglected and oppressed us all alike . . . transported from your native country, from wives, sweethearts, &c., mean and cowardly—so belay that my shipmates, and unite yourselves heart and hand, and endeavour to regain your lost rights and liberties, and no doubt we shall see in a little time, the shattered constitution of old England hoisting its true colours. I wish you not to mistake me, I would have thundering justice strike terrors to the heart of the plundering villains—that corrupt den of th——s, who are robbing the industrious class of society of millions yearly and wallowing in luxury whilst we are starving in the midst of plenty . . . [Brave Jack Tar!] . . . transport you to Canada!? . . . never ceasing taxation would get at you . . . I therefore advise you the general union in the common cause . . . remain with your families and exert yourselves to regain your rights and liberties. Some of these lubbers, who do not know what hunger is, have struck up bills this morning, advising you to starve and be content, and leave it to your superiors to judge for you. This I am certain, however, that it is nothing but cowardice that has produced this starvation, and nothing but courage and perseverance will be of benefit to us; so, like Britons, we must let our tyrants know that all they can say or do, will not satisfy us, without our just demands are complied with, viz.: a complete restoration of our rights and liberties, and these we are determined to have. [He opposed the petition, to cries of] Bravo, bravo!

'Mr J. T. Saxton, from the crowd,' the *Observer's* report goes on, 'then requested permission to address the meeting . . . ascended the hustings amidst loud cheers.' Dr Read[1] reports part, but only part, of his speech. Mr Saxton also had this to say:

No man, he said, was better qualified to appreciate the character of the English Government than a British sailor . . . hardship of neglected tars for many years had been the theme of our Lancashire poets . . . [wooden walls of Old England . . . bravery of seamen &c., . . . sailors begging their bread, like our friend Walker, &c.] . . . Their petition breathed throughout every line of it a feeling of despondency and forlorn hope . . . the abominable doctrine of passive obedience and non-resistance. He [Saxton] said they should seek for redress through a channel completely opposite to that which they were pursuing . . . join with the [radical reformers] Annual Parliaments, Universal Suffrage and Election by Ballot . . . without these blessings misery and death . . . He asked the meeting whether they were disposed to petition? [loud cries of No! no!] Will you then stand by the People and demand your rights?' [Yes! yes! from a thousand throats]. No other speaker, [the report gravely concludes] came forward.

1 Read, p. 23.

A vote was called for, and a long series of resolutions (ten in number) agreed upon. No. 10 was:

That the Union of Manchester be requested immediately to join the National Union, now in contemplation; the principles of which are imbodied in the 7th Resolution which was unanimously agreed to at a Meeting held at Hurst, near Ashton, on 14th June, 1819.

'During the meeting many attempts were made by a horde of wicked incendiaries to throw the business into confusion; but the trick being discovered, and the blackguards foiled in their designs, everything proceeded in its due course.' The 'loyalist' press reports of this meeting might well be studied with profit: in fact the *Observer* does it instead:

The *Observer*[1] reported an article in the *Manchester Mercury* on 23rd June, which said: 'These assemblings of the distressed and disaffected, the idle and the mischievous, are rapidly multiplying themselves. There is to be one next Monday at Stockport. It can no longer be reproached to these agitators, but they are covertly pursuing iniquitous objects under the pretext of seeking relief from their distresses.'

[John Thacker Saxton added to this paragraph:] 'How the base apostate writhes and spits his venom. The wretch will have an extra dose when he observes in our paper of this week a notice of a Blackburn Meeting on the same subject . . .'

'From now on,' Dr Read says, 'the magistrates' alarms were to be given no time to cool.' 28 June saw the great Stockport meeting, 'probably the greatest of the Radical meetings in the area in 1819 apart from Peterloo itself.' As such, it deserves a closer scrutiny than it has already received. Dr Read continues: 'As at Manchester, the last of the Stockport hand-loom weavers had recently gone over in despair to the Radicals', developments which he describes fully, ending with a description of the 'memorial' sent by the weavers to the Government in June 1819; the *Observer*, as usual, adds enlightenment on (a) magisterial-radical relations, and (b) a meeting which resulted in the two principal speakers—a baronet and a minister of religion—receiving prison sentences.

The *Observer*[2] records that earlier in June, 'in consequence of a requisition being presented to the rector of Stockport [the Rev. Mr Prescot] to call a public meeting on the subject of reform, the rector wishing to evade that, directed an investigation to be made into the condition of the weavers, with the professed intention of ameliorating their condition.' The investigation took place, but the radicals felt that

[1] *Manchester Observer,* 26 June 1819.
[2] *Manchester Observer,* 3 July 1819.

it was all a plan to divert them from their 'grand object of Parliamentary reform'; another meeting was called by the weavers and it was decided to spurn any idea at relief in orthodox ways; nothing but a radical reform in the people's House seemed likely to benefit them. 'This was their determination; and they would either have it or perish in the attempt.' The *Observer* published the text of their demand to the magistrates and commented:

The above is the substance of their memorial to the magistrates and by them forwarded to Lord Sidmouth last Monday, and they expect in return a quantity of Lord Castlereagh's bayonets. We believe those two words Radical Reform were rather obnoxious to the magistrates, and they wished to have them struck out; but the weavers put them in as the two corner-stones of the foundation, and would not, by any means, agree to their removal; therefore the magistrates agreed to send it as it was. A numerous meeting of weavers on Monday heard the result of the deputies' visit to the magistrates seemed well satisfied that no alteration had been made to their memorial.

Emboldened, perhaps, by this success, a requisition was sent to Mr Prescot to call a public meeting for, as they put it:

the purpose of taking into consideration what constitutional and legal steps are necessary to be adopted to get our Petitions &c to the Throne, and of making a solemn Appeal to the People of Great Britain praying them to join us in forming A NATIONAL UNION; also the propriety of considering whether the People do or do not possess [as Mr. Cobbett has suggested] the power of destroying the Bank-Bubble—being convinced 'that the main question to be decided is whether we shall submit to an additional burthen of Taxes, or Borough-monger Usurpers shall submit to a RADICAL REFORM.

The *Observer* quite seriously informed its readers that the rector had refused to call the meeting! One was therefore convened for Monday, 28 June, to be held at Sandy Brow, and Sir Charles Wolseley, the radical baronet was to attend.

Sir Charles arrived in Stockport on the Sunday night, and addressed a communication to the rector notifying him of his intention of attending the meeting, and noting:

that it having been rumoured that there is an intention on the part of some ill-disposed individuals to endeavour to create a riot, he hopes Mr. Prescot will on this information take those measures best calculated to frustrate such evil designs.

The following day a deputation waited on the rector, who received them in Stockport parish church. The *Observer* takes up the tale:

The deputation found the Reverend gentleman surrounded by a host of peace officers; and after he had looked in their direction, then at the deputation, again at the letter—a significant glance he cast at Mr. Birch, the police officer —all seemed consternation and alarm [Guy Fawkes might have been there with his match ready to fire the gunpowder and blow up the whole sanctuary]; —he then read the letter.

He assured the deputation that he could render no other assistance than that of sending an armed force to the meeting. Mr. Fitton manfully remonstrated against military interference, and assured the worthy Rector, that, if he would attend in his own person, every respect due to his situation would be strictly preserved. 'No, no,' says the Rector, 'fine talking, when stones and sticks are flying, to think that it is in the power of two or three individuals to stop the torrent!' Mr. Prescot's son pleaded with his father not to expose himself . . . to which opinion the Reverend gentleman instantly acceded, and politely wished 'good morning, to the deputation.

It hardly appears necessary to refer the reader back to the rector's touching faith in his fellow-men, (a) in his complaisance in respect of the weavers: no doubt believing the precept he had often uttered, of 'leading into the way of truth all such as have erred and are deceived'; (b) in not realizing, in his appeal to Harrison in front of the Wind-mill rooms, that the 'leader' into the way of truth, however unwittingly, was Mr Harrison; and (c) in his retort, 'Fine talking when stones and sticks are flying', which was the realization that it was he who had erred and had been deceived! It is difficult to believe that the radicals really expected to get the magistrate-rector on their platform under a requisition such as they published, especially after his recent experience. It is the last glimpse of this unusual (as some writers would suggest) clerical magistrate. His brief public appearance does his office, both as magistrate and cleric, credit.

'In the meantime,' the *Observer*[1] relates, 'the meeting assembled, with upwards of 20,000 people on Sandy Brow.' The crowd was told that Sir Charles was coming, and Mr Knight before retiring from the platform exhorted the people to good order, to which the crowd made an odd response:

Immediately after these observations, [reports the *Observer*] one of Nadin's gang was pointed out to some bystanders, who had been very officious in searching an individual on the road from Manchester to Stockport, and he was immediately 'served out' with a hearty sousing from John Bull, and was carried off the ground incapable of further mischief.[2]

[1] *Manchester Observer*, 3 July 1819.
[2] At the trial of Sir Charles and the Rev. Mr Harrison ten months later it was alleged that 'the constable was nearly put to death'. *Manchester Observer* 15 April 1820.

Sir Charles Wolseley had come, he said, 'for the purpose of giving my sanction to the proceedings of the Friends of Radical Reform, having had previous intimation of the menaces that had been held out to intimidate them in the performance of the greatest of all duties: viz. their political salvation; determined to see the brave men of Stockport have fair play . . . [he was not] indifferent to the importance of the spot of ground [Sandy Brow] on which we stand[1]—to the victory that has been achieved by the prowess and valour of my fellow-citizens who, naked and unprepared in the exercise of their rights, were attacked by a lawless banditti, every one of whom ought, if the law had been administered with impartiality, to have been committed for a breach of the peace; but the infamy, however, recoiled upon their own head, and instead of wresting from your hands your Cap of Liberty, they have rendered the name of Sandy Brow sacred to the cause of Liberty' [Cries of 'Bravo, bravo! hoist the Cap', vociferated from thousands]. Sir Charles announced the Cap was sent for.[2]

He said that here again their enemies had been defeated . . . I suppose there must be a number of police officers in this meeting [warned them not to be the first to break the peace]. Allow me to tell them, as chairman, that they must take the consequences on their own shoulders, and that it will be my duty to take cognizance of every transaction that is calculated to disturb the harmony of this great assembly of people.

Sir Charles said he also wished 'to address a few words to that set of vermin that Sidmouth has sent as a curse throughout the land, I mean the spies and informers. If there be any present let them step forth and

[1] Henry Hunt was not 'indifferent' either during his trial to the importance of Sandy Brow, for there was a curious (and to the casual reader inexplicable) anxiety on his part to prove that Moorhouse—the only one of the accused who had connections with Stockport—was not at Sandy Brow at this meeting. After Hunt had proved his point he let the matter drop. It is the only reference in the trial to Sandy Brow.— *State Trials*, p. 199.

[2] It is instructive to note the pre-Peterloo radical attachment to the Cap of Liberty and the complete *volte-face* in post-Peterloo days. At Hunt's trial the Cap was pointed out as an ancient symbol peculiarly British, perhaps with not much effect. At the Wolseley and Harrison trial shortly afterwards, Charles Pearson, the radical lawyer defending, said: 'A cap of liberty and a flag had also been descanted upon very strongly on the other side; yet he would wish to leave such topics out, being unwilling to waste the time of the jury upon such trifles. . . . He felt rather at a loss how such a subject as the cap of liberty ought to be treated. His learned brother had objected to the cap of liberty; but it would be recollected that a demur had taken place about its use and it was said that one gentleman did object to it. It was not a symbol of revolution; indeed it was a bauble not worth a wise man's notice. But to the mass of mankind, these symbols had a different effect: they are the playthings of men, and men are like children in their turn. Some men are as much pleased with rattles, trifles, rosaries and garters. But, after all that has been urged against this trifling symbol, the cap of liberty, if we inquired into history . . . [an emblem of the constitution, etc.]' *Manchester Observer*, 15 April 1820.

hear me distinctly—let them take down the words the chairman shall utter in the first instance, and then they may calculate upon a luxuriant bounty for their day's labour.'

Let them [went on Sir Charles] tell Sidmouth, Castlereagh, and the mountebank George Canning, that there is no love lost between themselves and the PEOPLE OF ENGLAND, for their hatred to the labouring classes; we, the *'lower orders'* may in just retaliation declare that we not only hate, but we despise and abominate *them* all alike, and that we do not intend to suffer our hatred to exhaust itself in *idle* words, but to use our endeavours to bring them speedily to an account for their manifold and aggravated misdeeds. [Cries of 'Bring them to trial! Bring them to trial!']

Then, with a cliché which might have been used if Sir Charles had been laying a foundation stone: 'After a few other remarks, "I will not further trespass on your time, but proceed to the business of the meeting." The Cap of Liberty was hoisted . . . Sir Charles took off his hat requesting three hearty cheers . . . the air was rent with the acclamation of the people.'

The Rev. Joseph Harrison's speech was alleged to contain the reference '. . . Whether or not the seat of royalty was or was not occupied by a pig or a man . . .' and he was also indicted for uttering in a 'sermon' preached on Sunday 15 August, at Stockport,[1] the sentiments: 'Can laws, proceeding from such a source [the House of Commons] be called the law of the land, or is it fit we should obey them?' Sir Charles made his famous 'Bastille' speech.[2] John Thacker Saxton too was in the forefront as orator as well as writer; as orator he said, amongst other things:

. . . The system of that infernal Monster Pitt, was at length coming to a close—in the course of a few months we might fairly anticipate the mortal blow, which would be succeeded by a glorious funeral . . .

To the *Observer's*[3] report he added the 1819 equivalent of a banner headline: 'BRAVE, GALLANT, AND INVINCIBLE STOCKPORT,' and Sir Charles announced the reading of 'An Appeal to the Nation by the Inhabitants of Stockport . . . on Sandy Brow . . .'

The trial of Wolseley and Harrison took place ten months later, and

[1] *Manchester Observer,* 15 April 1820.
[2] Read, p. 110.
[3] *Manchester Observer,* 3 July 1819. There were two radical *Observer* newspapers being published in Manchester during the months of June and July 1819: the second one being *Wardle's Manchester Observer* (No. 1, Vol. 1) appeared on 5 June. *Wardle's Observer* report of the Sandy Brow meeting in its issue of 3 July is milder than that of Saxton's.

made very little stir in the country because Hunt, Bamford and the others had just been found guilty of conspiracy (the charge they faced after Peterloo) and the country was resounding with the echoes of their sensational trial. The *Observer*[1] did, however, devote considerable space to the minor case. Witnesses stated that during the Sandy Brow meeting a rumour flew round that the cavalry were coming, and that many men in the crowd waved their sticks; one alleged that he saw several of the reformers in a public house with large sticks who 'wished that the cavalry might come for they were prepared for them'. Another alleged that Sir Charles said that not only was Sandy Brow consecrated to the cause of liberty, but he trusted that 'Sandy Brow would prove more famed in history than the field of Waterloo'. Sir Charles had expressed his hope too soon.

[1] *Manchester Observer*, 15 April 1820.

VI

The Magistrates, the Government
and the Radicals (1)

The communications which passed between the Manchester magistrates and the Government from the end of June 1819 until 16 August and after have long been before the world. They were first presented to Parliament in November 1819, were printed, and had a wide circulation as *Papers Relative to the Internal State of the Country*. In isolation the magistrates' fears expressed in these letters appear excessive; in the context of Manchester affairs, as we have related them here, they acquire a different hue. That these meetings could cause alarm has hitherto seemed almost unbelievable; but they were meetings with a difference. Mr Thompson has this to say:

The effect on the reformers' morale of each successive demonstration was instantaneous. With each breach of the walls of deference, the waters of insubordination swept through. The morale of each individual weaver or shoemaker was higher from the reassurance of numbers, the pageantry, the rhetoric. If the open organization of the people had continued on this scale it would have become impossible to govern. . . .[1]

Mr Thompson may have reason to demur that the quotation is wrested from its context; his contention is that the reformers were emerging not as revolutionaries but as constitutionalists. There is, however, a quaint ambiguity in the passage 'it would have become impossible to govern', for that seems to be precisely what both the Government and the magistrates felt. It is not in the scheme of the present work to even try to prove that the radicals were following revolutionary courses, but they ought not to have been surprised that their actions and menacing language seemed to suggest to the magistrates that they were.

In June, Norris was complaining that since the Act prohibiting large public meetings or 'seditious assemblies' was repealed[2] the magistrates

---

[1] Thompson, p. 682.
[2] The Act (57 Geo. III cap. 19) 'for the more effectually preventing seditious meetings and assemblies' had not been repealed. It had *expired* on 24 July 1818, after being in force from 31 March 1817.

had lost their main power;[1] to which complaint the Government was pointing out that the power in that Act to suppress seditious assemblies was only a temporary measure, and that they still had powers against riots and unlawful assemblies in their hands. The joint-magisterial letter of 1 July, after Sandy Brow, takes on a new interest; there are others in a similar vein:

Five Magistrates of Lancashire to Lord Sidmouth. 'New Bailey Court House. 1st July, 1819. . . . far from wishing to yield to unnecessary alarm; but when we entertain serious apprehensions, we cannot refrain from making them known to your Lordship. We feel a difficulty in stating any specific facts upon which legal responsibility will attach to any particular individuals at present; but upon a general view of the subject, we cannot have a doubt that some alarming insurrection is in contemplation . . . cannot but applaud the hitherto peaceful demeanour of many of the labouring classes, yet we do not calculate upon their remaining unmoved. Urged on by the harangues of a few desperate demagogues, we anticipate at no distant period a general rising, and possessing no power to prevent the meetings which are weekly held, we, as magistrates are at a loss how to stem the influence of the dangerous and seditious doctrines which are continually disseminated.

To these meetings, and the unbounded liberty of the press, we refer the principal weight of the evil which we apprehend. We believe, on Monday next, a meeting will be held at Blackburn, and on the following Monday, at Manchester, at both of which Sir Charles Wolseley is to preside. As the law now stands we cannot interfere with these meetings notwithstanding our conviction of their mischief and danger . . . [anxious to preserve the peace] but upon this important point we are unarmed.[2]

> J. Sylvester   R. Wright
> W. Marriott   C. W. Ethelston
> J. Norris.

Sir Charles, however, did not come to either Blackburn or Manchester, although he arrived in Manchester for the 9 August meeting which was abandoned. On 12 July at a massive demonstration at Birmingham he was elected 'Legislatorial Attorney' for that unrepresented city,[3] which Mr Thompson says 'pointed the way to an even more dangerous development: a National Convention, appointed by Radical Suffrage, challenging Parliament.' It was a 'development' which the Manchester radicals proposed to imitate, later, on 9 August. Henry Hunt was to be invited to attend, and Joseph Johnson, the radical brushmaker with a shop in Shudehill and who lived at Smedley Cottage,

---

[1] *State Trials*, App. B, p. 1372.
[2] *Papers Relative to the Internal State of the Country* 1819, p. 1.
[3] *State Trials*, App. B, p. 1374.

was at the beginning of July in correspondence with Hunt on the proposed visit. Dr Read deals fully with this: with Hunt's vanity and stage-management of this appearance, although, in this correspondence, the matter of an 'election' had not been broached. Johnson, however, had written:

Trade here is not worth following. Everything is almost at a stand still, nothing but ruin and starvation stare one in the face. The state of this district is truly dreadful, and I believe nothing but the greatest exertions can prevent an insurrection . . .[1]

Which, to say the least, is hardly the comment of a man conspiring towards one! Johnson was a right-wing radical.

Meanwhile the local authorities in Manchester began to act. They called their famous Police Office Meeting on 9 July 'for the purpose of adopting effectual measures for the maintenance of public peace at this important crisis'. The meeting and its proposals were widely advertised in the local press headed by the signatures of over fifteen hundred townsmen. They:

regret the commercial difficulties and embarrassments which, in their melancholy consequences unhappily afflict the working-classes as well as their employers, whose interests are mutually connected [not peculiar to Britain . . . in Europe in U.S.A. also] . . . Indignation and abhorrence at revolutionary principles now so studiously disseminated . . . in the press; the scandalous reflections upon the administration of Justice; menaces against the Prince Regent and Constituted Authorities; the numerous assemblies in populous districts where these principles are openly avowed; the continued employment of Delegates and Missionaries who subsist upon the contributions of the poor they are deluding; the Plan of Sectionary Divisions, and other well-known arrangements for preparing large bodies to act in concert; the training of these local Divisions; the preparation of Pikes and other weapons; and the approaching formation of a General Union to overthrow the Constitution of the country, under the pretext of a radical Reform of Parliament . . . [It was resolved that a Committee be formed].[2]

In addition to this, the Government began to act as well: on 7 July Lord Sidmouth wrote to the Lords Lieutenant of Lancashire, Cheshire and Warwickshire, stating that 'in view of the many public meetings in Manchester and places adjacent, the presence of their lordships in their counties was desirable.' To Lord Derby (Lord Lieutenant of Lancashire) he said: 'It is earnestly hoped that the power of the civil authorities will

[1] *State Trials,* App. B, p. 1373.
[2] *Manchester Gazette,* 17 July 1819.

be fully sufficient, but as a measure of precaution, your lordship is desired to give immediate directions to the several corps of the Yeomanry cavalry in County Lancashire to hold themselves in readiness to attend to any call for support and assistance, which in case of necessity they may receive from the magistrates.'[1] On 10 July Norris was asking Lord Sidmouth for an Act to prevent 'these meetings', which 'would give great relief to all parts of this agitated country'; the alarm, he said 'was excessive'.[2]

As a result of the Earl of Derby's initiatory moves, there came about the formation in Manchester of an 'armed association'—a kind of Home Guard to which weapons were to be eventually made available; recruiting was, however, slow. The weapons were never issued and never left the custody of the military authorities. As a result of Lord Derby's move, Dr Read alleges, the sabres of the Manchester and Salford Yeomanry were sent to the cutlers.[3]

The radicals' reactions to these preparations were fierce and immediate, except that they reserved their censure of the Earl of Derby till after 16 August and this, in the main, on account of his letter of 2 August putting into operation the Watch and Ward Acts:

We had never before conceived that the Earl of Derby was the complete tool of the administration, but his bare faced tergiversation in relation to the disturbances which he and his coadjutors *foresaw* because they were predetermined, has marked his character with a stain which all the Lethean waters of the vile Boroughmongers will not be able to wash out. The measure of Watching and Warding . . . appears to have originated with his lordship, was but the prelude to the tragedy which was shortly afterwards to be exhibited. We are not fond of looking on the dark side of human nature, but we are afraid that the unities to be discerned in this bloody spectacle of death, was not the effect of accident: the place, time, and action must have undergone a rehearsal, and we confess that the performers in the piece, from the Earl of Derby down to Joe Nadin, were perfect in their several parts.

Like other radical allegations, this charge against the Earl of Derby was quite unwarranted. It was based on an official document: 'Earl Derby (on 2 August ordered the general session of the Justices to take place on 12 August to put into action the Watch and Ward Acts'; a document quoted in *Peterloo Massacre* p. 195, and which preceded the castigation quoted above. Lord Derby wrote to Lord Sidmouth (15 August) telling him:

[1] *State Trials*, App. B, pp. 1373–4.
[2] Ibid., p. 1374.
[3] Read, p. 116; but see below, pp. 261–63.

. . . that in consequence of a representation made to me by the select committee of Magistrates assembled in Manchester (and perfectly agreeing with them on the expediency of the measure) I issued a precept for a special meeting of the magistrates to consider of the propriety of a general execution of the Watch and Ward Act.[1]

The radicals' *dramatis personae* was not quite so distinguished as they thought.

The *Observer*[2] commenting on the Police Office meeting, and especially on the recruitment of special constables, referred to a Police Office declaration intended for:

. . . the signatures of such GREENHORNS as they could catch. Of course, a list of these animals was procured to countenance the TRICK. Numbers, however, have since been to us, and expressed their contrition at having been induced to sign against the PEOPLE, and indeed, it will afford us much pain to be compelled to place their names in the list of those we shall feel it our duty to record in the EXTRAORDINARY BLACK BOOK, which will speedily be ready for publication, for the Information of the Public. This shews the propriety for every Man 'to look before he leaps.'

It is laughable to see our wiseacre Police Association have recourse to *Signatures* in behalf of their measures—were we to adopt only one-hundredth part of their stupid exertions, we could overwhelm them in the proportion of a *Thousand to One*. Away with your shuffling, before we devour you stump and branch . . .

One of the magistrates' letters to Sidmouth stated that four principal inhabitants of Bury had volunteered the information of 'their utter inability to resist the torrent of disaffection without military aid; and that persons proper to serve as special constables were so intimidated that without the presence of some military they doubted their inability to induce them to come forward to be sworn on the day appointed . . .'[3]

A letter in the *Observer*, again on the Police Office meeting:

. . . Do you suppose the people will bear these frequent insults without resenting them? No, surely not! If you value not your own lives, for the sake of your wives and children forbear; lest they should become also a sacrifice. Every breeze from heaven seems to whisper 'to your Tents O Israel?' Be cautious how you provoke a people's vengeance, for if you once raise the *storm*, your puny efforts to arrest its progress would be blasted in the heightening of its career.[4]

[1] *Papers Relative to the Internal State of the Country*, p. 26.
[2] *Manchester Observer*, 17 July 1819.
[3] *Papers Relative to the Internal State of the Country*, p. 18, dated 10 August.
[4] *Manchester Observer*, 24 July 1819.

Dr Read, in surveying the pre-Peterloo radical scene, quoted one of John Thacker Saxton's flights of oratory with the observation:

But all this was merely in the realm of words, and due allowance must be made for the excitements of the moment. Radical language often outran Radical intention; the considered intentions of the Radicals were much more restrained than their occasional outbursts might suggest . . . [and in another passage] Leaving aside then these occasional aberrations of language, it is clear that the Radical reformers in 1819 were expounding a highly detailed and peaceable programme of reform . . .[1]

It is perfectly possible now to see that they were expounding such a programme, but it is arguable as to its being a peaceable one. But they were 'expounding' it to their contemporaries, a very great number of whom just didn't believe them; they believed, as the Police Office manifesto said, they were 'planning to overthrow the Constitution of the country, under the pretext of a radical reform of Parliament'.

Some of the letters passing between the Magistrates and the Government in those pre-Peterloo weeks concern the radicals' alleged arming themselves with pikes. As, however, no charges of any kind were made by the magistrates on this score, pikes do not affect the issue. Their first report after Peterloo said, 'There was no appearance of arms or pikes, but great plenty of sticks and staves . . .'[2]; and although Lord Sidmouth did say in Parliament (in November 1819) '. . . persons carrying with them caps of liberty, pikes bearing the appearance of having been dipped in blood, and flags inscribed . . .'[3] etc., the point was never pursued save that Opposition replies seized on Sidmouth's slip to give it emphatic denial. The only evidence at all brought forward of the radicals being armed at Peterloo was provided by the 'independent' witness, the Rev. Mr Stanley, who, when he was called to give evidence at the second trial, gave it against the magistrates. In his privately circulated account of the transactions[4] he states that he saw 'nothing like arms', but that afterwards he was shown a 'couple of short skewers or daggers fixed in wooden handles', which a constable had taken in the fray. This, of course, was not introduced during his evidence at the trial. During the pre-Peterloo period, however, the possibility of secret arming on whatever scale must have added its quota to the magistrates' alarms, and they were obliged to take due note of the evidence.

[1] Read, p. 46. Cf. also Jeremy Bentham's statement (below p. 87).
[2] *Papers Relative to the Internal State of the Country*, p. 28.
[3] *Parliamentary Debates*, XLI, 1819-20.
[4] Bruton *Three Accounts of Peterloo by Eyewitnesses* (1921), p. 22.

A more important element of alarm before Peterloo was caused by the secret or open drillings; Bamford insisted that there was nothing secret about them, but that the radicals, having often been taunted with the charge of their being a ragged mob,[1] were anxious to acquire 'expertness and order while in moving bodies'. Dr Read deals fully with the charges of secret drilling, calling them 'the final addition to the magistrates' many alarms'.[2]

Bruton,[3] on the other hand, accepts Bamford's explanation without reservation: 'there seems to be no reason why the explanation should not be accepted . . . It is easy for those of us who know the beautiful green uplands to which Bamford refers, to believe his statement that "to the sedentary weavers and spinners these drillings on the open moors were periods of healthful exercise and enjoyment". His description of them is one of the most charming passages in all his writings . . .' Bruton then adds: 'The authorities saw fit to take quite another view of the drills.'

The point to be made in this work on the drillings was made by Dr Read: they were the final addition to the magistrates' many alarms. Bruton, in rounding-off the radical version of Peterloo with his account, might have been surprised that the future historian of the working class 'saw fit' also 'to take quite another view of the drills'. Mr Thompson was making the point that the Blanketeers of 1817 were country weavers who, he says, were again dominant in 1819:

These were the men[4] whose nightly drillings, of which Bamford has left idyllic and over-innocent descriptions, were the prelude to Peterloo. [The mill-hands of Manchester had neither the time for such preparations, nor the secluded moors upon which to undertake them.] These were the people, too, whose great orderly contingents—from Lees and Saddleworth, Middleton and Rochdale, Oldham and Bury—filled so large a part of St. Peter's Fields on 16 August 1819. And, just as the more extreme 'physical force' party in the provinces waited upon London for a signal, so many of the upland weavers waited impatiently for Manchester to commence the insurrection. Fury, not only against the authorities, but also [one suspects] against this apathetic Babylon of the factory-system, nourished the talk in 1817, and again in 1819, of starting the insurrection by making a 'Moscow of Manchester' . . .

If Mr Thompson, after his impressive researches into radical source material for his history, could not wholly accept Bamford's 'idyllic and

---

[1] Bamford, I, pp. 176–7.
[2] Read, pp. 124–6.
[3] *Story of Peterloo*, p. 15.
[4] Thompson, p. 647.

over-innocent descriptions' of the drillings, even though he was really referring to 1817, is it surprising that the magistrates of 1819 could not accept them either?

The magistrates' disbelief in the theory that Bamford was to put forward later is expressed in Norris's letter even as late as 12 August: To Lord Sidmouth (re drillings in the neighbourhood): '. . . Many more may be added to the number, but I apprehend those which I now send will be sufficient to assure your lordship of this alarming practice. They affect to say that it is for the purpose of appearing at Manchester in better order &c., on Monday next; but military discipline was not requisite for this purpose, and that it is impossible not to feel a moral conviction that insurrection and rebellion is the ulterior object.'[1]

Amongst these pre-Peterloo documents there was a sober and restrained 'Address from the Grand Jury of Lancashire, at the Quarter Sessions at Salford, to the Magistrates' expressing[2]:

. . . united concern and abhorrence [of] . . . that foul and restless spirit of sedition which has so long been maturing its desperate designs, and has so frequently disturbed the public peace, assuming at the present moment a tone of defiance, and pursuing a system of organization which unquestionably indicate an approaching effort to involve this country in all the horrors of a revolution . . . We are well assured that the magistrates and local authorities of the district will adopt every measure of precaution . . . for public safety . . . expedient . . . [the] immediate establishment of armed associations . . . whilst we thus feel the urgent necessity of providing for the public security against every lawless and treasonable attempt of the abettors of revolution, we are not insensible to the distress which prevails among the labouring classes of society, in consequence of the present serious depression of our commerce. We know that the wants and privations which the families of the industrious labourer now endure owing to the low rate of wages, are extremely severe; and we feel it our duty to recommend the adoption of every possible means for their relief . . . [What they believe to be the reasons for the depression] It is evident therefore to the plain reason and understanding of every honest man, that any attempts to disturb the public tranquility and to seize this occasion of carrying into effect revolutionary designs against the state, can only serve to increase and embitter our present misfortunes; to interrupt the regular course of trade; and to retard the return of better and more prosperous times; and we fervently hope that such of our misguided countrymen as may have been seduced from their allegiance will yet seriously pause: and consider that if they persevere in the wicked course they are now pursuing, they will inevitably bring upon themselves the just and severe punishment of the offended laws of their country.

[1] *Papers Relative to the Internal State of the Country*, p. 19.
[2] Ibid., p. 8.

Meanwhile the radicals, through the *Observer*, were still inveighing against the results of the Police Office meeting and the activities of the authorities, giving the impression that they had their opponents on the run. On 17 July[1] loyalist flesh was once more made to creep:

The destiny of England is near at hand. The situation is drawing near, when a constitutional stand against the corruptions of the day, is to be made. The reign of oppression is near to its close, its dying embers are fast receding from our sight; and the spirit of freedom is rearing her head in lofty triumph over the departing tyrant that has so long usurped her place.

The crouching aristocrats have taken the alarm; hurry and bustle with them, appear to be the order of the day. Soldiers are pouring in from all quarters; special constables are swearing in; the feather-bed cavalry are ordered to hold themselves in readiness, and sharpen their swords; and a declaration is now handing about for signatures, to protect their constitution and properties: from whom, think you? why, truly from that grunting herd, styled the Swinish Multitude; ... (the constitution) is in danger of being upset by ... animals who are said never to be in their glory, but when wallowing in filth and mire . . . a hungry pig will not stand on ceremonies: if a meal stand in an earthenware mug before him, he will not miss it on account of the risk he runs of destroying the vessel in which it is enclosed . . . In the Police [Office] Declaration it is said: 'We the undersigned being impressed with the danger that threatens the community . . .' [is the community, I wonder, the privileged few who are allowed to live in luxury from the hard earnings of the millions?] . . . Do the declarers think that their efforts to support a tottering fabric will be of any avail? Do they really suppose that the signatures they are endeavouring to obtain can intimidate the reformers? . . . The die is cast, upwards of a million have within these few days declared their determination to be free; and who can prevent them? . . . It would be well if the declarers would take warning before it is too late. [The article was signed 'Alfred' and dated: Manchester, 13 July.]

'Alfred's' letter was not the only one; in the same issue was the often-part-quoted letter which has been used as evidence to show that the radicals had developed an utter contempt for the Manchester and Salford Yeomanry Cavalry. It is worth quoting in its entirety. The writer was William Fitton, of Royton, erstwhile champion of Sandy Brow, and protester to the Rev. Mr Prescot when that reverend gentleman offered him the 'protection' of a military force for the second Sandy Brow meeting, but who had been content to preside at the dinner in the Wind-mill rooms, 'protected by Military, outside the building, with fixed bayonets; which had only the effect of giving life

[1] *Manchester Observer,* 17 July 1819.

and interest to the occasion.' Mr Fitton addressed his letter 'To the Pig-Tailed Gentry of Manchester':[1]

I believe it is not quite unknown to you, that I have for a considerable time past, held you in the most sovereign contempt. Your uniform opposition to the best interests of the state, by giving your support to the late wicked, and unprincipled War, against France, together with your most decided support of the present corrupt system since the termination of that war, has operated to produce this feeling in my mind against you.

But what has increased it to a much greater degree, is your late meeting, in the Police Office, to agree to a memorial to Old Mother Sidmouth, requesting the old lady to use her influence in procuring another suspension of the Habeas Corpus Act, in order that you might have another opportunity of gratifying your political spleen, against men, who are as much your superiors in talent, as in political honesty: this only increased my indignation, but not my surprise, for I have long known there is no act of meanness, no measure of dishonesty, of which you are not capable. Men may, for a long time, act improperly, and badly, from error; you however have not this plea as an excuse; for adversity in that case takes wisdom, points out, and produces a different line of conduct; no adversity of a country however great, no misfortunes however terrible, even among your friends or trading associates, produces among you sympathy for their sufferings or a wish to alleviate them. No! Blindly attached to the System of that monster Pitt, and conceiving all political excellence to consist, in supporting that ruinous system, as I before observed, you hesitate at no means, however unjust, at no measure however wicked, for the accomplishment of your object.

You are ever found the ready tools of oppression, in all its various shapes, hence the mountebank Canning; the bloodthirsty C——; the old Lady Sidmouth; the canting Vansittart; and the calculating Jenkinson, with his 'stern path of duty', ever employ you in your subordinate capacity, to carry their infamous schemes into complete effect. If they want a green-bag, who so fit, because who so willing, to furnish it, as the mean-minded, dastardly-souled, Pig-Tailed Gentry of Manchester? If they want some false statements, against honest but unfortunate men; some wretches who think perjury no crime, who so fit to furnish it as the Pig-Tailed Gentry of Manchester, with the all-potent Nadin as their assistant?

Reason has been so often employed, and so often failed, in bringing you to a proper mode of conduct, that it is a quixotish idea, to suppose that it will ever prevail; yet we might almost expect that fear would do what reason cannot. If you were not as stupid as you are base, I would ask you whether you do not think your repeated acts of provocation, might possibly rouse the vengeance of an insulted, injured and indignant population? Indeed, it almost appears, that this sentiment does begin to prevail, amongst your dandy

[1] *Manchester Observer*, 17 July 1819.

whiskered heroes: alias, stupid boobies, alias Yeomanry cavalry, inasmuch, as that it is currently whispered, that they are anxious to get home and get spared; that is get discharged from the dangerous service in which they are engaged, by procuring substitutes; Oh! is this their loyalty then? What, they smell danger, do they? They have heard rumours among the poor weavers' pikes, have they? And now shrink back! Brave fellows! And well they may; for half a dozen hungry, angry weavers would eat a whole corps of Yeomanry fellows. Pig-Tailed Gentry, I have something of greater consequence to attend to, and shall therefore take my leave of you, that if you (as I much suspect) have no greater respect for me, than I have for you, there is no love lost between us.

July 12 1819   WILLIAM FITTON.

It might be thought that there was, in William Fitton's letter, a hint of frustration: that despite all the blusterings and threatenings by the radicals, those 'stupid' authorities had not yet succumbed, and a baffled Fitton cogitates on 'where they go from here'. His letter lacks the direct intimidatory tones of 'Alfred's' or the confident denunciatory tone of John Thacker Saxton's leading articles. There seems to be an anxiety lest the radicals should be checkmated.

Things however were moving as a result of the determined loyalist steps following the Police Office meeting. On 23 July there was a general meeting of magistrates at the New Bayley Court House, Salford, at which thirty-one magistrates from Lancashire and Cheshire attended. It was probably an unprecedented number; Wilbraham Egerton (Cheshire) was in the chair. The resumé of their communiqué issued to the press after the meeting said:

A very disturbed spirit in the manufacturing districts. Special constables should be appointed. Peaceful inhabitants should form Voluntary Associations under the Magistracy for action, and should apply to the Lord Lieutenant for arms. A select committee to be formed consisting of the following magistrates: Thos. W. Tatton, Trafford Trafford, William Hulton, John Entwisle, Ralph Fletcher, William Marriott, Richard Marsh, James Norris, Thos. Dunham Whittaker, D.D., Rev. John Holme.

There are some curious omissions in the list of names of magistrates forming this committee. This may seem to be of little consequence when this committee acted for so short a time. It is, however, of very great consequence indeed when it is remembered that the word 'acted' means taking the vital (to quote Mr Thompson) 'decision to disperse the meeting by force' this 'foreseen', this *pre*-determined' step.[1] That

[1] p. 74 —and nearly all the histories since that date.

decision was taken during that span of less than three weeks, or it was taken after 11 o'clock on the morning of 16 August, or it was not taken at all.

The first notable omission is that of the Rev. William Robert Hay, who was to share, with William Hulton and the Rev. Charles Wickstead Ethelston, most of the odium for that 'decision', and who for a time was the *bête noire* of the whole transaction. The committee had been deliberating for fourteen days before Hay was called in on 5 August.[1] His sworn evidence:[2] Mr Hay was not a member of the committee, because he was obliged to return home into Yorkshire; he withheld himself from them until he found it necessary to come to Manchester on 5 August, owing to the meeting (prohibited) on the 9th. He gave them what advice and assistance he thought requisite, wishing not to interfere with their general arrangements. Mr Hay was the stipendiary chairman of the Salford Quarter Sessions, attending four times a year, but lived at Ackworth, Yorkshire.

Because the *State Trials* edition of the Redford *v* Birley trial is abridged at this point,[3] the Rev. Mr Hay's evidence on when he joined the magistrates' committee is overlooked. It appears in full in the Farquharson (Manchester printed) edition. The omission has doubtless led to some of the misapprehensions about Hay's part in these pre-Peterloo activities. Farquharson's text is as follows:

The Rev. Wm. Robert Hay cross-examind by Mr. Serjeant Cross.

Q. . . . We understand from Mr. Hulton, that you occasionally assisted the committee of magistrates?

A. I did.

Q. Though you were not yourself one of them?

A. I was not one of them, because I was obliged to return home into Yorkshire, and could not give constant attendance; and therefore, I withheld myself till I found it necessary to come to them.

Q. On what day preceding the 16th of August did you arrive in Manchester?

A. As soon as I heard that the magistrates had forbidden the meeting that was to take place on the 9th, I immediately set out; and I believe that was on the 4th: and I slept at Wakefield, and got, in good time the next day, to Manchester.

Q. That would be the 5th August?

A. That would be the 10th or 11th day before the meeting of the 16th.

---

[1] *State Trials,* App. B, p. 1381.
[2] *Redford v. Birley* (Farquharson), pp. 426–7.
[3] *State Trials,* p. 1179.

Q. Did you remain there, Sir, to perform the duties of a magistrate, till after the meeting was over?

A. I remained there till the afternoon of the 17th.

Q. During all that time were you employed in concerting measures for the public safety.

A. I gave what attendance I could to the gentlemen of the committee. I had constant access to them, and I gave them such advice and assistance as I thought was requisite, wishing not to interfere with their general arrangements.[1]

The next curious omission is that of the Rev. C. W. Ethelston; he was not a member of the committee, but as a Manchester magistrate, a Fellow of the Collegiate Church, and rector of St Mark's, Cheetham Hill, he was present in Mr Buxton's house on 16 August, signed the warrant and because of his powerful voice was recruited to read the Riot Act which, it was generally alleged, no one heard. As a resident Manchester magistrate, the omission of his name from the committee lends a little more point perhaps to Richard Cobden's later argument[2]

Recollect that the massacre of the 16th August, 1819, could not have occurred if Manchester had been incorporated . . . —and why? Because the united magistrates of Lancashire and Cheshire, who then entered the town to hold their bench at the Star Inn, take command of the police, and order the soldiers to cut down and trample upon unarmed crowds, would, in such a case, have no more jurisdiction over Manchester than Constantinople.

There are, so far as is known, no minutes of the proceedings of this fateful committee. A glimpse of its work was given by William Hulton in his evidence at the two subsequent trials. He was appointed chairman at its first meeting; not, as Hunt tauntingly had suggested, because no one else would take the chairmanship, but at the unanimous wish of the committee. He had, as has been seen, some claims; not least of those being his activity as a magistrate (although in a subordinate role) in similar times of disturbance and riot seven years previously. His late 'principal', Col. Fletcher of Bolton, was also on the committee, but perhaps advancing years, or, a former alleged reputation (amongst the radicals at any rate) of 'arch-fiend' precluded him in favour of the young and vigorous Hulton.

The 'disturbed state of the country' was the only topic; they knew 'that in every town and in almost every village, there were union societies, conducted by committees corresponding with each other by

1 *Redford v. Birley* (Farquharson edn.), p. 426.
2 Read, p. 206, quoting Cobden *Incorporate Your Borough* (1838), pp. 5–6.

means of delegates' and there was a 'general panic throughout the district'. The frequency of meetings varied from that time until 16 August; before the 9th they had held meetings almost daily; the reports coming in produced a rapid increase of alarm for the public safety.[1]

[1] *State Trials*, p. 1172.

VII

The Magistrates, the Government
and the Radicals (2)

Before 23 July, when the joint committee of Lancashire and Cheshire magistrates was formed, preparations were going forward between the committee of the Manchester Patriotic Union Society, with Johnson as their correspondent, and Henry Hunt for the proposed Manchester August meeting. The date however had not yet been settled; at first, it was intended for 21 August[1] (Hunt to Johnson): 'I think by management the *largest assemblage* may be procured (on) 21 August that was ever seen in this country.' A letter from Johnson to Hunt (written 10 July)[2] showed that the date was brought forward to 2 August, and he enclosed an invitation, and told Hunt he had received letters from Sir Charles Wolseley and Major Cartwright stating that they meant to attend. 'Write by the first post,' said Johnson, 'your letter was two days longer on the way than it ought to have been.' Such a passage was a reminder of the slow communications between Manchester and the capital; the time between the dispatch of a letter to London and a reply being received in Manchester seemed to be normally about four days. The passage gave intelligence of another fact: the reformers' letters were being intercepted.

The 12 July meeting at Birmingham, at which Sir Charles was elected 'legislatorial attorney', brought swift reaction from the Government. Their decision was communicated to Norris, in a letter dated 17 July, that persons involved in such elections were 'guilty of a high misdemeanour and should be prosecuted for conspiracy'.

[17 July; Hobhouse to Norris, conveys the decision] Lord Sidmouth therefore hopes that, if such an election should be attempted at Manchester, measures will be taken for bringing the offenders to justice. From the opinion of the Law Officers it follows that a meeting held for the purpose of such election is an unlawful assembly. But if the meeting is not convened for the unlawful

---

[1] *State Trials*, App. B, p. 1373.
[2] Ibid., p. 1374.

purpose, the illegality will not commence until the purpose is developed, and of course after the crowd has been collected; when it must be a question of prudence and expediency, to be decided by the magistrates on the spot, whether they should proceed to disperse the persons assembled. Lord Sidmouth has no doubt that the question will be judiciously decided by the magistrates of Manchester.[1]

It was an important communication, because the Manchester magistrates were shortly to be faced with an identical situation; they leaned heavily on that letter, more heavily than Lord Sidmouth intended.

There was, however, a further complication developing, and one generally overlooked. The law officers of the Crown were deliberating how far Hunt had become compromised by his active participation in the great Smithfield meeting in London on 21 July—the meeting at which the Rev. Joseph Harrison was arrested on the hustings, and where alleged seditious resolutions had been proposed and carried, with Hunt as chairman. Although Hunt probably did not realize it then, what he *had* done at Smithfield was to be associated with his alleged intentions later when he arrived in Manchester.[2] In the meantime he was preparing, in his correspondence with Johnson, for his second and more sensational visit to Manchester. The date was finally settled for Monday, 9 August.

Dr Read[3] relates the sequence of these national Radical meetings with precision:

After Birmingham the next meeting in this series was held at Hunslet Moor, near Leeds, on July 19th. Knight, Fitton, and the local middle-class Radical Edward Baines, were the principal speakers. The meeting agreed to 'the election of a representative to parliament, whenever a proper one could be met with'. The numbers attending were perhaps not so large as the reformers had expected, only four or five thousand according to *The Times*; but, despite this, the decision to prepare for the election of a Legislatorial Attorney on the Birmingham model made the meeting an important event in the progress of the Radical agitation.

Two days after the Leeds meeting the Radicals held a rally in London itself, at Smithfield. Some ten thousand people were present according to *The Times*, and Hunt was the principal speaker. Among the other Radical leaders present was Harrison from Stockport who was actually arrested while the meeting was in progress for his speech at Stockport on June 28th. The meeting passed eighteen resolutions, and these assumed an especial importance later because they were used by the prosecution at Hunt's trial as evidence of his dangerous intentions at Manchester. The most important point which

[1] *State Trials*, App. B, p. 1375.
[2] Ibid.
[3] Read, pp. 112–13.

3. Henry Hunt, Esq.

they made was to claim that because the House of Commons had 'not been fairly and freely nominated or chosen by the voices or votes of the largest proportion of the members of the State,' any laws which it enacted or taxes which it imposed were not in equity obligatory upon those who were unjustly excluded from the franchise. The meeting resolved therefore 'that from and after the 1st of January, 1820, we cannot conscientiously consider ourselves as bound in equity by any future enactment which may be made by persons styling themselves our representatives, other than those who shall be fully, freely, and fairly chosen by the voices or votes of the largest proportion of the members of the State.'

Such language [goes on Dr Read's account] as this certainly seemed to threaten anarchy; and the government and magistrates were not disposed to believe, as Bentham suggested a few days later in the *Observer*, that the language of the reformers far outran their intentions.

The authorities worst fears seemed only to receive confirmation when on July 23 Birch, the constable bringing Harrison back under arrest from Smithfield, was shot at and seriously injured in Stockport. A reward was immediately offered for the discovery of the intended assassin and the Radicals were naturally accused of the deed. In fact, the culprit was a silk weaver who had acted entirely on his own initiative. Hunt wrote to Johnson saying he was 'sorry for the Act; it will give the Villians of the Press such a handle'. . . . A week after the Birch affair appeared the first public announcement of the intended Peterloo meeting. The present intention was to hold the meeting on August 9th:

The Public are respectfully informed, that a MEETING will be held here on Monday the 9th of August, 1819, on the area near ST. PETER'S CHURCH, to take into consideration, the most speedy and effectual mode of obtaining Radical Reform in the Commons House of Parliament; being fully convinced, that nothing less can remove the intolerable evils under which the People of this Country have so long, and do still, groan: and also to consider the propriety of the 'Unrepresented Inhabitants of Manchester' electing a Person to represent them in Parliament; and the adopting Major Cartwright's Bill.

H. HUNT, Esq. *in the Chair.*

Major Cartwright, Sir Charles Wolseley, Mr. Charles Pearson, Mr. Wooler, and Godfrey Higgins, Esq., have been solicited, and are expected to attend.

[Names of eleven signatories]

The Boroughreeve, Magistrates, and Constables are requested to attend.

The Manchester magistrates' committee were here faced with an identical problem like the one envisaged in Lord Sidmouth's letter of instruction already quoted (written by Hobhouse) on 17 July: the proposed 9 August meeting, to them, was plainly illegal and they promptly decided to suppress it before it assembled, by placarding the town with a prohibitory notice,[1] couched in these terms:

[Royal Coat of Arms] New Bailey Court House, Saturday 31 July, 1819. Whereas it appears by an advertisement in the 'Manchester Observer' Paper of this day that a PUBLIC and ILLEGAL MEETING is convened for *Monday the 9th day of August next,* to be held on the Area near St. Peter's Church in Manchester: We, the undersigned Magistrates, acting for the Counties Palatine of Lancaster and Chester *do hereby Caution all Persons to abstain,* AT THEIR PERIL,[2] from attending such ILLEGAL MEETINGS.

William Hulton	J. Holme
J. Norris	R. Marsh
John Entwistle	Trafford Trafford
W. Marriott	Ralph Fletcher.[3]
Thos. Wm. Tatton	

'On 30 July' Dr Read reminds us, 'the government acted again. A proclamation was issued in the name of the Prince Regent[4] condemning seditious assemblies and libels and the practice of drilling. This proclamation was posted up by the magistrates in Manchester on 3 August. The magistrates seem, however, to have acted against the proposed Radical meeting of 9 August even before they knew of the proclamation, for on the same day as its first announcement [31 July] they pronounced the intended meeting illegal.' The magistrates, it is probably more correct to say, in prohibiting the 9th meeting, were acting on something more definite than the proclamation, following Sidmouth's letter of the law as laid down on 17 July. But the letter was not quite so explicit as they had taken it to be. The Government was studying the proposal for the 9 August meeting with an intensity not visualized by the everyday Justices of the Peace in Manchester. Missives were being passed to and fro between the Home Office and the Law Officers of the Crown,

[1] The Magistrates, by this decision to prohibit the meeting, appear to have thought it a wiser course than 'deciding on the spot' whether to, or whether not to, disperse the meeting in accordance with the terms of Sidmouth's letter of 17 July. The banning of the meeting, to them perhaps, seemed less likely to lead to a breach of the peace than the alternative. Even after Peterloo, this same committee of Magistrates adopted a similar course by banning a meeting at Bolton (see below, pp. 326–32).

[2] Much derision, was hurled at the magistrates for their phrase 'To abstain at their peril from attending . . .': that the wording was an instruction to *attend* the meeting. James Scarlett, K.C., in prosecuting Hunt, observed that 'it was an idiom well justified by our language, although it was criticised, because not understood by those who are not acquainted with the idiom . . .' (*State Trials,* p. 412).

[3] *Manchester Gazette,* 7 August 1819.

[4] *State Trials,* App. B, p. 1376.

Lord Sidmouth asking them to report to him 'whether in the event of such meeting becoming illegal by the parties proceeding to the election of a representative in Parliament, or by debating of any other illegal question, it will be competent for the magistrates to use force in the dispersion of such meeting'. Such legal niceties as whether the meeting proposed to 'elect', or merely met to consider the 'propriety of proceeding to such an election' were being churned over in Whitehall on 3 August,[1] and on that and on the next day the following letters were dispatched to Manchester:

[Hobhouse to Norris] 3 August. The Attorney-General having advised me that he sees great difficulty in pronouncing beforehand the meeting of the 9th to be illegal, considering the words of the advertisement by which it is called together, Norris is asked to call the attention of the magistrates to this circumstance with a view to their reconsidering the resolution to which they came on Saturday [31 July] of preventing the assembly. Lord Sidmouth deems it highly important that the magistrates should upon this point act strictly within the law.[2]

[Hobhouse to Norris] 4 August. Lord Sidmouth having further considered the question which was the subject of yesterday's letters, desires me to say that reflection convinces him the more strongly of the inexpediency of attempting forcibly to prevent the meeting of Monday. Every discouragement and obstacle should be thrown in its way, and the advertisement from the magistrates will no doubt have a salutary effect in this respect. But his Lordship thinks it would be imprudent to act up to the spirit of the advertisement. He has no doubt that you will make arrangements for obtaining evidence of what passes; but that if anything illegal is done or said, it may be the subject of prosecution. But even if they should utter sedition or proceed to the election of a representative, Lord Sidmouth is of opinion that it will be the wisest course to abstain from any endeavour to disperse the mob, unless they should proceed to acts of felony or riot. We have the strongest reason to believe that Hunt means to preside and to deprecate disorder. I ought to have mentioned that the opinion which I have expressed for Lord Sidmouth is supported by that of the highest law authorities.[3]

The Manchester committee of magistrates had committed their first blunder. They had read too literally the 17 July instruction, and acted with promptitude, but they called down upon themselves a mild rebuke from their superiors.

The signatures affixed to the 'Abstain at your peril' notice show who comprised the committee on 31 July. There was only one professional

1 *State Trials*, App. B, p. 1377.
2 *State Trials*, App. B, p. 1378.
3 *State Trials*, App. B, p. 1379.

legal mind amongst them, James Norris. Sidmouth's rebuke soon altered that, and Mr Hay 'found it necessary to come to Manchester on 5 August', to give them 'what advice and assistance he thought requisite, wishing not to interfere with their general arrangements'. But their bold step, so it seemed, had paid off! They made their explanations to the Government:

[Norris to Sidmouth] 4 August. I am sorry to find by the latter part of Mr Hobhouse's letter that any doubts are entertained as to the propriety of declaring the intended meeting on Monday [9 August] to be illegal in consequence of the peculiar wording of the advertisement. The magistrates had taken into their consideration that circumstance, but unanimously agreed that it could not alter the possible meaning of the parties to elect a representative at the time and place, and I trust the opinion of the Attorney-General when obtained, will bear us out in that.[1]

The Attorney-General's opinion did not, as it happened, 'bear them out', but events were moving too fast for the slow cogitations of the Attorney-General (Sir Robert Gifford); his decision was not arrived at until the day after Peterloo. In the meantime the Royal proclamation against seditious assemblies, election of 'representatives', drillings, etc., was posted on Manchester's hoardings on 30 July, and the *Observer*[2] reported with some zest the previous Monday's gigantic meeting at Rochdale:

Writhe and foam away, King Sidmouth, your majesty's command[3] seems to pass by unheeded. The people, on Monday last, assembled in greater numbers at Rochdale than ever were known since the first stone was laid in that ancient town; for the express purpose, too, of declaring their unalterable determination to shake off their ponderous chains. It is now of no use dwelling a moment to consider of it. Reform must come, or Revolution, with all its dreadful consequences will ensue. Whose fault is it? . . . etc.

All the now familiar features were to be observed. A crowd of fifteen to twenty thousand persons. William Fitton again harangued the crowd; he referred to a 'threat' by several 'sham-valiants' in the town and neighbourhood to seize and take away the Cap of Liberty; the meeting was justified in preserving it. An attempt, he said, had been made, similar to this some months since at Stockport, when he, Mr Fitton, had the honour to preside; the consequence was, the assailants

---

[1] *State Trials,* App. B, pp. 1379–80.
[2] *Manchester Observer,* 31 July 1819.
[3] The oblique ambiguity of these three words, in view of the Royal proclamation, probably did not 'pass by unheeded' also to the less enthusiastic readers of John Thacker Saxton's prose.

were vanquished in an instant, and the Cap and Banner were preserved, to the utter confusion of the ragamuffins, who had too lightly been persuaded to [en]counter that fruitless and ridiculous attack. Perhaps the most novel feature of the meeting was an attempt to bring recalcitrant towns to a due sense of shame that they were outside the radical ranks. 'An Address to the Inhabitants of Wigan and its vicinity. . . : Hear of the united exertions that are now making in various parts of the kingdom, and take shame to yourselves for having delayed so long to declare yourselves openly on the side of Reform.' The 'Ancient and Loyal' borough of Wigan responded with a will; but it was after the Peterloo band-wagon had started to roll.

The *Observer*'s chagrin on the set-back to their uninterrupted progress by the 'abstain at your peril' notice was reserved for their next issue (7 August). Therein appeared that famous and often-part-quoted letter 'To the Official Gentlemen of Manchester'. Mr Thompson quotes it as evidence to clinch Francis Place's testimony that the Manchester magistrates and Yeomanry were a 'greater set of brutes than you form a conception of'; and cites the passage: 'I defy the bloodthirsty partisans of Danton, Marat, Robespierre, to furnish a more despotic, tyrannical crew . . .' The letter was written by 'W. Walker' who is not precisely identifiable; whether he was the same 'Walker' who was a 'young man not long returned from sea' who harangued the earlier weavers' meeting in the garb of a sailor, who seems to be the W. C. Walker whom Norris stigmatised as 'the Thistlewood of this part'[1] is not known, but his language is trenchant enough for any part, and is more to be considered as an example of the evidence which increased the 'excessive alarms' of the natives of Manchester than of anything else.

TO THE OFFICIAL GENTLEMEN OF MANCHESTER. It is surprising you should attempt to irritate the minds of a suffering people, by such a cruel and tyrannical mode of conduct as you of late and still continue to adopt. At a time when thousands of your fellow-creatures are starving for want of employment, who are willing to work if they could get it; when thousands now are partly employed, cannot earn what is sufficient to drag on a miserable existence! when the whole nation loudly calls on its rulers for reform and retrenchment; I say, when a whole nation has so far degraded themselves as to supplicate, petition and remonstrate, but all in vain; for our prayers, petitions and remonstrances have not been attended to, but have been trampled under foot, and the petitioners disdainfully treated with scorn and derision, by the very persons who ought to be their representatives! When

[1] Read, p. 157, quoting H.D. 42/197. Thompson (p. 698) suggests that W. C. Walker was a Government spy.

the channel of communication betwixt the people and the throne, has been, and is still, blocked up by an insidious Sidmouth and the borough-mongers. That Sidmouth who has and for some time past, and is still, pursuing the ignominious career of a *maure pas*, who by the very same conduct plunged Louis the Sixteenth into an embarrassed abyss, out of which he never could extricate himself. When the people of Manchester and its vicinity, after all the insults they have received for years past, not only from the Government, but from you also, whilst they have been only pursuing legal means of peaceably obtaining a reform: you have so far forgotten yourselves as to dare them at their peril to seek redress in any constitutional manner; pray, who are you, who dare thus to threaten a whole country at their peril?

I would advise you to place your mirror before you, look seriously, and if you remain still in doubt of what you really are, ask yourselves the question, Who am I? Common sense will say although thou art one of the pig-tailed tribe, still thou art a man, and a tyrannical man, which is one of the worst species of the human race; and though few in number, you have dared to threaten hundreds of thousands at their peril to legally attempt to seek redress; but your threats are in vain, we are men as well as you; we were born free, we know what are our rights and we are determined they shall be restored to us.

You have declared yourselves armed associates of the notorious borough-mongering system, both by act and deed. Nay, I may even say armed associations, for you have threatened at their peril; you have either misunderstood the implication of the word, and trusting to the timidity of a long injured, patient, suffering, and starving people; or have been jovially indulging yourselves with the juice of the grape, or you must be downright fools, to think to frighten thousands, nay, millions of enlightened Englishmen, who openly declare themselves to be naked, but staunch Radical Reformers; not armed associates, and enemies to liberty, but friends to their country and constitution; and men, determined to sit down with nothing but their rights. Oh! ye *buveurs* of human blood. But gentlemen, I again tell you your late and present conduct is, and has been such, that I defy the bloodthirsty partizans of Danton, Marat, Robespierre, to furnish a more despotic, tyrannical crew. Nay, I challenge Spain, with all its holy tribunals of inquisition, to match you with the despotic measures you have adopted and do still continue to adopt over a peaceable, suffering, and long-injured people.

You have not only supported the unjust measures adopted by H.M. ministers, but you have even surpassed them, by usurping a power which was not even entrusted to them; and which neither law nor reason can sanction. Gentry, I pity you, and your *dernier resources*, but whilst the world laughs at your *foiblesse*, I hope Englishmen will not forget to enter you into the Black Book; nay, I hope they will record your actions in their hearts; and should you, on Monday next, commit another *faux pas*, by interrupting the peaceable proceedings of the day, I hope they will patiently put up with your insults as they have hitherto done, being assured the day of retribution cannot be far off. I conclude by assuring you, and all mankind, that I have long been, and will remain as long as blood flows in my veins, with the utmost of my exertions A RADICAL REFORMER, an open and avowed enemy to tyranny and oppression, and to subscribe myself, your as you deserve.

WM. WALKER.

Loyalist fears were no doubt played on by this letter, but the committee of magistrates, who had just seemingly 'got away' with their premature precautions, read between the lines. Questions must surely have assailed them: did this Wm. Walker know anything of the anxious correspondence passing between Manchester and Whitehall, for by his references to a *faux pas*, and 'usurping a power which was not even entrusted to them . . .' there was a hint that he did. But more particularly, the letter was published on 7 August, and Mr Walker referred to the meeting on 'Monday next'! Were the Reformers, after all, secretly intending to carry on with the meeting in spite of the prohibition, in spite of the postponement until the 16th, advertised in the same issue of the *Observer*? In fact, this was the fear in their minds, and it was this fear that Scarlett, prosecuting Hunt later, expressed as having existed; he was, calling attention to the immensity of the Peterloo meeting:

Can any man doubt that such a multitude must inspire terror and alarm? Not from their demeanour upon the field, not from their dispositions betrayed by any acts they did, or any expressions they uttered; no, but by their secret organization . . . by their appearing to be under some secret leader? The very mystery in which that organization is involved is a proof of the danger, and necessarily excites the mind to alarm and terror . . .[1]

Not only were the columns of the *Observer* newspaper eagerly scanned for pointers and portents for the immediate future, but for every word, too, written by Hunt. Every 'private' letter he seemed to write was treated as a 'hand-out' to the Manchester press, radical and loyal alike. In a pre-public relations era, with no apparent organization, Hunt's advance publicity must be rated almost perfect. One letter[2] contained a passage suggesting that the people 'if assailed are prepared to resist the acts of those who first break the peace':

By natural inference, then, [said *Wheeler's Manchester Chronicle*, 31 July] those who assemble here on the 9th of August are to *come armed*. What other construction does it admit of? If our Magistrates see occasion to interfere for

[1] *State Trials*, pp. 425–6.
[2] See below, p. 106.

lawful purposes, the ignorant and misled strangers who may pour into the town on that day are previously publicly admonished to *come prepared* for resistance! It would be highly improvident of our Police not to give the town assurance of internal safety, by a special armed provision for the occasion, that this demagogue may feel himself hemmed in on every side if he dare to offend the laws.

For the gall-dipped pen of John Thacker Saxton, the magistrates' 'abstain at your peril' notice was a gift from the gods. From it stemmed his:

IMPORTANT COMMUNICATION TO THE PEOPLE OF ENGLAND. Contending, as we are, single-handed, against the base and mercenary hireling Newspapers of the day: there is a consolation to find that their puny efforts to stifle the voice of Truth, recoils only on the apostate heads of our opponents. They have deceived, insulted, and betrayed the suffering People of England—they are, however, at length discovered, and the public have abandoned them—down they are falling, and all the weight of flimsy power and base authority cannot save them from tumbling into the mighty precipice that yawns for their destruction. We fearlessly proceed with our duty, in honestly recording the very important occurrences of the past week. We are aware that we speak at the cannon's mouth—the match is already lighted, ready to throw our suffering country into one common Chaos. AT OUR PERIL we are told to complain, and the din of war, in the days of peace, is the only solace a dying nation is to receive for all her great and weighty sacrifices.

Our country, however, must NOT be allowed to perish at the Shrine of TRAITORS; the Hell-hounds of corruption, must be diverted from their scent—the mask must be rent asunder by the all-potent arm of Truth, AND WE WILL DO THE DEED, even though we stand alone and expire in the struggle.[1]

The conduct of the phalanx of corruption, forces upon us the task of remarking upon, and consequently analizing [*sic*] the imbecile efforts of this extra-judicial junto of Ministerial tools, to thwart the legitimate assembling of the People in support of their inalienable and yet unalienable rights; the standing army of Britain having been brought in aid of the Civil Power—to overawe with the point of the bayonet, and by the mouth of the cannon, this dearest boon of English Liberty, under the pretence of preserving the peace, when it had never been broken. It is vain to say the People are tumultuous— for where is there an instance where any popular Meeting has been otherwise than orderly or constitutional? We know the PEOPLE well: and we are sure, if they are not provoked and driven to desperation, from the contempt

---

[1] 'It was part of the essential rhetoric of the movement . . . to hint, warn, or bluster about the ultimate recourse of the people to physical force.' (Thompson, p. 625).

and ill-treatment of their Rulers, that their conduct will always prove such as to render abortive the incendiary plots of any SET OF MEN.

A Requisition was issued at the conclusion of the past week for a Public Meeting; its tenour and meaning will be seen, by referring to the Advertisement in our last Journal'[1] 'This notice brought forth a flaming Posting Bill, bearing the signatures of Nine County Magistrates, which from the obscurity, or rather nonsense of its Phraseology, we submit to our readers, more as an article of curiosity than of importance. The following is really a literal copy—with the exception of a Rampant Lion and Unicorn, which we acknowledge very appropriate emblems, to lead off this fierce and terrifying document' [Copy of 'At your peril' bill.]

Thus it will be seen that this anomalous placard, purporting to be issued by the Magistrates of Manchester and Cheshire, cautions 'all Persons, at their Peril, to ABSTAIN FROM attending the meeting'; It follows, of course, at their Peril they are OBLIGED to attend the Meeting. We will not, however, further notice the blunders of this sapient group—that task we leave to those who have leisure and inclination to finish their repast upon Trifles.

The steady and discreet conduct of the Requisitionists upon this occasion will add immortality to their names when the actions of their oppressors will be remembered only with execration and abhorrence. No sooner did they imagine, that in consequence of an objectionable clause in the Advertisement, whereby they might inadvertently lead their townsmen astray, than they dispatched off Mr. J. T. Saxton to Liverpool, where the County Quarter Sessions were holding, for the purpose of obtaining Counsel's opinion on the legality of the Notice they had issued. This prudent step proved satisfactory at least to the general friends of Liberty in Manchester . . . [and] it appeared that the objectionable clause was that part in their Notice which suggested the propriety of choosing Representatives, contrary to the usages and practice of the existing establishment of the country.

On Mr. Saxton's return from Liverpool on Tuesday evening, the thousands of anxious enquirers as to the result of his mission, could not be immediately pacified; he consequently issued early on Wednesday morning the following ADDRESS TO THE REQUISITIONISTS, which was posted throughout the town, and universally distributed.[2]

In this notice Saxton related his mission to Liverpool and the result of his enquiry to Counsel, which said: 'under those circumstances it would be deemed justifiable in the Magistrates to prevent such a meeting.'

In recommending you to withdraw your Notice, [Saxton's placard went on] and relinquish your intention of meeting your neighbours on the important subject intended to have been discussed on Monday next, I deem it necessary

---

[1] See above, p. 88.
[2] *Manchester Observer*, 7 August 1819.

to state to you and the public, that in the opinion of the most enlightened friends of Liberty in Liverpool, your Requisition is perfectly legal and constitutional; they are, nevertheless, induced to recommend this pause in your proceedings, merely in consideration of the cruel threats of violence issued in a Paper from the Bench of Magistrates, since the publication of your Notice, and of the evident preparations now making to carry those threats into execution. I am acquainted with your necessities—I know the honesty of your intentions—and the lawful means you are desirous of pursuing; but in a question of absolute right, you are not prepared to defend yourselves; I therefore do not deem it advisable under the present circumstances, to subject the persons of yourselves or your friends to the illegal and unconstitutional violence which your oppressors and contemptible tools have prepared for the occasion.

Up to this point John Thacker Saxton was partly admitting defeat; but there was a Victory to be snatched from its jaws:

The formidable preparations [he went on] which your tyrants have made to meet you, their unarmed and suffering victims, is the highest compliment in their power to bestow upon you; it is more even than you could hope to gain by the Meeting; you may therefore relinquish the objectionable parts of your requisition without regret, or even the shadow of a defeat. Colonel Williams, a County Magistrate had the honest boldness on Monday last at the Liverpool Quarter Sessions, to advocate your Cause, and the Cause of the Lancashire Reformers before his brother Magistrates: he confounded the whole Bench; not one man being disposed to reply to the Constitutional arguments of this faithful and sincere friend of his Country.

I beg leave, to conclude with reminding you, and all the friends of Liberty and Justice, that our Cause grows and gathers strength with the plunderings of our enemies; whilst their rapacity must not only destroy the means of their own existence, but ere long turn them to the destruction of each other.

J. T. SAXTON.

The Requisitionists, 'less sanguinary than their opponents' resolved not to risk a breach of the peace, and immediately on being acquainted with the result of their application, they published the following posting-bill on 4 August:

PUBLIC MEETING. We, the undersigned inhabitant householders of Manchester [re the 9 August meeting] . . . prudent to state such meeting will not take place . . . and to relinquish their intention of attending . . . but to request the Boroughreeve and Constables to convene another . . . Requisition now lies this day only for signatures . . . at the *Observer* Office, 49, Great Ancoats Street (Requests the meeting 'on as early a day as possible.')

The new Requisition, the *Observer* reported, when opened, was signed in three hours by nearly a thousand names. The doors of the office were surrounded by hundreds who could not have access to sign. Mr Saxton glowed with pride:

The pimps of authority witnessed this spontaneous movement of the People; here was no begging for signatures—no scouring the streets and alleys and wretched brothels for the dependent and alarmed minions of Power—nor reminding servile Publicans with the approaching Licence-day—no discharge of servants—no promises—no bribes—no threats—no undue influence—no renewing Accommodation Paper—no Nadin's hypocritical smiles to coax, nor frowns to intimidate—no promises of bushels of potatoes to the hungry and dying poor, to enable them to linger another week under the scourge of oppression—all, all, was fair above-board—THE HEART AND SOUL OF THE PEOPLE were with us, and with their honest hands, they placed on record their honourable Names. Names that Posterity shall cherish, and little children exalt their uplifted arms, while their tongues lisp in accents of praise and thankfulness.

'It cheers us to say', the exultant rhapsody went on, 'that the gilded reptiles were unable to overawe this simultaneous expression of public opinion. Here then is once more food for triumph; let the friends of Radical Reform but persevere; let them be firm and fear not!—the Victory is their own—their enemies will shrink before the voice of all —powerful TRUTH, and eventually gnaw the File, flowing with blood, from their own envenomed Tongues.'[1]

A further news paragraph from this faithful chronicler of those vital pre-Peterloo days occurs in that same number of the *Observer*:

On Monday night last, the neighbourhood of Great Ancoats Street was thrown into a state of alarm, by the appearance of the military, with Nadin and others at their head, the cause so far as we can learn is as follows: It is usual after the fatigues of the day, for a number of working-people to assemble at the New Cross, to discuss politics, &c. In the course of the fray, the runners made themselves very active in defacing and tearing down the Posting Bill for the [9 August] public meeting, and putting up opposition

---

[1] How plain facts can bring reality to a highly-coloured narrative is given by the editor's note in the State Trials edition of Hunt's trial. Moorhouse's counsel was under the misapprehension that the Manchester magistrates had consulted counsel in Liverpool on the legality of the 9 August meeting. The *State Trials* editor added this footnote:

'The defendant Saxton published an advertisement on August 4th, 1819, stating that the opinion of Mr. Fletcher Raincock, of the Northern Circuit, had been taken, and that he advised that the meeting should not be held.' (Quoting Dom. Papers, Geo. 3, p. 321.) *State Trials* 280 (note).

The same footnote, placed against the context of Saxton's articles on this very matter, would seem, it is suggested, a little inadequate.

ones in their stead. Some abusive language passed betwixt them and the people, and at last the runners were fairly driven away; they now arrived again with Nadin at their head, and were driven away by the people; in a short time they returned with a body of military, the Riot Act was read, and the people ordered to disperse; they then paraded through the neighbouring streets, striking and wounding any Persons who did not or could not get out of the way.

The Magistrates, regretful of their menacing language of the earlier 'abstain at your peril' bill, had adopted a more reasonable tone. The new posting-bill read:

August 9th, 1819. Englishmen! The Illegal Meeting appointed to be held this day in Manchester has been Postponed. Thus the wicked and seditious men who are endeavouring to mislead you have avoided the punishment due to a violation of the Public Peace.

Time is afforded for Reflection:—Abhor, Reject the Itinerant Advocates of Treason; whose counsels, if followed, would be destructive of that LIBERTY which they pretend to establish. It is only by obedience to the JUST and EQUAL LAWS of your *Country*, which protect alike the Poor and the Rich that you can preserve to yourselves the Blessings of a FREE CONSTITUTION. 'Fear God, Honour the King'.[1]

It is instructive to follow in detail this riot at New Cross as related in the 'loyalist' press; the riots lasted three nights, the police and the 'runners' were attacked with paving stones by a mob assessed at 2000. Its bearing on the events of 16 August is however more important than hitherto realized, for this riot was given as the reason by the constables, and more particularly by Joseph Nadin, the deputy constable of Manchester, for refusing to serve the warrants at the Peterloo meeting without military support.

[Nadin's evidence as his excuse for refusing to execute the warrant on 16 August]. I durst not do it, from the reception I had received a few days before, and that, on attempting to execute a warrant. The Boroughreeve and constables, and me, and two or three beadles, were called to New Cross. The paper-sticker was posting bills. We had sent a bill-sticker and two of our men with him . . . We went to the place, where it was said our men were in the house, and they were stoning the house; we went through the mob . . . when a shower of stones came upon us . . . Mr. Moore and Mr. Clayton got away, and Andrews with me, and the two beadles could not get away well. We got on the outside and turned down Oldham Street, and then Mr. Moore and Mr. Clayton were bringing in the Military.[2]

[1] (Eng. MS. 1197/19 John Rylands Library).
[2] *State Trials,* Redford *v.* Birley, p. 1165.

Bruton[1] deals with these pre-Peterloo details very briefly. In recounting Saxton's seeking legal advice at Liverpool, his account goes on: 'He returned with this important ruling, "that the intention of choosing Representatives, contrary to existing law, tends greatly to render the proposed meeting seditious". Accepting this ruling, the Reformers at once abandoned the meeting, and carefully revised their programme.' It has been observed earlier that Bruton treats the background to Peterloo 'rather naively'. His authority, no doubt, for so doing was to be found in a statement made in defence of Hunt, Bamford, and the others in the subsequent trial:

A meeting was certainly intended to be held on that day [9 August] at Manchester; but you find that there was something objectionable in the advertisement announcing the meeting to take place on that day, which, being pointed out to those that intended to hold the meeting, they very properly acquiesced in the remonstrance of the Magistrates, and the meeting did not take place.[2]

[1] *Story of Peterloo*, p. 17.
[2] *State Trials*, p. 277.

VIII

Henry Hunt in Manchester, August 1819 (1)

On 31 July, the same day as the great Rochdale meeting, there was evidence of a widening alarm in towns adjacent to Manchester. *Wheeler's Manchester Chronicle* of that date published a declaration from the town of Oldham, signed by about 400 inhabitants, expressing concern at 'the sense of danger which threatens the community'; another from Bolton, with 300 signatures; and others from Bury and from Leigh and Pennington. The view was being put forward that 'It is manifestly one thing to petition and remonstrate, and another thing to insult and menace . . .' As late as 3 August, Norris and the magistrates were not sure whether their prohibition of the 9 August meeting was to be ignored or not:

August 3rd. Norris to Lord Sidmouth: If the meeting takes place there must be a serious contest, I fear, for which we are preparing ourselves as best we can.[1]

The interception of the letters passing between Manchester and Hunt evidently continued, for apart from the publicity some of these letters received in the *Manchester Observer*, such as the one sent to Hunt by the General Committee of the Stockport Union for Promoting Human Happiness inviting him to visit Stockport, there were others which found their way into Government hands. The Stockport letter assured Hunt that, 'The idea of your arrival strikes terror to the very foundation of the borough faction in this part of the country';[2] others from Johnson were a little less confident:

August 1st. Johnson to Hunt. Sending you a posting bill sent forth by our sapient magistrates in consequence of the advertisement in the *Manchester Observer* calling the 9th August meeting. You will see what the knaves are about, and by trick mean, if possible, to prevent the meeting. Have the goodness to send me the best advice you can get from yourself and friends on this in my opinion *ultra vires* bill.[3]

[1] *State Trials,* App. B, p. 1378.
[2] *State Trials,* App. B, p. 1377.
[3] *State Trials,* App. B, p. 1376–7.

August 3rd. Hunt to Johnson. [before Hunt knew that the meeting had been prohibited] I am sure the people will be quiet and orderly, unless some of the hellish agents and spies of the police should venture to create a riot; but if it be so, may the blood and consequent vengeance be upon the heads of those who begin it.[1]

August 3rd. Johnson to Hunt. To-day they have posted a Proclamation from London, in consequence of which I shall alter the advertisement for the meeting, and call one for the purpose of taking into consideration the *propriety of petitioning* the House of Commons, or something else. I have not made up my mind on the subject, but I shall do it to-day. I suppose it is considering the propriety of electing a member for Manchester that they call 'illegal'. We must therefore alter it.[1]

The radicals did not use the phrase 'propriety of petitioning' the House of Commons as Johnson was suggesting; and unless Henry Hunt had changed between January and August 1819, no one, who remembered the sentiments delivered in Manchester in January, ought to have expected he could have agreed to it. His tirade against 'such infamous conduct as petitioning' even Johnson ought to have recalled. Only *after* 16 August, and then insidiously, was the pretence of 'petitioning' put into their arguments when avowing to the world their peaceable intentions. Bamford, for instance, pleaded in his defence at his trial in 1820 (referring to the 'demands' on their banners): 'Why should we demand that which we were going to Manchester to petition for?'[2] In the Redford *v.* Birley trial, 1822, counsel for Redford said: 'The people of Manchester wished to have their petitions more effectively attended to. They thought that when a great body of the people met to petition the Commons House of Parliament. . . .' When memories had grown dim on such obscure matters, even Hunt gave himself the liberty of renouncing his past and strengthening his case by referring to the crowd who were 'legally and peaceably assembled to petition for Radical Reform' etc.[3]

In Manchester, during those last ten days before the fateful 16 August, the atmosphere was dramatic, with the magistrates and the loyalists on the one hand uncertain and anxious about the next radical move; the radicals on the other displaying eagerness for the latest news of their great champion, even then on his way from London to stand at their head on what seemed likely to be the greatest day in radical history, although the news of this only reached Manchester at the weekend of

[1] *State Trials,* App. B, p. 1378.
[2] *State Trials,* p. 284.
[3] *An Address from Henry Hunt, Esq., to the Radical Reformers of England.* No. 11, 1831; Letter from Hunt to the *Morning Herald,* 29 June 1828.

7 August. For the first part of his journey, Hunt was quite unaware of the momentous happenings in Manchester. He received the first inkling of it at Coventry, where he penned what he thought fit to call 'Proclamation the Third'; the title ironically referring to the two proclamations already seen in Manchester: the 'Royal' one, and the 'Abstain at your peril' placard. The *Observer*, in printing Hunt's proclamation provided another example of that ingenuous reporting which made their opponents suspicious afterwards when probing for 'intentions' on the part of the radicals.

Even the ascription tended to heighten the sense of the dramatic, addressed as it was 'To the Reformers of Manchester and its Neighbourhood,' headed 'Coventry, on my road to Manchester, August 5th, 1819.'

Since I last addressed you, [began Hunt] I see by the newspapers that the Ministers have published *their Proclamation*, in the name of the Prince Regent, vowing vengeance against all future meetings for Reform. I now see by this day's *Courier* that the Magistrates acting for the counties of Lancaster and Chester have also published *their Proclamation*, denouncing our Meeting on the 9th for Reform as an *illegal Meeting*, and they caution all persons to abstain AT THEIR PERIL from attending such illegal Meeting; as the Chairman appointed to preside at that Meeting, I do hereby publish this *my Proclamation*.

First, I shall attend at the time appointed to preside at the said Meeting, under the full impression that the Meeting is not only legal, but perfectly constitutional, it being called for the purpose of considering the best means of promoting that great object, Reform of the Commons House of Parliament.

Second, if any proposition should be offered which is illegal, as Chairman of that Meeting, I hold myself responsible, and therefore I certainly shall not submit it to the Meeting.

Third, there is no law that empowers a Magistrate to disperse a Meeting convened for such a purpose, unless the Magistrates of Manchester intend to act upon the law which expired in July 1818.

Fourth, The Magistrates having ordered all persons *to abstain at their peril,* which means in plain English that those who stay away from the Meeting will do it at their peril, of course all those who are under the influence of the said Magistrates will certainly attend under pain of their high displeasure.

Fifth, If anything seditious or illegal should take place at the said Meeting, surely the law in the hands of the present Attorney-General, aided by a packed Lancashire Special Jury, is quite strong enough to meet such an offence, unless the Magistrates mean to dispense with all law, and resort to open force at once; which should they the Reformers will at all events know what they have to trust to.   Yours &c., H. Hunt.

The sense of authority which Henry Hunt could put into his communications, penned probably alone in his room at a Coventry inn, giving the impression that he had a powerful organized movement behind his pronouncement, is remarkable. The confident note as to his deep knowledge of the niceties of the law is also remarkable; in all probability he had carefully gone into all aspects of the case, either with or without Johnson's queryings, referred to in an earlier letter, before he left London. But the Manchester magistrates, still remembering the rebuke from the Government for acting prematurely read Hunt's proclamation with a sense of premonition. Hunt was calling their bluff. Mr Thompson[1] sums it up:

The policy of open constitutionalism was proving more revolutionary in its implication than the policy of conspiracy and insurrection. Wooler and Hunt achieved, without any secret 'correspondencies' or system of delegates, a position in which they could call out a national movement . . .

The magistrates and loyalists of Manchester would not, in any case, have recognized that which they feared, as 'constitutionalism'; they were under the impression, too, that 'correspondencies and systems of delegates' were active; moreover they did not know how much was 'open' or how much was 'secret'; and in this event they feared that that which was alleged to be open was only a blind to cover that which was secret. Hunt's proclamation, they believed, meant a show-down.

It was not the magistrates only who were nonplussed. John Thacker Saxton was nonplussed too. Hunt's proclamation needed 'interpretation' in the following week's Manchester Observer:

We announced the postponement of the Manchester Meeting in our last journal, and on the day of publication we received from Mr. Hunt the following communication, which we had no doubt had been obstructed in its delivery by the agents of power, purposely to keep it from the public, through the extensive medium of the Manchester Observer. The bold—the manly—the noble spirit which it breathes prompts us to lay it, without comment, before the public . . . at the time this Proclamation was written, it appears that Mr. Hunt had not been apprized that the intended meeting of the 9th had been postponed; or rather, that it had been abandoned altogether, for reasons already assigned, and that another, for the 16th had been appointed in its stead. Without keeping this in view, some of the passages will be quite unintelligible.

How 'unintelligible' this announcement was to be for some of John Thacker Saxton's readers even that gentleman himself did not know;

[1] Thompson, p. 682.

those readers were the Manchester magistrates. They believed, not without good reason, that the alleged abandonment of the 9 August meeting was a feint, and that Hunt really was calling their bluff, for bluff it had now become after Sidmouth's second letter, of not acting up to the spirit of their advertisement. As it turned out, despite the magistrates' fears to the contrary, the meeting had been abandoned, although they did not rid themselves of their fears until the afternoon of 9 August. Owing to the terms of Saxton's announcement a second suspicion then assailed them,[1] that although the meeting was put off until the 16th, it was only a *postponement*; in other words, although the election of a 'legislatorial attorney' was dropped from the notice convening the meeting, the idea had not been abandoned altogether, but had only been postponed from the 9th to the 16th; the use of the word 'postponed' in Saxton's announcement only strengthened that suspicion.

But leaving out of account the complications envisaged in Manchester, the Proclamation was perhaps anything but unintelligible to Henry Hunt, with the recent Smithfield meeting on his mind. For even though he was avowing that he would insist on presiding at an allegedly illegal meeting because he did not think it was illegal, he was making clear to all the world that if anything illegal was done at that meeting, as chairman he would not allow it to be discussed. By doing so he was putting himself on the right side of the Law, and was avoiding as much as in him lay becoming enmeshed in the net which was surely being laid to entrap him by the Government. Hunt stoutly maintained in subsequent weeks and months that he was within the law, and that he had every respect for the law. His display of brinksmanship in defying the custodians of the law in Manchester was, however, later to be used as an argument against his protestations of respect for the law, in spite of his assertion that he did not become aware that the 9 August meeting was called off until he arrived at Bullock Smithy, outside Stockport on 8 August. James Scarlett, in prosecuting Hunt, months later, had this to say:

Hunt learned at Coventry that the meeting was put off . . . at Bullock Smithy, too . . . I ask a man of sense to say, and understanding about this: whether he can say that the object of this man in coming to Manchester was to inspire respect to the local magistrates or to preach up disaffection, and excite the mob to resistance to those placed in authority over them? What does he do? He makes a speech to the persons assembled, many of whom he had brought from Stockport . . . they state . . . [with variations] that he

[1] English MS. 1197/86. J.R.L.

was sorry to find that they had resolved in obedience to the magistrates, to postpone the meeting that the magistrates considered it illegal, but he did not; that they were no more fit to be magistrates, or no more worthy of being called magistrates than so many tailors to be called a man; that it wanted nine tailors to make a man, and nine magistrates to make that [abstain at your peril] proclamation; which he treated with contempt and scorn.[1]

Long before Scarlett was to pin the above indictment upon him, Hunt had said (on his final appearance before the magistrates after Peterloo, on 27 August), referring to the 16 August meeting:

I did not attempt to follow, nor was it the opinion of those who took part in the proceedings of the meeting, that we ought to attempt to follow the example of Birmingham in the election of a representative. I had written to Mr. Johnson to this effect long before the intended meeting [9 August] was prohibited in Manchester; the Royal Proclamation had declared it illegal, and, though I did not think it illegal, I thought it a foolish and absurd scheme. It was my opinion, that to follow such an example, at such a time, would have been unjust to the people of Manchester . . . I have declared that I would not have put such a question as chairman, long before the first meeting was prohibited.[2]

Hunt had a long memory, but his words were on record that he had said that he 'would not have put the question' *after* the meeting was prohibited, even if he did not know, as he averred that he did not know, the meeting had been abandoned. Hunt had indeed written to Johnson replying to the invitation to preside at the 9 August meeting at which it was intended to follow Birmingham's then proposed example of electing a 'representative'; Hunt's letter does not seem to bear out his 27 August opinion that it was a 'foolish and absurd scheme':

20th July, London . . . Consequence of absence from home and some delay at the post office, yours of the 10th, containing the flattering invitation of the Committee to preside at the intended Public Meeting . . . on August 9th . . . did not reach me until Saturday last. If by my humble, though un-ceasing, exertions to procure for the People of England, their undoubted right to elect their own Representatives, I have secured the confidence of the brave Reformers of Lancashire, that is an ample reward for my trouble; and it is most grateful to my feelings to know that in proportion to the vindictive hostility heaped upon me by the common enemies of the human race, I experience the esteem and protection of such men as the Reformers of Lan-cashire . . .[3]

[1] *State Trials,* p. 412.
[2] *Peterloo Massacre,* p. 44.
[3] *Manchester Mercury,* 3 August 1819.

The complications arising out of Henry Hunt's visit to Manchester in August 1819, have never been understood; there were further and more serious complications to arise for those Manchester magistrates before 9 August. Further to Hunt's protestations that he had always treated the authorities and magistrates with respect[1] his sentiments in that letter of 20 July 1819 were 'confided' to Johnson:[2]

Our meeting here takes place at Smithfield to-morrow, and you may easily conceive the agitated state of the tools of corruption on this occasion. The Lord Mayor Atkins, who is as busy a fool as your Boroughreeve, is capering about like 'a parched pea upon a drum-head' mustering all his turtle-fed forces; and would create a riot, or do anything, however ridiculous, to be dubbed a knight, if he were not restrained by orders from those at Head Quarters who are too cunning, and have too much at stake, to run the risk of losing it to gratify the vanity of such a coxcomb. He is supported by horse, foot, and artillery; but the Boroughmongers tremble when they reflect that those who *wield* the *sword* and the bayonet, as well as those who *point* the *Cannon* and apply the *Torch* are the *Fathers*, Brothers, and Relations of the People of England, who are struggling as much to secure for *them* their Rights, as they are to obtain Liberty and Justice for *themselves*. Notwithstanding all the dreadful note of preparation, I have full confidence we shall have an excellent meeting, and that I have the pleasure of meeting my friends and have the honour of presiding again at Manchester on the 9th of August.

From what I can learn of the disposition of the People of the Metropolis, they are resolved to conduct themselves peaceably and orderly, but if assailed, they are prepared and determined to resist the acts of those who may first break the peace . . . H. HUNT.

'Confided to Johnson': it appeared in all the Manchester papers at once. There was a feeling abroad in Manchester that their intended 'representative', if Manchester followed the Birmingham model, was to be Henry Hunt.

Hunt arrived at Stockport on Sunday, 8 August, receiving a tumultuous welcome from throngs of people (and caused something of a panic in the magistrates' minds). Cab proprietor James Moorhouse was his host, for which he was later to find himself arraigned in court with Hunt. Johnson came out from Manchester to welcome the Great Champion. It was at Stockport that Hunt alleged he was first informed of the prohibited 9 August meeting; but it would appear that at Stockport he was informed of something else, which apparently gave him much concern. No longer were the local radicals a cowed mob, such as

[1] *State Trials*, pp. 324–5.
[2] *Manchester Mercury*, 3 August 1819.

the one he addressed in January, to be encouraged to action, to be threatened out of the 'infamous conduct of petitioning', or vague references to 'if the day should arrive when we are called upon to act as our ancestors have done before us, to fight for our liberties . . .' There is ample evidence from Stockport itself that the radicals of Stockport believed that that day had arrived, or nearly so. On Monday, 9 August, Hunt went in a triumphal procession to Manchester; Sir Charles Wolseley was with him, faithful to his promise to attend the great Manchester meeting, although he did not stay for the 16th. There was a demonstration outside the *Observer* office, when cheers three times three were given; when they arrived at the Exchange a great burst of exultation was repeated. Another large demonstration met at Red Bank, which Hunt addressed, and then on to Joseph Johnson's house, Smedley Cottage, where Hunt was to stay quietly for the next seven days.

It would be an exaggeration to say that Hunt's arrival almost brought the business centre of Manchester to a standstill, but the arrival was not lost on the watching loyalists. *Wheeler's Manchester Chronicle* (14 August) reported:

The expectation of this man, and his subsequent arrival, brought a great influx of strangers into the town. There was a general laxity of business. Seditious language was unreservedly expressed in the streets, and an excitation of the worst passions of the workpeople was very manifest. Yet, Mr. Hunt preaches Peace, and talks of not offending the laws. For what purpose, then, does he come? Is his presence here a natural occurrence? Does he come to assist the Magistrates and the Police? Do the Reformers stand in need of his presence, or of any abilities he may possess? Has there ever appeared to be such a want of sagacity in their radical pursuits, that they cannot arrange their own measures, or express their objects? Certainly not. Their writings and political productions negative all such assumptions. Mr. Hunt is bound to give some satisfactory reason, if in his power, for approaching a great manufacturing town under such an *understanding* with its population as to take their minds off all natural pursuits, and to create a general excitation to an *expected something* which militates against the comforts of society. Let him look to this.

Every man is a responsible being, accountable for his actions. Why is it that all respectable persons *shun* him? There is no other man in the habit of causing sensations such as he causes when he visits this town. Surely there is something mysterious in it, something that does not admit of an *honest* explanation. Let him look to it. The Magistrates, Boroughreeve, Constables, and Special Peace Officers were at their posts; the Military, Horse and Foot, were under arms; and every respectable inhabitant was ready to assist, as soon as required.

The most formidable critics of the magistrates *after* Peterloo were the writers in the *Manchester Gazette*, more particularly Archibald Prentice and John Edward Taylor, later founder of the *Manchester Guardian* (1821). When critics became traducers in the following months, Taylor was not amongst their number, although Bruton has alleged him to be one of the most virulent of those traducers by attributing to his 'editorship' the rabidly radical *Peterloo Massacre* published in fourteen weekly parts from the end of August 1819.

Nothing is more noticeable in the contemporary newspaper reports of this pre-16 August period of 1819, than the contrast between the radical (the *Observer*) and the other Manchester newspapers (particularly the *Manchester Gazette*) in the use of language. On the one hand there is a complete lack of restraint in the use of terms, and on the other, a careful measured, and restrained choice of words, giving precise meaning to that which they intended to convey. The greatest exponent of the latter type of writing was John Edward Taylor, and it is on this score that it may be stated categorically that he was not the 'editor' of *Peterloo Massacre*. The *Manchester Gazette* (possibly from the pen of Taylor) published its 'To Reformers and Anti-Reformers' on 7 August. They approved of the magistrates' measures thus far, but with some reservations:

> Upon the present occasion, Government have acted with much greater propriety than in 1817. Every one must approve of the vigorous execution of the existing laws rather than the renewal of those practices of secret arbitrary imprisonment which disgraced that year. If sedition is preached at public meetings, let it be duly punished; but a wise policy would endeavour, rather by temperate and conciliatory conduct, to detach the people at large from those who have assumed the station of their leaders, than to maintain a hollow and insecure tranquility by the exhibition of military force . . .

Taylor's language has more than once been strained to fit certain theses, as for instance in the sentence: 'to maintain a hollow and insecure tranquility by the *exhibition* of military force.' The operative word is, of course, 'exhibition', and it is not pedantic to point out that to *exhibit* and *overawe* with military force is not inconsistent with another sentence used in the same article: 'The poor are not to be reasoned with, but *terrified* into quiescence.' It hardly bears the inference drawn from the article by Dr Read: 'On the one side, they [the middle-class radicals] believed were the unreasoning poor [and] on the other were the unreasoning authorities too ready *to rush in with the sword*'.[1]

To distinguish what was said and written before 16 August, and what

[1] Read, p. 72.

was said and written after that date, is of paramount importance in discovering the truth of Peterloo. The Manchester middle-class radical organ's 'manifesto' went on:

. . . Anxiously desirous as we are of rational and moderate, but, at the same time, *radical* reform in the representation of the people, from a deep and sincere conviction of its importance to the best interests of the State, we think most of the recent proceedings of our professed reformers exceedingly unwise and injurious. The bustle and loss of time occasioned by their constant succession of meetings—the violent resolutions generally passed there—the intemperate harangues of the travelling speechmakers—the very questionable character of many, if not most of these persons—the highly objectionable matter which finds its way to the public through that part of the press which is under their control—all these are things which do infinite mischief—which utterly precludes moderate men from wishing them success—and throw all the timid into the ranks of their opponents . . .[1]

Just how many of the 'timid', or even the not so timid, were to be thrown into the loyalist ranks by the events of the next ten days, was to become a matter of some dispute, even by Taylor himself. After 16 August he challenged the suggestion of a general alarm amongst the inhabitants of Manchester, because by that time to admit to such alarm was to condone the extreme measures which it was alleged had been taken because of it. The article proceeded:

The Saxtons, the Harrisons, the Wolseleys, the Knights, the Johnsons, the Fittons, and the Ogdens, are not men by whom anything really valuable to the cause of civil liberty is to be achieved—they are not men by whom the intellect of the country will submit to be led—they are not teachers whose dogmas will be admitted as the gospel of political truth, or whose characters afford a goodly testimony in favour of the doctrines they profess. Some of them, indeed, we do not hesitate to consider as men whose activity in the cause which they support, arises from anything rather than a sincere and conscientious attachment to the principles of Reform. We do not mean to apply hard terms to any of our countrymen, and shall therefore not accuse them of wishing for tumult and revolution; but we sincerely believe, the attainment of that reform for which they profess to be so anxious would be their destruction. They *live* by ranting and railing against abuses—remove the abuses and they must perish, for *they will not work*. They have appealed not to the reason but to the passions and the sufferings of their abused and

1 'But whatever his [Hunt's] object, if the form and mode of assembling the vast numbers, if the organization, the secret and undiscovered hand that trained them—if all these circumstances conspired together to produce alarm and terror in the minds of peaceable men, the meeting was unlawful.' (Scarlett, prosecuting Hunt; *State Trials*, p. 428).

credulous fellow-countrymen, from the scanty and hard-earned pittances of those whose ill-requited industry they extort for themselves the means of a plentiful and comfortable existence. '*They toil not, neither do they spin,*' but they live better than those that do . . .

Henry Hunt on St Peter's Field on 18 January 1819, had half seriously, half jokingly, perhaps, told his auditors, 'Whenever I appear in public they honour me with the attendance of soldiers . . .' He had been more than honoured on his arrival in Manchester on 9 August to find the town literally an armed camp. *Wheeler's Manchester Chronicle,* 7 August, reported:

The probable occurrence of such a meeting [August 9] had engaged the serious attention of the Rt. Hon. the Earl of Derby, the active and vigilant Lord Lieutenant of the County; of the Magistrates, of the Boroughreeve, of Constables, and the whole of the Civil Authorities. Government had also not been inactive in its contemplation; but they had directed to the town and neighbourhood of Manchester and Salford a formidable force of Artillery, Cavalry, and Infantry, under the superintendence of General Sir John Byng, military commander of the District; and Sir John had regulated in person a proper distribution of the extensive armament. A very great addition to the Civil Power had also been provided by swearing-in extra constables . . .

    These public agitators are therefore very properly thrown back upon their resources, and the probability is, that Manchester, Salford and neighbourhoods, will for several days more be kept in a state of anxiety by the continued determination of ill-disposed subjects to disturb the public peace. The steady and undeviating attention of the Magistrates and Police, will, however, be continued, and nothing will be left to chance. The armed force will be kept together; the special constables will be on the alert with their wonted spirit; and to make personal security, and the safety of property be beyond all doubt, the extensive and strong powers of *watching and warding* are about to be carried into effect. [They then referred to the order of the Earl of Derby, as *Custos Rotulorum* of the county, which has already been referred to (p. 74). The article concluded]: The Public will not feel it improper to be again apprised, that it is a *well-established fact* that numerous bodies of men continue to be trained to military exercise in various districts within a few miles of this town. To suppress so dangerous a procedure the summary powers of the watch and ward are peculiarly well adapted.

To say that Henry Hunt was frightened is probably an exaggeration; although he did say that he 'dreaded any mad attempt to produce disturbance'. He knew of the drillings, he knew of the militancy of the meetings, he knew of the Epic of Sandy Brow; and he knew of the dragons' teeth which had been sown in bluster and bravado, which, in these probably unprecedented circumstances, could well bring forth a terrible crop.[1] The dangerous doctrine which had been hinted at only a twelvemonth ago, that 'tyranny only needs to be resisted to be conquered,'[2] was still being preached to its admiring readers by the inimitable John Thacker Saxton; and as recently as just prior to Hunt's leaving London, when Saxton harangued the crowd on St Peter's Field on 'the abominable doctrine of passive obedience and non-resistance.'[3]

Not for nothing did Henry Hunt stay quietly at Smedley Cottage during those next few days. He was expected both by the radicals and the magistrates to appear at a radical meeting held at Leigh, thirteen miles west of Manchester, on Wednesday, the 11th; he did not go. Remembering all this, Sir John Byng's letter, from his HQ of the Northern District in Yorkshire, to the Home Office, on 14 August, takes on its proper significance: 'I have no fear of any disturbance on Monday; on the contrary they are much alarmed at our precautions!' Dr Read has described Sir John Byng as 'the only man in important office who did not share the excessive alarms of the magistrates';[4] he took his 'precautions' nevertheless, which up to that date was all that the magistrates had done.

[1] 'I was, nevertheless, ultimately prevailed upon to stay, from a conviction that my presence would promote tranquillity and good order, and under the assurance that, if I did quit the place, confusion and bloodshed would, in all probability, be the inevitable consequence. The manner in which those in authority had treated them, had irritated to the highest degree the people in and near Manchester, and they had also been excited to acts of desperation and violence, by some of those who professed to be their leaders.'—*Henry Hunt's Memoirs*, Vol. III, pp. 605–6.

[2] *Manchester Observer*, 25 July 1818.

[3] That the idea of passive obedience and non-resistance was an abominable doctrine seems indigenous to Stockport. Mr Knight at the Blackburn meeting in July 1819, said: 'That soon after the arrest of Drummond, Bagguley and Johnston, the doctrine of passive obedience and non-resistance was so disgustingly inculcated and enforced in the old-established Sunday school at Stockport, that the more intelligent part of the scholars could no longer endure it but absented themselves and applied to the Political Reformers requesting they would commence a Sunday school, and they would join and assist them therein; and this was the history of that highly valuable Institution.' [In a toast to the Union of Stockport. *Manchester Observer*, 10 July 1819.]

[4] Read, p. 115.

IX

Henry Hunt in Manchester, August 1819 (2)

Hunt issued two 'manifestoes' during that week of tension, one dated 12 August, to inform the editors of the London press on the state of affairs in Manchester and which was widely copied in the local papers; the other, the well-known (but again only in part) 'proclamation' which he addressed 'To the Inhabitants of Manchester and Neighbourhood'. The letter to the press referred to the 'drillings . . . done in open day, and not secretly':

All this is known to the Magistrates, who appear, in their wisdom, to be providing arms, at least for their armed associations. I have no doubt that those who are instructing these poor men are in the employ of the ***** of Bolton, as well as his compeer, the *****. I am supposed to have some influence in these parts over this description of persons, and you may rely upon it, I have done, and will continue to do all in my power to dissuade them from continuing any foolish measures . . .

He had earlier in his letter referred to the distress of the weavers, who, for want of better employ,

many of them pass a considerable portion of their time in what they call playing soldiers, or, in other words, learning to march, wheel, &c., and other manoeuvres practised by the military. The parties (one third of them at least) having either served in the militia, the local militia, or the regulars, I am informed, make a respectable drill, in the most orderly manner possible. As this fact is notoriously known in this neighbourhood, I am well convinced the Government agents (of whom there are a sufficient number here) must have long since informed their employers, and I am surprised that it is only hinted at in the ——— and other ministerial papers. A gentleman informed me yesterday that he saw 1,400 men formed in line, marching, &c., &c., on Sunday morning last, and that 800 of them marched a considerable distance before they were dismissed. This was all done in open day and not secretly; they have drums, fifes, and bugles, but no arms whatever; nor do I believe that they know or think that they are offending any law whatsoever . . .[1]

[1] *An Impartial Narrative of the late Melancholy Occurences in Manchester* (1819) (quoting *Manchester Gazette*).

Here was Henry Hunt at his most detached: using his 'influence in these parts over this description of persons', and doing, and will continue to do all in his power to dissuade them from continuing any foolish measures! Here was no 'daring' the magistrates, as he had done in January, then reminding his auditors of the 1817 Blanketeers' meeting, where those magistrates had 'introduced soldiers to insult, assault and shoot, an injured people. . . . They dare not, my friends [do it now]; they are grown wiser from their fears.' That, however, was January; it was now four days only before 16 August! Hunt's memory was prodigious; he may well have recalled his own words of three years previously:

. . . But if the fatal day should be destined to arrive, he assured them that if he knew anything of himself, he should not be found concealed behind a counter, or sheltering himself in the rear.[1]

Hunt's letter to the press went on:

I have been invited to take a ride on Sunday to review them [the drillers]; no one but a Manchester spy would give me credit for walking with my eyes open into such a trap.

Hunt had no intention of walking into any traps during that week, and he was even bold enough before the week was out to seek out the magistrates in their offices and offer to give himself up if a warrant was out against him. He continued:

At the Reform meeting held at Leigh yesterday, it was reported, two of the speakers had warrants issued against them by Mr. Fletcher, of Bolton, and they were arrested without opposition. We have our Meeting here on Monday next, and the preparations for a riot (to be produced, if any, by the agents of the Police) are equal to those made by the Lord Mayor previous to the meeting in Smithfield. I have no doubt but we shall conduct the proceedings with great quietness and order, although I dread any mad attempt to produce disturbance, as the people here, although disposed to peace, are much more determined to resist any illegal attack made upon them; however, I shall do my duty, and I hope to keep them firm and quiet.

H. Hunt

Bamford's testimony on Hunt's disquiet, that he was 'apprehensive lest the people from the country should bring arms to the meeting' is the other side to the picture portrayed in Hunt's letter, that he feared a riot produced by the 'agents of the Police'. Hunt did not express his true fears.

Hunt's proverbial vanity is well exemplified in this belief of his that

[1] Thompson, p. 625, quoting Hunt's speech, 15 November 1816.

he had it in his power to control thousands of people by merely raising his hand or his voice; he might well have profited by the reaction of the magistrate rector of Stockport on a former occasion, when similar assurances were given to him by Mr Fitton, 'Fine talk when stones and sticks are flying. . . .'

Scarlett animadverted on this point at Hunt's trial:

One of the arguments of the law, one of the reasons, in the wisdom of the law, for prohibiting such meetings, is, that, whatever such a meeting may be at the beginning, no man can answer for the result; for who is the man that can command, by merely holding up his finger, 80,000 men? Will the law or the Constitution permit any individual to have that power? Is it safe, is it reasonable, that any one subject in this kingdom of England shall assume to himself the power of governing a multitude of fifty or sixty thousand persons at his pleasure? And do you think Mr. Hunt would be less dangerous to this community if he could indeed, as he more than insinuates, successfully organise and keep in discipline 50,000 men whom he could carry about like a wild beast with a muzzle, saying: 'I can keep him at peace or let him loose at my pleasure'? Should we all enjoy, with peace and tranquility, our liberties, if that were so? He may dream of the powers of his eloquence; he may think that he is that person pictured by the poet, who in the midst of a violent commotion of the people, when arms are furnished by their fury, and when stones and other missiles begin to fly, upon merely erecting himself to speak, would soothe the passions of the multitude, and make them listen with the utmost attention and silence to his commands'

> Iste regit dictis animos, et pectora mulcet.

He is mistaken if he dreams that he is that person; nor, if there is any who possesses that power, ought he to be allowed an opportunity of exercising it in this country.[1]

Henry Hunt, however, persisted; and there is no doubt that he desperately desired a peaceable meeting. It is not so sure, whether he really believed that the danger to that peace would come from his own side or, as he continually repeated 'for the record', the other. In the light of this theory, his second, and better known 'Proclamation' takes on its proper significance:

(1) To the Inhabitants of Manchester and Neighbourhood. Fellow-Countrymen: Our enemies are exulting at the victory they profess to have obtained over us, in consequence of the *postponement for a week* of[2] the PUBLIC MEETING intended to have been held on Monday last.

---

[1] *State Trials*, p. 401.
[2] On the Rev. W. R. Hay's copy of the original proclamation, preserved in John Rylands Library, at Manchester, this paragraph mentioning the 'postponement' is pencil-marked for emphasis. (See before, p. 104.)

TᴇE
INHABITANTS
OF
Manchester
And Neighbourhood.

FELLOW COUNTRYMEN,

Our enemies are exulting at the victory they profess to have obtained over us, in consequence of the postponement, *for a week,* of the PUBLIC MEETING intended to have been held on Monday last.

The Editor of the London Courier, (although he admits that we are only *checked* not *subdued*) appears to be as much rejoiced as if *he,* and his *coadjutors,* had for a time escaped unhurt from the effects of an Earthquake or some other great National Calamity; his *blood-thirsty imitators* of the local press of Manchester, cannot disguise the fears of their employers, although I am informed that they attempt to do it, by resorting to the most vulgar and impotent abuse. To reply to any of their malignant and contemptible efforts, would only tend to drag them forth, for a moment, from their natural insignificance and obscurity; therefore you will bestow on their petty exertions the most perfect indifference ; for as they are beneath your anger, so you will not even suffer them to attract your notice.

You will meet on Monday next my friends, and by your *steady, firm, and temperate* deportment, you will convince all your enemies, you feel that you have an *important* and an *imperious public duty* to perform, and that you will not suffer any private consideration on earth, to deter you from exerting every nerve, to carry your praiseworthy and patriotic intentions into effect.

The eyes of all England, nay, of all Europe, are fixed upon you ; and every friend of real Reform and of rational Liberty, is tremblingly alive to the result of your Meeting on Monday next.

OUR ENEMIES will seek every opportunity by the means of their sanguinary agents to excite a RIOT, that they may have a pretence for SPILLING OUR BLOOD, reckless of the awful and certain retaliation that would ultimately fall on their heads.

EVERY FRIEND OF REAL AND EFFEC-TUAL REFORM is offering up to Heaven a devout prayer, that you may follow the example of your brethren of the Metropolis: and by your *steady, patient, persevering,* and *peaceable* conduct on that day, frustrate their HELLISH AND BLOODY PURPOSE.

Come, then, my friends, to the Meeting on Monday, *armed* with NO OTHER WEAPON but that of a self-approving conscience ; determined not to suffer yourselves to be irritated or excited, by any means whatsoever, to commit any breach of the Public Peace.

Our opponents have not attempted to show that our reasoning is fallacious, or that our conclusions are incorrect, by any other argument but the *threat of Violence,* and to put us down by the force of the *Sword, Bayonet,* and the *Cannon.* They assert that your leaders do nothing but mislead and deceive you, although they well know, that the eternal principles of *truth* and *justice* are too deeply engraven on your hearts ; and that you are at length become (fortunately for them) too well acquainted with your own rights, ever again to suffer any man, or any faction, to mislead you.

We hereby invite the Boroughreeve, or any of the *Nine wise Magistrates,* who signed the Proclamation declaring the meeting to have been held on Monday last, *Illegal,* and threatening at the *same time* all those who *abstained from going* to the said Meeting ; we invite them to come amongst us on Monday next. If we are *wrong* it is their duty as *Men,* as *Magistrates,* and as *Christians,* to endeavour to set us *right* by *argument,* by *reason,* and by the mild and *irresistible precepts of persuasive truth* ; we promise them an attentive hearing, and to abide by the result of *conviction alone.* But once for all we repeat, that we despise their THREATS, and abhor and detest those, who would direct or controul the mind of man by VIOLENCE or FORCE.

I am, my Fellow Countrymen,

Your sincere and faithful Friend,

Henry Hunt.

Smedley Cottage, Wednesday, August 11, 1819.

J. WROE, PRINTER, OBSERVER OFFICE, MARKET-STREET, MANCHESTER.

4. To the Inhabitants of Manchester and Neighbourhood

(2) The Editor of the London *Courier* (although he admits we are only *checked* not *subdued*) appears to be as much rejoiced as if he, and his *coadjutors*, had for a time escaped unhurt from the effects of an Earthquake or some other great National Calamity; his *bloodthirsty* imitators of the local press of Manchester, cannot disguise the fears of their employers, although I am informed that they attempt to do it, by resorting to the most vulgar and impotent abuse. To reply to any of their malignant and contemptible efforts, would only tend to drag them forth, for a moment, from their natural insignificance and obscurity; therefore you will bestow on their petty exertions the most perfect indifference, so you will not even suffer them to attract your notice.

(3) You will meet on Monday next, my friends, and by your *steady, firm and temperate* deportment, you will convince all your enemies you feel that you have an *important* and an *imperious public duty* to perform, and you will not suffer any private consideration on earth to deter you from exerting every nerve, to carry your praiseworthy and patriotic intentions into effect.

(4) The eyes of all England, nay, of all Europe, are fixed upon you; and every friend of real Reform and of rational Liberty, is tremblingly alive to the result of your Meeting on Monday next.

(5) Our *Enemies* will seek every opportunity by the means of their sanguinary agents to excite a *Riot*, that they may have a pretence for *Spilling our Blood*, reckless of the awful and certain retaliation that would ultimately fall on their heads.

(6) EVERY FRIEND OF REAL AND EFFECTUAL REFORM is offering up to Heaven a devout prayer, that you may follow the example of your brethren of the Metropolis; and by your steady, *patient, persevering* and *peaceable* conduct on that day, frustrate their *Hellish and Bloody Purpose*.

(7) Come then, my friends, to the Meeting on Monday, *armed with no other Weapon* but that of a self-approving conscience; determined not to suffer yourselves to be irritated or excited, by any means whatsoever, to commit any breach of the Public Peace.

(8) Our opponents have not attempted to show that our reasoning is fallacious, or that our conclusions are incorrect, by any other arguments but the threat of *Violence*, and to put us down by the force of the *Sword, Bayonet*, and the *Cannon*. They assert that your leaders do nothing but mislead and deceive you, although they well know, that the eternal principles of *truth* and *Justice* are too deeply engraven on your hearts; and that you are at length become (fortunately for them) too well acquainted with your own rights, ever again to suffer any man, or any faction, to mislead you.

(9) We hereby invite the Boroughreeve, or any of the *Nine Wise Magistrates*,[1] who signed the Proclamation declaring the Meeting to have been

[1] Henry Hunt's fondness for The Nine allusion—referring to the nine magistrates who signed the 'abstain at your peril' placard—was continued: he likened them to the

held on Monday last, *Illegal,* and threatening at the *same time* all those who *abstained from going* to the said Meeting; we invite them to come amongst us on Monday next. If we are *wrong,* it is their duty as *Men,* as *Magistrates,* and as *Christians,* to endeavour to set us *right* by *argument,* by *reason,* and by the mild and *irresistible precepts of persuasive truth*; we promise them an attentive hearing, and to abide by the result of *conviction alone.* But once for all, we repeat, that we despise their *Threats,* and abhor and detest those, who would direct or control the mind of man by *Violence or Force.* I am, my Fellow-Countrymen, your sincere and faithful Friend, HENRY HUNT, Smedley Cottage, Wednesday, August 11th, 1819.[1]

The paragraphs in Hunt's original Proclamation were not numbered. As it is an important document showing Hunt's 'intentions', it is interesting to see how it was received. The *Manchester Gazette* printed (without comment) paragraphs 1, 3, and 7; Dr Read prints paragraphs 3 (in part, but gives ellipses showing omissions), 5, and 7. *Wheeler's Manchester Chronicle,* too, only printed part of it; its comments show which parts it did not print—in their issue of 14 August:

On Thursday, Mr. Hunt appeared before the public again by his proxy, 'An address . . .' Sold at the *trifling sum* of one penny each. In it he says (re 1): This is very intelligible language. No one can mistake its meaning. Again (re 3) Why so? it may be asked. Is there something in all this which must not meet the eye? (re 4): What is it that *all Europe* is expecting? (re 5): This is strange language. To whom does Mr. Hunt in *reality* address it? This requires a little explanation. Perhaps the following passage (8) may solve the question. So it is clear, then, as the sun at noonday, that *Mr. Hunt's opponents* are the *Government of the Country:* for they alone have the power to put in array such warlike instruments, and *they have* put them in array in the town and neighbourhood, because Mr. Hunt and his Colleagues have arranged preparations for *such* a meeting of the disaffected on Monday next, as every one, particularly of the lower orders, has been carefully taught to believe will bring about some *great event*; some change in their condition. The Rich are to become the

---

proverbial Nine Tailors in his speech on his arrival in Manchester. References to The Nine served for radical propaganda purposes long afterwards (as will be seen), giving the impression that the 'diabolical' Nine had been constant actors throughout the whole tragedy which ended in the denouement on St Peter's Field. Three of the original Nine were not even present on the 16th of August; another was not in the magistrates' room where the 'decisions' were taken. Two of the most notorious of The Nine of post-Peterloo propaganda (the Revs. Hay and Ethelston) were not even members of the magistrates' committee when the original Nine signed the placard. It could be inferred, from the wording of Hunt's proclamation, that the Boroughreeve was a magistrate. He was not; although some later reports gave the impression that he was.

[1] Eng. MS. 1197, J.R.L.

Poor, and the states of society are to be fundamentally altered: to be *radically reformed*. The belief has certainly gone forth to such an extent, that it is openly spoken of in our streets . . . Perhaps Mr. Hunt can explain this mystery, and inform his *opponents* how such a *general belief* has obtained in this town and neighbourhood!

Mr Hunt's publicity being what it was, he could hardly complain if the national press did not let him have it all his own way; the whole nation knew Hunt was at Manchester. An 'anecdote' from the *New Times* (London) newspaper was reprinted and posted in the streets of Manchester:

HUNT'S GENUINE BEER. Hunt's first appearance in public life was as a *public brewer*. In January, 1807, we find him advertising in the 'Bristol Gazette', that he had established a brewery at Clifton: 'The Families of Clifton and Bristol,' says he, 'are respectfully informed that they may now be supplied with *genuine* Table Beer produced from the best Malt and Hops, and wholly *exempt from any other ingredient* whatever.' He afterwards offered to make a voluntary Affidavit to the same effect. On consulting the Records of the Court of Exchequer however, we find that a very few months after the date of the above Advertisement, seventy gallons of *other ingredients* were seized from Henry Hunt, of Clifton '*genuine* Brewery': and were condemned, Michaelmas Term, 1817. This awkward little accident, it seems, gave the Bristol men a sort of distaste for Mr. Hunt's *genuine* Beer, and no great relish for his affidavits; and the consequence was, that he shut up his brewery, and turned *genuine* Patriot.[1]

One of the Manchester newspapers[2] remarked that Saturday's *Observer* (14 August) was full of Mr Hunt; Mr Hunt's Visit; Mr Hunt's Letters; Mr Hunt's Peaceable Demeanour; and Mr Hunt's Propriety of Conduct. The writer had his doubts. On the foregoing placard, he said:

I never heard such a tale!!! Sure this can never be our Orator, Henry Hunt. He, good man!! is honestly labouring day and night to keep our Constitution pure and unadulterated. The Brewer was day and night infusing poison into the Constitution of all his fellow subjects.

The same writer referred to 'another placard which had been posted in the streets, though copies were almost all torn down or defaced by some of the Hackney Chairman's followers, almost as soon as they were affixed.' Hunt had referred in his Proclamation (paragraph 2) of the attempts to defame his character. The placard complained of was as follows:

[1] *Exchange Herald,* 17 August 1819.
[2] Ibid.

To the Friends of Reform. There are diversity of opinions, as to the means of effecting a Reform, and it behoves you to pause before you adopt the proposition of any one, lest that person should happen to be 'A Tub to amuse a Whale'; and by directing your minds to his ideas, prevent the exercise of your *own*.

I was led to this reflection by the regularity which marks your conduct, which has furnished your opponents with arguments against the wisdom and justice of your cause. They say 'You embrace this cause of Universal and Popular Representation, and yet you pin your faith on the opinions of a person of whom you know little or nothing but what he chooses to say of himself.'

I do not wish to insinuate anything against the character of your intended chairman; but certainly there are some suspicious circumstances attached to his connection with your Cause. I would not by any means have you treat him unkindly, but I would put you on your guard, so as to induce you to satisfy yourselves that all is right, before you implicitly confide in him. In giving this caution, I do not advert to his private character, for it is nothing to us, whether he is a good husband or a bad one; whether he does or does not live in open Adultery with the wife of another Person;—though to be sure, it would strengthen your Cause, if you could with truth boast of the Virtues of your leaders. It is nothing to you, if he did make Oath that he used nothing but Malt and Hops in his Brewhouse, or that almost on the eve of the Oath, he should stand convicted of using Unwholesome Drugs in the fabrication of the Beer which he sold to the inhabitants of Bristol;—for though he might be a little careless in what he *swore*, he may be very conscientious in what he *says* to you; and you know, *you* did not drink the Beer which the law pronounced pernicious. You must not therefore suspect him because his *Private Life* is said to have been a little incorrect.

But I must say, it behoves you to consider one thing in his *Public* Character. He has repeatedly told you, that he will devote his Fortune and his life to the Cause of Reform; and yet has he not given you to understand, that he expects to be reimbursed for the expense of attending your Meeting? Really, this marks his Character doubtful; for the Expense can be of little importance to him, if he is what he declares himself to be—an Independent Man of Property and Estate. However, we should not judge him too harshly on that account, for, as we have been given to understand, he has not been immaculate in his private life, he may have injured his Fortune by irregularities, and it may be necessary for him to have recourse to your generous credulity.

But there is another point worthy of cool consideration. In absence, he writes boldly, and urges you to *action* and *resistance*; and yet, when he speaks in public, he advocates *peaceable demeanour and obedience to law*. This looks like Personal Fear, if it is not Double Dealing. Is this the result of a white feather? —or rather, has he not some secret understanding? Is it not, moreover, strange that Sir Charles Wolseley, the Rev. Mr. Harrison, Mr. Fitton, and Mr. Knight—to say nothing of Messrs. Bagguley, Drummond and Johnston, &c, should be apprehended for words spoken at Public Meetings, and that Mr. Hunt, who, at the late meeting in Smithfield, recommended you to resist the Payment of Taxes, should escape? He may be a very honourable man; but on the face of these Truths, which are so well known to be correct, there is a just ground for hesitancy; at least, so it appears to A PATRIOT, Manchester, August 14th, 1819.[1]

Whatever effect such innuendo might have had in a different context of events, it had no immediate effect on Henry Hunt; he was to ride it all out in triumph, for the present. It was only later that the scales began to drop from the eyes of the admirers of St Henry of Ilchester; even from the eyes of Bamford and Johnson, his Manchester lieutenants.

★   ★   ★

It is much to be regretted that posterity is deprived of Samuel Bamford's pre-Peterloo observations in prose, and has to rely on his observations in verse. Bamford's *Passages in the Life of a Radical*[2] does indeed deal with Hunt's visit to Manchester, in January 1819, but it is, as has been seen, almost solely devoted to the theatre incident. Passed over, too, by Bamford, are all the meetings at Stockport, Ashton, Rochdale, etc. After the close of his description of the fracas at the theatre, he writes:

Amongst the meetings for reform held in the early part of the summer of 1819, were the one which took place on Spafields, London, at which Mr. Hunt was chairman; and another held at Birmingham, at which Major Cartwright and Sir Charles Wolseley were elected to act as legislatorial attornies for that town, in parliament. [sic].

It would seem that these movements in the country, induced our friends at Manchester to adopt a course similar to that at Birmingham, and it was accordingly arranged that a meeting for that purpose should be held on St. Peter's Field, on the 9th of August. But the object of that meeting having been declared illegal by the authorities, it was countermanded, and another was appointed to be held on the 16th of the same month.

Such are Samuel Bamford's 'passages' dealing with the history of those eventful months; he does, of course, deal with the 'drillings' in some detail, and prints a selection of the Government's documents concerning them. Posterity has therefore to rely, in the main, on his observations in verse. Not that they are not plain enough, and perhaps to his mind they were just. The radicals were entitled to use 'Nature's

[1] *Exchange Herald,* 17 August 1819.
[2] Bamford, Vol. I, 169.

ammunition' if assailed. His 'Stockport Lads', whom he commended in verse for drubbing the Yeomanry, for interfering with their meeting, had a record for such prowess even before he wrote.

One of the more enlightening 'passages' in his *Life of a Radical*[1]— written of course some time afterwards, and not published until twenty years later—relates, however, to a conversation Samuel Bamford had with Henry Hunt at Smedley Cottage:

On the afternoon of Friday, the thirteenth of August, I saw Mr. Hunt, at the residence of Mr. Johnson, at Smedley. Tuke, the painter, was amending Mr. Hunt's portrait, which indeed it wanted. In the course of conversation, Mr. Hunt expressed himself as apprehensive lest the people from the country should bring arms to the meeting on the following Monday; and he desired me to caution those from Middleton from so doing. He also shewed me a letter on a placard, addressed to 'The Reformers of Manchester and its Neighbourhood,' where he entreated them to come to the meeting 'armed only with a self-approving conscience.' He said that if the soldiers did attack the people, and take their caps of liberty and their banners, still, he hoped, they would proceed to the meeting, and not commit any violence.

I must own that this was new, and somewhat unpalatable advice to me. I had not the most remote wish to attack either person or property, but I had always supposed, that Englishmen, whether individually or in bodies, were justifiable by law in repelling an attack when in the King's peace, as I certainly calculated we should be, whilst in attendance at a legally constituted assemblage. My crude notions, which wonderfully coincided with those of the magistrates before quoted [Bamford had been quoting selected documents from the papers placed before parliament in November, 1819], led me to opine that we had a right to go to this place; and that consequently, there would not be any protection in law, to those who might choose to interrupt us in our right. I was almost certain there could be no harm whatever in taking a score or two of cudgels, just to keep specials at a respectful distance from our line. But this was not permitted.

Bamford is apparently sincere; but he knew, Hunt knew, that it was not now a case of 'keeping specials at a respectful distance' but that in the background was a host of armed men. The narrative continues:

Still I scarcely liked the idea of walking my neighbours into a crowd, both personally and politically adverse to us; and without means to awe them, or to defend ourselves. Was it not a fact that a numerous body of men had been sworn in to act as special constables?—was not an armed association formed at Manchester? and had not weapons been liberally distributed?[2] and what could

---

[1] Bamford, Vol. I, p. 191.
[2] The weapons never left the custody of the military authorities.

we do, if attacked by those men, with nothing to defend ourselves?[1] But Mr. Hunt combatted these notions, 'Were there not the laws of the country to protect us? would not their authority be upheld by those sworn to administer them?—and then, was it likely at all, that magistrates would permit a peaceable and legal assemblage to be interfered with? If we were in the right, were they not our guardians? If wrong, could they not send us home by reading the riot act? Assuredly, whilst we respected the law, all would be well on our side.

Had Samuel Bamford not known, which he undoubtedly did, that his own 'Stockport Lads' did not usually go home when the Riot Act was read, but attacked; as they had done with stones and brickbats after the Riot Act was read, in July 1818[2] and *routed* the 'Cavalry'; that they had routed the 'Cavalry' again with similar weapons in February 1819, at Sandy Brow. On that same day, (a fact not mentioned in the *Observer* report) they had, so the loyalist press alleged,[3] used the same 'nature's ammunition' on the military from behind a cover of women and children, and had later 'violently opposed and overpowered the constables' when ordered to disperse. Another radical bard had put on Bamford's mantle and laureateship at Stockport after Sir Charles Wolseley's visit, one Isaac Murray:

And Stockport's sons shall be thy van, thy country's rights to save,
Should Tyrant's vengeance thee assail, thou'lt Stockport's courage prove;

---

[1] Extract from Samuel Bamford's Petition to Parliament (printed in the *Manchester Observer*, 11 December 1819):
'. . . That your petitioner and his neighbours arrived at the proposed place of general meeting in Manchester for the purpose afore-said, in the greatest hilarity and good order, intending mischief to none, and suspecting none towards themselves, therefore, wholly unprepared with means of offence or defence, and many of them affording an indubitable pledge of their sincerity, by taking in their company their wives and female relatives . . .'
[2] [The magistrates ordered out the cavalry during a Stockport lockout] '. . . and went to the scene of pretended disturbance, when one of the magistrates read the Riot Act, and began to harangue the people, telling them they had Bagguley, Drummond, and Johnston among them, and that they were the persons who had caused the whole of the riot, not for the purpose of procuring an advance in the price of labour, but to gratify their hellish inclinations, by throwing the country into a state of rebellion; but he hoped the people would have more sense than be led away by the doctrines of such wicked incendiaries. He had no sooner uttered this infamous lie, than a volley of stones from the people obliged the officious gentleman to retreat for safety. The cavalry were then ordered to disperse the people, but as tyranny only needs to be resisted to be conquered, they soon found themselves inefficient to the task. Some of them were pelted with stones; others were dismounted; many retreated homeward; and one fled up Hillgate with the quickness of lightning, calling out murder! murder . . .' (*Manchester Observer*, 25 July 1818).
[3] *Manchester Mercury*, 28 February 1819.

She'll safe from harm her Wolseley keep, wrapt in his country's love,
Their base designs* should they this day, attempt as they have said,
E'er they thy sacred person touch, THEY'LL CLIMB O'ER ENGLISH
DEAD.

The capitals are the *Observer's*[1] and so is the asterisk, with a footnote:
*'To disturb the Meeting and seize by force the Cap of Liberty.' All the
foregoing, and the dangerous doctrine printed in the *Observer*, Bamford
knew; had he not known this, and that he himself by his undoubted
gifts had fostered incitement and resistance, his sincerity would have
been unchallenged. Whatever may have been Bamford's private
thoughts, Henry Hunt's arguments prevailed. At his trial, Bamford
said:

. . . I advised them not to insult any person, but rather to suffer any insult
on that day, as their opponents would be glad of a pretext to accuse them of
riot and disorder; that I entreated them to bear towards every one a spirit of
good will . . . I cautioned the people against offering any resistance, if such
an attempt should be made, as I preferred an appeal to the laws of my country
rather than to force; that I insisted no sticks should be taken, and that in
consequence several were left by the way; that we went in the greatest
hilarity and good humour, preceded by a band of music, which played
national airs; and that our fathers, our mothers, our wives, our children, and
our sweethearts were with us . . .[2]

Bamford's simple testimony on the crowd's demeanour on 16 August
convinced the court when he gave it in March 1820; it convinced even
the Crown prosecuting counsel, and it has convinced posterity. Perhaps
most important of all, it convinced Samuel Bamford that the Old Adam
in him had been put away:

> But, come my lads, some other day
> We'll pin them, e're they sneak away,
> And they shall either play or pay
> When Hunt returns again.

Hunt's insistence in his 11 August 'proclamation' that the people
should come to the meeting 'armed with no other weapon but that of a
self-approving conscience; determined not to suffer yourselves to be
irritated or excited, by any means whatsoever, to commit any breach
of the Public Peace' was plain; nothing could be plainer. But it could
not expunge completely the reiterated radical doctrine, expounded by
William Fitton at Rochdale to a crowd of 15,000 to 20,000 persons on
26 July:

[1] *Manchester Observer*, 3 July 1819.
[2] *State Trials*, pp. 285–6.

. . . Various measures had been adopted by His Majesty's Government to stifle the complaints of a suffering, he might almost say, a perishing people; but it appeared that every effort was unavailing, as from the numbers that had assembled on the present occasion, it was clear to every one who had been in the habit of attending similar meetings at Rochdale, that the increase of friends to the cause of Radical Reform was in the proportion of thousands to hundreds. Indictments had been preferred against some of the best friends to the country, for the purpose of bringing them to trial, under the alleged charge of sedition and conspiracy:—these futile efforts, he was happy to say, afforded no terrors to the honest man; as they would see by his side the persecuted Mr. Harrison, who had been arrested upon the hustings in London, on Wednesday last, upon charges that were indeed too contemptible to notice. (Applause). He felt it his duty, as Chairman of the Meeting, to observe, that indictments might also that day be preparing against several of his patriotic friends with whom he had then the pleasure of being sur-rounded—the same honourable notice the Boroughmongers were about to confer upon himself;[1] and it was not improbable that warrants might be served upon the parties, even before the expiration of the present Meeting; as, according to New Bayley Law, and New Bayley Grand Juries, Bills had only to be preferred, to be found, as a matter of course. However, he was sure that all his friends were armed with justice, and were strangers to fear; he would therefore earnestly request that under any circumstances, where the laws of the land were about to be enforced, that the people would not attempt to impede the officers of justice, as he could assure the assembly that the means the friends of liberty possessed of rebutting every charge, would most assuredly confound their opponents, and more fully expose the machinations of their enemies. . . . On the other hand, he begged to remark, that several threats had been held out by some *sham-valiants* in the town and neighbourhood of Rochdale, to seize and take away the Cap of Liberty. Under such circum-stances, he considered the Meeting were justified in preserving it, if they thought proper; as such a seizure would certainly amount to a theft, and indeed, depraved and obdurate as were the Borough-tyrants, they had not yet the hardihood publicly to countenance direct and open robbery. An attempt, similar to this, was made some months since at Stockport, when he had the honour to preside, the consequence was, the assailants were van-quished in an instant, and the Cap and Banner were preserved, to the utter confusion of the ragamuffins, who had foolishly been persuaded to encounter that fruitless and ridiculous attack . . .

William Fitton's reasoning to this point could not be challenged. It was the identical reasoning also of James Norris, the Manchester stipendiary magistrate. It was, however, beyond the wit of the wisest and most

---

[1] Fitton was arrested the same night (26 July) and on the following day put in bail. Harrison had been bailed out on the day of the meeting. *Aston's Exchange Herald*, 3 August 1819.

prudent radical to determine, whether the 'officers of justice' were to be 'impeded' or not, because they would not know, or could not know, whether those 'officers of justice' introduced themselves into the crowd to arrest or to assault. More important still, the radicals did not know that the much-played-up incident of the attempt to seize the Cap of Liberty at Stockport, in February 1819, was a display of overzealousness by the local constables of Stockport, condemned as such by their superiors, the magistrates at Manchester, and consequently never likely to occur again. It was the one fatal radical misapprehension.

It was this dilemma which was slowly looming up before the perspicacious mind of Henry Hunt. It can only be guessed whence Hunt feared the spark would come which could cause the seemingly inevitable explosion; for he did fear it. He probably did not in his wildest dreams at that point believe that he would be able to manipulate that explosion to turn defeat into victory. The Rev. Mr Stanley, watching Hunt curiously after his arrest on 16 August, thought he could 'perceive a smile of triumph on his countenance'. For days, for weeks, before 16 August, it had been suspected that the drillers on the moors were the danger; even Hunt had suspected it. The 'spark' had not come from that quarter.

X

Excitements and Anxieties, 9-16 August 1819

In reviewing the situation as it stood in that fateful week before 16 August, cognizance must be taken of the radicals' persistent charges that the magistrates intended, or were likely, to use violence against their meeting. So persistent are these charges that they sound convincing. But the truth is that no violence had been used against them since the Stockport Sandy Brow meeting in February, when a 'troop of cavalry', mounted constables armed only with staves, attempted to seize their cap of liberty. Their conduct was deplored by the Manchester magistrates at the time, and such conduct was not repeated. It was however referred to at every radical meeting thereafter.

Dr Read, nonetheless. piles up his evidence against the magistrates relentlessly, beginning with Hunt's visit to Manchester in January: 'Violence on the Peterloo scale was probably far from their minds, but an unhappy beginning had been made. As yet, however, the magistrates remained calm.'[1] Dr Read presents however, for most of the January– 9 August period, evidence only of their 'excessive alarms'. He continues:

Unfortunately, Byng was almost alone in his calm appraisal of the situation. The local magistrates were fully supported in their alarms by the local 'loyalists'. On July 9th they met at the Police Office in Manchester and passed the series of alarmist resolutions which have already been discussed. They also established a Committee in Aid of the Civil Power. This Committee, consisting chiefly of former town's officers, was very active in Manchester in the weeks just before Peterloo: its members (rather than the magistrates) were 'the original instigators' of the massacre, wrote Taylor, 'men of the most violent party feelings.' At a meeting of the Committee on July 16th it was resolved to form an 'Armed Association' for the protection of life and property in the town . . .[2]

It will be seen again that this passage from John Edward Taylor's indictment has been strengthened by substituting the word 'massacre' for the word which Taylor actually wrote, 'tragedy'; but in fact,

[1] Read, p. 107.
[2] Read, p. 116, quoting Taylor's *Notes and Observations* (1820) pp. 173–4.

Taylor was hinting darkly at the 'power behind the magistrates', because he could not bring himself to believe that there were any amongst the magistrates capable of doing what had been done, and with the motives then being universally attributed to them. The exact quotation was:

But though there can be no doubt that the Magistrates sanctioned the proceedings of the 16th of August, I am inclined to believe, that it is not to them that we are to look as the original instigators of the tragedy of that day. There is a Committee appointed . . . etc.

As pre-Peterloo evidence against the magistrates' 'decision' it is not very convincing. There is a further piece of evidence quoted. Dr Read says:

Exhortations . . . to gather evidence of Radical meetings and plottings were a constant theme in the letters sent out from the Home Office in the fortnight before Peterloo. Sidmouth and Hobhouse clearly had the very sensible idea of getting the Radical leaders quietly into prison by using the normal processes of the law and without making any spectacular gestures. Unfortunately their policy met with little response from the Manchester magistrates: they did not think a policy of accumulating evidence sufficiently vigorous. 'The remedy for the present state of things', wrote Norris six weeks before the massacre, 'must be (*in the first instance*) more violent than informations or indictments.'[1]

Chronology in dealing with pre-Peterloo matters is very important. This Norris quotation was written on 30 June. A number of strong measures was shortly to be taken, among them increasing the number of troops in Manchester, the Armed Association proposals, Watching and Warding, and the setting up of a special committee of magistrates whose duty it was to relieve Norris himself of an inordinate burden of responsibility. Dr Read's quotation goes on:

There was thus a great and very important difference between the attitude of the Home Office and the attitude of the Manchester magistrates before Peterloo. Both sincerely believed that the Radicals were plotting eventual revolution, but their ways of thwarting that revolution were very different. Hobhouse pressed for the collection of damaging evidence: Norris on the other hand had given up all hope by the end of June of putting down the reformers by mere informations or indictments. The Home Office expressed the need for the greatest caution in the use of the military: Norris was for putting his trust in 'martial law' and more troops. The Home Office suggested a monitory and conciliatory Address to the lower classes': the magistrates made no such gesture.

[1] Read, p. 120.

In fact, the magistrates did make such a gesture, reference to which is contained in a letter written by Lord Sidmouth's secretary, Hobhouse, dated 11 August, a copy of which is printed in Appendix B to the *State Trials*[1] volume containing Hunt's trial. This letter is far more important than many others printed in that appendix, because it is the last one sent by the Home Office to the Manchester magistrates *before* 16 August. It was the Home Office last-minute instruction, and had more bearing on the proceedings of that day than perhaps is realized. The first paragraph reads:

Lord Sidmouth's thanks for the letter of the 9th inst. From another quarter he has received a very judicious placard put forth on that day against 'the itinerant advocates of treason' . . .

This undoubtedly refers to the placard put out by the magistrates, dated 9 August[2] and couched in more conciliatory terms than their 'abstain at your peril' notice. Whatever may be thought of the effectiveness of this placard as a 'monitory and conciliatory Address', it is not correct to say that 'the magistrates made no such gesture'. Mr Norris may indeed have 'given up all hope by the end of June of putting down the reformers by mere informations and indictments', but he hadn't given up hope (or so he said) of preserving the *peace* even up to the night of Sunday, 15 August, although he added 'it is scarcely possible to expect it'.

Dr Read continues emphatically:

. . . But once the meeting had assembled the magistrates were no longer bound by the detailed moderating advice of the Law Officers. They were left much more to their own discretion. And because, as we have seen, fundamentally they were out of touch with the desire of the Law Officers and of the Home Office for moderation, this discretion was not exercised with the restraint which their superiors clearly desired. In the weeks before the Peterloo meeting moderation had been forced upon the Manchester magistrates from above, but on the day of Peterloo itself they were left free to give rein to their own immoderate alarms. Ominously, on August 3rd the 'loyalist' *Manchester Mercury* newspaper reported that the Cheshire magistrates had 'come to a determination to act with decision, and to *suppress all Seditious Meetings as they assemble.*' It was this policy, not the one advocated by the Home Office, which produced the Peterloo Massacre.

While behind the scenes the magistrates and the Home Office made their regrettably ill-attuned preparations for the great meeting, an atmosphere of great excitement was developing in Manchester . . .[3]

[1] pp. 1380-1.
[2] See above p. 98.
[3] Read, p. 122.

The question of an 'operative word' in a sentence thrusts itself forcibly upon the attention again. The italics in the penultimate paragraph are not Dr Read's; they belong to the writer of the *Manchester Mercury*. The word 'suppress', it is suggested, in the context used by the quotation conveys one meaning only; it is *suppress* by military execution, a method advised against by the Home Office, but, according to Dr Read, and according to the radical interpretation of Peterloo, machinated by the irresponsible (to put it at its mildest) Manchester magistrates. The *Manchester Mercury*'s use of the word 'suppress' simply will not bear the weight of the meaning placed upon it by Dr Read's paragraph; the full quotation reads:

The Cheshire Magistrates have come to a determination to act with decision, and *suppress all seditious Meetings immediately as they assemble*: and if the civil power be not sufficient, then to read the Riot Act, and call in the aid of the military. This is as it should be.[1]

Given in full it is not very important as evidence to show the magistrates' malignant intentions.

How vitally important *intentions* were before 16 August has been seen. It is certain, because there is abundant evidence, that Hunt, Bamford and Johnson (to name only those three) had no wanton intention to cause a riot, although it must be admitted there was a remarkable exhibition of what modern idiom has termed 'brinkmanship' displayed; the great majority of their followers on St Peter's Field did not want it either. But it can scarcely be argued, in the face of the evidence set out in this narrative, that amongst that vast crowd on that fatal ground there were not those who shared Bamford's pre-Peterloo opinion that they were entitled to resist, or even take the initiative and attack. Attack, that is, in the spirit of William Fitton's 'half a dozen angry weavers would eat up a whole corps of Yeomanry fellows', or of giving them a Saxtonian 'sousing',[2] little considering the effects of so doing in a field surrounded with troops and in the middle of a tightly-massed crowd of people.

So far, this recapitulation has left out of account the Manchester and Salford Yeomanry Cavalry. Nothing in this investigation has been discovered in the way of evidence to indict even an element of them with the 'give it 'em, lads' spirit displayed by the Bamford school; except that which Dr Healey said he had heard prior to the Ashton meeting, 'that a reward of £50 had been offered' if a Cap of Liberty was seized;

[1] *Manchester Mercury*, 3 August, 1819.
[2] See above p. 56.

a fact he had got 'from one of the Yeomanry cavalry'.[1] The officers in the fracas with Hunt in January were regulars. Indeed, the lack of evidence in the *Observer's* columns is remarkable, for there was no reluctance in those pre-Peterloo months to bring forward any stick with which to beat the Yeomanry, whom it regarded with contempt. Even *after* Peterloo, John Edward Taylor had to say in their favour:

With respect to the conduct of the Yeomanry on the 16th of August, I am decidedly of opinion that considerable misapprehension has existed. That the greater part of the corps are actually incapable of acting with deliberate cruelty, it gives me pleasure to state my belief . . .[2]

But he then had much to say regarding their alleged excesses. In spite of the lack of pre-Peterloo evidence, there must have been a 'give it 'em, lads' faction amongst the Yeomanry, if only in retaliation for the merciless lampooning they received from the radical press.

A solitary broadside song-sheet, issued after Peterloo, has survived in the Manchester Public Library collection of Peterloo broadsides: (p. 131).

The song-sheet could be taken as evidence of this 'give it 'em, lads' school. It is to be feared that they had little stomach for singing, however, in those tragic post-Peterloo months. There is one flaw in it, which might suggest it did not emanate from the Yeomanry at all, an error of fact which could not have escaped them. They didn't 'assemble in St James's Square[3] and march to Peterloo'; they galloped from Pickford's yard in Portland Street; the broadside could therefore have been the production of some enterprising ballad-monger. That it did not have a wide currency is self-evident. It would have been seized on by their opponents as additional evidence against them.

★   ★   ★

There has been no convincing evidence up to the present of the magistrates' premeditated intentions to suppress the meeting by military execution. The one fact that the radicals could bring against them was that by their ill-conceived placard, 'abstain at your peril', they had threatened to use force. In that age of the careful, the meticulous, use of the language, it was a mistake of the first magnitude. Even Lord Sidmouth was to expostulate:

Every discouragement and obstacle should be thrown in its [the meeting's] way, and the advertisement from the magistrates will no doubt have a

[1] See above, p. 61.
[2] *Observations*, pp. 175-6.
[3] Their H.Q. was in St James's Square.

THE ANSWER

TO

PETER-LOO!

ON the sixteenth day of August, eighteen hundred and nineteen,
All in the town of Manchester the REBELLY CREW were seen,
They call themselves reformers, and by Hunt the traitor true,
To attend a treason meeting on the plains of Peter-Loo.

Those hearers at their patron's call came flocking into town,
Both Male and Female radical, and many a gapeing clown,
Some came without their breakfast, which made their bellies rue ;
But got a warm baggin on the plains of Peter-Loo.

From Stayley-Bridge they did advance with a band of music fine,
And brought a cap of liberty from Ashton-under-lyne ;
There was Macclesfield and Stockport lads, and Oldham rougheads too,
Came to hear the treason sermon preached by Hunt at Peter-Loo.

About the hour of one o'clock this champion took the chair,
Surrounded by his aid-de-camps, his orders for to hear,
And disperse them through that REBELLY MOB, which around his
    standard drew ;
But they got their jackets dusted on the plains of Peter-Loo.

They hoisted up treason caps and flags, as plainly you may see,—
And with loud acclamations shouted Hunt and liberty ;
They swore no man should spoil their plan, but well our Yeomen
    knew ;
They assembled in St. James's Square, and marched for Peter-Loo.

The Rochdale band of music, with harmony sublime,
Had placed themselves convenient to amuse Hunt's concubine ;
But soon their big drum head was broke, all by our Yeomen true;
They dropped their instruments, and run away from Peter-Loo.

When the Yeomen did advance the mob began to fly,
Some thousands of old hats and clogs behind them there did lie ;
They soon pulled down their *Treason Flags*, and numbers of them
    flew ;
And Hunt they took a prisoner on the plains of Peter-Loo.

Now Hunt is taken prisoner and sent to Lancaster gaol,
With seven of his foremost men, their sorrows to bewail ;
His mistress sent to the hospital her face for to renew,
For she got it closely shaven on the plains of Peter-Loo.

Success attend those warlike men, our Yeomen Volunteers,
And all their Gallant Officers who knows no dread or fears,
Likewise the *Irish Trumpeter*, that loud his trumpet blew,
And took a cap of liberty from them at Peter-Loo.

Now to conclude and make an end, here's a health to GEORGE our
    KING,
And all those Gallant Yeomanry whose praises I loudly sing ;
May Magistrates and Constables with zeal their duty do ;
And may they prove victorious upon every Peter-Loo.

5. The Answer to Peterloo

salutary effect in this respect. But his Lordship thinks it would be imprudent to act up to the spirit of the advertisement.[1]

To the magistrates' critics, as distinct from their traducers, this apparent threat to use violence on a meeting was *prima facie* evidence that they had (as Lord Sidmouth's secretary put it) 'acted up to the spirit of the advertisement'. It could never be explained away *after* Peterloo.

One of Samuel Bamford's less admirable ventures into verse appeared in his collected edition of 1864 entitled 'Lines to a Plotting Parson', consisting of five rather innocuous verses, originally written in 1820, and directed at the Rev. William Robert Hay, the co-opted stipendiary magistrate on the Select Committee who acted at Peterloo. He figures in almost every account of Peterloo as having received the valuable living of Rochdale as a 'reward' for his services on 16 August. Dr Read even termed it a 'provocative appointment'.[2] Bamford's five verses in their 1864 version are toned down in their asperities, and the poem truncated as it is from the original version seems to have little point. The 1820 version of fifteen verses had plenty. It was one of the bitterest, most vituperative pieces of writing in all the Peterloo canon, because it was aimed at an individual, and it was a work of which Bamford was not very proud later.[3] Its opening verses shew little promise of what is to follow:

> Come over the hills out of York Parson [Hay]
> Thy living is goodly, thy mansion is gay,
> Thy flock will be scattered if longer thou stay,
> Our Shepherd, our Vicar, the good Parson [Hay].
>
> O fear not, for thou shalt have plenty indeed,
> Far more than a shepherd so humble will need;
> Thy wage shall be ample, two thousand or more,
> Which tithes and exactions will bring to thy store.
>
> And if thou *should'st* wish for a little increase,
> The lambs thou may'st sell, and the flock thou may'st fleece;
> *The market is good and the prices are high,*
> *And the butchers are ready with money to buy.*
>
> Thy dwelling it stands on the ridge of a hill,
> And the town lies below it, so quiet and still;
> With a church at thy elbow for preaching and prayer,
> And a rich congregation to slaver and stare.

[1] *State Trials*, App. B., p. 1379 (Hobhouse to Norris, 4 August).
[2] Read, p. 184.
[3] Raines, *Vicars of Rochdale* (Chetham Soc., NS. 11, Part II, p. 300).

And here, like a good *loyal* priest thou shalt reign,
The cause of thy patrons[1] with zeal to maintain.
And the poor and the hungry shalt faint at thy word,
As thou doom'st them to hell[2] in the name of the Lord.

And here is a Barrack with soldiers enow,
The deed which thou willest all ready to do;
They will rush on the people in martial array,
If thou but thy blood-dripping cassock display.

And Mea[ghe]r[3] shall ever be close by thy side,
With a brave troop of Yeomanry ready to ride;
For the steed shall be saddled, the sword shall be bare,
And there shall be none the defenceless to spare.

Then the joys that thou felt upon St. Peter's Field,
Each week or each month some new outrage shall yield,
And thy eye which is failing shall brighten again,
And pitiless gaze on the wounded and slain.

Then thy Prince too shall thank thee, and add to thy wealth,
Thou shall preach down sedition and pray for his health;
And Sidmouth, and Canning, and sweet Castlereagh,
Shall write pleasant letters to dear Cousin [Hay].

Each dungeon now silent shall sound with a groan,
For the captive shall mourn in its darkness alone;
And the chain shall be polish'd which now hangs in rust,
And brighten'd the bar which is mouldering to dust.

And the tears of the virgin in torrents shall flow,
Unheeded her tears, and unpitied her woe;
The blush of her cheek like a rose-bud shall fade,
For the youth whom thy villainous arts have betrayed.

---

[1] The minute and insignificant change of the word 'patrons' of the original edition, to 'patron' in the 1864, is not so insignificant as it appears; The original 'patrons' referred to the Government: the radical version being that they had conferred upon Hay the living as a 'reward' etc. It was pointed out that the living was not the Government's to give, but the Archbishop of Canterbury's; which was countered by: then the Government had prevailed upon the Archbishop, etc. Finally it was officially denied in the House of Commons* that the facts were as the radicals had stated, but that it was to redeem a promise made to Hay by the Archbishop two years *before* 1820; yet the contrary continued to be proclaimed. What is more, it still is. Bamford added a footnote to his 1864 edition: 'The vicarage of Rochdale is in the gift of the Archbishop of Canterbury, and it was conferred on the Rev. W. R. Hay shortly after his distinguished services in the affair of St Peter's Field, in 1819'.(!)
* *Parl. Deb.* NS. V, 15 May 1821, p. 716 et seq.
[2] 'Doom'st them to' changed to 'threatens with' in 1864.
[3] The Yeomanry Trumpeter.

For spies they shall lurk by the window at night,
Like bloodhounds, to smell out the prey of thy spite;
And laugh shall be hush'd, and the townsmen shall meet,
But none, e'en his neighbour shall venture to greet.

And now, gloomy famine shall stalk thro' the land,
No comfort the poor shall receive at thy hand;
And the widow shall curse thee whilst life doth remain,
And the orphan shall lisp back her curses again.

And the night wind shalt sound like a scream in thine ear,
And the tempest shalt shake thee with terrible fear,
And the zephyr, which fans thee, shall bring thee no cure;
It will whisper a tale which thou can'st not endure.

And the day shall arise but its joys will be fled,
And the season of darkness shall add to thy dread;
And a mark of affliction thou ever shalt be,
And none shall partake of thy trouble with thee.

Middleton, January 12th, 1820.   B.[1]

The Rev. W. R. Hay was considered to be something of a stoic; he had to be. If Bamford's Sandy Brow lines are to be considered as an incitement to throw stones, his 'Lines to a Plotting Parson' were an incitement to throwing stones of another kind. It wasn't to be the 'zephyr' which would 'whisper the tale' Hay could not endure, but the writers of anonymous letters. Hay considered that he had been the recipient of more of these than any man living or dead, letters which he kept during his lifetime tied up in bundles.[2] The 'tale' otherwise wasn't whispered: it was shouted from the housetops, from the platforms, and in the columns of most newspapers in the realm. On being asked, soon after Peterloo, if he meant to prosecute one editor for a particularly scathing piece of scurrility, he retorted with perfect nonchalance, 'Why should I give myself the trouble'; but he did give himself the trouble of writing to the offending editor:

Sir—In return for the calumny with which you have honoured me (for your censure is panegyric), I send you the sentiments of a great man (if I mistake not, Lord Verulam) for your perusal. 'Convinced, as I am, that every man has his failings, and that few are exempt from malice, I shall never be ready to confirm a report to the prejudice of my neighbour's honour; if he prove

[1] Another truncated version is quoted in Raines' *Vicars of Rochdale*, p. 300; the complete version appeared in the *Manchester Observer*, 26 February 1820.
[2] Raines, MS. 36 (p. 276), Chetham's Library.

guilty, I shall be sorry to encrease the burden of his sufferings, by my reflections; if he be proved innocent, I shall be happy to think I was not one of his
calumniators.'[1]

Parson Hay tied up innumerable bundles of papers and manuscripts,
filled commonplace books with the *bon mots* and jotting of a lifetime,
and meticulously packed scrapbooks with news-cuttings, most of which
are in Chetham's Library, Manchester, and some of which concern
Peterloo. One bundle escaped Chetham's net, and has only fairly
recently (1957) found its way into that other famous Manchester library,
the John Rylands Library. Against the day when that 'tale' which it was
alleged by Bamford that Hay could not endure would be told in its
entirety, he gathered together these papers concerning Peterloo, even
transcribing all of Hunt's letters to the press which he could find, preserving 'placards', broadsides, and other ephemera which probably
exist nowhere else. The bundle was part of the bequest made in 1957,
in memory of A. P. Wadsworth, one time editor of the *Manchester
Guardian*, and had been preserved by the family of J. T. Smith, of
Rochdale, to be gathered in by A. P. Wadsworth's wide-ranging book
and manuscript collecting net. It is catalogued 'English MS. 1197'.
Perhaps the most enlightening document in the collection is a copy report
given by Hay to Lord Sidmouth, on 7 October 1819.[2] It is a post-Peterloo
document, and might be considered disingenuous; but facts can be
checked. For pre-16 August it is valuable:

Your Lordship will have received from Mr. Norris, from time to time, previous to the 11th July, various statements respecting the private movements of
the disaffected. On that day he came over to see me [probably at Ackworth,
in Yorkshire] and on the next day went over to see Sir John Byng. It was
clear from Mr. Norris's accounts, that some support would be necessary for
the Magistrates here, and that it would be proper that other districts should be
put upon their guard. Our Sessions commenced here on the 19th, and one of
the first measures adopted by the Bench was to issue circulars, to the Magistrates of the neighbouring parts of Cheshire, and to the more distant districts
of Lancashire to attend on the following Friday. A very numerous attendance
was then given. I hope to be able hereafter to furnish your Lordship with the
names—Mr. Egerton was in the Chair, and amongst other proceedings a
select Committee of the Magistrates from both Counties was appointed—the
names of which were privately communicated to your Lordship.

At our Sessions it appeared that some spirited Resolutions had been passed
at the lately held Knutsford Sessions, at which Lord Stamford attended—that

---

[1] *Manchester Gazette*, 25 September, 1819.
[2] Eng. MS. 1197/67, J.R.L.

these had been privately communicated to Lord Derby, who, in strong terms expressed his approbation of them.

The Knutsford Sessions had been held on 13 July, and one of the 'spirited resolutions' was:

That it appears that various Public Meetings have lately been held in this and the neighbouring counties, at which evil-disposed and designing persons, taking advantage of the depression of trade, and the consequent distress, having wickedly disseminated inflammatory doctrines; and under the false pretext of Parliamentary Reform, have vilified the constituted Authorities, inciting thereby the ignorant and unwary to insurrection and the commission of crimes which may endanger their personal liberty and lives.[1]

Cheshire armed associations were proposed, special constables to be enrolled, and all the other measures which were to be copied in Manchester. Hay's report proceeds:

From the Information received, the Sessions signified to the Grand Jury the necessity they felt for an armed association and such proposition was also forwarded to your Lordship and Lord Derby.

The select Committee of Magistrates met from time to time, after the first two meetings, three of the members were *unable to attend*, and the remainder continued to act regularly,[2] the name of Mr. Wright[3] being added to the Committee. These Magistrates, of course, amongst other matters received informations in respect of different particulars connected with the views of the disaffected. It was soon made known that a Meeting in which great stress was laid by the disaffected was fixed for the 9th of August, but when the purposes of the Meeting were published, the Magistrates issued a Notification of their Sense that it would be an unlawful Meeting and of their Intention to stop it. After consulting Counsel, one Saxton, an assistant to the editor of the *Observer* gave notice that the Meeting was abandoned, but in that Notice there was a peculiar expression which caused the Committee to doubt whether or no the abandonment was real.

This 'peculiar expression' was, of course, the gloss which Saxton gave to Hunt's 'proclamation' issued from Coventry, that it might appear to some of his *Observer* readers as 'quite unintelligible'. It was just that to the magistrates, and is another example of that fear (alarmist or real) that they were being outwitted by some secret organization. It lends point to Norris's 3 August letter to Sidmouth[4]: they were

---

[1] *Papers Relative to the Internal State of the Country*, p. 3.

[2] These were probably the Rev. Thos. Dunham Whitaker, and the Rev. John Holme, who in the 1820s was acting as magistrate in the Oldham area, both from the Blackburn Division of the county, and Richard Marsh, of the Warrington Division.

[3] Of Flixton.

[4] Quoted on p. 100.

shadow-fighting, in spite of their prohibition of the 9 August meeting. They had a shock too, when Hunt and Sir Charles Wolseley turned up at Stockport on the evening of 8 August. The meeting, they felt, was 'on':

The unexpected arrival of Hunt with Sir Charles Wolseley at Stockport on the Evening of the 8th, [goes on Hay's report], and their proceeding to Manchester in the forenoon of the 9th, and in going through the streets with an evident wish to court popularity, strengthened our suspicion. In truth, Information was brought to us that Emissaries had been dispatched to their friends to order attendance at St. Peter's that afternoon at 4 o'clock; this however proved unfounded.

The parties proceeded to Johnson's at Smedley with a Seeming Intention to stay there; and as Meetings were to be held at Leigh and other places, the Magistrates thought that they meant to travel about to these Meetings for the whole week, and to harass the Military by attendance previous to the 16th on which day the Meeting postponed was to be holden.[1] These circumstances were communicated to General Byng. However the apprehension was false. Sir Charles Wolseley left Smedley, and Hunt was principally engaged in writing and other Business.

This communicating with General Byng clears up another pre-Peterloo misapprehension. Dr Read says[2]:

Despite this 'painful uncertainty' [Norris's hope that 'peace may be preserved, but under all circumstances it is scarcely possible to expect it; and in short, in this respect we are in a state of painful uncertainty' in his letter of 15 August], Hay had written to Lord Sidmouth only five days before saying that there was now no need for the presence of General Byng in Manchester as the situation had improved.[3] Thus almost on the eve of the great meeting the magistrates, either through folly or through vanity, had dispensed with the assistance of the man who had restrained their alarms at the Blanket meeting and who had peaceably dispersed the weavers' parade in 1818. This was perhaps the most important single decision leading to the bloodshed at Peterloo. [and Dr. Read adds a footnote]: Byng, at his headquarters in Pontefract, had no expectation of trouble at Manchester: 'I have no fear of disturbance

[1] It is, of course, necessary to remind the reader of the terms of the Prince Regent's Proclamation of 30 July, which charged all Sheriffs, Justices of the Peace etc. to 'make diligent inquiry . . . and bring to justice . . . all persons who have been or may be guilty of uttering seditious speeches and harangues, and all persons concerned in riots, or unlawful assemblies, which, on whatever pretext they may be grounded, are not only contrary to law, but dangerous to the most important interests of the Kingdom.' The interpretation of this *Order* was to have an extremely important bearing on the events of the period ending at two o'clock on Monday, 16 August. This is a point usually overlooked.

[2] Read, p. 124.

[3] Read, quoting H.O. 42/191.

on Monday', he wrote to Hobhouse; 'on the contrary they are much alarmed at our precautions'.[1] His attitude contrasts with that of Norris as expressed in his letter [Norris hopes for peace, but doubts it] of the 15th quoted above. There seems little doubt that if Byng had been present at Manchester on the 16th the arrests would have been made without bloodshed.

The Rev. W. R. Hay did indeed tell Byng that his presence at Manchester was no longer necessary but it was not for the 16th—it was for the weekend of the 9th, when the magistrates had sent an SOS to him on hearing of the arrival of Hunt and Wolseley at Stockport, for they feared that their banning of the 9th meeting was to be flouted, which would have meant insurrection. Norris's letter[2] used the words 'serious contest'. It was the magistrates' relief when this feared danger had passed which caused Hay to write to Byng; it was neither 'folly' nor 'vanity' but just plain relief, and this misinterpreted letter was sent probably by messenger, on Monday the 9th, as soon as it was obvious the feared meeting was 'off'. It must have been a message of the briefest nature, for Byng was not quite sure what had happened. General Byng's reply written from York is in Hay's bundle of papers:

York, 8 a.m. August 10, 1819. My Dear Sir. I received your letter late last night about $11\frac{1}{2}$ p.m. having been some time in Bed with a violent Headache occasioned by the intense heat of the day. My first intention was to get into the Mail then about to leave this for Liverpool, but I found myself quite unequal either to write to you by it.

Upon consideration it appears to me either that the Meeting dispersed quietly and my presence is unnecessary, or that something may have occurred to require the movement of such disposable Force as I may be able to collect in this part of my District. I have therefore resolved to send this by express, which will arrive in time for your answer to be sent by the Mail leaving Manchester for this at an early hour to-morrow, and if express is necessary I shall receive your reply to-morrow morning. I have the fullest confidence in the Officer commanding the Troops in and near Manchester, and if no serious disturbance occurs I am not aware of any particular service my presence can render. I must request you to believe that I stay not here from the unworthy motives of seeing the Races, for circumstances have occurred to prevent my receiving any interest or pleasure, and I should return Home, but until I hear again I think myself better placed here, where I have a Regiment at my disposal, and am with the Lord Lieutenant of the West Riding, who will if wanted I am sure authorize the assembling of his two excellent Yeomanry Corps. Yours . . . J. Byng.

I will trouble you to give me as full information as you can, that I may

[1] Byng to Hobhouse, 14 August 1819, H.O. 42/192.
[2] Quoted on p. 100.

better be able to decide on the necessary arrangements, all my attention is at this moment being particularly *called to other quarters*.[1]

Parson Hay's reply was sent the day of receipt, written cryptically because it was being forwarded by the Mail:

Police Office, Manchester. 8 o'clock. Tuesday 10th August 1819. I have just been favoured with your Letter of this morning which has arrived in the fair course of the Orderly Messenger. At the time I took the liberty with the concurrence of the Magistrates here to request your attendance in aid of the civil power—I certainly did not wish it to be understood that we desired it with a view to any one individual act or meeting. It appeared to us then that from the appearance of the parties who had so very unexpectedly come down, from other circumstances that the probable intention was to traverse different districts for above a week—that this was a sort of service which you might not have originally contemplated—that therefore a sort of continuance of service might be required which would ultimately interfere with the arrangements you had made and which your presence alone could order or regulate. Such was the aspect of things at the moment at which I applied to you. I am happy to say that that aspect has been materially altered from the reports which we have since received and in such a degree as to do away with the propriety of applying to you in any further instance with the same view as in the first instance we felt it to be our duty to do. I have therefore merely sent this by the course of post not conceiving that either an express or an orderly is requisite, &c., &c. W. R. Hay.

The details of these tortuous and complicated improvisations as the situation changed are self evident: a mobile force of troops to cover the whole area, if necessary, such as General Byng appeared to have kept at his disposal; all now it seemed, were not required. The magistrates thought their bluff had been called by the reformers; but it was a 'scare'.

On Tuesday, 10 August, the magistrates reported to Lord Sidmouth that there were drilling parties operating in the area between Bolton and Bury, and that representations had been made by some of the principal inhabitants of Bury stating that they 'doubted their ability to resist the torrent of disaffection without military aid; and that persons proper to serve as special constables were so intimidated that without the presence of some military, they doubted their ability to induce them to come forward to be sworn on the day appointed for that purpose, viz. Friday next.'[2] There was the meeting at Leigh, eight miles from Bolton, to take place on Wednesday the 11th. To concert measures for action at this

[1] Eng. MS. 1197, J.R.L.
[2] *Papers Relative to the Internal State of the Country*, p. 18, dated 10 August 1819.

meeting the magistrates of the Bolton and Warrington divisions met at Hulton Hall on the Tuesday. It was the first direct reference to William Hulton's activities before the fateful day.

Their report on the Leigh meeting was forwarded to Lord Sidmouth the same day:

During the morning a great concourse of the lower orders of people were waiting for the arrival of Mr. Hunt, whose presence was anxiously expected, in consequence of which the meeting was delayed until past two o'clock. Mr. Hunt, and none of his partisans forthcoming, it was deemed necessary to commence the proceedings of the day. Two carts were lashed together in the market place, [a fine open space of ground], when Mr. Battersby, [an itinerant preacher], Mr. Thomas Cleworth, and a Mr. Bamber [one of the society of Friends] with several others ascended the platform . . .[1]

There were in fact several speeches made, according to the reports in the local press, and the crowd was estimated at about 3,000; the report states 300:

After the business was opened by Mr. Battersby . . . Mr. Turner, [a magistrate], at the head of the police, made their appearance, and took Mr. Thomas Cleworth into custody upon a warrant of the Magistrates. About 300 people were concentrated; and the officers took their man without opposition, and this vigilant step threw dismay in the ranks of the reformers, many of whom I saw dispersing in all directions.

The press had reported that there was a move to resist by some of the audience, but they were persuaded against it by the speakers. The Leigh meeting was the first Lancashire meeting actually 'suppressed'.

Hunt, whilst he was confined in the New Bayley prison during the days after 16 August, in writing to his friends in London, gave his version of his movements during his stay at Smedley:

I arrived at Mr. Johnson's house on Monday, and was never two miles from it during the whole week, although I had repeated, and kind invitations, not only in Manchester, but the neighbourhood; and that was on Saturday previous to this bloody business. It was reported that the Magistrates had issued a warrant against me for some supposed or real offence, in order to put it in execution by apprehending me at the Meeting on Monday. Now *mark this*: That they should not have any such pretence for interrupting the proceedings, I drove into Manchester, and waited upon the Magistrates, who were sitting at the New Bailey, and informed them that as I had heard there was a warrant issued by them against me, I thought it my duty at once to wait upon them to say, that I was, and should be at all times, ready to meet any charge they may have against me, without giving them the least trouble! They

[1] *Papers . . . Internal State of the Country* p. 19.

politely answered that they knew of no such thing, or any such intention! Therefore, I retired, perfectly satisfied, in my own mind, that it was only an idle report. This fact cannot be too generally known. Recollect that I received this answer from two of the very Magistrates (one of them a Clergyman) who signed the warrant against me on Monday![1]

Hunt did not know that on this incident his account would practically coincide with the Rev. Mr Hay's report:

On Saturday the 14th Hunt came with Johnson to the New Bailey and inquired for Mr. Norris or me. We were not there—Mr. Tatton and Mr. Trafford were; applying himself to Mr. Tatton, Hunt said: 'I understand that there is a warrant against me.' Mr. Tatton replied: 'I am not aware that there is one.' Hunt said: ' I merely have to say that if there is a warrant out against me I am ready to deliver myself up'. Before dinner Mr. Norris returned home and found Johnson writing a note to him. On Mr. Norris appearing, Johnson stated that the purpose of his Enquiry was to know whether any Warrant was out against Hunt. Mr. Norris answered: 'I have issued none, nor do I know of any.'

Apart from the confusion of persons[2] involved there is no matter of conflicting facts here. The warrant was not, of course, issued until the morning of 16 August, and it was not for the arrest of Hunt only, but of Hunt, Knight, Johnson, and Moorhouse; and it would appear that the decision to make the arrests had certainly not been taken on the Saturday, although the magistrates were being pressed by the Government. When the following letter from Whitehall was received in Manchester it is not known; it could have been received on the Friday and considered by the magistrates then, or it may have received consideration on the Saturday, for on those last few days they were in continuous session. Hulton later said that for the last few days, because of this continuous sitting he did not return home, although he lived only twelve miles from Manchester:

August 11th. Hobhouse to Norris. Lord Sidmouth's thanks for the letter of the 9th instant. From another quarter he has received a very judicious placard put forth on that day against 'the itinerant advocates of treason.' Upon the subject of Hunt's arrest, his Lordship thinks that if you find good grounds for issuing a warrant it will be advisable not to forbear from doing so, in the expectation of his giving you a better opportunity, unless some other reason for your forbearance presents itself. We know that all the demagogues feel extremely sore on the subject of criminal prosecutions, and that Hunt in

---

[1] *Manchester Observer*, 28 August 1819.
[2] Hunt, at his trial, said: 'There were Mr. Wright, Mr. Tatton and two other magistrates present at the time.' (*State Trials*, p. 323).

particular observes extreme caution for the sake of avoiding them. It is therefore very desirable to take the earliest opportunity of proceeding against him. Lord Sidmouth is extremely happy that Dr. Hay[1] affords you the benefit of his assistance until after the 16th.[2]

Hunt had certainly given no opportunity so far to the magistrates for issuing a warrant, and he probably knew it; although at the back of his mind would be the doubt as to how much he had been implicated by the alleged illegal resolutions of the Smithfield meeting some weeks before. This very matter was still being churned over by the Law Officers of the Crown even up to 17 August[3] when they sent to Lord Sidmouth their considered opinions on it. That the implications of this Smithfield meeting were well known in Manchester is certain from the facts stated in the placard 'To the Friends of Reform' issued on 14 August.[4] Not only then were there upper and nether millstones grinding away at the magistrates in the above letter and the implications of Smithfield; but there were 'side' millstones as well in the Royal Proclamation, already seen, and the alarm of a considerable part of local opinion. Not to mention the sanctions imposed upon them by their precipitancy—going faster than desired by Government—in the matter of the prohibited 9 August meeting; and, finally, that 'the *avowed object* of the second meeting (the 16th) was legal'. Mr Hay's report from the magistrates continued:

The Committee continued to meet, and did so on Saturday, the 14th, Sunday, and Monday. Prior to the Saturday, different points had been discussed as to the propriety of stopping the Meeting and the manner of doing so. They were of opinion that Multitudes coming in columns with Flags and Marching in military array were even in the approach to the Meeting a tumultuous

---

[1] He was not 'Dr' Hay.

[2] *State Trials,* App. B., pp. 1380–1.

[3] 'If it can be proved that Mr. Hunt spoke or took part *in support* of the resolutions [at Smithfield], we think that he, as well as any other person acting in a similar way, may be made the objects of a criminal prosecution, but before any such prosecution is instituted, we think that the whole of the evidence affecting him and such other person should be more fully and particularly stated.

R. Gifford

Lincolns Inn, August 17th, 1819.'   J. S. Copley.

Gifford was Attorney-General. He died 1826; in a biographical note he was described as 'discreet and moderate, not putting the formidable machinery of state prosecutions in motion without necessity, and with the strongest probability of obtaining a conviction.'—(*Legal Observer,* November 1831). Such a character is borne out by the above extract, and by the Law Officers' decisions after the arrest of Hunt and his companions. (qv) Quoted by *State Trials,* App. B, p. 1376.

[4] See above p. 120.

assembly; and it was for a little time under consideration whether each Column should not be stopped at their respective entrances into the Town, but this was given up—it was considered that the Military might then be distracted and it was wished that the Town should see what the Meeting was, when assembled, and also that those who came should be satisfied they were assembled in an unlawful manner. In truth, our Information was such that we could have little doubt, but that the parties would assemble in an illegal ['unlawful' crossed out] manner.

There would seem to be little doubt too that, in the foregoing, the magistrates were thinking along the lines of the recent Prince Regent's Proclamation.

In addition to the general Information [the report goes on] of training, from time to time, there was a specific Information of the training to be at White Moss on the 15th, early in the morning; we had also information that the parties were told it would be the last training that would be necessary before the meeting. Your Lordship will be aware that it was at this meeting on the 15th that Murray and Shawcross met with the treatment which was at the time detailed to you.

This White Moss incident has been related before. Dr Read deals with it, Bamford does too; but details from radical sources as reported by the *Observer* have not, it is believed, appeared since 1819. Dr Read's account[1] is as follows:

. . . the magistrates of Manchester could not by this stage have been calmed by any assurances. The seal was set on their fears when early on the morning of the 15th two of their spies were beaten up while watching drilling on the White Moss near Middleton. Taylor afterwards pointed out that one of the spies, Murray, had been one of the gang which had broken into Hunt's private room in January. It was for this, he argued, and not because the Radicals were dismayed at their sedition being discovered, that Murray had been attacked: the Radicals had no seditious intentions. This explanation of the White Moss incident was not known to the magistrates, however, and it would not have been believed by them if it had. The White Moss affair, Bamford believed, caused the magistrates finally to decide 'to return a full measure of severity to us on the following day'. Their worst fears had been confirmed, 'it being considered,' wrote a contemporary,[2] 'as a presage of what might be feared, when the many thousands who were expected should actually assemble'.

The *Manchester Observer*, (21 August) reported:

[1] Read, p. 126.
[2] The 'contemporary' is quoted as *Impartial Narrative*, p. 31; the latter's account was copied from *Wheeler's Manchester Chronicle*.

. . . Mr. Murray, the gingerbread maker, has been most seriously injured; this active constable has made himself obnoxious, by the diligent discharge of his duty, and which is always the case in every situation where the duties of those situations are improperly discharged. Mr. Murray, then, not wishing to rely upon common report, repaired to White Moss, about five miles distant from Manchester, accompanied by a beadle or two, to make observations on those who were 'training'. He was soon recognised as no reformer; and as soon pinioned by a few men, and corrected for his heinous offence without mercy; not contented to give him a common castigation, he was made to recant his former opinions; he begged pardon on his bare knees: we understand he made his obeisance ten times; and in this prostrate condition promised, on his *word,* to be *good* for the future; and on this solemn promise he was suffered to depart. After his arrival home, he was visited by no less than four surgeons, who declared that his brain was not affected; the skull, it seems, was proof even to *clogs.* He is now convalescent.

The Eve of Peterloo, as seen by the writer in *Wheeler's Manchester Chronicle,* adds a few more details to this incident which 'set the seal' on the magistrates' fears:

On the previous Saturday it was observed that strangers of a low description began to drop into the town. This was more particularly the case in the evening. On Sunday morning an occurrence took place which gave a shock to the feelings of all who heard it. Two residents[1] had gone very early in the morning to . . . White Moss, not far from Middleton, to see what they had so often been told of the Radical Reformers going through military movements. Unfortunately, they were recognized and underwent the most barbarous treatment. A number of these ruffians detached themselves from the rest, beat these persons inhumanly with large sticks threw them down, jumped upon them, kicked them over the head and face, made them beg for their lives upon their knees, forced them to abjure their King, and withdraw their allegiance, and finally threw one of them in a ditch bottom in a state of lifelessness, and left the other insensible with a horrid remark 'that they were done for'. One of the miserable men was also cut desperately in the face by them with a sharp instrument.

This outrage gave but a melancholy foretaste of what was to be expected from the assembling of such characters in the centre of the town on the following day. The solacing satisfactions of the *Divine Day* were diminished by the obtrusion of painful anticipation as to how the following day would *terminate.* Night drew on and strangers passed into the town in accumulated numbers.

Murray in his evidence later said that after the 'beating-up' he was taken to Manchester on Sunday morning in a chaise, arriving at his

[1] Murray was a confectioner with a shop in Shudehill, as well as a special constable.

house in Shudehill about eleven o'clock. Two of the magistrates, Mr Norris and Mr Tatton, after church, took a deposition[1] at his bedside, which was then considered by the rest of the Committee at the Star Inn, where their sittings were held. The magistrates' report, as sent by Hay, proceeded:

Under this Information [re the White Moss 'drillings' being the last, etc.] and being satisfied that in point of Law [the Meeting] if assembled as it was expected, would be an illegal Meeting, we gave notice to Lieut.-Col. L'Estrange, the commanding officer here, of our wish to have the assistance of the Military on the 16th; and in the Evening of the 15th the arrangements in respect of the Military were made; what the arrangements were, were unknown to the Magistrates. Our advice and assistance as Friends had been wished for in this respect, but we declined giving them. They were made between him and other Officers and Gentlemen in our room—so that we were total Strangers to what was settled.

Bruton's damaging inference, that the magistrates had chosen to retain the control of the Manchester and Salford Yeomanry to themselves[2] made on very slender evidence,[3] is refuted in other Peterloo documents. It has double refutation here in the magistrates acting 'correctly' almost to a fault. They persisted all along in saying that they had nothing to do with the military arrangements. The references to the 'Gentlemen' no doubt means the members of the Committee in Aid of the Civil Power mentioned by Taylor. If therefore any 'decisions' of the nature attributed to the magistrates, or, hinted at by Taylor, attributable to this 'secret' committee,[4] were taken before the 16th, this was the moment that they were taken. Taken with the connivance of Lieut.-Col. L'Estrange, who had the full confidence of General Byng? The suggestion is untenable.

There had been one report to the Home Office sent out on the 14th; it was from Stockport: it was an 'alarmist' one:

The lower orders are in a dreadful state, not by distress, for there is work for most that may be willing, except the weavers, who are badly off, and yet not perhaps the worst of the reforming crew; I mean they are quite bold and insulting, and reckon a speedy and radical change to give them complete power over us. A man has come to me from the neighbourhood of Oldham, and states that the person he worked for judged prudent to discontinue till

---

[1] *State Trials*, p. 215.

[2] *Story of Peterloo*, p. 26.

[3] On the strength of Lieut. Jolliffe's letter printed in Bruton *Three Accounts* (1921) p. 50; a statement decisively refuted by official documents.

[4] Taylor *Observations*, pp. 174–5.

things are settled. The tenants of a gentleman near this town refuse to pay their rents till they know the issue of Monday's meeting. J. Lloyd.[1]

J. Lloyd had been one of the leaders of the mounted constables at Sandy Brow. His son had been 'violently attacked' by the mob in Stockport on the same night.[2]

There was, however, a more important letter sent from Manchester to Lord Sidmouth on the Eve of Peterloo. It was from James Norris, and was headed 'Manchester, August 15th, 1819. 11 o'clock p.m.':

My Lord—The Magistrates, the military, and civil authorities of Manchester have been occupied nearly the whole of this day in concerting the necessary arrangements for the preservation of the peace to-morrow, and for the safety of the town in case riot should ensue. We have been much occupied in taking depositions from various parts of the country; and although the Magistrates, as at present advised, do not think of preventing the meeting, yet all the accounts tend to shew that the worst possible spirit pervades the country; and that considerable numbers have been drilling to-day at distances of four, six, and ten miles from Manchester; and that considerable numbers are expected to attend the meeting. I hope the peace may be preserved, but under all circumstances it is scarcely possible to expect it; and, in short, in this respect we are in a state of painful uncertainty . . . J. Norris.[3]

George Lamb, M.P., a Whig, was in Manchester a few days after the 16th on a fact-finding mission. Of James Norris, whom he called his 'learned friend', he said, 'a more kind-hearted man did not walk the earth. If the proceedings of the 16th of August were authorized by him —if his judgment were not overruled by the opinions of those with whom he acted—then must Mr Norris have changed his character on that day.'[4]

The whole Select Committee of Lancashire and Cheshire Magistrates in a few hours ahead, on that Eve of Peterloo, were to have their characters forcibly changed for them.

[1] *Papers Relative to the Internal State of the Country*, p. 23.
[2] *Manchester Mercury*, 23 February 1819.
[3] *Papers Relative to the Internal State of the Country*, p. 27.
[4] Reported in *Exchange Herald* 23 November 1819 ('soon after 16 August'), and quoted in Lamb's speech in the House of Commons 26 November 1819. (*Parl. Deb.*, XLI, p. 309).

XI

The Fateful Morning, 16 August 1819

The 16th of August 1819. The *Manchester Observer's*[1] report: 'The morning was extremely fine, and well calculated to produce the attendance of an immense assemblage'—suggests that there was at any rate one aspect of the day which could be free from controversy. Alas, even in respect of this almost incontrovertible statement, there were to be discrepancies. Hunt was to say that the platform (carts with planks covering them) had been so arranged so that 'he would be speaking against the wind'; Bamford in his unforgettable account was to say: 'The sun looked down from a sultry and motionless air . . .'

Commentators agree, by and large, on what occurred before the arrival of Henry Hunt, but even in this period there were to be misapprehensions which brought later accusations of perversion. The minutes between a quarter past one o'clock and twenty-five minutes past are vital, for it is about these ten minutes that such truth as was spoken about Peterloo was spoken. What happened later, even minutes later, is a tragic tangle. The Furies had taken over, and men's passions were unleashed. It was a tangle of the most dire kind, which generations could not unravel, because men's judgments, sincere though they were, were clouded by righteous indignation.

But is was yet early morning, and in the streets of Manchester numbers of bill-posting men were pasting a notice on every available notice-board and spare wall:

The Borough Reeves and Constables of Manchester and Salford most earnestly recommend the peaceable and well disposed inhabitants of the two towns, as much as possible, to remain in their own houses, during the whole of this day, Monday, August 16th inst., and to keep their children and servants within doors.

Alongside it was the other notice, now ten days old, and already out of date in some details; both were to remain as mute witnesses to the tragedy when the hours of darkness fell.

---

[1] *Manchester Observer*, 21 August.

A requisition having been presented to the Borough Reeve and Constables of Manchester, signed by above 700 inhabitants house-holders in a few hours, requesting them to call a Public Meeting 'to consider the propriety of adopting the most legal and *effectual* means of obtaining a reform in the Commons House of Parliament' and they having declined[1] to call such a Meeting, therefore the undersigned requisitionists give notice that a Public Meeting will be held on the area near St. Peter's Church for the above mentioned purpose on Monday the 16th instant, the chair to be taken by Henry Hunt, Esquire, at 12 o'clock. Major Cartwright, Mr. Wooler, Mr. Pearson, Mr. Carlile, Dr. Crompton, Mr. Edward Rushton, Mr. J. Smith, Mr. Thomas Smith, will be invited to address the meeting, Manchester, 6 August, 1819.

Apart from the fact that some of the supporting speakers did not turn up, there was another advertised feature of the meeting, which since the first reports has escaped all notice.[2] Henry Hunt, Esq. was an hour and a quarter late in keeping his appointment with his enthusiastic auditors. It was to have some bearing on the scenes which were to follow.

To establish the facts about some disputed event, recourse is had in modern times to the ciné projector, which can be run in slow motion or stopped at some given point. In those times, the nearest equivalent was the press report, written immediately after the event. There are many press reports of that day. There is however no need to use them all, as the controversial details are not really reached until after Hunt's arrival. *Wheeler's Manchester Chronicle* of 21 August and *The Times* of 19 August are as good as any, and they certainly had the advantage over most other papers in that their reporters were present. One of the greatest traps in trying to assess correctly the happenings of 16 August is that most of the press reports were merely 'lifted' from other papers' columns; and there are some remarkable, if not ludicrous, inferences which have been drawn on that day's reporting, most notably that of Bruton's:[3]

It is a curious and interesting fact, that the future editors of two Manchester newspapers not then founded, both of whom were present in St Peter's fields on the 16th of August, 1819, finding that the reporter for the London *Times* had been arrested at the hustings, and fearing that therefore the accounts in the London papers would be one-sided, unfairly condoning the action of the magistrates, determined to send a report to London themselves, which duly appeared in two leading London papers. These two men were John Edward

---

[1] They did decline, although Bruton in his short account (quoted above on p. 24) said 'they appear to have made no reply'.

[2] Humphrey House in his article in the *News Chronicle* 16 August 1939 mentioned it; reprinted in *All in Due Time* (1955) p. 46.

[3] *Story of Peterloo*, p. 7.

Taylor, the founder and first editor of the *Manchester Guardian*, and Archibald Prentice, founder and editor of the *Manchester Times* . . .

To Bruton's comment, Haslam Mills[1] adds:

On the evening of the same day John Edward Taylor wrote a full account of the occurrence to a London paper. Archibald Prentice, who was not only Taylor's colleague on the *Gazette* but his nextdoor neighbour in Islington Street, Salford, wrote a full account for another paper. Both narratives left Manchester by the night coach, and, appearing in print within some 48 hours of the affair, got ahead of and were never overtaken by the official version . . .

A more 'curious and interesting fact' is that Prentice was *in* Islington Street, Salford, when the climax of that day was reached[2] and that Taylor, who had been on the 'field' earlier had left the scene before the beginning of the tragic moments.[3] But this 'fact' pales against the other 'fact' that an 'official version' was not published until months later, when details began to be stated in Parliament; that the 'official' version which came out at Hunt's trial in March 1820, for reasons which will later be apparent, was trounced; and that, in actual fact, it was not until three years later, at the trial of Redford *v.* Birley, that anything like an 'official' version could be disentangled from the mass of evidence which was presented there and elsewhere. No wonder the versions of Taylor and Prentice were 'never overtaken'.

At length *Monday* arrived, [says *Wheeler's Chronicle*][4] early in the morning the various responsible Authorities were on the alert. The Magistrates, the Boroughreeves and Constables of Manchester and Salford, an immense body of Special Constables, many of them of the first consideration, and the various force of military and artillery were in motion for their appointed duties. The latter consisted of our own Yeomanry Cavalry, under Major Trafford; the Prince Regent's Cheshire Yeomanry were under Lieut.-Col. Townsend; the 15th Hussars from the Barracks, under Lieut.-Col. Dalrymple; a detachment of the 88th Foot, now stationed in the King Street Barracks, under Col. McGregor; some pieces of Royal Horse Artillery, under Major Dyneley; and a detachment of the 31st Foot, under Lieut.-Col. L'Estrange, the able, intelligent, and active officer who commanded the whole and made all the necessary arrangements for the occasion. [Details of the 'Keep within Doors' notice printed on very large sheets of paper and in bold characters.]

At 11 o'clock in the forenoon, the following Magistrates assembled at a gentleman's house in Mount Street, which commands an immediate and uninterrupted view of the whole area near St. Peter's church, in which the

---

1 *The Manchester Guardian—a Century of History*, 1921, p. 28.
2 Prentice, *Recollections*, p. 159.
3 Taylor, *Observations*, p. 167 (quoted below p. 306.)
4 21 August 1819.

meeting was to take place, viz.: the Rev. Mr. Hay, the Rev. Mr. Ethelston; Mr. Wright; Mr. Marriott; the Rev. Mr. Mallory; Mr. Hulton; Mr. Tatton; Mr. Fletcher; Mr. Sylvester, and Mr. Fielden. The special constables assembled on the ground soon after; the Military were halted in various suitable stations, retired from the public ground.

There was one ironical fact not reported in any account of that day, that the field, the 'area near St Peter's Church' was, in 1818, *rented* out to the Manchester and Salford Yeomanry Cavalry as an 'exercise ground'.

Hay's private report to Lord Sidmouth gives a hitherto unknown angle to the morning's proceedings:

In the morning of the 16th we requested that the Town's Constables and the Special Constables should be in attendance, but they, none of them, knew in what particular Instance or for what particular purpose, they might be employed ['applied' crossed out]. They attended in consequence. The Magistrates got to the Ground and were in a house fronting the Area of St. Peter's, whence we could have a full view of what passed at the Hustings, though we could not hear.

A special constable was later to be killed in the mêlée; one of his friends bemoaned the fact that his dead friend imagined that he thought he knew how the special constables were to be employed.[1] 'The Magistrates would certainly protect the Civil Power; "Yes, yes", said the constables, "we shall be protected; we are only called to surround the hustings and take the leaders, and if the Military are wanted they are here".' It gives a hint of what was in their minds. Not all the special constables were on the 'field', a great many were set to guard the factories, and some (mounted) were posted on the roads leading into the town to bring in reports of the columns of reformers marching in.

The Radical Reformers, [goes on the *Chronicle* report] now began to make their formidable appearance. They marched in regiments under regular leaders, and all the appalling insignia, *Caps of Liberty*, &c., which had been long preparing for what they considered to be a most glorious day. As they progressively advanced to the hustings they were received with the loudest acclamations, with huzzas and the clapping of hands. About 11–30, a strong party marched up in files of four or five abreast, with various colours and banners; one inscribed 'No Corn Laws' surmounted with the Cap of Liberty. This was from Stockport. At a quarter before twelve another body marched in from Deansgate, in files, with two colours, and a bugle, surmounted with the Cap of Liberty. Another party followed from the same street, with *women in single files*, and men on each side in double files, with a flag inscribed with a motto, and 'Union *Female Society* of Royton.' Another party

[1] *Manchester Gazette*, 28 August.

marched in from St. Peter's-road direct up to the hustings. Another party marched in at twelve o'clock, with a band of music and a flag, accompanied with a cart for the hustings, in which *women were riding*. At this moment the hustings were filled with men, eight flags or banners flying , several thousands standing round *with hats off*. George Swift, a Reform orator, now addressed the meeting, and on ending his speech 4 or 5 huzzas were given by order. At 12.30 another cart, with planks; and a large chair, were brought to add to the hustings.

The most perspicacious observer on that day was not a local reporter but John Tyas, the writer for *The Times* who had been sent to 'cover' the meeting, and whose article, which was to appear in the historic issue of *The Times* on 19 August, was written in part in the New Bayley prison;[1] for he was taken into custody by an over-zealous constable soon after the arrests of the orators. Tyas wrote colourfully:

The place appointed for the meeting was a large vacant piece of ground on the north side of St. Peter's-place. At half-past ten o'clock about 250 idle individuals might be collected within it. About half-past eleven the first body of Reformers arrived on the ground, bearing two banners, each of which was surmounted by a cap of liberty. The first bore upon a white ground the inscription of 'Annual Parliaments, and Universal Suffrage'; on the reverse side: 'No Corn Laws'. The other bore upon a blue ground the same inscription, with the addition of 'Vote by Ballot'. After these flags had been paraded over the field for some time, it was thought fit by the leaders of the party who had brought them, that they should remain stationary. A post was accordingly assigned to the bearers of them to which shortly afterwards a dung-cart was brought, into which the standard bearers were ordered to mount, and from which all the standards arriving afterwards were most appropriately displayed. Numerous large bodies of Reformers continued to arrive from this time to one o'clock, from the different towns in the neighbourhood of Manchester, all with flags, and many of them drawn up five deep, and in regular marching order.

A club of Female Reformers, amounting in numbers, according to our calculation, to 150, came from Oldham; and another, not quite so numerous, from Royton. The first bore a white silk banner, by far the most elegant displayed during the day, inscribed *Major Cartwright's Bill, Annual Parliaments, Universal Suffrage, and Vote by Ballot*. In one compartment of it was Justice holding the scales in one hand, and a sword in the other; in another a large eye, which we suppose was impiously intended to represent the eye of Providence. On the reverse of this flag was another inscription; but in the

[1] 'The most important and, notwithstanding the strong [Whig] bias of his politics, the most intelligent and accurate of the witnesses in Mr. Hunt's behalf.'—Horace Twiss, Tory M.P. in the House of Commons on 15 May 1821. (*Parl. Deb.*, NS. Vol. V, p. 786.)

hurry of the day we found it impossible to decipher what it was, and can only say that there were upon it two hands, both decorated in *shirt ruffles*, clasped in each other, and underneath them an inscription *Oldham Union*. The latter (i.e. the females of Royton) bore two red flags, the one inscribed *Let us* [i.e. women] *die like men, and not be sold like slaves*; the other *Annual Parliaments and Universal Suffrage*. The Radicals of Saddleworth brought with them a black flag to the field, on one side of which was inscribed *Taxation without Representation is Unjust and Tyrannical; Equal Representation or Death;* on the other side, *Union is Strength—Unite and be Free. Saddleworth and Mossley Union*. The Reformers from Rochdale and Middleton marched to the sound of the bugle, and in very regular time, closing and expanding their ranks, and marching in ordinary and double quick time, according as it pleased the fancy of their leaders to direct them. They had two green banners, between which they had hoisted on a red pole a cap of liberty, crowned with leaves of laurel, and bearing the inscription, *Hunt and Liberty*. Another band bore a banner, in which Britannia was represented with her trident, leaning on a shield, upon which was inscribed the motto borne by Sir William Wallace, *God armeth the Patriot*.

In this manner the business of the day proceeded till one o'clock, by which time we should suppose that 80,000 people were assembled on the ground. During this period we found it impossible to approach the wagon, though very desirous to do so, as a young lad, not more than 17 or 18, was addressing the meeting with great vehemence of action and gesture, and with great effect, if we may judge from the cheers which he every now and then extracted from his audience, who were now beginning to be impatient for the arrival of Hunt and the other orators who were to follow in his train, like satellites which attend on some mighty planet.

The Reformers who had up to this time arrived in the field demeaned themselves becomingly, though a posse of 300 or 400 constables, with the Boroughreeve at their head, had marched in a body into the field about 12 o'clock, unsupported by any military body to all outward appearance. Not the slightest insult was offered to them. The people did indeed rush to behold them, but this was probably occasioned by an idea that they were another body of Reformers. As soon as they saw who they were, they turned away from them with a smile; and, attracted by a crowd which was advancing from another corner of the area, went to meet it crying, 'Let us keep peace and order, and go to welcome this body, which is one of ours.' As we stood counting the members of the Oldham Female Reform Club in their procession by us, and whilst we were internally pitying the delusion which led them to a scene so ill-suited to their usual habits, a group of the women of Manchester, attracted by the crowd, came to the corner of the street where we had taken our post. They viewed these Female Reformers for some time with a look in which compassion and disgust were equally blended, and at last burst out into an indignant exclamation—'Go home to your families, and leave *sike-like as these* to your husbands and sons, who better understand them.' The women who thus addressed them were of the lower order of life.

It has already been observed that, contrary to some opinions, there never was an 'official' version of the happenings of 16 August until some considerable time later, and also that many of the press reports were merely 'lifted' from other papers' columns. Two reporters' versions of day's proceedings are free from all suspicion on the latter score because they appeared in print ahead of every other, on the following day, Tuesday, 17 August. These reporters' papers were *Aston's Exchange Herald* and the *Manchester Mercury*—both loyalist Manchester journals; both reported that the Riot Act was read at 12 noon; a mistake which not only confounded confusion on that later-much-disputed feature of the meeting, but which earned for the reporter of another newspaper dismissal by his employers, possibly because his report maintained that it was not read. The radicals later seized the opportunity to publish the alleged suppressed report he had written.[1] The *Manchester Mercury* in its issue of the week following (24 August) further developed the theme of this alleged reading of the Riot Act at 12 o'clock; it was later dropped like a hot brick.

It has already been seen from *Wheeler's Manchester Chronicle* report that at twelve o'clock 'the hustings were filled with men, eight flags or banners flying, and several thousands standing round with their hats off, and one, George Swift, a Reform orator, addressing the meeting.' It has been seen, too, that the magistrates from their vantage point could see but could not hear. What is more important, however, is that the meeting was timed to begin at twelve o'clock. The *Exchange Herald* reported thus:

Soon after 12 o'clock the Magistrates and a body of constables repaired to the ground to which the Brigaded Reformers had marched, and in consequence of Depositions made before several of His Majesty's Justices of the Peace by many of the most respectable inhabitants of the towns of Manchester and Salford, in which they stated their apprehensions of Riot and Tumult as the probable consequences of such an assemblage of persons from distant townships marched thither under banners of so explicit of rebellious intentions, the Riot Act was read, but it did not appear to be much attended to by the more infatuated crowd, who continued to scowl and laugh at the constables in attendance, &c.

The *Manchester Mercury*'s report in their 17 August issue was very brief,

[1] *Peterloo Massacre*, p. 56.

but it also reported the reading of the Riot Act at 12 noon. The other paper's alleged suppressed report, later published by the radicals, read:

About twelve o'clock, Mr. Clayton, the Boroughreeve, followed by, I should think, four or five hundred special constables, came into the midst of the multitude: at first, there was a considerable pressure upon them by the crowd, but an admonitory cry of 'order, order!' having been raised by some of the leaders, it speedily abated, and, in a few minutes, the special constables seemed no more an object of particular notice than any other persons present. They formed themselves into two continuous lines, which reached from the waggon outwards towards a gentleman's house on the south side of St. Peter's Field, which commanded a view of the whole scene, and in which, I was informed, the Magistrates had taken up their station. I kept very close to Mr. Clayton, during the whole time he remained on the ground on this occasion, anxious to gather from the first authority, the course things were likely to take. I did not lose sight of him for a single moment, until he left the ground to report the state of matters to his brother magistrates. I can there-fore state, as a positive truth, that during this perambulation, the Borough-reeve never addressed one word to the people as to any illegality in their meeting, any disorder in their conduct, or any thing else whatever, and that he never read any thing either printed or written.

The suppressed account is important for two reasons: first, it seems to prove that the magistrates did not, as the reporter of the *Exchange Herald* averred, accompany the special constables to the ground; but the Boroughreeve did. There is no evidence at all in magistrates' statements on that day or later wherein they said they did. Second, it proves that the dismissed reporter believed that the Boroughreeve was a magis-trate, which he was not; the same misapprehension could well have been in the mind of the *Exchange Herald* reporter as well. He could well have imagined that the cries of 'Order, order!' meant that the Riot Act was being read; he may or he may not have been aware that only a Justice of the Peace could read the Riot Act. Whatever the explanation, the 'fact' that the Riot Act was read at 12 o'clock was reported in those first-published accounts of what happened on St Peter's Field. The confusion which was to arise from the reporting of this 'fact' neither paper could foresee. Happily, neither the *Exchange Herald*'s nor the *Manchester Mercury*'s evidence on the subsequent events of that day are vital to an understanding of what occured; they are quite subsidiary. The blunder of the reporting of the 12 o'clock reading did not, as may well be imagined, bring any benefit to the magistrates' case. Henry Hunt was later to use the non-reference to the reading of the Riot Act in his trial with dire effect:

Where is the Riot Act? The Riot Act? If they had ever brought a witness into the Court to have proved the reading of that, the learned counsel knows that [his testimony on it] would have been kicked out of court. . . .[1]

The magistrates' case (probably submitted to the Birley defending counsel) contented itself with stating what was finally brought out in evidence in Redford *v.* Birley, 1821:

As the reading of the Riot Act has been by many disputed, it may be not amiss to state (although the Magistrates do not consider it forming any necessary feature in the case) that the Proclamation was read twice before the apprehension of Hunt (by the Rev. C. W. Ethelston from the window of Mr. Buxton's house, and by Mr. Sylvester from the ground).[2]

The *Exchange Herald* had perhaps taken too literally the time stated on Hunt's posting-bill advertising the meeting to begin at twelve o'clock. At that hour the platform was full of orators, and an enormous crowd had already gathered. Hunt was, in fact, only leaving Smedley Cottage at 12 o'clock, two to three miles away from St Peter's Field. The *Herald* report continues:

At one o'clock another procession passed the Exchange, escorting Hunt to the place of meeting; for the Great Man, perhaps to enhance his consequence, made the would-be legislators wait for him, although their Advertisement stated that the chair would be taken at 12 o'clock. The leader of this band bore a large club, and he was followed by some hundreds of men and boys who marched in columns with military step, to the music of a regular band, dressed in gay uniforms. By the colours which were displayed, the van, at least were from Oldham. After them was borne a board elevated on a pole, and as if in downright mockery, on both sides was painted 'Order, Order'. Almost immediately before the barouche, in which Hunt rode, was borne the same Flag and Cap of Liberty, which were displayed in his first visit to Manchester.[3] On the box of the carriage was seated a woman! bearing a Flag: and in the open carriage stood the main Pivot of Mischief; several other persons were seated in it, but we did not learn their names. The carriage was followed by many hundreds of men and boys in the order above described, with colours flying. They marched through Deansgate, in which, and in all other streets through which they passed, the shops were shut up.

On arriving at the Hustings, Mr. Hunt and his friends ascended it, amidst the shouts of the greatest assemblage of people ever collected together at one point in Manchester. We understand the Travelling Orator had begun to address the Reformers, when an hour having expired, after the reading of the Riot Act, the Warrants of the Magistrates were carried into effect . . .

[1] *State Trials*, 306.
[2] Eng. MS. 1197/89.
[3] The January meeting.

The reporters were impatient; Mr Tyas reports that after an hour had elapsed after the supposed time of start the crowds began to get impatient, too, and even although Tyas considered that he was witnessing a novel and entertaining sight, he made his way from the ground to go and meet Hunt's procession. The impatience was no doubt also to be noticed in the magistrates' room, a hundred yards away from the tantalizing hustings. What was a novel and entertaining sight to Mr Tyas was something far different to those Justices of the Peace with anxious forebodings because of what had occurred previously, and what might happen on this momentous day. And they were not alone. If, as John Edward Taylor had said, the reformer's doings in the past few weeks of July were driving 'all the timid' into the ranks of the loyalists, there was a considerable augmentation of those ranks in the first fortnight in August. The Rev. Mr Hay's report continues:

The area of St. Peter's is computed to be 14,000 square yards. This space was occupied very closely near the hustings, and in other parts more or less so. We compute the numbers of those collected who took part in the meeting to be about 30,000 [Hulton's estimate later was 50,000–60,000; the radicals' estimate was 150,000!] of these at least 20,000 were strangers to Manchester. We saw 5 or 6 columns march in—there were from 2000 to 5000 each, if not more; they marched in quick time, with martial music, banners and ensigns, the Representations on several of the banners have been communicated to your Lordship. Each column as it came marched directly to the Hustings, as they came up were received with 3 cheers—their banners were arranged in front, and they were cheered again. This took place in every Instance. After the others had arrived Hunt came with his party and the same reception took place.

Prior to Hunt's appearing on the ground, one Owen came to us and gave information as to the parties in Hunt's company—his Information was taken in form and a warrant filled up in consequence and signed by ten Magistrates. Before this, the Magistrates had as long been in their own view convinced that the Meeting was in Terror of his Majesty's subjects, but they had also taken Confirmation of about fifty Inhabitants who swore to the same effect. In addition to this the Shops at the Lower part of the Town at a quarter of a mile from St. Peter's had been shut all morning, and but a very few could be prevailed in [sic] the afternoon to take down their shutters. . . .

Tyas, too, was impatient for Hunt's arrival; his narrative continues:

We had waited up to one o'clock on the field of action for the arrival of Mr. Hunt; but as he had not then made his appearance, we determined to go and meet the procession, which it was said was to attend the Orator. We met it just by the Exchange, where the people were cheering most loudly, and Hunt and Johnson joining in the cheers. They were seated in an open landau, along with Carlile, Knight and others, and had moved in grand procession from Smedley Cottage, past New Cross and Shude-Hill, preceded by a large body of male, and followed by a scarcely less numerous body of female Manchester Reformers.

At the trial of Hunt, later, it was alleged that his procession had made demonstrations by hissing and groaning at a few selected places on his route: at Murray's (the injured special constable's) house in Shude Hill, at the Star Inn, where the magistrates had held their meetings, and at the Police Office[1]. Tyas's account continues:

Before them were carried two boards, on which were inscribed, *Order, Order*; these were followed by two flags for annual Parliaments and universal suffrage, and also by Hunt's old flag and cap of liberty, of Westminster notoriety, 'Hunt and Universal Suffrage.' This latter was held by a female Reformer, seated on the *dicky* of the landau, which had the honour of carrying the illustrious band of patriots, whose name[s] we have just mentioned. It was now to be exhibited in the last of its fields.

It was just opposite to the Exchange, as was before mentioned, that the individual who furnishes this report met the procession in full march; from the numbers whom he had already seen collected on the field, and from those whom he then saw proceeding to increase them, he felt convinced of the impossibility of getting into any position in which he could hear the proceedings of that day, unless he received some personal accommodation from Mr. Hunt himself. He had never previously spoken to that individual, nor would he have thought of addressing him upon this occasion, had he not known that every gentleman connected with the London press had gladly availed himself of similar assistance at the Smithfield meeting. As to espousing the political principles, or advocating the wild doctrines of radical reform, supported by Mr. Hunt, it is the very last thing, if he knows himself, that he should ever be induced to do; he holds them in as utter abhorrence as the most loyal subject of his Majesty possibly can hold them, and will always be ready to express that disgust in the warmest and most indignant terms. Mr. Hunt, on this individual's asking to be admitted, immediately acceded to his request. He decided to stand as close as possible to the landau in which he was riding, and promised to take care that every accommodation in his power should be paid to his convenience. He followed in the train of the Orator till he arrived in the field of action.

The enthusiasm excited among the crowd by the presence of the Orator was certainly beyond anything which we ever before witnessed; and the cheers with which he was hailed were loud and lasting. When he had taken his stand upon the hustings, which were formed of two carts lashed together, and boards spread over them, he expressed considerable disapprobation of the manner in which they were formed, and of the place in which they were

[1] *State Trials* p. 190.

situated. This will not excite surprise, when we state, that it was so arranged that the speaker had to talk against the wind; and also that on Mr. Hunt's last appearance at Manchester, the hustings were so slightly built as to yield to the pressure of the superincumbent crowd, though fortunately no accident happened from their giving way.

Bamford's description, in his *Passages*, of the sun looking down 'from a sultry and motionless air' must be dismissed as verisimilitude. There was some wind, as Tyas said, and repeated later in his court appearance. The *Manchester Gazette* too, reported 'a sudden breeze of wind' clearing away the cloud of dust after the mêlée.[1] Tyas's narrative clears away, too, a misapprehension which has grown up on this very point—of movement of the hustings. It has been said by Dr Read:[2]

From the magistrates' house to these hustings the two hundred special constables formed a double line through which, it was hoped, the magistrates could communicate with the speakers. Nadin, the Deputy Constable, moved up and down this line until Hunt made his appearance. When Hunt arrived he found that the position of the hustings was such that he would be speaking against the wind; they were therefore moved a few yards and apparently out of contact with the line of constables. This was afterwards claimed by the authorities as a most sinister development.

The movement of the hustings was just as 'sinister' as it was made out to be; they were moved before Hunt arrived,[3] and without his knowledge. On his arrival the *Gazette* reported there was some delay before Hunt quitted his vehicle, without attributing a reason. *Wheeler's Chronicle* reported, 'When Hunt mounted the hustings, he *commanded* the different musical instruments which were piled upon them to be removed; and in a very peremptory tone also commanded all persons to leave the hustings who did not intend to address the meeting.' In any case, it was hardly the moment to manhandle the two lashed-together carts, with or without musical instruments and spectators, a distance of about eight yards, and in that dense mass of human beings.

George Swift, the radical responsible for the erection of the hustings writes of:

the cordon or wall of men round the hustings . . . the inside of this circle we had filled with women from the Union schools, music, and flags.[4]

---

[1] 'The flags waved as they were moved by the wind' (Hay's evidence: Redford *v.* Birley, p. 432).
[2] Read, p. 128.
[3] Hay's Report qv., Eng. MS. 1197/86. See also below p. 159.
[4] *Swift's Narrative* (Manchester Central Library).

The radicals' alleged suppressed report:

[Hunt] seemed by his look and gestures, in some displeasure. Several persons descended from the stage, and I understood it was in consequence of Mr. Hunt's insisting that everybody should go down except those who were necessarily there. I remarked one person, with spectacles, making a great bustling effort to get up, who had afterwards serious cause to regret the success of his importunity. He addressed himself to Mr. Tyas, the reporter for *The Times*, who had got a place close by Mr. Hunt; and Mr. Tyas whispered some words to the latter gentleman, who nodding his assent, the person I allude to was permitted to take a place among the elect. I saw him immediately afterwards with book and pencil in hand, taking notes, and hence concluded that he was like myself, what is technically called—a Reporter.[1]

The Rev. Mr Hay's version states as follows:

The Constables in the first instance were formed on one side of the Hustings; and an alley of them was formed up to the House where the Magistrates were—agreeably to a plan which will hereafter be forwarded to your Lordship. As soon as the Reformers came I saw the situation of the Special Constables; they moved the Hustings twice.[2] The first movement was about 8 yards distance; by this means they got between the Special Constables and the Hustings, and pushed them back; the second movement was merely to arrange the fronting of the Hustings. These men were 10 or 12 deep, linked together, their hats off and evidently placed to prevent the Special Constables from having access to the Hustings.

A special constable named George Brown, with one or two others amongst those who were nearest the hustings, was cut off from the rest of the constables by this movement. Brown could be considered as a valuable witness on (*a*) the cutting-off of the constables; and (*b*) the linking of arms by the Reformers round the hustings. On (*b*) Hunt, at his trial, was to tear William Hulton's solitary evidence to shreds, and score his greatest triumph. It was a triumph which ought only to have been a temporary one, but it was not. Confirmatory evidence only came to light in April 1822.

[1] *Peterloo Massacre*, p. 56.
[2] Birley trial stated the second cart came at 12 noon; the *Chronicle* reported 12.30.

XII

The Setting for Tragedy

Henry Hunt's speech on that memorable afternoon was well reported. It has been said that even what he did say in those few minutes 'caused great dispute'. Bruton's prime witness (and a prime witness in this account) has been cited as saying: 'I should think no-one beyond ten yards from the hustings could hear'. As the assertion was from the Rev. Mr Stanley, who was a hundred yards away on the second floor of Mr Buxton's house, this is not surprising. But John Tyas was on the hustings and there were other reporters nearby, including the one from *Wheeler's Manchester Chronicle*. Tyas wrote:

After the different persons who intended to address the multitude had taken their position [on the hustings] and silence had been obtained, Johnson came forward, and proposed that Henry Hunt be appointed their Chairman. Here a short pause ensued, as if Johnson expected that some person would have come forward to second his proposition. No person, however, doing so, Johnson proceeded to call upon them to carry the question by acclamation. The meeting did so, and Henry Hunt was declared Chairman, amid cheers of 3 times 3. The noise continuing longer than usual, Hunt found it requisite to entreat his friends to preserve tranquility. He commenced his address by calling the assembly 'gentlemen', but afterwards changed the term to 'fellow-countrymen'. He had occasion, he said, to entreat their indulgence. (Noise continued). Every man wishing to hear must himself keep silence. (Laughter, but no silence.) 'Will you', said he, addressing himself to the mob, 'be so obliging as not to call silence while the business of the day is proceeding?' (Silence was then obtained.) He hoped that they would now exercise the all-powerful right of the people; and if any person would not be quiet, that they would put him down and keep him quiet'. (We will.)

On this part of the speech the reporters differ; *Wheeler's Manchester Chronicle* report it as follows:

. . . I must beg that none of you will call 'Silence', as such call is generally attended with uproar and confusion. ('Then come off the hustings, and don't you make confusion!' from one of the mob.) I hope, Gentlemen, that if any of your enemies attempt to interrupt the proceedings, or cause a riot or disturbance, that there are some amongst you who possess enough courage to put them down and keep them down. ('Why, that's killing them,' from one of the mob; but not sufficiently loud for the demagogue to hear.) . . .

For the honour which they had just conferred upon him [went on Tyas's report] he returned them his most sincere thanks; and for any services which he had or might render them, all that he asked was, that they would indulge him with a calm and patient attention. It was impossible for him to think that with the utmost silence he could make himself heard by every member of the numerous and tremendous meeting which he saw assembled before him. If those, however, who were not near him were not silent, how could it be expected that those who were at a distance should hear what he should say. (A dead silence now pervaded the multitude). It was useless for him to recall to their recollection the proceedings of the last ten days in their town; they were all of them acquainted with the cause of the late meeting being postponed; and it would be therefore superfluous in him to say anything about it, except, indeed, it were this—that those who had attempted to put them down by the most malignant exertions had occasioned them to meet that day in more than two-fold numbers. (Hear.) (Knight here whispered something into Hunt's ear, which caused him to turn round with some degree of asperity to Knight, and to say, 'Sir, I will not be interrupted: when you speak yourself, you will not like to experience such interruption.') They would have perceived, that since the old meeting had been put off, and the present one had been called—though their enemies flattered themselves with having obtained a victory, they showed by their conduct that they had sustained a defeat. (Loud and long applause.) In the interval between the two meetings, two placards had been circulated, to which the names of two obscure individuals were attached; the first was signed by Tom Long or Jack Short, a printer in the town whom nobody knew . . .

At this stage of the business the Yeomanry Cavalry were seen advancing in a rapid trot to the area . . .

In what occurred in the few minutes after this point in time are the clues to the solution of the enigma of St Peter's Field. There are several prime witnesses, and several minor ones. Of the prime witnesses, some have been cited by other writers; one was heard for a moment, and then dismissed imperiously. He was Capt. Hugh Hornby Birley, the officer who led the Yeomanry on to the field. The authority who dismissed him was Bruton.

'Finally,' writes Bruton,[1] 'let us hear the officer who led the charge in person'. Bruton then quotes part of a speech explaining what happened on St Peter's Field, made by Birley and culled from a local newspaper, leaving unquoted one of the most important clues to the solution of the

[1] *Story of Peterloo*, p. 32.

whole Peterloo problem; and ends the quotation with, 'but there is no object in quoting further from an *apologia* which at the best is a very lame affair.' Whether Birley's evidence is 'lame' or not is beside the point. Placed as he was, on horseback in the middle of the multitude during those vital minutes, his evidence is important.

The next prime witness is Bruton's prime witness, the Rev. Edward Stanley, whose privately-issued narrative was reprinted by Bruton[1] in 1921, coupled with Stanley's sworn testimony at the Redford v. Birley trial (1822). He has been regarded as the most damaging independent witness against the magistrates. He was admirably placed during those vital moments at a window on the floor above the magistrates' room in Mr Buxton's house overlooking the whole area.

John Tyas, *The Times* reporter, is another witness; and, again, usually regarded as hostile to the magistrates, appearing in both Hunt's trial and Redford v. Birley for the radicals. He was on the platform until the arrests were made.

The next, and *the* prime witness is William Hulton, 'Peterloo Magistrate', who was presently to step from, as it were, the wings into the centre of the post-Peterloo stage, into the fierce light of notoriety. The solitary magisterial witness in Hunt's trial, he was to receive the full onslaught of Hunt's devastating defence, and the half-credulous summing-up of the Judge, then to be assailed in and out of Parliament by critics and traducers Left, Right and Centre, using those words in their strictest political sense; only to come forward, unabashed, and repeat his apparently discredited testimony in the second trial in 1822. When all the other magistrates had lapsed into sullen, or maybe discreet, silence, after the resurgence of the radical version, William Hulton stubbornly refused to accept what others felt to be inevitable—that theirs was a lost cause—and persisted in his protestations, in one instance being almost studiously provocative. Until, in the end, maybe on reading Bamford's *Passages*, where Bamford repeated what Hulton must have considered exploded arguments, from the sheer tedium of having to go through all the refutations again, he lapsed into silence. Or perhaps, even Bamford was not the last straw; it might well have been Prentice's *Recollections* (1851) when William Hulton's lifespan had yet thirteen years to run:

Reverend W. R. Hay, who was rewarded with a living of £2400 a year for his services in 'putting down' the Reformers; Reverend W. C. Ethelston, whose reading of the Riot Act nobody ever heard; Stipendiary Magistrate James Norris, who sought from government a power beyond the existing law; Hugh Hornby Birley, who led the attack upon a defenceless multitude;

[1] Bruton, *Three Accounts*, pp. 1–43.

Joseph Nadin, who harshly apprehended those who were to be harshly punished under judge-made law;—all these have gone to their graves, without an assault, without an insult . . . [And then, on Hunt's trial] Mr. Hulton, of Hulton, amongst other evidence, swore that he *had seen from the windows where he stood, a number of men close to the hustings, with their arms locked together* . . . [and, after referring to Hunt's staggering questions which he put to Hulton, Prentice added gravely] The witnesses for the defence were generally of a more respectable class than those who were called for the prosecution.[1]

If there was such a thing as a 'transparent' witness in the trials, it was William Hulton. He referred to the marching and wheeling of the bands of reformers as 'beautifully exact', and to the Yeomanry as being 'in a certain degree of confusion, their horses being raw and unused to the field'. In the first trial the Judge suggested that Hulton's eyes might have deceived him on certain points; even the counsel (Scarlett) against Hunt, thought Hulton might 'have confounded the period when brickbats and stones were thrown.'[2] In the second trial it was the opposing counsel, who did not doubt Hulton's veracity, but again suggested he might have been misled by his sight. Hulton stuck to his story. He gave no testimony at either trial (wittingly) on the question of the reading of the Riot Act. In the first trial because Hunt studiously refused to mention the Riot Act as such, and then score his point; in the second trial it was left to the other magisterial witnesses to give evidence on that fact, which by then was not quite so relevant.

The final prime witness is another reporter, of the *Manchester Observer*, from the columns of which so much of the evidence for this account of pre- and post-Peterloo days has been taken. It could not have been John Thacker Saxton, because he was in prison; but it is curious that evidence supporting the magistrates' case should be found from such a source; and which was even to be reprinted in the arch-anti-magisterial organ *Peterloo Massacre*.

There are also minor witnesses on which to test the magistrates' case: Edward Baines of the *Leeds Mercury*, on the platform; Lieut. Jolliffe, introduced by Bruton; the isolated special constable, George Brown; and some of Hunt's witnesses. The scene is back to the magistrates' room.

There was to be plenty of evidence from the press reports on Peterloo from all angles except one: what occurred in the magistrates' room in Mr Buxton's house in Mount Street. The fact was even remarked on by

[1] Prentice pp. 169; 184–6.
[2] *State Trials,* p. 425.

the *Manchester Gazette* reporter in recounting what happened to Hunt after he was arrested:

When Hunt entered into the presence of the magistrates he displayed considerable agitation. What passed before the magistrates we only know from report, and we wish to confine ourselves to facts.

It is not thought that John Edward Taylor was the reporter for the *Gazette* on that day, because he had left St Peter's Field before this incident; he was to add his theories later.

It is a fact, however [wrote Taylor], that early in the forenoon on August 16th persons supposed to be acquainted with the intentions of the magistrates distinctly asserted that Mr. Hunt would be arrested on the hustings, and the meeting dispersed. I myself was more than once told so, but could not conceive it possible that there was any foundation whatever for the report, provided (of which I entertained no doubt) that the meeting were peaceable.[1]

There were, then, 'inspired reports' abroad of what was to happen in Manchester; which was not surprising in view of the previously announced decision of the Cheshire magistrates to 'suppress all meetings immediately they assemble' (and it must be remembered that about half of the magistrates present in that room were Cheshire magistrates). What, of course, has to be remembered, too, is that the words 'disperse' and 'suppress' were to bear much different overtones after half-past one o'clock on 16 August.

What occurred in that room was to remain anybody's guess for some months to come, until hints were given in Parliament in November 1819, that the veil was to be lifted a little further by the publication in November of Mr Hay's letter written late in the evening of the 16th; it was not, however, until Hunt's trial in March 1820, that William Hulton narrated his story as evidence. The narrative was to be changed only in detail at the second trial in 1822, when he admitted an error in the calculation of the distance between Mr Buxton's house and the hustings; and he added a few points of little moment, such as his observing through a pair of opera glasses the linking of arms and the moving of the hustings.

No reader of the evidence given at the two trials—that of Hunt in 1820 and the other of Redford *v.* Birley in 1822—can help noticing that Hulton gave the most complete picture—from the magistrates' point of view of course—of what happened on that fatal field. Hunt's masterly cross-examination seemed to discredit Hulton in the eyes of the court, in the eyes of the judge, and in the eyes of the country, both in

[1] *Observations*, p. 55, footnote (N) to Hay's letter.

parliament and in the press. It discredited Hulton so completely that it over-shadowed all attempts to retrieve his reputation. Even though the second trial of 1822 vindicated the magistrates' case in several points, two at least of the contemporary 'authorities' on Peterloo—Bamford and Prentice—write as though Redford *v.* Birley had never taken place. But Redford *v.* Birley is not the only touchstone on which to test Hulton's evidence, as will be seen. He testified at Hunt's trial as follows:[1]

. . . [We] first assembled at the Star Inn, and then adjourned to Mr. Buxton's house, which overlooked St. Peter's Area. We assembled between ten and eleven o'clock, and received information on oath relative to the approach of large bodies of people. As Chairman of the bench of magistrates for the counties of Lancaster and Chester, much of my time was taken up in writing, but I frequently looked out of the window and saw large bodies of men approach. They first came by Mosley Street towards St. Peter's Square, with banners and music. They were apparently divided into sections, and had persons walking at the side, who from time to time seemed to give the word of command. This observation more particularly applied to the first body, for the others were too far off to be so minutely observed. All the bodies, however, proceeded regularly, and in a remarkable manner, for they did not march straight to the hustings, but wheeled when they received the word of command. The persons in command went up to the hustings and deposited their colours. They were regularly received with loud huzzahs. The men appeared to me to be beautifully exact in coming to the hustings, but I could not mark their motions afterwards. The division which advanced from Mosley Street, by St. Peter's Square, marched with particular precision. I could not see what sort of order was kept by the division which came with Hunt. I should think, having seen regiments reviewed, the first division consisted of 4000 to 5000 men; they had music but I do not know whether they had any drums. I observed the division which escorted Hunt; he was in a carriage, in which I believe were also Johnson, Moorhouse, and Carlile. The extraordinary noise which was made on the approach of Hunt induced me to walk to the window and mark what was going forward; the hustings were moved in the course of the morning: this he knew, because it had been the desire of the magistrates to form a line of constables from the hustings to the house where the magistrates were, but I observed that a number of men had rushed in, seized their arms together, and surrounded the hustings. I could perceive from the window different people coming forward to address the meeting; from the situation in which I was placed, I had a view over the whole of St. Peter's area; the number of persons assembled was estimated at 50,000; the meeting did undoubtedly inspire terror in the minds of the inhabitants. I received depositions on oath to that effect, and I myself marked the extraordinary way in which the people approached.

[1] *Hunt Trial* (edn. Pratt), p. 54.

Hunt, at this point during his trial, demanded the production of the depositions; they were not available, and the judge told Hulton he must not state the opinions of others. Hulton continued:

Many gentlemen stated to me that they were greatly alarmed, and looking to all the circumstances, my opinion was that the town was in great danger. The population of Manchester and Salford . . . 100,000 souls; . . . Manchester was a large place and contained many shops and warehouses. The magistrates in consequence of these proceedings deemed it necessary to issue a warrant for the apprehension of the supposed leaders, which was given to Nadin, either in the presence of one of the chief constables of the town, or else it was handed to him by the constable. I cannot say whether the warrant was brought back after it had been made out. In giving the warrant to Nadin, he said he could not execute it without military aid.

Hunt objected to hearing what Nadin said, and Hulton continued:

He refused to serve the warrant without military aid, and made use of this remarkable expression—[Here Hulton was interrupted by the Judge on the same score.]

In the second trial Hulton's evidence on the identical point was objected to again, and although Nadin was then called to the witness-stand to speak for himself (he was not called in the first trial, with damaging results to the magistrates' case), what he did say lacked the dramatic flavour which Hulton probably intended to give. The incident is brought out in Hay's unpublished narrative:

The warrant was filled up about the time of Hunt's arrival. Mr. Andrews, one of the Town's Constables came into the Magistrates' Room, & told Mr. Hulton that it co[ul]d not be served without Military aid. Nadin was in the room. Mr. Hulton laid hold of Nadin by the arm & asked him whe[the]r it was not possible for the Police aided by the Special Constables to execute that Warrant. Nadin replied neither with these Special Constables, nor with 10 times the Number, nor with all the Special Constables in England. Mr. Hulton asked him, cannot it be executed with[ou]t Military force? Nadin answered it cannot. Mr. Hulton said then you shall have military power & for God's sake don't sacrifice the lives of the Special Constables. . . . The warrant was del[ivere]d into the hands of Mr. Moore, The Town's Constable—he delivered it over to Nadin the deputy constable.

Perhaps it was as well (for Hulton) that Hunt objected to hearing what Nadin had said, for he would almost certainly have had this ingenuous reply of William Hulton's to exploit to the full; Hay had prepared this report to the Government with the magistrates' (including Hulton's) full concurrence. Its implications, however, are not entirely one-sided. Hulton continued:

The reason Nadin gave was perfectly satisfactory. I then wrote two letters, the one to the Commander of the Manchester Yeomanry, the other to Col. L'Estrange, requiring them to come to the house where the magistrates were, which they accordingly did. A troop of the Manchester Yeomanry soon arrived from the Mosley Street end. The troops came at a quick pace, and formed in a line under the wall of the magistrates' house.

Here the magistrates are seen entrusting to the civil power, the town's constables, not only military support, but the responsibility, in concert with the military officers, for its use. At that moment it was quite unknown to the magistrates that the support, in the first instance, would be confined to the local yeomanry; but, more important, it was not then even considered that the military support was anything more than coercive backing to enable the constables to arrest the leaders. Hulton's concern for the safety of the special constables is understandable—many were still strung out in a double file across the field up to within a few yards of the hustings.

A hitherto unquoted original source for details of these vital minutes is given in the Yeomanry's Narrative[1] relating to the disposition of the Yeomanry:

One troop with part of the 15th King's Hussars under the command of Lt.-Col. Dalrymple in Byrom Street (on the north side of Deansgate, with which troops were the military commander, Lt.-Col. L'Estrange and Mr. Trafford, the magistrate); the remainder of the Corps, consisting of two troops, were under the command of Major Trafford, in Portland Street, which is a few hundred yards to the eastward of the ground.

The names of Major Trafford, the Yeomanry commander, and Mr Trafford, the Cheshire magistrate, were to be hopelessly confused in the press reports. The former was, of course, in the mêlée, and at the hustings; Mr Trafford, the magistrates' representative, was with Lt.-Col. L'Estrange, and was with him on the fringe of the crowd when the dispersal order was given. The Yeomanry's narrative relates how 'About a quarter after one o'clock a letter was received (in Portland Street) from Mr. Hulton' [quoted] . . . 'A similar direction *was sent at the same instant* to Lt.-Col. L'Estrange, who was waiting under the direction of a magistrate (Mr. Trafford) in Byrom Street . . .' The underlining of the words in the manuscript in the Hay papers is by Hay himself, to which he added this note: 'I know had been previously sent by 3 to 5 minutes.'

[1] *Narrative . . . Manchester Yeomanry*, Eng. MS. 1197/26, J.R.L.

In spite of this, the local Yeomanry arrived first on the spot, owing to the regular troops having to make a detour to get to the ground. Hulton's evidence continues:

The moment they appeared, the crowd set up a tremendous shout. They groaned and hissed, and those men who had sticks shook them in the air. I saw those sticks lifted up in a menacing manner. I had a full view of the whole. I can positively swear that I saw the sticks flourished in this manner, and I even heard the expressions of some of the people who were near the military. Whilst the cavalry were forming, some of those persons who were nearest to them turned or advanced towards them. After the mob had set up this shout the cavalry waved their swords.

Hulton was now in the thick of his disputed and (later) discredited evidence. The Rev. W. R. Hay, in his hurried report sent on the evening of the 16th, (which was the document on which the magistrates' most trenchant critic, John Edward Taylor, based most of his criticisms) contained a reference to 'a most marked defiance acted by the reforming part of the mob'. Hay was undoubtedly referring therein to that which Hulton described more fully as the tremendous shout, the flourishing of sticks, and the 'turning and advancing towards' the Yeomanry. Taylor dismisses this 'defiance' by referring to:

what that journalist of undoubted and unbounded loyalty, Mr. John Wheeler, in the *Manchester Chronicle* of August 21st, more candidly designates as 'cheers'. I heard them, and certainly am not aware that they differed from those which Mr. Hunt has been in the habit of frequently instructing his followers to give, when no idea of 'defiance' could enter into his mind.[1]

Taylor heard the shout although he was not on the field: he could have heard, too, the shout set up a few minutes before, when Hunt arrived, which even Tyas mentioned. The effect of that shout in the magistrates' room can be imagined when, in the Redford-Birley trial. Hulton was asked if he had ever heard such a shout before. 'Never since I was born;' said Hulton, 'and I hope I never shall again.' Taylor perhaps underestimated the effects of the Hunt-inspired 'shouts'; he could have forgotten Saxton's description of the nine distinct shouts outside the Exchange months earlier 'like nine vollies of artillery'. The 'defiance' of turning and advancing towards the Yeomanry Taylor did not see, but his colleague on the *Manchester Gazette*, who reported the meeting from a vantage point outside the fringes of the crowd (or, so it would seem from his inaccuracies as to what was happening near the hustings), saw something which could be construed as partly bearing

[1] *Observations*, p. 58 (footnote (R) to Hay's letter).

out the 'turning round' part of the 'defiance', for he said: 'The persons on the side of the crowd now faced about and cheered in return.'

There were other witnesses to corroborate Hulton's flourishing of sticks and sticks waved in the air. Dr Read sums up the evidence thus:

The question of the use of sticks by the reformers was a topic on which the evidence was later to conflict hopelessly. Bamford, as already indicated, had ordered his Middleton men not to bring sticks: other contingents, however, appear to have done so. They were only such sticks as country people carried with them when out-of-doors and they were mostly borne by old people, but the authorities and 'loyalists' were immediately convinced that they had been brought to the meeting for violent purposes (p. 137).

And on p. 130 where Dr Read is describing the account given by Francis Philips of the procession of a-thousand-and-a-half Stockport reformers, he says:

Philips was careful to add that nearly half the men carried 'stout sticks'.

Francis Philips also, in addition to 'carried stout sticks', added 'many had them shouldered, and one man particularly attracted my notice, from his audacious appearance, having on his shoulder a club, as thick as the wrist, rough, newly-cut, with bark on, and many knots projecting . . .'[1] a sentence which is usually dismissed as hyperbole. John Thacker Saxton was on the hustings with Hunt, but it is not believed he sent his usual report to the *Manchester Observer*. No one seemed to remember, not even the magistrates, his report of the Ashton-under-Lyne meeting only eight weeks previously, where he wrote:

. . . We witnessed such a display of powerful nobbed sticks as we never recollect to have seen before—these weapons of self-defence we are convinced were not for the purpose of breaking the peace, but to preserve it against those privileged violators of the Law, who, under a fancied security of protection from the Borough-despots, are ever ready to disturb the harmony of the people when assembled in the exercise of the Rights of Englishmen.[2]

It was Bamford's old doctrine writ large, a doctrine he had repudiated at the behest of Henry Hunt. The magistrates had no conception of the reformers' gradations of doctrine; they interpreted what they saw by their own old-fashioned lights. Hulton saw sticks 'flourished' in a defiant manner; modern commentators are prepared to admit 'walking sticks'. Philips and his contemporaries saw the stout sticks as weapons of

[1] Philips, *Exposure of the Calumnies* (1819) p. 20–21.
[2] *Manchester Observer*, 19 June 1819.

aggression, and Saxton's sticks were weapons of self-defence. A quantity of these stout cudgels were carted over to York[1] to produce as evidence at Hunt's trial, but Scarlett, or whoever was responsible for the conducting of the prosecution did not produce them. Henry Hunt was to make the most of it:

The bludgeons then, . . . Mr. Scarlett's bludgeons, Mr. Hulton's bludgeons . . . are only to be found existing in the mind of the learned counsel and his solitary witness. They know well that they had no other existence. . . . He is yet the only man who dares to swear to the . . . brandishing of sticks, to the face about of the people against the military.[2] . . . He only speaks to the hissing and hooting. I shall contradict that man. Why was he not corroborated by his brother magistrates, nine of whom were with him in that room where he saw all these indications of violence . . . etc.

The field as it was at the moment the Yeomanry galloped round the corner of Cooper Street to form up outside the wall near Mr Buxton's house: Hunt was still speaking; he had made his ironic, or, alternatively as some reports say, indecent references to the magistrates. The double line of special constables, with enough space between them for two men to walk abreast, still existed, stretching from somewhere near the magistrates' house to where the line was alleged to be broken by the solid phalanx of men who surrounded Hunt's platform. The magistrates' case was that the line had been severed by the movement of the carts before Hunt arrived, and by linking arms the phalanx were determined to stop any approach by the constables to the hustings. That by the movement of the hustings a few of the special constables were separated from their fellows. The full 'flavour' of Hunt's demolition of Hulton's evidence on this point can only be ascertained by the paragraphs reported when he cross-examined Hulton at York.

Hunt: Are you sure, sir, you have stated the facts?
Hulton: I declare that I have related everything exactly as I saw it.
Hunt: Did you see me so distinctly as to know me?
Hulton: I could not see distinctly so as to know you on the hustings. I mean that I could not distinguish your person from that of another.

---

[1] Hunt Trial, (Pratt edn.), p. 66.
[2] 'In order to create a disturbance, as Sir Charles had apprehended before he came to the meeting, some boys were *set on* to fight. Other boys rushed towards them, and created a momentary and very partial confusion . . . Those in the centre remained firm, and evinced their resolution to do the duty of the peace officers, in not allowing the peace to be broken, by elevating their hands and sticks. Order, of course, was immediately restored.'—*Wardle's Manchester Observer*, 3 July 1819, report of the Sandy Brow, Stockport, meeting of 28th June.

Hunt: How far do you think you were from the hustings?

Hulton: The hustings were, I believe, about 300 or 400 yards from the window where I stood; but though I saw a map of the place with the admeasurement, I cannot speak exactly to the fact.[1]

Hunt: Then, am I to understand that, although you could not distinguish me from another, you could perceive that the people were linked arm in arm round the hustings?

Hulton: I could not distinguish you from another, but I could perceive the persons locked together round the hustings, because they formed a complete *cordon*, and were bare-headed. I believe solemnly that those people near the hustings were locked arm in arm.

Hunt: You saw them linked?

Hulton: I saw them linked, I believe, by the arms. They were as close together as ever they could be, and were distinguished from the rest of the crowd.

Hunt: You swear this notwithstanding the distance?

Hulton: Though the distance was so great as to prevent me distinguishing an individual on the elevated hustings, still I and others could see the persons beneath locked together.

Hunt: From your own knowledge, you swear this?

Hulton: I swear this from my own knowledge and observation, and not from what I was told.

Hunt: Can you, sir, standing in that elevated situation, and looking round on the comparatively small number of persons in this court, see whether their arms are locked? (Here a very considerable tumult of approbation was manifested, partly in the galleries, but principally in the lower part of the Court. His Lordship strongly commented on such impropriety of conduct, and a man was immediately brought into the witness-box, who was accused of having joined loudly in it. His Lordship after a suitable admonition, committed him to the Castle gaol.)

Hunt: You will now look round to the benches, where that crowd is elevated, one above another, and say whether you can see what they are doing with their arms?

Hulton: Must I answer that, my Lord?

Judge Bayley: You may declare whether the opportunity you had of viewing the meeting on the 16th of August was better than that which you have of seeing the people now present.

Hulton: I had a much better opportunity of seeing the persons at the meeting than I have of observing those in the Court.

Hunt: Could you see the arms of the persons then ?

Hulton: I could see them wedged, and, I believe, linked together.

Hunt: Could you see any part of their arms?

Hulton: I could distinctly see the outside men linked.

1 Hulton was badly mistaken on this point; the distance was about 100 yards.

Hunt: Then, from the appearance of the others, you believed the rest were linked?

Hulton: I have no doubt of it. I described before what I will state again, that I saw a body of men ten deep, whom, on my oath, I believe to have been linked arm in arm, and many of whom I had an opportunity of ascertaining were so linked. There was a space within this circle, which admitted the hustings, and also some of the mob. I could distinguish the circle from those who were nearer the hustings, because the men who composed it were bare-headed . . .[1]

The linking of arms was a small point of detail in a scene teeming with incident, but Hunt pressed it hard. It was the weak spot in the dyke, the dyke which protected the land which, figuratively, was the magistrates' case; through which the flood-waters of doubt came rushing in. The land remained flooded in spite of the later patching-up of the dyke. Henry Hunt never let go his triumph; he boasted years later how he grilled Hulton in the witness-box and caused him to perjure himself. He denounced him as a perjured man in court, using this apparent instance of Hulton's telling the court 'that as truth which has not the least shadow of probability', to cast doubts on every other part of Hulton's testimony. It brought from Scarlett, the counsel prosecuting Hunt, the weak re-joinder that a man who alleged he saw things in that vast scene of incident was not necessarily perjured because what he saw was not seen by others. Hulton's evidence also brought from the Judge, in his summing up, the commiseration that perhaps in the anxiety of the moment his eyes might have deceived him! Samuel Bamford, in his defence, played on this incident: 'the soldiers ready to fight for Mr Hunt; with bare heads and with arms locked—a fighting posture forsooth . . . that "cordon" impenetrable to everything, save the newly-ground sabres of the Manchester yeomanry cavalry', which comes down to this day as one of Bamford's more-convincing 'passages' in his *Life of a Radical*. That other contemporary authority of Peterloo, Archibald Prentice, reprinted the Hunt-Hulton encounter on locked arms verbatim in his *Recollections* to shew the hollowness of the magistrates' case.[2]

In fact, Hunt in his speech of defence, made less[3] of the incident of

---

[1] *State Trials*, pp. 256-7.

[2] That Prentice should lay such stress on Hulton's alleged 'perjured' testimony is remarkable. The inference being that no such thing as a locked-together cordon of men round the hustings existed and was a figment of Hulton's imagination. Remarkable, because the cordon not only existed, but was admitted by Hunt as existing, except that he claimed that it was open at that point where the line of constables was. The existence of the cordon was admitted by others as well.

[3] Hunt trial, (Pratt edn.), p. 94.

locking arms than either Bamford or Prentice—there was other evidence of its taking place from witnesses whom Hunt did not even cross-examine;[1] for Hunt alleged merely that the motives assigned for locking arms and removing the hustings were completely fallacious, that the hustings were broken down on a former occasion (his January meeting) and that the only object they had in locking arms was to 'preclude the recurrence of similar accidents, not, as was stated, to prevent the cavalry or "corruption" coming in.' 'I can prove', Hunt said, 'that all those who surrounded the hustings were locked together, except at that part where an approach was opened for the constables.'

In 1822, at the Redford v. Birley trial the radicals' counsel said: 'As to the locking of arms,—not that I think it matters the snap of my finger, how they were locked—everybody knows that it was a means of preventing the hustings from being knocked down . . .'[2] There was, however, one eye-witness, whom Hunt did not cross-examine, nor was he heard on this point at all until 1822, when it had ceased to matter. When Hunt's trial came on Richard Carlile was in prison on another charge, but on 16 August 1819, he had ridden to St Peter's Field with Hunt in his barouche, he had been with him on the platform, and he printed accounts of what he saw in his rabidly radical journals. He was reticent on some aspects of what he saw, until later. In 1822, Carlile was incensed that Hunt had charged Manchester reformers with cowardice. He wrote to Hunt (publishing the letter in his *Republican*) a refutation of the charge, harking back to the memorable 16 August:

They did not run away when the Yeomanry appeared on the field, they were received with loud and long cheering, and when they formed for an advance to the hustings, the brave fellows, at a considerable distance round the hustings, linked themselves as compact as possible to assist you in the best manner they could, unarmed, and you stood and saw the yeomanry cut their way through them, which occupied some minutes to do, to get at you on the hustings.[3]

[1] *Hunt Trial*, pp. 61–64.

[2] Redford v. Birley (Farquharson), p. 550.

[3] *Aston's Exchange Herald*, 23 April 1822, quoting a 'late number' of *The Republican*. Henry Hunt's method of disposing of Carlile's statement on the brave fellows linked together round the hustings was by way of point-blank denial. On 24 April 1822, in his Letter to the Radical Reformers, Hunt wrote: 'The story of the "linking of arms" is well told; but it is a wanton, barefaced falsehood, invented by Hulton, to justify himself, and adopted by Carlile for a much baser purpose'. To support him in his denial, Hunt quoted a letter he had received from Robert Wild, one of the acquitted radicals in the 1820 trial. 'The fact is,' wrote Wild, 'there was no linking of arms for more than an hour before your [Hunt's] arrival, and then it was done to preserve room round the hustings for the accommodation of the females and bands that might

Scarlett in prosecuting referred to the 'dexterity' of Hunt's defence. There was no small amount of dexterity used in the public discussion of the trial afterwards. It has been seen how, when the warrant was made out, Joseph Nadin, the deputy-constable, refused to serve it without military aid. Such was Hulton's evidence. *The Times* (30 March 1820) made the most of the conclusions which could be drawn from Hunt's trial by using them devastatingly to refute the Government explanation of the event of Peterloo given earlier. The Solicitor-General, *The Times* recalled, had told the House of Commons that 'Nadin, the officer, saw the meeting, and found that it would be impossible to execute the warrant by the civil power alone'. This statement, went on *The Times* writer, was not only proved to be false by the evidence, but was 'invalidated by the Judge himself, who informed the jury, before summing up, that "there was no evidence of Nadin's inability to execute the warrant", whilst the man was in York, to have proved such inability, if he dared to have sworn to so atrocious an untruth'. Judge Bayley did say that there was 'no evidence' given by Nadin on this point, but not quite in the same sense as the columnist of that day inferred. The Judge said:[1]

. . . As to Nadin's refusal to serve the warrant, that was an extremely good reason for Mr. Hulton, and a complete justification to him for acting as he did in granting to Nadin that assistance in executing the warrant. But what Nadin's reason was, and whether that was the reason upon which we should be warranted in acting, we are left considerably at a loss, because we have not the testimony of Nadin in that respect. . . . If Nadin knew facts which satisfied him that he could not execute the warrant at that place, Nadin should have been put into the box as a witness in order to have shewn that fact to you.

That the 'Thunderer' made such a point on such slender evidence at that time is not surprising; many points were made on even less evidence, and the enterprising columnists of that day could be forgiven for it, *if* the spate of words had remained buried deep in the files of con-

---

attend, and for no other purpose; and no one but *Hulton of Hulton* and *Richard Carlile* have ventured to say to the contrary; no, not even the celebrated *Joe Nadin* himself, who is so far and so justly famed for swearing★★★★'.

Wild's candour in writing thus is suspect, even though he was writing under the influence of Hunt's 'triumph' at York. Joe Nadin did not 'venture to say to the contrary' at York because he was not called as a witness, but he had sworn most vehemently at the Oldham inquest to that effect. Hunt was completely disingenuous. At the date on which he wrote his letter, he knew Wild's testimony was completely invalid, but, in addition, both Joe Nadin and many others had given sworn testimony in Redford *v.* Birley, and the fact was even admitted by the radical counsel.

[1] *State Trials*, pp. 458–60.

temporary newspapers. There were, however, later 'exhumations'. Samuel Bamford, for instance, was to 'lift' practically the whole of that article, even though both that point, and other points, had become completely untenable by subsequent disclosures in Redford *v.* Birley and elsewhere. They serve as props to support Bamford's *Passages* in 1844.[1] Samuel Bamford had, however, some inhibitions: one paragraph in *The Times* article he only printed in part. It was:

The authors of the falsehoods shrunk from owning them at York, as an unnatural father does from acknowledging his illegitimate offspring, dreadfully sorry that the sins of former days should stare him in the face, when he would least have wished to meet with them.

The words underlined do not appear in Bamford's *Passages in the Life of a Radical.*

[1] Bamford II, p. 99.

XIII

The Fusible Elements

Joseph Nadin refused to serve the warrant for various reasons, one being, as has earlier been seen, the rough treatment he had received a few nights before in the New Cross fracas. Most commentators on Peterloo report that he had walked up and down the line of constables before Hunt came, but few say that he testified that at the end of the line of constables was not the hustings, as maintained by Hunt, which were free and open to provide access for the constables if necessary, but a strongly linked and determined band of reformers. 'They were linked ten or twelve deep in the part where I was'[1] observed Nadin; and there can be no mistaking which part that was. One of the Town's Constables, John Moore, testified similarly: he 'could not restore the communication [of the constables with the hustings] without ill-blood, without creating some uneasiness, and therefore I abstained. I could not do it without force.' This testimony was in Redford *v*. Birley.[2] It was Nadin who, after the Yeomanry had arrived, went into the crowd again to draw the special constables back from the thicker part of the crowd; a stone thrown into the spot where he and the constables had lately been, possibly helped to strengthen his mind, which was already made up, that he 'durst not' serve the warrant without military aid.

Capital was made in the House of Commons, and elsewhere, that it had been the magistrates' contention that the deputy-constable had preceded the Yeomanry into the crowd, whereas it was later stated that Nadin had not done so, but had followed them, to which fact he actually testified; Jonathan Andrew, the Town's Constable, did however precede the Yeomanry.[3]

The weapon of military aid had been placed in the hands of the civil power, the constables; they in turn called on the military to aid them, *not*, be it emphasised, to disperse the meeting, but to assist them to make the arrests. The Manchester and Salford Yeomanry were on the

[1] Redford *v*. Birley, p. 372.
[2] Ibid., p. 360.
[3] Ibid., p. 262.

scene first; Col. L'Estrange with the 15th Hussars, the Cheshire Yeomanry, and the other troop of the Manchester Yeomanry were still a few streets away, hurrying to the scene. With Col. L'Estrange rested the command and the *plan*. Hunt had been interrupted in his speech, the alleged shout of defiance had been given, the Yeomanry, in 'some disorder' waved their sabres over their heads. The Yeomanry's statement:

On their arrival in front of the house where the magistrates were assembled they found the Boroughreeve and Constables of Manchester in attendance, who stated to the officers that the troops had been sent for to enable them to apprehend Hunt and others who were upon the stage as they could not execute the warrants without military force. They doubted whether the strength of the Yeomanry was sufficient to justify them in proceeding before the arrival of the other troops, but they assented to the opinion of the squadron officer that the approach which was then open along the front of the special constables might be filled up if the advance was delayed.[1]

Jonathan Andrew, the Town's Constable, testified:

I went up to Captain Birley and stated that we had a warrant. I desired him to surround the hustings, in order that we might take the orators off the stage. . . . We set off together; I advanced before him, on the right of the constables, with Mr. Moore and, I think, Mr. Nadin, the deputy constable. Kept in advance of the Yeomanry as long as I could. I believe I walked the whole way—was not on horseback—but was prevented from keeping in advance the whole way by the interruption of the people. When obstructed, the Yeomanry passed me, but got to the hustings as soon as I could; kept up with the Yeomanry as close as I possibly could.

There was some dispute over the fact of the drawing back of the special constables. Andrew swore that they were 'not drawn back by order' but 'they might have gone a little way'.[2] Nadin swore that he had drawn the constables back to let the Yeomanry come down. The fact surely emerges that there was no grand strategy here. Only some were drawn back.[3]

In the House of Commons debate of 1821 Scarlett, in opposition to the Government, told the House:

Mr. Hulton stated that he never gave them [the Yeomanry] orders to ride into the meeting and attack the multitude. He [Scarlett] was not able to give any satisfactory information to the House how it happened that the Yeomanry did ride into that meeting. He had, however, been given to understand

[1] Eng. MSS. 1197/26, J.R.L.
[2] Redford *v.* Birley, p. 265.
[3] qv. Suppressed account, p. 183 below.

that they had done so upon the representation of one of the constables. Mr. Hulton declared that he knew nothing at all of their advance until he saw them engaged with the multitude.[1]

There is yet no evidence that the magistrates intended to disperse the meeting by force, which again it must be emphasized is, in varying degree, the contention of almost every writer on Peterloo. Dr Read,[2] for instance, in detailing the events of the day, carefully says:

That the Manchester Yeomanry appeared first on the field was the last link in the chain of events leading up to the massacre. . . . The employment of these troops to *arrest* Hunt was the final misfortune; if experienced hussars had been used instead, men skilled in manoeuvring into and breaking up a crowd without violence, there would probably even then have been no bloodshed. . . .

This is a fair interpretation. The word *arrest* is not italicized by Dr Read. It cannot, however, be reconciled with his statement on p. 100:

It is important to contrast the way the Blanket Meeting was broken up with the method employed at Peterloo two years later. Assuming the need to *disperse* the meeting at all, the action of the authorities was as restrained in 1817 as it was violent in 1819. For this there were probably three main reasons. First, the Blanket Meeting was much smaller than Peterloo, only one-fifth the size; this clearly made the dispersal of the assembly a much easier matter. Second, in 1817 the *dispersal* was effected not by ill-trained volunteer yeomanry as in 1819 but by disciplined regular cavalry used to doing such work with the minimum of violence. And, finally, in 1817 General Sir John Byng, the cool-headed commander of the Northern District, was present in person to control the situation. He was not present at Peterloo because the magistrates had told him that he was not needed.

The answer to the crucial question—for what purpose did the Yeomanry go into the multitude?—is that it was to give support to the constables in making the arrests, not to disperse the meeting. To the question— what did they do when they got there?—the answers are conflicting:

On the cavalry drawing up they were received with a shout of good will, as I understood it. They shouted again, waving their sabres over their heads; and then, slackening rein, and striking spurs into their steeds, they dashed forward, and began cutting the people.

'Stand fast,' I said, 'they are riding upon us, stand fast.' And there was a general cry in our quarter of 'Stand fast.' The cavalry were in confusion; they evidently could not, with all the weight of man and horse, penetrate that compact mass of human beings; and their sabres were plied to hew a

[1] *Parl. Debates*, N.S.V. 1821, 832 et seq.
[2] Read, p. 133.

6.
A plan of
St Peter's Field
in the town
of Manchester
(the 'official' plan)

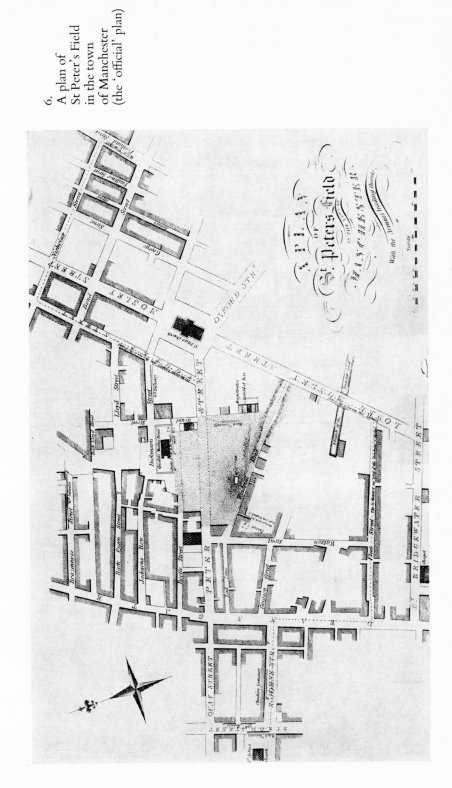

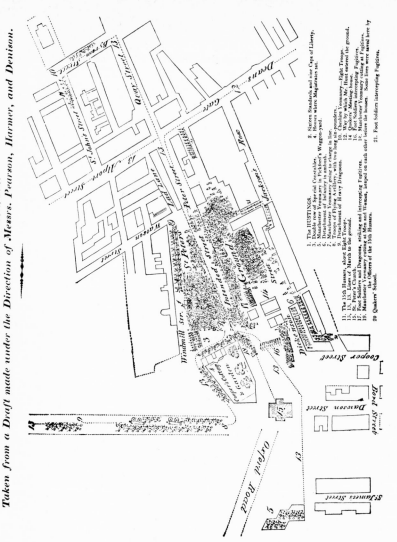

Map of St. Peter's Field, Manchester.

AS IT APPEARED ON THE 16th OF AUGUST, LAST:

Taken from a Draft made under the Direction of Messrs. Pearson, Harmer, and Denison.

1. The HUSTINGS.
2. Sixteen Standards and nine Caps of Liberty.
3. Double row of Special Constables.
4. Houses where Magistrates sat.
5. Manchester Yeomanry in Pickford's Waggon-yard.
6. Detachment of Infantry in ambush.
7. Manchester Yeomanry going to charge in line.
8. Troops of Flying Artillery, with two long six-pounders.
9. Detachment of Heavy Dragoons.

10. Cheshire Yeomanry—Eight Troops.
11. The 15th Hussars, about Eight Troops.
12. Way by which Mr. Hunt entered the ground.
13, 13, 13. Lines of March to the ground.
14. Quakers' Meeting-house.
15. St. Peter's Church.
16. Foot Soldiers intercepting Fugitives.
17. Foot Soldiers and Dragoons, striking and intercepting Fugitives.
18. Manchester Yeomanry cutting at Fugitives.
19. Manchester Yeomanry cutting at Men and Women, keeped on each other before the houses. Some lives were saved here by
20. Quakers' School.
21. Foot Soldiers intercepting Fugitives,

7.

Map of St Peter's Field, Manchester, as it appeared on the 16th of August (published by the *Manchester Observer*, 23 October 1819)

way through naked held-up hands, and defenceless heads; and then chopped limbs, and wound-gaping skulls were seen; and groans and cries were mingled with the din of that horrid confusion. . . .[1]

That, with varying emphasis, is the radical description of the 'charge' of the Manchester Yeomanry. What did the various eye-witnesses see? Hunt had asked Hulton to refer to what took place whilst he stood looking out of the window. 'Did any portion of the people,' ran Hunt's question, 'when I was advancing' (meaning when he arrived in his barouche) 'turn round and give a shout of defiance to the constables?'

Hulton: Not that I know of. The shouts of applause that were bestowed on you had great influence with me in signing the warrant, because you brought with you a great accession of strength to the numbers already collected. . . . The first deposition, not against you, Mr. Hunt, but with respect to the alarm of the town, was made about half-past eleven or twelve o'clock. The last deposition was made immediately after you had ascended the hustings; it was made by a person named Owen . . . [The warrant] was placed in the hands of Nadin . . . when the warrant was made out I had a very strong idea that its service would be a task of great difficulty. Neither I nor any of my constables, to my knowledge, called on the people to make way for the constables to approach the hustings. . . . Then the cavalry, in forming, waved their swords and advanced to the hustings. If I were called on to state their pace in which they advanced, I should say it was something of a trot, or rather prancing; the horses were fidgeting in consequence of the noise, and they were not in good order. I saw none of the cavalry galloping. The pace I wish to describe was between walking and trotting. I believed they advanced to the right of the constables; but the line of the constables, had, I believe, previously been broken. . . .

The space which the cavalry made in their approach was immediately filled up by the people. I cannot say that it was filled up by the constables on the right, and the people on the left endeavouring to escape. I only know that the space was filled up. I think decidedly the space was filled up for the purpose of closing them, and cutting them off.

[A seemingly sympathetic question from the Judge: 'Do you think it was done to pull them off their horses and injure them?' brought from Hulton: 'I certainly do, my lord.'] The impression made on my mind at the time was, that the people closed in order to injure the Yeomanry. There might be some constables that mixed with the people. I could not see them. I do not know that the closing was effected by the rushing in of Nadin and the constables. I believe the people wished to close on the cavalry. I will swear that many of the people did not fly when the first body of the cavalry rode amongst them. They fled when they saw the second. The moment Col. L'Estrange advanced with his squadron, the general flight took place.

[1] Bamford, *Passages from the Life of a Radical,* Vol. I, p. 206 et seq.

I saw very few children in the crowd. I cannot undertake to swear that I saw one. There were a good many women undoubtedly. I heard the women particularly busy in hissing and hooting the cavalry when they first appeared. When the Yeomanry advanced to the hustings I saw bricks and stones flying. I have not stated that they were levelled at the Yeomanry, nor can I swear it. I wish to convey to the jury: those stones and bricks were thrown in defiance of the military. I saw them attacked, and under that impression I desired Col. L'Estrange to advance. . . .

It is interesting to note how Bruton used this part of Hulton's evidence. The above extracts are from Pratt's edition of Hunt's trial, which for the sake of condensation prints only some of the questions made by the person cross-examining, but all of the answers of witnesses. The result is sometimes an apparently scrappy narrative. Bruton[1] uses the above passage in discussing 'missile weapons':

There is no method of discussing the question except that of quoting the various testimonies. Mr. Hulton stated that his reason for thinking the Yeomanry in danger, was that he saw sticks flourished in the air and brickbats thrown about. *He afterwards said at the Trial*: 'I have not stated that bricks and stones were levelled at the Yeomanry and I can't swear it. They were in defiance of the military.'

The words italicized are not italicized in Bruton's passage, but their insertion gives the impression that Hulton was, under cross-examination, 'trimming' a statement he had perhaps made earlier, or at least contradicting that he had made such a statement. Hulton's statement arose through his side-stepping of Hunt's masterly cross-examination. The corresponding passage (*State Trials*, 260–261) is as follows:

Hunt: Were there not many children in the crowd?
Hulton: I saw very few children in the crowd. I cannot undertake to swear that I saw one.
Hunt: There were a good many women?
Hulton: There were a good many women, undoubtedly. I heard the women particularly noisy in hissing and hooting the cavalry when they first appeared. When the yeomanry advanced to the hustings, I saw bricks and stones flying.
Hunt: At the yeomanry?
Hulton: I have not stated that they were levelled at the yeomanry, nor can I swear it. I wish to convey to the jury that those stones and bricks were thrown in defiance of the military. I saw them attacked, and, under that impression, I desired Col. L'Estrange to advance. . . .

Bruton's intentions may have been quite innocent, but the effect of this passage was to weaken Hulton's position. Bruton was not the first to

[1] *Story of Peterloo*, p. 34.

exploit this 'ambiguity' in Hulton's evidence. John Cam Hobhouse used it successfully in the House of Commons debate:[1]

. . . All those who have read the trial, must be aware that Mr. Hulton's evidence stood almost, if not quite, alone, and quite contradicted by a cloud of witnesses. And yet, supposing Mr. Hulton to have deposed to nothing but actual facts, to what did he depose? Did he depose to this previous assault on the military? No such thing. The learned member for Peterborough [Scarlett] found it necessary to exculpate Mr. Hulton from having so deposed, contrary as it was to all the other witnesses; for he said, 'Mr. Hulton had not sworn that sticks and stones were thrown at the cavalry, but it appeared to him that they were raised up'. So that, after all, Mr. Hulton's evidence is good for little or nothing to the gentlemen opposite. . . . [Cam Hobhouse then quoted Stanley's narrative about the non-use of missiles to clinch his argument].

The House was indeed at the 'heart' of the transaction in this discussion, for Hobhouse was able to triumphantly lead on to his conclusion:

. . . Yet, what the ministers of the Crown, with all their power, have been unable to allege—what the magistrates of Lancashire, with all their local information, were unable to adduce—what the learned counsel for the prosecution, with all his talent and address, was unable to prove—namely, that the first aggression came from the people—this discovery was reserved for the learned gentlemen opposite, who boldly assumes that all-important fact as a thing notorious and admitted on all sides. Sir, I repeat the direct contrary is the fact; the Yeomanry attacked the people without warning, without provocation . . . [And the argument was back to the beginning!]

To counter Hulton's statement on the use of 'missile weapons' Bruton quotes Stanley, his principal witness:

Mr. Stanley, on the other hand, says: 'I saw nothing that gave me an idea of resistance, except in one or two spots where they showed some disinclination to abandon their banners; these impulses, however, were but momentary; their sticks, as far as came under my observation, were ordinary walking sticks. I have heard from the most respectable authority *that the cavalry were assailed by stones during the short time they halted previous to their charge.*[2] I do not wish to contradict positive assertions. What a person sees must be true. My evidence on that point can only be negative. I certainly saw nothing of the sort, and my eyes were fixed most steadily upon them, and I think that I must have seen any stone larger than a pebble at the short distance at which I stood and with the commanding view I had. *I indeed saw no missile weapons used throughout the whole transaction,*[3] but, as I have before stated, the dust at

---

[1] *Parl. Deb.*, 2nd series, Vol. V, 15 May 1821, pp. 803–4.
[2] *not* Bruton's italics.
[3] Bruton's italics.

the hustings soon partially obscured everything that took place near that particular spot, but no doubt the people defended themselves to the best of their power, as it was absolutely impossible for them to get away and give the cavalry a clear passage till the outer part of the mob had fallen back.

What Stanley here said was, that if any stones larger than a pebble had been thrown at the Yeomanry whilst they were lined up in front of Mr Buxton's house, or nearby, he must have seen them. Indeed he must; but no one ever said (so far as this investigation can discover) anything of the kind.[1] Stones and brickbats began to fly, or so it was alleged, when the Yeomanry were in the middle of the crowd, and Stanley's evidence on that stage of the transaction was negative—'the dust partially obscuring everything that took place near that spot. . . .' Stanley was challenged in the witness-box as to his use of the word 'apparently'; his 'no doubt' towards the end of his written narrative (above) is equally inconclusive. Stanley's evidence, so confidently set forth by Bruton, on the non-use of 'missile weapons', to strengthen the radical interpretation of Peterloo is weaker than it appears. Bruton was not the first to quote it; it has been in use a long time. John Cam Hobhouse, as has been seen, in the House of Commons, in 1821, was quoting Stanley's narrative to prove the non-existence of stones and brickbats. The evidence has carried weight ever since.

The newspaper reporter, who was dismissed, wrote his account and it was not published by his paper; it was however published by the editor of *Peterloo Massacre* (No. 4). 'The report of one' its editor said, 'who, we may suppose, was not predisposed to speak with much favour of the Radical Reformers, will furnish ample testimony. It is the production of a feeling mind released from the shackles of dependence upon a dependent newspaper.' On the incursion of the Yeomanry into the crowd the report says:

. . . A body of cavalry were galloping into the field from Peter-street. I was told by the persons next me, that they were the Manchester Yeomanry. They pulled up under the range of houses on the south side, in one of which . . . the magistrates were stationed. Mr. Hunt called out in a most empahtic manner to the mob, 'not to be alarmed, but to stand firm', and, taking off his hat, 'let us give them,' said he, 'three cheers.' Three loud cheers were accordingly given, and except some persons on the outskirts of the assemblage, who scampered off on the approach of the troops, the whole body of people remained compactly congregated around the hustings. The cavalry cheered

[1] No one, that is, except Nadin, who testified to a stone being thrown (qv above p. 176), and it was before the Yeomanry advanced. Stanley's misapprehension could have arisen from the passage in Philips *Exposure of the Calumnies* referred to on p. 223 below.

in return, waving their swords round their heads. For a moment, I thought they had ranged themselves under the house where the magistrates were seated, in order to be at hand should any event subsequently occur to render their services necessary. As yet, I had seen, I had heard, nothing to make the imagination of danger enter into my head. I had a constable at each elbow—constables all around me—in one moment more, however, I was fearfully undeceived. I heard the bugle sound—I saw the cavalry charge forward sword in hand upon the multitude, I felt on the instant, as if my heart had leaped from its seat. The woeful cry of dismay sent forth on all sides, the awful rush of so vast a living mass, the piercing shrieks of the women, the deep moanings and execrations of the men, the confusion—horrid confusion, are indescribable. I was carried forward almost off my feet, many yards nearer the hustings than I had been. I was running into the centre of the danger, but I could not help it—I had no choice—I had not a moment to choose. I found myself at last pushed up against the landau which brought Mr. Hunt to the field. I know not what rational hope I could have in seeking shelter under it, but under it I went, and coiled myself fast round the pole. A minute more, the cavalry were around me, trampling down and cutting at all who could not get out of their way. . . .

The reporter from his worm's-eye view reported further carnage, but as a witness to what occurred when the Yeomanry entered the crowd he has his value. By the time he saw the hooves of the horses arriving at the hustings, for it is difficult to imagine that he could see much else, the moment of the 'flash-point' was passed. The writer ended his account with this heartfelt assertion:

I have now brought this brief narrative to an end, and I declare, before God and my country, that it is, in every word, a true and faithful picture of what fell under my personal observation; whether this may have been the reason which has induced its suppression, and lost me the confidence of my employers, I leave the world to determine.

This suppressed account has been before the world since September, 1819, to testify to what occurred on St Peter's Field. 'I leave the world to determine' is still valid.

Hulton had stated (the former being brought out in cross-examination):

When the yeomanry and constables approached the hustings, I saw brick-bats and stones flying in all directions. I saw what appeared to be a general resistance. In short, when Col. L'Estrange arrived at the magistrates' house, with the 15th and the Cheshire Yeomanry, I conceived the Manchester Yeomanry to be completely beaten. The crowd closed the moment the Yeomanry had entered; and when Col. L'Estrange arrived, and asked what was to do, so convinced was I of their perilous situation, that I exclaimed 'Good

God, Sir, don't you see they are attacking the Yeomanry?' My idea of their danger arose from my seeing sticks flourishing in the air, as well as brickbats thrown about. I believe the Yeomanry went in about four abreast, but their horses being raw, unused to the field they appeared to me to be in a certain degree of confusion. They must penetrate through the crowd to get to the hustings, and as far as they advanced, the crowd closed in around them. I saw distinctly from the window where I stood an immense body of people between the house and the Yeomanry, when they advanced to the hustings. In a few minutes some of the party were taken into custody. On my saying to Col. L'Estrange 'Good God, Sir, they are attacking the Yeomanry?—disperse the crowd', he advanced, and the dispersion of the crowd took place. . . .

Hulton believed that the Yeomanry advanced four abreast. The Yeomanry's Narrative has so far received scant notice. It says:

The squadron advanced six abreast along the front of the line of special constables, accompanied by the Boroughreeve and constables and deputy-constable of Manchester, and met with no obstruction from the persons immediately near them, 'till they had approached within some yards of the hustings. There the line of special constables which they believe originally extended from the house where the magistrates were sitting, to the hustings, was broken off by the crowd. As the column approached, the crowd drew back, and opened a passage for the trumpeter and officers who led the way, sufficient to admit six men abreast but they closed in again, immediately upon the rear of the officers, and the first rank of six which followed them was obliged to proceed in single file to avoid riding over the persons who had so broken in upon the line of march, some of the Yeomanry pursued the back of the officers who passed behind the stage and round by the front, whilst others advanced by the front to meet them. By this means the hustings were surrounded and the warrant of the magistrates was executed by the constables so aided by the Yeomanry cavalry according to the directions they had received.

Up to this point, comparing what the Yeomanry said with what Bamford said is like describing scenes on different planets. Yet, it must be remembered that the Yeomanry's Narrative was a considered statement to the Government on what happened, not an *apologia* in the columns of a newspaper. It proceeds:

Up to this point of surrounding the hustings no violence whatever was used on the part of the Yeomanry cavalry. A shout of defiance was set up against them on their coming on the ground which was answered by a shout from the special constables and the Corps. It has been asserted amongst other falsehoods that the squadron cut at the mob right and left as they advanced to the hustings. They struck no blow at any individual 'till they were assailed by the mob. Before the column had actually reached the hustings, stones and other missiles were thrown at them and this mode of attack was afterwards increased to such a degree that it became necessary in self-defence to resist it.

Before taking the sequence of events further, what did other eye-witnesses see? John Tyas was on the platform with Hunt and the other radicals. His narrative, quoted earlier, had ended with: 'At this stage of the business the Yeomanry Cavalry were seen advancing in a rapid trot to the area;' It continues:

. . . their ranks were in disorder, and on arriving within it, they halted to breathe their horses, and to recover their ranks. A panic seemed to strike the persons at the outskirts of the meeting, who immediately began to scamper in every direction. After a moment's pause, the cavalry drew their swords, and brandished them fiercely in the air: upon which Hunt and Johnson desired the multitide to give three cheers, to show the military that they were not to be daunted in the discharge of their duty by their unwelcome presence. This they did, upon which Mr. Hunt again proceeded. This was a mere trick to interrupt the proceedings of the meeting; but he trusted that they would all stand firm. He had scarcely said these words before the Manchester Yeomanry cavalry rode into the mob which gave way before them, and directed their course to the cart from which Hunt was speaking. Not a brick-bat was thrown at them—not a pistol was fired during this period: all was quiet and orderly, as if the cavalry had been the friends of the multitude, and had marched as such into the midst of them. A bugle-man went at their head, then an officer, and then came the whole troop. They wheeled round the waggons till they came in front of them, the people drawing back in every direction on their approach . . .

Edward Baines junior, of the *Leeds Mercury*, was also a reporter on the platform, and also an anti-magisterial witness in both trials; his evidence was that he saw the Yeomanry advance about ten yards into the crowd, and 'thinking at the time they were coming to take prisoners from the hustings, I leaped down from them. . . .' He would not have thought they were coming to take prisoners if Bamford's version is true.

Another of Hunt's witnesses from Hollinwood testified:

When the Yeomanry came on the field the people looked confused. When the soldiers drew their swords and cheered I began to feel alarmed . . . the Yeomanry in their advance passed within a yard of me. I kept my eyes fixed upon them as they proceeded to the hustings. There were not any large stones, brickbats, or sticks hurled in the air as they advanced. The people did not close in on the cavalry as they passed; they endeavoured to get out of the way and escape. I heard no expression of alarm at the meeting before the military came . . . When the Yeomanry advanced I thought they were going to take somebody from the hustings. I stood near the line of constables while I remained on the ground . . .[1]

John Smith, of the *Liverpool Mercury*, had been invited to speak at the meeting, but had refused. Amongst much testimony hostile to the magistrates' case he said: 'Up to the moment of their [the Yeomanry] reaching the hustings, I did not feel, nor did those around me express, any alarm. . . .' The evidence of John Smith has been regarded as important. In Hunt's trial, he had testified as above. Such testimony modified a statement which he made in a letter addressed to the Earl of Derby, dated 18 August, 1819:[2].

. . . Hunt was beginning to address his countrymen when the volunteer cavalry of the town, many of whom but a few days before had made the most violent declarations, rushed upon the people, cutting right and left, taking forcible possession of the conductors of the meeting, and then proceeding by direct charges upon the multitude to force them from the ground.

Smith, in his evidence in Redford *v.* Birley, reverted to his original statement to the Earl of Derby. The value of his evidence is perhaps less than that for which it has been given credit. He was not (as Dr Read says, who followed Haslam Mills's view of Peterloo as the provincial *debut* of the English reporter—Read, p. 132)—on the platform, but in the crowd. His 'not feeling any alarm' evidence occurs in Hunt's Trial (Pratt edn., p. 108.)

One of Redford's witnesses[3] was in his house on the second floor in Windmill Street, saw the Yeomanry form a line outside Mr Buxton's house. When asked at what speed they went down, he replied: 'They came as fast as they could for the crowd. When they got to the hustings they formed round it; when they cleared the hustings they made a charge on the people. . . .' His wife at the same window testified, amongst much that was hostile:[4] 'saw no stones thrown; they showed more cowardice than that . . . they threw their sticks away.' Another of Redford's witnesses saw the Yeomanry riding in at 'a quick trot at first; but as they approached the hustings, their progress appeared to be impeded. They appeared to me to urge their horses forward in consequence of the crowd they had to get through, then some of them waved their swords to and fro, threatening rather than striking, to clear the way; when they arrived at the hustings, some of them appeared to

[1] Hunt's Trial (Pratt edn.), p. 136.
[2] Quoted *Peterloo Massacre*, p. 15.
[3] Redford *v.* Birley, p. 116.
[4] Redford *v.* Birley, p. 119.

surround them—to go round them; and I saw some striking there, at the persons or at the poles of a flag. . . .'[1]

One of the principal radical witnesses at both trials was John Shuttleworth, a wholesale cotton and twist manufacturer, and a prominent member of that group which Dr Read describes[2] as middle-class radicals. He swore repeatedly at the Redford *v*. Birley trial that he saw the Yeomanry striking with their swords when they were yet 20 yards away from hustings. He testified:

Saw the line of constables drawn back . . . they left an open space of perhaps 30 or 40 yards in front of the Yeomanry troop. As soon as this place was cleared I heard Mr. Birley say something and in a few moments after the Yeomanry proceeded towards the hustings. The first two or three files went off in order, but the remainder of the troop galloped after them in considerable confusion; the speed of the horses was increased as they passed through the open space, until they got to the compact part of the crowd, they assumed a circular appearance, and I saw them striking the people; I continued watching until they got up to the hustings, and then I left the ground.[3]

On the disputed point of striking and cutting before the Yeomanry reached the hustings Shuttleworth's evidence was seized on by the defence counsel for this comment:

He is the only man who has ventured to swear to that fact. Others tell you they cut one way or the other, but whether by way of menace merely, or in order to cut and wound, they would not say: other persons say they saw swords go up and down, with what view, they cannot tell. The only individual who has ventured to go to that length, is Mr. Shuttleworth; and he certainly did state that; and he is decisively contradicted by a man who was on the spot, and one of the persons, who says, that he himself received a blow from one of the mob in going up to the hustings,[4] and he swears that no such thing as cutting took place.[5]

The latter testimony was from a former member of the Yeomanry who was giving evidence against the magistrates. Another witness on the radical side was a young man who was later to assume a leading place among the middle-class radicals; he was Robert [Hyde] Greg,[6] Manchester merchant, who testified that he did not see the Yeomanry 'do anything' on their way to the hustings.

[1] Redford *v*. Birley, p. 146.
[2] Read, p. 59.
[3] Redford *v*, Birley, p. 155.
[4] The 'blow' was received later.
[5] Redford *v*. Birley, p. 242.
[6] Redford *v*. Birley, p. 164.

In Redford *v*. Birley the radicals' last witness was the Rev. Edward Stanley, whose evidence, in spite of its being proved erroneous in one minor point of detail—the order in which he stated the troops came on to the ground—has usually been regarded as most damaging to the magistrates' and the Yeomanry's case. He was proved wrong, too, on a more important matter, when he averred that the constables apparently surrounded the hustings, but by 1822, as has been observed, this was not claimed to be important by the radical counsel. He was to be produced as the principal witness for Bruton's account of Peterloo in 1919; and in 1921 not only did Bruton reprint Stanley's privately-circulated account, which had been issued some months after Peterloo, but included in the same volume the whole of Stanley's evidence verbatim from the Redford *v*. Birley trial. Bruton in 1919 introduced Stanley thus:

One of the most valuable of all the individual narratives is that given by the Rev. Edward Stanley (1779–1849), father of Dean Stanley, and brother of the first Baron Stanley of Alderley, who came upon the scene quite unintentionally and by pure accident, and watched the proceedings from beginning to end from the room immediately above that in which the magistrates were assembled. Stanley was at the time rector of Alderley; he afterwards became Bishop of Norwich. His testimony—which was accompanied by a small sketch-plan—is specially valuable because he was pre-eminently a statistician; he became, indeed, one of the first presidents of the Manchester Statistical Society. Moreover, he saw everything from the point of view of a stranger from outside; and his efforts to be impartial and to confine himself to measured language is almost laboured.

Stanley, in his narrative, details incidents which happened after the orators ascended the platform; he could hear but could not distinguish the words. He heard that the soldiers had been sent for, and from a back window watched the messengers going for the cavalry. He returned to the front window:

. . . anxiously awaiting the result; a slight commotion among a body of spectators, chiefly women, who occupied a mound of raised, broken ground on the left, and to the rear of the orators, convinced me they saw something which excited their fears; many jumped down, and they soon dispersed more rapidly. By this time the alarm was quickly spreading, and I heard several voices exclaiming: 'The soldiers! the soldiers!'; another moment brought the cavalry into the field on a gallop [a footnote explaining his version of a gallop] which they continued till the word was given for halting them, about the middle of the space which I before noticed was partially occupied by stragglers.

Stanley shews, on his sketch-plan, this 'raised ground on which many spectators had taken a position; a commotion amongst them first announced the approach of the cavalry'. His comment that this raised ground was to the rear of the orators corrects the impression given by his plan which shews the hustings facing, not end-on to, the magistrates' house, as they really were. He continues:

They halted in great disorder, and so continued for the few minutes they remained on that spot. This disorder was attributed by several persons in the room to the undisciplined state of their horses, little accustomed to act together, and probably frightened by the shout of the populace, which greeted their arrival. Hunt had evidently seen their approach; his hand had been pointed towards them, and it was clear from his gestures that he was addressing the mob respecting their interference. His words, whatever they were, excited a shout from those immediately about him, which was re-echoed with fearful animation by the rest of the multitude. Ere that had subsided, the cavalry, the loyal spectators, and the special constables, cheered loudly in return, and a pause ensued of about a minute or two.

An officer and some few others then advanced rather in front of the troop, formed, as I before said, in much disorder and with scarcely the semblance of line, their sabres glistening in the air, and on they went, direct for the hustings. At first, *i.e.*, for a few paces, their movement was not rapid, and there was some show of an attempt to follow their officers in regular succession, five or six abreast; but, as Mr. Francis Philips in his pamphlet observes, they soon 'increased their speed', and with a zeal and ardour which might naturally be expected from men acting with delegated power against a foe by whom it is understood they had long been insulted with taunts of cowardice, continued their course, seeming individually to vie with each other which should be first.

The reference to Philips's pamphlet shews that Stanley's narrative was not in circulation much before December 1819, and the assertion was made by Birley's counsel when he cross-examined Stanley in 1822, that perhaps it owed something to the many conflicting reports which were in circulation before that time; but this was to be expected. There had been, however, revisions made in Stanley's mind if not in his printed narrative by the time Redford *v.* Birley came on in 1822. Bruton appeared quite oblivious that these discrepancies existed. The printed narrative continues:

Some stragglers, I have remarked, occupied the space in which they halted. On the commencement of the charge, these fled in all directions; and I presume escaped, with the exception of a woman who had been standing ten or twelve yards in front; as the troops passed her body was left, to all appearance lifeless; and there remained till the close of the business, when, as it was no great distance from the house, I went towards her. Two men were then in the act of raising her up; whether she was actually dead or not I cannot say, but no symptoms of life were visible at the time I last saw her. [Stanley adds a footnote here: 'I am particular in mentioning these minute circumstances, because in this and some other points in which I could not be mistaken, I have been strongly contradicted'.]

As the cavalry approached the dense mass of people they used their utmost efforts to escape: but so closely were they pressed in opposite directions by the soldiers, the special constables, the position of the hustings, and their own immense numbers, that immediate escape was impossible. The rapid course of the troop was of course impeded when it came in contact with the mob, but a passage was forced in less than a minute; so rapid indeed was it that the guard of constables close to the hustings shared the fate of the rest. The whole of this will be intelligible at once by a reference to the annexed sketch.

On their arrival at the hustings a scene of dreadful confusion ensued. The orators fell or were forced off the scaffold in quick succession; fortunately for them, the stage being rather elevated, they were in great degree beyond the reach of the many swords which gleamed around them. Hunt fell—or threw himself—among the constables, and was driven or dragged, as fast as possible, down the avenue which communicated with the magistrates' house; his associates were hurried after him in a similar manner. By this time so much dust had arisen that no accurate account can be given of what further took place at that particular spot.

It will be noticed that up to this stage in his narrative, Stanley has not made any reference to the alleged attack—the cutting and wound- ing of the people by the Yeomanry on their way up to the hustings. At a later point he returns to it, in a footnote. He says:

It has often been asked when and where the cavalry struck the people. I can only say that from the moment they began to force their way through the crowd towards the hustings swords were up and swords were down, but whether they fell with the sharp or flat side, of course I cannot pretend to give an opinion.

Bruton quotes this footnote of Stanley's to prove his point that the Yeomanry were using their sabres on their way up to the hustings, and at the end of Stanley's inconclusive statement, adds:

. . . Lieutenant Jolliffe decides this point for us when he says: 'The Hussars drove the people forward with the flats of their swords; but sometimes, as is almost inevitably the case when men are placed in such situations, the edge was used, both by the Hussars and by the Yeomanry.'[1]

Lieut. Jolliffe, one of the three writers of Bruton's *Three Accounts of Peterloo*, was a singularly ill-chosen witness to prove whether the

[1] *Story of Peterloo*, p. 30.

Yeomanry were 'cutting' as they went in, because at that moment Lieut. Jolliffe had not arrived on the scene. What he saw, he described vividly:

[As the Hussars drew up with Col. L'Estrange] It was then for the first time that I saw the Manchester troop of Yeomanry; they were scattered singly, or in small groups over the greater part of the field, literally hemmed up and hedged into the mob so that they were powerless either to make an impression or to escape; in fact, they were in the power of those whom they were designed to overawe, and it only required a glance to discover their helpless position, and the necessity of our being brought to the rescue. As I was at the time informed, this hopeless state of things happened thus: A platform had been erected near the centre of the field, from which Mr. Hunt and others were to address the multitude, and the magistrates, having ordered a strong body of constables to arrest the speakers, unfortunately imagined that they should support the peace officers by bringing up the troop of Yeomanry at a walk. The result of this movement, instead of that which the magistrates desired, was unexpectedly to place this small body of horsemen [so introduced into a dense mob] entirely at the mercy of the people by whom they were, on all sides, pressed upon and surrounded.

The context of the Jolliffe's earlier quotation (above) which was used by Bruton belonged to dispersal proper, after the order to do so had been given by Hulton. Bruton's use of Jolliffe as a supporter of his thesis is questionable, in another instance as well, as will later be seen. Stanley, in his footnote, however, is firmly of the opinion that the Yeomanry were 'striking' with their sabres from the moment they came into contact with the crowd, but unsure whether with the flat or the sharp side.

Not unnaturally, after Shuttleworth's evidence of striking by the Yeomanry before the hustings were reached, Stanley was cross-examined by Birley's counsel. Stanley's testimony under oath was not the testimony given in his narrative:

Did you watch the advance of the cavalry from their place up to the hustings?
I did.
Did you see either sticks, or stones or anything of the kind used against the cavalry in their advance up to the hustings?
Certainly not.
Did you see any resistance whatever to the cavalry, except the thickness of the meeting?
None.
Do I understand you to say you saw them surround the hustings, or not?
Surround I could not say, for the other side of the hustings, of course, was partially eclipsed by the people upon it.

But you saw them encircle part?

Encircle part.

Did you see what was done when they got there?

Yes.

Will you tell us what it was that you saw done?

I saw the swords up and down, the orators tumbled or thrown over, and the mob dispersed.[1]

In his printed narrative the 'swords were up and the swords were down' on their way up to the hustings. On oath, Stanley testified he saw 'swords up and down' when they got to the hustings. Bruton ignored, or, more likely, failed to perceive, the differences in the testimony which he himself had caused to be printed!

[1] Printed in Bruton's *Three Accounts*, p. 29.

XIV

Flashpoint

Capt. Birley's testimony on these vital moments was heard twice, first through the medium of Lord Stanley, a Whig opponent of the Government in the House of Commons, in the debate in November 1819, and again, from Birley himself on the occasion of the King's Birthday celebrations in Manchester, in 1820. Lord Stanley explained to the House thus:

He could assure the House, as he was informed, the use [of the Manchester Yeomanry] arose from pure accident . . . Orders were issued to bring some of the troops round to the point where the constables were stationed, and the Manchester Yeomanry being the first were moved forward. The crowd was so great that doubts were expressed whether the civil power could be effectually aided without some additional troops. The officer who commanded the Yeomanry, seeing an open space leading to the hustings, near the line of constables, and fearing from the motion of the crowd, that it would be blocked up, pushed forward to occupy it. At this time there was obstruction, and the soldiers advanced six abreast, until they got rather nearer the hustings. Here the line of constables was broken by the crowd, who, however, retired, and made way for the trumpeter, officers, and first part of the body. In a short time, however, the crowd closed and obliged the remainder of the troop to move forwards [to] the hustings in single file, contrary to the wish of the commanding officer, but the reason why the Yeomanry did so was to avoid riding over the people. Some followed the officer directly up to the hustings, while others went round, by which means the cart was surrounded, and the warrant of the magistrates executed. At this period, considerable tumult prevailed, and a struggle ensued between the constables and those persons in the cart, who, wished to save the caps of liberty, banners &c. Some of those who resisted were taken into custody, and the soldiers cut with their sabres. In doing this, it was possible that some persons had been hurt, but not intentionally. This was an answer to those who stated that Yeomanry cut right and left in their approach to the hustings . . .

He understood from [Capt. Birley] that the real state of the case was, that a part of the Yeomanry, when they approached towards the hustings were separated from the rest—that the individuals so separated from the rest were closed in on, and then assailed with stones and sticks, in consequence of which some of them faced around, in order to defend themselves. The situation in which these individuals were placed was perceived by the magistrates, who, on seeing what was going forward, thought it their duty, without delay, to order Col. L'Estrange to move forward troops in support of them . . .[1]

Capt. Birley's statement was made in commenting on the report which John Tyas had sent to *The Times*:

Mr. Tyas says the crowd drew back in every direction on our approach. He appears to have fixed his eyes upon the leaders of the column as we went round by the back to the front of the hustings. It was impossible therefore for him, though elevated by favour of Mr. Hunt, *above six feet high*, to see what was passing in the rear. I observed, as I approached the stage, a movement in the crowd about the spot from which all accounts agree in stating that the first attack was made upon the Yeomanry. That movement appeared to be intended to throw an obstacle in the way of our advance. Up to that moment the Boroughreeve had walked by my side, but I then quickened my pace in order to prevent any interruption. There was ample space for a front of six men wherever we passed, but I am assured by those who formed the very first rank of six, that they were obliged to break off into single file before they reached the stage. The mob must therefore have closed in immediately behind the officers who led the squadron.

Mr. Tyas accuses the Yeomanry of cutting, to get at the flags, after Hunt and Johnson had been taken into custody—of losing their command of temper after brickbats had been hurled at them. There is ample evidence to prove that this species of attack had begun before the hustings were surrounded . . .[2]

There is one radical eye-witness account of Peterloo hitherto unused because it was unknown before the year 1956, but used by Dr Read to illustrate one small point of detail regarding the hustings, for the erection of which the writer of the narrative, George Swift, was responsible. Dr Read used a reference from Swift also to illustrate the happenings after the critical moments of the day—during the dispersal. Any genuine eye-witness account of what occurred before the dispersal is more important than a dozen narratives of what took place when the 'free for all' began. George Swift, one of the lesser radicals put on trial with Hunt, but acquitted, has already been noticed in the press reports at 12 o'clock on the hustings haranguing the crowd, not on radical policies or reform, he alleged, but to ensure the safety of the hustings. After his arrest he wrote a letter to his brother retailing what had happened on that day, and dated it 16 August from the New Bayley prison; that it contains information which could not possibly have been

[1] *Parl. Deb.*, XLI (1819–20), p. 325.
[2] *Wheeler's Manchester Chronicle*, 29 April 1820.

acquired on that day is of small moment; it is still one of the earliest accounts extant. He wrote:[1]

. . . Mr. Hunt now set himself off to advantage, he had 130 thousand people under command, he gave a signal for a general cheer and ordered the people to stand fast. 'If they want me,' said Mr. Hunt, 'let me go—don't resist, don't rush'—pointing to a place near him, 'if them fellows won't be quiet put them down and keep them down,' and again exerted himself as a Masterpiece in managing a public assembly. The cavalry formed in front of a range of buildings at the top of the area. After a pause of about two minutes they dashed towards us as well as they could, closing in as they got farther into the crowd. Their swords was lifted up and struck down all the way but I could not at that distance see whether they cut any one or not. They was a considerable time getting through the dense crowd considering the distance so short. They came to the cordon or wall of men round the hustings but no resistance was made to their progress there more than at any other place. The inside of this circle we had filled with women from the Union Schools, music and flags. The cavalry surrounded the hustings and made a full stand for the space of one minute and then turned round to the unoffending multitude . . .

The whole enigma of Peterloo is to a large degree soluble by determining what the Yeomanry did when they went into the crowd. If they went in, as Bamford and Hunt aver, and cut their way to the hustings to disperse the crowd, then the corollary is drawn that the magistrates intended to suppress the meeting in that manner regardless of the consequences. That the Government supported them, and were the power behind the magistrates; or, alternatively, connived after the event. That as a 'massacre' it is rightly named. The 'decision to suppress the meeting by force' had, or had not, at this stage of the narrative been taken; i.e. *before* Hulton gave his decisive command to Col. L'Estrange.

If the radical interpretation of Peterloo is true, then it was the most fatuous 'attack' ever made in history; with men from their own side strewn out in front of the attacking force; with men, armed with constables' staves, walking in front or on the side; with attacking forces going in, sabre in hand, six abreast on horseback, so placed that only the two outside men in each rank could use their sabres. If it is still thought that the evidence so far presented of these few minutes is one-sided, there is a witness still to be heard—the radicals' own organ, the *Manchester Observer*. No hurriedly got-together report, it was published on the Saturday, 21 August, after the fateful Monday, and its testimony

[1] Swift, p. 13.

ought[1] to be impeccable. The headline over this report reads 'Manchester Political Meeting':

No sooner had this thirty sworn and signed the Manchester Magna Charta[2] than the Boroughreeve was called upon to mount his charger, and lead on the special constables in the rear of our *should have been protectors*. They were led on by an *Irishman*, trumpeter to the corps; but the populace were so compact and stood so firm that they could not reach the hustings without halting. Few, if any of the meeting, even yet, supposed that this martial display was intended for anything more than securing Messrs. Hunt, Johnson, Knight, and Moorhouse, for whom they had warrants. Mr. Hunt was called upon to deliver himself up, which he offered to do to a Magistrate, but not to the Manchester Yeomanry Cavalry. A Gentleman in the Commission presented himself, and Mr. Hunt acknowledged his authority, and departed for the rendezvous of the Magistrates; where Mr. Johnson and Mr. Saxton were taken, and from thence conducted, along with Mr. Hunt to the New Bayley prison; Mr. Knight escaped, but was afterwards arrested at his own house;[3] and Mr. Moorhouse was soon after taken into custody at the Flying Horse Inn. As soon as Mr. Hunt was secured followed a scene so truly bloody and horrific . . . etc.

Apart from such minor errors of detail, as the Boroughreeve mounting his horse, when he was said to have dismounted and walked into the crowd, and a 'Gentleman in the Commission' taking Hunt, whereas Nadin 'took' him, the report is not what might have been expected from the ultra-radical Manchester newspaper. Dr Read[4] uses a quotation to emphasise a point: ' "We are not likely to be surprised at any thing nowadays", commented J. E. Taylor in the *Peterloo Massacre*.' Such a quotation is not inappropriate here.

It will be recalled that the Yeomanry's Narrative, quoted earlier, had claimed:

They struck no blow at any individual till they were assailed by the mob. Before the column had actually reached the hustings, stones and other missiles were thrown at them and this mode of attack was afterwards increased to such a degree that it became necessary in self-defence to resist it.

The Narrative continues:

About this time the troops from Byrom Street had arrived upon the Ground under the command of Lieut.-Col. L'Estrange. At this moment the

---

[1] It was not.

[2] A reference intended for the sworn affidavits that the town was in danger.

[3] In the reprint of this article, in *Peterloo Massacre* pp. 10–11, some time afterwards, this sentence read: 'Mr. Knight escaped unhurt, but was afterwards arrested at his own house.'

[4] Read, p. 149.

Magistrates, who from the house where they were stationed had a full view of the Stage, were so impressed with the danger to which the Squadron from Portland Street and the Constables were exposed that they called out to Lieut.-Col. L'Estrange to disperse the mob . . . [A long dissertation on drillings of the mob, how the mob had entered the town etc.] . . . Knowing all this it was impossible for the Yeomanry who were so attacked not to feel the necessity of defending themselves and of protecting those members of the Corps who whilst engaged in assisting the Constables to secure the persons named in the Warrants and the Banners had their backs turned to the Mob and were exposed to considerable danger. It is evident that any delay which would have given time for the Mob to have organized themselves for resistance would not only have endangered their own lives and those of the Constables but would have subjected the town and its inhabitants to such serious mischief as cannot be calculated. . . .

It may be considered doubtful whether indeed the Yeomanry had, in that moment of crisis, thought out so carefully the implications of their actions as explained in their narrative, but they had some justification, if they were attacked, to repel the attack.

. . . They did not conceive that as soldiers they had lost their right of self-defence as citizens, or that they could be considered as doing their duty by remaining inactive under such circumstances of danger. . . .

That attack on the Yeomanry, if made, is to be considered as the 'flashpoint' from which stemmed the inevitable explosion. Anything could happen after that; and in fact did. The *Manchester Observer* (June 2nd, 1821) got to the heart of the matter:

. . . Were they [the Ministers] so ignorant as not to know that in an affair of the most common assault, the *minutiae* of how the affair commenced, and who struck the *first blow*, is always inquired into; and that he is held to be the aggressor who commenced the assault?

'The heart of the matter', because the success or failure of the radical version of Peterloo pivoted on whether this fact of striking the first blow could be pinned on to the Yeomanry or not. Once that fact was established the rest of the radical version dropped easily into place with or without embellishments. By that period in time, (June 1821) however, the *Observer* writer was confident enough to state:

. . . the peace never was at any time broken by the people, but that it was broken by the Yeomanry who we can prove sabred and trod upon many persons in their way up to the hustings . . .

That a large part of the troop of Yeomanry did reach the hustings without striking a blow is proved, conclusively, by evidence from hostile witnesses. That the greater mass of the people stretched out in

front of the hustings, to a great extent on the sides as well, were peaceably inclined and had obeyed the injunction of Hunt to come 'armed
only with a clear conscience', is indisputable. But what of those of
Bamford's school of doctrine, publicly repudiated it is true, that 'there
could be no harm whatever in taking a score or two of cudgels, just to
keep specials at a respectful distance from our line. . . .' Or William
Fitton's reiteration to a crowd of from fifteen to twenty thousand
persons at Rochdale, on 30 July of the 'threat' by several 'sham-valiants'
in the town and neighbourhood to seize and take away the Cap of
Liberty; the meeting was justified in preserving it. There were six of
these hallowed symbols hoisted before the eyes of the crowd on St
Peter's Field. An attempt, said Fitton at Rochdale, had been made,
similar to this some months since at Stockport, when he had the honour
to preside; the consequence was, the assailants were vanquished in an
instant, and the Cap and Banner were preserved, to the utter confusion
of the ragamuffins, who had too lightly been persuaded to counter that
fruitless and ridiculous attack. Or something even more apparently
sinister than the 'give it 'em, lads' doctrine of Bamford and Fitton, which
was later to be voiced by Richard Carlile:

I know not what the Manchester men are to think, when you [Hunt] compliment them with running away! If you had been as bold and as honest as
one half of them, that massacre would not have taken place, or, at least, it
would have been a massacre of a very different kind. If any *fight* had been
offered on the part of the military, it would have been at the risk of a *fair
battle*, a circumstance that, in my opinion, would have kept the Magistrates
and the Yeomanry in a different humour. There was a general expectation of
an attack from the military, and the Reformers were anxious to come to that
meeting *armed*, but your veto put a stop to it, and brought them to be
massacred unarmed. It was offered to you that fifteen thousand men should
come armed with pikes; and your saying that you would not meet them
under any such conditions, alone put a stop to the matter, and led to the
disastrous result that followed[1] . . .

Carlile, writing on 18 August 1819, wrote rather differently:

. . . Nothing but the uniform and steady determination of Mr. Hunt to use
no other weapons than our oppressive legislators themselves have sanctioned,
nor to encourage the use of any other weapons where he had any influence
could have saved the lives of those Yeomanry and Police from a people
goaded to desperation by an outrageous attack on their lives.[2]

[1] See above, p. 173.
[2] Carlile to Lord Sidmouth, quoted in *A Report of the Manchester Meeting* (Manchester: John Leigh, 1819, p. 18).

The pertinent passage in Carlile's letter is: 'Where he [Hunt] had any influence'[!]

Scarlett, in prosecuting Hunt:

When they [the Magistrates] found that, in defiance of their own prohibition [of the 9th meeting] a man had come down from London to preside at this meeting, that the people were arming round Manchester, that they were then directed, by that man, not to come armed, thereby proving that an armed meeting was probably in contemplation, were they wrong in assembling a military force, lest occasion might require it? Was it not their duty to make the constables take their part upon the field to prevent excess, if excess should take place?[1]

There were no pikes, unless, following Stanley's evidence, 'skewers or daggers with wooden handles' be regarded as substitutes for pikes. There was however some evidence of the tactics of Sandy Brow in attempts to cut the saddle-girths and accoutrements of the horses.[2] The fact remained that, after Peterloo and its appalling consequences, it was hard for anyone to believe that any attack had come from the mob. John Edward Taylor (December 1819) wrote:

. . . That any person should gravely assert, or, asserting, expect to obtain credit, that an unarmed multitude, amongst whom were many women and children, should attack a body of cavalry, armed with swords and pistols, is indeed to me astonishing[3]

Taylor did not believe it; Prentice did not believe it; and even James Scarlett did not believe it, from the way he spoke in Parliament, and even from his stray remarks in prosecuting Hunt.[4] Scarlett denied that any part of Mr Hulton's evidence had been shaken. 'Mr Hulton has probably confounded the period when the brickbats and sticks were thrown.' That was, Scarlett said, the explanation of the alleged contradictions. The inference being that missiles were thrown after the *dispersal* order had been given, or after the Yeomanry attacked the crowd; when, it was rightly argued, the crowd were justifiably defending themselves. From this incredibility stemmed the doubts, from doubts, sheer unbelief, and with unbelief the way was open for any Huntean travesty of that days' transactions to be put across to the public, such as the one he issued in 1831, allegedly replying to some remarks made by Hulton in a letter to Lord Althorp:

[1] *State Trials*, p. 417.
[2] *State Trials*, pp. 1201–2.
[3] Taylor, *Observations*, p. 168.
[4] *State Trials*, p. 425.

This, then, is the account of this cowardly and bloody slaughter of the 16th of August, 1819, given by the ex-Magistrate Hulton—William Hulton, of Hulton, near Bolton, in Lancashire; the fellow who acted as chairman of the magistrates who were assembled in Buxter's [sic] house on that lawless day, and who, it is said, gave the order to the drunken Manchester Yeomanry to CHARGE a peaceable and an unarmed multitide of men and women, and children, who were legally and peacefully assembled to petition for a Radical Reform of the Commons House of Parliament, and a Repeal of the Corn Laws, which drunken and infuriate Yeomanry, with newly-sharpened sabres, cut down, rode over, and trampled upon, indiscriminately, men, women, and children, by which cowardly and blood-thirsty acts, fifteen persons were killed, and upwards of four hundred badly wounded . . .[1]

The doubts, as expressed by Taylor and others, were to remain: they were to be allayed in some minds by Hunt's trial in 1820, but increased in others; and even the sheer weight of testimony brought out by the Redford *v.* Birley trial in 1822, that such an attack was not only feasible but had been made, failed to remove the suspicion that something was unexplained. The report of that trial, with its six-hundred and thirty-two pages, has trundled on through history, an also-ran in competition with the versions of Hunt and Bamford.

There is, of course, no radical testimony in either trial of any attack on the Yeomanry, although there is, naturally, a cloud of Crown witnesses to that effect in Redford *v.* Birley in 1822 in contrast to William Hulton's solitary evidence against Hunt in 1820. Dr Read's summing up on this point was:

. . .To what extent stones were really used was another point of dispute. Bamford admitted that when a number of Middleton people were pressed back by the yeomanry they defended themselves with stones. This, however, was excusable. *The Times* reporter said emphatically that not until the yeomanry attacked the flags were any brickbats or stones thrown, and then only a few. On the other hand, the authorities made a great point of stressing that they had had the field cleared before the meeting but yet that afterwards a load of brickbats and stones was removed from it. This seems to confirm that a few stones at least were thrown by the crowd and that some at least had been specially brought to the meeting by the reformers.[2]

The 1819 equivalent of the borough surveyor had, in fact, had every stone cleared from the ground at 8 o'clock on the morning of the 16th, and certified to that effect.[3] It seems, rather, to confirm that not 'a few

[1] *An Address from Henry Hunt to the Radical Reformers* No. 11. 1831.
[2] Read, p. 137.
[3] *State Trials*, p. 1187.

stones' but all of them had been thrown by the crowd; and not 'some at least' but all of them had been 'specially brought to the meeting by the reformers'.

When John Tyas was giving evidence at Hunt's trial on what occurred before the Yeomanry made the arrests, he referred to his original notes. His evidence did not vary from his written account except in one instance: he was recounting the moment when the 'cheers' were given by the crowd on the line-up of the Yeomanry. Pratt's edition[1] of Hunt's trial says:

. . . The cheers were given. Whilst this was doing Mr. Hunt desired that some persons on the waggon might be removed, as they were neither speakers or writers, and were creating a disturbance. This I did not mention in the report, not thinking it material . . .

The State Trials edition gives the point more prominence, attributing the reproof given to the disturbers to Johnson:

. . . Whilst this was doing, a circumstance occurred on the hustings which I did not think of sufficient consequence to mention in my note, that Mr. Johnson desired the proprietor of the waggon to take down from the hustings those persons who were not speakers, and who had only been making a disturbance.[2]

This edition goes on to report that Scarlett brushed the comment aside, saying it was of no importance, and proceeded with his cross-examination on the 'cheers'. The incident, does, however, suggest a disruptive element in the crowd actively opposing the Huntean mode of proceeding—that of passive resistance.

George Swift's narrative on this neglected incident is particularly valuable. There has been a much-quoted part of Hunt's speech, a part made much of in the Redford v. Birley trial, to prove Hunt's aggressive intentions towards the special constables and the Yeomanry and to the military in general. The proof adduced against Hunt, in the light of what is known, is not very convincing. One version was: 'Stand firm and keep our enemies at a distance'; or, as *Wheeler's Chronicle* reported '. . . put them down and keep them down'. There are too many asserters that words of that kind were used by Hunt to dismiss the testimony completely. Swift, however, says that Hunt was addressing himself to the disruptive element among his own supporters. In Swift's context, the words were:

[1] Hunt Trial (Pratt edn), p. 117.
[2] *State Trials*, p. 357.

. . . [Hunt] ordered the people to stand fast. 'If they want me,' said Mr. Hunt, 'let me go—don't resist, don't rush',—pointing to a place near him, 'If them fellows won't be quiet put them down and keep them down' . . .

George Swift was standing on the hustings between Saxton and Edward Baines, the reporter. The latter was to be quite impressed by Hunt's repeated cry of 'Stand firm' (as other reporters have it), or 'Be firm' as Baines reported. 'Mr Hunt, stretching out his arms,' testified Baines at the 1820 trial, 'cried "Be firm". His face was then in the direction of the cavalry—the words were addressed to the whole crowd.' In Bamford's vivid prose occurs the passage: ' "Stand fast," I said, "they are riding upon us; stand fast." And there was a general cry in our quarter of "Stand fast". . . .' Hunt's cry was 'Stand firm!'

The cry might have been, and probably was, quite unfamiliar to Hunt. The cry must have struck a thrill of pride (or, at that moment, more likely, one of horror) into the heart of John Thacker Saxton standing beside him, the words were his own anent Sandy Brow:

'Stand firm!'[1] was the order of the day, and the air in an instant was darkened with nature's ammunition, brickbats, stones and mud. The *Gentry* on horseback had by this time quitted their bridle reins, (some of which, it is said, were cut), and the necks and manes of the horses were every vestige they could contrive to lay hold of, to enable them to keep saddle. The horses, with tenfold more sense than their riders, unwilling to face 'the pelting storm', galloped from the field . . .[2]

Hunt and Bamford had not, in spite of all their protestations, converted all the militants to whom Carlile referred; there may have been a mere score or two only in that vast crowd. A few of them only were needed to provide the 'flash-point' that led to the explosion. The drilling weavers on the moors, on Tandle Hills, on White Moss, or from Middleton, with Samuel Bamford at their head, were not the danger; and the two cryers of 'peace, peace!' knew it. All evidence points to the militants assembled near Windmill Street. It was in that area that the Stockport contingent had taken their places—in the rear of the hustings.

Birley described 'a movement in the crowd about the spot from which all accounts agree in stating that the first attack was made on the

[1] There was a radical significance to the cry: 'Stand Firm'. On the occasion of Hunt's visit to Manchester for the anniversary of Peterloo in 1830, the *Manchester Times* reported an alarm was raised on the outskirts of the crowd, when women and boys, 'fearing a renewal of the scenes of 1819 began to retire; but the men, who seemed to have made up their minds for the worst, called out "Stand firm!" and confidence was restored . . .' *Manchester Times*, 21 August 1830.

[2] *Manchester Observer*, 20 February 1819.

Yeomanry. That movement appeared to be intended to throw an obstacle in the way of our advance.'[1] Jolliffe has a reference[2] to baulks of timber in the middle of the field, but Birley was referring to the attack. He does not identify the spot, and his reference to 'all accounts' must refer to contemporary opinions then current rather than to published accounts. Birley's statement was made, however, before Redford *v.* Birley, and from that trial evidence must be sought. Roger Entwistle, Manchester solicitor, had testified[3] at Hunt's trial that he saw danger the moment he saw parties come in from Stockport; they arrived with sticks, some 'very large'; he followed the Stockport contingent on to the ground and took up his place near them, and was ten or twelve yards behind the hustings whilst Hunt was speaking. He saw stones and brickbats thrown at the Yeomanry when they were fifteen yards from the hustings. He was adjacent to Windmill Street.

One of the special constables who was forced back by the linked men round the hustings[4] saw attempts to knock the Yeomanry off their horses by the use of sticks, during their advance to the hustings; saw brickbats and stones thrown from Windmill Street;[5] another also alleged that he heard from where he stood: 'We'll settle them all before three o'clock'.[6] Another saw sticks elevated so high above the horses' backs and in the act of striking, causing the horses to swerve. 'I never removed my eye' he testified, 'from the hustings till the cavalry surrounded them . . . the moment that the head of the column of the Yeomanry approached the side of the hustings next to Mr Buxton's house, I observed a brickbat hurled from the high ground along Windmill Street. . . .'

It has already been observed[7] that Hunt, at his trial, was anxious to prove that James Moorhouse, his erstwhile host at Stockport, and one of the lesser radical leaders arraigned with him in court, was not at the Sandy Brow meeting some weeks before 16 August, nor had he spoken there. Moorhouse was indeed the only possible link between what had happened at Sandy Brow and what might happen at St Peter's Field. Saxton had a reporter's alibi. The two occurrences were never linked, and Hunt seemed to go out of his way to ensure they were not. Moorhouse, however, was arrested, not indeed on the hustings, but at the

---

[1] See above, p. 193.
[2] Bruton *Three Accounts*, p. 55.
[3] Hunt Trial (Pratt edn.), p. 34.
[4] Redford *v.* Birley, pp. 456–62.
[5] Redford *v.* Birley, pp. 501–2.
[6] Ibid., p, 459.
[7] See above, p. 68. footnote 1.

Flying Horse inn later in the day. At his trial in 1820, Hunt, in cross-examination, drew from a Crown witness an admission that Moorhouse was not at Sandy Brow;[1] his cross-examination of this witness came to a rather abrupt end, curiously it might be thought, because he was eliciting admissions favourable to Hunt's case. 'Hunt: Did you hear me address the people? What did I say? Witness: I heard you address the people, and request them "to be quiet and peaceable". Hunt: What was the general conduct of the people before the arrival of the military? Witness: With the exception of one or two persons, who forced their way through the constables, I saw nothing but peace and quietness among the people until the cavalry arrived.'[2] The witness was very near the hustings; the disturbance began near the hustings amongst Hunt's own 'supporters'. Hunt did not put any more questions.

That Hunt desired to get a denial from the witness that Moorhouse was not at Sandy Brow at all seems inexplicable. Scarlett, the prosecuting counsel for the Crown, had probably never heard of Sandy Brow; doubtless he was puzzled as well. Indeed, from the amount of evidence brought by the Crown against Moorhouse, he hardly seemed worth their powder and shot. He was, of course, acquitted. The charges brought against Hunt, Moorhouse, and the rest were for conspiring to disturb the peace, excite discontent . . . with unlawful assembling. The links between Hunt and Moorhouse were thin: Hunt saw that they were kept thin. Scarlett maintained that it was no part of his case to consider what happened after the arrests. Neither the alleged attacks on the Yeomanry, nor, alternatively, the similarly alleged attacks by the Yeomanry on the people, affected his case. Hunt indubitably made the most of this, and by his own almost unaided efforts turned the trial of himself into a trial of Hulton and the magistrates. It did not affect the jury's verdict, but it affected the verdict of the country. It was from a Crown witness that Hunt elicited the admission that Moorhouse was not at Sandy Brow. Hunt mustered fifty-four witnesses on his side—he boasted that he had sent eighty-three home after his case was closed. They were from every area around Manchester, especially from the 'drilling' areas, but only two were from Stockport. Those two were called only to prove that Moorhouse was not on the hustings. One of these witnesses, and Moorhouse, had alibis for the vital moments of the meeting: when the Yeomanry came on the field, they were in the Windmill public house. Neither witness was cross-examined by Scarlett.[3]

[1] Hunt Trial (Pratt edn.), p. 14; State Trials, p. 199.
[2] State Trials, p. 202.
[3] Hunt Trial (Pratt edn.), pp. 148–9.

James Moorhouse's activities on 16 August may be thought to be remarkable. He had headed the Stockport procession of radicals with his own coach in which he rode; this coach it was alleged by the same witness was the same 'coach' in which Hunt and his party rode to the hustings. Further evidence disproved that it was the same coach; but in any event, Moorhouse rode with Hunt in his carriage in triumphal procession to St Peter's Fields, and was seen to dismount with Hunt at the foot of the hustings;[1] indeed, Crown witnesses swore that they had seen Moorhouse on the hustings, and offered the information as evidence at the preliminary hearings after 16 August.[2] Hunt went to the remarkable length of attempting to bring in bills before the Grand Jury against these three witnesses for perjury at the subsequent Lancaster Assizes. The Grand Jury threw two of the bills out, but one was successful. All of which seemed to shew that Hunt was making a great pother about a very insignificant point. A point which he, or his legal advisers, decided to take so far and no further; because when the bill was brought in, and the alleged perjurer appeared at Lancaster with a body of supporters, they were informed by the judge that his accusers had not put in an appearance.[3] Hunt's seemingly inexplicable conduct with regard to Moorhouse may have puzzled many. Hunt, at his trial, months after the non-appearance at Lancaster of the accusers said: 'He (the witness,

---

[1] *State Trials*, p. 202.

[2] A Crown witness at Hunt's trial was still prepared to swear that he saw Moorhouse on the hustings. Hunt Trial (Pratt edn.), p. 49.

[3] It was against Richard Owen (whose name appeared on the warrant against Hunt, Moorhouse, and others, on which the arrests were made) that the 'true bill' was found for perjury by the Grand Jury. Whatever may have been the reason in Hunt's mind for believing Owen perjured, both Owen and his supporters who journeyed to Lancaster to defend themselves were firmly of the opinion that it was for Owen stating that Moorhouse had been seen on the hustings. They were adamant as to the correctness of their testimony. (*Wheeler's Manchester Chronicle*, 22 April 1820). It would seem therefore that Moorhouse had been on the hustings before the commencement of the meeting, before descending and going into the Windmill Inn. It will be seen, too, that the *Gazette* reporter was under the impression that Moorhouse was 'taken' from the hustings.
   A Radical commentary (*A Narrative of the Manchester Massacre by the Editor of the 'Black Book'*, p. 36) says: [Richard Owen's] 'evidence [at the preliminary hearings after Peterloo] was a tissue of the most atrocious falsehoods and contradictions. A bill was found against him for perjury at Lancaster; therefore his testimony cannot be worth recording'.
   Dr Read (pp. 145–6) quoting the *Manchester Observer*, 18 September and 13 November 1819): 'The Grand Jury, however, refused to find true bills against any of them [two of the Manchester police for perjury, and against several of the Manchester Yeomanry for cutting and maiming] The only true bill was found against Richard Owen, the chief of those who had deposed as to their alarm on the 16th, and even this eventually came to nothing.'

who was one of the alleged perjured witnesses against whom a bill had been thrown out) also swore that he saw Moorhouse on the hustings—a man who was never there, who never intended to be there . . . who, I believe, did not even think of attending at the meeting . . . I am obliged to answer and explain as to Moorhouse.'[1] Hunt, it would seem, did not wish to have any parallel drawn with what had happened at Sandy Brow, Stockport not quite so recently and very recently, and what had occurred on St Peter's Field. Out of over a hundred witnesses for his case, there were only two from Stockport, one of them with an alibi for the time when the Yeomanry came on to the field, and the Stockport leader safely with him in the Windmill public house. Hunt and his advisers were apparently aware, even if those from Stockport were not, that in cold print in the July 3rd, 1819, issue of the *Manchester Observer* were the lines:

> And Stockport's sons shall be thy van,
>   thy country's rights to save,
> Should Tyrant's vengeance thee assail,
>   thou'lt Stockport's courage prove;
> She'll safe from harm her Wolseley keep,
>   wrapt in his country's love.
> Their base designs* should they this day,
>   attempt as they have said,
> E're they thy sacred person touch, THEY'LL
> CLIMB O'ER ENGLISH DEAD.

(* To disturb the Meeting and seize by force the Cap of Liberty.)

Change the word 'Wolseley' for 'Hunt', and it was a pretty piece of circumstantial evidence for getting at the truth of what the later *Manchester Observer* was to call 'the *minutiae* of how the affair commenced'.

It was the last thing in the world that Henry Hunt desired. He had, up to that moment, strained every nerve to avoid such a situation. After 16 August he strained every nerve again to prove to the world that the results of Peterloo were through no fault of his or his followers. All the blame lay with (1) the Government (2) the Magistrates and (3) the Yeomanry, in that order. Once establish the guilt of the Yeomanry, and the rest followed. Hunt, assisted by the easily-aroused social conscience of the nation, convinced the world, or the greater part of it. The results of that day's proceedings were dreadful in any case, no matter who were to be made the scapegoats of the nation's wrath.

[1] Hunt Trial (Pratt edn.), p. 91.

The time would surely come, of course, when the hollowness of the Huntean case would be revealed, as its props were struck away one by one by exposure and refutation. Men's memories, however, were short, and there were to be others in the future who would boil up indignation again with a recital of the old 'facts'. The radical version would be born again. Reference has been made earlier[1] to Samuel Bamford's use of *The Times* article of 30 March 1820, which he quoted almost entire to strengthen his *Passages* and his case. That the trial of Redford v. Birley had occurred after the article had appeared, and years *before* Bamford published his *Passages*, affected him not a whit. The Bamfordian version of Peterloo took no cognizance of refutations. *The Times* was commenting with asperity on what had been stated in Parliament in November 1819, by the Government in support of the magistrates. The Government's case had been blown sky-high by what had been 'revealed' by Hunt's trial. What the impact of that trial was, and how general was the belief that this was so, is seen from a short paragraph in the London *Examiner*:

[Mr Hunt has] succeeded in dissolving, with a few words of his mouth, all that cloud of pretended horror and atrocity on the part of the people, which the Magistrates raised, and which the Ministers kept up, in order to cover the violence of their own proceedings[2]

The passage from *The Times* article quoted by Bamford was:[3]

But we now come to the greatest dupe. It is needless to copy here all that Lord Castlereagh has said, and, we believe, would have sworn, if he might, with respect to the Manchester meeting; such was the credit which his eager simplicity reposed in the basest, falsest, and most perfidious of informers. [Bamford here made an unimportant editorial alteration]. 'The truth was,' he said, 'that the Magistrates did not determine upon dispersing the meeting until it had assumed the character of tumult and sedition' * * * 'As soon as the character of the meeting had declared itself, the Magistrates put the warrants into the hands of the constables; and it was not until they had declared their inability to execute them, that a military force was employed at all'.

All this is totally false; more than twenty witnesses swore at the trial, and none contradicted them, that the meeting never assumed the character of tumultuous.

Close quotes, and no ellipsis; no indication in the *Passages* that Bamford had silently pruned away what *The Times* columnist must have thought

[1] See above, p. 175.
[2] Quoted by the *Manchester Gazette*, 8 April 1820.
[3] Bamford II, p. 100.

to be the irrefragable conclusion to his paragraph. Why? Bamford was writing with his tongue in his cheek; he did not believe in the full radical version of Peterloo. After the passage: 'that the meeting never assumed the character of tumultuous', *The Times* article went on:

. . . that the yeomanry never were assaulted by stones, brickbats, or bludgeons; that there were no stones, brickbats, or bludgeons at the meeting; and that witnesses must have seen if such weapons had been used, or even been there.

The radical attitude towards the evidence of the throwing of stones and brickbats showed some flexibility. First, it totally ignored that they had been thrown; then, when that view became untenable, they said that stones were thrown in self-defence to repel the military attack made upon them. It was Richard Carlile, however, who, when it was known that St Peter's Field had been cleared of stones before the meeting provided the most ingenious suggestion. It had been done, he said, to render the crowd utterly defenceless in readiness for the premeditated massacre![1]

Hunt and Bamford could proclaim, after 1820, that Hulton had perjured himself. Hunt still proclaimed, after Redford *v.* Birley, that the cloud of witnesses there must have done the same. It was then, however, not quite so convincing. Many of their own radical witnesses failed to substantiate the version of Peterloo they proclaimed. Of those radical witnesses whose testimony did support the Hunt–Bamford version, James Scarlett's excuse for Hulton holds equally good: they probably confounded the period when the attack was made.

John Tyas's account has been taken to the point: 'They [the Yeomanry] wheeled round the waggons till they came in front of them, the people drawing back in every direction on their approach.' It continues:

After they had surrounded them in such a manner as to prevent all escape, [!] the *officer* who commanded the detachment went up to Mr. Hunt, and said, brandishing his sword, 'Sir, I have a warrant against you, and arrest you as my prisoner'. Hunt, after exhorting the people to tranquility in a few words, turned round to the officer, and said, 'I willingly surrender myself to any civil officer who will show me his warrant.' Mr. Nadin, the chief police officer at Manchester, then came forward and said, 'I will arrest you; I have got informations upon oath against you,' or something to that effect. The military officer then proceeded to say that he had a warrant against Johnson. Johnson also asked for a civil officer, upon which Mr. Andrew came forward, and Hunt and Johnson then leaped from off the waggon, and surrendered

[1] See above, p. 31.

themselves to the civil power. Search was then made for Moorhouse[1] and Knight, against whom warrants had also been issued. In the hurry of this transaction, they had by some means or other contrived to make their escape.

The description is that of an honest chronicler. Birley, however, in his statement made a perfectly valid point in his assertion: 'He [Tyas] appears to have fixed his eyes upon the leaders of the column as we went round by the back to the front of the hustings. It was therefore impossible for him, though elevated, by the favour of Mr Hunt, above six feet, to see what was passing in the rear.' Keeping the apparent conflicting testimonies in mind—Shuttleworth's insistence that he saw striking fifteen yards from the hustings; Birley's account of the attack on the isolated half-dozen Yeomanry—the 'conflicting' reports do not seem to be so utterly irreconcilable after all. What cannot be reconciled, however, are those accounts put out by (a) the *Manchester Observer* (not the one quoted, but another quite at variance with it, and even the *Observer* cannot have it both ways); and (b) the *Manchester Gazette* which was factually inaccurate on what happened at the hustings and in the crowd, as will be seen; and from which report stemmed the doubts of Taylor, and the stubbornly unalterable view of Prentice, that other 'prime authority' who clouded the understanding of generations, neither of whom were present.

The magistrates' almost laconic statement, as given by Hay, to Lord Sidmouth:

Mr. Hulton on learning that the civil power was inadequate to execute the warrants sent Notices by 2 Gentlemen to the Military in diff[eren]t situations, informing them of such inadequacy & requesting their presence in front of the Magistrates' house. Mr. Andrew & Nadin were now tog[ethe]r, Mr. Andrew headed the Yeomanry on foot towards the Hustings, but as the Yeomanry advanced on a trot, they got first to the Hustings, surrounded them & Mr. Andrew found himself mixed with them directly; he bro[ugh]t Johnson off, Nadin seized Hunt.

The Cavalry on coming up to the House had to form, prior to their forming, we observed the Mob to wave their hats and sticks to defy them. They formed. Whilst they were forming & before they went up, Mr. Ethelston read the Riot Act out of the window, Mr. Sylvester went down stairs, proceeded as far as he could into the Crowd, & read the Riot Act, but before he had quite finished he was ['got' crossed out] pushed down by the Mob ['crowd' crossed out]. As the Cavalry were advancing Mr. Hulton saw the Cavalry were assailed by brickbats & several pistols were fired. Col. L'Estrange & Col. Dalrymple at this Instant rode up & with Mr. Trafford

---

[1] Tyas, too, was possibly under the impression that Moorhouse was on the hustings.

(a Magistrate who attends the Commanding Officer) & asked what they were about; Mr. Hulton said 'Don't you see they are attacking the Cavalry? Disperse the Mob'—they were instantly dispersed. The Cavalry had been attacked about $\frac{1}{4}$ of a minute before Col. L'Estrange came up—from the time of forming the Cavalry to the dispersion of the Body of the Mob about $\frac{1}{4}$ hour did not elapse.

If anything in the whole of the transactions of that day was later to confound confusion it was the evidence on the reading of the Riot Act. Dr Read[1] sums up succinctly:

Another question which gave rise to much discussion at the trials and elsewhere was whether the Riot Act had been read before the second body of troops was ordered to charge the crowd. The reformers and their friends doubted whether it had been read at all, and declared that if it had been then certainly the people had never heard it. There seems little doubt that the Act was read: it was emphatically stated by the magistrates at the trials that it was read twice. Admittedly few people probably heard it, and the statutory hour was not allowed to elapse before the meeting was dispersed. But the whole discussion was somewhat academic, since, if the action of the magistrates was justifiable at all, it could be justified without benefit of the Riot Act; an illegal assembly can be dispersed under common law without any of the Riot Act formalities.

The question was anything but academic after the transactions of 16 August. It gave rise to doubts and suspicions on the part of the critics of the authorities second only to the unbelief that an attack had been made by any section of the crowd. In any case, it was not, as Dr Read says, 'emphatically stated by the magistrates at the trials that it was read twice'. Hunt, at his trial, made the non-reference to it one of his biggest sticks with which to thrash the prosecution. In Redford *v.* Birley, of course, it was stated emphatically, but its perfunctory mention before that time dissipated any benefit to the magistrates' case that its mention gave in 1822. Tyas's account knew nothing (understandably, as will be seen) of it; Stanley's narrative knew nothing of it; neither did Hulton's evidence at Hunt's trial. It had a seemingly casual mention in Hay's report to the Government made on the evening of the 16th, but not made public until after the Parliamentary debate in November. Up to that time the only references to the reading of the Riot Act occurred in three local newspapers: the *Chronicle* (which had the reading of it in the right place), the *Mercury*, and the *Exchange Herald*, the latter two's veracity being immediately suspect by their misapprehensions on the 'reading' of the Riot Act at twelve o'clock, and the quickly-afterwards

[1] Read, p. 138.

refutation of this by the publication in *Peterloo Massacre* of the sacked reporter's suppressed account. From the *Billinge's Liverpool Advertiser*, 23 August 1918:

Although on several points the truth has been completely elicited there remain some, which have not been, and probably never will be so stated as to be universally agreed to. The most important of these points, and the one most involved in difficulty, is the fact of the reading of the Riot Act. It is admitted by all that the reading of this Act an hour before the attack was indispensable to the justification of those who made it or ordered that attack: and of the fact of its reading, we collect the following contradictory evidence, which is so unpliant as to defy all attempts at reconciling it . . .

The article then mentioned the various press reports of the twelve o'clock reading, together with another report in a Liverpool paper 'written by a special constable who was in the crowd' who saw the civil officers go up to the platform at 12 o'clock but could not hear what was said. The enterprising journalist drew the inference that, since the way to the platform was open, the claim of the constables that it was impossible to serve the warrants was false:

In the midst of such conflicting testimony, the only course we can with propriety pursue is to wait patiently till further and positive information is drawn forth in the investigation which must ensue.[1]

Other comment was less kind. The *Statesman* unburdened itself thus:

The first great hinge on which the portal opening to their [the magistrates'] acquittal or condemnation will, and must, turn, is the fact of the reading of the Riot Act, and also the proof of its necessity. It will not be enough that it was read from a distant window, or gabbled over in the corner of a field. It might have been read from the motive of preventing mischief, and not as a colour or pretext to conceal the approach to mischief—no *ruse de guerre* will do here. It was no open rebellion which called out the discretion of the Justices, and the power of the military . . . [peaceful meetings, etc.] . . . The chief or senior magistrate among those who have been thus acting, should have thought of the consequences of spilling one drop of citizens' blood . . . &c.[2]

Given the premises the writer had assumed as his narrative progressed, it was an easy matter to lead on to his conclusions: '. . . And these are the Military, which the local civil power let loose upon the miserable, half-starved men, women, and children (for so they are designated) assembled together. Here is a victory for you!'

[1] Quoted by *Peterloo Massacre*, p. 23 et seq.
[2] Ibid.

John Edward Taylor's *Observations* in December 1819, which contained such incisive criticism of the magistrates' case that it outweighed all the more calumnious criticism of the more radical wing, did more in influencing moderate opinion against the magistrates and the Government than any other source. It has done so ever since. His criticisms however were directed only on what was known of the magistrates' case in December, 1819 namely, Hay's hurriedly-composed letter written on the night of 16 August (released as an official document in November), the reports of the debates in Parliament, and Philips' *Exposure of the Calumnies* of November. On the Riot Act he wrote:

In the composition of his [Hay's] despatches announcing the victory obtained over the starving populace, the reverend stipendiary chairman of the Salford Quarter Sessions seems to have thought it almost needless to say a word with respect to the reading of the Riot Act. It is just noticed, but evidently only *en passant*; and being placed in immediate collocation with the dispersion of the meeting, we must necessarily suppose the two circumstances to have been simultaneous: where then is Lord Castlereagh's authority for asserting that the Riot Act was read, not once, but three times? Who told him that a magistrate, in attempting to read it, was trampled under foot? Or, that they sent a third magistrate to read it at the hustings, in order that no man might be ignorant of the fact of its having been read? Let him, if he *can*, produce one man, above the character of a *lag*, or a police officer, who will pledge his veracity for the fact; and I now assert my fullest conviction, that not one respectable person can be found, who will vouch of his own knowledge, that the Riot Act was read once in any manner, comprehending even a tolerable approach to the form prescribed by the Statute.[1]

The reading of the Riot Act would seem to be on a par with all the other empirically made decisions of that day. It has been said[2] that the magistrates were out of touch with Home Office instructions. Home Office instructions were doubtless pounding in their ears in those vital last minutes: on Hunt's arrest—'not to forbear from doing so, in the expectation of his giving you a better opportunity'. (11 August). 'But if the meeting is not convened for the unlawful purpose, the illegality will not commence until the purpose is developed, and of course after the crowd has been collected; when it must be a question of prudence and expediency, to be decided by the magistrates on the spot, whether they should proceed to disperse the persons assembled.' (17 July); or, finally (4 August) 'Lord Sidmouth is of opinion that it will be the wisest

[1] Taylor, *Observations*, p. 58 Note (т) on Hay's letter.
[2] Read, p. 122.

course to abstain from any endeavour to disperse the mob, unless they should proceed to acts of felony or riot. . . .'

Events, however, were moving too swiftly for the Lancashire and Cheshire Justices of the Peace in that upper room. But the necessary premise to be accepted for the promulgation of this view is, that they should be believed when they stated that they had no intention of dispersing the meeting with the sword; it hardly needs to be reiterated that there is no evidence that it was their intention. From their own observations and the pressure of the Home Office, they decided to make the arrests; such arrests had been made before—in the face of a great meeting at Smithfield, in the face of a smaller one on St Peter's Field two years earlier, and in the face of a smaller meeting still at Leigh five days before. Reluctantly, they had granted to the civil power (the constables) military support, and when it was granted they knew not how that support would be given, but they suspected that it would mean the incursion of the cavalry into the crowd as had been done at the Blanket Meeting; hence Hulton's anxiety for the special constables who were the magistrates' own responsibility. The military plan was with the Commander, Col. L'Estrange whose squadrons arrived after the Manchester Yeomanry. There is one last and vital misapprehension of Dr Read's[1] to be cleared up here:

The Manchester Yeomanry however, unskilful as they were, soon got into difficulties in the crowd and began striking out. The magistrates themselves seem to have half-realized that this would happen, for there was some discussion among them whether to wait until the hussars arrived before proceeding with the arrests. It was decided, however, that as many of the special constables had already been withdrawn, the gap down which the troops were to pass might fill up if there were any delay. After a brief pause, therefore, the Yeomanry wheeled and (accompanied by Nadin) rode through the crowd towards Hunt and the hustings.

Whether the Yeomanry were 'striking out' or not is ascertainable from the evidence of witnesses; what is not so ascertainable is why the inference is drawn from the Yeomanry's Narrative, which is not quoted, that the 'magistrates themselves seem to have half-realized that this would happen, for there was some discussion among them whether to wait until the hussars arrived before proceeding with the arrests.' There was no discussion between the magistrates; the discussion was between the officers of the Yeomanry and the Boroughreeve and Constables of Manchester:

[1] Read, p. 133-4.

On their arrival in front of the house where the magistrates were assembled they [the Yeomanry] found the Boroughreeve and Constables of Manchester in attendance, who stated to the Officers, that the Troops had been sent for to enable them to apprehend Hunt and others who were on the Stage as they could not execute the warrants without a Military force. They doubted whether the strength of the Yeomanry was sufficient to justify them in proceeding before the arrival of the other Troops but they assented to the opinion of the Squadron Officer that the approach which was then open in front of the special constables might be filled up if the advance was delayed.[1]

The decision on the next move in that inexorable game was with the little knot of men on the pavement outside Mr Buxton's house,[2] and by this time the magistrates were as helpless as the rest in being swept along in that now fast-flowing current towards what Dr Read calls 'the climax of the whole day', when a bewildered commander-in-chief Col. L'Estrange shouted up to an equally bewildered chairman of the magistrates: 'What am I to do?' ('Lord Sidmouth is of opinion that it will be the wisest course to abstain from any endeavour to disperse the mob, unless they should proceed to acts of felony or riot. . . .' Hobhouse's quill had scratched those fateful words in the quiet recesses of 10 Downing Street). Through that window in Mount Street, Hulton could see the isolated Yeomanry being attacked. Riot in his eyes was in being: 'Good God, Sir, don't you see they are attacking the Yeomanry; disperse the meeting!'

The cry has reverberated down the century and a half since it escaped from the lips of that thirty-one-year-old magistrate. Most commentators have given it short shrift; a few saw poignancy in it. Horace Twiss, in the House of Commons debate, in 1821:[3]

. . . It was no deliberate act; it was no preconceived plan; it was the impulse of the moment, when but that moment was given to think and to act . . . I believe, in my conscience, that here was no excess of jurisdiction; but let the order have been more or let it have been less prudent, I, for one, can never consent to put men of humane and honourable characters upon their trials as criminals, for having exercised their best discretion in circumstances of such difficulty and such danger, such doubt, and such alarm.

Hunt, at his trial, could not resist scoring a point against Hulton in respect of his order to Col. L'Estrange:

Hunt: Why did you leave the window?
Hulton: Because I gave my orders to Col. L'Estrange.

[1] Eng. MSS., 1197/26, J.R.L.
[2] State Trials, p. 1152.
[3] Parl. Deb. N.S., Vol. V, 1821, p. 791.

Hunt: Was the carnage too horrible to look at?

Hulton: I would rather not see the advance of the military.

Hunt: Then you gave orders for that which you had not the courage to witness?

Hulton: I gave orders to Col. L'Estrange to advance to the support of the Yeomanry; I never thought it would be necessary to disperse violently, as I thought they would disperse it by the apprehension of those named in the warrant; and I will add, that we had no previous intention of dispersing the crowd . . .[1]

If Bamford's version is to be believed, that the Yeomanry penetrated 'that compact mass of human beings; and their sabres were plied to hew a way through naked held-up hands, and defenceless heads; and then chopped limbs and wound-gaping skulls were seen. . .' then Hulton must have witnessed, before he left the window, enough for any stomach to stand.

[1] *State Trials*, p. 262.

XV

The Explosion—and After

When the Yeomanry were still outside Mr Buxton's house, the Riot Act, the magistrates averred, was read by the Rev. Mr Ethelston with his head and body thrust out of the window in the magistrates' room, with the equally reverend Mr Hay ready to catch on to his coat-tails to prevent him from falling out. John Edward Taylor's 'fullest conviction, that not one respectable person can be found, who will vouch on his own knowledge, that the Riot Act was read once in any manner, comprehending even a tolerable approach to the form prescribed by the Statute' was probably unshaken even by this (for that colourful description of the reading of the Riot Act only came out in Redford *v*. Birley, 1822). After 16 August Taylor had ceased to regard the Mr Ethelston or Mr Hay as coming within the terms of his reference of 'respectable' persons, or the reading of the Act as coming within the 'prescribed form'. The odium attached to Mr Hay has already been remarked upon; Mr Ethelston was to receive his full measure of that odium. Mr Sylvester, a magistrate, went into the crowd, furnished with one of the small printed cards which each magistrate in that upper room had been given, containing the short form of words which is the Riot Act, intending to read it in the crowd. He did not get far, he was knocked down in the rush, and made his way back to the magistrates' house with a dirty coat, having been, so it was alleged on his behalf in the Redford *v*. Birley trial, trodden under foot.

With what zest were later radical speakers to tear into shreds the Government spokesmen's narration of these facts, later to be embodied into sworn testimonies in Redford *v*. Birley. Sir Francis Burdett, in the House of Commons debate, 15 May 1821: first on the evidence of stones and brickbats:

From whence then, had the stones come, unless the noble lord [Lord Castlereagh], with certain philosophers, held that they fell from the moon; and assuredly that was a much more probable conjecture than that the people should have brought them in their pockets. This flight to the moon, however, was not high enough for the noble lord: he mounted with bolder pinion, and ventured to add, not only that the magistrates did not and would not interfere with the meeting until it assumed the formidable shape of tumult and treason; but that even then they were determined to act according to the strictness of the law; that one magistrate read the Riot Act from a window in the first instance, but as that was not held to come up to what was required, another magistrate notwithstanding the tumult and formidable appearance of the meeting, like another Decius, devoted himself to his country, plunged into the midst of the danger to read the Riot Act, and was trampled down by the people. That was not all: the self-devoting magistrates multiplied like Falstaff's men in buckram, and a third actually made his way to the hustings [to read the Riot Act there]. All, [concluded Burdett] had proved to be utterly false in a court of law . . .[1]

The 'court of law' then, of course, was Hunt's trial, when Scarlett, the Crown prosecuting counsel, left out of his case all mention of the Riot Act and the question whence the attack had come.

Lord Castlereagh's reference to that other magistrate who forced his way to the hustings in order to read the Riot Act was not, as Burdett supposed, another flight of imagination on the part of the magistrates or of the Government. It was no doubt mentioned in the conversations between the magistrates' delegation and the members of the Cabinet a few days after 16 August: there is no record of it in any of the known (by this investigation) documents of the time. What is known of it comes, as does much else, from hostile sources—radical evidence intended to damage the magistrates' case, and submitted before the Coroner at the allegedly notorious Oldham Inquest.[2] The magistrate who forced his way through the crowd with his card, probably in the wake of the Yeomanry, for he took no part in the arrests, was the then equally notorious Col. Ralph Fletcher of Bolton, the radicals' 'arch-fiend'. Whether he read the Riot Act near the hustings matters not. Lord Castlereagh on behalf of the magistrates said that he was sent for that purpose, but it was never referred to afterwards by them, and would have remained an unsolved mystery had not the radicals brought it forward to make capital out of the incident for their case at Oldham. As evidence to show the diabolical nature of Manchester magistrates in general and of Col. Fletcher in particular, it fell completely flat. For the best or the worst that could be brought out of the incident in cross-examination was the rather ludicrous spectacle of an irate Col. Fletcher berating and belabouring some of the crowd with his cane across their backs, telling them to go away. He did not, the witness maintained in

[1] *Parl. Deb.*, NS., Vol. V, p. 722.
[2] *Oldham Inquest* (Dowling edn.), pp. 510–16.

spite of searching questions from the radical counsel, seem to be hurting them! Thenceforth, it was one of the few instances of magisterial delinquency to remain unexploited by the radicals. Even John Edward Taylor, who carried on a campaign against Col. Fletcher in his paper, right up to the latter's death in 1832, did not refer to it in his *Observations* (1820).

After Hulton's order for the dispersal, almost anything could have happened; but there were still to be some doubtful inferences drawn by later commentators.

As soon as Hunt and Johnson had jumped from the waggon, [went on John Tyas's report] a cry was made by the cavalry, 'Have at their flags'. In consequence, they immediately dashed not only at the flags which were in the waggon, but those which were posted among the crowd, cutting most indiscriminately to the right and to the left in order to get at them. This set the people running in all directions, and it was not until this act had been committed that any brickbats were hurled at the military. From that moment the Manchester Yeomanry Cavalry lost all command of temper. A person of the name of Saxton, who is, we believe, the editor of the *Manchester Observer*, was standing in the cart. Two privates rode up to him. 'There', said one of them, 'is that villain Saxton; do you run him through the body.' 'No,' replied the other, 'I had rather not—I leave him to you.' The man immediately made a lunge at Saxton, and it was only by slipping aside that the blow missed his life. As it was, it cut his coat and waist coat, but fortunately did him no other injury. A man within five yards of us in another direction had his nose completely taken off by a blow of a sabre; whilst another was laid prostrate, but whether he was dead or had merely thrown himself down to obtain protection we cannot say.

It will be seen that a few moments later, to ensure his own safety, Tyas put himself into the hands of a friendly constable who placed him under arrest. Whilst 'languishing' (the common description used in the radical version of the events of this day) in the New Bayley prison with Hunt, George Swift, and Saxton, Tyas was preparing his MS. notes for the compositors of his paper, assisted, according to Swift's narrative, by the other three. Swift maintained that Saxton had sustained a slight wound, but Tyas does not refer to it. He could not, of course, know what kind of a reputation Saxton had earned for himself amongst the Manchester Yeomanry, with his countless taunts at them in the columns of the *Observer*, and his boasts of defending the Cap of Liberty with his life. The fact surely emerges, that in spite of all the alleged excesses taking place, Saxton escaped, and, according to Tyas, unhurt. Tyas's report in *The Times* was seen by the world, but few would see, or take note of, a paragraph published in *The Times* some weeks later:[1]

It is but justice to state, that the individual belonging to the Yeomanry Cavalry, who took Saxton, the Reformer, into custody, was not either of the two wretches who held the brutal conversation about running him through the body. We are glad of this opportunity of removing suspicion from a gentleman who on that occasion acted so unlike many of his corps, and against whose conduct in this instance a very unfounded charge of cruelty had been raised.

There were, in September, few indeed who acknowledged that there were any 'gentlemen' at all amongst the Manchester Yeomanry, although *The Times* squeezed out of its paragraph all it could to back its original assertion. On the seizure of the flags, the special constables were as active as the Yeomanry, notably the almost legendary Richard Owen, whose name generally emerges only as a signatory to the deposition which was quoted for the arrest of Hunt; he is credited with the capture of the noted black flag, so frequently mentioned in the accounts of Peterloo.

Tyas's report of these moments should be compared with that given by Capt. Birley, already quoted in part:

Mr. Tyas accuses the Yeomanry of cutting, to get at the flags, after Hunt and Johnson had been taken into custody—of losing their command of temper after brickbats had been hurled at them. There is ample evidence to prove that this species of attack had begun before the hustings were surrounded.[2] The temper of the Yeomanry and of all the troops employed in the dispersion of the meeting is sufficiently marked by the fact, that, notwithstanding the fury with which they were assailed—notwithstanding that a Yeoman was struck from his horse senseless, and to all appearance, lifeless—not more than one death can be ascribed to a sabre wound . . .

It was futile, at that date, to base arguments on the casualties. To argue whether they were few or many only brought forth further cries of protest. Such an attempt evoked from John Edward Taylor a scathing retort. Taylor was commenting on Francis Philips's *Exposure* which said: 'It appears almost miraculous that soldiers could be employed, and do so little injury'.

Soldiers, [said Taylor] at the Blanket Meeting did none; . . . that the military *could* have done more mischief, will not however be questioned. Instead of using their sabres they might have fired their pistols. But it is to

---

[1] *The Times,* quoted by *Manchester Gazette,* 11 September, 1819.

[2] That evidence, of course, had not been heard by the time Tyas's account was published.

be remembered that this was the first or (taking the Blanket Meeting as a precedent) only a second experiment, and it was not prudent, either for the Magistrates or military, to proceed too far, lest they might unfortunately find, to their cost, that they had calculated too securely upon the favour and *complaisance* of the law. I have no doubt, however, that if the records of the various courts of law (I would rather have said justice)—of the Grand Jury— of the Manchester Magistrates . . . and of the House of Commons, had exhibited any previous instance of such an extraordinary, though *of course* fortuitous concurrence of decisions favourable to the Magistrates and Yeo- manry, the carnage of the 16th of August would have been much more dreadful and extensive, than that which the whole kingdom has even now joined in reprobating.[1]

To utter an *apologia* on the question of casualties was immediately to be brought up against the dilemma posed by Canning in the House of Commons on 24 November 1819:

Undoubtedly, Sir, the meeting at Manchester, was attended with great and grievous calamities. Much suffering was occasioned by it to all classes of the inhabitants of that place; and the loss of lives which occurred in the dispersion of the assembly must be deplored by every mind that has the smallest tincture of humanity. But I know how cautiously I must deal with matters of this kind. I know well the nature of the artifices too successfully practised by those who endeavour to pervert the public judgment by the slander of individual characters. *Experto credite.* The process is of this kind:—An incendiary narrator of what passed at Manchester affirms, perhaps, that 'one hundred persons were slain.' Suppose, indignant at this extravagant falsehood, I answer, 'No, no, not a hundred, the number of sufferers was six only.' '*Six only*!' is then the exclamation, 'O barbarian! it is thus that you trifle with the sacrifice of human life!' This, Sir, is the common trick. It consists in first putting forth a monstrous exaggeration of calamity for the express purpose of inviting contradiction; and then holding up to public indignation the man who reduces the exaggeration to reality, as if he were the unfeeling defender and approver of whatever part of the calamity he does not deny . . .[2]

In a few hours after the mêlee any kind of vindication of the conduct of the magistrates was immediately equated with the condoning of the calamities of that doleful day. Theirs soon became a lost cause. It re- quired a hundred and forty years before it was possible for a comment to be made such as that made by Dr Read:

. . . The successful designation of Peterloo as a 'massacre' represents another

---

[1] Taylor, *Observations,* p. 183.
[2] *Substance of the Speech of the Rt. Hon. George Canning . . . Nov. 24. 1819,* London: 1820.

8. A Representation of the Manchester Reform Meeting dispersed by the Civil and Military Power

9. To Henry Hunt, Esq., a dedication plate from Richard Carlile

10.
Manchester Heroes

piece of successful propaganda. Perhaps only in peace-loving England could a death-roll of only eleven persons have been so described.[1]

But even Dr Read still called it a *massacre*.

James Scarlett, in prosecuting Hunt in 1820, made, as has been seen, the excuse that Hulton 'confounded the period when the brickbats and stones were thrown.'[2] He was not alone in that respect, for it is feared that Scarlett himself did the same thing. A year after Hunt's trial had occurred, the House of Commons was still debating the events of 16 August. Scarlett, as an Opposition speaker, with all the facts at his command which he must have elicited in preparing himself for Hunt's trial, had still not brought himself to believe that any attack had come from the crowd. That this was so, is obvious from his speech in Parliament. He was referring to Tyas's account of affairs at that point just quoted:

['Have at their flags'] That was the moment at which Mr. Hulton conceived them [the Yeomanry] to be in real danger . . . had they stopped then no real damage would have been done, but they then began to attack . . .[3]

That was not, according to the evidence which has been presented here, the moment Hulton conceived the Yeomanry to be in danger; it was not the moment that either the Yeomanry or Birley had in mind; nor the moment that even radical witnesses saw as the 'flash-point': that moment was just prior to the arrests. Modern commentators refer to the 'official' version being overtaken by the versions of those of the 'other side'. The 'official version' had not got across to the public, had not even got across to the prosecuting counsel at Hunt's trial nearly two years later. It gives some idea of the morass the whole question was in after 1819:

Seeing all this hideous work going on, [Tyas's report went on] we felt an alarm which any man may be forgiven for feeling in a similar situation: looking around us, we saw a constable at no great distance, and thinking that our only chance of safety rested in placing ourselves under his protection, we appealed to him for assistance. He immediately took us into custody, and on our saying that we merely attended to report the proceedings of the day, he replied, 'Oh! oh! You then are one of their writers—you must go before the magistrates.' To this we made no objection; in consequence he took us to the house where they were sitting, and in our road thither, we saw a woman on the ground, insensible, to all outward appearance, and with two large gouts of blood on her breast. Just as we came to the house, the constables were

[1] Read, p. vii.
[2] *State Trials,* p, 425.
[3] *Parl. Deb.* NS. Vol. V, p. 834.

conducting Hunt into it, and were treating him in a manner in which they were neither justified by law nor humanity, striking him with their staves on the head. After he had been taken into the house, we were admitted also; and it is only justice to the man who apprehended us to state, that he did everything in his power to protect us from ill-usage, and shewed us every civility consistent with his duty.

Tyas's account, faithful though it was, contained one great gap: it had no knowledge of the 'climax of the whole day'—the arrival of the hussars and the dispersal proper after Hulton's command was given. It was a fatal flaw having some bearing on the conflicting reports which later circulated. He saw the incursion of the Manchester Yeomanry on to the field, and a few minutes later some of the carnage, and a few minutes later still, when he came out of the magistrates' room: '. . . On casting our eyes at the place where the immense multitude had lately been assembled, we were surprised, in the short space of ten minutes to see it cleared of all its former occupiers, and filled by various troops of military, both horse and foot.'

The Rev. Mr Stanley was still at his window; he had described Hunt's arrest, and although he said that by this time so much dust had arisen at the hustings 'that no accurate account can be given of what further took place at that particular spot,' he proceeds:

The square was now covered with the flying multitude; though still in parts the banners and caps of liberty were surrounded by groups. The Manchester Yeomanry had already taken possession of the hustings, when the Cheshire Yeomanry entered on my left in excellent order, and formed in the rear of the hustings as well as could be expected, considering the crowds who were now pressing in all directions and filling up the space hitherto partially occupied.

The Fifteenth Dragoons appeared nearly at the same moment, and paused rather than halted on our left, parallel to the row of houses. They then pressed forward, crossing the avenues of constables, which opened to let them through, and bent their course towards the Manchester Yeomanry. The people were now in a state of utter rout and confusion, leaving the ground strewed with hats and shoes, and hundreds were thrown down in the attempt to escape. The cavalry were hurrying about in all directions, completing the work of dispersion, which—to use the words given in Wheeler's *Manchester Chronicle*, referred to by Mr. Francis Philips[1]—was effected in so short a space of time as to appear as if done 'by magic'. I saw nothing that gave me an idea of resistance, except in one or two spots where they showed some disinclination to abandon the banners; these impulses, however, were but momentary, and banner after banner fell into the hands of the military power . . .

[1] In Philips's *Exposure of the Calumnies*, published November 1819.

Bruton describes Mr Stanley's efforts to be impartial as 'almost laboured'; but how much of some parts of the narrative is Stanley's and how much is borrowed is doubtful. In the above extract he admitted his borrowing from Philips. He must have borrowed also, which he does not admit, his version of the order in which the second wave of military came on the field, for only in Philips, who copied from *Wheeler's Chronicle*[1] are the Cheshires shown (wrongly) as preceding the hussars. He did not, of course, proceed with Philips's further quotations from *Wheeler's Chronicle*, or from the paragraph preceding his borrowed facts. It read:

. . . but before the Cavalry could reach the hustings, they were assailed with stones and insulting language[2] . . . Till thus assailed no Yeomanry-man used his sword, each man having confined himself to waving it over his head. Now the duty of self-preservation obliged them to strike, but in very few instances to cut . . . [Surrounding the hustings; arrests, and the coming of the Cheshire Yeomanry and the Hussars; Philips again curtailed *Wheeler's Chronicle* report considerably, but he went on] Many of the Cavalry were severely bruised, principally with stones previously provided. One gallant youth, Mr. John Hulme, was struck in the face with a brick . . . (he was struck from his horse and stabbed in the back with a sharp instrument . . .)

Stanley's account proceeds:

During the whole of this confusion, heightened at its close by the rattle of some artillery crossing the square, shrieks were heard in all direction, and as the crowd of people dispersed the effects of the conflict became visible. Some were seen bleeding on the ground and unable to rise; others less seriously injured but faint with loss of blood, were retiring slowly or leaning upon others for support. One special constable, with a cut down his head, was brought to Mr. Buxton's house. I saw several others in the passage, congratulating themselves on their narrow escape, and showing the marks of sabre-cuts on their hats. I saw no firearms, but distinctly heard four or five shots, towards the close of the business, on the opposite side of the square, beyond the hustings; but nobody could inform me by whom they were fired. The whole of this extraordinary scene was the work of a few minutes. [A comment on the non-use of the infantry posted in some streets, though they might have impeded the retreat of the crowd].

The rapid succession of so many important incidents in this short space of

[1] *An Impartial Narrative* (1819) p. 34, in which this fact also occurs is a copy of the *Wheeler's Chronicle* report.

[2] Philips had here modified the *Chronicle's*: 'assailed with heavy vollies of stones, shouts of defiance, and the most coarse and insulting language.' This particular passage, could well have been 'the most respectable authority that the cavalry were assailed by stones during the short time they halted previous to their charge', where evidence suggests the biggest shouts were given. See above p. 182, note 1.

time, the peculiar character of each depending so much on the variation of a few instants in the detail, sufficiently accounts for the very contradictory statements that have been given; added to which it should be observed that no spectator on the ground could possibly form a just and correct idea of what was passing. When below, I could not have observed anything accurately beyond a few yards around me, and it was only by ascending to the upper rooms of Mr. Buxton's house that I could form a just and correct idea of almost every point which has since afforded so much discussion and contention.

The most striking point about Mr Stanley's narrative is what it does not say. He has no mention of the reading of the Riot Act, for instance; but this is of small moment. Indeed, when he was cross-examined in the Redford v. Birley trial, he testified that he did not hear it read; and he was, of course, not alone in testifying to not hearing it. He noticed (again in his court appearance) that the hussars were wearing their Waterloo medals; and he remarked (in his narrative) on the 'excellent order' of the Cheshire Yeomanry, as compared with the confusion in the ranks of the Manchester Yeomanry. That comparison could be put down to his pride, as rector of Alderley, of the men from his own county. But that he could stand at that upper window, and notice the Waterloo medals, and not observe, or even *hear*, in spite of all the confusion of that moment, the bewildered shouts of Col. L'Estrange from the street to Hulton a floor below, underneath the very window where Stanley stood, is beyond comprehension. And this could not possibly come amongst the disputed facts of the day. The reader of the Rev. Mr Stanley's narrative must come to his own conclusion, but there is a possible explanation, namely his digression on the woman he described as lying in the wake of the advance of the Manchester Yeomanry. His narrative relates that, in compassion, he went down to succour her 'at the close of the business'. By the time Hunt had been brought into the magistrates' house, a fainting woman had also been brought into Mr Buxton's. Hulton was questioned whether he had seen her; the 'business' of dispersion must still have been going on whilst Hunt was in that room. It could account for the mysterious lacuna in Stanley's evidence, that he went downstairs to her before the 'close of the business'.

Because of this lacuna there is no proper distinction shewn in Stanley's account between the two separate 'charges' (if the Yeomanry's incursion into the crowd is to be called a charge); his privately issued account is challengeable, as has been seen, in important details; he alone thought the double cordon of special constables stretched from near the house where he stood, not only up to the hustings but part way round them as well (as his sketch-plan shows).[1] The account was in circulation in influential quarters some months after the affair. Both Sir Robert Wilson, and John Cam Hobhouse referred to it in the House of Commons debate in 1821, and quoted it as evidence on the then burning question of the use of 'missiles'. In the pre-Redford *v.* Birley era it added its quota, although not 'published', to the confusion. How it was used to confound the magistrates' case after the second Parliamentary debate in 1821, may be inferred by this quotation from the *Manchester Gazette* (24 May 1821). The Government, by that time, was being relieved (in more moderate circles at any rate) of some of the burden of 'guilt':

. . . The only points upon which there could be any defence put up by the magistrates, was that the warrants against Mr. Hunt could not be executed, and that the military were first attacked by the people assembled. Now this is fully disproved by a person whom no one can charge with being one of the Radicals or abetting their cause—a clergyman, who was ready to depose at the Bar of the House of Commons that there was a free passage up to the hustings maintained by a powerful line of constables, and that the military first attacked the multitude. This being the case, and we have no doubts of its truth, on no one but the Magistrates or Yeomanry (as the Government disclaims all previous knowledge of the transaction) can the blame of that event be attached.

Thus the opinion of the left-wing of Dr Read's 'middle-class Radicals' in 1821. After Redford *v.* Birley in 1822, Stanley's original narrative would carry less weight; indeed, some of it was dead. Bruton's resuscitation of this evidence in 1921 to give it pride of place in his *Three Accounts* has given to it an importance it does not deserve. Happily, Bruton gave also the 'revised' Stanley version alongside it, but not with the results Bruton expected.

Cognizance should be taken of the other reporters' versions who were present that day on St Peter's Field: Edward Baines, of the *Leeds Mercury*. His testimony is incomplete owing to his having jumped down from the hustings whilst the Yeomanry were still only a few yards into the body of the crowd. John Smith, as has been seen[2] whatever may have been his first impressions recorded in his paper, thought fit to modify them under oath at the Hunt trial. There remained, of course,

---

[1] The same misapprehension was fostered by Prentice, writing thirty years later (p. 159) who said: 'The numbers of special constables had been greatly increased, 200 additional having been sworn in for the occasion; a portion were stationed round the hustings, and another formed a line of communication thence to a house in which the magistrates were assembled.'

[2] See above p. 186.

the Manchester reporters, and whilst each had their narratives coloured to some extent by their party leanings, their facts should be noted. The *Chronicle* has been, in part, quoted. It noted the reading of the Riot Act twice, by the Rev. Mr Ethelston and also by Mr Sylvester. It confused the Traffords, by asserting that Mr Trafford, the magistrate who was with Col. L'Estrange, led up the Yeomanry, whereas it was Major Trafford;[1] it recorded the on-the-way-up-to-the-hustings attack on the Yeomanry; the incursion of the second wave of troops; and it proceeded:

A scene of confusion and terror now existed which defies description. The multitude pressed one another down; and in many parts they lay in masses, piled body upon body. The cries and mingled shouts, with the galloping of the horses, were shocking. Lt.-Col. L'Estrange, the commander of the troops received a tremendous blow on the forehead with a brick, which for a moment deprived him of sense, and he had nearly fallen from his horse. Many of the most respectable Gentlemen of the town were thrown down, ridden over, and trampled upon. One special constable, Mr. Ashworth, of the Bull's Head, in Market Place, was killed dead on the spot . . . [other casualties] . . . Under the circumstances, these accidents were unavoidable: not the smallest blame is attached to the Military, by those who were the temporary sufferers. It was scarcely to be anticipated that great numbers of the Reformers would come to the meeting prepared with offensive weapons; but it was the case. A class of them were dressed as brewers' servants usually are, with long brats that contain pockets. These pockets were filled with stones. Therefore it is manifest that if the Law found occasion to interpose, a regular system of prevention had been arranged to defeat its object . . .

They referred to Hunt as The Great Delinquent, of his being taken to the magistrates' house, 'dragged by Nadin and others', and to the capture of the flags.

The Rev. Mr. Hay came forward [went on the *Chronicle* report], he said he respected the feelings of the good and the loyal, but as Hunt was now a prisoner, and in the hands of the Law, he hoped that no expression would be given which could endanger the man's personal security; but that he would be satisfied to let him pass to the New Bayley prison with their *silent contempt*. This address was highly applauded, and its purport assented to; but, still . . . a general hiss could not be repressed.'

It reported the cry of 'Let him walk', the cavalcade which escorted him, and Hunt's smile of contempt.

[1] There was some dispute later whether or not Major Trafford was with the troop of Manchester Yeomanry when they advanced to the hustings. In Redford *v.* Birley (439) he testified that he was. *Manchester Observer* writers before 1822 seemed to doubt; it is perhaps not important.

The *Exchange Herald* was the first paper to print details of the meeting in its issue of 17 August and its reference: 'We understand the Travelling Orator had begun to address the Reformers, when an hour having expired, after the reading of the Riot Act, the warrants of the magistrates were carried into effect . . .'—referring, of course, to the twelve o'clock alleged reading of the Riot Act—which no doubt gave a wide impression of that report wilfully misleading opinion. As the *Herald* went to press on the evening of 16 August, its report was necessarily brief, but it had its facts in order, that is apart from the misapprehension of the 12 o'clock Riot Act: the Yeomanry and the police 'dashing' into the crowd to make the arrests. 'At the moment the seizure was made by the Yeomanry, the 15th Hussars' etc., then appeared and the ground was very soon cleared. It added: At the moment of surrounding the hustings, a shower of brickbats and paving-stones were hurled at the Yeomanry, several of whom were struck . . .' It reported more killed than there actually were.

The *Mercury* was out the same day (17th), but its report was of the briefest nature. The following week this paper published a long article on the implications of the Riot Act, and showed some indignation at the wilful misrepresentations of the London and other 'disaffected' provincial papers, whom they rebuked. The storm in other papers on the alleged non-reading of the Riot Act prompted the *Mercury* to publish a 'we are informed' paragraph that the Act was read in several conspicuous stations, and a keeping to their story that the statutory hour was allowed to elapse before the meeting was dispersed. Such assertions were never made again.

The Saturday, 21 August issue of the *Manchester Gazette* report, the paper on which both Taylor and Prentice were writers, was probably considered more accurate than the other three loyalist papers, because its details agreed with what people *thought* had happened on St Peter's Field. Its reporter was not on the hustings or near the hustings. With both Taylor and Prentice away from the scene during the vital moments. it could have been a 'composite' report, partly from one writer standing on the fringe of the crowd near the magistrates' house, and partly borrowed from other papers. The writer was ready to swear, for instance, to the accuracy of his remarks on what occurred when Hunt was brought in. Concerning the construction of the hustings, it was 'we believe'. It reported the mistaken notion that a *magistrate* arrested Hunt;[1] it named Moorhouse as being taken from the hustings when he was not

[1] *Impartial Narrative* allegedly quoting the *Manchester Gazette's* report some weeks later, changed the word 'Magistrate', as the report had it, to 'a Civil Officer'.

there; it knew nothing of the broken line of special constables; and did not hesitate to print, in that issue of the Saturday following 16 August, the most apocryphal story of the whole day:

. . . It is reported that a number of the Cheshire Yeomanry were killed by the populace on Monday evening. Whether this be true or not we hope to ascertain before going to press.

It was not true, nor was it denied in their further issues. On some of the details of the day, the *Gazette* appeared to borrow from Tyas's report which had appeared two days before (the 19th).

Taylor's and Prentice's reports are famous as being sent off to London from Manchester by the night coach on that fatal Monday, thus outstripping the 'official' version! And not only the 'official' one but John Tyas's report as well, which did not leave Manchester until the Tuesday. It is not definitely known, of course, in which London papers the reports of Taylor and Prentice appeared, but there is an affinity in detail between two of the correspondents' reports printed by *The Times*, (both received by them and also quoted from other papers), and the long report printed in Saturday's *Manchester Gazette*; and also the strain in which Taylor and Prentice wrote afterwards. The suspected Taylor/Prentice report in *The Times* reads:

[Arrival of the Yeomanry] The greater part of the persons who were at the outskirts of the assembly on that side instantly ran away; but the main body remained compact and firm, and finding the soldiers halt under the houses, faced round to and cheered them. But a few moments had elapsed, when some orders were given to the troops, and they instantly dashed at full gallop amongst the people, actually hacking their way up to the hustings. A cordon of special constables was drawn from the house occupied by the Magistrates towards the stage, and these fared as ill from the attacks of the soldiers as the people at large. A comparatively undisciplined body, led on by officers who had never had any experience in military affairs, and probably all under the influence both of personal fear and considerable political feeling of hostility, could not be expected to act either with coolness or discrimination; and accordingly, men, women, and children, constables, and Reformers, were equally exposed to their attacks. Numbers were trampled down, and numbers were cut down.

When they arrived at the hustings, the standards were torn, or cut from the hands of those who held them. Hunt was taken along by the constables to the house where the Magistrates were sitting, crying out 'Murder!' as he was every instant struck by the bludgeons of numbers of constables who surrounded him. An attempt was made to knock his hat off, but unsuccessfully; and just as he was going up the steps, a person, who shall be for the present, nameless, with a club of large size, struck him with the force of both hands a blow on the head, which completely indented his hat, and almost levelled him with the ground: of this I can produce evidence on oath.

Whether the Riot Act had been read, I am not enabled positively to say; but I affirm, from actual observation, that not the slightest breach of the peace had been committed, or appeared, as far as I can judge, likely to take place; and, most certainly, instead of an hour being allowed after proclamation, for the people to disperse, not twenty minutes had elapsed, after Mr. Hunt came upon the ground, before the carnage began.

What are the charges on which Hunt and the rest are arrested, I know not. Rumour says *High Treason*, of which carrying the cap of liberty is stated as an *overt act*!

The 'facing round of the people'; the constables faring as ill as the rest (although a well-placed 'probably' occurred at this point in the *Gazette* report appearing on the Saturday); Hunt's cry of 'Murder'; the both-hands blow on the head; all are peculiar to the *Gazette's* report on the following Saturday. But *The Times*' 'letter from Manchester' in its historic issue is an indictment of the Manchester Yeomanry only; no other troops being mentioned. More important still, they are reported as 'actually hacking their way up to the hustings'. A *Gazette*-writer's report it certainly is, but between the Monday night and the more sober reflections of the ensuing days in writing for the Saturday issue of the *Gazette*, 'hacking their way up to the hustings' was modified to 'instantly charged up to the hustings'. True, Saturday's report says that 'Numbers . . . were trodden under foot or sabred,' but a modification it is; and they added the vital information missing from the one sent to London of the use of other troops, and an admission of resistance from the crowd:

. . . About two minutes after the attack of the Manchester Yeomanry on one side, the Cheshire Yeomanry—a detachment of Dragoons and of the 15th Hussars charged on another, thus adding to the dangers and horrors of the scene . . . and after the commencement of the attack some brickbats were thrown at the Yeomanry; one of whom was struck in the face, so that he let go the reins and falling from his horse fractured his skull . . .

The Taylor/Prentice report, containing the cardinal radical 'fact' of the Yeomanry 'hacking their way to the hustings'—the only report which said so—appeared in *The Times* of 19 August. Its contents were swallowed by an eager nation thirsting for news. The *Manchester Gazette* with that 'fact' modified by Taylor/Prentice and correcting any impressions which might have been made by a 'solo' Manchester Yeomanry action, showing that other troops had been involved as well, and that there had been resistance—appeared in the *Gazette* on Saturday, 21 August. Saturday's *Gazette* had a small circulation in and around Manchester. In any case, every newspaper in England was full of Peterloo reports by then.

John Tyas had been taken to the magistrate's house. His report continues:

In the room into which we were put, we found the Orator, Johnson, Saxton, and some other individuals of minor note, among whom was another woman in a fainting condition. Nadin, the constable, was also there. Hunt and Johnson both asked him to show them the warrant on which they had been apprehended. This he refused to do, saying that he had informations upon oath against them, which was quite sufficient for him. Hunt then called upon the persons present to mark Nadin's refusal. Shortly after this transaction, Mr. Hay, the chairman of the Magistrates,[1] came into the apartment, and asked Hunt if he was afraid to go down to the New Bayley; if he was, he himself would accompany him, and look after his safety. Hunt, who we forgot to mention had received a slight sabre wound on one of his hands said, that he should have no objection to the Magistrate's company; he certainly did not like either a cut from a sabre, or a blow from a staff, both of which had been dealt out to him in no small quantity. Mr. Hay shortly afterwards went out, having first made a reply to Mr. Hunt, which some riot out of doors prevented us from hearing.

Tyas was surprised, as has been seen already, that the whole ground where the meeting had been held was in so short a time cleared of the multitude, and was occupied solely by the civil and military power. That was the one moment when all reporters on the happenings of that tragic day could agree, where their narratives touched each other in their common humanity. Touched for a moment; hardly ever to touch again. Samuel Bamford gives us a peerless glimpse of that moment:

In ten minutes from the commencement of the havock, the field was an open and almost deserted space. The sun looked down through a sultry and motionless air. The curtains and blinds of the windows within view were all closed. A gentleman or two might occasionally be seen looking out from one of the new houses before-mentioned, near the door of which, a group of persons, (special constables) were collected, and apparently in conversation; others were assisting the wounded, or carrying off the dead. The hustings remained, with a few broken and hewed flag-staves erect, and a torn and gashed banner or two drooping; whilst over the whole field, were strewed caps, bonnets, hats, shawls and shoes, and other parts of male and female dress; trampled, torn, and bloody. The yeomanry had dismounted,—some were easing their horses' girths, others adjusting their accoutrements; and

[1] A natural assumption, of course, by Tyas; but Hulton was the chairman.

some were wiping their sabres. Several mounds of human beings still remained where they had fallen, crushed down and smothered. Some of these still groaning,—others with staring eyes, were gasping for breath, and others would never breathe more. All was silent save those low sounds, and the occasional snorting and pawing of steeds. Persons might sometimes be noticed peeping from attics and over the tall ridgings of houses, but they quickly withdrew, as if fearful of being observed, or unable to sustain the full gaze, of a scene so hideous and abhorrent.[1]

That this passage was so graphic may be due to the fact that it was a long time in the writing; other compositions were dashed off more hurriedly. Tyas's report was written largely within the confines of the New Bayley prison, but others had more opportunity to mix sacred fact with free comment. The London *New Times* (18 August) writer told that when Hunt was brought into the magistrates' house, 'he betrayed the most abject cowardice and dismay; every limb trembled and his voice was faint'. Even if this were his condition, it should have occasioned no surprise, in view of what he had just experienced. Honours, however, were even, for Hunt was later to describe Hulton's condition at that moment in almost identical terms. One reporter in the London *Courier* allowed his 'imagination' to range thus:

Had it not been for the interference of Mr. Nadin, the deputy-constable, whom these men [the radicals] have particularly calumniated, it is certain that Hunt would not now have been alive, for the military were determined to cut him to pieces. The loyal inhabitants of Manchester and loyal they certainly are, felt themselves imperatively called upon to rescue the town from the odium cast on it by the toleration of these meetings. It is solely from such feeling that they have acted; and, in so doing, they have certainly set an admirable example to the community at large; for, though irritated to a very high degree, they have conducted themselves on this unhappy occasion with the greatest temperance and forbearance.[2]

Such comment was like tossing a bag of gunpowder into a blazing building. The facts that the hustings had been surrounded with Yeomanry and that Hunt was still alive were forgotten.

A Magistrate came into the room, went on Tyas, and bade the prisoners prepare to march off to the New Bayley. Hunt was consigned to the custody of Col. L'Estrange, of the 31st Foot, and a detachment of the 15th Hussars; and under his care, he and all the other prisoners, who were each placed between two constables, reached the New Bayley in perfect safety. The staffs of two of Hunt's banners were carried in mock procession before him.

[1] Bamford, Vol. I, p. 208.
[2] Quoted in *The Times*, 19 August 1819.

After these individuals had been committed to the custody of the Governor, they were turned into one common yard, where the events of the day formed the subject of conversation. Knight and Moorhouse, who had been taken a short time after them, were afterwards added to their company. After 5 o'clock the Magistrates directed the Governor of the prison to lock each of them up in a solitary cell, and to see that they had no communication with each other. This was accordingly done.

The closing of the New Bayley prison gates on this ill-fated band of captives was to affect each of them differently. That they had three hours' 'freedom' together was perhaps surprising in that allegedly ruthless age, not only to converse on the events of the day, but with writing materials, so that Tyas was able to begin his famous 'dispatch' with the help of Hunt, Swift, and Knight. Whether the other three were able to influence his report unduly matters hardly at all, for it was completed in the quietude of his own cell, Hunt was later to describe his incarceration as languishing in a dungeon cell; Johnson, his companion, was to point out:[1]

Your [Hunt's] imprisonment in the New Bayley: What was it? Your servant was allowed access to your room (the best lodging in the Keeper's old house) whenever he pleased. You were supplied with hot meals regularly from Smedley Cottage [Johnson's home] though the distance is full three miles; and your servant was allowed to carry them to you the moment of his arrival.

Johnson was in a 'back cell where refractory felons were kept for a short time as a great punishment'; but even Johnson was able to bribe a turnkey and also get messages to his wife. Tyas wrote:

The writer of this article was one of the parties thus imprisoned. Except that it was imprisonment, he has no reason to complain of the treatment he received. He was in custody from 2 o'clock on Monday till 12 o'clock on Tuesday. As soon as the magistrates were acquainted with the circumstances under which his apprehension had taken place, they immediately ordered his release, and expressed in very polite terms their regret for the inconvenience to which he had been subjected . . .

With Tyas imprisoned, suggests Bruton, Taylor and Prentice sent their famous dispatches to forestall any misleading account from official sources. *The Statesman* (quoted *Manchester Observer* 21 August) saw it thus:

We have learned, we were going to say with surprise, but no event can surprise us from such a quarter, that Mr. Tyas, who was among those arrested on the hustings, is the Gentleman sent by *The Times* to report the proceedings

[1] Johnson, Jos. *A Letter to Henry Hunt Esq.*, Manchester, 1822, (p. 13).

of the Meeting. That the Manchester Magistrates should deem it necessary, in order to produce a proper impression in London, thus to interrupt the Report, and imprison the Reporters of those Morning Papers, which they might apprehend were not likely to approve of their ultra measures, is an instance of the exercise of magisterial discretion such as we do not desire to see repeated.

The irony of that comment lies in the fact that *had* John Tyas's report reached his paper before those of the Taylors and the Prentices, the writing of history might have been different. The ancient beatitude was to receive a new twist: 'Blessed are those that have not seen, and yet have *been* believed'. Tyas had 'seen'; he was fated *not* to be believed.

A modern commentator[1] has said:

State prosecutions were commenced, not against the perpetrators, but against the victims of the day—Hunt, Saxton, Bamford, and others.

To refer to the 'perpetrators' now is as irrelevant as the *Manchester Chronicle*'s 'Great Delinquent' then. All the actors in that tragedy were victims. The radicals on the platform, the militants in the crowd, the peaceable in the crowd, the Yeomanry, the constables, the magistrates in their room, and the captives in the New Bayley, were each and severally as much the victims of the tragic chain of circumstances as the dead special constable lying in the Bull's Head, the wounded in the infirmary, and Mrs Partington, crushed to death, lying at the bottom of the cellar steps. The *Statesman* sardonically wrote of a Victory; there were no victors and no vanquished, only victims. The Fates had, moreover, not yet finished with these victims; physical violence had ended, but the great verbal back-lash of Peterloo was to come. With the prison gates of the New Bayley shut, the spate of minute-by-minute narratives became a trickle. The story of the hours remaining in that day were soon to be passed over. Lieut. Jolliffe wrote:[2]

Carriages were brought to convey the wounded to the Manchester Infirmary . . . For some time the town was patrolled by the troops, the streets being nearly empty, and the shops for the most part closed. We then returned to the barracks . . .

On the roads out of Manchester the fugitives were fleeing to their homes. About half-past three in the afternoon General Sir John Byng was in the town[3] to receive the report from his local commander, Lt.-Col. L'Estrange, whose written report was begun at 8 o'clock that night.

[1] Thompson, p. 684.
[2] Bruton, *Three Accounts*, p. 56.
[3] *Parl. Deb.* Vol. XI, 3rd series, (1832) p. 251 et seq.

General Byng returned to his head-quarters at Pontefract, from which his endorsement of this report went out the following day, direct to Lord Sidmouth:[1]

. . . most sincerely regret that the employment of military in aid of the civil power should have been necessary; but I trust it will appear to your lordship, that the utmost forbearance, consistent with their duty, has been evinced by Lt.-Col. L'Estrange with the troops under his command; and I hope it will meet with your approval his having employed the corps of Cheshire and Manchester Yeomanry Cavalry, who, at the request of the magistrates had assembled with the greatest alacrity in full numbers, and had placed themselves at the Lt.-Col.'s disposal. By the latest accounts I understand the town of Manchester has become more quiet. I shall await here a further report, and shall hold in readiness to move, at the shortest notice, all the disposable force under my orders. John Byng, Maj.-Genl.

The report of Lt.-Col. L'Estrange is more important in assessing the events of that day than it has hitherto been given credit for. First, because of the time it was written—at eight o'clock on the Monday night —making it one of the first-written accounts; and second because it was uninfluenced by the rapid developments of the succeeding days:[2]

Sir, The magistrates assembled here in consequence of the disturbed state of the district, directed me to have the troops in readiness to assist the civil power in case of necessity, at the time of the meeting proposed for this day. In concurrence with their wishes, and after consultation with them, the military were prepared and arrangements made, such as then seemed calculated to meet any occasion, in which the aid of the troops might be required to assist the civil power. The magistrates were in attendance near St. Peter's Church: and Mr. Trafford, a Justice of the Peace for the counties of Chester and Lancaster, was appointed to remain with the cavalry.

It will be seen that Col. L'Estrange makes no distinction between the voluntary Yeomanry and the Hussars—both were 'cavalry' under his direct command.

Early in the afternoon, the civil power finding it necessary that the troops should act in aid of them, it was deemed expedient that the cavalry should advance; and a warrant was executed, preceded by the civil authority under which two persons Hunt and Johnson, named therein were arrested; as were also two other persons named Saxton and Sykes[3] who were active, as I am told on the hustings. This service was performed with the assistance of the cavalry. The infantry was in readiness, but I determined not to bring them in

[1] *Papers Relative to the Internal State of the Country*, p. 30.
[2] Ibid., pp. 30–31.
[3] An error for Tyas?

contact with the people, unless compelled to do so by urgent necessity; not a shot therefore has been fired by the populace against the troops. I have, however, great regret in stating that some of the unfortunate people who attended this meeting have suffered from sabre wounds, and many from the pressure of the crowd. One of the Manchester Yeomanry, if not dead, lies without hope of recovery; it is understood he was struck with a stone. One of the special constables has been killed. The Manchester Yeomanry, under Major Trafford, and the Cheshire Yeomanry under Lt.-Col. Townsend, who had come on a very short notice from the county magistrates (many of them from a great distance) were most active and efficient in discharge of their duty. The committee, now sitting, consider it necessary to keep all the troops ready, though every means will be adopted to prevent the necessity of their acting.
George L'Estrange Lt.-Col. 31st Regt.
Major General Sir John Byng, K.C.B.

The world at large did not see this report until the end of November 1819, by which time its issue, with other documents, was thought necessary by the Government to help placate the intense bombardment of criticism directed at them. The references both by Gen. Byng and Col. L'Estrange to the short notice and the inconvenience under which the voluntary units assembled, ought to have been considered (though they were not) an excuse for the return of thanks by the Prince Regent and Lord Sidmouth a few days later. As an act of common courtesy, at the least, it had been the usual custom on similar occasions from time immemorial. But this was not a 'similar occasion'.

Even whilst Col. L'Estrange was writing, a precautionary routine measure, so Lt. Jolliffe tells us,[1] was being taken:

About 8 p.m. one squadron of the 15th Hussars (two troops) was ordered on duty to form part of a strong night picket, the other part of which consisted of two companies of the 88th Regiment. This picket was stationed at a place called the New Cross at the end of Oldham Street. As soon as it had taken up its position, a mob assembled about it, which increased as the darkness came on; stones were thrown at the soldiers, and the Hussars many times cleared the ground by driving the mob up the streets leading from the New Cross. But these attempts to get rid of the annoyance were only successful for the moment, for the people got through the houses or narrow passages from one street into another, and the troops were again attacked, and many men and horses struck with stones. This lasted nearly an hour and a half, and the soldiers being more and more pressed upon, a town magistrate, who was with the picket, read the Riot Act, and the officer in command ordered the 88th to fire (which they did by platoon firing) down three of the streets. The firing only lasted a few minutes; perhaps not more than thirty shots were fired;

[1] Bruton, *Three Accounts*, p. 56.

but these had a magical effect; the mob ran away and dispersed forthwith, leaving three or four persons on the ground with gunshot wounds. At 4 a.m. the picket squadron was relieved by another squadron of the regiment. With this latter squadron I was on duty, and after we had patrolled the town for two hours, the officer in command sent me to the magistrates (who had remained assembled during the night) to report to them that the town was perfectly quiet, and to request their sanction to the return of the military to their quarters.

At a quarter past nine on that Monday night, one of the magistrates sat down to write his official report of the day to Lord Sidmouth. What was in that report was not made known to the public until four months later, again with embarrassing effects on the magistrates' case, since it became an easy target for the incisive prose of John Edward Taylor. James Norris had penned the eleventh-hour report to Lord Sidmouth on the night of 15 August[1], and it might have been thought fitting that he should have indited this. It was however signed by William Robert Hay.[2] It begins:

Manchester, August 16th, 1819; quarter past nine. My Lord.—Mr. Norris being much fatigued by the harassing duty of this day, it becomes mine now to inform your lordship of the proceedings which have been had in consequence of the proposal put forward for a meeting.

The curious may ponder on the ingenuous admission to be made three years later by the Rev. Mr Hay, when under cross-examination at the Redford v. Birley trial. Said Hay:

I saw Mr. Norris very late in the evening. I had been engaged out of doors; I came in very late, and I ought to have written the account which he was obliged, in a great hurry, to write, I being so fatigued . . .[3]

They were both fatigued! The report goes on:

. . . The special committee have been in constant attendance for the last three days, and contented themselves till they saw what the complexion of the meeting might be, or what circumstances might arise with coming to the determination only, which they adopted in concurrence with some of the most intelligent gentlemen of the town, not to stop the numerous columns which were from various roads expected to pour in, but to allow them to reach the place of their destination. The assistance of the military was of course required, and the arrangements in consequence made with them of such description as might be applicable to various circumstances. About 11 o'clock

---

[1] See above, p. 146.
[2] *Papers Relative to the Internal State of the Country*, pp. 28–29.
[3] Redford v. Birley (Farquharson), p. 433. The *State Trials* edition is abridged slightly at this point.

the magistrates, who were very numerous, repaired to a house whence they might see the whole of the proceedings of the meeting. A body of special constables took their ground, about 200 in number, close to the hustings; from them there was a line of communication to the house where we were. Mr. Trafford Trafford was so good as to take the situation of attending Col. L'Estrange, the commanding officer. From eleven till one o'clock the various columns arrived, attended by flags, each by two or three; and there were four, if not more, caps of liberty. The ensigns were of the same description as those displayed on similar occasions, with the addition, that one had a bloody pike represented on it; another 'Equal Representation or Death'. There was no appearance of arms or pikes, but great plenty of sticks and staves, and every column marched in regular files of three or four deep, attended with conductors, music, &c. The most powerful accession was in the last instance when Mr. Hunt and his party came in. But long before this, the magistrates had felt a decided conviction that the whole bore the appearance of insurrection; that the array was such as to terrify all the King's subjects, and was such as no legitimate purpose could justify. In addition to their own sense of the meeting, they had very numerous depositions from the inhabitants, as to their fears for the public safety; and at length a man deposed as to the parties who were approaching, attended by the heaviest column.

On a barouche-box was a woman in white, I believe was a Mrs. Gant from Stockport, and who it is believed had a cap of liberty. In the barouche were Hunt, Johnson, Knight and Moorhouse, of Stockport; as soon as these four parties were ascertained, a warrant was issued to apprehend them. The troops were mustered, and Nadin, preceding the Manchester Yeomanry Cavalry, executed it. While the cavalry was forming, a most marked defiance of them was acted by the reforming part of the mob; however they so far executed their purpose, as to apprehend Hunt and Johnson on the hustings; Knight and Moorhouse in the moment escaped. They also took on the hustings Saxton and Sykes, who is the writer to the *Manchester Observer*, and which Saxton had been addressing the mob. The parties thus apprehended were thus brought to the house where the magistrates were. In the meantime the Riot Act was read, and the mob was completely dispersed, but not without very serious and lamentable effects. Hunt, &c., were brought down to the New Bayley; two magistrates and myself having promised them protection, preceded them; we were attended by special constables and some cavalry. The parties were lodged in the New Bayley; and since that time have been added to them Knight and Moorhouse.

On inquiry it appeared that many had suffered from various instances; one of the Manchester Yeomanry, Mr. Holme, was after the parties were taken, struck by a brickbat; he lost his power over his horse, and is supposed to have fractured his skull by a fall from his horse. I am afraid that he is since dead; if not, there are now no hopes of his recovery. A special constable of the name of Ashworth has been killed—cause unknown; and four women appear to have lost their lives by being pressed by the crowd; these, I believe, are the fatal effects of the meeting. A variety of instances of sabre wounds occurred, but I hope none mortal; several pistols were fired by the mob, but as to their effect, save in one instance deposed to before Col. Fletcher, we have no account. We cannot but deeply regret all this serious attendant on this transaction; but we have the satisfaction of witnessing the very grateful and cheering countenances of the whole town; in fact they consider themselves as saved by our exertions. All the shops were shut, and, for the most part, continued so all the evening. The capture of Hunt took place before two o'clock, and I forgot to mention, that all their colours, drums, &c., were taken or destroyed; since that I have been to the Infirmary and found myself justified in making the report I have; but Mr. Norris now tells me, that one or two more than I have mentioned, may have lost their lives.

The parties apprehended will have their cases proceeded on to-morrow; but it appears there may arise difficulties as to the nature of some of their crimes, on which it may be necessary to consult government. The whole committee of magistrates will assemble to-morrow as usual. During the afternoon and parts of the evening, parts of the town have been in a very disturbed state, and numerous applications made for the military. They have been supplied, but in the Irish part of the town, been obliged to fire, I trust without any bad effect as to life, in any instance. At present everything seems quiet; the reports agree with that, and I hope we shall have a quiet night. I have omitted to mention, that the active part of the meeting may be said to have come in wholly from the country; and that it did not consist of less than 20,000 men, &c. The flag on which was 'Equal Representation or Death' was a black one; and, in addition, on the same side, had 'No borough-mongering—Unite and be Free' at the bottom, 'Saddleworth, Lees, and Mossley Union'; on the reverse 'No Corn Laws:—Taxation, without Representation, is Unjust and Tyrannical'. On the Middleton flag was 'Let us die like men, and not be sold like slaves'; reverse 'Liberty is the birthright of man'. I close my letter at a quarter before eleven; everything remains quiet—many of the troops have returned to the barracks, with the consent of the magistrates. I have to apologise to your Lordship for the haste in which this is written, but I trust that the haste will naturally be accounted for. I have the honour to be &c., W. R. Hay.

'Everything remains quiet . . .' It was the quietness, the stillness, before a storm, the greatest storm of controversy that has ever shaken England. The distant rumble of its thunder is still occasionally heard. Doubting John Edward Taylor, was, as yet, unaware of this letter; four months were to pass before he was to turn his incisive criticism on this easiest of the compilations on the transactions of that day. It was to turn that part of Taylor's *Notes and Observations* more into a logomachical exercise than a critical one.

Lieutenant Jolliffe's claim that the magistrates were still 'assembled' at 4 a.m. probably means that as a body they had not yet dispersed. They had much to do. Dr Read says:[1]

The authorities and 'loyalists', full of alarms, were feverishly active for several days after the massacre. On the 17th Hay, the Chairman of Quarter Sessions, and Thomas Hardman, a former Boroughreeve and a leading 'loyalist', were sent off to London to justify the massacre . . .

'Justifying the massacre' did not enter their heads; it is exceedingly doubtful whether, at that stage, they even imagined that it would be very shortly dubbed as such, but the deputation to the Government was planned to leave Manchester on the evening of the 17th. The Rev. Mr Hay seemed a fairly obvious choice; so was Thomas Hardman, for he had been one of a similar deputation in 1812[2] after the disturbances then. In 1819, he was a man getting on in years, but he had acted as a special constable and was on St Peter's Field on duty at the meeting. 'Feverishly active' hardly appears to be the right description in arranging for this deputation to be 'sent off to London', when they did not leave Manchester until at least thirty hours after the close of the meeting. James Norris wrote to Lord Sidmouth on the night of the 17th:

. . . Mr. Hay and Mr. Hardman having left town this evening on a mission to your Lordship and to government, it is unnecessary for me to give you any information up to the period when they left, as they are fully informed. Since their departure the town has continued to assume a gloomy aspect as the night has approached, and at this hour (a quarter from ten), all the civil and military authorities are in action throughout the town. Great numbers are assembled this evening, from about 8 to 9, about the New Cross, but did not do any act of violence, though evidently of the description disposed to do so. Soldiers are placed there, and bodies of special constables with orders in the first instance for the constables to act, and afterwards, in case of need, the military to disperse the mob. The Riot Act was not read this evening when I first went up (about six o'clock) though some stones had before been thrown at one or two houses, and a few at the military; yet I found matters peaceable and quiet, and the offending parties straggling about, and at considerable distances, and I hoped they would disperse; but the numbers considerably increased at the distances, and I found it necessary to communicate with Col. L'Estrange &c. The military have in consequence been strengthened in that quarter, and at present everything, I believe, remains quiet, although it can alone be attributed to the full exertion or appearance of the military strength . . . J. Norris.[3]

[1] Read, p. 142.
[2] Philips, iv.
[3] *Papers Relative to the Internal State of the Country*, p. 31.

On that same day, Tuesday, the 17th, Hobhouse, at 10 Downing Street, was replying to Norris's letter which he wrote late at night on the 15th:

> . . . I am directed by Lord Sidmouth to thank you for your letter of the 15th inst., and to express the anxiety he feels for the arrival of to-morrow's post, though he himself does not admit the existence of risk, thinking the designs of the disaffected more deeply laid.[1]

Sidmouth's thinking was largely correct; the 'designs of the disaffected', of which Henry Hunt was the pivot, were more deeply laid. Hunt had not anticipated that the meeting of the 16th would end like this. Nor had the magistrates; nor had the Government.

[1] *State Trials,* App. B, p. 1381.

XVI

The News Breaks

The nation, which knew of the momentous meeting at Peterloo, now waited anxiously for news of the outcome, as can be sensed in the brief leader in *The Times* of Wednesday morning, the 18th:

. . . We kept the press open until a late hour this morning in the hope of receiving minute accounts . . . the Riot Act was read, and the troops called upon by the Magistrates to enforce their orders that the crowd should at once disperse. Hunt himself was taken prisoner—and we add, with unfeigned sorrow, that several lives were lost.

The troops that were employed were the Manchester, Macclesfield and Chester Yeomanry. The 15th Light Dragoons were likewise in the field, but were not called into action.[1] The local troops, it is said, behaved with great alacrity. The consternation and dismay which spread amongst the immense crowd cannot be conceived. The multitude was composed of a large proportion of females. The prancing of the cavalry and the active use of the sabre among them, created a dreadful scene of confusion, and we may add of carnage . . . killed eight; wounded eighty to a hundred.

Such is the brief or general outline . . . what actual violence or outrage was perpetrated—what menaces were uttered, or symptoms exhibited, which induced the Magistrates to read the Riot Act, and to disperse the meeting by force of arms, we cannot possibly state' . . . [A reminder to its readers how limited were these Magistrates' powers on Riot Act, &c., and the leader asked:] Can they be justified?

During Wednesday the reports came pouring into London and into *The Times* office; to that paper from all sources except one: that of their own reporter. Their columns were open, waiting to receive it. *The Times* of 19 August 1819, was to be a historic one. The publishers were to be proud of it: they still are. In *The History of 'The Times'* (1935) vol. I (p. 235) the writers preened themselves on this historic issue:

The Times was never weary of denouncing the activities of Sherwin, Wooler, and Orator Hunt, and the Radical reformers generally. It denounced the

---

[1] The first erroneous reports on the troops used in the action were 'confirmed' rather than contradicted by *The Times*'s 'official' report the next day.

intention of holding the assembly at Manchester; though, since the Radical re-formers persisted in that intention, *The Times* expressed its hope that 'nothing will occur to divide the blame of any tumult with the parties who *prima facie* have provoked it.' (August 17th, 1819). Seven out of the twelve columns of leading matter in the issue for August 19th were given to the completest of all press accounts of the massacre of Peterloo. The reports were written by one of the best of the paper's reporters. He was on Hunt's platform at the time of the charge and was arrested in the course of his duties . . .

The writer of that particular chapter in *The History of 'The Times'* could be forgiven for his slight inaccuracies, for there was an immense field to cover. He did not notice that the reports were not written by 'one of the paper's best reporters'—only one of the reports; albeit the longest one. Nor did he notice that the pontifical leader in that historic 'Thunderer' issue (which he quoted) was quite at variance with what *The Times*'s 'one of the best' reporters said. *The Times* leader told its eagerly waiting readers that 'the Yeomanry Cavalry of the town of Manchester charged the populace sword in hand, cut their way to the platform, and with the police at their head, made prisoners of Hunt' etc.; whilst Mr Tyas wrote: '. . . during this period all was quiet and orderly, as if the cavalry had been the friends of the multitude, and had marched into them as such . . .' *The Times* leader had been written before Tyas's report had arrived (the leader writer said so) and such are the exigencies of newspaper offices it was probably too late to change it. *The Times* historian of 1935 did not notice it; that hardly mattered. What did matter was that the waiting nation, eager to learn about what occurred on St Peter's Field, did not notice it either. The 'Thunderer' had summed up the conflicting reports in its leader, and given its readers the benefit of its summing up:

. . . whatever . . . an observant mind may suspect as to the real objects of the few [Hunt and Co.] who thus played upon the passions and misfortunes of a suffering multitude,—all such considerations, all such suspicions, sink to nothing before the dreadful fact, that nearly a hundred of the King's unarmed subjects have been sabred by a body of cavalry in the streets of a town of which most of them were inhabitants, and in the presence of those Magis-trates whose sworn duty it is to protect and preserve the life of the meanest Englishman . . .

That 'dreadful fact' *The Times* leader had communicated to the nation. What had occurred at Manchester, the leader writer had reduced to the simplest possible language: the Manchester Yeomanry had cut their way through the crowd. It is hardly necessary to reiterate that once such a 'fact' was established, then the inference was drawn that the magistrates intended to suppress the meeting; that the Government were the power behind the magistrates; and that it was a massacre. *The Times's* 'dreadful fact' *was* thus established; all that now was necessary was to fill in the details. The nation was roused in a day to an intense indignation, such as it had seldom felt before, or has felt since. The way was wide open for the expression of that indignation in any printable, and almost un-printable, denunciation.

Elsewhere in the *History of 'The Times'*[1] the writer was recalling William Cobbett's long-standing antipathy to that paper. Against itself, *The Times* history quoted an extract from Cobbett's *Political Register* for 1823. Cobbett had written:

. . . One cause of the faith which people give to these newspapers is pro-duced by the reporters. People see them with book and pencil in hand. They afterwards read with astonishment that which they have heard. They think that men capable of taking down with so much accuracy what others say, must be wonderfully clever men. And this is really the case. It is a fact *indis-putable*. But like many other indisputable facts is made to lead to most erroneous conclusion. The conclusion generally is: if the reporter, who is employed by the proprietor be so clever a man, what must the proprietor himself be! . . . The reporter comes, unless he be a supple knave, and brings his true report. The vile hunk of the proprietor, then garbles, guts, swells out, cuts short, or otherwise manages the report according to his interest . . . so that the report which you see in his paper frequently bears no resemblance to that which has been brought him by the reporter.

The Times editor or proprietor had done none of these things, except to tone down (so Tyas said at the trial) some hard things he had said about the Yeomanry during the time they were attacking (or repelling attack) during the dispersal proper. The editor/proprietor had simply ignored that which his own reporter had written. Naturally then, it could be countered, he 'distilled' from the other reports the 'fact' feat-ured in his leader. It was the most curious distillation in the history of newspaper reporting. There were ten reports of the happenings at Manchester, in addition to that of John Tyas; they are summarized below. In only one of these ten was contained the 'fact' which *The Times* leader established. It was the one from Taylor or Prentice.

(1) From the *Manchester Mercury*, which, apart from saying that the Yeo-manry 'advanced in full charge through the multitude and surrounded the orators upon their own stage', gave no details of their aggressive action before the arrests.

(2) from *Aston's Exchange Herald*: 'No aggressive action before the arrests.'

[1] pp. 251–2.

(3) from *The Courier*: the same.

(4) Extract of another Letter: 'But before any of these worthies had time to speechify the Manchester Volunteer Cavalry charged up St. Peter's Street, surrounded the scaffold and took Hunt', etc. [prisoner] 'together with their flags.'

(5) Another Letter: [re Yeomanry's appearance]: 'instantly the mob assailed them with stones and sticks and attempted to unhorse them.'

(6) Extract of another letter in the *Courier*: [already quoted p. 231]: '. . . military determined to cut him [Hunt] to pieces'.

(7) Extract of another letter in the *Courier*: '. . . at half-past one the magistrates deemed it expedient to read the Riot Act, and instantly after, the platform was surrounded in a masterly manner . . . the whole of this grand manoeuvre would have taken place without bloodshed, had not the mob assailed the military and civil authorities with every resistance in their power, and particularly missiles. Consequently the cavalry charged in their own self-defence . . .'

(8) Another Letter (from the *Star*): [This was the suspected Taylor/Prentice letter, but certainly from a *Manchester Gazette* writer—referred to pp. 228–29] in which occurs the passage: 'actually hacking their way up to the hustings.'

(9) Private Letter: '. . . when a body of cavalry rode up through the crowd, brandishing their drawn swords, surrounded the hustings, and seized Hunt and his associates.'

(10) 'The proceedings had scarcely commenced, when the Manchester and Cheshire Yeomanry with the regular cavalry stationed here, made their appearance. In a few moments five caps of liberty, with eight or ten flags, bearing various inscriptions, were torn down, and hundreds of people trampled under the feet of the horses. Indeed, the special constables shared a harder fate than tens of thousands on the ground.'

Eleven reports printed in that historic issue of *The Times*; in only one was that 'dreadful fact' of cutting their way to the hustings mentioned. *The Times* own reporter, when his report came through, contradicted it. It still passes unnoticed. Dr Read says:

The middle-class Radicals, J. E. Taylor and Archibald Prentice . . . knowing that Tyas, *The Times* reporter, had been arrested for being on the hustings . . . had both written reports of the meeting, and sent them off to two London papers. As a result, a full and honest account of the massacre was quickly available in the capital; when released, Tyas confirmed the accuracy of the two accounts.[1]

It was honest enough; but one 'accuracy' which Tyas's report confirmed was the *inaccuracy* in both on a vital point: their complete

[1] Read, p. 143 (quoting Prentice, p. 163, as his authority).

ignorance on what Dr Read himself calls 'the climax of the day'. They knew only of the use of the Manchester Yeomanry to disperse the meeting.

The Times leader, be it said in its favour, was already in type; and they distilled one anti-radical 'fact' which was quickly forgotten, it is supposed, because that too contradicted Tyas. The relevant portion of the leader read:

. . . the Yeomanry Cavalry of the town of Manchester charged the populace sword in hand, cut their way to the platform, and with the police at their head, made prisoners of Hunt and several of those who surrounded him— seized the flags of the Reformers—trampled down and cut down a number of people, *who, after throwing some stones and brickbats at the cavalry in its advance towards the hustings,* fled on all rides in the utmost confusion . . .

The italics are not *The Times* leader writer's. After the leader they inserted another 'short', and added Tyas's two-and-a-half-column-long report; the short leader stated:

Express from Manchester. Just as our paper was going to press, we received from the gentleman deputed by us to report the proceedings at Manchester, the following account. It comprises not only copious details of what took place on Monday, and brings up those of Tuesday to a late hour, but contains, besides, some very important occurrences in other parts of the great manufacturing district, to which we direct the serious attention of our readers.

The Times had done its duty; its issue made history. The nation was informed; the leader said so, in these terms:

. . . In *The Times* of Monday we concluded an article which severely blamed Hunt as a moral agent, by expressing an anxious hope that no person (thereby meaning the magistracy) would so conduct themselves as to share with that brawler the reproach of any evil consequences which might follow the assemblage of so large a body of discontented labourers . . . The hope we expressed was an indirect, though sufficient intimation of the fears of which we could not divest ourselves on that subject; and our readers are now as qualified as ourselves to form an opinion as to what extent those melancholy forebodings have been justified.

The Times' readers were 'as qualified' as the editor, perhaps more qualified, because they had more time, to distil the truth from that paper's eleven reports. The ironical fact may again be recapitulated: that the one report (that by Taylor or Prentice of the *Manchester Gazette*) was to modify its 'dreadful fact' of 'actually hacking their way up to the hustings' between Monday, 16 August and Saturday, 21 August to 'instantly charged up to the hustings'.

How widely this discrepancy between *The Times*'s statement in its leader and that of the account written by its own reporter became known after this time is not determinable. James Scarlett had re-read Tyas's evidence more carefully, but still not carefully enough, hence his references to it in the House of Commons.[1] It did not, however, ultimately pass unnoticed in Manchester. Hugh Hornby Birley was addressing the King's Birthday celebration dinner in Manchester after the conclusion of Hunt's trial. Amongst his remarks, after referring to the 'unmerited obloquy' he and his fellow-members of the Manchester Yeomanry had lain under, he went on:

. . . To be marked out for abuse by certain persons who live amongst us, affords indeed some evidence of merit, and for their censure no solace was required. Yet even they did not venture to put forth the calumnies which have been so widely circulated, until the example had been set by the un-principled part of the daily press. That powerful instrument, invaluable as it is when honestly directed, has acquired an ascendancy over the public mind, which, from its liability to abuse, is much to be lamented. The generality of readers adopt, without examination, the opinion of their favourite news-paper. The Editor of *The Times* seems to have felt secure of this when he ventured, in his observations on the dispersion of the meeting of the 16th of August, to assume as fact what was contradicted by the statement of his own reporter . . .[2]

Bruton, in his researches for his study of Peterloo in 1919, unearthed the foregoing quotation from *Wheeler's Manchester Chronicle*, 29 April 1820. He quoted part of Birley's speech, and ignored Birley's references to *The Times* report, dismissing the whole as 'at the best a very lame affair'.

The *Manchester Gazette* 28 August 1819, (reprinting other press reports) quoted *The Examiner*:

They assembled peaceably; and the speakers were proceeding as quietly as the ridiculed meeting at Smithfield, when, according to all accounts but ONE (which every succeeding account has contradicted) a body of military dashed through them sword in hand, trampled down opposition, bruised and wounded many, and bore off the flags and the speakers to the county gaol . . . [The Riot Act] . . . Who heard it? . . . The account sent up to *The Times* newspaper by a gentleman who obtained a place for convenience sake on the hustings, and who in the infinite hurry of the government-officers was arrested with the leaders of the meeting, says that nobody knew anything about the Riot Act . . . [On Hunt's danger of being cut to pieces, and the *Examiner* writer was away, with his 'Cry havoc! and let slip the dogs of war.']

[1] See above, p. 221.
[2] *Wheeler's Manchester Chronicle*, 29 April 1820.

The curious may ponder over the *Examiner*'s report, and over, too, the possible thoughts of the editor or reporters of the *Manchester Gazette* in reprinting it, after they had, the week previously, modified their 'hacking their way to the hustings' to 'instantly charged up to the hustings'. Or, perhaps, the *Gazette* staff believed that by modifying their report they had fallen into line with the rest. That the journalists of 1819 could put out such reports is almost incredible: quoting Tyas and garbling Tyas. Tyas was not 'arrested with the leaders of the meeting'; he gave himself in charge of the constable after the arrest of the leaders to ensure his safety; Tyas did report that the Yeomanry were 'sword in hand', but did not say anything about trampling down opposition, bruising and wounding many, until *after* his celebrated 'Have at their flags' passage. It was on such newspaper reporting as the *Examiner*'s that the nation was 'informed' as to what had occurred on St Peter's Field.[1]

How much the public were misled by the press reports is nowhere better illustrated than by the following. And not the public only, the Lord Chancellor of England was not completely informed when he wrote to Sir William Scott in August 1819. Lord Eldon was of opinion that High Treason was involved:

Can any man doubt, connecting Birmingham and Manchester together, that these meetings are overt acts of conspirators, to instigate to such specific acts of treason or some of them? I can't doubt it. But how ridiculously shall I be reasoning in Parliament if the prosecutions are for misdemeanour! An unlawful assembly, *as such merely*, I apprehend can't be dispersed; and what constitutes *riot* enough to justify dispersion is no easy matter to determine where there is not actual violence begun on the part of those assembled.[2]

What Lord Eldon did not know when he wrote that letter, was that the meeting was not dispersed *until* what the magistrates considered an actual riot was in being.

Meanwhile, during those days after 16 August, the newspapers all over Britain were full of the details of the momentous happenings at

[1] The *Examiner*'s report inspired Shelley's *Mask of Anarchy*. H. Buxton Forman in *The Mask of Anarchy* (facsimile of the holograph manuscript—Shelley Society, 1887) pp. 12–13 says that Shelley sent the MS of the poem to Leigh Hunt for publication in *The Examiner* before November, 1819. 'It never saw the light till 1832; for [Leigh] Hunt, prudent for once, thought that, if given to the public in 1819, it would have a very different effect from that for which the poet designed it.' It was published by Leigh Hunt in 1832 as *The Masque of Anarchy*. Forman (page 66) continues: 'The spelling of the word *Mask* in the title was already settled; for Shelley himself wrote the heading of the Hunt manuscript, and put *Mask*, not *Masque*."

[2] Quoted: State Trials edition, Trial of Hunt, p. 424.

Manchester, each quoting other papers' reports to obtain full coverage. The Manchester papers were, of course, full of it; all the Manchester papers, that is, except one, the *Manchester Observer*. For weeks the *Observer* columns had been spilling over with news of the intended meeting. On the date when, it might be thought, its columns could not have been long enough to report the crowded happenings of the week (for it came out on Saturday) its coverage was probably the most modest in the country. Out of its eight pages of thirty-two columns, the first page of four columns being as usual given up to advertisements, only five columns contained news of the principal events of the week; it printed two separate accounts concerning the meeting and its aftermath: a reporter's account and a leading article. The former (astoundingly) was headed 'Manchester Political Meeting'!

Part of that report on the 'Manchester Political Meeting' has already been quoted to show that its writer did not agree with Bamford's version of the Yeomanry's first incursion into the crowd. The leading article told, however, a very different story. The reader may wonder what possessed this extremely radical Manchester newspaper to present two versions, one of which *must* have been wrong. The conclusions are inescapable: (1) The *Observer* leading article (unlike that of *The Times* of 19 August) had been written after the reporter's version; (2) Five days after the meeting it was still not certain whether the Huntean (and later Bamfordian) version could be sustained. It could! Not only had *The Times* newspaper come down on their side, but, probably more important still to them, that local denigrator—that 'snaffling hypocrite' (the *Observer's* description) John Edward Taylor was on their side too. The *Manchester Gazette's* modified report was still unknown to them, as both papers were published on the same day. The verbal back-lash of Peterloo cracked in that second version in the *Observer's* leading article.

That the contrast between the two *Observer* versions escaped remark can only be attributed to the fact that in the welter of reports published at the time it was unnoticed. There were to be further embellishments later it is true, but in this leader-report the radical version was launched:

The Borough mongers and their abettors, have at length filled up the measure of their iniquity to the brim! The hand trembles, the heart shudders at the melancholy catalogue of cool-blooded murder which must this week occupy these columns hitherto devoted to the purposes of peace and to the best interests of mankind. We last week ventured to predict that the fears of the timid were unnecessarily raised, respecting the contemplated meeting for reform on Monday, and assured our readers, that the dwellings and persons of the inhabitants of Manchester would be perfectly safe, provided no illegal interference was attempted by the madness of official men. Our predictions were correct: our assurances warranted by our observation. We knew the temper of the Radical Reformers of Manchester, and we were well acquainted with the tried firmness and prudence of the Man who was invited to preside over their deliberations. Unfortunately, however, we did not know, or rather we did not let ourselves believe, the horrible malevolence of those abettors of corruption, who are haplessly now in power to murder and destroy.

The morning of the 16th was hailed with exultation by the many thousands, whose feelings were powerfully excited on the occasion. At an early period numbers came pressing in from various and distant parts of the country, to witness the greatest and most gratifying assemblage of Britons, that was ever recorded in the annals of our history. From Bolton, Oldham, Stockport, Middleton, and all the circumjacent country; from the more distant towns of Leeds, Sheffield, &c., &c., came thousands of willing votaries to the shrine of sacred libery; and at the period when the Patriotic Mr. Hunt and his friends had taken their station on the hustings, it is supposed that no less than 150,000[1] people were congregated in the area near St. Peter's Church.

Had the day been suffered to pass over with that serenity and peace which the principles and the cause of the assembly entitled it to, we should have aimed at giving an account of the flags and other civic emblems which the people from different towns were distinguished, and we could feel happy in thus procrastinating the tale of woe; but we must hasten to the barbarous narrative, however abhorrent to our own minds, or however harrowing the detail may prove to our readers.

Mr. Hunt ascended the hustings about half-past one o'clock, and after a few preliminary arrangements, proceeded to address the immense multitude, recommending peace and order for their government, and not as one of our vile prints asserts with language and suggestions of desperate and malevolent character'. Whilst thus engaged, and without the shadow of disorder occurring or likely to occur, we were surprised, though not alarmed, at perceiving a column of infantry take possession of an opening in the immediate propinquity of the assembly; but had hardly time for a volition of thought on the subject, when our fears were raised to horror, by the appearance of the Manchester and Salford Yeomanry Cavalry, who came galloping into the area, and proceeded to form in line ready for action;[2] nor were they long delayed from their hellish purpose—the special constables were called in from their previous stations—the bugle sounded a charge—the leaders

'——— cried havoc,
And let loose [sic] the dogs of war!'

---

[1] Discussed below, p. 251–52.

[2] This, in one column; and in another: 'Few, if any of the meeting, even yet, supposed that this martial display [the riding into the crowd of the Yeomanry] was intended for anything more than securing Messrs. Hunt, . . .' etc. See above, p. 196.

and a scene of murder and carnage ensued which posterity will hesitate to believe, and which will hand down the authors and abettors of this foul and bloody tragedy to the execration of the astonished world. Men, women, and children, without distinction of age or sex became the victims of these sanguinary monsters; for 'all are not men who bear the human form'. Mr. Hunt, on perceiving the intention of these infuriated peace-keepers, advised the company around him to retire, and hoped that such gentlemen as they might incline to arrest, would surrender without resistance.

It is impossible for us to ascertain the extent of loss in lives and limbs which has been thus wantonly and inhumanly occasioned—people flew in every direction to avoid these hair-brained assassins, who were supported by detachments from the 15th Hussars. The latter, however, did not deal out death and wounds with the same liberal hand as our brave townsmen, whose ardour we are told they were frequently, in the course of Monday and Tuesday, obliged to restrain, by bestowing the epithet of 'cowardly scoundrels' on some of the most valiant. [On the arrests] . . . The area where the immense multitude were assembled, was completely cleared in about 20 minutes from the commencement of this lawless attack. The mischief was still not suffered to rest here. As the authorities had succeeded in 'kicking up a riot' they were resolved to 'keep it up after they had kicked it up', (we ought to ask pardon for speaking lightly on this heart-rending subject)[1] and accordingly parties of horse continued to patrol the streets, and succeeded in sometimes provoking the people to resistance. (Followed by details)

These *Manchester Observer* versions of events were reprinted in leaflet form in the shortly-to-be-issued *Peterloo Massacre*. There were some curious corrections. One has been noticed[2]—on Knight's arrest. There was another in the following paragraph:

. . . We do not think, nay, we are quite confident, that out of a population of 120,000 inhabitants, and as many strangers in addition, that a hundred

[1] The reference to 'kicking up a riot . . .' really needed no apology, but another *Observer* article did: in another column of the paper, so near the tragic day, an *Observer* writer, alone amongst all other commentators attempted to raise a laugh at the Yeomanry's expense. It could only, surely, have excited disgust. Immediately following their first 'version' was the paragraph:

We have to inform our readers that we have received orders for a few handbills of rather a curious description; and are afraid from the circumstance of the person who brought the order, not bringing his name, that a hoax was attempted upon us. Having, however, a particular dislike to a hoax upon ourselves, we shall be obliged if any of our readers can give us any information on the subject. The handbill wanted runs thus:

'To be Sold by Auction, at the Police Office, on Saturday next, at 12 precisely, 39 pairs of cavalry men's breeches: they are perfectly clean on the *outside*. N.B. They will be sold without reserve, as the parties are declining business. Also to be sold at the same time, 56 Constables' Staffs.'

[2] See above, p. 196, note 3.

persons could be found, who could solemnly affirm it as their opinion, that there was any intention on the part of the Reformers, to commit the slightest breach of the peace; nor five, who would make oath, that the meeting would have not have been dispersed by the troops from the barracks, (had the Riot Act been read, and had the Magistrates' order been confined to them, after the usual time allowed by law for dispersion had elapsed,) without the least injury to any individual.

It is scarcely conceivable that anyone would possibly challenge the *Observer*'s rodomontade, but the careful editor of *Peterloo Massacre* altered 'that a hundred persons could be found . . .' to 'that ten persons could be found.' They were more sure of themselves when *Peterloo Massacre* appeared than they were in the first flush of success for their case!

The 21 August *Manchester Observer* was to be the first time, Dr Read reminds us, that the new word Peter Loo appeared in print. It explains, also, the puzzling discrepancy between the radical estimate and other estimates in the number of people assembled on St Peter's Field. Dr Read[1] has a summary of the various estimates. He says:

The report of the meeting in the *Manchester Observer* (21 August, 1819) said that 153,000[2] people were present at Peterloo; Hunt claimed 150,000 (ibid, 18 September, 1819) and the *Annual Register* gave 80,000 (*Annual Register*, 1819, General History, 106). Hulton, however, the chairman of the committee of magistrates, gave the total as 50,000–60,000 (*State Trials*, 225) and this latter figure was accepted by Prentice (159), in most other respects a severe critic of the magistrates.

They were all, of course, estimates, and even if Prentice did accept Hulton's estimate, the estimate did not, happily, come amongst the controversial facts of the day. The *Annual Register*'s authority was plainly Tyas's account in *The Times*. Both Hunt's and the *Observer*'s were merely errors in arithmetic: the latter did a simple sum.

The site was . . . 170 yards by 70 yards, which gives 25,000 square yards exclusive of all the avenues, which were filled by the wondering spectators. As nine persons will stand in one superficial square yard; and as the whole of the above space would most undoubtedly have been not only filled, but closely filled; and it been either prudent or possible, for persons to have existed in such an indissoluble mass, we may fairly reckon, at only six to the yard, that the aggregate number would be 153,000.

Or perhaps it was not quite so simple a sum; for the total area, as assessed

[1] Read, p, 131.
[2] The second *Observer* report said 150,000.

by the magistrates—who had doubtless more accurate sources of information than the *Observer* writer—was only 14,000 square yards! Richard Carlile's 'estimate' was a crowd of 300,000.[1]

In such a manner were the people of England informed of the 'facts' of Peterloo, solely and entirely from the columns of the daily and weekly press. Parliament was not in session. No statement was made by either the Government or the magistrates. Any clue to what was the 'official' version had to be gleaned from the newspapers supporting the Ministry. The press had a field-day. On the 21st, also, the Government and the Prince Regent sent their letters of thanks to the magistrates and to the military authorities for their 'prompt, decisive, and efficient measures for the preservation of the public tranquility'. The press had another field-day.

Tyas and the other captives had been left 'languishing' in the New Bayley prison on the night of Monday, the 16th. John Tyas was set free at 12 o'clock on the following day. He has another glimpse of post-August 16th Manchester before he retires from the scene:

When we were once more allowed to enjoy that freedom of which we had been for a moment deprived, we took a walk through most of the principal streets of Manchester, and found that they were at that time (twelve o'clock) completely under military disposal. Soldiers were posted at all the commanding positions of the town, and were to be seen extended at full length on the flags in various directions. At 3 o'clock they had, however, all of them returned to their quarters, and the town was to all outward appearance once more in a state of tranquility.

At seven o'clock, when we quitted Manchester, all was quiet in the town. A report had, however, reached it that there was a serious riot at Oldham, and in consequence some troops of the Cheshire Yeomanry were sent to quell it.

In our road to Stockport, our attention was forcibly struck by the numerous groups of idle men, who were congregated together along it. They appeared ready for any wicked or desperate purpose; and we have reason to believe that before the evening was concluded they were engaged in an attack upon the magistracy of Stockport. About a mile from that place some hundreds of them were assembled near a petty public house. A new hat, a tea-kettle, and some other articles of little value, were displayed at the window, as is customary to display the prizes at walks or feasts in this part of the country. This was to serve as a pretext for their meeting together; but that it was only a pretext we learned to a certainty during our stay at Macclesfield . . . [disturbances at Macclesfield] . . . When we left the town, which was at four o'clock in the morning (Wednesday the 18th), tranquility

[1] See above, p. 31.

was perfectly re-established; 30 or 40 rioters were in custody, and the gentleman who had gone with the express to Stockport, had returned with the
intelligence, that though a battle between the military and the rioters was
momentarily expected, a troop of infantry had started from Stockport, and
when he left them within an hour's march of Macclesfield. At Stockport
the magistrates were assembled at the Warren Bulkeley Arms, before which
the soldiery was drawn out as that was the first point against which the rioters
had declared their intention of making an attack. Similar riots were expected
at other places; almost all the military being stationed at Manchester . . .

Thus with a glance at the aftermath in Stockport, ended John Tyas's
invaluable evaluation of these momentous events.

XVII

The Nation's Scapegoats

Meanwhile, within the walls of the New Bayley prison, the captives languished, each with his own thoughts. Posterity is privileged to have a glimpse into the thoughts of more than one of them. First, into those of Joseph Johnson. Whether he was aware of a paragraph which had found its way into the columns of that 21 August issue of the *Observer* is not known, but it illustrates his concern:

Sir John Byng, who commands in the north of England, apprizes the Commanding Officers of regiments that an attempt has been made to circulate seditious papers among the troops, some of which have been delivered to a corporal and private soldier of the 88th Regiment, and concludes with offering a reward of ten guineas to 'any non-commissioned officer, drummer, or soldier, upon *whose evidence*' any person guilty of such crime of seduction shall be convicted by law.

It will be recalled that Mr Hay on writing to the Government, on the night of 16 August, had asked for their advice on the framing of charges against the prisoners, who in the meantime had been remanded by the magistrates on a charge of High Treason. It was not long before one of the Crown solicitors, a Mr Bouchier, was in Manchester to advise the magistrates. It will be remembered too that the letters passing between Johnson and Hunt in the earlier period had been intercepted. Johnson relates how he was closely questioned by Bouchier on this correspondence.[1] Johnson could not recall much, but Bouchier, to Johnson's surprise, read him an extract from one of his letters to Major Cartwright.[2] 'It was,' said Johnson, 'deploring the great distress in Manchester . . . and concluded by expressing my belief that insurrection was inevitable without an alleviation of their distress.' Johnson said he would give up his correspondence to the Government. Bouchier asked him to do so, as he did not wish to put Johnson's family to inconvenience by searching his house; he was prepared to give him a little time to produce

---

[1] In *A Letter to Henry Hunt, Esq.*, published 1822, p. 14.
[2] It was couched in the same terms as the Johnson to Hunt letter (see p. 73).

it. Again a gentle manner of proceeding for such a 'ruthless' age. Johnson reminded Hunt (in his pamphlet) of a letter he had received on the morning of the 16th with a parcel (of what he did not say) from Dr Watson, the London radical leader. 'After reading it,' said Johnson, 'I intended to destroy it,' but it was still at Smedley Cottage. 'You know,' said Johnson to Hunt, 'the contents of this Letter, for you read it. It alluded in very *particular* language to the soldiers, and to *one* regiment which was then in Manchester.' The 88th regiment was in Manchester. Johnson alleged that he managed to bribe someone to get a message to his wife, and the parcel and letter were destroyed.

Security from inside the New Bayley was apparently less stringent than the security from outside. One of the radicals describes the rigours of this prison confinement in different terms:

. . . The only individual (except the magistrates themselves and their officers) who had been permitted to have intercourse with him [Hunt] is his man-servant . . . Mr. Johnson's family have made many efforts, to no purpose, to obtain an interview with him. A younger brother, who manages his business during his absence, was significantly told after having applied several times to see the prisoner, that he had better not shew his face again on such an errand, lest he got taken up.[1]

Johnson's narrative should be placed alongside Hunt's own version told years later[2] at one of the anniversary celebrations of Peterloo:

. . . That while confined in the New Bayley, one of the persons who was taken prisoner with him, and with whom he had corresponded freely and in the openness of his heart, previously to the meeting of the 16th of August, was induced by bribes and threats to agree to give up his letters of correspondence, so as to enable the magistrates to prefer a charge of high treason against him. He could not have believed this if the person himself had not confessed it in the presence of Sir Charles Wolseley and Mr. Pearson, who were then in this town. He wrote to his wife to deliver up the letters, and if they had been given up, although there was nothing treasonable in them, he believed he should have been executed for high treason at Lancaster. The attorney of that individual, who was a gentleman of the old tory school, had previously got them from his wife, and when she applied for them, he, though a rank old tory, said, 'This is too disgraceful, and I shall never give up one of them'. Sir Charles Wolseley and others were ready to give bail for him, but he was put into a post-chaise, and driven to Lancaster, where they followed him the next day and put in bail . . .

[1] *A Report of the Manchester Meeting*. Manchester: John Leigh, n.d. [1819], p. 28.
[2] *Manchester Times*, 21 August 1830; Hunt's version of this incident is dealt with at some length in his *Memoirs*, Vol. III, p. 621, et seq., to which Johnson's pamphlet is a reply.

In contrasting the two accounts of Johnson and Hunt, we must note that Hunt very conveniently forgot that probably most of his letters to Johnson had been published, and that, even if they had not, they were being intercepted by Government agents. More important still, he surely cannot have imagined that the more critical members of his audience were unaware that he was the only one then facing a charge of high treason. His fellow-captives, including Johnson, were in the same plight. *An Impartial Narrative* (1819) reported that Hunt would not give bail. He would not give it, he said, even though no more than a farthing were required. In consequence of this determination, and the near approach of the Assize at Lancaster, he was sent off to the Castle at that place, in a coach guarded by troops. Knight, Saxton, Bamford, Wylde, Swift, and Healey were with him. Johnson and Moorhouse had given bail and were released. A comparison of the various narratives on this incident is of interest. *An Impartial Narrative* pp. 54–55:

Johnson and Moorhouse immediately procured bail, and were liberated . . . We understand that notices of bail were given for Mr. Hunt and Mr. Knight. Mr. Hunt complained, when he was asked by the magistrate in court, whether he had provided bail, that he was not allowed to be visited by a respectable solicitor in town, whom he had sent for some days ago. The Chairman mentioned that he would now be sent for if he desired it. 'No, no' said Mr. Hunt, pointing to Mr. Pearson, 'here is now my solicitor'. From this circumstance, and from knowing that two individuals, whose securities were unimpeachable, had offered to become his bail, we concluded that we should see him immediately out. After consulting, however, with his solicitor, he had taken a different view of the matter, and we were told that he said to the magistrate that he would not give bail, even though no more than a farthing were required.[1] In consequence of this determination . . .

A different story occurs in *Narrative* (editor of the *Black Book*), p. 38 —quoting a letter from Hunt to a friend:

Johnson and Moorhouse were bailed out immediately, and good bail was offered for me; but as I was very hot with the exertion of four hours in the most crowded court, I retired to change my linen to attend for that purpose; and before I had done this I was informed by the turnkey that he was very sorry, but that there was an order come that I must be ready to go to Lancaster Castle in *three minutes*. I had not time even to take a cup of tea, or get clean linen, before I was hurried down to the yard where I met my fellow-prisoners who had not yet been bailed, and who had been *handcuffed and ironed*! and we were crammed some *in* and others *on* a coach . . .

[1] *The Times* (30 August) reported the same detail, and was quoted in the same day's issue of *The Courier* (an evening paper).

Samuel Bamford's *Passages* on this point (I, 273) were compiled from *An Impartial Narrative* (pp. 54–55) or so it would seem, for they are an almost verbatim copy. Like other Bamford quotations, they contain some excisions. He does not mention that Hunt would not give bail, 'even though no more than a farthing were required', but ended his quotation at the point where Hunt says 'Here is now my solicitor'. Bamford then proceeds with his own narrative:

From the bar I was conducted to the yard of my former cell, where I was joined by several of the other prisoners, and we were taking what should have been our dinners, when an order suddenly came that we were to prepare to set off for Lancaster Castle. Our meal was soon dispatched, and we quickly bundled up a few things. We were then taken to the turnkey's lodge, and each hand-chained, after which we were placed on a four-horse coach, in the inside of which were Mr. Hunt, Mr. Knight, Saxton, and Nadin. Outside . . . myself, Swift, Wilde, Healey and Jones, with a number of constables armed with pistols; we were also escorted by a strong detachment of hussars, and thus, amid the huzzas of an immense multitude, we drove off.

The *Manchester Observer* (4 September 1819) saw the matter of Hunt's bail thus:

It now appears that Mr. Hunt intended to have given bail in Manchester on the day after his commitment, and not to have gone to Lancaster; for bail was proposed and only time demanded (this next day) to enable the parties to complete it; but their wisdom or folly we do not know which, determined that he should be sent off on the evening of the day of his examination; and that he had only three minutes allowed to prepare for his journey. Some of his fellow-prisoners were handcuffed; but on Mr. Hunt's joining them previous to stepping into the coach, which was to convey them to Lancaster, shame, or fear, dictated the propriety of releasing them, which was done, and they were sent off, not exactly like felons (the irons being taken off) to the county jail . . .

There is plenty of evidence to show Henry Hunt's thoughts during his confinement in the New Bayley, for his restless spirit found release in writing instead of talking. The Manchester press of that day thought he must have had a bad conscience. He had nothing of the kind. His conscience was clear. He wrote to his friends, he wrote to the magistrates, and he wrote to Lord Sidmouth; to all of them protesting his innocence. To Lord Sidmouth he wrote[1] demanding his release—an act of justice, even to a political enemy. He told him he was in Manchester 'in consequence of an invitation to take the chair at a public meeting

[1] Quoted *Peterloo Massacre*, p. 19.

intended to have been held on Monday, 9 August, 'to take into consideration the most *legal* and effectual means of obtaining a Reform of Parliament', in consequence of which all hostilities to the holding of the meeting appeared to have been withdrawn by the magistrates, and I was prevailed upon, much against my inclination, to stay here to preside at the meeting to be held yesterday, the 16th . . .' He closed with the postscript: 'There are 100,000 witnesses to prove the truth of what I have stated.'

To the magistrates he demanded to be brought in as a witness in the forthcoming inquest (on Thursday, 19 August)

. . . on those persons who had lost their lives on Monday last in consequence of the dreadful attack of the military upon an unarmed and peaceable multitude, and as I was present and saw the commencement of this illegal and unconstitutional act of violence, and can identify some of those who first committed a breach of the peace, I demand as an act of common justice, that I may be permitted to be present . . .[1]

He went on:

And as I have seen quite enough already to convince me that the real murderers are endeavouring to wipe the bloody stain from their remorseless, guilty souls, by casting imputations and suspicion upon others that they know had no hand, directly or indirectly, in the foul and cowardly deed, I am bold to say, that such inquest will be esteemed in the eyes of God and man, *worse than suspicious*, unless all the parties who are imprisoned, or said to be instrumental in the act, be permitted to be present and interrogated before the Jury and the Coroner. You will recollect, Gentlemen, that you have no common case in hand, and that the eyes of the whole country will shortly be fixed with scrutinizing penetration upon every step you take in this bloody affair . . . Be assured that there are thousands of witnesses, and many of them of the first respectability and fortune, in this town, who will prove that not one finger was raised against the peace officers, the military, or the Magistrates, upon the ground where the meeting was held; and that no resistance whatever was made to the bloody murderers, till the Yeomanry had driven individuals to the wall, and they resisted to protect their own lives. As for the Manchester Yeomanry, they were all in disorder before the charge; and if the people had chosen to resist, the men who had the flag-staves would have unhorsed and taken them every one prisoners, if they had thought proper. But the people had been instructed not to resist. Whether this was wise *advice* or *not* remains to be proved.

To his friends on 21 August Hunt appeared almost elated. He had sized up fairly accurately the position he was in. He had a clear

[1] *Manchester Observer,* 28 August 1819.

conscience; all the moves he had made before 16 August, and all the moves he had made on that day, were faultless, and were on record. *He was not responsible for the tragic conclusion:*

. . . I am in *tip-top* spirits. What should make me otherwise? I sleep as sound as a bell, and feel more pleasure in five minutes' reflection than the Manchester Bench of lamblike Magistrates will obtain consolation during the remainder of their lives. The blood of the poor murdered people sits heavy on ✱ ✱ ✱ 'Let the galled jade wince; my withers are unwrung!' I fear that it will never be forgiven, and that there will be too great a disposition to demand 'blood for blood'. Our enemies will not now, I hope, say anything more about assassination; they have taught the people how to assassinate by wholesale; they have struck the first blow and have taken the advantage of attacking a peaceable multitude, who had studiously come to the meeting unarmed, by a large military force, the Regulars keeping guard while the Yeomanry Cavalry ✱ ✱ ✱ all they could get at, and in their disorder ✱ ✱ ✱ alike friends and foes. I believe their friends suffered most. I have not heard of one Reformer suffering yet, that I know or ever heard of . . . Be assured, my good fellow, that they have not the shadow of a shade of pretence for charging me with *High Treason*. But they are in a dreadful scrape; and they will flounder on farther into the mire every struggle they make.[1]

To another friend he said: 'It is much more easy to bear with the inconvenience of a dungeon, than it is to conduct a public meeting.'[2] Hunt verily believed in the radical interpretation of Peterloo, but there were to be other embellishments added later. The 'drunken Yeomanry with their newly-sharpened sabres'—sharpened, it was alleged, specially for the meeting.

It is difficult to track down the genesis of the drunken Yeomanry aspersion. It had no place in the early reports, even in the *Observer*. Dr Read,[3] perhaps conscious of this, says:

. . . These [the Yeomanry] were local men, ardent in their politics, who had suffered much from the taunts of the Radicals. There was thus a strong presumption from the first that they would not show much moderation in a crisis. Their prejudices had been further aggravated by the fact that during the morning, while gathering in the taverns to have their boots cleaned and their horses curried, they had become half-drunk.

The source given for the latter part of this statement is 'Marshall, 168', not a very impressive source, for Dr Read himself says 'Marshall [a work published in Syracuse, U.S.A., in 1946] is written in tiresome

---

1 *Manchester Observer*, 28 August 1819.
2 Ibid.
3 Read, p, 133.

pseudo-scientific jargon, and the author tends to excessive generaliza-
tion.' Moreover, on turning to 'Marshall, 168', no authority for the
statement is given.[1] Tracing the allegation back is tedious. It probably
originated from Richard Carlile, who claimed to have been an eye-
witness, but whose account of some of the happenings on St Peter's
Field agrees with no other witness's accounts whatsoever.[2] Writing in
his paper, the *Republican* (27 August), he said:

. . . The passions of the Yeomanry Cavalry and Police, were inflamed by
strong and spiritous liquors, their reason and reflection (if ever they possessed
either) was first eradicated by these means, and then they became fit agents for
the *Nadins*, the *Withingtons*, the *Traffords*, and the *Fletchers* of Manchester . . .

This version does not appear to have been arrived at immediately. His
'eye-witness' account, dated 18 August, and given in a Letter to Lord
Sidmouth, does not refer to the Yeomanry being drunk at the meeting,
but the letter proceeds:

I will now, my Lord, quit the dreadful scenes of St Peter's Field, and examine
the conduct of the police and Yeomanry in and about the streets of Manchester. Intoxicated with the idea of having dispersed so great an assemblage
of persons, they began to increase that intoxication by the use of strong
liquors, and taking them in the aggregate, they were evidently in a state of
intoxication . . .[3]

(He goes on to describe their conduct afterwards). Axon (1886) speaks
of 'hot-headed young men who were more or less intoxicated'; this he
changed in his article in the 11th edition of Encyclopedia Britannica to
'the drunken yeomanry cavalry were then turned loose'. Axon, however, was a noted temperance advocate. No attempt was made to prove
the charge of drunkenness at the trials, although Hunt did refer to the
'drunken and infuriate Yeomanry'.[4] The charge was again introduced

[1] Marshall (168) reads: 'Some of them appear to have refreshed themselves and
fortified their loyal spirits with liquor.'

[2] Quoted above at p. 31.

[3] *A Report of the Manchester Meeting* (pp. 18, 21).

[4] 'I wish to shew', said Hunt in defence at his trial (Pratt edn., p. 37), '. . . that the
fears which were entertained were quite erroneous, and not justified by the conduct of
the meeting. I wish to shew, that though an attempt was made, by sending a few
straggling and drunken soldiers amongst them, to try their tempers, and to excite
them to a breach of the peace, or to put them to death . . .' The final six words almost
appear to have been an afterthought! That Huntean interpretation of the incursion of
the Yeomanry into the meeting was, it is believed, not repeated. It was the *Observer*
(21 August) versifier's interpretation:

'Now send to th' Cavalry, and tell them that,
(As the reformers will not make a riot,)
They must, when all is peaceable and quiet,

by radical witnesses at the Oldham inquest in October. One said:[1]

. . . The cavalry did not appear to me to be in a good humour; they appeared angry; they looked pale. I think there was a good deal of intoxication amongst them, because they rolled on their horses; he did not think they were very good horsemen.

Another:[2]

. . . Soldiers then came—the first could hardly sit on his horse, he was so drunk; he sat like a monkey . . . he was fuddled, I reckon.

The calibre of the testimony is, however, better to be judged by the same witness's statement:

. . . I saw three pigeons fly out of a window, and then the curtain was dropped, and I suppose that was the signal. 'What reason', he was asked, 'have you to suppose so?' 'Why, because the soldiers and constables directly began together playing their music with their swords and truncheons.' 'What do you mean by music?' 'Why, the soldiers began cutting and slaying, and the constables began to seize the colours, and the tune was struck up; they all knew of the combination.[3]

The newly-sharpened sabres became an issue, and came into prominence too during the proceedings of the Oldham inquest,[4] but only after a newspaper paragraph had appeared in the (London) *Star*, which reported that Mr ——, the cutler, in Manchester, had been employed to sharpen the Yeomanry's sabres a 'day or two before the meeting' of 16 August. Harmer, the radical barrister, introduced the cutler as a witness to give evidence. The 'day or two' was finally extended to a month before, for the cutler said he had sharpened sixty-three sabres by the week-ending 17 July.[5] This became asserted as proof that, as a result of the letter of Lord Sidmouth to Lord Derby telling him to 'give immediate direction to the several corps of yeomanry cavalry in the county of Lancaster to hold themselves in readiness' that their sabres were sent for

---

Prance in among the People,—lay them flat,—
Help constables to take the leaders,—
Those cursed *peaceful* meeting breeders;
And bid them then disperse the mob,
By hundreds down to mow them; . . .'

[1] *Oldham Inquest*, p. 169.
[2] Ibid., p. 75.
[3] Ibid., p. 79.
[4] Ibid., p. 151.
[5] Ibid., p. 161.

sharpening.[1] It was Philips[2] (in November, 1819) who sought proof to counter the *Star's* assertion of 'a day or two before the meeting . . .' giving as his proof that which Dr Read stated. It is interesting to note how Bruton used this evidence:

The sharpening of the swords, by the way, was fully acknowledged by the other side. Thus Mr. Philips writes [p. 17]: 'The simple history of all the tales we have heard of sharpening sabres is briefly this. On the 7th of July the Government issued orders to the Cheshire and Manchester Yeomanry Cavalry, through the Lords Lieutenant, to hold themselves in readiness, and consequently most of the Manchester Cavalry sent their arms to the same cutler which the corps during the last war had employed, to put them in condition'. All these details are important as aggravating the bitter feelings which already existed, and we shall see later that when this improvised corps advanced into the crowd, using their sharpened swords, they were in some cases individually recognised by those at whom they struck.

Which was a rather novel way of using Philips' refutation of the *Star's* innuendo. John Edward Taylor was reduced to inferring (*Observations*, p. 180) that if the sabres were not sharpened for the 16 August meeting, then they were sharpened for some meeting! In fact, the swords were not even sent to the cutlers as a result of Lord Derby's order, because that order was not given locally until 13 July, and the ever-vigilant reporter of the *Manchester Observer* had noticed (in the issue of 10 July) that the swords were sent to the cutlers. They had been sent because they were in poor shape. The relevant passage is as follows: (*Manchester Observer*, 10 July).

We have just heard from unquestionable authority that a number of our valiant Yeomanry Cavalry have, during the last four days, had their sabres freshly ground, in order to stop the mouths of the disaffected rabble—the whole corps, we understand, are going through a course of medicine, and the Parson is busily employed in preparing this august body for speedy dissolution. Sir John Falstaff could not devise more effectual preparations than these.

We have just heard that the Police Office is full of Pikes taken from the disaffected—another burning plot, no doubt. Hubble, hubble, toil and trouble.

Capt. Birley finally said:

If any blame attaches for sharpening the swords, I must take it all to myself. At drill a sabre was drawn to screw a flint, and seeing the state it was in, I looked at the sabres, and finding them not serviceable, I directed them to be taken to be put in order.[3]

[1] Read, p. 116.
[2] Philips, *Exposure*, p. 17.
[3] *Exchange Herald*, 30 November 1819.

This must have been sometime before the 6th of July when the *Observer* heard about it. What was perhaps Henry Hunt's final comment on this sword-sharpening controversy was made by him in the House of Commons, 15 March 1832.[1]

. . . It had been stated that the swords of the Yeomanry were not sharpened for the occasion, but the wounds they had inflicted on defenceless men and women, proved that the statement was not true . . .

Recurring again and again in the radical version of Peterloo is the theme of expectation, even anticipation, that the Yeomanry were bound to act as they were alleged to have acted because of the taunts and insults hurled at them by the radicals. It is a novel idea that the radicals should use their own vituperation against the Yeomanry to prove that the Yeomanry attacked so wantonly. The *Manchester Mercury* (24 August), unaware that they were writing about the Manchester 'Massacre', tried to put in a plea for the Yeomanry:

. . . But the constitutional feeling and humanity of the Magistrates are attested by what they have done, and by what they have forborne—abstaining from harsh measures to the last; when force became necessary, what force did they employ against the rioters? Not a standing army of stipendiary soldiers, but the voluntary unpaid arms of their fellow-townsmen, their neighbours, their employers, their natural guardians, leaders and protectors—who know their distresses, and commiserate their sufferings, but who also know, that far from being relieved, they can only be involved in a deeper misery, by the malignant schemes of those in whom they madly repose confidence . . .

The writer in the *Mercury* was still unaware that a 'massacre' had taken place.

If there had been vituperation before 16 August directed against Yeomanry it was as nothing to that which came afterwards:

MANCHESTER Y——Y VALOUR

Sad sixteenth of August! accursed be the day;
    When thy field, oh, St. Peter! was crimson'd with gore;
When blue-mantled bullies, in hostile array,
    Struck down to the earth the defenceless and poor.

Yes, yes! it was valour to gash the unarmed,
    To bear down the aged—the cripple—the child;
It was manly to vanquish the female, alarmed,
    To mangle her bosom was gentle and mild.

[1] Hansard, Vol. XI, 3rd series, p. 251, et seq.

Ye cowardly brutes! may the Lancashire fair,
 With merited scorn, your base doings repay;
May they scoff at the coward, whose half-soldier air
 Serves this counterfeit lion the more to betray.

May the ghosts of the murdered your slumbers infest,
 And drops of their blood be found in your wine;
Thus, sinking in heart, and by conscience opprest,
 In remorse, and in fear, may you sicken and pine.

(*Manchester Observer*, 18 September, 1819)

Very early in the post-Peterloo days, radical accusations were made that the Yeomanry had dealt out wounds with a more liberal hand than the regular cavalry. The press, after discovering, contrary to the impression they had given in the first place, that the dispersal was not confined alone to the Manchester Yeomanry, made this higher responsibility for wounds a feature of their attack. On 23 August, Sir John Byng wrote to Hobhouse:

Private ✱ ✱ ✱ From what I heard the 15th Hussars hit only with the flat, while the Yeomanry *cut* with their swords. It would be invidious to make such a distinction, and yet it is hard for the 15th to be reflected upon, and it may be easily accounted for, that the assemblage formed an erroneous opinion that the yeomanry either could not or would not act, that they were therefore insulted, and by some despised, while to the 15th no such conduct was offered. This is, I have no doubt, nearly the truth, and if given would justify both.[1]

There is much that is written on this very point. It has been seen how Bruton in his *Three Accounts* (1921) used Lieutenant Jolliffe's evidence to prove that the Yeomanry were cutting with their swords when they went into the crowd, whereas Jolliffe had not at that moment arrived on the scene. Introducing Jolliffe's account, he writes:

. . . It seems clear, from the evidence which was given before the Relief Committee after Peterloo, that there was not the same feeling of resentment against the Hussars as against the local Yeomanry; in fact, it was more than once asserted that troopers of the Hussars actually restrained the Manchester Yeomanry from excessive violence.

Jolliffe's account, therefore, actually counters Bruton's assertion:

The Hussars drove the people forward with the flats of their swords, but sometimes, as is almost inevitably the case when men are placed in such situations, the edge was used, both by the Hussars and, as I have heard, by the Yeomen also; but of this

---

[1] *State Trials*, App. B, 1382.

latter part I was not cognizant, and believing though I do that nine out of ten of the sabre wounds were caused by the Hussars, I must still consider that it redounds to the humane forbearance of the men of the 15th that more wounds were not received, when the vast numbers are taken into consideration with whom they were brought into hostile collision; beyond all doubt, however, the far greater amount of injuries were from the pressure of the routed multitude . . .

That part of the paragraph in italics is the only part used by Bruton in his earlier version, *The Story of Peterloo* (1919). Even Prentice only truncated the extract from Jolliffe by leaving unquoted the last eighteen words.

Bruton,[1] on what authority he does not say, appears to be responsible for the now widely accepted belief that John Edward Taylor was the editor of *Peterloo Massacre*; that he, said Bruton, 'constituted himself the protagonist among the champions of the "Reformers", and opened the battle in a series of fourteen weekly tracts entitled "The Peterloo Massacre", the first of which appeared just a week after the event'.[2] We have already given some reasons for doubting this attribution. That the *Peterloo Massacre* emanated from the office in Manchester of the rabidly radical *Observer*, in whose columns Taylor had been called a poltroon and a snaffling hypocrite, is the least of the reasons why Taylor could not have been its editor. One has only to consider the quality of the writing which appeared in it to realize that Taylor could not have been its editor. Dr Read wrote:[3]

The Radical press increased its circulation immensely: 'odious and blasphemous publications', declared the Cheshire Grand Jury, 'poured forth throughout the country'. Such 'garbage' Taylor commented, would not have flourished if the people had not been so ill-treated. (Referring to his *Observations* pp. 68–69, which read: [Since] 'the dispersion of the meeting of the 16th of August, the circulation of *The Republican*, in this district, increased *three-fold*. It seems, therefore, that military execution is but an ineffective recipe for the cure of "blasphemy". That there have been many other vile periodical publications issued, I have no doubt; but if the feelings and passions of the people had not been strongly excited, by the ill-treatment they have received, they would have rejected the garbage with disgust . . .)'

For publishing the following 'libellous' advertisement announcing the sale of *Peterloo Massacre*, Wroe, the printer, received a prison sentence:

[1] *The Story of Peterloo*, p. 7.
[2] Dr Read accepts this attribution to J. E. Taylor unreservedly (Read, pp. 136, 164).
[3] Read, p. 141.

Peterloo Massacre. Just published No. 4, price twopence, of *Peterloo Massacre*, containing a full, true, and faithful account of the inhuman murders, woundings, and other monstrous cruelties exercised by infernals (miscalled soldiers) upon an unarmed and distressed people, who were constitutionally assembled to consider of the best, most legal, and most efficient means of alleviating their present unparalleled sufferings, when they were broken in upon by bands of armed ruffians, who murdered many, and cut and maimed hundreds more in a horrid manner.[1]

The *Manchester Observer* writers felt the indictment unjust. They wrote (6 November 1819):

. . . the power which our magistrates claim, *jure divino*, from their political god, Lord Sidmouth, of constructing sedition out of our most simple effusions, even from the remarks in advertising a book for sale.

And on 22 January, 1820:

. . . And yet, for selling copies of the *Manchester Observer* which announced 'an authentic narrative of these afflicting woundings, maimings and deaths' for publication, *four* of our people are indicted to stand their trials for a libel . . .

Much of what was most vituperative in *Peterloo Massacre's* columns was lifted from other papers, but an editorial delivered itself of a tirade from which the following is a choice example:

. . . These miscreants, not content with fattening upon the labour of the poor, (who like Pharaoh's lean kine are now to be eaten up), will not allow us the privilege of grumbling, but at the peril of being *slaughtered*; we peaceably and *constitutionally* assemble, to seek for bread, and we are accommodated with *steel*. Our *wives*, our *little ones*, are put to the mercy of an armed banditti, more ferocious than the Arab of the wilderness, more callous to feeling than the cannibals of the Isles. We verily believe, that had these vile *military* violated the chastity of our females, on the field of St. Peter, in the open face of that accursed day, the friends who set them on, would have advocated their cause, and endeavoured to cover their delinquency. They would have told the poor victims, (as the Lancashire Grand Jury told others) that they went there for the purpose.

But as we before asserted, their guilty and blood-thirsty course is finished; they have arrived at the goal without winning the race: retreat, they *cannot*—proceed they *dare not*. The gulph is before them—let but the oppressed people propel them one step, and their oppressors are swallowed up for ever![2]

[1] *Manchester Observer*, 4 September 1819.
[2] *Peterloo Massacre* No. 8, p. 113.

The foregoing should be compared with the literary style of John Edward Taylor, who wrote (*Observations*, p. 46):

There is a disgusting, flippant, and passionate vulgarity in the style of Mr. Lloyd, who is clerk to the magistrates at Stockport, as manifested in this and in his preceding letter, which marks him as a person by no means qualified to convey accurate and unimpeachable information with respect to the subjects on which he writes. His indecent phraseology of the '*lower orders*', and the '*reforming crew*' . . .[1]

There is still more convincing reason to reject utterly the attribution of *Peterloo Massacre* to John Edward Taylor. It occurs in an article (p. 24) quoted from the *Statesman* of 19 August, 1819 which reads:

The Manchester Magistrates have lamentably and unhappily thrown multitudes of individuals into sorrow and mourning, and the whole kingdom into consternation and dismay. They have also carved out work enough for the Bench and Bar to occupy both for some time to come at least. They happen too to be *manufacturing* Magistrates, which makes their case the more affecting to their characters; and that circumstance ought to have instilled a greater wariness into their conduct. They are opposed by interest against the complaints and bewailings of the poor weavers who constituted a very great majority of people which formed the unarmed mass of population, into which the yeomanry cavalry so heroically charged on a gallop sword in hand! They should have been slow to strike, where it was so obviously natural for the profit in trade, and the passion in authority, to influence their minds, if not their movements. But they have done the deed—and a fatal one it is . . . The Manchester Magistrates, full of their own self-conceit, but inflated with their accidental power, impatient for the contest which was to chase away the high-priced notion of liberty, and to cheapen the already too high priced labour of the loom, have fleshed their swords of their young trained bands in the bodies of Britons assembling to regain their lost RIGHTS —we will not say *privileges* . . . The chief or senior Magistrate among those who have been thus acting, should have thought of the consequences of spilling one drop of *citizen's* blood . . .

The editor of *Peterloo Massacre* '. . . trusted no apology was necessary for the insertion of these views.' Taylor, had he been editor, would have realized the utter futility of so trying to influence readers of his paper, or even any informed Manchester or Lancashire body of readers; for not only were there no manufacturers among the magistrates, but also that the Chancellor of the Duchy of Lancaster had made it a rule that none who were engaged in the cotton trade should ever be

[1] Taylor was commenting on the eve-of-Peterloo letter quoted above, p. 145–46.

appointed as magistrates. It was, according to Dr W. Cooke Taylor, the standing plaint of many, and the middle-class radicals' self-appointed spokesman, Archibald Prentice, allegedly quoting Dr Cooke Taylor, wrote:

[Prentice, p. 153] A rule had been established by the Chancellor of the Duchy of Lancaster, that no manufacturer should receive the commission of the peace; consequently, the magistrates were either landowners or clergymen. The Lancashire squires viewed the manufacturing population with a jealousy which may have been unreasonable, but certainly was not unnatural; they saw persons suddenly becoming their rivals in wealth and influence by a course of industry and economy, which hereditary prejudices led them to despise; and they feared that these new men would displace the ancient families. The clergy were identified in feeling with the landlords, by habit, education, and social intercourse; for a very large proportion of the manufacturers belonged to the dissenting sects. With such feelings they allowed the meeting of the 16th of August to assemble, hoping, by a *coup d'etat*, to strike terror into the reformers, and perhaps, disposed to show their contempt for spinners and weavers by arresting the leaders in the midst of the assembly. [It is not possible to discover, in Prentice's (second edition) context, where Cooke Taylor's quotation ends.]

The *Statesman's* smear could very well pass in other parts of the country where they were not so well informed about the custom of appointing Lancashire magistrates, and George Canning, with his knowledge as Member of Parliament for Liverpool, was quick to point out the fallacy of such argument, in the House of Commons debate in November, 1819. It is hardly possible to believe that the real editor of *Peterloo Massacre* was unaware of this Lancashire custom; if he was, he would be better informed after George Canning's speech:

. . . 'It was impossible to overlook,' said Canning, 'those flagrant misrepresentations of fact, by which the public mind had been worked up into a fearful state of irritation. It had happened to him' [Mr. Canning] 'to take the Reports of a part of the daily press on these transactions in the gross; a course of reading which brought exaggerations and contradictions into view, much more clearly than a perusal from day to day. The first thing that had convinced him of the extreme caution with which the testimony of these records was to be received, was an allegation, that the Magistrates of Manchester were necessarily actuated by hostile feelings towards the people, from the circumstances of their being generally "master-manufacturers". His connection with Liverpool . . . [refutation] . . . How many persons must have read the assertion, who, perhaps, to that hour, were not aware of its untruth! How many persons in the country, remained even up to the meeting of Parliament under the influence of that alarming but delusive impression!

Was it not obvious that such impression must materially have influenced the Resolutions of any meeting where it was received as true' . . .[1]

The point to be drawn is that Taylor knew it, and therefore would not have 'edited' a publication reiterating it. The 'meetings' referred to by Canning were the county meetings of protest which were held throughout the country, the prototype for which was the celebrated meeting of the Common Council in London. 'How many persons, in the country,' ejaculated Canning, 'remained even up to the meeting of Parliament under the influence of that alarming but delusive impression!' How many, indeed. It required more than Canning's celebrated diction to convince them, and convince generations after them. Says Mr Ziegler:

. . . The petition of the Common Council was certainly more concerned with dramatic effect than prosy accuracy. But with all its hyperbole it still reflected the feelings of the people more faithfully than the robust defence of Sidmouth or the modulated regrets of George Canning.

But the most cogent reason of all for rejecting Bruton's attribution of the editorship lies in Taylor's use of words. It will be recalled that attention has been called[2] to a modern commentator's quotation from Taylor which reads:

This Committee, consisting chiefly of former towns' officers, was very active in Manchester in the weeks just before Peterloo: its members (rather than the magistrates) were 'the original instigators' of the massacre, wrote Taylor, 'men of the most violent party feelings' . . .[3]

The words within the single quotation marks only, were used by Taylor. He did not use the word 'massacre'; he used the word 'tragedy'. In the whole of his *Notes and Observations* . . .[4] consisting of 224 pages, he never once uses the word 'massacre': he refers to the tragedy, melancholy occasion, the violent and rapid incursion of an armed force into the midst of a peaceable multitude, and the bruises, the tramplings, the fractures, the sabrings that ensued. He writes of a dreadful occasion, the Yeomanry who were active, a scene of military execution and horrifying scenes. On p. 184 he writes of 'the carnage of the 16th of August would have been much more dreadful and extensive', and only in one place does he mention 'murder', and then in the context of quoting the law of collective responsibility for murder, in a reference

---

[1] Parl. Deb. XLI (1819–20), p. 199.
[2] See above, p. 126.
[3] In part quoting Taylor's *Observations*, p. 173.
[4] London, 1820.

to the Oldham inquest and not the word 'massacre' only. In the whole of his book, Taylor never once uses the then already-well-established sobriquet Peterloo, except in a footnote on page 116, where the word occurs in a witness's affidavit, which Taylor quotes. Both publications: Taylor's *Observations* and *Peterloo Massacre* were issued concurrently: the latter was issued in the weeks between August and the beginning of December, and the former's preface is dated 18 December. The two publications side by side are as black to white; Taylor has been made a Jekyll and Hyde.

The stature of John Edward Taylor is increased rather than diminished by the removal of this spurious attribution. It was unworthy of the man described by A. W. Ward,[1] whose account knew nothing of it. His view of Taylor's *Observations* for the most part will stand:

. . . [It] is a masterly exposure of a miserable chapter in the history of our national policy, and an unanswerable plea for trust in the people. It concludes with a prescient appeal to the middle classes to profit by their recent discovery 'that they *must* interfere with domestic politics, because domestic politics *will* interfere with them'.

Taylor *ought* to have written his 'masterly exposure of a miserable chapter in the history of our national policy' at a date a little further removed from the main incident in his theme. He deserved, too, better targets to attack than Hay and Philips.

[1] In D.N.B., XIX, 449.

XVIII

The Radical Protest Meetings

Solely on the evidence learned from reports in the newspaper press, and the discussion they engendered, the protest meetings began to add yet more heat to the already boiling indignation of the nation. There was the famous Crown and Anchor meeting in London on 21 August when T. J. Wooler, editor of the radical *Black Dwarf* declaimed thus:[1]

. . . He was not aware, even under the present system, bad as it was, that there could have been found beings so atrocious, that, like a conclave of fiends, they could deliberate and arrange as for a drama or tragedy, scenes infamous and horrid as those which they had witnessed at Manchester. If the scenes of slaughter were not so near, a rational man might justly refuse to subscribe his belief to them . . . [a tirade against the Government] . . . They had suppressed the meetings of the people . . . they had proceeded step by step in their iniquitous system, until they had plunged into a depth of blood which it was impossible for them to wade through . . . [The Government had employed soldiers] . . . He would not pollute that manly name by applying it to a set of beings, who were intended for murderers and assassins; who under the sanction of an order from the magistrates, could satisfy their appetite for slaughter by murdering their fellow-countrymen . . . The proceedings at Manchester exhibited every mark of deliberate intention to shed blood. The intended meeting of the 9th was objected to as illegal . . . [people ordered to abstain from attending; another meeting; far more attending] . . . and from all the preparations which were made, a person might have reasonably inferred that it was the magistrates' wish to congregate all the reformers together from the neighbouring towns, in a small place, and butcher a few, as a terror to the rest. (applause) . . . The Yeomanry ought to be excommunicated from society, to be pointed at wherever they went, saying, 'There goes the assassin or murderer of so many unarmed people'. . . . For his part he should not be satisfied until a special commission was sent down to punish every one who had been guilty of violence towards those who were legally assembled. Were he in Manchester he would placard them about once a month, until they were brought to justice. (Loud and continued cheering). He was convinced that when future

[1] *Manchester Observer*, 28 August 1819.

historians recurred to this blood-thirsty page, they would consider the actions to be such that nothing but demons could have planned and none but devils executed.

Richard Carlile's 'brave fellows . . . linked together' round the hustings had not yet been described in his trenchant prose, but he stoked up manfully in that post-Peterloo blaze (*Republican*,[1] 27 August):

The massacre of the unoffending inhabitants of Manchester, on the 16th of August, by the Yeomanry Cavalry, and Police, at the instigation of the Magistrates, should be the daily theme of the Press until the MURDERERS are brought to justice . . . the Bloodhounds of Manchester . . . or some charge of High Treason must be trumped up against those who were connected with that meeting. In the latter case, the Magistrates will be enabled to imprison all those who are likely to be called as evidences against them, for seven months, and perhaps by that time get them all destroyed; for those men who could direct their bloodhounds to attack and destroy a peaceable meeting at noon day, are capable of directing the dagger or the poison cup to the cell of their prisoners . . . Shall it be said of England, that a Prince, a Duke, or a Magistrate, shall murder their fellow-citizens with impunity, whilst a man who resisteth his oppressors, and kills him to save his own life, is executed as a murderer? Forbid it, Nature! But this is now to be attempted at Manchester. The wholesale murderers say, that before they began to use their sabres, a pistol was fired and a brickbat thrown. This is false! . . .

Carlile gave his version of the state of post-Peterloo Manchester thus:

The murders which have been lately committed at Manchester at the instigation of the Magistrates, have rendered the town prominent in the cause of Despotism and Liberty. Those Magistrates are evidently sensible that their lives are forfeited to the offended laws of their country, and are endeavouring to carry everything with a high hand whilst they continue to receive the thanks and approbation of the Regent and his Ministers. The Magistracy of Manchester have banished Justice from that town, and hold even common decency in contempt. They study to irritate rather than to allay the outraged feelings of the inhabitants. Capt. Nadin and his banditti of Police, are hourly engaged to plunder and ill-use the peaceable inhabitants; whilst every appeal from those repeated assaults to the Magistrates for redress, is treated by them with derision and insult.

This state of things cannot continue long—the very soldiers who are compelled now to act at the discretion of any Police-Officer, must soon become disgusted with their conduct. Every man in Manchester who avows his opinions on the necessity of Reform, should never go unarmed—retaliation is become a duty, and revenge an act of justice.[2]

[1] *Republican*, Vol. I, No. 1, 27 August, 1819, p. 3.
[2] Ibid., p. 83.

The *Manchester Observer*, 28 August:

PETER-LOO

This is the field of Peter-Loo.

These are the poor Reformers who met, on the state of affairs to debate; in the field, of Peter-Loo.

These are the butchers, blood-thirsty and bold, who cut, slash'd and maim'd, young, defenceless and old, who met, on the state of affairs to debate; in the field of Peter-Loo.

This is *Hurly Burly*, a blustering knave, and foe to the poor, whom he'd gladly enslave, who led on the butchers, blood-thirsty and bold, who cut, slash'd and maim'd young, defenceless and old, who met on the state of affairs to debate; in the field of Peter-Loo.

These are the just-asses, gentle and mild, who to keep the peace, broke it, by lucre beguil'd, and sent *Hurly Burly*, a blustering knave, a foe to the poor, whom he'd gladly enslave, to lead on the butchers, blood-thirsty and bold, who cut, slash'd and maim'd, young defenceless and old, who met on the state of affairs to debate; in the field of Peter-Loo.

Manchester Observer, 11 September, at the end of an article entitled 'Manchester Politics':

. . . the most infamous tragedy that ever stained with human blood the land of freedom, with horror we hear of the applause given to persons who have been the means of the death and mutilation of so many human beings, our fellow-creatures and fellow-countrymen. As yet it is not ascertained who got up the tragedy; [!] who converted armed men into executioners; who were the conspirators against the privileges of the People, directed the aggression and commanded the cruel assault. When they are known (we again repeat it) we will record their names and fix the charge. They shall not smell sweet and blossom in the dust; the wrongs which they have heaped upon society will adhere to them like the leprosy; and they will become, as they deserve, objects of loathing and disgust. Power will not protect them, influence cannot conceal them; time will disclose the secret; and then they may call on the heavens to hide, and the hills to cover them, but the outstretched arm of Offended Justice will seize these children of blood, even at the uttermost bounds of the earth. He must be lost in apathy, or rendered stoical by interest, whose heart is not fired by indignation at the recital of the carnage. He who tamely witnesses any infringement on the liberties of the People, deserves to forfeit his rights as man; and his privileges as a Briton! We shall cry aloud and spare not.

Looking again at the foundations upon which the structure of the radical interpretation of Peterloo is erected, it is essential to remember that before Dr Read wrote his book, the responsibility for the massacre was accepted as lying with authority in general, the Government and the magistrates. Dr Read's book exonerated the Government, but his conclusions have since been challenged by Mr E. P. Thompson, who reverts to the already established interpretation. Of those early days after the transactions of the 16 August, Dr Read says:

. . . Turning now to the attitude of the magistrates on August 16th itself, they had two main charges levelled against them. One, that they deliberately let the Peterloo meeting assemble so that they could attack it; the other that the Riot Act was not read by them, or if read at all was not acted upon correctly with an hour elapsing before the dispersal of the meeting.[1]

Leaving aside the fact that the *main* charge levelled against them was that they had attacked a peaceable meeting, Dr Read goes on to show that the magistrates made no reply to the charge, or the charges. He says: 'Only after the passage of nearly three years with the case of Redford *v*. Birley was any fact of their defence put before the public.' It cannot be too often reiterated that there was nothing brought out by Redford *v*. Birley which had not been 'put before the public' by Government spokesmen earlier. But they were not believed. Dr Read goes on:

. . . If the magistrates could remain silent after Peterloo, the Government, by contrast, could hardly escape without fully explaining its position. At heart, ministers were far from enthusiastic about the fatal ardour of the magistrates . . .

In the first place, there could have been no official 'enthusiasm' for the tragedy. To assume that there was is the one flaw in the radical interpretation of the event. Mr Thompson says:[2]

Lord Liverpool declared that the action of the Manchester magistrates was 'substantially right', although it was not altogether 'prudent'. There remained no alternative but to support them. [And in another paragraph (p. 683)] If the Government was unprepared for the news of Peterloo, no authorities have ever acted so vigorously to make themselves accomplices after the fact . . .

There is the assumption that at this time—the early days or weeks after Peterloo—the 'guilt' of the magistrates (in Dr Read's case) and of the Government and the magistrates (in Mr Thompson's) was established, established by the facts read in the newspapers; facts which may be summed up by the knowledge that the Yeomanry had 'hewed their way through the crowd'. Dr Read goes on:

[1] Read, p. 182.
[2] Thompson, p. 684.

That the government felt bound to support the Manchester magistrates in general terms was perhaps not surprising. What was less defensible was the haste and gullibility with which they rushed to their defence in detail. Thus the thanks of the Prince Regent were conveyed to the authorities at Manchester within five days of the massacre, long before there could be even the appearances of an unprejudiced inquiry by the government into the facts of the situation. Soon afterwards came the Regent's over-assertive reply to the Common Council of London, and in January, 1820, the provocative appointment of Hay, the Chairman of the Salford Quarter Sessions, to one of the richest livings in the country.

The 'provocative appointment' of Hay in January, 1820, could not have affected the indignation which gathered in the immediate post-Peterloo weeks; the other measures did. The thanks of Lord Sidmouth (a fact not generally known) were conveyed to the magistrates even earlier: in a letter written on 18 August. This was, however, 'suppressed' as will be seen. The Prince Regent's 'over-assertive' reply to the Common Council of London should, however, be placed alongside the not less 'over-assertive' communication which prompted it. Alderman Waithman in moving the series of resolutions sent to the Regent had said:

. . . The Manchester magistrates, without waiting for the observance of the forms of which the [Riot] Act prescribed, directed the Yeomanry Cavalry to surround the hustings. These gallant heroes performed the exploit in a most valorous manner. They dashed on towards the hustings, cutting their way indiscriminately through a vast multitude of unoffending and inoffensive men, women, and children, whose loud and piercing cries for mercy and protection were answered by the cuts of sabres or the tramplings of horses. When the first accounts of this horrible scene had reached the metropolis, the Ministerial hirelings were loud in their boasts of the triumph which had been obtained. This gallant charge of the Manchester Yeomanry Cavalry was extolled as a master-piece of policy . . . &c. . . . His Royal Highness the Prince Regent, through, he had no doubt, the gross misrepresentations of others, had been induced to sanction, and not only to sanction, but to applaud and express his thanks, for the conduct of the Manchester Magistrates and of the Yeomanry Cavalry—conduct which no dispassionate man could contemplate without feelings of indignation.[1]

The Alderman's indignation was unfeigned, as was that of the people of England. The resolutions did not mince words. The relevant clause in the series of resolutions read:

. . . [The Common Council] had 'learnt with grief and astonishment that

[1] *Manchester Observer,* 18 September 1819.

while the meeting was so assembled, and when no act of riot or tumult had taken place, the Magistrates issued their warrants for the apprehension of certain persons then present, for execution of which, although no resistance was made on the part of the people or those against whom the warrants were issued, they immediately resorted to the aid of the military; when, without any previous warning of their intention, the Manchester Yeomanry Cavalry, rushing forward, opened a passage through the multitude, furiously attacking by force of arms, peaceable and unoffending citizens, whereby a great number of men, women, and children, and even peace-officers, were indiscriminately and wantonly rode over, and many inhumanly sabred and killed.'

The common indignation of the Common Council was not to be moved by the plea of one who suggested a pause:

A Mr. Brown 'hoped the Court would not be led away by the pathetic descriptions which they had heard, but would discharge their duty as became men who wished to view matters on both sides before they gave their decision. He would freely avow his opinion, that if the magistrates of Manchester, or the Yeomanry Cavalry, had acted in the manner which had been described they ought to be punished for it in the most exemplary manner; but then, on what authority did those accounts rest? On the authority of newspapers; no two of which had agreed as to the circumstances which they detailed. Would the Court then, upon such conflicting evidence, sit in judgment over men and condemn them unheard? Would they judge his Majesty's ministers, and pass a censure on all from the evidence which was before them? It should also be observed, that from all the evidence which could yet be collected, a conclusion might be drawn quite the reverse of that which the resolution had adopted. A Grand Jury of a county had ignored bills against some of the Yeomanry Cavalry for some of the acts for which they were condemned! and however respectable the individual alluded to[1] might be, he could not let it outweigh in his mind the credit which was due to a Grand Jury on their oaths. He then contended, that it would be unjust to pass any opinion which might prejudice the public mind against men whose conduct might soon become the subject of legal inquiry.

Mr Brown was one of the few amongst the minority of forty-five against seventy-one of the Common Council who did not believe all they read in the press. There have been many like him since his day. The resolution sent by the Common Council was typical of all the county meetings, the city meetings, and the towns meetings which were called all over the country. *The Times's* 'dreadful fact' was established. The nation's wrath was swift and fierce. If the 'dreadful fact' was a fact, the wrath, as Mr Brown said, was justifiable.

[1] A previous speaker.

To the Common Council's 'over-assertive' resolution came the Prince Regent's 'over-assertive' reply:

Gentlemen: I received with feelings of regret the Address of the Lord Mayor, Aldermen and Commons of the City of London. At a time when wicked and designing men are endeavouring by every species of device, and the most insidious arts, to alienate the minds of the people from his Majesty's government, from the Constitution of this realm as by law established, it is to the great vigilance of the Magistracy that we can alone look for safety. With the circumstances which took place previously to the Meeting on the 16th of August, at Manchester, you are not acquainted, and of the conduct which was adopted on that occasion you are not rightly informed. If, however, the laws have been violated by those who are entrusted with their execution, the ordinary Tribunals of the country are open for redress; and to institute any extra-judicial enquiry upon these subjects would be manifestly contrary to the principles of common justice.

What the Prince Regent (or the Government) knew, and what the Manchester magistrates and their supporters knew, was one thing. How to convince the people of England that they were 'not rightly informed' was another. They were already convinced that they were. As each day passed, how to find a way out of the morass into which the Government and the magistrates had stumbled, grew more difficult. Even when they at last believed they had reached firmer ground, the mud still clung to them. How accurately Henry Hunt had summed up the position during his confinement in the New Bayley: 'But they' [the magistrates] 'are in a dreadful scrape; and they will flounder on farther into the mire every struggle they make'. 'With the circumstances which took place', said the Regent's reply, 'previously to the Meeting of the 16 August, at Manchester, you are not acquainted.' It was a foretaste of what was to happen at the beginning of the next Parliamentary session. Parliament was to be hurriedly (for those days) recalled in view of the emergency; the letters and documents relating to what had transpired prior to 16 August, were to be given to the nation to make them 'acquainted'. These documents were even to include extracts from the *Manchester Observer*. They fell flat. Taylor was to reprint them in his *Observations* with caustic comments on some of them. The Government's borrowings from the *Manchester Observer* were perhaps not extensive enough!

Mr Thompson[1] hints at the possible suppression of Peterloo documents:

. . . if any 'Peterloo decision' was reached by Sidmouth and the magistrates

[1] Thompson, p. 683-4.

it is likely to have been reached privately in the week before the meeting. And it is highly unlikely that any record would have been left in the official Home Office papers for subsequent inspection . . .[1]

Mr Ziegler, it may be reiterated,[2] demurs, thinking it unreasonable to suppose that Home Office control—which in this case meant collusion between them and the magistrates to decide to disperse the meeting by force—was 'strict enough to dictate the whole pattern of blunders which led to the disaster'. Collusion between conspirators in these latter more enlightened days may be easier with modern aids in communication, but in 1819 collusion between men two hundred miles apart had to be committed to paper. Total destruction of evidence may have been complete at one end; but what of the other? There was some suppression at the Lancashire end, politely requested by London. Amongst William Hulton's papers there is a letter from Lord Sidmouth's secretary (Hobhouse), headed 'Whitehall, 23 August, 1819':[3]

Sir—I am directed by Lord Sidmouth to acknowledge the receipt of your letter of the 20th inst., in which, as Chairman of the Select Committee of Magistrates of the two counties of Lancaster and Cheshire, you by their direction, request permission to publish Lord Sidmouth's letter of the 18th instant. in which his Lordship expressed his approbation of the conduct of the Magistrates at Manchester on the 16th.

As Lord Sidmouth's Letters of Saturday last to the Earls of Derby and Stamford conveyed the most gracious Approbation of His Royal Highness the Prince Regent of the conduct of the Magistracy at Manchester, and expressed the great satisfaction which His Royal Highness had derived from their prompt, decisive, and efficient Measures, to preserve the Public Tranquility; which must be of far greater Value than any thing only proceeding from Lord Sidmouth himself, his Lordship presumes that it can no longer appear to the Magistrates to be of any Consequence to give Publicity to his Letter of the 18th inst., and his Lordship would accordingly prefer that it should not be published.

But his Lordship sees no objection to a Publication of his Letter of the 21st. I have the honour to be,

Sir . . . H. Hobhouse.

Wm. Hulton Esq., Manchester.

[1] Mr Thompson was not the first to suspect secret collusion for the same sinister ends. Prentice (p, 157) made the same suggestion when he commented on Norris's eve-of-Peterloo letter to Lord Sidmouth. 'Can it be,' wrote Prentice, 'that whilst thus writing to Lord Sidmouth officially, there was a private resolution, perhaps directed by him, to allow the meeting to assemble and to disperse it with the swords of the Yeomanry, notoriously known to have been sharpened for the occasion?'

[2] See above, p. 37–39.

[3] DDHu/53/57 L.C.R.O.

Lord Sidmouth had not had to wait, as Hobhouse's earlier letter had suggested, for the Wednesday (18 August) post for news; Hay's letter to the Government had reached Ministers on Tuesday night. There was a full Cabinet meeting of all those Ministers who were in town on Wednesday, which met the delegation from Manchester.

On Wednesday, also, two letters left London—one to Hulton as chairman of the magistrates, and another to Sir John Byng as commander-in-chief. Research into Hulton's papers in Lancashire suggests that not only did Hulton obey Sidmouth's request not to publish the letter, but that the letter was destroyed. It would appear, however, to be reasonable to conclude that it was not an incriminating letter. Had it been, Hulton would hardly have asked permission to publish it. There remains, how-ever, the other letter dated 18 August—a copy of which still reposes in in the Home Office 'Private and Secret' file—a part of which letter Mr Thompson considers, in pursuing his argument of the destruction of incriminating documents, as suspicious.[1] Such an argument presupposes a wider circle of conspirators than the Government and the magistrates; it had to include General Byng and, presumably, his local commander Lt.-Col. L'Estrange. The 'suspicious' letter was to Sir John Byng.

This present investigation has relied, generally, on printed sources for the Home Office papers; it would appear to be naive to expect that anything hostile to the magistrates' case would have remained unquoted in the intensive search which has been made to strengthen the radical interpretation of these events.[2] The relevant part[3] of Mr. Thompson's suspicious letter deserves fuller investigation. It reads:

(To) Sir John Byng, Pontefract. *Private.* My dear Sir. As my letter of the 17th was written from my own impressions only of Lord Sidmouth's Sentiments, and not by his Authority, it is right that I should now communicate to you, that he not only *entirely approves* of your absence from Manchester, but on several accounts is *glad* that you were not there. Your presence would have given too much importance to Hunt, and would have given an appearance of a Predetermination in Government to subject the People to Military Execu-tion. Your confidence in Col. L'Estrange appears to have been, as Lord Sid-mouth had no doubt it was, judiciously reposed; and his Judgment has in Lord S.'s mind been evinced by his employing the Yeomanry in the Van agreeably to the Plan on which I know you intended to act. I trust there will

[1] Thompson, p. 683.

[2] That there are Home Office documents, hitherto unquoted, to strengthen the present thesis, is apparent; as may be instanced by Hay's long report quoted above (p. 138) and subsequently.

[3] A later part of the letter deals with General Byng's attempts to stop the sale of alleged seditious literature to the troops under his command.

be no occasion for you repairing to Lancashire again, as I hope a decisive Blow has been given to the treasonable and seditious spirit prevailing there . . .[1]

It seems ironical that Sidmouth was glad that Sir John Byng was *not* at Manchester, as his presence, so Sidmouth thought, would have 'given an appearance of a Predetermination in Government to subject the People to Military Execution'. Ironical, because a modern theory has been that *had* Sir John Byng been present the 'massacre' would not have occurred.

Against this letter, Mr. Thompson's footnote on the question of suppression of documents reads:

Dr. Read places great weight (p. 120) on a letter of Sidmouth's twelve days before Peterloo, advising the Manchester magistrates to 'abstain from any endeavour to disperse the mob'. But if any 'Peterloo decision' was reached by Sidmouth and the magistrates it is likely to have been reached privately in the week before the meeting. And it is highly unlikely that any record would have been left in the official Home Office papers for subsequent inspection. The 'Private and Secret' correspondence between Hobhouse and Byng and Norris (in H.O. 79.3) is curiously ambiguous. Several letters (which have the air of being 'for the record') deprecate 'hasty' or forcible action against the crowd (folios 479, 480, 483); but there is an air of anticipation without precedent, a private address is given to Norris (Chairman of the Manchester Bench) for correspondence (folio 489), and two days after Peterloo Hobhouse records Sidmouth's satisfaction in the judgment of Col. L'Estrange in 'his employing the Yeomanry in the Van, agreeably to the Plan on which I know you intended to act' (folio 510). My opinion is (a) that the Manchester authorities certainly intended to employ force, (b) that Sidmouth knew—and assented to—their intention to arrest Hunt in the midst of the assembly and to disperse the crowd, but that he was unprepared for the violence with which this was effected.

The first question which is suggested by Mr Thompson's suspicions of the 'Private and Secret' (H.O. 79.3) Home Office file surely is: Why place letters 'which have the air of being "for the record"' in a highly-confidential dossier like H.O. 79.3? They could have gone into the general disturbance correspondence of the Home Office papers which would be produced more readily for inspection, if needed. The deprecation of 'hasty' or forcible action against the crowd is fully covered in the correspondence for the 9 August meeting (quoted above pp. 89, &c.) The 'air of anticipation without precedent' was surely a reflection of the intense anxiety felt both in London and in Manchester as to the outcome of what was to be, up to that date, the greatest radical

[1] H.O. 79/3/509–10–11.

meeting in history. The 'private address' given to Norris for correspondence may have meant no more than a relaxation of office routine during the time Parliament was in recess; it has already been seen that some Ministers were out of town.

What there can be in the least sinister in the plan to 'employ the Yeomanry in the Van' is not known. Even in the 'corrupt' House of Commons, Ministers were anxious to avoid the criticisms of their ever-watchful opponents across the floor of the House. Lord Castlereagh dealt with this very aspect of 'employing the Yeomanry in the Van', in replying to the criticisms of Tierney, the Opposition leader in the debates in November, 1819:

. . . It was not until the constable could not execute the warrant without military support that the magistrates granted that military support. The Right. Hon. Gentlemen [Tierney] asked Why, if it was not meant to provoke, why were the Manchester Yeomanry called in? I formerly used to hear the Right Hon. Gentleman say, that the Yeomanry were the only constitutional force. It only proves the resources of the Right Hon. Gentleman's mind. He is always able to show that we do wrong even though we sometimes follow the suggestions of the Right Hon. Gentleman. But it does happen that the magistrates of Manchester had nothing to do with the selection of the Manchester Yeomanry; for they had nothing to do with any part of the military arrangements. So far they are not responsible for the execution any further than in giving the orders, according to law; the rest is with Col. L'Estrange, and in conformity with the Right Hon. Gentleman's former opinions, the Colonel conceived the Yeomanry would be more constitutionally employed upon such an occasion than the regular troops. So much, Sir, with respect to the intention of the magistrates . . .[1]

The quick eye of the *Manchester Observer* leader-writer spotted the seeming incongruity of Lord Castlereagh's statement:

Lord Castlereagh acknowledges that the Manchester Yeomanry were employed in dispersing the meeting on the 16th, and that they were selected for that service by Colonel L'Estrange; whilst Mr. Bootle Wilbraham, who boasts of the accuracy of his information, asserts that it was by mere chance that the Yeomanry were early engaged in the business of the day, occasioned by the regular cavalry having mistaken their route, but that the latter arrived soon enough to render it doubtful who were most active in dispersing the assembly.

The incongruities of the ministerial statements are so numerous as to place them beyond criticism.[2]

[1] *Aston's Exchange Herald*, 30 November 1819, report of Parl. Debate, XLI, 94-95.
[2] *Manchester Observer*, 27 November 1819.

It need hardly be said that whatever plan had been in Lieut-Colonel L'Estrange's mind before the meeting was rendered nugatory by the chance of how things actually occurred.

With 'suppression' in Lancashire of the Sidmouth to Hulton letter dated 18 August, which could not have been incriminating in view of Hulton's desire for its publication in the press; with a copy of another letter of the same date still lying in the Home Office file, which a modern investigator considers suspicious, which is not suspicious when considered in its proper context; with all this, it would seem not unreasonable to conclude that there was no collusion between the Government and the Manchester magistrates with sinister ends in view; especially when both believed that they had nothing to hide.

Indignation rising in the country; silence from the magistrates; and silence from the Ministry until November, when Parliament was recalled. Dr Read,[1] writes:

Finally, the account of the massacre given by ministers to parliament was far too obviously biassed in favour of the authorities; Castlereagh quite blithely acknowledged that the principal sources of government information were Hay, the Chairman of Quarter Sessions, Byng, the Commander of the Northern District, L'Estrange, the officer-commanding at Manchester, and Hardman, a leading local 'loyalist', without seeming to consider it important that all these persons were associated with the very authorities whose conduct was under discussion. In the days of a limited professional system of law and order the government was perhaps right to support the sometimes inept but usually well-meaning labours of an amateur magistracy; but they might at least have given that support with a greater appearance of impartiality.

The Government was criticised in and out of the House for relying on a 'professional' system of law in the shape of stipendiary magistrates, of whom there were two on that final committee of magistrates. In modern days they are criticized for relying on 'amateurs'. Byng and L'Estrange ought, at least, to have been above suspicion, even if the others were not. In the first place, it was the 'transaction' generally, not merely the conduct of the magistrates, which was the subject under discussion. The Government knew, though their critics and traducers did not, that through garbled newspaper commentaries on inaccurate reports, the nation was being misled in its interpretation of the events of Peterloo. Well might Sidmouth say in the House:

. . . There never was a transaction in which the public were interested, or respecting which they were solicitous, in which there had been so much mis-

[1] Read, p. 184.

representation, falsehood, and exaggeration as respecting the proceedings of that day . . .[1]

On the storm raised by the sending of letters of approbation and thanks by the Prince Regent and the Government, they explained that after the Law Officers gave their opinion:

the magistrates were completely justified by the necessity under which they acted, under the necessity which compelled them to act . . . the presumption was in favour of the truth of their statements; and were the Ministers in such a case to say after hearing them. No, we cannot approve of your proceedings; there is every appearance that you acted with proper temper and decision; there is a certainty that you exposed your personal safety in the performance of your duty, but facts may afterwards come out against you, and on this vague anticipation of probable contradiction, we will refrain from thanking you till we have heard the statement of your accusers.[2]

Sidmouth, however, could no more still the storm which had broken than Canute could hold back the tide.

For a full three months the storm of British indignation raged. On Whig platforms noble lords and lowly radicals rubbed shoulders, declaiming together. At the York meeting, a Mr. W. Hargrove addressed the Lord Mayor and Gentlemen of that city:

. . . We perhaps may be blamed, we even have been blamed, for thus meeting, but in my humble opinion, to be silent on such an occasion would be criminal—it would constitute an invitation to tyranny; and then, whilst under the iron heel of despotism, Infamy would sit grinning on the blood-stained sword, and Cruelty would tarnish the boasted honour and former valour of the British Soldier, the great national character of Englishmen would be changed—our fair Temples of Religion, of Science, and of Commerce, would moulder in the dust, and the land of our fathers, the land of liberty, the land of former plenty, would soon become but a Den of Tyrants and a Wilderness of Slaves![3]

At the great Birmingham meeting charges were more specific; Mr Edmonds[4] had raked through, so it would seem, every indictment recorded in the columns of a hostile press.

. . . Murder has been committed, Mr. Edmonds declared, under peculiar and aggravating circumstances—under the authority of the guardians of the law . . . under the authority of a Secretary of State's warrant, they have

[1] Parliamentary Debates XLI (1819–20), p. 22.
[2] Ibid., pp. 24–25.
[3] Quoted in *Manchester Observer*, 2 October 1819.
[4] George Edmonds was tried at Warwick in August 1821 for his part in the legislatorial attorney election at Birmingham. (*State Trials*, N.S. I, p. 795).

driven men to madness and suicide—they have refused free Britons what is allowed to the vilest of criminals, a fair trial by the established laws of the country. The reformers have been accused of revolutionary designs; but can all the atrocity laid to their charge equal this? Did Robespierre, Danton, or any of the monsters who disgraced the French Revolution, surpass the Manchester magistrates? Did they not beguile the people to meet in immense multitudes? Did they not betray them into ambush, and then attack them, sword in hand, and murder indiscriminately, men, women and children? In their defence can they say that the meeting was illegal? If so, why did not they proclaim it to be contrary to the laws, as a declaration of this kind would have been attended to, the Reformers having relinquished their design of assembling at the meeting advertised the week before merely in observance of their edict. This might have been done again, had they not wished to prepare a banquet of human flesh for the special bloodhounds . . . [on the Riot Act being read in a private room] . . . He believed the transaction was preconcerted, and circumstances all conspire to prove it. The place intended for the Theatre of the bloody carnage was previously cleared of what might be stumbling-blocks to the Cavalry. The Infirmary was prepared for the reception of those who might be lacerated, plaisters were ready spread for the wounds meant to be given; and the half-bred soldiers were cutting at a straw to try if their swords were sharp enough to hack the flesh from English bones.' The meeting at Birmingham was, concluded Mr. Edmonds, to express their abhorrence at the murder of their countrymen—to wash their hands of the iniquities which were thought worthy of receiving THE ROYAL APPROBATION . . .![1]

At Sheffield: 'God preserve them from Manchester Politics; Manchester Cavalry; Manchester Juries; and above all from Manchester Magistrates!'[1]

In neighbouring Liverpool, with the Earl of Sefton in the chair, the Rev. William Shepherd, the dissenting minister, left his study of Italian literature to denounce the happenings in Manchester and those responsible:

. . . They were now assembled,' he said, 'round the graves of their slaughtered countrymen. They were now met to consider the propriety of addressing the Prince Regent, and of imploring inquiry into the melancholy events of the 16th of August. As for the Manchester magistrates, it might be worth while to consider who and what they were. First came the Rev. Mr. Hay and Mr. Norris, justices who received wages for their magisterial services. These stipendiary magistrates were a foul excrescence on the body politic, were unknown to the British Constitution, and borrowed from the tyrannic system of ancient France. (cheers) Mr. Hay might have some sympathy with the

[1] *Manchester Observer,* 30 October 1819.

Reformers; for he thinks that 'there is something rotten in the State of Denmark'. Yes, gentlemen, he is extremely discontented, as I am informed, with the smallness of his salary. (loud laughter). He only receives the insignificant sum of £500 for four journeys in the year to Manchester, deems this sum sadly too small for his valuable services (laughter) and thinks it would be a noble reform to raise it from £500 to £800 a year. (cheers). The rest of the Bench consisted of retired manufacturers, who, like candle-snuffers at the theatre, were used to eke out the fag-end of a procession. What would they think of one of them, who, though a leading man among these sapient justices, had sat many years on the Bench before he knew that a potato was a vegetable? (laughter continued) . . .[1]

The Rev. Dr Drake, vicar of Rochdale, was still above ground receiving his emoluments in August, 1819, only to depart this life in September. The Rev. Mr Hay, in October, was still four months away from receiving his 'reward' for his activities on 16 August. In the meantime, he had to be content with satirical castigations from Mr Shepherd, author of *Every Man his own Parson* (1791), or *The Fatal Effects of Religious Intolerance* (1816).

The press in the Rev. Mr Shepherd's Liverpool added its own tribute:

'Priest, butcher, and chairman, and patron of spies,
He slays and he preaches, he tries and he lies;
For a sermon, a charge, or a tale of a tub,
Who shall vie with this reverend political scrub?
No wonder such merit succeeds; 'tis but giving
The wages of labour, when —— gets a living.'
—*Liverpool Mercury*, 11 February, 1820.

Mr Hay, however, was probably more concerned with unpublished tributes to his probity, of which the following is an example:

Dear Sir—I hereby give you notice that it is in contemplation to pop you off between this and the next Sessions, and that arrangements are made for that purpose.

Your motions are closely watched, and as soon as an opportunity offers, a Ball will be sent through your head. I would not be the hand to do it, but would *glory* in hearing of an *arbitrary* scoundrel *being levelled with the dust*. The fittest place for all Rascals who tread upon the *rights* of the *people*, and set all Laws human and divine at defiance.

This will be a glorious day, and thousands will rejoice and be glad. It is contemplated with pleasure and is sure and certain to be performed to the glory of the Lord and the thanksgiving of thousands. I write merely that you *set your house in order, and pray to God* to forgive your lawless conduct. He that

[1] *Manchester Observer*, 9 October 1819.

inflicts without Law shall also suffer without Law and remorse. The DEED
may be considered as DONE. A friend to Order.

Rev. Mr. Hay, Manchester . . .[1]

To distil their full flavour contemporary documents and contemporary opinions should not be taken out of their context. John
Doherty is seen[2] in 1830 as 'at the heart of the great movements of the
northern workers for general unionism, factory reform, co-operative
organization, and "national regeneration" ' ; Doherty saw in 1827 Mr
Hay, as a:

. . . magistrate who, he said, in the bloody tragedy of Peterloo caused a
drunken and infuriated body of soldiers to cut down the people and drench
the streets with their blood. This man, he added, after murdering his fellow-
subjects—murdering them in open day, had been preferred to a clergyman's
dignity with £2000 a year, instead of being sent to India with Oliver and
Castles.[3]

Henry Hunt paid a visit to Rochdale during the election campaigns
in August, 1832. He asked his audience how far Parson Hay lived from
where they were meeting, and on being told about a quarter of a mile,
he said: 'Let us give a shout that will make him shake in his chair!' A
shout, reported the *Manchester Guardian*,[4] was accordingly set up; but
it was a very feeble one. It was too late to intimidate Mary, the wife of
the Rev. William Robert Hay who had died on the 18 February, 1832.
Canon Raines,[5] tells us that Mrs Hay once observed:

That she entirely agreed with a gentleman who had just left the vicarage, that
Manchester was built on a *volcano*, and that the time would certainly arrive
when the *reform mania* would produce its legitimate results in the over-throw
of society, in general plunder and universal despotism!

The reaction to the events of 16 August had, it seemed, produced 'reactionary' prejudices. Seldom, it may be argued, were they more
justifiably formulated.

The nation shewed no loss of appetite for knowing what had occurred
on St Peter's Field; in that free-for-all period they did not lack in-
formants. One gave them his

*Manchester Massacre!! An Authentic Narrative of the Magisterial and Yeomanry
Massacre at Manchester; with Remarks on the Illegal Conduct of the Magistrates in*

[1] Eng. MS. 1197/50, J.R.L.
[2] Thompson, p. 774.
[3] *Wheeler's Manchester Chronicle*, 1 September 1827.
[4] *Manchester Guardian*, 1 September 1832.
[5] *Vicars of Rochdale* (Chetham Society, N.S., II Pt II, p. 319).

suppressing the Meeting, and their proceedings towards Mr. Hunt; also anecdotes of the Yeomanry Cavalry and Police; Biography of the Magistrates. London: John Fairburn. pp. 48.

A succinct 'history' of the events leading up to 16 August was given at p. 6:

Nothing would do. The people felt their power. They saw that justice and humanity, without violence, must ultimately triumph. They met at Stockport, Birmingham, Manchester, Leeds, and almost in every other part of the kingdom. Every account bore testimony of their unprecedented sufferings; matchless patience; peaceable, constitutional and enlightened deportment. Their enemies foresaw the result, and were sorely afraid. They were taunted, ridiculed, and stimulated; but still the Reformers would not turn from their object; their patience seemed to increase with the provocations they received. Then it was that the rage of their oppressors increased tenfold; it was turned into madness; they could neither *cajole* nor force them into *outrage*; and the memorable struggle, in which the people were determined to observe the law, and their opponents that they should violate it, ended in the bloody field of St. Peter's.

We have endeavoured to find some parallel to this sanguinary deed. We have thought of all we have read. We have thought of all the crimes of fanatic zeal, civil strife, and ruthless war. We have thought of the murderous Sylla, who butchered six thousand Romans in cold blood; but then he had conquered them in battle, and besides, it was in the midst of a furious civil war. We have thought of the bloody Bartholomew; but then it was religion maddened into frenzy; and, besides, the horrid deed was not perpetrated in open day, but in the shades of night. We thought of all the unfortunate excesses of the French; but then they had long suffered, their rights had long been withheld, and, besides, they were enraged at the base traitors who fled their country to introduce foreign hordes to extinguish their rising liberties and glory. In short, we could find no parallel; when we reflect that 100,000 persons were assembled—lawfully and peaceably assembled—in open day—without arms—accompanied with nothing but emblems of peace—dressed as for some village holiday—suspecting no harm—anticipating no danger; when we reflect that this immense assemblage—congregated in one mass—men, women, and children—all at once—without notice or alarm of any kind, was attacked, and indiscriminately butchered; and when we reflect that thirteen magistrates, three of them ministers of religion, which breathes nothing but humanity, sworn to preserve the peace and life of the meanest citizen, could assemble, in a conspicuous place, to arrange, execute, and behold the murderous scene; we say, when we reflect on all these circumstances, that the cowardly, lawless, and inhuman massacre of Manchester is unparalleled in history.

The editor then quoted Tyas, and the *Chester Chronicle*, which report, incidentally quoted the 'charge' of the Yeomanry as 'instantly made a passage and surrounded the hustings'. Carlile's eye-witness account cleared away any doubts which might have arisen from the former extracts. Details of the imprisonment of the captives, and of the Rev. Mr Hay's departure for London:

. . . This reverend gentleman, after complimenting the calico heroes for their brilliant exploits on the memorable day, immediately posted to London, with the first intelligence of the glorious victory of Peterloo. His object, most probably, as is usual in such cases, was to reap some new honour; probably an archdeaconry, or even a bishopric. Whatever might be his motive, he appeared to have been disappointed, and retired to his seat in Wakefield.

The magistrates were overjoyed with their captures, that they appeared at first entirely at a loss how to make the most of them. Sedition was at first thought of; but then that only subjected the offenders to fine and imprisonment. Rioting indeed was a good thing, but then perhaps it might be commuted into transportation. Justice *Hulton* seemed to fix his mind on murder; that was hanging to be sure without mercy. But even this was not enough. So at last our wiseacres determined to satisfy themselves with *High Treason*. The crime seemed quite to their minds, because it embraced every kind of punishment—hanging, quartering, beheading, digging out the bowels, burning, and, in fine, every thing they could wish or desire. We shall be rather particular in our account of the examinations. They are very important for many reasons: first, because they show what sort of persons are in the *commission of the peace*. We would not, however, have it taken for our opinion, that all Justices of the Peace are such egregious coxcombs as Justice Hulton; nor that they are all as grossly ignorant as Justice Trafford, who did not know the difference betwixt a fee and a fine on a recognizance; nor do we think, on an average, they are as ridiculously insolent and overbearing as Justice Norris.

Secondly, these examinations show how pernicious a thing a little power is in the hands of men whose characters exemplify the most intolerable pride and ignorance, united with a total insensibility to the sufferings of the people. Thirdly, they will show what a foolish thing it would be for the people of England to suffer Justices of the Peace, indiscriminately, on the authority of Lord Sidmouth's circular, to hold to bail for libel; a crime which the wisest men in the kingdom cannot define. Lastly, they will exhibit a singular contrast of the talents, and virtues of the *Radical Reformers*, accused of being illiterate, vicious, and visionary, with the mild Christian virtues, brilliant endowments, refined eduction, of the loudest and most vehement champions of the National Church, the Monarchy, and the Constitution, *as by law established*.

[A footnote added] 'after Parson Hay had completed his mission, and brought the doleful intelligence that the Reformers were neither to be drawn, quartered, burnt, nor have their bowels taken out, nor even hanged, according to the particular desire of *Dandy* Hulton'* (*'better known by the name of Miss Hulton—'the glass of fashion and mould of form in Lancashire') 'This was grievous intelligence surely. We hear no more of Parson Hay after his return from London. Having witnessed the cutting and slashing of the 16th, he seemed to have no relish for the tame things likely to follow.'[1]

It would be vain to argue that the foregoing was devoid of truth; it contained a very pertinent truth. It was, that there was a crime which the wisest men in the kingdom, then, could not define!

In this post-16 August festival of invective and denunciation, tempered sometimes with indignation, there was a rather belated contribution not reported until February, 1820. It shows, amongst other things, how ineffective was the Government's attempt to placate the torrent of criticism by its efforts in Parliament in November. The Prince Regent's 'over assertive' letter had not only failed to convince the Common Council of the City of London that they were not correctly informed; it had failed to convince his own Royal brother! The *Manchester Observer*[2] reported that at the Norfolk Fox Dinner. (Charles James Fox, of course,) H.R.H. the Duke of Sussex proposed a toast to the Norfolk Yeomanry:

. . . It was not the gallant Yeomanry of Norfolk who would have galloped into a peaceable meeting assembled for peaceable purposes, there to cut down men, women, and children. Neither were there in Norfolk, Magistrates who would have given orders to such an effect; and if they had been given, the Yeomanry of Norfolk would have paused before they executed them . . .

To the Manchester loyalists, Royal castigation must have seemed the last straw.

[1] *Manchester Massacre*, p, 32.
[2] *Manchester Observer*, 5 February 1820.

XIX

The Loyalist Case and Radical Reactions

Archibald Prentice's *Historical Sketches and Personal Recollections of Manchester* (2nd edn 1851) has been called[1] invaluable as a general study 'providing a framework for more unprejudiced investigation'. It is most certainly that. Prentice, conscious of all the scurrility reproduced here could write in 1851:

Reverend W. R. Hay, who was rewarded with a living of £2400 a year for his services in 'putting down' the Reformers; the Rev. C. W. Ethelston, whose reading of the Riot Act nobody even heard; Stipendiary Magistrate James Norris, who sought from government a power beyond the existing law; Hugh Hornby Birley, who led the attack upon a defenceless multitude; Joseph Nadin, who harshly apprehended those who were to be harshly punished under judge-made law;—all have gone to their graves, without an assault, without an insult . . .

We have suggested[2] that the time would come when the hollowness of the Huntean case would be revealed, as its props were struck away one by one by exposure and refutation. The rotten props of scurrility were soon kicked away by the later propagators of the radical version of events. Prentice gave the impression they had never existed. He says[3]:

No time was lost in endeavouring to create a prejudice in the minds of the public against those who were doomed to be victims of an arbitrary government, for in a few weeks[4] Francis Philips issued a pamphlet which he was pleased to entitle, 'An Exposure of the *Calumnies*[5] circulated by the Enemies of Social Order, against the Magistrates and the Yeomanry Cavalry of Manchester.' To counteract this slanderous production, an able work was written and compiled by the late John Edward Taylor, entitled 'Notes and Observations . . .' (1820) . . .

'No time was lost' says Prentice; a great deal of time was lost during

[1] Read, p. 225.
[2] See above, p. 207.
[3] *Recollections*, p. 178.
[4] Prentice had been writing about the November Parliamentary debates.
[5] The italics were Prentice's.

this post-Peterloo period in stating the magistrates' case, because they made *no* attempt at public justification at all:

. . . The good points, [says Dr. Read], on their side (and there were a few) were never heard, only the loud and repeated charges of their critics. Even those inclined to support the authorities regretted their silence. 'I think,' wrote Wilberforce, 'the magistrates have been unjust to themselves in not publishing what might be called their case. The bulk of the people will not forbear forming an opinion, because they are told that hereafter the grounds of a just opinion shall be supplied to them.' Even Bootle Wilbraham, the spokesman of the magistrates in the Commons, had to admit in 1821 that 'the country had, perhaps, been led to draw an inference unfavourable to the magistrates of Lancashire, on account of the silence they had thought proper to preserve'.[1]

This 'silence' was not, of course, observable amongst the magistrates' supporters in Manchester. The local loyalist press were most active in attempting to counteract the effects of the storm of criticism coming from other parts of the country. As early as 28 August the proprietors of *Aston's Exchange Herald* put out a small eight-page weekly publication *The Patriot*, which according to its original prospectus, contained 'Information on Political, Moral, Commercial, Agricultural, and Economical Subjects, combined with a due portion of Amusement'. It only lasted until just after the end of the year, and it is instructive to note that by the time the bound volume appeared its title-page read '*The Patriot*: a periodical publication intended to arrest the progress of Seditious and Blasphemous Opinions, too prevalent in the year 1819'. At the beginning its tone was mild and benevolent, breathing sweet reasonableness, in the manner of a parish magazine. Even in October when the clamour from without was at its height it did not depart from its measured language. One, 'Civis' wrote:

I perceive by the daily accounts in the newspapers, that the most active exertions are making to assemble meetings in different parts of the country, for the purpose of censuring the conduct of the Manchester magistrates; and it is not without considerable surprise that I hear that these proceedings are sanctioned by some persons of real weight and importance. The conduct of the magistrates must now undoubtedly become the subject of legal investigation; and the justice of the concluding paragraph in the Prince Regent's firm and manly reply to the Common Council of London, I should have thought, must be clear to the meanest apprehension, that under such circumstances the premature establishment of an extra-judicial enquiry is contrary to the clearest principles of public justice.

[1] Read, p. 181.

The magistrates themselves, it is clear, are prevented by a due regard to the dignity of their office from appearing personally before any other than two tribunals; one of which, the Prince and his advisers, they have already so thoroughly satisfied as to the legality and propriety of their conduct, as to have received their public thanks; and before the other they will ere long appear to receive that descision which a Jury of their country may think proper to award. In the meantime, since it is evident that attempts are making with the most zealous and unceasing perseverance to prepossess and prejudice the minds of the people by statements sometimes partial and exaggerated, and sometimes altogether false, it becomes necessary that we should endeavour to counteract these unfair and illiberal attempts, by truly stating and candidly investigating the circumstances of the case[1] . . .

In later issues *The Patriot* was further incensed by the 'attempt' to 'excite a general odium against this highly respectable [Yeomanry cavalry] corps':

. . . To disprove a general and sweeping assertion is always a very difficult and tedious task: but whenever their calumniators have ventured to state any specific instances of cruelty, they have met with instant refutation. All the respectable inhabitants of the town who were present on the occasion, agree in declaring that the yeomanry did not use their swords until they had been attacked by repeated vollies of stones and brickbats. They then charged the mob . . . It was with a view of protecting their [the magistrates'] characters from that ungenerous and unjust calumny with which it has been attempted to overwhelm them, that I have been induced to enter into an examination of the proceedings of 16th August; and I trust that I have not unsuccessfully endeavoured to . . . &c.

'Civis' fell into only one error; he attempted to justify the military. As the Prince Regent retorted to the London Common Council, 'he was not rightly informed'. The magistrates' case, stated and re-stated, was that they had no intention to disperse the meeting by force. 'Civis' was under the impression they intended, however, to 'disperse' the meeting. 'To attempt to disperse such an immense assembly . . . by means of a few hundreds of special constables would evidently have been ridiculous and absurd. . . .' 'Civis' was not a magistrate writing under a *nom de plume*; he was therefore quite entitled to conclude that what he had written:

. . . justifies us in placing the fullest confidence in their future exertions for the preservation of public peace; and entitles them to the countenance of every well-disposed inhabitant of this town, and to the gratitude of the country at large.

[1] *The Patriot*, No. 7, 9 October 1819.

The Patriot was preaching to the converted, and its impact on public opinion was probably very small, and confined to the Manchester area. It is, however, an important piece of evidence in assessing that August–December 1819 scene in Manchester. It proves that there was no guilt-complex amongst those who were defending the magistrates. It became, in fact, a casualty of one of the Parliamentary measures which that turbulent age had brought into being. With the passing of the Six Acts it ceased to exist. To the end, however, it maintained its stand:

The steadiness with which these calumniated persons have borne in silence the unmerited reproaches heaped upon them, rather than injure the public service or interrupt the course of public justice by an authorised refutation of the charge, will doubtless be remembered as no small addition to the claim they have upon the gratitude of the nation.

The tide of public indignation has already turned against the really guilty —those unprincipled incendiaries, who having inflamed the minds of the populace, and urged them into illegal acts which involved them in danger and punishment, have since contrived by ceaseless calumnies, and measured falsehoods, to avert the scorn and abhorrence of the nation from their own heads, upon those by whom their villainies have been detected and their success prevented.[1]

Gradually the indignation of the loyalist sympathisers grew, as they realized that men, and seemingly otherwise fair-minded men at that, could believe what they apparently did believe. On 4 September, *Wheeler's Manchester Chronicle* wrote as follows:

The calumnious violence with which circumstances relating to the meeting . . . are treated by the public press is much to be regretted. Magistrates, men of the most pure minds, and certain portions of the Military who acted on the above day only to benefit their Country, are dealt with in the most slanderous manner. The Manchester Yeomanry come in for more than ordinary proportion of every kind of insinuation, and direct charges also, that can tend to degrade men in the eyes of an Englishman. That they have received the high sanction of the Prince Regent, who has declared that they have done their duty to his satisfaction, and with humanity, is at present attempted to be held as nothing. Certain of His Royal Highness's subjects contend, that they can form a more correct conclusion. Hence the most painful suggestions are thrown out; and the personal friends of Hunt have gone the length of having posted on the walls of the town, in large characters, language of a terrible description against the Yeomanry, for having performed a painful yet important duty.

The object of these endeavours is too obvious to require explanation. That

[1] *The Patriot* No. 16, 11 December 1819.

assertions are made without due regard to truth cannot be doubted, and this is even scarcely denied by those very prints which have been most zealous in propagating the slanders . . .

The report is worth quoting because it shows that some attempts were made to scotch the rumours, or allegations, at the source. How successful they were remains a moot point; they did not convince John Edward Taylor, nor did they convince the country, whatever their effect in Manchester. The report went on:

The conduct of these persons has not been confined to endeavouring to traduce a so loyal and constitutional force as the Yeomanry. They have attempted to 'damn with false praise' the Regular Troops stationed here, thereby wishing to create a belief amongst their own vitiated admirers, and to extend the belief to the country in general, that whilst the Voluntary Cavalry exceeded their duty, the Regular Troops did *less* than theirs. Let such men neither deceive themselves, nor mislead those whose credulity they would turn to the worst and most *interested* of purposes . . . [the impossibility of swerving a British soldier from his allegiance] . . . Truth is a very soberminded quality, and must ultimately prevail. Investigations are to ensue which will draw out complete evidence. By that men must stand or fall. In the meantime it is not quite consistent with the true notions of British justice to condemn parties who cannot yet have an opportunity of being fully heard. Clamour, in such a case, can only be characterised as vulgar abuse. [Copy of placard]:

> Whereas on the 16th of August, an individual who was present at the Area of St. Peter's Church, was attacked by one of the Manchester and Salford Yeomanry, and severely cut in the hand by the sabre, and also received a sabre wound in the elbow; and, after several unsuccessful cuts at his head, was wounded in the brow by the same Yeoman; the name of the Yeoman not being known, one of the Hussars, who addressed him in the following manly language: 'You bloody rascal, that's murder: if you do as much again, I will split you down!' is requested to forward a communication to Mr. Charles Pearson, solicitor, at Mr. Johnson's, Shude Hill, in order that means may be taken to identify the Yeoman in question; and the Hussar will receive the grateful thanks of the individual who is indebted to his protection for the preservation of his life.—J. Wroe, printer, *Manchester Observer*

In consequence of the appearance of so scandalous a publication, [the report went on] every individual soldier of the 15th Light Dragoons was ordered out on parade by their commander Lieut.-Col. Dalrymple, and the bill read to them. Any one of them who might have used the above expressions was desired to stand forward, and explain the circumstances stated in it. A sufficient pause of time was then allowed for the purpose, but no one did come forward, and there cannot be a doubt of the whole being a false statement.[1] Perhaps it was too much to hope that any man would stand forward; and, perhaps as well, it was too much to claim that the man's not standing forward proved that it was a false statement. There is, however, no indication in the comment of a loyalist guilty conscience; on the contrary there is the sense of dismay that some should think as they did, and an implied certitude that truth would eventually prevail.

Another comment[2] before Parliamentary explanations began to be made, on the uncertainty caused by the absence of an 'official version':

Mr. Buxton's house commands a complete view of the ground, and the magistrates were assembled in an upper room, to observe the meeting, and to direct the necessary proceedings. Most of these gentlemen being highly respectable in private character, their veracity would be relied on, if they would come forward and state, when and by whom the Riot Act was read, and whether the early dispersion of the meeting by the Yeomanry and regulars was not owing to some mistake; because the confusion that ensued, exposed to danger the special constables equally with the Radicals and spectators . . .

Another letter to the same paper: 'To the Radical Reformers of Manchester and Neighbourhood'[3] seemed to get nearer to a true view of the situation than any other:

It is very difficult for you to consider the events that have lately taken place with coolness and impartiality. But, as men who profess public principles, and who declare, that they are actuated by a pure love of liberty, it becomes you to take a dispassionate view of the circumstances which led to the dreadful scenes of the 16th of August.

You assembled that day to state your opinion of national grievances: and the manner in which these grievances should be redressed. You marched in military order with banners flying, and presented a formidable picture of the discontented state of the country. This appearance intimidated the weak minded; and it is asserted that numbers of respectable individuals made affidavits to the magistrates, that they apprehended riots, and consequent destruction of property.

I am no apologist for the conduct of the magistrates. Had the outrage commenced on the part of the Reformers, it was their bounden duty to repress it; if it did not, and if the Yeomanry Cavalry did, previously to the reading of the Riot Act, and in the manner required by the law itself, trample upon the people, and wound the inoffending inhabitants, then, their conduct will certainly undergo a severe scrutiny; and their countrymen will severely condemn it. In the meantime, by the regard you have for the laws of your

1 *Wheeler's Manchester Chronicle*, 4 September 1819.
2 *Manchester Gazette*, 13 November.
3 *Manchester Gazette*, 25 September.

country, which have *hitherto* protected you, abstain from all purposes of revenge and recrimination. It was the passion of fear which led to the perpetration of cruelty. The inhabitants of Manchester were terrified by your formidable appearance. They instigated the magistrates to the measures that were pursued. But the conduct of the magistrates will be brought before the bar of public opinion.

The People of England will not coolly submit to the exercise of military despotism, as you have seen from what is passing in London, Westminster, and Southwark. The affair of the 16th of August will undergo Parliamentary inquiry; and the voice of the nation will be heard through their representatives. It is not by violence that you will obtain the sympathy of your countrymen. Violence, on your part, will have no effect but to justify the conduct of the magistrates: it will intimidate all honest, all cautious, and all well-meaning men. For however they may feel for your injuries, they would wish the law, and not yourselves, to redress them.

Reverence for the laws should be a sacred principle with the friends of freedom. If you are not governed by law you must necessarily be governed by *force*.

Return peaceably to your professions. Trust your cause to the influence of public opinion. Take no part in the quarrel, except in an appeal to justice. You are misled by flatterers, who inflame your passions, and make you distrust the wholesome and constitutional safeguards of your liberty. The freedom of the Press, and Trial by Jury, and not the desperate counsels of theoretical politicans, will best secure you against oppression. I am, your Friend, and the Friend of Parliamentary Reform, Aristides.

There were Members of Parliament who tried to seek out the truth by inquiries on the spot. George Lamb's unbelief with regard to his learned friend, James Norris, has already been referred to. J. G. Bennet, M.P. for Shrewsbury, was also in Manchester before the November debates; he may have been over-influenced by the denunciations in most of the newspapers of the dastardly magistrates of Manchester:

'Can you give me an account of the *character* and *situation* of the Magistrates who signed Hunt's warrant?' he asked John Shuttleworth, the radical leader, in a letter on November 18th.[1]

It is not believed that his inquiry got very far.

The 'slanderous publication' referred to by Prentice was Francis Philips's *Exposure of the Calumnies* . . . which appeared in November, 1819. Perhaps because it was 'slated' by John Edward Taylor almost immediately on its appearance, and treated by later commentators in the manner of Prentice, it has always been dubbed as biased, a defence of the indefensible, and damned with faint praise. Bruton called it 'an

[1] Read, p. 168.

able pamphlet', and then practically ignored it. Dr Read calls it 'well argued within the limits of the "loyalist" case, but an occasional bluster has to do service for logical argument'. Most have probably accepted Hunt's dictum,[1] that Philips was 'a man who has done more falsely to prejudice this case perhaps than any other man in the country. . . .'

Philips had every reason to use the word Calumnies. Taylor[2] remarked on Philips's passage on the 'depraved licentiousness of the press', that it involved 'matters of opinion quite as much as fact', and for that reason 'I shall not notice [it]'. Philips had written:

. . . Nothing we can conceive, can possibly be more indecent, ungenerous, and unjust, than the rash and malignant charges which have been made against gentlemen of the highest respectability and most unblemished character, upon no better ground than the incorrect and exaggerated statements which have appeared in the public newspapers, the violent aspersions contained in seditious libels, or the very questionable testimony of those who are notoriously the authors and abettors of every public tumult.

Whatever indulgence we might be disposed to allow to the conscious exercise of private opinion, we cannot but consider as utterly unwarrantable and presumptious the unmerited obloquy and abuse which have been so intemperately lavished upon our highly respected magistrates, by public bodies of men expressly convened for this purpose in various parts of the Empire . . . [The justification for their action] . . . and it will be obvious to every one who gives the subject a calm and dispassionate attention, that the Magistrates, and others of our fellow-townsmen, who have been so wantonly assailed with insult and abuse, are solely withheld from vindicating themselves from these calumnious aspersions by a firm and magnanimous sense of public duty, by a determination not to suffer any personal feelings of injury and insult to betray them into those premature disclosures which might defeat the salutary ends of public justice.[3]

Philips's use of English was already in 1819 twenty years out of date, but he acknowledged his unworthiness for the task he had undertaken. He had travelled round the country, he said, and had been able to counteract some of the criticism, but had been asked again and again why the facts of the magistrates' case were withheld from the public. He had replied:

. . . That it would be derogatory to the dignity of the Magistrates, who felt in the fullest degree the consciousness of rectitude, who had received the unanimous thanks of a most respectable and numerous meeting [in Manchester] and the approbation of their Sovereign, to descend to a defence of

[1] *State Trials*, p. 305.
[2] *Observations*, p. 178.
[3] Philips, p. xxiii.

their conduct. [But could not someone, he was asked, do it for them?] I felt the just reproof; I regretted extremely that no one more competent had engaged in the undertaking, and determined to employ my first leisure moments in the defence of truth and justice.

His gallant effort was announced for publication on 4 November: 'two shillings per copy (twelve for twenty shillings); profits arising to be given to the Manchester Infirmary'. A second edition was out before the year was ended, but Philips still possessed copies twelve years later and sent one to Lord Althorp—then Chancellor of the Exchequer—to give him the 'true facts'. Lord Althorp, in 1819, was a back-bencher opposed to the Ministry, amongst that Opposition which all the measured eloquence of Lords Liverpool, Castlereagh, and Sidmouth, and George Canning failed to impress. The whole weight of that combined oratory—and it was formidable—could not budge the balance of that 'dreadful fact' lying heavily on the other side of the scales. It is no wonder that Francis Philips failed, where others so much more talented were to fail. Lord Sidmouth gave up in despair, and busied himself with his defences in the form of the Six Acts. Philips might be compared to Dame Partington with her Mop (five years before her time), who was 'excellent at a slop or puddle, but should never have meddled with a tempest'. The 'explanations' of the Ministers did not convince; the dossier of incriminating documents flung down on to the table of the House of Commons did not convince either, documents which have come down through history as *Papers Relative to the Internal State of the Country presented to both Houses of Parliament, by command of His Royal Highness The Prince Regent, November, 1819.*

In Manchester, with the Government's dossier before him, with the extensive reports of the Parliamentary debates just concluded, and Philips's *Exposure* at his finger-tips, doubting John Edward Taylor turned his incisive mind to a refutation of almost every facet of what had been revealed by the 'official version' of events.[1] Taylor would, surely, have been surprised to know that 'history' would credit his 'version' of the happenings of that day, sent off with such haste on the night of 16 August, as having overtaken the official version which he was then studying. He never made, so far as can be discovered, any such claim. But Prentice did. Prentice said (p. 160):

It was known that some ['some' equalled two] of the reporters who were on the hustings, amongst them Mr. Tyas, of the London *Times*, when the sanguinary attack was made upon the assembled multitude, had been taken into

[1] (Taylor, J. E.) *Notes and Observations . . . on the Papers . . .* [and] *A Reply to Mr. Francis Philips* 8vo, pp. xvi + 206, Manchester: 1820.

custody, and it was feared that no relation of the events would reach London, except what might be sent by directions of the magistracy, and coloured to justify their conduct. Mr. John Edward Taylor undertook to write to one London paper that evening, and I to another. Our narratives appeared in print on the following day, and bearing greater internal evidence of truth, they received credence in preference to the accounts sent to government and the government press, and raised a strong feeling of indignation which was deepened in intensity, and spread to all parts of the kingdom, when the reporter of the *Times* rescued from durance, corroborated all our statements and added details of still deeper atrocity than those which we had described . . .

Prentice does not say to which London newspapers their reports were sent.

For the first time, new light was thrown on what had transpired between the magistrates and the Home Office in the days before Peterloo, by the publication of the magistrates' correspondence. There was, these seemed to prove, no intention to disperse the meeting by force; there was detailed evidence of the drilling. Most important, however, was the report under the signature of W. R. Hay, written on the night of 16 August. Taylor had the whole of the Government's dossier reprinted, turned his penetrating criticism on Hay's report, on Norris's eve-of-Peterloo letter to the Government, and, finally, gave a blistering commentary on Philips's *Exposure*. The result was the most formidable, and seemingly unanswerable indictment of the Government and magistrates in all the Peterloo canon.

First, it should be emphasised, there were certain things which Taylor did not believe. He did not believe there had been, that there could possibly have been, any aggression from the people. He was intensely sceptical on the alleged reading of the Riot Act; but he could not accept a 'blanket' indictment of the magistrates, nor even of all of the Yeomanry, pinning his faith on the suggestion that a few fanatics amongst the Yeomanry had been the main culprits. What he does not say is that he had modified his first (or his paper's first) impression of the Yeomanry actually 'hacking their way up the hustings' to something less incriminating. As we have seen he never used the word 'massacre'—a word then being freely bandied about—but he implies criminal negligence on the part of the magistrates. His comments are worth quoting in extenso:

. . . That I write under circumstances of considerable restraint, will be sufficiently obvious.[1] It is an ungracious task, at all times, publicly to blame

[1] He was perhaps the only journalist in the country at that time who did.

those who are our neighbours and fellow-townsmen; but at the present time to start a doubt of the humanity, of the prudence, of the impartiality, of the constitutional spirit, or of the sound judgment, of the magistrates, will almost be held seditious. However nauseous and fulsome the adulation which may be offered as incense to their vanity, it may yet be imprudent to reply to it; and when the rage of political hostility has instigated human passions to a deep and stern vibration, the 'small, still voice of truth' prompting to manly and independent investigation, is scarcely ever heard amid the storm. . . .

The comments which I have made upon the parliamentary documents will exhibit my opinion of the conduct of some of the magistrates in individual cases. [Mainly on Hay and Norris. qv.] With respect, specifically to the transactions of the 16th of August, it is generally understood, and I am assured it is capable of proof, (though for that I do not pledge myself) that there was considerable difference of opinion amongst the magistrates themselves, as to the propriety of calling in the military *unless some actual breach of the peace were committed*.[1] Certainly, my estimation of the character of some individuals amongst them has been very erroneous, if the deeds of that day received their *unanimous* approbation.

But, however, that fact may be, that there are amongst the magistrates, individuals of the most violent political character—men, who are most unwilling to concede to those who differ from them the liberty of manifesting their opinions, and sometimes use language on the bench more fit for the orgies of a Pitt Club—is beyond dispute . . .[2]

Taylor here made one of the most damaging references ever to be made to the magistrates. It concerned the Rev C. W. Ethelston, the clerical magistrate who read the Riot Act, who was one of the signatories to the warrant arresting Hunt, but who was not one of the Select Committee of Magistrates. Mr Ethelston's language on the bench was: 'I believe you are a downright blackguard reformer. Some of you reformers ought to be hanged, and some of you are sure to be hanged—the rope is already round your necks.'[3] Both Mr Thompson and Dr Read use the reference. The former puts it in this context:

. . . A writer in the *Manchester Observer* in the week before Peterloo addressed the 'official gentlemen of Manchester': 'I defy the bloodthirsty partisans of Danton, Marat, Robespierre, to furnish a more despotic, tyrannical crew.' A month after Peterloo a clerical magistrate afforded himself the privilege of the Bench to address the accused: [Quotation, as above].[4]

---

[1] What Taylor refused to believe—because it had already been stated in the House of Commons by this time—was that the constables had refused point blank to make the arrests without military support.

[2] *Observations*, p. 171.

[3] Ibid.

[4] Thompson, p. 685.

Dr Read, after giving a short biographical account of Mr Ethelston, says:

As a magistrate he was very easily alarmed, and during the Peterloo period he seems to have believed everything told him by his spies, whom he employed on a large scale. [giving a Home Office reference for the foregoing.] In spite of his cloth he showed little Christian charity towards the Radical Reformers: 'Some of you reformers ought to be hanged', he told two of them brought before him for drilling in 1819, 'and some of you are sure to be hanged—the rope is already round your necks.'[1]

What Taylor did not mention were the circumstances in which Ethelston's outburst was made. Dr Read says they were radical reformers brought before the magistrate for 'drilling'. The accused, one David Kay, was not being charged with drilling, but with [a] murderous attack on Murray at White Moss during the weekend before the fateful Monday. *Wheeler's Manchester Chronicle* (2 October 1819) reported:

David Kay was apprehended on Wednesday se'night, and brought to the New Bayley, under an escort of two Dragoons, charged with being engaged in a violent assault at White Moss on the morning preceding August 16th.

The *Manchester Observer* (2 October) reported that Kay denied that he had struck the complainant, but did not deny that he was at the meeting. The *Observer* reporter then wrote that the complainant was 'a person whose name we could not hear'. A quick reference to their files might have helped them, for they had reported gleefully on 21 August that Murray, 'after his arrival home, was visited by no less than four surgeons, who declared that his brain was not affected; the skull, it seems, was proof even to *clogs*. . . .'[2] Taylor, in making this reference, forbore giving a primary local source for this case—which surely would have been put into its proper context by a Manchester paper; his 'authority' is *The Times*, of 27 September. Even the *Manchester Observer* put its animadversions on the case in its context. If *The Times* did, Taylor did not say so.

Taylor continued his indictment of the magistrates:

. . . That there are some, whose circumstances render it but too probable that they look to the good things at the disposal of Ministers as the reward of their devoted services, is also undeniable. [Taylor here added a footnote, referring to though not naming, William Hulton] One of this class of worshipful persons, to whose name the epithet 'Miss' is frequently affixed, and who a few years ago gave an excellent specimen of the correctness of his taste,

[1] Read, p. 77.
[2] See above, p. 144.

by *quoting Greek to a Manchester Pitt Club*, hit upon a notable expedient for putting down Mr. Hunt. He proposed to take him into custody, on his return from Lancaster, as a *vagrant*, on the ground that he had *no visible means of subsistence*; to confine him seven days in the New Bayley, flog him, and pass him out of the parish. His colleagues, however, were not quite so far gone as to fall in with his plan.[1]

Taylor was seemingly somewhat at a loss to find evidence of malignancy in Hulton. Hulton's quotation, probably from an old Statute book, of the method adopted to deal with vagrants during the seventeenth century hardly deserved notice, made, as it must have been, sardonically. Hulton remained the butt of Taylor's sarcasm for many years after 1819. Hulton once referred to himself as 'one of the foolish country squires' who had been mentioned in some article. Taylor for ever after dubbed him the 'self-styled foolish squire'. Taylor's indictment went on:

That there are some, the avowed founders and patrons of Orange societies, the organizers and supporters of a system of *espionage* of extent far greater, and of consequence more tremendous, than in any other district in the kingdom, is also too true; whilst that there are *any* distinguished for the possession of clear and comprehensive judgment, of sound constitutional information, of liberal and enlightened opinions, of superior acquired knowledge, or of great natural talents, I have yet to learn.

The 'founders and patrons of Orange Societies' was a direct reference to Col. Ralph Fletcher of Bolton. Whatever part Col. Fletcher might have taken in the Luddite troubles several years before, he was in 1819 playing only a minor part. The incident[2] in which Col. Fletcher figured, near the hustings during the mêlée, was well known to Taylor, for he had studied the Oldham inquest proceedings; the incident could not be further exploited.

But though there can be no doubt [Taylor went on] that the magistrates sanctioned the proceedings of the 16th of August, I am inclined to believe, that it is not to them that we are to look, as the original instigators of the tragedy of that day. There is a committee appointed, I know not how, and consisting of I know not whom; but which arrogates to itself the title of the 'Committee to Strengthen the Civil Power'. Judging of this body from its conduct, I am led to believe that it consists principally of the waning remnant of the few apt successors of those whose bigotry and prejudices caused the riots of 1791 and 1792 . . .

Taylor then goes on at length on the operations of this committee,

[1] *Observations*, pp. 172–3.
[2] Pp. 217–18 above.

quotes some of its letters giving the names of both the secretary and the chairman, which appear plainly on the letters, and crediting them with alleged disruptive tactics to crab the 'public welcome' to Hunt after his preliminary appearances at Lancaster; tactics, which Taylor also admits could have been intended to help to preserve public order. He hints that members of this committee could have been the 'affidavit makers' on 16 August. He then discovered, after he had written his notes, that some of them were members of the Yeomanry.[1] He makes no charges, but only hints at the power of this 'secret' committee. In another part of his *Observations*, he refuses to believe in the vague accusations of a named Home Office 'informer'.[2] He says:

I must therefore, be excused for withholding my credit from the stories of the 'man from Oldham', and 'the tenants of a gentleman near this town', &c. If the poor are to be calumniated as they have been on such authority, and, on the credit of those calumnies, cut down,—God help them I say!

Which is not an inappropriate comment on Taylor's own fulminations on the Committee to Strengthen the Civil Power.

He continues:

With respect to the conduct of the Yeomanry on the 16th of August, I am decidedly of the opinion that considerable misapprehension has existed. That the greater part of the corps are actually incapable of acting with deliberate cruelty, it gives me pleasure to state my belief; but it is at the same time necessary to add, that by far the greater proportion of those cases, in which it is ascertained by what body of military wounds were inflicted, the Yeomanry Corps are named.[3]

It is hardly necessary to point out that *all* of the wounds, *all* of the sabrings and *all* of the tramplings, were inflicted by the Yeomanry; or at least that is what the Taylor/Prentice letter to *The Times* told the waiting nation on 19 August. The report was mistaken, of course, and corrected later, but that correction did not undo the damage done in the first place.

In order to account for this, it may be remarked, that they were first upon the field—they alone went up to the hustings, they alone took the flags and caps of liberty—and they alone were known to, and consequently can be identified by, the people. It is also beyond question, that there are in the corps individuals, whose political rancour approaches to absolute insanity; who before

---

[1] *Observations*, pp. 174–5.
[2] Taylor was commenting on the letter from J. Lloyd, of Stockport, already noticed above—pp. 145–6.
[3] *Observations*, pp. 175–6.

the meeting threatened what they would do; and who, reeking from the field, boasted of the feats they had achieved; who have openly avowed that their intention was to assassinate Mr. Hunt; and expressed their regret at not having effected their purpose.[1]

Taylor is here again in company with his own 'man from Oldham' and 'the tenants of a gentleman near this town'. A small point, but the Yeomanry did not alone take the flags and caps of liberty. Probably they were 'known' to a few people in that vast crowd, but they had certainly been the target for vituperation in the columns of the *Manchester Observer*, which had been avidly read by a great number of the crowd for weeks before Peterloo. It *was known* that there were in the radical ranks 'individuals, whose political rancour approaches to absolute insanity; who before the meeting threatened what they would do'—known because it was set out in cold print in the columns of the *Observer*, and had the writers in the *Observer* had such evidence concerning the Yeomanry in those weeks before Peterloo they would not have hesitated to print them. The 'intention to assassinate Mr Hunt' was vain boasting, before and after the event, because the Yeomanry had every opportunity.

It is not necessary, however, to grant Taylor's point that there might be such individuals amongst the Yeomanry; he grants it himself:

My decided opinion, therefore, is, that a few individuals inflicted all the wounds which have been attributed to the Yeomanry as a body. It is also true notwithstanding the extraordinary disclaimer of Col. Dalrymple[2] that in several instances both officers and privates of the Hussars did interfere to stop the carnage [He is assured of this by many persons vouching for it.]

Taylor never entertained the idea that a 'few individuals' such as he suggested could be found amongst the Yeomanry could, with equal logic, have been found amongst the crowd. He was 'saddened' by the reports of the forming and cheering of the Yeomanry outside Mr Buxton's house after the field was cleared.[3] A slightly different complexion was put on this incident by *Wheeler's Manchester Chronicle*.[4]

Only occasionally does Taylor allow his carefully formulated sentences to run riot. The one passage most untypical of his fair, meticulous style occurs where he is ridiculing Francis Philips's playing-down the small number of casualties[5] where he sardonically suggests that the

[1] *Observations*, pp. 175-6.
[2] The parade of all the men of the 15th Hussars—see above, p. 294.
[3] *Observations*, p. 176.
[4] See above, p. 226.
[5] Fully given on pp. 219-20 above.

Yeomanry could have done more damage by firing their pistols. Apparently sincerely seeking some explanation of the tragic events, he says:[1]

Had the people on the 16th of August committed any act of riot, the measure of dispersing them according to the form of law, would have excited no disapprobation; but when they had done nothing obnoxious to the known laws on one hand, nor were the provisions of the law, which would have operated in their favour, observed on the other, it is not to be wondered, that the public mind should be revolted by the treatment to which they were subjected . . . That the magistrates, who acted on the 16th of August have not obtained the approbation of persons [who believe in the rule of law administered without prejudice and passion] must be admitted by all; nor can I conceive that any circumstances will be developed, either on the trial of Mr. Hunt, or upon any other occasion, which as it respects them, shall convert 'censure into praise, and detestation into gratitude'; or which, indeed, shall operate any change in the matured and deliberate judgment of the public at large.

Taylor, in using the words 'convert censure into praise and detestation into gratitude' was paraphrasing Philips; but he only paraphrased part of the quotation. In his pompous style Philips had written:

And is it possible that the Magistrates and other Public Functionaries, who so well deserved, and who received the thanks of Government, and of their fellow-townsmen, can at once change their nature and their character? Can humanity at once become barbarity? Can wisdom become folly, and prudence insanity?

Blush for your credulity all ye, who have listened to the slanderous falsehoods, so industriously circulated by the vilest of the vile; recall your hasty judgment; await with patience, till *all* the truth can be developed, nor doubt that in the end, your censures will be converted into praise, your detestation into gratitude.[2]

Doubtless the reference to the thanks of either fellow-townsmen or the Government only incensed Taylor the more; nor did he believe he had been listening to falsehoods. He had not, so far as he knew, made any hasty judgments; and he believed he was developing the truth. He replied to Philips's assertion that he could not for the life of him see how his censure could be converted into praise. . . . Yet he ignored the few words in Philips's passage which were really challenging: 'Can humanity at once become barbarity? . . .' Here was no sadistic tyrant wreaking his vengeance, but a body of men whom Taylor knew, or

---

[1] *Observations*, p. 204.
[2] Philips, *Exposure*, p. 3.

knew of, and they were being accused of *planning* a cruel attack by the military on a peaceful assembly. Perhaps Cromwell's impassioned appeal to his fellow-men was not so well known in 1819.[1]

Taylor did not spare Philips:

Like Mr. Philips, I did not see 'one person struck with the sabre', though it was not the 'dust' which prevented it, but a more potent reason; inasmuch as I had left the ground some minutes before the Yeomanry came. The number of sabre wounds that I have seen since, is, however, ample proof that many were given. And several persons, whose credibility is not to be impeached, at least by Mr. Philips's negative evidence, have distinctly sworn either that they were wounded themselves, or saw wounds inflicted upon others, before the cavalry arrived at the hustings.

This assertion did not, although it has long been imagined that it did, prove that Bamford was right. The alleged attack on some of the Yeomanry—the isolated group—was made before the main body of the troop got to the hustings.

There is no evidence, which deserves serious refutation, to prove that any stones were thrown at the cavalry before they reached the hustings; though it is assumed by Mr. Philips as a point established that 'no lives would have been lost, if opposition had not been made to the civil and military powers'. What! did Mr. Ashworth oppose them? Did Mrs. Parkinson [*sic*] oppose them? But I ask for proof that such 'opposition' was made.[2]

Taylor's crushing rejoinder carried a lot of weight. There was, however, to be proof produced of opposition on that day; and proof from some unlikely sources.

Wheeler's[3] story of the 'long brats with pockets' is too ridiculous to obtain credit; [went on Taylor] like the Parliamentary tales of the two cart-loads of stones and the thrice-read Riot Act. It bears falsehood upon the face of it . . .

That paragraph shows how moderate opinion scouted the already-made Ministerial explanations. But Taylor had now become the captive of the propaganda he had successfully put across in the first press reports. He then went on at length on the impossibility of anyone believing that an attack could have come from the crowd. He practically sums up his whole case in the following passage:

[1] 'I beseech you, in the bowels of Christ, think it possible you may be mistaken.' Cromwell's *Letter to the General Assembly of the Church of Scotland, 3 August 1650.*

[2] *Observations*, p. 167.

[3] *Wheeler's Manchester Chronicle,* 21 August 1819.

But by what right were the Yeomanry brought upon the field? I think I have, in my remarks upon the parliamentary documents, proved that the meeting was legal. That it was peaceable, I presume, will not now be questioned. If therefore, the object were merely to arrest Mr. Hunt and his companions, why, but for the very determination to produce the consequences that ensued, were such instruments employed, or such a period chosen? Mr. Hunt might doubtless have been found with ease when the meeting was over, and none of his companions who were named in the warrant, were likely to abscond to avoid its being served upon them; indeed, it is morally impossible that they could in any way be aware of its existence. Nor is the execution of a warrant for misdemeanour (the warrant does not, I am assured, allege *any* distinct fact of illegality), a matter of such importance as to justify the putting in danger the lives of such an immense multitude of people. But, even if Mr. Hunt and his companions be guilty to the full extent to which crime is imputed to them, I cannot think that the consciences of the Magistrates would have been less at ease, whilst I am sure that the feelings of the country would have been less outraged, if the yeomanry had not been ordered to assault the people; and to arrest Mr. Hunt, without assaulting them, was under the then existing circumstances absolutely impossible.

Again, if it were after mature deliberation thought necessary to arrest Mr. Hunt during the meeting, why was not the civil power in the first instance employed? No attempt was made to execute the warrant by its agency, and it would have been thought time enough by any discreet, or humane, or constitutionally disposed persons to call in a military force, when the civil power had been found unable to do its duty, or had been obstructed in the performance of it.

Taking, therefore, all the circumstances together, I cannot but conclude, that it was *ab initio* intended to dissolve the meeting by force, and that the arrest of Mr. Hunt and his associates was merely the pretext by which the attack was to be justified.[1]

No one could accuse Taylor of being unfair as he stated premise after premise and led up to his conclusion. No one ever attempted to answer him directly; but some of his premises were to be proved fallacious in the parliamentary debates and more particularly in the trials. Taylor was much stronger in argument on the legal aspects of Peterloo than on the incidents of the day. Nevertheless he treated Philips's statement on these incidents in a devastating way:

In describing the advance of the cavalry towards the hustings, Mr. Philips says, he 'did not see a sword used'. I am not aware that any person has ever asserted that he did. He 'solemnly believes, that had the crowd given way to them [the Yeomanry] no cuts would have been given'. I know of no law,

[1] *Observations*, pp. 168–9.

which authorizes a yeoman to sabre me because I may not give way to him quite as soon as he wishes that I should. Besides, the density of the crowd, and the suddenness and impetuosity of the irruption of the cavalry rendered it impossible for the people to open a passage. There is an unconscious simplicity about the remainder of the sentence, which is quite amusing: 'a great dust arose, when they quickened their speed, so that I could not distinguish all that passed; and certainly did not see one person struck with a sabre'. Why not? Mr. Philips shall answer for himself. 'Because I could not distinguish all that passed.' The letting-off of this negative evidence, reminds me of the story of an Irishman, who, when half a score of persons swore that they had seen him commit a theft, claimed to be acquitted upon his trial, because he could produce ten times as many who did not see him; like Mr. Philips, I did not see 'one person struck with a sabre . . . &c.[1]

The involved legal questions posed by Taylor were not to be easily answered. Indeed, the questions were a great deal easier to formulate than were the answers. On Norris's eve-of-the-meeting letter Taylor's questions came out pat:

. . . At that time [eleven o'clock on the 15th August] Mr. Norris states, the magistrates did not think of preventing the meeting; from which I conclude they considered it to be legal. Before their subsequent interference can be justified, it must therefore be shown, either that some circumstances, *not then anticipated*, had occurred, to change the character of the meeting, or it will follow, that the magistrates, with a full knowledge that it would be illegal, determined not to prevent it; a supposition which their notice with respect to the proposed meeting on the 9th, renders inadmissable[2] . . .

It took the trial of Hunt, two parliamentary debates, and appeals to the judges to convince many of the illegality of the meeting. Even then Taylor was proclaiming the unfairness of associating Hunt's conduct at Smithfield and his conduct at Manchester.[3] To those who would ferret out the legal aspects of 16 August, recourse must be made to the opinions of the judges at both trials and on the appeals.

John Edward Taylor was easier to follow in his dissection of the long report, sent to the Government on the night of 16 August, under the signature of William R. Hay. In view of the curious contradictions given by Hay in the witness-box at the trial of Redford *v.* Birley, the question of 'authorship' of this document is a matter for doubt. It would appear to this investigation, more likely that it was written by James Norris rather than Hay; but it was possibly a joint effort. The

[1] *Observations*, p. 167.
[2] *Observations*, p. 53–54, Note (M).
[3] *Manchester Guardian*, 20 April 1822.

circumstances under which this famous dispatch was written, Taylor did not know; they were rather pathetic. Hay's own admission in April, 1822 is revealing:

[Hay said he saw Mr. Norris late in the evening;] I saw Mr. Norris very late. I had been engaged out of doors; I came in very late, and I ought to have written the account which he was obliged, in a great hurry, to write; I being so fatigued. When he wrote the letter —[Here Hay was asked another question by the counsel: 'Did you mention to Mr. Norris this important fact of stones being thrown?'] Hay answered: 'We had no power; there was not time to do any thing, but write the best account, in a hurry, we could. We could merely save the post; and I was unable to keep a copy of the letter. And I think it right to state, that there are in the letter some things over-stated with regard to four women reported to be dead, but it was the best account we could give, and such as was reported to us to be true.[1]

Thus was composed a document which, in a few months time, was to be issued as the 1819 equivalent of a White Paper. This letter was to receive more scrutiny than possibly any other document of the period, to be quoted in Parliament, on platforms, in newspapers; finally to be subjected to the penetrating criticism of John Edward Taylor's *Observations*. Hay's letter[2] contained over twelve hundred words; Taylor's comments over sixteen hundred. Some of Taylor's criticisms have already been noted: on the 'defiance' of the crowd when Hunt arrived; on the reading of the Riot Act. Many of Hay's passages were to be given an inordinate amount of prominence—far more than they warranted, and probably far more than Hay even expected, because they were of the man-bites-dog variety; more than Hay expected, because he and his supporters had to explain them away. He said, in 1822, that there were things over-stated, mentioning the four women victims; but perhaps the smallest matter to be exaggerated was his reference to the banners:

. . . The ensigns were of the same description as those displayed on similar occasions, with this addition, that one had a bloody pike represented on it; another 'Equal Representation or Death' . . .

When Lord Sidmouth was describing the scene in the House in November, he used this account to embellish his narrative:

. . . When they [the magistrates] saw an immense assemblage of individuals, marching in military array, coming in large bodies from a distance, and declaring their object to be neither more nor less than the total subversion of the constitution or perish; more persons carrying with them caps of liberty, pikes

---

[1] Redford *v.* Birley (Farquharson), p. 433.
[2] See above, pp. 236–8; *Observations*, pp. 55–61.

bearing the appearance of having been dipped in blood, and flags inscribed with the most seditious sentences; all in his humble estimation, ought to have placed presumption on the side of the magistrates . . .[1]

With both Hay's letter and Sidmouth's speech before him, Taylor launched his broadside:[2]

This admission confines any legal offence which the banners can be presumed to have created to the two which Mr. Hay has particularised. With respect to the pike, either Mr. Hay was so far blinded by his fears as to mistake a sword in the hand of an emblematical figure of Justice for a 'bloody pike'; or there is no foundation whatever for his assertion. With respect to the latter, certainly such a flag was carried; but before I can admit that there is any legal offence in it, I must be informed what 'Equal representation' means; and be convinced that it is not a *lawful object of pursuit*. The exhibition of such flags is however, very foolish and in bad taste, because to some persons it gives offence; yet it affords no justification for delivering over an unarmed crowd to military execution. Mr. Hay's distinct statement that, 'there was no appearance of arms or pikes' forms a contrast with Lord Sidmouth's assertions in the House of Peers, not much to the advantage of his Lordship's veracity. Unless, indeed, as ministers had, after this letter was written, the assistance of the personal narratives of Mr. Hay and Mr. Hardman, the noble Secretary should have happened to make the statement on their *verbal* authority. In that case the merit of the *embellishment* belongs to them.

Henry Hunt was to play the 'bloody pike' incident even harder in his trial:

. . . Who that read the learned counsel's speech, and heard his allusions to a bloody dagger, encompassed and surrounded by the people of the Manchester meeting—a dagger too which has now been seen through the public prints by nineteen-twentieths of the empire—who, I say, but must not think, that the vile criminal so impugned, is a monster, a low-bred, vulgar villain, a desperado of low life, plodding violence and rapine, treason and murder—instigating his fellow-creatures to hurry on with him in his career of desperate and atrocious criminality! What proof is there in evidence to entitle the learned counsel to draw this 'air-drawn dagger', save indeed the evidence of one uncorroborating witness—a man, too, bearing the rank of high life, a Gentleman and a Magistrate; he, of all, only dared to utter this breath of slander, and to implicate us, or any part of the meeting, in any acts of tumult or violence . . .[3]

Mr Hay's 'bloody dagger' had perhaps added a little verisimilitude to his own narrative, but it was to be used entirely for Mr Hunt's benefit.

[1] Parl. Deb. XLI (1819–20), p. 23.
[2] *Observations*, p. 56, Note (o).
[3] *Hunt's Trial* (Pratt edn), p. 80.

But it had not been mistaken, as Taylor had imagined, for the sword of the blind figure of Justice. It was the tip of the Bury contingent's banner-staff purporting to represent a *fleur-de-lys*. The maker of it did not possess yellow or gold paint, so he painted it red![1]

Taylor, in his meticulous and penetrating criticism of Hay's letter, missed nothing; he made no allowances for the fact that several things were stated which Hay could only have learned from the reports of others. He comments tartly on 'official accuracy' and 'deviations from the truth': Hay had written:

. . . They also took on the hustings, Saxton, and Sykes, who is the writer to the *Manchester Observer*, and which Saxton had before been addressing the mob.

Taylor said:

In this sentence there are *only three* deviations from the truth. In the first place, there was no such person as Sykes arrested; in the next, the *Manchester Observer* has not, and never had any writer of that name; and in the third, Saxton had *not* been addressing the people.

Hay had probably, in copying the name, misread 'Tyas' for 'Sykes'; the second point was a grammatical error. Hay was undoubtedly aware that Saxton was the *Observer* writer, and meant to say so, because he had signed his name on the warrant for the arrest of Saxton. It was probably reported to the magistrates that Tyas also was an *Observer* writer, and in the hurry he was packed off to gaol with the rest; as Tyas himself reported, he was released as soon as the magistrates discovered who he was. On the third 'deviation from the truth' though again in the event a small matter for Saxton was acquitted, Taylor was wrong: Saxton had been speaking to the crowd before Hunt arrived.[2]

The believers of the theory that John Edward Taylor was editor of *Peterloo Massacre* may contrast Taylor's statement: 'I hope I am not disposed to be uncandid towards Mr Hay. . . .' with the *Peterloo Massacre* style; it occurs in Taylor's comment on Hay's sentence: 'We cannot but deeply regret all this serious attendant on this transaction; but we have the satisfaction of witnessing the very grateful and cheering countenances of the whole town; in fact, they consider themselves as saved by our exertions'. Taylor came back:

I hope I am not disposed to be uncandid toward Mr. Hay, but I can only view the expressions of regret which occur in the commencement . . . as the mere common-place cant of affected humanity, which it would not have

[1] *Hunt's Trial* (Pratt edn), p. 151.
[2] *State Trials*, pp. 453–4.

been *decent* to omit; and which are in perfect keeping and congruity with the nauseous vanity of the remainder of the sentence. Never was there a grosser attack, never a more groundless aspersion, on the character of the inhabitants of Manchester. Mr. Hay is not to confound his affidavit-making friends with 'the whole town'. For myself, I never witnessed such a strong, though, from motives of prudence, restrained expression of horror, astonishment, and dismay, as on that dreadful occasion.

Hay had written: 'there may arise difficulties as to the nature of some of their crimes, on which it may be necessary to consult Government'. On this paragraph Taylor made one of his most telling comments:

It seems the magistrates could not tell what to do with Mr. Hunt when they had got him. Why, then, this breathless haste to apprehend him? Why, then, place the safety of so many thousands of persons in jeopardy, to take into custody a man of whose escape from the reach of public justice, they will not *pretend* to have been afraid? Why was he, *at all hazards*, to be seized and committed upon some undetermined charge, the evidence to substantiate which was *subsequently to be sought*?[1]

To Taylor, with no knowledge of the background of Hunt's arrest except the evidence before the public in November 1819, the arrest was inexplicable. He came to the conclusion, as did thousands of others, that the arrest was the pretext for the violent dispersal of the meeting. There were those who knew differently, and 'those' did not include only the magistrates and the Government. Privately, amongst the arrested radicals on the hustings, there was later to be some apportionment of blame, particularly by Hunt on the extra severity of his sentence compared with the others. He blamed it, so he told Johnson,[2] on the fact that Richard Carlile, the 'blasphemer', was on the hustings at the invitation of Johnson; Hunt had never intended that he should share the same platform with such a notorious figure. He had written to Johnson telling him how 'astonished' he was on seeing Carlile walk into Johnson's house on the morning of 16 August. 'Mr Carlile attended,' wrote Hunt, 'as I conceived, at the Manchester meeting as a spectator, the same as the rest of the multitude of 200,000 who attended. He was never consulted about the resolutions or any other measure that was to have been submitted to the Meeting; in fact, he had nothing to do with it. Mr Johnson and some others invited him, for which I am indebted, at least, twelve months of my time'.[3] Johnson

---

[1] *Observations*, note (v), p. 60.
[2] *Letter to Henry Hunt*, p. 11.
[3] *To Radical Reformers* . . . [from Ilchester Gaol] 26 July 1821, p. 9.

retorted that Carlile was there at the invitation of the Manchester committee, so that it was not his (Johnson's) fault that Hunt had an extra eighteen months imprisonment: 'It was owing to your very stupid resolutions at the Smithfield meeting, which Mr Judge Bayley allowed the Jury to receive as evidence against us at Manchester, that either you or I was imprisoned at all'. It has been said that Taylor could not separate what happened before Hunt's arrest and what happened after. But Johnson could.

Taylor was, without doubt, the most serious contemporary critic of the Manchester magistrates. He continued as such, although some of his later criticisms lacked the strength of his original position. His tart comments on Hay's 'official accuracy' and 'deviations from the truth' have been noted in two instances. There were others. Hay had written:

On a barouche-box was a woman in white, who I believe was a Mrs. Gant, from Stockport, and who it is believed, had a cap of liberty. To which Taylor replied: 'There are two mistakes in this short sentence. In the first place Mrs. Gaunt[1] is not from Stockport; and in the next she was not on the barouche box.—So much for official accuracy!

A woman had been arrested on the 16th because she had been found in Hunt's carriage during the *mêlée* by a constable. The constable who took her imagined, because she was there, that she had been the woman who had ridden to the meeting on the box in Hunt's procession. The unfortunate woman had been kept in the New Bayley several days on the strength of that supposition before being finally released. She had actually been put into the carriage in a fainting, some said wounded, condition by a sympathetic person for safety. It was a miserable blunder, but Hay could hardly be blamed for reporting what had been reported to him. He had also reported that four women had lost their lives; a mistake which he was to point out when he was cross-examined in 1822.

Taylor was commenting on Hay's description of the events leading up to the arrests. He said:

But it has also the additional ingredient of falsehood in its composition. Mr. Nadin did *not* 'precede the Manchester Yeomanry.' On the contrary, he himself swore at the Oldham Inquest, that he *followed* them . . .[2]

The facts about this 'falsehood' have been given earlier.[3]

---

[1] Hay had written 'Mrs Gant'; Taylor gave the correct spelling: 'Mrs Gaunt'.
[2] *Observations*, p. 58.
[3] See above, p. 176.

None of the 'untruths' quite deserved the emphasis Taylor was to give them in his later criticisms of the magistrates. The long leader in his newly-founded paper, the *Manchester Guardian*, which he wrote after the second Parliamentary debate in May 1821, shows how uncompromising was his position as critic in that year. Horace Twiss, in that House of Commons debate ('a person whose name,' wrote Taylor in his leader, 'we dare say, few of our readers ever heard of before,[1] but who talks as decidedly of the Manchester meeting, as if he knew something about it') had referred to the *rioters* at Manchester. Taylor wrote:

In answering such statements as these, we should be in danger of forgetting our natural and necessary moderation, if we did not feel them to be as contemptible as they are false. The hon. gentleman (for so we are bound to call him), in the unequalled amplitude of his assertions, subsequently thought proper to state that 'Mr. Hay's letter to government written on the evening of the 16th of August stood at that moment uncontradicted in any point.' No less than six distinct untruths have long ago been pointed out in that document; not intentional, we dare say, but which, in addition to its numerous collateral misrepresentations, render it little respectable as an official statement; as a literary composition, it is disgraceful.

It has been said[2] that that part of Taylor's *Observations* dealing with Hay's letter was more of logomachical exercise than a critical one.

It has been shown how Prentice, in the second flowering of the radical interpretation of Peterloo, kicked away the rotten props of scurrility to give it a respectability it had lacked before. He did even more; he deliberately undermined the reputation of his erstwhile journalist colleague, by suggesting that Taylor had turned his back on the cause he had fought for so stoutly. Taylor indeed came at last to realise the hollowness of the Huntean version of the events of 16 August: but not until 1832, thirteen years after the event.

In November 1822, Taylor wrote a trenchant leader in his paper, inspired by the occasion when the members of the Manchester Yeomanry presented Birley, their commander, with a sword as a token of their respect. Taylor, according to Prentice had this to say:

[1] Horace Twiss, in spite of Taylor's assertion that he dared say few of *his* readers ever heard of before, was to have undying fame amongst the millions of readers of Thomas Babington Macaulay's famous description of the moment when the House of Commons passed the second reading of the Reform Bill in 1831. Twiss, as a member for one of the corrupt boroughs and who was to lose his seat, showed his reaction by the expression on his face: 'the face of Twiss', wrote Macaulay, 'was as the face of a damned soul'. (Trevelyan *Macaulay*, 1, 208). It has been, ever since, a particularly tempting quotation for other writers.

[2] See above, p. 238.

Whether, however, we are to be classed with the 'designing or the deceived', 'the ignorant or the ill-disposed,' we have no hesitation in avowing our firm and unchangeable opinion, that the strongest censures which have been applied to the magistrates and Yeomanry, for their conduct on the 16th of August, are not stronger than they deserve; and that the sanction of all the special juries, and of *all the judges in the kingdom*, would be quite insufficient to wash out the 'damned spot' of blood with which that event has been tainted. [To the foregoing, Prentice added his comment]:

Yet, not withstanding the stain of this 'damned spot', ten years had not elaspsed ere the editor of the *Guardian* went, hand-in-hand, and arm-in-arm, with Mr. H. H. Birley, in the attempt to impose a member of Mr. Birley's choice upon newly-enfranchised Manchester! Let no man talk of an unchangeable opinion whose opinion is founded on present expediency.[1]

From this extract one would suppose Taylor's opinions in 1822 to be as uncompromising as before, but in that same *Guardian* article (30 November 1822) the reader may sense the feeling that Taylor was writing with less of the original conviction of his *Observations*. He gives the impression that the facts are piling up against him:

. . . That the verdict at Lancaster, and the opinions expressed by the judges of the Court of King's Bench, on the motion for a new trial, were favourable to the yeomanry, is not a matter to be disputed, and if the corps are disposed from this circumstance, to lay the flattering unction to their souls, that the killing of ten or a dozen, and the wounding of five or six hundred, of their fellow-creatures, is an affair of which the real characteristics can be at all affected by the opinion of special jurymen, or time-serving lawyers, let them do so . . .

The Redford *v.* Birley trial and the opinions subsequently expressed by the judges worried John Edward Taylor; but they did not worry Prentice. His version of the events following on 16 August never even mentioned them! Prentice's suppressions are almost unbelievable. He had referred to Taylor's *Observations*:[2]

. . . Numerous other tracts appeared on the subject, but this by Mr. Taylor will always be not only an important local record, but valuable as containing a detail of the lawless tyranny which at that time prevailed amongst officials of all ranks and degrees from Lord Sidmouth down to the deputy constable Nadin. We now come to the trials . . .

Prentice's Peterloo 'trials' include the preliminary hearings of Hunt and the others and their trial proper, ending with tilts at Bamford and

[1] Prentice, p. 239.
[2] Prentice, p. 178.

Hunt. On p. 232, philosophizing on the writing of history and the events ignored and unnoticed by historians, Prentice says:

. . . Mr. Wheeler in his history of Manchester, makes a great leap from Hunt's trial at York in 1820, to the bank failures at the end of 1825. There lay a happy period some time between . . .

Prentice's leap does not cover quite so long a period, but it is a very much more remarkable one, for he leaps from Hunt's trial in March 1820, to the part-quotation of Taylor's *Guardian* article in November 1822. Redford *v*. Birley (April 1822) (which, incidentally, was the main theme of Taylor's animadversions) did not exist for Archibald Prentice! It has already been said that Prentice clouded the understanding of generations, but his smear on Taylor has had unhappy repercussions. It caused J. L. Hammond, in his life of C. P. Scott, of the *Manchester Guardian* to write thus:

. . . At the time of Peterloo John Edward Taylor and Archibald Prentice were giving vigour and spirit to its [*Manchester Gazette*] pages. Taylor wrote the manifesto of the Radical party on the events of that memorable day, and the immense effect of Peterloo on the minds of the English people was largely caused by his success and that of Prentice in despatching accounts of the conflict to the London papers before the official version became public . . . [On the founding of the *Guardian*] . . . Once he found himself in the saddle, Taylor was more active as a journalist than as a politican. It is true he was one of the first members of the Anti-Corn Law Association founded in 1838. But Peterloo was becoming a fainter memory, and his friend Archibald Prentice complained that Taylor had moved from the left to the centre and from the centre to the right. This estimate was pretty near the truth. The paper was hostile to Cobbett and to Fielden. In 1849 it denounced Mrs. Gaskell's *Mary Barton*, and more than once it was at odds both with Cobden and Bright. But Taylor produced a paper that was better in all respects than its predecessors in the journalism of the provinces.

The future history of the *Manchester Guardian* will take care of the paper's reputation; but to show that Prentice's estimate of Taylor was 'pretty near the truth' by pointing out that Taylor's paper, in 1849, denounced Mrs Gaskell's *Mary Barton* seems remarkable. Taylor had been dead five years.[1]

[1] Dr Read deals with this alleged 'left to centre and from centre to the right' move by Taylor in his book *Press and People* (1960), p. 85:

[The purchase by Taylor of two Tory newspapers] brought to a head a quarrel between Taylor and several of his former political friends. He was accused of losing his enthusiasm for reform. The Potter brothers, wealthy Unitarian merchants who had subscribed to instal Taylor in the *Guardian*, wrote to him in 1826 telling him how disappointed they were in him. 'The tone and temper of your Paper', wrote Richard

Prentice has been cited so often and for so long as one of the prime authorities on Peterloo. The *Victoria County History of Lancashire*[1] in its short account of Peterloo cites five authorities as its source material; one is Hunt's trial, the other four are 'Prentice'. Taylor *ought* to have written his 'masterly exposure of a miserable chapter in the history of our national policy' at a date a little further removed from the main incident in his theme; but he did not live long enough to witness how his erstwhile colleague added his miserable contribution to that miserable chapter.

Potter, 'has in my opinion altered from what it formerly was, and by no means meets my views of Politics. That you have materially "softened", I apprehend is undeniable: it is in everyone's mouth'. Taylor replied that it was not his politics but political circumstances which had changed. Since the coming into office of the moderate tories, Canning, Peel, Huskisson 'the whole spirit and conduct of Government' had changed. Even 'the tone and temper' of the tory party in Manchester had greatly improved since 1821: 'they are much less intolerant and overbearing; and . . . no small part of this change is owing to my exertions'.

Taylor's change in views was probably sincere. It is unlikely that he had altered his political attitude simply to retain the support of his new tory readers. . . . The politics of the *Guardian* by the mid-1820s can be described as moderate liberal. It wanted (to use a favourite adjective of the paper) only 'practical' change. 'He who makes it a boast', wrote Taylor, summing up his new attitude, 'that, in mature age, and on every subject he retains entirely unmodified the ideas of his youth, is far more likely to have a claim to the title of obstinate, than to the merit of being regarded as consistent'.*

* Prentice's smears on Taylor are discussed below on pp. 474–5.

[1] *V.C.H. Lancs*, IV, p. 184.

XX

The Abortive Oldham Inquest
and Magisterial Activity

It is no exaggeration to say that in those last four months of 1819 English newspapers had the biggest bonanza of front-page news they had ever known, or were to know for some years to come. Sensation followed sensation; when the immediate repercussions of the day began to flag, came the Oldham Inquest, followed in November by the assembling of Parliament.

Dr Read[1] sums up the Oldham Inquest thus:

The approach of winter brought little relaxation of the tension in Lancashire. The inquest on one John Lees of Oldham, who died on the morning of September 7th from injuries received at Peterloo, was a particular cause of continued excitement.

Lees, of course, was not the only victim of the massacre: several other persons had also been the subjects of inquests. But the verdicts in these other cases had all been quickly arrived at, and were not such as to make legal proceedings possible. Some had been 'accidental death', another (on a child) 'died by a fall from his mother's arms', and another 'died by the pressure of the military being under the civil power'. In the case of Lees, however, the Radicals determined to make a special effort to secure acceptance in a court of law of the illegality of the action of the magistrates at Peterloo. Harmer and Dennison, two leading Radical solicitors, engaged themselves on the case without charge to the Lees family. Harmer's particular purpose was to prove that the meeting was peaceable and that the military cut down the crowd. The authorities were naturally anxious to prevent this, and it was around this issue that the long drawn-out squabbles, which aroused national interest, principally turned, with Farrand, the Coroner, doing his best to foil the Radicals at every stage.

It was one of the complaints of the Coroner, incidentally, that the radical lawyers, Harmer, of London, and Dennison, of Liverpool, had 'engaged themselves' on the case; it was some time before they were able to prove to the Coroner that they had been 'engaged' by the Lees family;

[1] Read, p. 147 et seq.

the Coroner remained unconvinced. Before the official Coroner (Farrand) took up the case Harmer referred to John Lees, the deceased:

who has met his death in consequence of the outrageous incursion of the military upon an assembly of unarmed and unoffending people . . . and I am ready to prove most satisfactorily, by a host of evidence, that there was no provocation, legal right, or even plausible pretence for the interference of the military upon that occasion.[1]

The 'authorities' who 'were naturally anxious to prevent this', in the first place, were not present; unless Farrand was regarded as one of them. However, Dr Read proceeds:

On the first day of the inquest proper, September 25th, Farrand quickly made his bias clear by declaring that no notes of the proceedings were to be published until the inquest and any subsequent legal proceedings had been concluded. Here was an attempt to prevent any publicity being given to the inquiry. Because they ignored this ruling the reporters of both *The Times* and the *Morning Chronicle* were subsequently excluded from the court. The Boroughreeve and Constables of Manchester briefed Ashworth, a barrister, to appear for them.

Farrand's fiat with regard to what should be published was completely ineffectual, as the columns-long press reports all over the country show. It seems reasonable to assume that Ashworth would not have been briefed at all, to come into the court in the middle of the proceedings of the *fifth* day of the hearing but for what had occurred on the fourth day. At the end of the third day, Harmer announced that he had fifty witnesses, at least; on the fourth day, on introducing a witness, Harmer had said:

If the attack were made without necessity—if there were no riot or disturbance to justify even the interference of a peace officer, yet a body of military are sent in to cut down and trample on the unarmed and unoffending people, so as to occasion death—it is murder. And I mean to state, that all those concerned, and who were present aiding and abetting, whether they be magistrates, soldiers or constables, are, in the eye of the Law, guilty as principals, of the murder.[2]

During the middle of the fifth day's proceedings Ashworth appeared, 'briefed by the Boroughreeve and Constables of Manchester.' Ashworth referred to a passage which had appeared in *The Times*:

while the Coroner was re-examining this witness Mr. Ashworth, a barrister,

[1] *Oldham Inquest* (Dowling), p. 4.
[2] Ibid., p. 91.

entered the room, followed by the learned notetaker whom Mr. Harmer, with impunity, charged on the preceding day, with taking notes for the Magistrates.

Ashworth: 'It is untrue. Nobody here takes notes for the Magistrates. The Magistrates are not represented here at all. They have no counsel here; they have no attorney here; they have no note-taker here. I have never seen the Magistrates either since this inquiry has commenced, or before it. So much therefore for the authority of this reporter, who presumes to state as a fact, that which is only mere guess . . . and now, Sir, comes a most infamous falsehood, "and at a full meeting of the Magistrates yesterday at the Star Inn, Mr. Ashworth had been instructed to appear at the Coroner's court." Good God, Sir, what sort of a statement is this? . . . This is an infamous falsehood, I say. The Magistrates never instructed me. I have no connection with the Magistrates on this occasion . . .'[1]

Dr Read proceeds:

Ashworth vigorously countered the attempts of the Radicals to prove that the Military attacked the crowd by arguing that until it could be settled exactly who had struck Lees (which it was impossible to do), it was not permissible to bring in more general evidence: 'Shew me a principal', he declared, 'and then I will accede to the possibility of there being accessories'. In this way, the authorities at Manchester sought to prevent any general discussion of their action at the meeting.

On the sixth day (2 October) Harmer demanded from the Coroner five hundred more witness summons-forms. Whether any discussion was prevented by the action of the 'Manchester authorities' is best answered by reference to the long printed report of the inquest. 'Despite all Ashworth's efforts', continues Dr Read, 'revelations prejudicial to the authorities began to be made.' The 'revelations prejudicial to the authorities' included many which were never heard again either in or out of a court of law. Dr Read continues:

On October 13th Farrand stepped in and adjourned the proceedings until December 1st. His excuse for this excessive adjournment was that the jury was fatigued by the long drawn-out nature of the proceedings; almost certainly, however, his real purpose was to prevent the accumulation of any further damaging evidence against the authorities.

Farrand had earlier had the inquest removed from Oldham to Manchester; the constable of Oldham advised it on account of disorder and threatened disorder. On the ninth day proceedings were held in Manchester. It was on the eleventh day (13 October) that Farrand 'stepped

[1] *Oldham Inquest*, p. 396.

in', and adjourned the inquest: 'It was at the request of the jury from indisposition that the inquest should be adjourned to a later period. Several of them have suffered so much from fatigue . . . he had, he said, sufficient reasons for myself in so doing; and if there is anything wrong in it, it will allow time for an application to be made to the Court of King's Bench, not only by those who think themselves aggrieved but by any other person who may appear here.'[1] Dr Read's account proceeds:

The Radicals were determined not to be baulked in this way, and they immediately applied to the Court of King's Bench for a mandamus to compel the coroner to proceed without further delay . . . Events in the King's Bench, however, took an unexpected turn. It was discovered that the coroner and the Jury had not viewed the body of Lees at the same time, and this, made all the proceedings at the inquest null and void. This error in procedure was entirely the fault of Farrand . . . but nonetheless he was in this way relieved from having to proceed further. 'The Coroner', as Prentice put it, 'by omitting to observe the law, had placed himself outside the law'.

It was Harmer who pointed out to Farrand that he had not viewed the body, and an exhumation was attempted secretly on 6 October early in the morning. The news was noised around Oldham, and a crowd of some thousands assembled; Farrand alleged that he and the Constable of Oldham were accused of trying to steal the body; Farrand believed that the crowds who attended the inquest were under the control of Harmer and Dennison, and he asked (27 November) the Court of King's Bench how he ought to proceed.[2]

The manner in which the Lees inquest was conducted, [said Dr. Read] aroused a storm of indignation not only in Radical circles but in all liberal circles in the country. Its mismanagement was one of the most frequent criticisms voiced at the many Whig meetings held during the autumn to protest against the massacre and subsequent events. Signatures were collected in Manchester protesting against the employment of Ashworth and saying that the signatories would not permit his fees to be paid out of the poor rates. Seven of the jury-men on the case subsequently wrote to the Coroner telling him that, had a verdict been asked for, they would have submitted one of murder.

In the Court of King's Bench, Mr Justice Best gave the court's decision:[3] 'No failure of justice will occur, because the case will go before the Grand Jury of the country—a body of men much better

[1] *Oldham Inquest* (appendix), p. 28.
[2] Ibid., p. 22 et seq.
[3] Ibid., 581. (Court of King's Bench Mich. Term, 60 Geo. III.)

calculated to examine so complicated a question, as that which may be submitted to them. I conscientiously feel no regret at being compelled to stop proceedings, which appear at the beginning to have been marked by so much irregularity on the part of the Coroner, and indecency on the part of others who attended the inquest, or in stopping a proceeding in which it sufficiently appears that the Jury have been so improperly tampered with. But I decide not upon these grounds. The ground I decide upon is, that from beginning to end every part of these proceedings is irregular.'

No attempt was made to bring the case before a Grand Jury by Hunt or his advisers. It was to add some point to the contention of Government spokesmen later when they asked why the radicals 'indulged in this theme of declamation when the laws were open to the aggrieved party.'

. . . Was it, [asked Lord Castlereagh in the House of Commons] because it answered better [the radical view] to keep this subject afloat as a topic of inflammatory declamation rather than put it into any train of legal inquiry? If there were any man, or body of men, under a charge of murder, and no person stepped forward to bring them to punishment, it was a reproach [to those who made the charge][1].

The radical retort to Lord Castlereagh's charge of not putting their case into any train of legal inquiry was, and had always been, that all such attempts had been blocked. They cited that bills were rejected by the Lancashire Grand Jury; that Manchester and Warrington magistrates refused to consider criminal informations; that the Oldham inquest was stopped; that Parliament refused inquiry; that the Court of King's Bench would not hear their pleas, and so on. The doors of justice were shut to every radical appeal. A complete investigation into all these alleged injustices would make an interesting study. A glance into some of these 'so far and no farther' demands for justice by Hunt and his legal advisers is revealing.

The Oldham inquest was second only in importance to the refusal of a Parliamentary inquiry. It had been stopped, claimed Prentice, by a legal quibble. The reasons for its termination have, perhaps, not been understood. Farrand, the coroner, in his final letter to Harmer[2] was somewhat at a loss to understand the radical Harmer's concern:

I cannot help remarking that this decision of the Court of King's Bench [in declaring the proceedings null and void] being entirely the result of your

[1] Parl. Deb., Second Series IV, p. 807, et seq.
[2] *Oldham Inquest*, p. 580.

own proceedings, it is somewhat extraordinary that you should wish to disturb it.

It was Harmer who had pointed out the flaw. The coroner and the judges claimed that the jury had been tampered with; it was certainly not anti-radical 'tampering'. The inquest had, in fact, been stopped at a most convenient radical point—when anti-radical evidence was being brought forward, and these witnesses complained of others being unheard. Twenty were waiting with evidence on 'stones, brickbats and sticks'.[1] Six important (it might be thought) anti-radical witnesses appeared after troops of Harmer's witnesses; they included Joseph Nadin, Roger Entwistle, and J. Platt (regarded as perjured by the radicals because of his evidence at Lancaster). Harmer then introduced another seven radical witnesses. The latter included one who testified that he heard one of the Yeomanry say 'there is that villain Saxton; run him through,' which in the printed report of the proceedings is italicized, apparently to make it clear that it corroborated John Tyas's report in *The Times*. It did. The words were almost identical. Tyas had written: 'There is that villain Saxton; do you run him through the body'. This passage has been cited in modern times[2] as convincing testimony, without adding the information that this witness, 'muttering to himself', was dismissed from the courtroom as an incredible one.

The printed report of the Oldham inquest was produced under radical auspices; the shorthand writer was employed by Harmer. It is a 600-page compendium of mainly anti-magisterial and anti-Yeomanry facts, and it was a best-seller. Comment on the Oldham inquest usually records the extensively signed protest from Manchester against Ashworth's fees being paid out of the poor rate; seldom is it mentioned that the cost of producing the printed report was met from the Metropolitan Relief Fund for the Sufferers at Peterloo.[3] Even a superficial examination reveals that the printed report is carefully, yet radically, edited by italicizing, as above, and elsewhere (p. 310). The coroner expressed suspicions as to the radical shorthand-writer's perversions (p. 580), and it would appear to be prudent not to take this report and the abridged report which appears in *Peterloo Massacre* as the sole authorities for what happened at Oldham. Recourse should be had to the extensive newspaper reports.

Turning to other instances of the alleged closed doors of justice, the non-appearance of radical accusers at Lancaster in the one case in which

1 *The Courier*, 6 December 1819.
2 Thompson, p. 686.
3 *Report . . . Relief of the Manchester Sufferers* (1820), pp. 64–65.

they had been successful in getting a true bill brought in before the Grand Jury (against Richard Owen for perjury) has been given.'[1] The bill against the constable, Platt, for stating that Moorhouse was on the hustings was thrown out. There was a sequel. On 11 November 1819, Hunt and his legal advisers appeared before the Court of King's Bench concerning their application before the Grand Jury of Middlesex against J. Platt, for 'having sworn before the Manchester magistrates on 27 August last, that on 16 August J. Moorhouse was on the hustings, waving his hat,' &c. Mr Justice Bayley informed Hunt: 'There are some acts which give Grand Juries extra power in certain cases, which happen out of the county, but perjury is not one of them'.[2] On 8 October, in that same Court of King's Bench, Hunt appeared in person to make a motion for criminal investigations against the Manchester magistrates; the court was at much pains to inform him that only a member of the Bar could bring in his case.[3] Hunt and his legal advisers were perhaps not so naive as these instances seem to prove.

Going to law, of course, was costly. Hunt's appearances in the Court of King's Bench were not, but on each occasion they were widely reported in the national press. Each appearance added to the accumulating claim that the doors of justice were shut. Costly though going to law was, the radicals had been prepared to spend, up to December 1819, on appearances at Lancaster and the costs of the long-drawn-out Oldham inquest, the sum of £1077 out of a Sufferers' Relief Fund which only totalled finally £3408. Some radicals objected,[4] but a further £810 was swallowed up in Hunt's trial. Only £1206 was distributed in relief to the sufferers in Manchester.[5]

The 'matchless opportunity' given to the Whigs of destroying the Government's reputation has already been referred to,[6] as well as the

---

[1] See above, p. 205 note 3.
[2] *The Examiner*, 14 November 1819.
[3] *Manchester Observer*, 13 November 1819.
[4] See below, p. 383 note 1.
[5] Parl. Deb. N.S. V (1821) 719 et seq, and *Metropolitan Report*, pp. 64–5.
Henry Hunt and other radicals, as has been seen, had different ideas as to priority in the matter of the relief of the 'Manchester Sufferers'. They were opposed to Harmer's tactics at Oldham and at Lancaster, and objected to his intervention as the Metropolitan (Rump) Committee's nominee. (See *Memoirs of Henry Hunt*, pp. 634–6). On p. 639, Hunt remarks on the Oldham inquest: '. . . at the end of the third or fourth day, the evidence was so conclusive, that the Jury were prepared to have returned their verdict of Wilful Murder! but, by some extraordinary fatality, by some accountable cause, Mr Harmer kept calling fresh witnesses, and the Inquest was adjourned from day to day, and from place to place, for a month, and after the last adjournment they never met again.'
[6] See above, p. 38.

surprise which modern commentators express at this opportunity not being pressed home. Dr Read deals with the removal of Earl Fitzwilliam and the suspicions it aroused. Fitzwilliam had replied to Dr Bardsley, of Manchester, when that ardent local loyalist had tried to explain to the indignant Earl that he, too, was not correctly informed on what had actually happened on St Peter's Field; the Earl was under the impression that the magistrates had wantonly used the military to disperse the meeting by force. What is more, he was incensed that this shocking act had received Royal approbation. Dr Read quotes part of Earl Fitzwilliam's reply:[1]

. . . it is the approbation given in the name of the Crown to the use, in the first instance, of a Military Body in the execution of a Civil Process that awakens my jealousy . . . Who will engage to restore to the Civil authority, powers once exercised by the Military? . . . its primary interference in Civil matters has been approved in that quarter [the Crown] to which alone it looks for approbation, the effect of which I cannot contemplate without alarm—it is this, that I am anxious to meet in the earliest stage, to prevent its assuming the dangerous form of acknowledged precedent.[2]

Here was perhaps, [continues Dr Read] the greatest fear of the Whigs after Peterloo, a fear sometimes overlaid in discussion of the details of the massacre but much more important to them than the actual events of August 16th, tragic though they were. The army, it seemed to Fitzwilliam and his friends, was being primed (as evidence at Peterloo) to act independently of the old constitutional authorities in preparation for its new role in support of 'a Government disposed to despotism' . . .

It must be assumed that Government explanations and other facts, as they came to light placated this Whig fear. Indeed, Dr Read's findings that the Government were not parties to the decision to disperse the meeting by force proves this to be the case. The radical version of Peterloo, however, as reiterated by Mr Thompson, gives them no such escape; they were merely going through the motions of protestation and in the end they 'coolly submitted to the exercise of military despotism'.

It is one of the weakest aspects of the radical interpretation of Peterloo to assume that these sincere and indignant Englishmen could have finally allowed their noblest instincts to be smothered by the passage of time.

What, however, were the Manchester magistrates thinking at the time these protests were being made? There is a long, and involved,

[1] Read, p. 194.
[2] Fitzwilliam to Bardsley, 17 October 1819 (*Manchester Guardian*, 15 August 1938).

incident which occurred in the early days of October 1819, which has never, since that time, been considered. It is the 'suppressed' Bolton Meeting on 13 October. The facts were well known at the time: the *Manchester Observer* made something of an attempt to exploit them, and John Edward Taylor commented on some of the Home Office documents which proved that pikes were being made to take to the Bolton meeting: proof which, in March 1820, in the case of The King *v.* John Knowles,[1] resulted in the accused receiving 20 months' imprisonment.

The Bolton meeting should be seen in the same light as that of the proscribed Manchester meeting of almost the same date: proscribed, not by authority, but by Henry Hunt. Radicals were, at the time, urging the calling of meetings in every town and village of the United Kingdom. Hunt was not so sure of the wisdom of this, for he said, in a letter 'To the Brave Reformers of Lancashire, Cheshire, Yorkshire, and the whole of the North of England and Scotland'[2] (dated 19 October):

Our enemies have declared open hostilities against us and the Laws of England. The infamous Authorities of Manchester, under the sanction of a corrupt and cruel Ministry, were the first to 'cry havoc and let slip the Dogs of War'; on the never-to-be-forgotten 16th of August, they polluted the history of the present age with the foulest stain, the *crimson gore* of their fellow men, women and children. Every exertion to bring the *instigators* and *perpetrators* of these cowardly murders to Justice, has hitherto failed . . . &c.

He was the last man in the world to urge reformers to refrain from meeting, but Hunt said he was afraid that spies were busy urging the people to meet:

I would urge a meeting in every *County, City, Town and Parish* in the United Kingdom, where they have not already met to express their opinions upon the Massacre at Manchester, and to take measures for bringing the Murderers and their abettors to Justice. But if anyone has been from London to advise or recommend a Meeting at Manchester under the present agitated state of the public mind, he must be a remorseless fiend indeed; no one will go to such a Meeting *unarmed*, after the cowardly murders and mutilations which were perpetrated on the 16th, and where is the man who would advise you to meet *armed*? I say, my friends of Manchester, *meet not*, till every effort has been made and failed to bring to Justice these Murderers; and then, and not till then, will there be any question whether you ought to *meet* or *not* . . .

It would not be unreasonable to suppose that Henry Hunt, although he does not say so, would have similarly advised the reformers of Bolton,

[1] *State Trials*, p. 497.
[2] *Manchester Observer*, 23 October 1819.

ten miles from Manchester, because of the same danger of 'attack'. On the other hand, the authorities of Manchester would have been equally confirmed in their opinion and would have prohibited such a meeting, firmly believing that 'mobs' provided with arms, were a danger to life and property. Prudent reformers likely to be 'attacked' would abstain from meeting; prudent authorities fearing an 'attack' would restrain as far as lay in their power the assembling of such meetings. Each side could draw their own modicum of satisfaction from their way of proceeding. At Bolton the 'danger' (to both) was as great as at Manchester, for in the Bolton Division of the County Justices were two of the magistrates most involved who had 'acted at Manchester'. The documents should be allowed to speak for themselves: they were published in the *Manchester Gazette*, 16 October 1819:

A Public Meeting of the inhabitants of the Towns of Great and Little Bolton having been called by certain individuals, to be holden on the area near the Commercial Inn, on Wednesday, the 13th inst., which meeting is convoked in direct opposition to the opinions of the Boroughreeves and Constables of those Towns, to the manifest inconvenience of those who attend the Annual Fair, on their lawful business, and to the great injury to the Trade of these Towns and neighbourhood.

We, the undersigned Magistrates for the county Palatine of Lancaster, residing within the Division of Bolton, earnestly recommend to all heads of families, and masters of manufacturing establishments, to warn all those under their influence and authority, that every person present at any disorderly and tumultuous assembly is liable to the same penalties as attach to the principals and instigators of such proceedings; and we hereby declare our firm resolution, that for the purpose of maintaining the public peace, we will apply all those powerful means which will be placed at our disposal, in the application of which we are sanctioned by the law of the land.

Ra. Fletcher	Jas. Watkins
William Hulton	Jos. Ridgway.

Bolton, October 11th, 1819.

Public Meeting . . . A placard appearing posted on the walls of the town, stating that the Public Meeting for Wednesday next[1] in this town, was in direct opposition to the opinion of the Boroughreeve and Constables of Great and Little Bolton. We the Boroughreeve and Constables of Great Bolton, flatly deny the assertion, as it was our joint opinion that the people should have a Meeting convened under the authority of the Towns-Officers, as in our opinion it would tend better to preserve the peace of the Town. Wm. Bowker, Boroughreeve; John Stanton, Constable. Bolton, October 11th, 1819.

[1] Original bill preserved at L.C.R.O. Preston (Hulton Scrapbook), DDHu.

It is not necessary to go through the involved and tortuous reasons which prompted the issue of still another placard, of the same date, which said: 'In consequence of an informality in calling a public meeting on Wednesday next; it is unavoidably postponed. The public may rest assured, however, that a Meeting will be held . . . in the course of next week.'

The *Manchester Observer* in their 16 October issue, unaware that they would later be coming down on the side of Henry Hunt's 'prudence', as regards the suggested Manchester meeting, did not let the occasion pass. Another big stick was in their hands with which to beat the authorities:

. . . The *powerful* means to which they [the magistrates] allude we are unfortunately no strangers to, and of the manner in which they threaten to apply these means we are equally well aware; but that the law of the land sanctions them in murdering peaceable inhabitants, legally assembled for a legal purpose, is a *lie*, and a lie of the blackest nature. That the late abominable atrocities at Manchester, under the authority of a Junta of which the Bolton division of magistrates formed a part, have received the sanction of my Lord Sidmouth, and, through him, the *high approbation* of the Prince Regent, there is no doubt; but we are equally sure, that the conduct of the projectors, aiders, abettors, and approvers of the hellish deed, from * * * * * * to the Beadle, have been guilty of High Treason against the People, and we would caution them, *at their peril* to repeat the horrid tragedy lest it should be *damned* in the first act . . . We trust the Boroughreeves and Constable of Great Bolton will have the courage to convoke a Public Meeting in that place on their own responsibility, and thus give townsmen the wished for opportunity of expressing themselves on the only subject which continues, and will continue, to occupy the public mind—'the late atrocious proceedings of the Manchester Magistrates and Yeomanry Cavalry' . . . [they added another piece of evidence of this atrocity] . . . An officer of the 15th Hussars (we believe Major Cochrane) informed him [J. W. Parkins, Sheriff of London] that in his endeavour to save the lives of the innocent people on Peter's Field, 'from the infuriated Yeomanry, his knees were ensanguined in the blood issuing from the wounded bodies of the victims of military execution.' A tale of horror but too truly told!

The curious may follow in the *Manchester Observer* how they and other radicals marched and counter-marched in this forgotten episode of the suppressed Bolton meeting, how one aggrieved reformer indignantly took the matter as high as the Whig Lord Lieutenant of the County, Lord Derby; and of the noble Earl's sympathetic reply.[1] The meeting, however, did not take place; and the reader may decide whether Henry Hunt or the magistrates gave the true reason; each had

[1] *Manchester Observer*, 6 November 1819.

some justification. The magistrates' reason may be seen, for the first time, in two hitherto unquoted and unused letters in the Rev. W. R. Hay's bundle of papers in the John Rylands Library, Manchester[1]

Earl of Derby to William Hulton (Copy, dated 19th October, 1819). Dear Sir. I was in hopes from the answers I received from Mr. Pilkington to the letter I lately addressed to him in answer to a communication made to me in the name of himself, of you, and Mr. Ainsworth, upon the subject of a proposed Public Meeting at Bolton, that the sentiments I expressed upon that occasion & particularly that part of those sentiments which stated my decided opinion that the Magistrates possessed *no legal* right to prevent or put a stop to any public meeting called for the consideration & full discussion of any supposed grievances, as long as the same was conducted in an orderly & peaceable manner, and did not come to any resolutions tending to subvert the Laws and Overturn the constitution of the Country, had met with your sanction and concurrence, and that consequently you as an *individual* magistrate concurred in that which I earnestly expressed that the Bench of Justices might see the business in the same point of view, & therefore be disposed to give no interruption without the strongest necessity, the grounds of which I was not acquainted with & could hardly conceive to exist to the quiet proceedings of this meeting. Under this firm conviction and earnest hope I should not have troubled you further upon the subject or ventured to obtrude any opinion or advice of mine upon the Bench of Magistrates collectively, to whose care & superintendence the Peace & Government of the Bolton Division is peculiarly committed, had I not this morning received a letter from Mr. Borron informing me that he had received a petition from one of the Boroughreeves and several of the inhabitants of the Town of Bolton addressed to the *Magistrates* of the *Warrington Division* who usually assembled *in Leigh*, in which they stated their apprehension of being disturbed in their intention of assembling for the exercise of the legal and constitutional right of the people in addressing the Prince Regent on the late proceedings at Manchester on the 16th of August, and calling upon them for *their attendance* to protect the people whilst in the exercise of their constitutional rights, being convinced that it would be unsafe to assemble without such protection. I understand Mr. Borron informed them that this business would probably be laid before me to which they heartily and cheerfully assented, adding that their most anxious wish was that everything should be peaceably conducted which they pledged themselves would be the case on the part of the meeting, if no official interference occurred on the part of the Magistrates. The answer to Mr. Borron has been that I should immediately communicate the purport of this information to you and the other Magistrates of the Bolton Division, which I accordingly request you to do, but that in so doing I should not think myself called upon, or that it was proper for me to interfere *further* than by

[1] English MS. 1197/73 and 1197/74.

stating to the Bolton Magistrates these *additional facts* which only *confirmed* me in the opinion I before ventured to give of the constitutional right of the people to assemble for the purpose of addressing the Prince Regent on their supposed grievances, and that in so doing they could not be legally disturbed as long as they conducted themselves peaceably and with the attention to the Laws of the Realm.

This, I repeat to you, is my considered opinion, but in stating it to the Magistrates & yourself, I do not think myself justified in any *further* interference with them in their discretionary exercise of the Power and Authority entrusted to them by Law . . . Derby.

Knowsley, October 19th, 1819.

Thus the letter from the *Custos Rotulorum* of the County of Lancaster, who is described in one prime document[1] in the radical interpretation of Peterloo, as 'the complete tool of the administration' whose 'barefaced tergiversation in relation to the disturbances which he and his coadjutors *foresaw* because they were pre-determined' which had 'marked his character with a stain which all the Lethean waters of the Boroughmongers will not be able to wash out'! To this letter, the chairman of the Select Committee of Magistrates replied:[2]

October 21st, 1819. Hulton Park. My Lord. The pressure of public business at this crisis is so great and the time of the Magistrates of the Bolton Division so portioned out for the due and proper execution of their office, that I shall be unable to give the deliberate opinion of the Bench, on the subject referred to in your Lordship's letter of the 19th inst., before Sunday or Monday next. On Saturday I will lay its contents before the select committee of Magistrates assembled at Manchester, without whose advice and concurment the Bolton Magistrates would not, under existing circumstances, be disposed to act on any public occasion. As however, your Lordship has appealed to me as an individual, I am unwilling that so long a time should intervene without a communication to your Lordship of my *firm* & *matured* opinion on the important occasion to which your Lordship refers. But previous to venturing a reply to your Lordship's Letter, it may not be irrelevant to recall to your Lordship's notice, the various publications which have been issued with regard to an intended public meeting at Bolton. A requisition was signed by certain individuals, without any description of their professions or places of abode, and presented to the Boroughreeves and Constables of Great and Little Bolton, requesting them to call a Meeting of the Inhabitants of those towns and their neighbourhood for the purpose of considering the late transactions at Manchester. A Counter Requisition was also presented, and the majority of the Towns Officers, the majority of a Corporate Body being

[1] *Peterloo Massacre*, p. 196.
[2] Eng. MS. 1197/74, J.R.L.

universally considered as speaking the sentiments of the whole, refused to convene the Meeting. Notwithstanding such refusal, the Requisitionists gave notice by printed placards of their intention to assemble, and then the Magistrates of the Bolton Division issued the caution which I have the honour to enclose. This contains their *unanimous* sentiments, and I venture to affirm, that they have, as yet, seen no cause to change them, nor are they likely to depart from opinions formed upon the most deliberate consideration.

On the same day that this caution of the Magistrates was published, the Requisitionists thought proper to postpone their Meeting with a *'flat denial'* on the part of one Boroughreeve and one Constable that they had objected to the Meeting. These Gentlemen go out of office tomorrow. I have felt it necessary to recapitulate thus far, in order to arrive at the time when Mr. Borron has chosen to address your Lordship.

In the sentiments expressed in your Lordship's letter to Mr. Pilkington, & 'particularly in that part of them which states your decided opinion that the Magistrates possess no *legal* rights to prevent or put a stop to any public meeting called for the consideration and full discussion of any supposed grievances as long as the same is conducted in an orderly and peaceable manner & do not come to any resolutions tending to subvert the laws and overturn the constitution of the Country' *I most fully & cordially agree.* I am not aware of any instance in which such a right has been invaded; & I am quite confident that no Magistrate with whom I have the honour of acting would *dare* to attempt so unjustifiable a measure. I hope your Lordship will receive this as a sufficient acquiescence on my part in the opinion and advice you have given to the Bench of Magistrates collectively.

Before the receipt of your Lordship's letter this morning the Magistrates of the Bolton Division were perfectly aware of the nature of Mr. Borron's communication to your Lordship & of his previous concert with Mr. Borron of Cockey Moor, & of the reception at his house of Mr. Battersby, the seditious orator from Leigh. The Petition which he states to have been presented to the Magistrates of the Warrington Division who usually assemble at Leigh, was certainly never shewn to Mr. Marsh, the only Magistrate who meets Mr. Borron. The former Gentleman was here on public business the day before yesterday, & expressed himself perfectly ignorant of Mr. Borron's proceeding. He shewed me the copy of a petition which had been forwarded to his Majesty's Secretary of State for the Home Department imploring instant Military Protection and expressing the well-grounded fears of the inhabitants of an immediate open insurrection. Mr. Borron either knows or *ought* to *know* that Pikes have been openly fabricated in the district committed to his peculiar care, and with the *intent of being carried to the Bolton meeting.*

The documents substantiating these facts have been sent to Lord Sidmouth. Mr. Borron offers to your Lordship a pledge on the part of certain persons that the Meeting at Bolton shall be peaceably conducted, if not officially interfered with. But who gives this pledge? Can the word of an infuriated leader of *Radical Reform* be accepted as a guarantee for public safety? & if it was not the pledge of some *leader* what effect would be produced by the promise of a few of their infatuated & rebellious followers? would their voice be listened to in a mob of twenty thousand people! For that such a tumultuous assembly would take place, unless they dreaded the salutary checks of the Law, there can be no doubt. Many persons from Yorkshire, Cheshire & the remote corners of Lancashire arrived in Bolton on the day of the expected Meeting, unconscious of its postponement, & at night a private of the 15th Hussars was shot while endeavouring to save some arms from seizure. You, my Lord, have expressed your 'Conscientious opinion'— You will pardon me if I express mine: no less founded on conscience, though not upon the same experience of the phrenzy of revolutionists under the ostensible pretence of popular deliberation, I am 'confirmed' in my opinion that such meetings as that contemplated at Bolton, the objects of which have been certified upon the oaths of incontrovertible witnesses were *illegal* in the best periods of English History, and remain so still.

However, if at the intended meeting at Bolton the resolutions proposed & the consequent discussion should relate only, as specified in the Requisition, to the affairs of the 16th of August, I, individually, would allow the people any possible latitude, because the part I took in the transactions of that day, would point out to me the indelicacy of interference when my own conduct was the subject of animadversion—so long therefore as there is no violent act of hostility on the part of the Mob, I should object to any opposition from the Magistrates. But pledged by my Oath, to protect the lives and property of those who are placed under my immediate superintendance, I hesitate not to declare, that the peaceable & loyal shall meet with as much vigorous support as they stand in need of, even though it may offend those who style themselves the friends of Radical Reform; and that so long as I remain in the Commission of the Peace 'those who are not bound by Laws or Morals *must and shall be bound by force.*'[1] I have the honour to be . . . William Hulton.

The Mr Borron, of Cockey Moor—not Mr Borron the Warrington magistrate—was the same person who had sent the witness to tell the coroner's court at Oldham what he knew of the alleged exploits of Col. Fletcher at the hustings on 16 August; with what success has been shown. The attempt to 'exploit' the matter of the suppressed Bolton meeting was not much more successful.

Hulton had said that the pressure of business at that time of crisis had portioned out his time. One office he had filled for some years was a casualty in that autumn of 1819. A letter 'addressed' to the editor of

---

[1] However uncompromising such a view might appear in the context of Hulton's letter, it was the identical viewpoint of 'Aristides': 'Reverence for the laws should be a sacred principle with the friends of freedom. If you are not governed by law you must necessarily be governed by *force*'. (See above, p. 296.)

the *Manchester Observer*, dated 6 October, concerned that office which William Hulton probably had to neglect. It ran:

Sir—The anniversary of the Bible Society belonging to this town, was expected to have been held in our Theatre as usual on this day. On making inquiry why it has not been held, I received for answer that the committee were afraid that the chairman W—— H——, Esq., of H—— P——, would not meet with the reception from the people which he has enjoyed on former occasions. In this town many pious persons lament most deeply that a cause like this should have at its head a character so objectionable. A chairman to a Bible Society, Mr. Editor, ought to be a man whose affections are ardently fixed on the sacred volume, and whose conduct eminently exemplifies the holy, the peaceable tendency of its doctrines; and if he sanction, or be accessary [*sic*] to the slaughter of defenceless men and women, and helpless infants, there are few but what will perceive the awful variance between his practice and the laws of the book which he professes himself wishful to circulate.

Had the chairman to the Bolton Bible Society remonstrated with the bloodthirsty magistrates, as Reuben did with his brethren, and said 'Shed no blood,' it would have been much to his honour as a man, and to his consolation as a christian. The shedding of innocent blood is no small crime. Among the six things which the Lord hateth, 'the hand that shed innocent blood' is one. The Jews shed the blood of an innocent Reformer, and what was the consequence? The vengeance of Heaven fell upon them, and is still endured by their offspring. Every man must admire the spirit in which our blessed Redeemer pronounced the beatitude 'Blessed are the merciful: for they shall obtain mercy'. 'Blessed are the peacemakers; for they shall be called the children of God.' And if our Chairman possesses not this spirit, he will find himself in the last day numbered, not with the few, as on the 16th of August, 1819, but with the many who shall be eternally shut out from the felicity of heaven.

Yours B. M., Bolton, October 6th, 1819.[1]

---

[1] *Manchester Observer*, 9 October 1819.

XXI

A Clamorous Parliament and the Trial of Hunt

Parliament met on 23 November. The cry of the Opposition 'prepared' with all the facts which had been learned from the newspapers, was for an inquiry. 'How,' replied the Prime Minister, Lord Liverpool, in the House of Lords, 'was a parliamentary inquiry to be instituted? It could only be done by suspending the functions of the courts of law, and by silencing all subordinate tribunals. But how can proceedings there be stopped? They are begun, and already far advanced.' He tried to put off the critics by explaining:

. . . The noble viscount [Sidmouth] had been spoken of as being the only party to the letter of thanks to the magistrates . . . whatever blame attached to it belonged to him and to others of H.M. Ministers who had sanctioned it . . . believed magistrates had done their duty . . . Good God! how was the government to be carried on—how was the country itself to exist—if these things were to be permitted . . . [the magistrates] . . . having arrested the individuals they presented three weeks afterwards, to the grand jury, bills for a conspiracy against such persons for what took place on that day. The jury found these bills; and therefore he did not feel it necessary to say one word more upon that subject; it would be, he thought, improper that he should. Well, the grand jury having found them, what happened? An individual, the agent for some of those who had suffered on that day, presented no less than five bills against so many of the Yeomanry. Was that not putting the question under judicial investigation? . . . [A defence of grand juries acting upon the evidence] . . . He did say however that while grand juries were to be upheld, their decisions were not lightly to be called in question, nor was the evidence upon which they had already decided to be re-examined in another place except upon the showing of a strong case . . .[1]

Lord Chancellor Eldon was brusque:[2]

It was complained that not only had the grand jury rejected bills, but that magistrates had refused to receive informations on oath. This latter conduct was either right or wrong; if right, why complain about it? if wrong, why

[1] Parl. Deb. XLI (1819–20), 44–45.
[2] Ibid., 39.

interfere with measures already under consideration in the Court of King's Bench? Another ground for complaint was the conduct of the Coroner in adjourning an inquest. But what was the fact? The coroner alleges that the jury had been tampered with, and that there is a fear that they might give their verdict on evidence not before them on oath. He therefore adjourned the inquest in order to have the opinion of the Court of King's Bench in a matter of such high importance. What was there unjust in this?

The House was soon telling the noble lords exactly what they thought was wrong, both in the Lords and in the Commons. Lord Castlereagh put in his most impassioned plea for them to listen to the facts:

. . . Nothing was further from the magistrates' intention than that the meeting should be dispersed as it was. The magistrates had no intention to disperse the meeting at all. I think the House will say that I am not asking too much charity for the magistrates of Manchester to suppose that they are incapable of such sanguinary proceedings; at least I trust such is the temper of the country, that they ought not to be accused, pending trial, by those who think proper to tamper with the public feeling. If the magistrates had the disposition which has been ascribed to them, why did they not put their purpose into execution on the 9th instead of the 16th, when they could at least, under the cover of attacking the meeting, have declared it illegal? . . .[1]

The details of the occurrence were gone carefully over by Ministers, by Castlereagh and the Attorney-General. A withering commentary on part of their careful testimony was afterwards written by *The Times* in a leading article on 30 March 1820, in the light of what was 'revealed' at Hunt's trial. It had described the Ministers' testimony:

. . . as totally and absolutely false; it was directly opposed to truth; it does not appear to have had verisimilitude or probability in its favour. It is no more descriptive of the proceedings at Manchester, on the part of the military, the magistrates, and the mob, than it is descriptive of the proceedings at Runnymede, in King John's time, further than there were magistrates, military, and a mob, at Manchester.

It would be difficult to find a more emphatic refutation. Subsequent revelations rendered *The Times* commentary completely nugatory, but the article was, nonetheless, put into ready-reference form for posterity as wholly valid by Samuel Bamford in his *Passages* (1844) unaltered and unchanged, save what Bamford decided studiously to leave out. The magistrates had one champion among the private members. He was the

---

[1] Speech reported in *Aston's Exchange Herald*, 30 November 1819. Parl. Deb. XLI, 93–94.

Rt Hon. Member for Dover, Edward Bootle Wilbraham. Dr Read tells us:[1]

Edward Bootle Wilbraham (1771–1853) was accurately described by the *Manchester Guardian* as 'the personage who seems to have a general retainer to defend the conduct of the magistrates' (May 26, 1821). Wilbraham lived at Lathom House, near Ormskirk, Lancashire. In 1819 he was M.P. for Dover.

John Edward Taylor, of the *Manchester Guardian*, ought to have known (and probably did know) that Wilbraham was not acting as a lackey. He was often in Manchester at loyalist gatherings; he knew intimately most, if not all, of the magistrates, on the committee of which were two relatives of his by marriage, and he was something of a near neighbour to William Hulton, as part of the Wilbraham estate in Westhoughton abutted on the estate of Hulton. Bootle Wilbraham, in the House of Commons, was defending his neighbours. He was probably not very effective, for he was regarded as one of the poorest speakers in the House.[2]

Not all the Opposition speakers in the House of Commons believed all they had read in the press. One Whig Member summed up his opinion with some clarity:

The noble lord [Castlereagh] had asserted that the magistrates never contemplated the dispersion of the mob by the military. Would the public give the noble lord credit for this important fact? Would they not require that it should be proved at the bar? As a lawyer, he agreed that the Riot Act need not be read before the dispersion of an illegal meeting, and he also agreed that if in a contest with constables in dispersing an illegal meeting, the civil power destroyed life, it was justifiable homicide; but he denied most firmly that, if persons continued on the ground after the arrest of the ringleaders, the yeomanry, by any law of this country, were authorized in cutting them down. Those who remained were guilty of a misdemeanour; and it was quite too much to say, that to prevent a misdemeanour life might be destroyed with impunity, though it was otherwise in cases of felony. It might be said that the yeomanry only endeavoured to arrest; but did they secure one individual, or did they take a single man to the New Bailey? Certainly not; and in this view of the question, supposing the meeting to have been illegal, the military had been guilty of a high offence in the deaths they had occasioned, and the wounds they had inflicted. What complexion, then, did the transaction take? The people met to petition. The magistrates issued a warrant to arrest certain individuals; and that being executed, the yeomanry disperse

[1] Read, p. 181.
[2] Tradition in his family.

the crowd at the edge of the sabre: three days afterwards the thanks of the Prince Regent were given, both to the civil and military authorities; and what was the unavoidable inference, but that opinions, however, absurd or preposterous, were to be put down by the bayonet, and that the ministers intended to act on a system of military coercion? Did not this demand inquiry? Did not this call upon the whole nation to insist that inquiry should be instituted . . . Where, but in that place which was the professed sanctuary of the rights of the people—the House of Commons. Where but before the grand inquest of the nation . . . &c.[1]

There were probably few of the members in the House on that day able to see the errors of fact in the careful statement of the honourable and learned member. There were minor errors and major ones; of the minor, the meeting was not called for 'petitioning'; of the major errors, the Yeomanry did not go in to disperse the crowd, nor to make the arrests; but the greatest 'error' was that the crowd, or part of it, had, according to the Government spokesmen's narrative, attacked the Yeomanry. The speaker was also seemingly unaware that other troops had been involved as well as the Yeomanry; even he had relied too much on the press reports.

There was, however, one matter of which the hon. and learned member was aware: it was that which has already been referred to, and of which Joseph Johnson, one of the accused, was aware also. It was that he could 'separate' what had occurred before the arrests and what had occurred afterwards. The hon. and learned member further observed:[2]

. . . from what he had heard he thought it likely that the motives of the persons who called it [the 16th August meeting] were criminal, and that many of the persons attending it had had criminal intentions. But many such meetings had been held before and since; and he was surprised that the persons attending these meetings had never been punished. In July last, a few days after the prorogation of Parliament, a meeting was held at Smithfield, at which it was resolved that the laws were not to be obeyed after January, 1820, and that no taxes were to be paid after that date; and having never yet heard of any proceedings to punish the persons who had passed those resolutions, he was surprised that a meeting should be put down by force, at which no such resolutions had been passed. The first meeting advertised [August 9th] would undoubtedly have been illegal, and on this account the object was changed, and the second Manchester meeting of the 16th of August took place. What followed? Hunt and his associates were arrested, and after the warrant had been executed, the people assembled were cut and trampled down by the yeomanry . . .

[1] Parl. Deb., XLI, 133.
[2] Ibid., 132.

The two foregoing extracts from one speech in that House of Commons debate in November were probably not particularly noticed either by most of those who heard it, or by those who read the speech afterwards. The speech was however noted with some satisfaction by Ministers, and especially by the Attorney-General Sir Robert Gifford.[1]

Sir Robert Gifford was concerned with the question of the legality of the activities of the radical leaders and had no intention of allowing the violence in which the Peterloo meeting ended to distract him from that inquiry. If one considers the events leading up to the Peterloo meeting, and right up to the moment of the arrest of Hunt, as (a) and the events thereafter as (b), Sir Robert Gifford had no intention of allowing (b) to interfere with (a), only in so far as (b) strengthened (a). The slow cogitations of the Law Officers of the Crown in the weeks before Peterloo have been related.[2] It will also be remembered that Sir Robert Gifford and Sir John Copley, the Attorney-General and Solicitor-General, had come to their considered decision on 17 August. Their opinion may be recapitulated:

If it can be proved that Mr. Hunt spoke or took part *in support* of the resolutions [at Smithfield] we think that he, as well as any other person acting in a similar way, may be made the objects of a criminal prosecution, but before any such prosecution is instituted, we think that the whole of the evidence affecting him and such other person should be more fully and particularly stated . . .

It might be imagined that this opinion, arrived at and signed on 17 August, whilst as yet none of the echoes of the din and clamour of events in Manchester had reached London, would have been overlaid and made irrelevant by events. It was not. Sir Robert Gifford, 'discreet and moderate, never putting the formidable machinery of state prosecutions in motion without necessity and with the strongest probability of obtaining conviction,'[3] was not to be deflected by 'the actual events of 16 August, tragic though they were'. On the contrary, he pushed on with his original plan 'of getting the Radical leaders quietly into prison by using the normal processes of the law and without making any spectacular gestures'.[4]

---

[1] It was noticed too by Henry Hunt. The part making an assessment of what occurred on the field of Peterloo Hunt tried to introduce into his defence at his trial. He was overruled by the Judge, after vigorous protests from the Crown prosecuting counsel, James Scarlett, for very good reasons. The speech in the House was that of the hon. and learned member for Peterborough, James Scarlett himself. *State Trials*, 381 *et seq.*

[2] See above, p. 142.

[3] See above, p. 143 note 3.

[4] Read, p. 120.

The despatch of Bouchier, the assistant solicitor to the Treasury, to Manchester, so that he could be present at the preliminary hearings against the arrested radicals on 27 August, has perhaps been misinterpreted. Henry Hunt completely misinterpreted it. In his *Memoirs* (III, 624) he gave his readers the impression that it was entirely owing to his brilliant cross-examination of witnesses, causing them to contradict one another, and his confounding the Manchester magistrates at every turn, that caused them, after a 'private conference' with the Crown Solicitor, to alter the original charge of High Treason to the lesser one of conspiracy. Hunt was wrong; the decision to bring the prisoners to trial on the lesser charge was made by the Cabinet two days before the final magistrates'-court hearings. Dr Read, although recognizing this, gives the impression that the Government stepped in to bring the blundering Manchester magistrates under control by taking decisions out of their hands. Dr Read says:[1]

Not surprisingly, after Peterloo the Home Office immediately gave up this attitude of trusting confidence [in the Magistrates of Manchester—of 'placing a heavy reliance on the good sense of the magistrates, inclining to give them detailed advice rather than definite instructions; which hopeful attitude was most unfortunate'] Bouchier . . . was despatched to Manchester to assist the magistrates in dealing with the situation, and the most complete surveillance was now exercised over the local authorities. The exact nature of the charge against Hunt was determined upon not by the local bench but by the government.

The evidence suggests, however, that, whatever had occurred at the arrest of Henry Hunt, it would still have been the Government who would have determined the charges to be preferred. It is known that Hunt, almost on his arrest, was demanding to know from the magistrates the nature of the charge. There were some exchanges not exactly recorded. Hunt averred that Hulton had suggested the charge might be one of murder, but Hulton denied this;[2] he was however remanded on 20 August on a charge of High Treason by the local magistrates. The charge being only a 'provisional' one pending the arrival of detailed advice from government, advice which Hay had requested in his letter written on the night of 16 August. Apart from Bouchier's arrival, Sidmouth had replied to the magistrates as follows:

Hobhouse to Norris, 25th August, 1819. Upon consideration of all the facts now before his Lordship [Lord Sidmouth] it appears to him most advisable, after consulting the Attorney and Solicitor General, to indict the prisoners

[1] Read, p. 184.
[2] *Wheeler's Manchester Chronicle,* 28 August 1819.

implicated in the transaction of the 16th inst., for a treasonable conspiracy to alter by force the constitution of the realm as by law established; and consequently his Lordship's wish that they should be committed for trial for that offence, but that nothing should be said to create a belief that an indictment for a more serious crime will not be preferred against them, in case the evidence to be hereafter procured should warrant it.[1]

The 'complete surveillance' after 16 August would appear to have remained similar to the surveillance before that date. The Attorney- and Solicitor-Generals were convinced that the news of how the 16 August meeting had assembled together with the meeting at Smithfield and that proposed for 9 August added up to treasonable conspiracy. They then looked at Peterloo itself from every angle: Hay's report; the Manchester delegation; Byng's and L'Estrange's reports; these were not enough to place before Parliament. A detailed report was required from the Yeomanry, and others from the magistrates. On 23 November they felt themselves sufficiently primed to present to the clamorous Opposition all, or nearly all, that they knew. To strengthen (a) they issued their 'White Paper' of documents.

On the illegality of the Manchester meeting he could speak with the utmost confidence. Without referring to information exclusively in possession of the government, and none of which had yet been communicated to the public; but taking the facts which were generally stated and admitted, he would not hesitate to declare, relying on the opinion of the great legal authorities, in whom he could place the most implicit confidence, that the assembly on the 16th August was not only illegal but treasonable.[2]

Thus Viscount Sidmouth in the House of Lords. In the House of Commons Lord Castlereagh was equally vehement:

. . . A meeting may not be illegal at the outset, but from circumstances may become so. I protest against the doctrines of the Rt. Hon. Gentleman [Tierney] that it never had a traitorous character [Mr. Tierney, across the table, denied his having so stated.] I beg pardon if I have mistaken the Rt. Hon. Gentleman; but I understood him, when he asked why Hunt was not arrested the day before (Hear). Why was the prisoner Harrison arrested in the midst of Smithfield? Why? because his arrest was attempted at Manchester, when he fled. He was taken as I trust all will be taken who offend against the law. Whenever Magistrates are charged with the execution, they are not to be deterred from that duty merely because the offender is surrounded with the paraphernalia of a mob . . .[3]

[1] *State Trials*, p. 173.
[2] Parl. Deb. XLI (1819–20), 23.
[3] Speech in House of Commons as reported in *Aston's Exchange Herald,* 30 November 1819.

With evidence to support them in regard to (a) the Government were in an impregnable position; but the House was hardly interested in (a), they wanted to know about (b). On that ministers were more vulnerable. There were miscalculations and blunders at Manchester which needed a lot of explanation. There had been the threatening placard regarding the meeting of 9 August; there was the fiasco of the alleged 12 o'clock reading of the Riot Act, details of which had got into the press; there was the (abortive) official reading of the Riot Act just before the constables and the Yeomanry moved in, and the inept attempt by two others to read it in the crowd and at the hustings; Hay's report lacked all mention of the central incident of the day, the alleged attack by part of the mob.

It is not known why the Government so resolutely set their faces against an inquiry; it is not believed that it was for the reason that they had something to hide, apart from a certain ineptitude. They were, however, conscious of their own rectitude; through their probing they had become convinced of the basic rectitude of the Manchester magistrates also. They said that they could not reverse proceedings already commenced. Lord Castlereagh continued,[1] on the lamentable loss of lives:

. . . Nothing can be more lamentable; but that does not go to establish, nor does it go to the presumption of the necessity of an inquiry into that transaction in this House. Because, though I apprehend it is the duty of the House to watch over the interests of the country, there may be calamities over which it can have no control; and I believe it is impossible for the Rt. Hon. Gentleman or any other member of this House to state a single instance of a Parliamentary inquiry into transactions in any degree resembling the transactions of August 16th. Strong allusion had been made to the transaction. This is not the place for the administration of justice. Justice is in this country administered with a firm, but with a merciful hand, and I cannot conceive that this House upon a transaction arising merely from local distress can by any possibility interfere. I am sure the House will go along with me in feeling an extreme delicacy in this state of the business in saying anything of the transactions at Manchester; so far as it may be supposed to affect any criminal proceedings depending in any court, or which may hereafter depend in any court upon that transaction, which has agitated so much the people of this kingdom.

Therefore I hope I shall be excused from completely answering some of the questions of the Rt. Hon. Gentleman. He has put a question which it is not imposed upon me to answer. There is a tribunal at which an answer may be given, if the view of prosecuting was for the purpose of public justice,

[1] See note 3 previous page.

and where statements can properly be made that affect the innocence or guilt of the parties, and where the one or the other may be made apparent . . . To adopt the mode of inquiry suggested by [Tierney] would be to abandon the proper means of justice.

Sir Robert Gifford, in replying in the debate, observed:

. . . Because the gentlemen on the other side might not have obtained information enough to satisfy them, that was no adequate ground for inquiry. He denied that a case of suspicion had been made out against the magistrates, and said that the presumption, after the decision of the grand jury at Lancaster, must be all in their favour. The question of the legality of the meeting would soon come before a court for decision; and he insisted that that was not only a competent, but the most competent tribunal.[1]

Lord Stanley, the son of the Earl of Derby, a Whig and in Opposition, made his plea for the hearing of the view of Capt. Birley:[2]

. . . It had lately been the practice to post up in the windows of the *Manchester Observer* the names of the persons wounded, and also the names of those soldiers by whom wounds were said to have been inflicted. Among others, the name of Capt. Birley was frequently mentioned. Now the fact was that Capt. Birley had, according to his own statement, never taken his sword from his shoulder, unless to make way for two poor women who were oppressed by the crowd. If that gentleman had seen the soldiers commit any of the acts so often talked of, he [Lord Stanley] had no doubt that he would have exerted himself to put a stop to them.[3]

The *Manchester Observer*, of 4 December 1819, commented on the proceedings in Parliament, and on Lord Stanley:

. . . But the ministers it appears have got a new and powerful ally in Lord Stanley (the son of our own dignified Lord Lieutenant). In a speech of considerable length, he contrives to vilify the character of the meeting and vindicate the conduct of the Yeomanry. He deals roundly in 'assertions'—did we not feel inclined to be courteous to high rank—we should have said 'lies'. We are happy, however, that we have obtained the honour of his lordship's particular notice, and will thank him or his humane friend and informant (Capt. Birley) to prove the truth of the following statement: 'In the windows of the *Manchester Observer* office were exhibited prints descriptive of the cavalry cutting at the people, and the names of individual Yeomen connected with those prints. The name of his friend Mr. Birley very frequently occurred there'. To the dreadful charge of having exhibited prints of Peter's Field, as it appeared on the bloody 16th of August, we must plead guilty—

---

[1] Parl. Deb. XLI, 135.
[2] See above, p. 193.
[3] Parl. Deb. XLI, 326.

but we defy it to be truly said that we ever descended to become aspersers of individual character. But this is of a piece with Lord Stanley's other averments . . .

From the printer and publisher of 'Hurly-Burly' (*Manchester Observer*, 28 August 1819)[1] it was cool comment. Lord Stanley, nevertheless, was for the suggested inquiry by Parliament. The government spokesman, Lord Castlereagh, still had faith in Englishmen:

. . . He trusted that the country would now see cause to give credit to those magistrates for what ought never to be denied to men in their situation, and presume them innocent till the contrary was proved. All he asked of his countrymen was, not to run them unfairly down, but to believe them innocent till something was established against them . . .[2]

The Opposition's cry was still for an inquiry. To counter-balance any effect the explanations of H.M. Ministers might have, on 29 November a petition of Henry Hunt's was presented, complaining of the misrepresentation of his conduct:

He complained of the Manchester magistrates, of the Juries, of the officers, and more pointedly and strongly of H.M. Ministers. Declared that the papers laid on the table were entirely false and prayed that he might be called to the bar of the House to prove his allegations. Recited his appeal to the people to 'come to the meeting of 16th August armed with no weapon but a self-approving conscience . . .' Hunt submitted 'that as the persons guilty of the outrages described in these affidavits, consisted of ten magistrates acting in the vicinity, having extensive local and family connections, and as the officers and privates of the yeomanry cavalry who perpetrated the cruelties were in like manner intimately connected with all or most of the persons exercising judicial and magisterial authority in the county of Lancaster, and were supported by a numerous train of dependants, unprincipled and desperate characters connected with the police, as it is notorious it must always be the case in police establishments . . . that the Grand Jury [at Lancaster] . . . were unavoidably actuated by the same party violence which had misled their brother magistrates at Manchester in committing those crimes which it is now become necessary under colour of law, to screen from inquiry and punishment . . .[3]

The Parliamentary report comments on this: 'Although 'no, noes' were heard in the House and there appeared a momentary disposition to divide . . . the petition was ordered to be printed.' Henry Hunt

[1] See above, p. 273.
[2] *Aston's Exchange Herald,* 30 November 1819.
[3] Parl. Deb. XLI, 1819-20, pp. 370-7.

could hardly complain that in that corrupt House of Parliament he did not get a fair hearing; and the press of the nation echoed with it.

As the forces ranged themselves for the famous trial, Hunt could not complain of the fate which placed a prosecuting counsel against him who was almost as critical of the Government and its policies after Peterloo as he was.[1] There is no place in Prentice's version of the trial for appreciation of this fact. Prentice saw only 'eager and vindictive attempts' on the prosecution's part to prove what they had to prove. Hunt at his trial commented sardonically on the absence of the Attorney-General and the Solicitor-General; he might also have added 'or any of the other Ministry-supporting K.C.s who could quite reasonably have been expected to have the brief for the prosecution in this famous case.' But the Crown prosecutor was James Scarlett.

There was some rancour shown towards Scarlett by Hunt during the trial proceedings, so much so that Scarlett, before judgment was finally given on 15 May 1820, rose 'to principally correct,' he said, 'a mistake under which Mr Hunt seemed to labour, namely that he [Scarlett] was selected to conduct the prosecution:'

There could not be a greater misapprehension. It was purely a matter of accident, from the circumstance of his situation at the Bar, and the absence of his senior, that he was employed in the case. As to any resentment he might be supposed to entertain towards Mr. Hunt, nothing could be more erroneous. He never entertained any towards that individual, of whom he knew nothing but what he happened to read in the public papers, and to suppose that he was selected to conduct the prosecution on account of this resentment, was really absurd. If such selection could have taken place on such an account, he could only have treated it as a personal insult towards him on the part of the Attorney-General. Adverting to the case under consideration, he entertained no doubt of the illegality of the defendants' conduct, who, he said, endeavoured to divert the attention of the Court and the public, by introducing matters which had nothing whatever to do with the offence with which they were called upon to answer. He insisted that whatever might have been the conduct of the Magistrates and Yeomanry of Manchester, it was wholly irrelevant to the question of the defendant's guilt or innocence of the crime imputed by the indictment.

[1] On 13 December Scarlett protested against the Seditious Meetings Prevention Bill, the provisions of which he described as being 'inimical to the liberties of the country'. (D.N.B. quoting Parl. Deb. 1st series xli, 1062–8). Scarlett to Lord Fitzwilliam (just before the verdict of Hunt's trial was given): 'If there is a conviction it will not touch the case of the Magistrates or the Yeomanry. The nature of the charges did not involve the propriety of *their* conduct, which will be still open to inquiry and in my opinion will call for inquiry as much as ever if all the defendants are found guilty.' (Dr Read, page 152, note, quoting Wentworth Woodhouse Papers, 52e).

Mr. Hunt in alluding to his trial at York ten years later, still said, 'that the gentleman who was to have been the leading counsel [Mr. Clarke] received six-hundred guineas to stay away from York Assizes, that Sir James Scarlett who was known to have a personal antipathy to him, might have the direction of the trial. After a trial of fourteen days, he was found guilty, one of the jury (as he afterwards acknowledged) being assured by the foreman, that the object of government was only to put down illegal meetings, and if they found him guilty he should not be called up for judgment.[1]

★   ★   ★

The trial of Henry Hunt, Bamford, Healey, and the others, which took place in March 1820, has been considered and reconsidered by generations since that time in the printed versions readily available. Some have considered it almost a travesty of justice. Prentice surely did. He inveighed against 'judge-made' law and justice; of the learned judge he wrote:

. . . There never was a man better fitted for the purpose than this judge. His appearance was prepossessing, tall, slender, and grave; mild in manner, but cunning in effect, and at the very time he led the people to suppose he was aiding the prisoner, according to the farcical notion of being his counsel, he was studiously entangling him in the meshes of special pleading, so as to secure his victim upon the altar prepared by Sidmouth and Castlereagh. For services rendered, this pious judge, and editor of an edition of the Book of Common Prayer, with notes, which teaches humility and mercy, was created a baronet on retiring from the Bench.[2]

Prentice was under the impression, wittingly or unwittingly, that Hunt and his associates were being tried for what had occurred on St Peter's Field. They were, but only for what had occurred up to the time when the warrants were issued for their arrest. On that the accused were charged; on that the accused were convicted. James Scarlett, as Crown prosecuting counsel, did everything in his power at the trial to make that clear. He carried it to such lengths as to make it appear that his own principal witness, Hulton, could be mistaken in his evidence; leaving his testimony uncorroborated when, as even the Judge remarked, corroboration should have been forthcoming.

Mr. Hulton, of Hulton, indeed did swear that the Yeomanry were assaulted and surrounded, but when this was totally disproved, the Judge kindly saved Mr. Hulton of Hulton, by stating that he must have been in such an agitation of mind, and such a local situation, as disqualified him from having a true

---

[1] Henry Hunt, on St Peter's Field for the first time after 16 August 1819, after his Preston election defeat in August 1830. (*Manchester Times*, 21 August 1830.)

[2] Prentice, *Recollections*, p. 190.

view, and no other Magistrates (though *they were all there*) was disposed of himself or was called by the Counsel for the Crown, to confirm Mr. Hulton of Hulton's evidence. Alas! Alas! Mr. Hulton of Hulton . . .[1]

Hunt used every weapon in his extensive armoury of circumlocution to impress the court. One incident did not impress Samuel Bamford—the moment when Hunt, with tears trickling down his face, denounced Richard Carlile. Bamford never forgave him. Hunt's flattery of the judge brought forth sharp retorts from that august personage almost in the manner of G. K. Chesterton to F. E. Smith. All Hunt's oratory was intended to delude the court and the public into believing that he was being tried for an offence which did not appear on the indictment— responsibility for all that had occurred on St Peter's Field—and that the real guilty parties were the wicked magistrates and the Manchester Yeomanry.

Henry Hunt has had many aiders and abettors since that day, notably, as had been said, Archibald Prentice.[2]

The attempt was made eagerly and vindictively, on the part of the prosecution, to substantiate a charge of sedition and conspiracy, by bringing evidence to establish some remote connection of that assemblage with a meeting that had previously been held at Smithfield, and with the trainings at White Moss; but the Judge, Mr. Justice Bayley, either saw that the evidence was insufficient, or that a conviction on such strained construction of the law would be odious to the country, and he laid main stress in summing up on the use of flags, as tending to incite the multitude.

A similar point of view as that promulgated by Prentice has been pursued since. Dr Read said:[3]

The summing up of the judge largely narrowed the case down to a discussion of the fourth count, the charge of unlawful and seditious assembling for the purpose of exciting discontent. In this context the drilling and the inscriptions on the Radical banners were all-important. Bayley drew the attention of the jury to these circumstances particularly in dealing with Bamford . . . [Quotation from the summing up.] . . . This drilling and these banners, it will be remembered, were particular causes of 'loyalist' alarm in Manchester, and they seem to have the same effect on the jurymen at York; for despite Bayley's obvious desire for an acquittal, they found the principal defendants . . . guilty on this fourth count. After a motion for a new trial had failed sentence was passed on May 15th.

[1] *The Times*, 3 April 1820.
[2] *Recollections*, pp. 189–90.
[3] Read, pp. 152–3.

The legend of Judge Bayley's 'obvious desire for an acquittal' persists against the evidence of Judge Bayley's own words. In the hearings on Hunt's motion for a new trial, on 13 May, Hunt said:

. . . After the great length of time that this important trial had occupied—after the attention which the Court had bestowed upon the mass of evidence which had been received in support of the prosecution—and after the decision of the jury (in opposition to the feeling and judgment of every man in the country, and he might add, he believed, of the Learned Judge)—

Justice Bayley:

I must not allow you to say that. If I had been on the jury, I must have found a verdict of Guilty, at least against you and some of the other defendants.[1]

Some of the defendants had already been acquitted. The public in 1819 (and there were many who gained the impression that the summing up and the whole proceedings were favourable to the accused) were misled; posterity has been misled, because they could not separate (a) from (b). Judge Bayley could; James Scarlett could; Joseph Johnson could; and there is no doubt that Henry Hunt could. During the hearings on Hunt's motion for a new trial, Hunt affected to have been taken by surprise by Scarlett's introduction of the Smithfield meeting resolutions in the trial. It was affectation. He was perfectly aware, as has been seen, of what Scarlett had said in the House of Commons on the Smithfield resolutions; so important did Hunt seem to regard it that he appeared to attempt to shake Scarlett's confidence on this very point (and score a point in his (Hunt's) favour). The relevant passage in the trials:

How comes it, [said Hunt] that the learned Counsel for the prosecution is placed in this situation [of prosecuting Hunt and the others] when one of the most important questions ever agitated in a Court of Justice, or submitted to the consideration of a Jury, is brought forward? How comes it that neither the Attorney-General nor the Solicitor-General are here? Perhaps you will be told because the defendant is little better than a country bumpkin, not worth while to combat, or some mere country squire; and they say, 'Oh, we can manage him.' Is this the case? No—if the Attorney-General were here, I'd call him, place him in that box, and make him prove he was consulted by the Lord Mayor and others, as to the legality of the Smithfield meeting; that he declared it was legal; and that between the 9th and 16th of August, Mr. Hay, of Manchester, also consulted him as to the meeting of the 16th.
Mr. Justice Bayley: That, Mr. Hunt, could not be allowed in evidence.
Mr. Hunt: My Lord, I would have tried the experiment.

[1] *Manchester Observer*, 20 May 1820.

Mr. Serjeant Hullock: No doubt of that.

Mr. Justice Bayley: If the Attorney-General had been here, whatever his opinion might be, he should take the law from me.

Mr. Hunt: *We* should have asked him many questions, and from Mr. Hay also.[1]

The 'we' at the end of the quotation is not, of course, in italics in the report; but Hunt had scored his point, though it doubtless did not affect Scarlett's opinion, the opinion he had voiced in the House of Commons. In spite of later commentators' opinions to the contrary, the connection with the Smithfield meeting was the most important factor in the conviction of Hunt. For Prentice to pretend, in 1851,[2] that there was only a 'remote connection' with White Moss and the affairs of the 16 August was sheer perversity.

There is a very good reason why modern commentators are led to believe in this long-held view of Judge Bayley's 'obvious desire for an acquittal'. It is that his assertion to the contrary does not find a place in the available printed reports of the trials. There is a long paragraph at the end of the report of Hunt's trial in the State Trials edition[3] which comments on the sources from which the printed report is compiled; it ought to convey a caution. It includes the sentence: 'No complete verbatim report of the evidence in the form of questions and answers appears to exist', and the learned editor goes on to say what other sources he has used; they include the older printed versions, Pratt and Dolby, *and* newspaper reports. There are minor variations between the State Trials edition and Dolby and Pratt[4] which illuminate certain passages. Neither Dolby's nor Pratt's editions include any reports of the proceedings on Hunt's motion for a new trial, which was heard on 1, 2, 3, 5, 6, 8, 13 and 15 May 1820; the State Trials edition report on these hearings is attenuated, covering only four columns;[5] it is quite inadequate for a full understanding of the trial. The newspaper reports are extensive, and the *Manchester Observer's*[6] particularly so; they correct, as has been seen, one misapprehension. There are others.

Chief Justice Abbott delivered judgment, and gave a long summing

[1] Hunt Trial (Pratt edn.), p. 87.
[2] Prentice, 183.
[3] *State Trials,* pp. 495-6.
[4] See above, p. 201. Both editions (Dolby's and Pratt's) were issued by the radicals as propaganda.
[5] *State Trials,* p. 490.
[6] 13 May 1820; 20 May 1820. The *Manchester Observer* (1820) printed an edition of Hunt's Trial in which these proceedings are given fully. This edition was presumably unknown to the editors of *State Trials,* and appears to have escaped notice by other writers.

up on Hunt's objections to the admission of certain evidence; he gave them in this order: 1. The conduct of the military; the evidence was not admissible. 2. On the Smithfield meeting; the evidence was admissible: 'that what was done under the auspices of the same man' [Hunt] 'at a meeting summoned professedly for the same purpose . . . was relevant to the matter in issue.' 3. Evidence on training and drilling and the assault on White Moss; evidence admissible. 4. On flags and banners; evidence admissible. Judge Bayley concurred.[1] If, therefore, Judge Bayley's summing up in the printed reports of Hunt's trial has appeared to give pride of place to the evidence on banners and flags, it was corrected on the motion for a new trial and given its proper place. Joseph Johnson's simple retort to Henry Hunt may be reiterated: 'It was owing to your very stupid resolutions at the Smithfield meeting . . . that either you or I was imprisoned at all'.[2]

Henry Hunt made much ado about the banners and flags, the 'bloody dagger', Carlile's presence on the hustings, and the other side issues which blinded his radical followers then and have blinded his apologists in later times. Those side issues did not blind his judges, nor the jury, nor James Scarlett, nor even Joseph Johnson. They did not blind Henry Hunt. One of the unrecorded pearls of Huntean candour—unrecorded, that is, in most of the printed versions of the trial—but contained in the *Manchester Observer's* (13 May 1820) report of the proceedings in Hunt's motion for a new trial, occurred during the hearings on Saturday 6 May:

. . . Mr. Hunt argued that, if the Smithfield resolutions were, as they ought to be, rejected, there would be against him no evidence at all.

They were not rejected.

Another point which Hunt understood very well during this hearing was the magistrates' version of the happenings on St Peter's Field, the version which he was doing everything in his power to undermine. He said:

[He] allowed the hissing and hooting at the Star Inn, but not towards the magistrates . . . It was in proof that the magistrates were not at the Star Inn at that time, and that they were not in the habit of meeting there. So far from the meeting of the 16th being illegal, there was originally no intention on the part of the magistrates to disperse that meeting. They never proposed to interfere until the meeting assumed an appearance *in terrorem*; even then, according to their own account, they only meant to secure the leaders; and it

[1] *Manchester Observer*, 13–20 May 1820.
[2] See above, pp. 312–13.

was not until they thought, or chose to think, the cavalry in danger, that they ordered the dispersion. He [Mr. Hunt] did not mean to hold that the people were justified in resisting the execution of a legal warrant . . .[1]

Henry Hunt was better informed than many of his contemporaries. Much has been said about what evidence was admissible, and what was not in the case against Hunt and his colleagues. Little or nothing seems to have been said on the evidence which Judge Bayley allowed in Hunt's favour. It was significant. The following exchange occurred between the Judge and Hunt on the fifth day:

Hunt said: I shall prove to you gentlemen of the Jury that during this transaction there was no resistance. I shall prove to you by those who sat immediately over—one, two, or three in a window—that those men so came in, and that, observing these persons looking over their bloody deeds, they drew their pistols and said 'Go from the window or we shall blow your bloody brains out. Drop the curtain'.

Judge Bayley: That cannot be evidence; that is the conduct of certain persons towards people in the windows. We must confine ourselves to the conduct of the crowd—to the circumstances which occurred to them.

Hunt: They were looking over.

Judge Bayley: At present it is in evidence, and you have a right therefore to contradict, that on the cavalry being ordered to go up to the hustings they were pelted, that there were stones, brick-bats, and sticks lifted up, and that there was a defiance, and that in addition to that they were surrounded; you may certainly be at liberty to go into evidence to show that when they advanced no such circumstance took place.

Hunt: I shall not endeavour to inflame the minds of any of my hearers after the decision of the noble judge. I shall not after what has fallen from the learned judge proceed. You shall find me, and he shall find me, always as willing to listen to any admonition or any direction he may give, as I am bold and determined in doing what I think is my duty to myself and to the public . . .[2]

Hunt, as has been seen, was perfectly aware of the magistrates' case, even though many of his contemporaries were not; his seemingly inexplicable attitude with regard to Moorhouse and the careful selection of witnesses from almost everywhere around Manchester, except Stockport, add to the significance of the above passage.

Henry Hunt used his trial, as he used all other of his appearances in the courts, as a platform and as a sounding-board to propagate his version of the transactions on St Peter's Field; all of his perorations were

---

[1] *Manchester Observer*, 13 May 1820. Hunt's assertion was made on Saturday, 6 May.

[2] *State Trials*, p. 328. The *Manchester Observer* report of the trial (p. 99) abridges, almost completely, this passage.

re-echoed in the nation's press. How well he succeeded may best be judged from the reactions to his trial in March 1820, by the country as instanced an example in *The Times* comment.[1]

Somewhere in the unexplored or unnoticed correspondence of the period may be discovered, perhaps, other reasons why the Crown thought fit to conduct the trial as it did, thereby exposing the Crown witnesses, and especially Hulton, to appear so utterly defenceless against Hunt's withering assault on his veracity. Scarlett did refer to it at the trial:

He [Hunt] says that I did not venture to call a single constable, or a single magistrate to corroborate Mr. Hulton's evidence; he has a right to make the most of this point, but shall I tell him the reason why? because I waited to hear to what points the Learned Judge meant to confine our attention. The moment the Learned Judge fixed that, why should I have called such witnesses? Whether the constables had made a right or an erroneous representation to the magistrates—whether the magistrates had or had not acted with propriety or impropriety—whether the yeomanry were right or were wrong—had acted discreetly or indiscreetly, you were told by the Court was extraneous to the present subject matter for your consideration . . .[2]

In such a manner did this critic of the Government in the House of Commons construe his brief in the trial of Hunt; and the Learned Judge, in summing up, had this to say of Hulton's evidence:

He believed Mr. Hulton to be a respectable man, who would not mislead them, but he must say, that such important evidence as he had given, ought not to be permitted to want that corroboration which it might have had from his brother magistrates who were in the room with him, and from Nadin the constable. It was due to the defendants to urge this want of corroborative evidence on such important facts, and if the omission were calculated to raise a doubt in the minds of the jury, the defendants were most certainly entitled to the benefit of that doubt.[3]

The 'doubt' if it did not immediately go to the benefit of the defendants in the minds of the jury, certainly went to their benefit in the minds of the country at large. In May 1821, in the House of Commons[4] James Scarlett did advert briefly to his mode of conducting the Crown case in that trial:

. . . It was perfectly fair to draw inferences from his [Scarlett's] manner of

---

[1] See above, pp. 345–6.
[2] Hunt's Trial (Pratt edn.), p. 159.
[3] Ibid.
[4] Parl. Deb., 2nd series, vol. V, pp. 831–2.

conducting the trial, but not from his silence in that House respecting his motives. Why Nadin and others had not been called, the House would not at least know from him. The public had a right to draw their own inferences. He had endeavoured on that occasion to follow the path of duty as on every other; and to effect this object by all means of a good conscience.

No contemporary observer of James Scarlett's conduct as Crown prosecutor in the court or as a severe Government critic in the House of Commons could doubt that through it all he had a good conscience. Nor may they have been unmoved by his assertion in that court:

I venture to maintain here, and I shall do every where, no matter what my opinion of the final events of that day may be, that if the magistrates had felt alarm for the public safety, from the information they had that training was going on, and had they not taken precautions to preserve the peace of the town, they would deserve to be dismissed, and punished as traitors to their functions! They did take precautions by placing, as was their duty, the military on the ground . . .

That view was to be reiterated in the House of Commons on what has been described as (a). It was later to be backed by judicial pronouncements, and to be received by moderate opinion as mitigating to some extent (b). For the moment, however, Henry Hunt's triumph was complete. The London *Examiner* voiced general opinion:

[Mr. Hunt has] succeeded in dissolving, with a few words of his mouth, all that cloud of pretended horror and atrocity on the part of the people, which the Magistrates raised, and which the Ministers kept up, in order to cover the violence of their own proceedings.[1]

To the public, the magistrates remained for the most part an impersonal 'they'. Hulton, their chairman, was the one member who had to bear by name the responsibility for their collective actions, to appear in court as their representative, to be taunted and have his evidence twisted and falsified by Hunt. On the locking of arms Hunt alleged that Hulton had perjured himself. This was to impress many, temporarily; it impressed Prentice at the time, and thirty years later; but it impressed only those who did not follow up their reading of the trial, to the point where Hunt almost nonchalantly dismissed as unimportant the point he had gained. He did not let go, however, his claim that Hulton was a perjured man, and called on the court to treat everything he had testified as tainted.

The Hunt-Hulton passage re the locking of arms has already been

[1] Quoted by the *Manchester Gazette*, 8 April 1820.

given. Other parts of the cross-examination and comments by Hunt were as follows:

Hunt: You say depositions were made before me, in the singular number; and a warrant issued by me in singular number. Were you Commander-in-Chief of the Magistrates on that day?

Hulton: I was President of the Lancashire and Cheshire magistrates. I did not know that I used the singular number. The warrant was signed by me and others . . .

Hulton: . . . they [the magistrates] were at that moment expressing fear themselves.

Hunt: What fears? Fears that the people would hurt the yeomanry, or the yeomanry destroy the people?

Hulton: . . . I saw some of the parties march into the field in beautiful order.

Hunt: And this thing which was so beautiful created alarm in your tender heart?

Hunt: The bludgeons then, the stones that were hurled at the yeomanry, Mr. Scarlett's bludgeons, Mr. Hulton's bludgeons, brick-bats and stones, are only to be found existing in the mind of the learned counsel and his solitary witness. They know well that they had no other existence. The learned counsel said he knew Mr. Hulton better than I do. I dare say he does, and I give him the joy of his acquaintance . . . He is yet the only man who dares to swear to the flinging of stones and brandishing of sticks, to the face about of the people against the military, their being attacked, and, as it were, cut off. He only speaks to the hissing and hooting. I shall contradict that man. Why was he not corroborated by his brother magistrates, nine of whom were with him in the room where he saw all these indications of violence? Why should testimony so important want the confirmation of his brother magistrates, who could, if the story be true, have corroborated every word of it? We know that the whole of the other nine magistrates were here on the first morning of the trial, we know that Mr. Hay was here, and Mr. Norris; we know that when witnesses were all ordered out of court they went out among the rest, from that box where they had taken their places. All went out; for what; To enable them to be called as evidence, and yet not one was brought to corroborate the most strong of all. All Lancashire did not furnish a brother magistrate to corroborate Mr. Hulton; of the whole police, who take oaths by the hundred every year, there was not one to prop up such an assertion of our guilty acts; no, not one soul could be found to swear after Mr. Hulton!
. . . [Hunt on the non-reading of the Riot Act]: Mr. Ethelston sent a message to the Oldham Inquest that he could prove that he read the Riot Act. He sent in the message but he could not dare go before a jury and swear to the fact. Where were Mr. Trafford, Mr. Tatton, Mr. Hay, Mr. Norris, Colonel Fletcher, Col. O'Estrange, and all the other gentlemen who were present, to prove the reading of any Riot Act? They knew what Mr. Hulton had

sworn, why have not these come forward either to corroborate his testimony, or supply his deficiencies? Mr. Hay, indeed, did not wait; he put himself into a coach, and drove off from York instantly; we were, I suppose, expected to follow him with a subpœna. I am too old a soldier to be caught by such a manœuvre. Nature has given me common understanding, and I have seen a great deal too much of the consequences of bringing a hostile witness into the box for an examination in chief. But if they had put him up at the other side, as they must have at first intended by bringing him here, then, indeed, I should have given a 'Jew's eye' for his cross-examination. This is the Mr. Hay who got a living of £2,500 a year for his conduct in this business. If Mr. Hulton gets his reward for his share in the service, there is no gift the Crown can bestow too great for his deserts. Mr. Hulton is truly a Gentleman; the boldest man I ever saw. I know and feel that when a man of rank and character speaks before a jury of Gentlemen to facts, his evidence is necessarily calculated to make a stronger impression on their minds than when the same information is derived from persons of meaner consideration. True, the rich and the poor man are equal in the eyes of the law; but still I can see the different impression which will be made by the same circumstances reaching your ears through a different channel.

It is, perhaps, natural and proper that more weight should, in such a case, attach to what falls from a man of rank and property. The common feelings of our nature, in a certain station in society, induces us to give a preponderating weight to the testimony of our equals, in preference to others, and makes us reflect that a person so placed has a great stake in maintaining his integrity, and that if he forgets what he owes to his own conscience and his God, he must expect, as the consequence, to forfeit the rank and consideration he holds in society, and what when such a man, be his rank what it may, becomes perjured, he falls to the earth. I shall bring the most unequivocal testimony before you that Mr. —— is a —— man [Pratt's edition inserts dashes; the State Trials edition does not print the passage: 'Perjured man'; the dashes are sufficient]. That he has told you that as a truth which has not the least shadow of probability. I know that you will not take this from my mouth. I am aware you will require the strongest evidence to convince you that a man of his station could be guilty of that which I charge him with. But if I do not prove what I say now, let me be the villain that I am not and he the innocent man . . . [then] . . . I shall call upon you to dismiss from your minds the whole of Mr. Hulton's evidence upon this point . . . You will decide whether the meetings of the people or of Gentlemen like yourselves, shall in future meet under any other better security, that they shall not be cut down by sabres, than the discretion of any hot-headed young magistrate. You will have to say whether in future it shall be lawful for any such person to send among a mixed meeting of men, women and children, a set of drunken infuriated yeomanry, to inflict upon them, while peacefully assembled, military execution . . .

Judge Bayley asked Hulton how long he had been a magistrate, and in his explanations to the court on the questions he had asked Hulton, he said:

Mr. Hulton had the appearance of a youth, and it had been insinuated that he was a young magistrate to take the chair, and therefore I was desirous of knowing, that it might assist your judgment in that respect, what length of time he had been acting as a magistrate.[1]

Hulton was thirty-two, and he had been in the Commission of the Peace for eleven years.

All sorts of calumnious statements were made in the House of Commons as to the conduct of the mob; it was asserted that they had marched into Manchester armed with sticks and clubs, and one gentleman of the name of Hulton, who, very lately, had again shown a disposition to make himself conspicuous on this very question, was called upon to prove this by being placed in the witness-box, where he underwent a seven hours' examination, three in chief, and four in cross-examination. Mr. Hulton, on that occasion, had thought proper to swear that the people carried sticks as big as muskets— he (Mr. Hunt) believed that he did not go the length of swearing that the people fired them off like muskets. This was a part of the evidence adduced before the Jury at York—a Jury, in the first instance packed by the Crown, and subsequently patronized by the Whig Club. He saw the hon. member for York shook his head when he mentioned the Whigs, but he begged leave to say, that he had always considered that Jury as a Whig Jury, because he certainly did think that it emanated from the Whig Club at York; for which reason he had always been of the opinion, that his conviction was a Whig conviction . . .[2]

Hulton (in evidence at York):

Several of those persons had large sticks, I won't say shouldered like muskets, but they had them up to their shoulders.[3]

The Judge in summing up had referred to one small instance in which Hulton had been mistaken—the distance of the hustings from Mr Buxton's house. At a later stage he said:

[After remarking on the lack of corroboration] and if you think it probable or possible that Mr. Hulton should have been mistaken as to any of the circumstances which he represents himself to have seen, that he may have had a wrong impression made upon his eyesight in a time of great confusion, in a

[1] *State Trials,* p. 459.
[2] Henry Hunt, House of Commons debate, 15 March 1832 (Hansard, Vol. XI, 3rd series, 251).
[3] Hunt's Trial (Pratt edn.), p. 60.

time of very great alarm, in a time in which probably he would be under a great degree of uneasiness upon the subject, if you think he may be mistaken as to any of these particulars, I am bound to state to you that, inasmuch as there were other persons standing by him at the time who could have confirmed his account, and who could have corrected his account if in any respect that account had been erroneous—if the other circumstances of the case make you think it possible that Mr. Hulton in any part of that representation may have been mistaken—then, in a criminal case you ought to say, Why were not the other magistrates called? . . .

If the defendants had been on their trial for what had occurred after their arrests, with such a defence, with such summing up, they would without doubt have been found not guilty. But the Jury, who had learned how to distinguish pre and post arrest events, found them guilty.

Hunt in his motion for a new trial before the Judges, observed that he could not hope to impress them as he might have impressed a jury. There were histrionics, made, not in the hope of impressing the Judges, but for the benefit of the outside world who were listening in. Hunt had been perfectly aware of what was relevant and what was not relevant, and he knew what was coming to him; there was one last Huntean harangue to the world outside before he disappeared from view:

. . . If it was evidence that the people resisted the military, the provocation which had produced that resistance must also be evidence. Mr. Hulton had sworn to the raising of sticks and the hurling of stones. He (Mr. Hunt) knew that Mr. Hulton's evidence had been overwhelmed and beaten down by the united testimony of a cloud of respectable witnesses. He felt that the jury could not have given credit to a tittle of it; but Mr. Hulton's evidence had gone to the jury; and the moment that Mr. Hulton's evidence was received, the defendants had a right to call evidence to show provocation . . .

They were told, 'Your meeting' [the 9th August] 'is for an illegal purpose'. They called another of a different nature. The requisition for that meeting was signed by seven hundred persons, strangers? They had lived and worked, some of them, twenty and twenty-five years in the same town . . . they were poor men; and if they committed any offence they were speedily detected and punished, and sent packing. They were not gentlemen; not like Mr. Hulton of Hulton; not men of property who might be steeped to the lips in infamy and crime, and yet lived unmolested and undisturbed in their mansions, who were above the reach of being driven from their homes or from society.

The Chief Justice: No man in England, Mr. Hunt, is above the reach of the law.

. . . But the Reformers met on the 16th of August. No doubt there was a feeling in the public mind: such a feeling might well be troublesome to government—it might go near to threaten some of those precious scenes of bribery and corruption, and drunkenness which distinguished our elections. What said the government? 'This will not do. We must make a law to put this down'. 'No', said the magistrates of Manchester', (no doubt in correspondence with some of the worthy gentlemen near Mr. Hunt)—'no; law is not necessary. You could not act at Smithfield; but we will put down the thing, and make an end at once!' Punishment! was punishment talked of for the defendants in this case? He (Mr. Hunt) knew the sort of men he had to contend with; and it was his misfortune that, by law, those persons were allowed to speak after him; but he would tell these learned counsel, that when they came to press, and press they would, for judgment against him, they should confine themselves to that part of the indictment upon which he had been found guilty, or he would take the liberty to interrupt them.

Punishment! If to be a sincere advocate in the cause of Reform was a crime, then he was guilty, and guilty he trusted he should remain. Punishment! In exercising the right of a citizen, he had seen his fellow-subjects struck down dead before his face; he had seen women cut down, mangled and trampled upon; he had himself been seized by the military, pinioned down, dragged along; he had narrowly escaped having his brains beaten out, and should not have escaped but for his own presence of mind: at the moment when his arms were pinioned to his sides, a major-general in the army had struck him from behind, a blow which had nearly felled him to the ground; that first blow had been insufficient for the purpose, and his hat had been snatched off, that the blow might be repeated with more effect. If the second blow had fallen upon his head, he should not now have been troubling the court. He freely confessed that he owed his life upon that occasion to Nadin. Nadin was the man who had again put his hat upon his head, exclaiming that it was 'a d——d shame to treat any man in such a manner!' He had been dragged into the house where the magistrates were, and had been carried before Mr. Hulton of Hulton. He had been committed to prison on a charge never substantiated—a charge of high treason; he had been dragged fifty miles to Lancaster, even while his bail were in the act of justifying; he had been subjected to expense, to danger, to inconvenience, and to insult; and now they talked of punishment. He really thought, at a fair computation, he had suffered at least, punishment enough . . .[1]

The Court heard him; the newspapers reported him. Henry Hunt was sent down for two and a half years. Johnson, Knight, Healey, and Bamford for one year. Moorhouse, Jones, Wild, Swift, and John Thacker Saxton were acquitted.

Over a year later, in the House of Commons, Sir Francis Burdett recalled the incident at the hustings when, as Tyas reported, one of the Yeomanry made a lunge at Saxton,

[1] *Manchester Observer*, 20 May 1820.

which luckily failed in its effect, [said Burdett]. Yet, 'that villain Saxton' was totally guiltless; he had been acquitted at York, there being no evidence against him. Such was the conduct of the Yeomanry that this innocent man might have lost his life! What said the law of England to this?[1]

Had (a) been more carefully studied, even Saxton might have been found guilty.

Samuel Bamford may well have had cause to ponder on an incident which he recorded himself some years later,[2] and feel thankful that the Crown prosecuting counsel was more concerned with (a) rather than (b):

. . . One morning [during the trial] I observed Mr. Scarlett reading some verses of mine (The Lancashire Hymn) in a *Manchester Observer* newspaper. In the evening, when I was passing along the corridor from the Court, I accidentally joined Mr. Scarlett and Mr. Maule, the solicitor for the Government. They both recognized me respectfully, and I returned the salute. Mr. Scarlett said he had seen some verses of mine which were certainly open to comment by the prosecution, but he should not make any use of them to my prejudice . . .

It is not believed that Scarlett was studying current numbers of the *Manchester Observer;* the 'Lancashire Hymn' had been published long before 1820. Other verses 'certainly open to comment by the prosecution' might have been his Sandy Brow lines which only received its title in Bamford's first published edition of his poems in 1821, when it became 'The Fray at Stockport'. The Sandy Brow verses were first published in the *Manchester Observer,* 19 June 1819. Scarlett's omission in not animadverting on Bamford's verses was all of a piece with his insistence on the relevance of (a) and the irrelevance of (b).[3] It had other repercussions. Members of Parliament were asking, in 1821, why facts favourable to the magistrates' case were not brought out in Hunt's trial—facts which were then being stated in the House of Commons debate at that time. Bootle Wilbraham explained how the learned judge thought proper to narrow the investigation down to certain limits:

There was, perhaps, another reason why it was not produced. The gentleman —an eminent solicitor—who was sent down to prosecute, did not address himself to the magistrates; but on his arrival at Manchester applied to a professional gentleman of great respectability, but unacquainted with most

---

[1] Parl. Deb., Vol. V., p. 726.
[2] *Passages*, II, p. 87.
[3] Scarlett did not believe that stones had been thrown before the arrests.

particulars of the transaction, and not at all connected with the magistrates . . .[1]

In such a manner were Hunt and his compatriots, so Prentice affirms, made the 'victims' and secured 'upon the altar prepared by Sidmouth and Castlereagh'!

[1] Parl. Deb., 2nd series, Vol. V, p. 746.

XXII

Stalemate and Satire

The verdict had been given; the actors departed from York. The case had filled the newspapers and soon there were to be available the printed reports of the trial. For the first time the much vilified 'they' who were the inarticulate magistrates were heard through their solitary spokesman. Immediately after the trial that solitary spokesman was heard again, in a letter to the *New Times* (London) newspaper:[1]

To the editor of the *New Times*. Hulton Park, April 9th, 1820. Sir—In the 'Remarks on the trial of Hunt and his accomplices' published in the *New Times* of the 6th inst., you found an argument on the supposition, that 'there may have been an erroneous impression on the mind of Mr. Hulton'.

I am always inclined to distrust the impression on my own mind; but for once I have escaped that liability to err, to which all human judgment is subject; as on *every point* alluded to in my evidence at York, I possess corroborative proof, on the oaths of numerous and unimpeachable witnesses. I remain, Sir, your obedient humble servant, William Hulton.

In Manchester, Hulton spoke freely at the King's Birthday celebration dinner, in reply to a toast to the select committee of magistrates:

. . . My first feeling is one of astonishment, that I should find myself in a situation invoking either the approbation or censure of my country. Originally placed in that state of life where domestic tranquility was my principal aim, domestic happiness my highest reward—I am now suddenly tossed on the stormy sea of politics, where, if I trusted to my own judgment as a pilot, I should be doomed to inevitable ship wreck; but where I find my best and unerring compass in your discrimination . . . [The magistrates' committee knew, when they took office] that in the fulfilment of their duties, their motives would be vilified and their actions misrepresented . . . I assert for each individual, that he will again evince the same patriotic energy should the exigencies of the times unfortunately demand the sacrifice . . . The *legality* of our past conduct has been pronounced by a verdict of twelve honest Englishmen, and we have no fear in submitting its *discretion* to a jury of three hundred . . .

[1] Quoted in *Wheeler's Manchester Chronicle*, 22 April 1820.

Throughout our populous neighbourhood, each day, each hour, affords some instance of returning reason, and by necessary consequence, of returning loyalty, on behalf of a generous, though deluded people. . . . We have been perpetually assailed with the cry, that the power of the Crown has increased, is increasing, and ought to be diminished. But who that has seen the tyranny of a mob—who that witnessed the scene of last autumn, can lay his hand on his heart and not confess, that he apprehended more from the overgrown and unconstitutional power of the people, than from the well-regulated and mildly-executed power of the Crown . . .[1]

Hulton was mistaken. The magistrates and the Government had not been vindicated. A few doubts had been removed in some minds by the trial of Hunt and his associates; in many minds these doubts had been increased. Vituperation did not cease; it took on a more refined form; in the columns of the *Manchester Observer* particularly so. Hulton perhaps imagined that his lofty disclaimer in the press would serve to redress the impression given by his demeanour in the witness box. Perhaps it did, in the long run, but for the present the waspish leader which appeared in the *Manchester Gazette*[2] ought to have persuaded him that it had not:

. . . As for William Hulton, of Hulton, Esq., all the most important of his statements are either left unsupported, or are flatly contradicted, both by every evidence for the defence, and by every witness for the prosecution, whose testimony related to occurrences on the field. Poor man! he has 'fallen from his high estate', and lies 'weltering', not in his blood, but in his oaths. He was, unintentionally to be sure, the most effective witness for the defendants; he could not refrain from an attempt to soar, and the fate of Icarus has awaited the imitator of his rashness and his folly. The achievements of Peterloo were the ladder by which he had hoped to elevate himself to the representation of the county of Lancaster; or, perhaps, the vamped up advertisement of his admirers was timed to help his testimony; but he must now be content with the humbler and less enviable distinction of having been a witness at York, whose solitary statement, 'warred with a world' of evidence, and was, therefore, terribly mauled in the encounter. We would not, however, be too severe in our remarks on this young Gentleman: we think his brethren of the Committee of Magistrates have treated him scurvily.[3] He ought at least to have had the *chance* of being confirmed by some of them; for there is now a load of testimony opposed to his single asserversations, against which the power of an Atlas could, with difficulty, struggle.

We feel for his situation quite as much as he does for the victims of his

[1] *Wheeler's Manchester Chronicle*, 29 April 1820.

[2] *Manchester Gazette*, 8 April 1820.

[3] There is a Taylorian ring in the style of this letter, and an admission (almost) in this paragraph that Hulton's evidence was not as false as Hunt had made it out to be.

impetuosity on the 16th of August. That *'faithful servant of his King, his Country, and his God,'*[1] the Rev. Mr. Hay should have helped him. We have no doubt that Mr. Hunt would, as he said, have given *'a Jew's eye'* for the cross-examination of this person; but we verily believe the Reverend Vicar of Rochdale would rather have given an eye of his own than have stood Mr. Hunt's fire in the witness-box. And as for Nadin, who also should have assisted the 'Squire', he was as sick at the bare idea of going into Court, as a clutch of his ever made a thief.

Before the trial, we had been called upon to suspend our judgment. We had been assured that when the case of the Magistrates came before the public, our 'censures would be converted into praise,—our detestation into gratitude'. We had been told on the authority of nearly a thousand of the 'loyal', that the Magistrates were restrained by an imperious sense of duty from a premature disclosure of circumstances, which would form a complete justification of their proceedings. But the Magistrates have given the lie to their friends, for the trial is over, and not one single new fact has been elicited. Nothing save the dubious statement of butcher Willey, whom two witnesses swore to be unworthy of credit upon his oath.

It is perhaps fortunate for the ultimate ends of justice, that the friends of the Magistrates talked so largely—so vauntingly as they did. It was difficult to conceive that there was no foundation for their pretences of postponed justification; but they had all the benefit of their assurances, as to what they could do—they have had what accused persons very rarely can have the opportunity of supporting the propriety of their proceedings, by their own corporal oaths, as to the circumstances which caused them. And how did they behave? Why, after Mr. Hulton's experiments, they shrunk away from the Court as 'a burnt child dreads the fire'. We know we may be told, with the same incredible assurance, which some of the London papers have already displayed, that the conduct of the Magistrates was not before the Court, and that therefore it was not necessary to call upon them; but, in effect, their conduct was under investigation, because whatever they could have proved to affect the character of the Meeting, or the criminality of the accused, would have been, as far as it went, a justification for themselves, their proceedings being professedly founded solely upon the dangerous character of the Meeting. In any other point of view, every word of Mr. Hulton's evidence was impertinent and irregular; and either he ought not have been examined at all, or the fact that none other of the Magistrates were, is a proof that their testimony would not have corroborated his. The Judge, indeed, dwelt strongly upon the circumstances of their not being called, and this in itself is a pregnant proof of the reasons why they kept back . . . [Cannot accept that the Meeting was illegal] unless it could be proved that the Meeting was *in terrorem populi* . . .

[1] An echo from one of Hulton's earlier letters printed in the press, although it did not refer to Mr Hay.

Dr Read[1] in his short biographical sketch of Hulton says:

In March, 1820, as a reward for his part at Peterloo, it was suggested to Hulton that he might stand for the representation of the county, and he agreed to take the next vacancy. 'This mark of esteem', wrote a contemporary, 'was intended to counteract the hostile deportment of his opponents'. Hulton never entered Parliament however . . .

The use of the word 'reward' is the only criticism which could be made of the paragraph. The 'mark of esteem' was made before the trial of Hunt, and a very extensively-signed memorial from freeholders all over the county[2] was carried to Hulton Park by a deputation. Hulton's reply is dated 10 March 1820, and from it was construed the *Gazette*'s taunt that his 'achievements of Peterloo were the ladder by which he had hoped to elevate himself to the representation of the County of Lancaster; or, perhaps the vamped-up advertisement of his admirers was timed to help his testimony'.

Gentlemen—A period of national disquietude and alarm has made us intimately acquainted with each other. An identity of feeling has established our mutual regard. Under painful and protracted anxiety, I have been supported by your kindness; and you now crown my very imperfect though zealous endeavours to serve you, by expressing a wish that on some future occasion I may be appointed to guard your high privileges, and watch over your vast agricultural and commercial interests in parliament. It is most congenial to my feelings that, to the invitation with which you have so unexpectedly honoured me, you have added a pledge to support our late Representatives, and thus overwhelm every effort to disturb the harmony of the county. When, however, you shall be deprived of the counsels of Mr. Blackburn, that faithful servant of his King, his Country, and his God,[3] I shall consider myself bound, in grateful obedience to your wishes, to present myself to the Freeholders of this great County. I will not hold from you my fears that I may be charged with presumption by many gentlemen whose talents, station, and property, give their claims a precedence to any of my own. Possessed of very limited pecuniary resources, I could not be justified in incurring expenses which might either endanger my independence, or abridge the comforts of a numerous family; but embolden by your offers of support, and confident in your zeal, I shall submit my humble pretensions to the decision of the Electors of the County of Lancaster.

My political principles are too well known to require elucidation. It therefore only remains for me to express, in very inadequate terms, my unbounded

[1] Read, p. 77.

[2] See also DDHu/53/61, L.C.R.O.

[3] Perhaps Taylor's seizure of this passage to discomfit Hulton was occasioned by the order in which that 'faithful servant's' allegiance was placed: 1. His King; 2. His country; 3. His God!

gratitude to those Gentlemen who, without my solicitation or previous knowledge have signed the address you have now presented to me. I have the honour to be, Gentlemen, your faithful and devoted servant, William Hulton, Hulton Park, March 10th, 1820.[1]

Whatever solace the writing of that letter gave to Hulton, it was soon to be submerged. Hunt's trial began six days later. After Hunt's trial, April brought its showers (of abuse) for the most part on the exposed head of Hulton:

Manchester Observer April 1st. We understand the Boroughreeve and some others of the 'authorities' of the town were assembled on Monday night, anxiously awaiting the arrival of the express from York with the verdict. We condole with these gentlemen on the disappointment they felt, when they received the intelligence. There was a report current yesterday that Mr. Hulton had resigned his commission. God forbid! What would become of 'Social Order' in the two counties of Lancaster and Chester, if the 'President of all the Magistrates' were to 'skulk' from his duty? . . .

An opinion begins to prevail that the conduct of the magistrates in dispersing the meeting will be subject to Parliamentary inquiry. The indignation of the Ministry is said to be aroused, and it is rumoured they are inclined to avert as much disgrace as they can, by sacrificing the authors of the shameful falsehoods which were attempted to be palmed on the world as to the character of the Manchester Meeting. We care not from what motive, so that justice is done on the instigators and perpetrators of the atrocious outrage of St. Peter's Field; though we confess it would be somewhat novel to see the Ministry performing any great public duty from fear of disgrace. Indeed, we suspect the rumour is not founded on any good authority. . . . We marvel why the Yeomanry were not on duty on Easter Monday. We saw appearances alarming enough to warrant their employment, we should suppose, in the opinion of Mr. Hulton. There was every essential requisite to excite 'apprehension'; and though our 'good coat' was not threatened to be torn from us, yet we felt too much dread of consequences to mix in the throng with money in our pockets. A body of Freemasons, marching in 'military array' with banners and other emblems of turbulence passed our office. Oh! if they had been Reformers, what terror would have been inspired! What depositions of danger would have been made! Mr. Francis Philips might have written another book, and have got rid of the edition as before by giving the copies away.

Other *Observer* comment was less kindly. Whatever impressions Hulton might have received of the 'day by day and hour by hour of returning reason' before his King's Birthday speech, they were soon to be erased. The *Observer* reported the King's Birthday celebration thus:

[1] Hay's Scrapbook, K 8, 206. Chetham's Library (cutting *Manchester Chronicle*?).

. . . A company more willing to be pleased surely was never assembled.
We are rather surprised at one omission in Mr. Hulton's 'eloquent address'.
He has, we believe, since the York trial, never put pen to paper, nor opened
his mouth, without assuring those whom he was addressing 'on his word'
that he was worthy of credit 'on his oath'. On this occasion he uttered not a
syllable in defence of his veracity; not a tittle of panegyric did he pronounce
on his corps of 'affidavit men' who can 'justify every point of his evidence';
of course who are ready to swear that this 'powerful advocate of order' could
see the rows of Radicals locked together round the hustings from a position
in which even the Judge felt the impossibility of the fact. Does he despair of
convincing the world, or does he deem the task accomplished? Capt. Birley
made a speech, too; 'eloquent' of necessity. Only one person was killed by a
sabre wound on the 'glorious' 16th of August, the 'day on which the honours
of the Constitution were vindicated'. The trash is too disgusting to follow;
we have neither space nor patience . . .[1]

A writer, signing himself 'Observer' addressed 'An Open Letter to
William Hulton Esq., of Hulton Park':

. . . I would furnish you with a proof of my impartiality by offering as an
extenuation of your conduct on recent occasions, all I can in your favour.
In so doing, I may in some measure reconcile your friends to the disappointment you occasioned them, by the failure of your efforts on the 24th of
April [King's Birthday Speech]. The space you have lately occupied in the
public eye, particularly since you received the humbling and mortifying
correction from the celebrated champion of Reform at York, must have had
its effects upon your very susceptible feelings; and that anxious attempt to
vindicate yourself through that pure channel of information The *New Times*,
as well as in your eloquent speeches shows how far your mind is from being
at ease. This would of itself account for your many incoherencies and pompous nothings. Some may think that you also wish to justify your conduct in
the eyes of the Reformers; but I am free to confess that I do not discover in
you any such weakness . . .

Another apology for your conduct may be found in your youth; and it
ought in justice to be observed, that like many other young gentlemen, you
have suffered from the contagious influence of pernicious company. This,
your *enemies* must admit, is rather a misfortune than a crime. At the commencement of your magisterial career hopes were cherished for your future
usefulness and greatness, which have since been sadly disappointed. Young
and inexperienced, and unsuspecting, it was your unhappy fate to be associated with a practised, cool, designing colleague,[2] who scrupled not to take
advantage of the fervour of your feelings, of the warmth of your temper, and
the ingenuousness of your open disposition. When I refer to your public

---

[1] *Manchester Observer*, 29 April, 1820.
[2] Col. Ralph Fletcher, of Bolton.

conduct in 1812, as it relates to all the circumstances connected with the destruction of Westhoughton Factory, and contrast it with that of the arch-fiend who was the prime instigator of that horrid event, I have much to offer in your favour. I well remember the interest you manifested for the unhappy sufferers at Lancaster, particularly the *child* that was executed; and I have also a perfect recollection of the strong indignation you evinced towards an abandoned *informer* at Chowbent, who wickedly encouraged the incendiaries, by promising to reward the most active among them with the greatest share of bread and cheese, in order that he might betray them to the Magistrates, when the deluded wretches should afterwards apply for the proffered bribe! But it was then your misfortune to be the dupe of a man who, I believe, kept you ignorant of his infernal scheme. Had he told you that the burning of a factory, and the sacrifice of a few human victims, formed a part, though a small one, of his *admirable spy system* would he not have chilled your blood with horror, and aroused every indignant feeling of your soul?[1]

Since the period of which I am now writing, it is almost eight years. What change may have been brought about in your mind during the interval, it may be difficult for me to ascertain with precision; but a general knowledge from the influence resulting from virtuous or vicious association, leaves me more to fear than to hope. I *may* be wrong; and I shall be glad to find that my apprehensions are groundless. *If*, however, it has been your misfortune to become the dupe of a man, whose character cannot be depicted in colours too black . . . Pause before you proceed . . . [On the evils of the spy system; how better things are ordered in America] . . .

I suppose that it is generally known that you are what is generally called 'an alarmist'. You are always afraid of the secret designs of the disaffected; and among other things, you fancy that your property is in danger . . . Pitt frightened poor John Bull . . . [on invasion] . . . Cock Lane ghost . . . &c. Some people have been surprised at the evidence you gave at York respecting the memorable events of [the 16th August] and can hardly believe that you saw the Reformers beating the Yeomanry Cavalry on St. Peter's Field. But surely it is not necessary to charge a man with perjury in such a case as this, when it can be so easily explained without impeaching his veracity. We have only to suppose your imagination to have been so completely bewildered, as to deprive you of all distinctness of vision, and the difficulty vanishes. . . . [Instances of optical deception—on 'Mr. Bootty going to Hell' when he had been seen to disappear into the volcano in Mount Stromboli] . . . you might, with as great propriety, swear that the Radicals overpowered *in your view* the valiant Yeomanry. And it was surely not your fault if your brother Magistrates *refused* to corroborate your testimony. By

[1] The former Westhoughton mill-owner (James Duncough) whose factory was burned down in 1812 was a Crown Witness at Hunt's trial. In reply to a question by Hunt he said: 'I never heard that the crime was perpetrated by the black-faced spies of Bolton, and, if I had, I would not have believed it,' (Duncough was abroad when the prosecutions of 1812 commenced). *State Trials*, 226.

so doing they must, I should think, have given you just cause to be offended at them. It looked like getting you into a situation in which they were either afraid or ashamed of being seen themselves. But when I contrast your *bold* (as Hunt would say) and manly conduct, with the *sneaking* behaviour of some others, surely I may be allowed to be your advocate and defender.

If the conduct of your quondam friends while at York, has induced you to form the resolution of resigning your commission in the peace, more mature reflection will, perhaps, cause you to change your determination. It would probably be more advisable for you to travel; and a change of scenery, such as the continent presents, would relieve your mind from the effects of those vexatious squabbles, which seem to be inseparable from party politics. Let me, however, advise you to keep out of Spain: there you would be stumbling on Spanish Radicals; and as they have succeeded in their efforts, it is ten to one but their sentiments would be more intolerable than those of the Reformers at home . . . I am your constant Observer. May, 1820.[1]

Gentle irony was not always the theme. In the *Observer*[2] a writer was referring to some malicious gossip about the *Observer* which had appeared in the *Courier*:

. . . It is a fair presumption that a statement is false because it has appeared in the *Courier*. If any living being would say, or if Mr. Hulton would swear, that he believed anything which that journal advances on its own authority, we might perhaps condescend to refute it.

In this chapter on the second blossoming of invective after Hunt's trial, the *Observer* on 2 September 1820, reported that the Editor had noted the receipt of an article 'To the Nine' by 'Caleb Lilburn'; but his 'excellent address' was thought 'almost too strong for the weak nerves of the gentlemen to whom it is directed. If we dare we will publish it, but some alterations will be absolutely necessary'. The Editor did dare, in his issue of 16 September:

TO THE NINE.[3] I had a strong mental scruple to satisfy before I resolved to do that which I am now doing. I doubted whether, in addressing a letter to you, I should not be committing an act of self-degradation. But I reflected that an honest man does not degrade himself by denouncing a villain to his face; that the judge does not degrade himself by speaking to felons or murderers when he pronounces their doom,—and I became fixed in my purpose to present you a view of your deeds in the time that is past, and part of your prospects in the time that is to come.

I must confess that my particular acquaintance with you commenced not

1 *Manchester Observer*, 13 May, 1820.
2 *Manchester Observer*, 12 August, 1820.
3 See above, p. 116 note 1, 117 note (continued).

long before that period when your names became universally celebrated. You were the representatives of lawless power before that time; and well did you sustain the character. Every man who, being within the sphere of your jurisdiction, dared to avow and promulgate political sentiments, was an object of your ceaseless hatred and persecution. It was no check on your hostility, that what he did was just and laudable. It was nothing to you that what he did was *legal*. You knew that the existence of a fearless public honesty, and the extension of correct political knowledge, were incompatible with the existence and the extension of the system of corruption and ignorance which you were employed to assist in consolidating; and your slender abilities were constantly exerted, as you thought, to consolidate it, by visiting with all the terror of your authority, the just, the laudable, the legal opponents of that system. Sworn to administer justice, you were to be seen one hour engaged in punishing the poor thief who had stolen a loaf, or a piece of meat, to satisfy the cravings of nature, and, in another hour, thrusting into your dungeons and ruining their families, men of unimpeachable character, who had incurred your vengeance as a consequence of the public spirit which led them to expose and execrate national robbers, the effect of whose peculations were felt by all except themselves or their agents.

In labours like these, however, you had, all over the kingdom, fellow-workers. You could not by these obtain any high distinction. Approval and reward you did receive—but only in common with hundreds of other candidates, to whose claims yours were not sufficiently superior to deserve an unshareable acknowledgment. This was galling to the high ambition of your souls, which panted to achieve something that should defy competition; something that should give you a monopoly of favour. At last you found your opportunity in the *   *   *   *   *   *   *   *
*   *   *   *   *   *   *   *   *   *   *   *
*   *   *   *   *   *   *   *   *   *   *   *

You beheld in that assembly a vast multitude of living, complaining sufferers, by that system of oppression, of which you had been, in your full measure, the active agents; and no doubt you witnessed the rout of them—unwarned, unoffending, defenceless as they were—with such feelings as fill the breast of the conscience-stricken murderer, when dawn chases the shades of night, which to all the innocent had been a season of pleasurable repose, but which, to his imagination, had teemed with the horrible visions of past iniquities and coming retribution. I know not whether you had, like his forbodings of a night which no dawn would dissipate, your fearful consciousness that your sanguinary measure could not avert the evil day which you dreaded; that it could bring but a temporary relief to the system for the benefit of which you devised it. Perhaps not. Perhaps the delight which thrilled your nerves was too exquisite, while the occasion of it lasted, to admit of alloy; else you might have perceived that you were acting like the unskilful physician, who administers to a wasting constitution, strong medicines, which while they relieve the patient, and light up his eyes with an unnatural glare for a moment, do also precipitate the dissolution of his frame, that might otherwise have lingered on and on through as many months as it has days now allotted for its duration. Perhaps you imagined that you had quenched in blood the sacred flame of freedom. You knew not that the last sigh of a victim in the cause of liberty is the breath which calls into being a thousand men impatient of their wrongs, where a thousand slaves, contented in debasement, had lain sluggishly prostrate.

A year has since passed over you, and surely, it must have brought you some accession of such wisdom as even fools cannot help learning from experience. Do you not see that you have spent your strength for that of which you will have to cry out, that, 'it profiteth not!'—It is true, that your ears have been regaled with the sweet sounds of approbation, spoken in the name of the great god of your idolatry; true, that at least *one* of you has received a more substantial meed; and true, that you have seen consigned to imprisonment the best and bravest of all those against whom your authority and the force of the system you had upheld had been leagued. But look at the times which are now, and try to exercise a little foresight upon the signs of them. Contemplate the rapid progress of the principles of freedom amongst our neighbouring nations; a progress like that of fire upon a sun-dried heath. Reflect on the emancipation of Spain, of Naples . . . . think of the agitation of France . . . But perhaps your minds cannot estimate the influence of continental example on England. Let me call you home.

There had long been wanted in England a centre of union to all the friends of liberty, who agreeing in the pursuit of our grand object, differed respecting trifles, and permitted their trifling differences to damp their zeal in the common cause. You have furnished them with a centre of very considerable attraction. When they saw acts which I dare not describe as I ought, perpetrated at the bidding of men vested with a little magisterial power; and saw redress denied to the living sufferers by these acts, and justice denied to the friends of dead victims of them; all men became sensible that the system under which such atrocities could be not only tolerated and unpunished, but *applauded*, was one along with which public safety could have no existence; and, though prohibited from expressing execrations in the loud voice of multitudes, yet did they the more deeply execrate that system, and the more solemnly, and sincerely did they resolve never to slacken in all the efforts they could make for its destruction. But there has arisen amongst us *now* an object whose power of attracting public sentiment and public feeling is less than universal . . . [The Queen pointed out as a rallying point for all the oppressed . . . she having declared that she will resist oppression 'with all the means which it shall please God to give her'] WHO SHALL calculate those means? With the despotism with which you must stand or fall her acquittal would be a death-blow . . .

Your masters who applauded and indemnified you, have staked their all upon the existing of a die which has but two faces, and both ascribed *Destruction*. If they are foiled in their purpose, their ruin is immediate; and if they effect their purpose, that ruin will assume *a shape*, which may not be all at once gigantic enough to crush them with all its tread, but *at the very first risings of which, all the false honours for which they and you have sold your souls will become nothing.*

I dare not explain myself; and if I dared, explanation to your tremblingly alive perceptions, would be needless.

Caleb Lilburn.

The writer's hopes for the arising of that 'rallying point' in the shape of the Queen's Case were soon to prove illusory, for after the short period of embarrassment it gave to the Ministry and its supporters, it fell away to nothing. The 'acts' which Caleb Lilburn 'dared not describe' were not outside the powers of description of another *Observer* writer, in an adjoining column of the same issue of the paper: the style—that of allegory. In it, 'facts' were not even needed; 'allegorical' Peterloo had no need for the crabbing and confining boundaries of facts. The radical version of Peterloo could soar to new heights, and plunge to new depths:

Wonderful Trance and Vision of the Major; a tale of a thousand years ago. [It ran for a week or two serially, bitterly gibing throughout at Capt. (later Major) Birley]. . . . The Major (then Capt.) happened to have the command of the two or three troops, of which the 666th or 'Devil's Own' consisted. All was prepared with the most dreadful and most treacherous secrecy. Rum and brandy were served out in *ad libitum* quantities, in various private out-houses and other buildings. As soon as they had succeeded in their endeavours to *'raise their courage to the sticking place'* the word was given; and at that moment the whole of these 'devils incarnate' with the Major at their head, galloped into a corner of the field. Their intentions were unknown, and they were received with *cheers*, as friends. They halted, however, in disorder; several nearly lost their seats; their faces were blanched with fear; their courage was ebbing fast; it was almost *neap-tide* with them;—one moment more and they were off. 'The wicked flee when no man pursueth; but the righteous are bold as a lion.'

To do the *Captain* justice, he was the only soldier in the corps; he saw the smock-coloured cheeks, and quivering, colour-forsaken lips of his companions-in-arms; he saw some actually turning their horses' heads for flight; he perceived that this was the critical minute, and, though ordered by his *civil* superiors, (who were close by, safe within bricks and mortar,) to stop an instant till the men recovered, themselves,—brandishing his sabre, 'Why wait a moment?' he cried; and setting the example of a horrid yell, which was followed by the whole of the corps, he led these *'hell-hounds'* into the midst of this assembly of *unarmed* men, women, and children.

It is proverbial that *'cowards are cruel'*; and the adage was never more completely verified than on that day. They appeared to be perfectly infuriated with *fear, rage,* and *strong drink*. They cut; they slashed in all directions. They trampled their helpless victims under the horses' feet. They came among the unoffending and terrified creatures like wolves among a flock of sheep. When they had completely scattered and driven them in all directions, they followed the trembling fugitives even into distant streets. *Six hundred* and upwards, were severely wounded; *thirteen* died, some of them being killed on the spot.

Oh! believe me, Mr. Editor, it was a sorrowful sight to behold innocent young creatures flying in all directions, their feet slipping in the plashes of blood that had streamed from the veins of their fathers or their mothers, their brothers or their sweethearts; to see mothers cut down and trampled upon, but still clinging to the infant that was sucking the mingled stream of blood and milk flowing from the same breast.

Will you credit it, Mr. Editor, that ere the dead were carried from the field; ere the wounded had time to collect their scattered senses, these miscreants had mustered again, and had indulged themselves in a yell of *fiend-like* exultation over their fallen, bleeding and dying countrymen;—and, in the midst of the horrid carnage, one of them was observed to brandish his sword, and was heard to exclaim, 'This is our *own* field of Waterloo!'

There, in that day's strife, you might have seen a fellow-creature, upon whose life the comforts and happiness of a wife and family of children depended, struck down by a cheesemonger's apprentice, who, perhaps the Saturday before, had been smiling in his face and cheating him in the price of half-a-dozen pounds of *Cheshire*. There you might have seen a monster in human shape cut down the woman, who, in days of yore, had been his foster mother, and had fed his worthless carcass from that bosom which he was now inhumanly lacerating. There was horror in the most horrible of shapes:— death, sudden and unexpected death, inflicted, *wilfully* inflicted upon a fellow-creature, unprepared perhaps, who had left his wife and smiling little ones at the dawn of day, and had promised to return before the setting of the sun;— alas! no more shall he return . . .

I see him still, as then I saw him lie:
   He leans upon his hand;—his manly brow
Consents to death, but conquers agony;
   And his droop'd head sinks gradually low:—
And from his side the last drops, ebbing slow
Through the red gash, fall heavy, one by one:
   . . . . and now
The arena swims around him; he is gone,
Ere ceas'd the *inhuman* shout rais'd by the FIEND who won . . .
. . . Butcher'd to make a Y——n's holiday . . .

In the 'Wonderful Trance and Vision of the Major' the radical version of Peterloo perhaps reached its nadir; nor did it include apologies to the author of *Childe Harold*.

Poetry, even Drama, were called to the aid of these second-wind propagators of the radical version. Nearly two years after 16 August 1819, the *Observer*[1] published 'The Wiseacres: or a Scene at York, written by Nobody Knows Who, and humbly and respectfully submitted to the public for the edification and amusement of all whom it may concern.'

Act the First. Scene — A room at an Inn. The Rev. Robert Rednose, Vicar of —— and Justass of the Peace, discovered in a ruminating mood, seated at a table partly covered with papers, and partly with empty glasses and decanters . . . One hand is employed in supporting his heavy, hanging head, and the other clenched as if unconscious of the grasp, a half-pint glass, which the beholder would suppose had a few moments before returned from the still imbrued lips of the Rev. Rednose. A long pause, a deep, desponding sigh, a wine-impregnated hiccup, another sigh, and then a soliloquy:

Rednose: Lie still my heart: lie still in calm repose;
(He now arose, hem'd, coughed, and blew his nose)
What means this heavy sadness at my breast?
This cank'ring worm, that robs me of my rest?
. . . Am I, who four times in th' revolving year,
Deal out my mandate from the Justice chair—
Am I to tremble, sweat, and groan, and grunt,
When cross-examined by this Henry Hunt?
. . . Conscience, avaunt! Robert's himself again.
(Rings for another bottle).

Enter the Rev. C. W. *Wisdom*, whistling the tune of 'Go to the Devil and shake yourself' . . . whirls around in an exulting manner.
(Rednose inquires why his *mirth*?) he asks:

Has anything's that passed in court to-day,
Given rise to that harmonious lay?
Or is it the effect of drinking . . .?
Rev. Wisdom: But come old buck (clapping him on the shoulder)
Arouse thyself and hear
That from this moment we have nought to fear;
Whate'er we had to tremble at before,
We've nothing now, the storm is past, 'tis o'er—
Bulton now's beneath examination,
Swearing away, old Boy, just like ——
Rev. Rednose: Bulton, well done! I knew thou'd do it neatly.

[1] *Manchester Observer*, 2 and 9 June, 1821.

Wisdom: Yes, by this glass (drinks) he's done it compleatly.
   He swears to things, which I, in point of fact,
   Ne'er saw myself, although I read the act.
Rednose: Adhere to that, my friend, the act, the act.
Wisdom: I'll stick to aught, provided I'm well back'd.
Rednose: You shall be back'd, the act I'll swear I heard
   And who will doubt a Vicar's word?
Wisdom: O, no, not one! (filling) come let's drink again.
Rednose: With all my heart, to that I'll say 'Amen'.
(A knock without).
(Enter Nailem, smiling even to fascination).
Wisdom: Well, Nailem, how does Bulton still go on?
Nailem: O, rarely, Sir, the thing's as good as done.
   He swears so *beautifully*, so concise,
   He's one of my sort like, not over nice;
   Whatever we can say will come too late.
Rednose: O no, Nailem! we must corroborate . . .
(Enter Flimsy, a Beadle).
Flimsy: Mathew Calfper's sent me down to tell
   That Squire Bulton goes on very well,
   And if he stands the *cross*, why Hunt's as fast as h——.
(Rednose calls on Nailem for a Song) . . .
Rednose: Here's a health to all Justasses
Both: They never mind what sorrow passes
   If with them the glass goes round.
Nailem: To all Justasses,
Wisdom: Here's a soaker.
Nailem: Fill your glasses;
Rednose: Mine's a choaker
All: Let the sparkling wine go round.
Nailem: May they live their days' full measure,
Rednose: May they live &c.
Wisdom: And no hemp cut short their pleasure,
All: For with them good things abound
   Here's a health . . . &c.
      (All drink, and huzzah). End of Act the First.

(In the second act the trio are still guzzling. Nailem twits Wisdom on: 'Did ye read the act . . .?.' Rednose twits Wisdom on his cases in the magistrates' court—*small* stuff; Wisdom reminds Rednose he nearly trapped a Radical . . .)
Wisdom: 'I ask you plainly, Rednose, was it fair,
   To thrust young Bulton into th' civic chair?

A man without experience, young in years;
'Tis said you did it, Sir, to calm your fears?
But I say 'twas a piece of speculation,
Calculated, Sir, to gull the nation—
You thought, if we succeeded, then you'd claim,
Your equal share of profit, and of fame;
But if we did not—if the project fail'd,
Rednose was free, and Bulton would be nail'd;
O, wary *Rednose*, deep your plot was laid,
Bulton is blam'd, and *you're* a Vicar made.

(The gibe went home. Rednose offers to fight Wisdom; Nailem comes between them . . . they desist. Steps are heard; all compose themselves). Someone from the Court with news. (Enter Swearought, a publican, formerly a Beadle).

Rednose: Well, Swearought, does Bulton keep to his text?
Or does he seem (I dread it much) perplex'd?
Swearought: O, not a bit! He's th' best I ever heard,
I've heard some hundreds, *but upon my word*
I ne'er heard one to equal him before,
He sticks to things, o'er, and o'er, and o'er.
Rednose: How pleas'd I am at what thou dost unfold;
This *Bulton*, surely, must be very bold.
Swearought: Bold, I believe you, if t' not been for him,
You would not now be filling to the brim.
But being fast, as if caught in a steel trap,
Your Worship would have merely sip'd a heel tap.
Wisdom: Swearought, thou'rt witty, but tell us what he's sworn.
Swearought: Why, then, your Worship, I might speak till morn:
He swore to 'marching beautifully exact,'
And how that you, Sir (to Wisdom) read the riot act.
Wisdom: Why, did he so? why then, if that be true
There's no denying: I must swear it too!
Swearought: He *also* swore 'bout broken limbs and bones,
Thousands of sticks and waggon loads of stones;
A walking-stick he'd call a mighty stake,
And all who shook 'em had 'em first to shake.
Rednose: There needs no ghost to tell us that, Swearought.
Swearought: Why, surely not, Sir, that is what I thought.
But first he swore to Peterloo they took 'em,
And then he said that 'all who had sticks
shook 'em'—
And then he said the Yeomanry were beaten,
And in two minutes they'd have all been eaten,
Had he not call'd L'Es *** e, and said 'Good G——!

Oh! save them, Sir, you see they're all in quod.'
Nailem: Well, and what then?
Swearought: Why, men, he turned his back,
  Because he would not see them cut and hack.
Rednose: O, Bulton, Bulton! thou'st drawn us from the mire:
Wisdom: I feel myself a man.
Nailem: Swearought, retire.
  (Exit Swearought) (Calls for another bottle &c.)
  End of Second Act.

There was still more of 'The Wiseacres' and had the circumstances under which it was written not been so tragic, it could have been passed off as a *jeu d'esprit*. There are curious inexactitudes in it: Hulton did not swear that 'Wisdom' (Ethelston) read the Riot Act; he offered no evidence of the reading of the Riot Act at either Hunt's or Redford *v.* Birley trials. The quips regarding 'Rednose's' (Hay's) thrusting him into the chairmanship of the magistrates are entirely beside the point, for neither Hay nor Ethelston were members of the committee when Hulton was appointed. The *non sequitur* on Hulton 'turning his back' has already been referred to.

XXIII

Truthseekers and Radical Bourbons

The original propagators of the radical version of Peterloo, like the Bourbons, learned nothing and forgot nothing; and they admitted nothing. They became an army fighting a perpetual battle. As their enemies routed them from one fortified position, they retired to another, and to another; and when their enemies had left the field and gone home, they sallied out once more reoccupying their old positions as though nothing had happened. To their enemies the battles had been fought and won, and the world knew it; to them they had never been fought at all.

It will be recalled that the Prince Regent's letter had castigated the Common Council of London for being 'not correctly informed' as to what had occurred on St Peter's Field. One of the points on which they had been misinformed was to the legality or illegality of the meeting. The Rev. Mr Hay was speaking on that point at the King's Birthday dinner celebrations at Manchester in April 1820:

. . . Proof had now been afforded by the highest authority in the land, that the law on which they had acted was not mere *Lancashire or Manchester law*, but the law of England; and by that law the meeting had been adjudged illegal . . . The adversaries of the Magistrates of Manchester had thought fit to blame his Majesty's Ministers for the 'breathless haste' with which they had conveyed to the Magistrates the approbation of their Royal Master. They certainly, on the contrary, had not been hasty to acknowledge the error of judgment or defect of knowledge which they had evinced; for from the month of August to the present time, although it had repeatedly been proposed, and by men of no common knowledge, to argue that the meeting was a legal one, the proposal had been as often abandoned; and it had in no instance occurred that such individuals, or any body connected with them, had acknowledged the false view they had taken of the question; through which view, and under whose sanction, numerous bodies had been induced to stigmatize the Magistracy. Thus the illegality of the meeting had been allowed by those very parties who were most anxious to argue in favour of its propriety.[1]

[1] *Wheeler's Manchester Chronicle*, 29 April 1820.

The Rev. Mr Hay had a point; but if there had been no recantations of the nature alluded to by Mr Hay, events as they occurred after Hunt's trial gave evidence that there was a change in the attitude of certain of the most prominent of those original critics of the magistracy and the ministry. Dr Read[1] writes:

Apart from the Peterloo Radicals most of the other Radical leaders also found themselves imprisoned or under threat of imprisonment by the middle of 1820. Burdett was sentenced to three months' imprisonment and fined £2000 for his address to the electors of Westminster occasioned by Peterloo. Wolseley and Harrison were sentenced to eighteen months' imprisonment for conspiring to cause a riot by their speeches at Stockport on June 28th, 1819, with an additional two years for Harrison on two other charges of seditious utterance; Wroe was imprisoned for twelve months with a fine of £100 for seditious publication, and Carlile received a three-year sentence with a fine of £1,500 for publishing the works of Tom Paine. Finally, in 1821, after long legal delays Wooler received a sentence of fifteen months' imprisonment and Cartwright was fined £100 for their parts in the Birmingham 'Legislatorial Attorney' meeting of July 12th, 1819.

The great working-class Radical effort of 1819 thus ended with most of its leaders in prison. The calm with which the people accepted the prosecution and conviction of their erstwhile heroes was due in part no doubt to the sudden engrossing of public interest in 1820 in the Queen's Affair. But even more it showed how superficial had been much of the working-class Radical influence over the popular mind. It held its grip only so long as economic distress was at its very worst: with a slight easing of popular suffering in 1820 came an immediate slackening of interest in Radical Reform.

Mr Thompson (p. 709) makes the reprisal measures of the Government sound even stronger: 'Thereafter the Government launched upon the most sustained campaign of prosecutions in the courts of British history. By the summer of 1820 Hunt, and four Manchester reformers (indicted for their part at Peterloo), Wooler, Burdett, Sir Charles Wolseley, the Rev. J. Harrison, Knight, Carlile, Edmonds, Wroe, Johnston, Bagguley, Drummond and Mitchell were all imprisoned.'

Some in this list were in prison before Peterloo; Wooler and Edmonds' trial did not take place finally until August 1821; Burdett, too, should not have been included in such a list.

Sir Francis Burdett had written his address to his Westminster constituents on 22 August 1819. He was charged at Leicester Assizes on 23 March 1820, with uttering a seditious libel on the Government; Hunt and his compatriots were being tried at the same time at York. Burdett

[1] Read, pp. 153–4.

was found guilty on that date, but it was not until February 1821, that his sentence of three months' imprisonment and a fine of £2000 was imposed. On 15 May 1821, released from incarceration, Sir Francis, M.P. for Westminster, introduced his motion in the House of Commons that 'this House will resolve itself into a Committee of the whole House to inquire' into the affair at Manchester on 16 August 1819.

There was nothing 'superficial' about the indignation of Sir Francis Burdett concerning the events of 16 August, nor was his concern expressed in his letter of 22 August 1819, of such a nature that the Queen's Affair, economic distress, or any other side issue could stifle it. The passage of time could not stifle it either; he was as indignant in 1821 as he had been in 1819, but his indignation was tempered with a certain willingness to admit that he was better informed in 1821 than he had been in 1819. In this he was different from some other critics. Sir Francis Burdett's indignant protest of 1819 is used by the propagators of the radical version of Peterloo to strengthen that version, even though Sir Francis himself was a hostile critic of Henry Hunt and his followers.[1] Because Burdett was not 'one of them', and yet could sustain his protests over such a long period, and at considerable cost to himself, his attitude to the affairs of 16 August deserves more careful study than it has hitherto been given. The cost to himself included a term of

---

[1] '. . . I have all along reprobated the temporising conduct of Sir Francis Burdett, ever since the verdict of guilty was pronounced against him; nay, I have censured him for his public conduct ever since he wrote that letter. The letter itself was most excellent, and did honour to his head and his heart; but he never followed it up. Even at the very meeting which the letter produced, which was the largest and the most enthusiastic that was ever assembled in Palace Yard; even at that meeting, he by no means acted up to the spirit of the letter. There was then an opening again for him to have made himself the most popular man in England, as he had been some years before; but *jealousy, the green-eyed fiend jealousy, his greatest enemy*, checked his zeal; and rather than contribute to the hard-earned practical popularity that *I* had obtained, by my unwearied exertions in the cause of public liberty, he sacrificed and damned *his own*, I fear for ever. I am well informed that, when a vote of thanks was moved to me, the enthusiastic shouts of his own constituents so far exceeded any thing he ever heard expressed towards himself that he turned pale, and his lips quivered and shook with envy and *jealousy*; . . . From that moment, he has never appeared earnest in the cause. His defence was any thing rather than that which the occasion required, and which he was so capable of making; it was so miserably weak, it was such a milk and water production, when compared to the letter, and was delivered in such a repentant manner . . . that it was impossible that the jury could have done otherwise than find him guilty. Then, instead of demurring in the first instance to the plea, his driving it off to the last moment, and at length attempting to creep out of the trial by a technical objection, was an act unworthy of the cause which he espoused . . .'
    Hunt's 'Letter to the Radical Reformers (from Ilchester Bastile 7th day, 4th month, 2nd year, of the Manchester Massacre without retribution or enquiry'. 3 December 1820), p. 1.

imprisonment, a fine of £2000, and the greatest individual subscription to the fund raised for the relief of the sufferers of Peterloo: out of a total of £3,408 raised, Sir Francis subscribed £210.[1] He led, too, immediately after his release from imprisonment, in May 1821, the Parliamentary agitation for inquiry. It was a debate which achieved two important objects: (1) it convinced many critics that the Ministry could no longer be implicated as 'parties to the decision to disperse the meeting by force'; nor could the magistrates be blamed for having done other than try to control a situation which was out of control; and (2) if excesses there were, as it was alleged, then the courts were open to try the case against the Yeomanry; nor was there any difficulty in the way, for several of the Yeomanry were named and known. The result of the Parliamentary debate of May 1821, was the famous case of Redford *v.* Birley, April 1822.

Sir Francis Burdett's place in the saga of St Peter's Field began on 22 August 1819:

To the Electors of Westminster: Gentlemen: On reading the newspapers this morning, having arrived late yesterday evening [at his home in Leicester] I was filled with shame, grief and indignation at the account of the blood spilt at Manchester. This then is the answer of the boroughmongers to the petitioning people, this the practical proof of our standing in no need of Reform. These the practical blessings of our glorious boroughmonger domination; this is the use of a standing army in time of peace. It seems our fathers were not such fools as some would make us believe, in opposing the establishment of a standing army, and sending King William's Dutch guards out of the country. Yet would to heaven they had been Dutchmen, or Switzers, or Hessians, or Hanoverians, or any thing rather than Englishmen, who had done such deeds. What, kill men unarmed, unresisting and Gracious God!! women, too, disfigured, maimed, cut down and trampled on by dragoons! Is this England? This a Christian land? A land of freedom? Can such things be and pass by us like a summer cloud unheeded? forbid it every drop of English blood in every vein that does not proclaim its owner bastard.

Will the gentlemen of England support or wink at such proceedings? They have a great stake in their country, they hold great estates, and they are bound in duty and in honour to consider them as retaining fees on that part of their country. Surely they will at length awake and find they have other duties to perform besides fattening bullocks and planting cabbages. They never can stand tamely as lookers-on, whilst 'bloody Neroes' rip open their mother's womb. They must join the general voice, loudly demanding justice and redress, and head public meetings throughout the United Kingdom to put a stop in its commencement to a reign of terror and of blood, to afford

[1] *Courier*, 30 December 1819.

consolation as far as it can be afforded, and legal redress to the widows and orphans and mutilated victims of this unparalleled and barbarous outrage. For this purpose I propose that a meeting should be called in Westminster which the gentlemen of the committee will arrange, and whose summons I will hold myself in readiness to attend. Whether the penalty of our meeting will be death by military execution, I know not; but this I know, a man can die but once, and never better than in vindicating the laws and liberties of his country.

Excuse this hasty address, I can scarcely tell what I have written. It may be a libel, or the Attorney-General may call it so, just as he pleases. When the Seven Bishops were tried for libel, the Army of James II, then encamped on Hounslow Heath, for supporting arbitrary power, gave three cheers on hearing of their acquittal. The King, startled at the noise, asked 'What's that?' 'Nothing, Sir?' was the answer, 'but the soldiers shouting at the acquittal of the Seven Bishops.' 'Do you call that nothing?' replied the misgiving tyrant, and shortly afterwards abdicated the government. 'Tis true James could not inflict the torture on his soldiers—could not tear the living flesh from their bones with a cat o' nine tails—could not flay them alive. Be this as it may, our duty is to meet, and 'England expects every man to do his duty'. I remain, Gentlemen, most truly and faithfully, your most obedient servant, Francis Burdett, Kirby Park, August 22nd, 1819.[1]

In the canon of writings on the radical version of Peterloo, the 22 August letter of Sir Francis had its due place; so too does the report of the great Westminster meeting of 2 September, with Burdett and Cam Hobhouse, (who in 1821 was the seconder of Burdett's motion in the House of Commons) as the two principal speakers. There was an attendance of some thirty thousand people at the Westminster meeting; it was peaceable, and the meeting declared the Manchester meeting to have been perfectly legal.[2] What does not find a place in that canon of writings, on which the radical version of Peterloo is founded, is the trial and the aftermath of the trial of Sir Francis Burdett.[3] The trial, coming as it did at the time of the great York trial of Hunt and the others, was naturally overshadowed. The *Manchester Observer* gave only the briefest of summaries, reporting that Sir Francis rested his defence, of having published a seditious libel, on the truth of his allegations, and for that purpose tendered evidence to substantiate their validity. Justice Best refused to receive it. His Lordship, in summing up, declared that the letter was a most seditious and scandalous libel, 'and the Jury without consulting a moment brought in a verdict of guilty.'[4]

[1] *Peterloo Massacre*, pp. 18–19.
[2] Ibid.
[3] *State Trials*, I, N.S. (Cols 2–170).
[4] *Manchester Observer*, 25 March 1820.

Sir Francis Burdett's letter had begun: 'On reading the newspapers this morning' (22 August 1819) 'I was filled with shame, grief' etc. Mr Justice Best observed to the jury:

. . . If you find [the letter] begins with a statement which the writer cannot know to be true or false, if you find it states many things not correct, if you find it appeals to passions . . . and not having a tendency to inform those who cannot correct abuses, it is a libel . . . Is [it] a fit and proper thing that a man of education and high station in life like Sir Francis Burdett should immediately assume there has been blood spilt at Manchester because he reads it in a morning paper? Is it fit he should assume it is true, and before it is possible whether he could ascertain whether it is true or false? We do not at this moment know whether it is true. They are now inquiring into what took place elsewhere. And yet, Gentlemen, the instant he gets the paper, thinks he is warranted to assume the fact there stated to be correct, and to write the letter . . .[1]

The judicial view that inquiry into what took place was being gone into elsewhere was, of course, a reference to Hunt's trial then proceeding. It was perhaps far-fetched to state that nothing was officially known of the transactions of 16 August until what was brought out on oath before the court at York; after the meeting of Parliament in November 1819, a considerable mass of evidence was before the public. In Sir Francis's trial, however, the point was brought out for the first time that the press reports appearing after 16 August were or could be erroneous. As the trial progressed into the following year, that fact was admitted by the defence. It was an admission of great importance. On 1 February 1821, James Scarlett had been briefed for Burdett's motion 'in arrest of judgment'. He asked: may not the blood spilt at Manchester have been spilt without the order of the Government? The Chief Justice [Abbott] replied that the libel had excited subjects of the King to believe that other subjects of the King had been inhumanly cut down, maimed, and killed by the King's troops on that day; what was more, the libel had been published. In the hearings which followed the defendant pleaded mitigation because of what he had read in newspapers, and requested permission to bring in affidavits to show that the statements in the news-papers were founded on truth; pèrmission was not given. Chief Justice Abbott said:

. . . Affidavits cannot be laid before the Court . . . It seems to me that we should do great injustice to the defendant if we were to allow ourselves to be induced, for the purpose of aggravating punishment, to receive any affidavits

[1] *State Trials*, I, N.S. pp. 51–2.

of falsehood of those representations on which he tells us he was induced to write that which he did. I think on the one hand, we cannot with justice to the defendant receive such affidavits, so, on the other hand, we cannot receive affidavits which go to show that a great part of the representation contained in those newspapers, which led the defendant to express his feelings thus strongly, was founded in truth. The affidavit made by the defendant himself stating that his feelings were strongly excited by the statements he had read in the newspapers was most properly laid before us.

Mr. Justice Bayley: I entertain no doubt that in this case any evidence of the truth of the facts charged in this information is inadmissible. If we were to accede to it, we should let in a most dangerous rule of practice, and one which would be a great disgrace to the administration of justice. The libel in question imports that troops had killed men unarmed, unresisting, and had disfigured, maimed, cut down, and trampled on women. If that were done, if unresisting men were cut down, whether by troops or not, it is murder for which the parties are liable to be tried by the law of the country; and I, for one, will ever uphold this, that a man shall come to his trial fairly and without any prejudice created upon the public mind in that respect . . .

Mr. Justice Holroyd:[1] It appears to me that it would not be proper for the Court to receive affidavits stating that there was no foundation at all for those accounts which were given in the newspapers, and upon which the defendant acted . . . The falsehood of these accounts does not form any ingredient in the crime for which the defendant is called up for punishment, and therefore it is not to be assumed that the accounts there stated were false, but only that, not knowing whether they were true or false, upon the reading of those papers, he, with the intent charged in the indictment (which is found by the jury) published this paper, containing a statement of the facts, or rather an assumption of the facts as represented in the newspapers, and expressing the irritated feelings of his mind upon the subject . . . The law of England says that libels are not to be published respecting persons accused, but they are fairly to come to their trial.

James Scarlett pointed out:

. . . the defendant wrote upon certain statements contained in the newspapers; from that hour to the present no authorized publication had ever contradicted the facts asserted in these papers; and therefore although the Government had good reason for knowing that the King's thanks ought to be applied in the way in which they have been applied, yet that knowledge can in no way bear upon the letter of the defendant, because that letter was written before the thanks were bestowed, at a time when the writer was not aware that the Government was connected with the action, and when he did not know but some military officer, without authority or previous instructions, had poured in his armed men, upon the defenceless multitude.

[1] State Trials, p. 164.

Scarlett emphasised the purity of Burdett's motives:

. . . He wrote under the impression of the moment . . . I have already protested against my client's being mixed up with the persons by whom the Manchester meeting was called. If I were permitted to advert to that which is now matter of history, I should say that at Westminster those persons were the most virulent opponents of the honourable baronet.[1] But let the conduct of those persons have been as mischievous as it may, still the question with Sir Francis Burdett was the same. Was the employment of an armed force, spoken of by the newspapers commonly in contradiction, but concurring on that point—was that act such an act as the people of England ought to silently submit to? My Lords, the employment of that military force, if not now *sub judice*, may come into that situation. My client does not mean to say that there may not have been grounds to justify the proceeding; all he says is, what I have said before, that up to this time no such grounds have ever been stated . . .

The sum total of Scarlett's pleas on behalf of Burdett was that his motives were noble ones. The Attorney-General acknowledged the purity of Sir Francis's motives, but said that it was the effect of the libel rather than the intention which should be looked at by the Court. He asked that no vindictive punishment be awarded. Scarlett had said:

Sir Francis Burdett always held certain principles . . . he is too old to change them . . . he bows implicitly to the judgment of the Court upon the terms of his letter; to the last moments of his life he will maintain the sentiments which it expresses . . . I know your Lordships will look at the question with that candour which belongs to you. I feel that however you may punish my client's expressions you will acquit him upon his motives.

The fine of £2000 and three months' imprisonment were imposed. The *Manchester Observer* briefly noticed Sir Francis Burdett's appearance in court in its 3 February 1821 issue. Reporting the later appearances of Sir Francis Burdett and Scarlett's pleas on his behalf, the *Observer* was disingenuous. Perhaps the second most important judicial utterance, after the doubts thrown upon the newspaper reports in this motion in arrest of judgment, was Judge Bayley's pronouncement:

. . . The libel in question imports that troops had killed men unarmed, unresisting, and had disfigured, maimed, cut down, and trampled on women.

---

[1] 'Equally blameworthy' [to Burdett's 'jealousy' and his 'milk and water' defence in the courts] 'was his sending his myrmidons of the Rump, with Alexander Galloway at their head, as a self-appointed treasurer, to paralize the subscription, and fritter that money away in all sorts of useless purposes, in order to prevent any of it being left to conduct that trial at York, for which the greatest part of it was subscribed; and in which unworthy purpose they were too successful . . .' (Hunt's 'Letter' *loc. cit*, 3).

If that were done, if unresisting men were cut down, whether by troops or not, it is murder for which the parties are liable to be tried by the law of the country; and I, for one, will ever uphold this, that a man shall come to his trial fairly and without any prejudice created upon the public mind in that respect . . .

From the radical viewpoint that pronouncement ought to have been of paramount importance; it would appear to have been the view which had been striven for ever since the early days after 16 August; it would appear to have been the pronouncement which Harmer was striving for at the Oldham inquest; it was shortly to be roundly asserted in the House of Commons during Burdett's imprisonment. The *Manchester Observer* did not even report it![1] Burdett was imprisoned. Scarlett's impassioned appeal, however, made good 'copy' for the *Manchester Gazette*'s leader:

. . . With respect to the letter which Sir Francis Burdett has written, [Scarlett had said] it should be observed that it expresses no opinion, much less calls for any approbation, of the conduct of those by whom the meeting at Manchester was assembled; it does not ask whether the unfortunate persons who are now suffering the sentence of the law, had or had not assembled such a meeting as the law ought to put down? It merely asks whether *the mode by which it was put down* be such as, without inquiry, remonstrances, or explanation, ought to be submitted to by the Gentlemen of England? . . . if the time ever should come when outrages like those of Manchester shall pass unheeded by persons of rank and consideration in this country, then I shall fear that the day of liberty is fast closing upon us.[2]

James Scarlett, the Ministry's severe critic in the House of Commons, the Crown prosecutor at Hunt's trial, the defending counsel in Burdett's later appearances before his judges, was still endeavouring 'to follow the path of duty . . . and to effect this object by all the means of a good conscience'. Henry Hunt demurred. From Ilchester Gaol, he wrote another of his 'Letters to the Radical Reformers . . .' dated 10 February 1821:

To be sure, miracles will never cease! I have just received the newspapers, which bring me the account of the last act of the farce that has been so long

[1] *Manchester Observer*, 10–17 February 1821. Perhaps the *Observer* did not see the significance of Judge Bayley's remarks. The intensely radical (London) *Examiner* did: their report toned them down (4 February): '. . . The libel set forth that certain troops had cut down men unarmed and unresisting; these acts, if the statement were correct, would subject such persons to a liability to be brought to their trials; and could that be done without exciting a prejudice against them after the reception of the affidavits in question?'

[2] *Manchester Gazette*, 17 February 1821.

performing in Westminster Hall, by Messrs. *Burdett, Scarlett, Copley, Gifford, Rump and Co.* I must not say one word about my lords, the pure and incorruptible Judges. Ha! ha!! ha!!! '*Westminster's pride, and England's hope*' has contrived by one means and the other—by fair means and by foul means by tampering and by begging, he has contrived at last to wriggle himself out of a gaol; for to say that to be sentenced three months to the King's Bench is any punishment at all, is childish in the extreme. Oh, how well have all the parts been got up. If the ministers had suffered their *shoy hoy*,[1] their grand, their long tried, their most efficient *shoy hoy* to have escaped without the farce of being brought up for judgment, without the farce of a sham sentence, they well knew that it would be such bare-faced deception, that they could never make use of him, that they could never play him off any more with any effect, even amongst his own dupes.

Gracious God! that *Hero of the Tower*, that '*Westminster's pride* and *England's hope*', should have come to this at last—that he should have sat listening while the Whig, Scarlett, *begged, prayed*, and *implored* the Attorney-General not to bring him up for judgment . . . Mr. Scarlett, I am also told, has received the most *substantial*, and the most convincing proofs, to induce him to swear by the private and public character of his honourable client. I am told that a thousand pounds was the price of the character that he gave the baronet, and what was of much more consequence, of the learned counsel's influence with the court . . . [On Burdett's riches—the fine meant nothing; of his Coutts' connections] . . . But that 'Westminster's pride' should so far disgrace and degrade his political character, as to submit to sit and hear his counsel, Mr. Whig Scarlett, make such tender advances to the coy, to the shy Attorney-General . . .

Then, Sir Francis, when you were brought up for what is called judgment, to listen to Mr. Scarlett while he bedaubed you, to pay a *hireling* to praise you up to the skies for those virtues, public and private, which he, the whole bar, the whole bench, and the whole court, as well as yourself, knew you did not possess. How much did you pay Mr. Scarlett for this? How much did you pay him for denouncing *me*? for having opposed and exposed you at the Westminster election? How much did you pay him for denouncing, in your name, me and those who attended the Manchester meeting, as well as the objects of the meeting? The world and posterity will judge of the sincerity of your political motives, by the sentences that have been passed upon us. Henry Hunt is sent to be incarcerated within the pestilential walls of a distant county gaol, deprived of almost every comfort for *thirty months*, and at the end of that time to give security not to attack the system of corruption for five years [!] that is, unless I will enter the ranks with you and do it as a *shoy hoy*, which rather than do, they know that I would rather remain and rot

---

[1] 'The "shoy hoys" were mere hypocrites who did not even want to obtain the Reform for which they clamoured. In the Radical Press Burdett is "the Don", Hobhouse "Sancho" . . .' Butler, *The Passing of the Great Reform Bill*, 84.

here. Sir Francis Burdett is committed to the custody of the Marshal of the King's Bench, in London, for three months . . . when May 8th comes . . . Mr. Scarlett, for *another thousand*, will swear with a solemn visage, that you are a paragon of virtue and consistency. Alas, poor 'Westminster's Pride and England's Hope', how low you must be fallen, to merit the praise of a hireling—and such a hireling as Mr. Scarlett!

And after the 'farce' was over, another Huntean letter dated 22 February:

. . . The farce of Sir Francis Burdett's punishment beats everything of the sort I ever knew. If ever there was what these Courts and Judges call a libel, the excellent letter of Sir Francis Burdett was a libel; and it was calculated to produce, in any other country but England, an open resistance to the bloody and tyrannical acts of the Government; because at the moment when it was written and published, the people were almost inflamed to madness, by every account of the bloody and cruel murders committed at Manchester. Every word of the letter was true; and therefore it was calculated to do the greatest mischief to the Ministers and Government. Notwithstanding all this, the Baronet has got off with a mere *nominal* punishment; and as for the fine, it is no more to him than the expense of swearing an affidavit is to me. Mr. Scarlett *begged* and *wept* 'salt tears', as I am told, and made it a *personal request* to the Judges to spare him. Mr. Scarlett is as good as a fifth Judge, and the other four dare not refuse his supplications.[1]

With Burdett serving his sentence, a petition from Nottingham was presented to the House of Commons on 20 February.[2] It was regarded as strongly worded (and was not printed) not because it attacked the ministry but because of its reflections on the administration of justice. It called attention, among other radical pleas, to:

. . . the carnage of the memorable 16th of August, a day of blood, which was not accounted for, demanded retributive justice. They prayed that the traitors and murderers of that day might be brought to condign punishment. The people on that day had done no wrong; why then should they have been butchered by armed yeomanry who received public thanks for their deeds of murder and of blood, from the ministers of the Prince Regent? . . .

Sir Robert Wilson (from the Opposition benches) spoke in favour of printing the petition. He recalled that Sir Francis Burdett was in prison, but persons, whom he (Sir Robert) was prepared to prove guilty of

---

[1] Hunt's attitude towards Sir Francis Burdett should be compared with the latter's appeal in the House of Commons on Wednesday, 24 April 1822, for a remission of Hunt's sentence. Sir Francis Burdett entered into an animated description of the whole series of miseries and the atrocious treatment endured by Hunt in Ilchester gaol. Burdett had visited Hunt at Ilchester, following which Hunt expressed some contrition. ('To the Radical Reformers . . . Ilchester Goal, 24 April 1822').

[2] Parl. Deb., Second Series, IV, 806–7.

murder if opportunity were allowed him, were not only at full liberty but were absolutely rewarded and encouraged, 'as far as impunity could encourage them, to repeat the offence.' Lord Castlereagh challenged Sir Robert and said he had better bring the charge before a competent tribunal. In this House of Commons exchange, which the *Manchester Observer*[1] reported fairly extensively, Lord Castlereagh's challenge finds its place. Lord Castlereagh, however, took the opportunity of re-iterating the Government's view, which the *Observer* reported thus:

Lord Castlereagh, for his part, gloried in the part which he had taken with respect to the Manchester transactions, in procuring the sanction of the government to those whose *bona fide* efforts on that occasion were dictated by what they considered, and what he believed to be, a sense of duty . . . [following on with remarks on the petition under discussion].

Lord Castlereagh's remarks were rather more pertinent than the *Observer* reported; he had this to say:

. . . [he] admired the strain of feeling in which [Sir Robert Wilson] thought proper to indulge, when he launched out in describing acts of the most extraordinary description, and at once charged ministers with protecting from punishment known violators of the law. Thank God the people of England lived in a country where the ministers could not, even if they were so disposed, protect any individual who offended against the laws from being amenable to their jurisdiction. The ministers here had no power to screen any man from the consequences of his act; the highest and the lowest were alike amenable to the law. Why did [Sir Robert] indulge in this theme of declamation when the laws were open to the aggrieved party? Was it because it answered better the views of the gallant member and others who thought with him, to keep this subject afloat as a topic of inflammatory declamation rather than put it into any train of legal inquiry? If there were any man, or body of men, under a charge of murder, and no person stepped forward to bring them to punishment, it was a reproach to the gallant general that he had not travelled out of his military character, and assumed the civil functions of a public prosecutor. With regard to the thanks which his Majesty had been advised to give to the Magistrates of Manchester, he should always glory in the share he had had in protecting men who had saved the country from the base attempts which evil-minded persons had made to subvert the constitution. The true reason why the conduct of the magistrates and yeomanry had not been brought before a jury was, that there existed no grounds for such a proceeding. Though ministers, in the line of conduct which they had pursued, had not the good fortune to possess the favourable opinion of the gallant general, they had obtained what they valued much more—the approbation of that House . . .

[1] *Manchester Observer*, 24 February 1821.

Stuart Wortley, who had been a dissentient at the famous York protest meeting in October 1819, and had protested from the platform at some of the proposed resolutions, observed:

. . . If the hon. Member [Sir Robert Wilson] had a charge against the magistrates of Manchester when would he prove it? This charge of murder was, he was convinced, brought on from time to time, for the purposes of inflammation, because if the object really was inquiry, it might have been attained by an action for common assault.

The charge of murder, in view of the recent judicial pronouncement, was after this period not to be bandied about quite so freely. Sir Robert Wilson was to figure as one of the principal Opposition spokesmen in the forthcoming two-days' debate in the House, after Sir Francis Burdett's release from prison; Sir Robert Wilson was to adopt a different tone.

In the later radical commentaries on Peterloo, the Bamford and Prentice versions, there is no mention of the famous Parliamentary debate of 15 and 16 May 1821. Henry Hunt does, however, refer to it (in prospect) in his 'To the Radical Reformers . . .' 22 February 1821:

On the 15th of May, the anniversary of my sentence, the mountain is to be in labour again, is it? Well, this is pretty well: '*Westminster's Pride and England's Hope*' is going to make a motion on the Manchester slaughter of men, women, and children, when fourteen were murdered, and 618 sabred and maimed, on the *16th of August*, 1819; the Hero to make a motion for an inquiry into this bloody affair, *one year and nine months* after the outrage! *one year and three months* after the famous trial at York, where the meeting was proved to be peaceable and the people non-resisting. *One whole year* after I was sentenced to be incarcerated in this dungeon, the magnanimous Hero of the Tower back-door has promised by his colleague, Mr. Hobhouse, to make a motion in the House! Gracious God, grant me patience! So 'Westminster's Pride' has had the address, or rather the impudence, to get all inquiry upon this most important affair—these unnatural murders, put off for three months! He has once more succeeded in preventing those active members, Sir Robert Wilson, Mr. Hume, Mr. Bennet, Alderman Wood, Mr. Creevey, and many others, from bringing this all-important measure before the House. He has done this in order to give him time to get out of prison, that he may damn it —for damn it he will, I am satisfied; however, time will prove all things, and we shall see. There is one thing which is quite clear—that the blood that was spilt at Manchester is unrequited; there has been neither inquiry instituted nor justice done the people; and while the murderers are walking at large, those who committed no crime are the victims of unheard of persecution . . . [Hunt pleads for the people of Manchester to send petitions to the House].

The debate did, however, get full coverage in the *Manchester Observer* of 19 and 26 May. Petitions arrived at the House from Manchester—a score or more; and there were two from Hunt himself. The presentation of these petitions (which were ordered to be printed) from the sufferers of the events of 16 August, inaugurated the debate. Sir Francis Burdett, opening the debate,[1] observed:

After the various petitions which have been presented to the House stating in terms as simple as they were incontrovertible, and as affecting as they were unaffected . . . he rose, not knowing to whom the blame of the transaction ought to attach, but with the intention of discovering that point by his motion; for, whether it was to the ministers, or whether it was to the magistrates, or whether it was to the yeomanry, who so particularly distinguished themselves on that occasion, that the great share of the blame ought to attach, or whether it was to attach to them all collectively, was more than he could tell at present, and was therefore a proof that some inquiry into the subject was necessary . . .

It was an approach towards the subject of an entirely different nature; nor was Sir Francis Burdett speaking with his tongue in his cheek—his *bona fides* were unimpeachable in view of his recent experience. He went over the familiar ground. Lord Stanley had earlier told the House of an attack from the crowd; Sir Francis hoped he would retract it. The House had been told of attacks by brickbats and sticks; the recent trial at York had refuted them:

Well might he have asked—(he would not say what answer he got to his question)—Is this a Christian land? Is this a land of liberty? Yes, he would repeat, it was a Christian land. Yes, he would still call it a land of liberty—one in which power however absolute might be the attempt to exercise it, had yet its limits[2] . . .

Why Hunt's arrest by magistrates who knew not with what to charge him? . . . Doubtless the Government, by whom the dreadful act was applauded, had consoled themselves with the hope that the terrible example of the massacre at Manchester would silence all public complaint; it had not done so. The people met as before and the Government were obliged to desist; unlike Macbeth they thought it better to stop where they had gone, than advance still deeper into blood. The justification which they had been told to await had been proved false:

. . . Unless that House had lost all respect for itself—unless it had thrown aside all regard for public liberty—unless gentlemen had not only dismissed

[1] Parl. Deb., N.S., Vol. V, 1821 (p. 719 et seq.).
[2] Ibid., p. 736–7.

all reverence for justice, but all feeling for their own character and estimation in the world—they would go into that inquiry, which he now demanded on the part of the people of England; they would now make good their professions, which some of them had expressed . . . It was impossible that an administration stained by the blood of the people—for so he must so contend the present administration was stained, until that blood was somehow atoned for . . . He could only say that, as far as he was concerned, he had, to the best of his power, endeavoured to do justice to the people, and to give ministers an opportunity to do justice to themselves . . .[1]

It was not the Sir Francis Burdett of 22 August 1819, in his letter to his constituents, even though he was now speaking with all the privilege of a member of Parliament. On the 'facts' which he knew he trounced the Ministry:

. . . If the gentlemen would take the trouble to read the evidence taken on the trials at York, they would find that, with the exception of Mr. Hulton, there was not a witness for the Crown who did not bear testimony to the peaceableness and orderly conduct of the people. Mr. Hulton was the only person who had seen the shower of stones which the noble lord [Lord Castlereagh] had said were afterwards collected in waggons. He [Sir Francis] hoped that the noble lord would take care of those precious stones—that he would cause them to be preserved in the British Museum, or some other public depositary, as a memento to the House to beware how it allowed itself in future to be misled . . . But even Mr. Hulton, who took the chair among the magistrates, because no other man could be found to fill it, did not state how the attack commenced; whether it was by order to the troops, or whether, without authority, they had fallen upon the unoffending multitude, excited by animosity or inflamed by intoxication. Surely, if there were nothing else, this demanded inquiry. Surely it ought to be ascertained, at least why and by whom the shedding of blood upon that day was occasioned. Mr. Hulton took upon himself to say that he saw the yeomanry beaten; and he ordered Col. L'Estrange with a party of the 15th Dragoons to support them; yet it was as notorious as the sun at noon, that not a single witness had corroborated this assertion; not even Nadin, the runner, who said, but only said, that he could not serve a warrant without the aid of the military, did not confirm it; even the Rev. Mr. Hay, who before and since the Manchester massacre had been in constant communication with Ministers, did not confirm it; only Mr. Hulton, had been gifted with senses differently formed from all the rest of mankind.[2]

There was a tirade against stipendiary magistrates; against the alleged reading of the Riot Act, and, because of what he knew of the trial at

[1] Parl. Deb., N.S., Vol. V, p. 738.
[2] Ibid., pp. 722–3.

York, he scouted all the previous assertions of Ministry spokesmen. Bootle Wilbraham went over the magistrates' case again; tried to prove that casualty lists were exaggerated; paid a tribute to the high character of William Hulton, and pointed out why the judge at York had limited the evidence which could be brought. There were other testimonies to the character of Hulton:

It did not by any means follow, that the magistrates, in availing themselves of the military power, could have contemplated the unfortunate scenes which afterwards took place . . . the magistrates' overbearing sense of duty, which in a complete degree justified the satisfaction expressed by the ministers of the Crown. Could it fairly be supposed, that the satisfaction expressed by ministers, meant anything like rejoicing at the events which had taken place? No, but it was a source of satisfaction that English magistrates would consent to take upon themselves such a responsibility at such a moment.[1]

One member, Mr Denman, on the York trial, said tartly: 'if the Government could have proved those circumstances' [the Riot Act, the stones, &c.] 'he had no doubt they would have done so.' The assertion brought the Solicitor-General to his feet:

. . . The previous speaker had insinuated, nay, boldly asserted that the magistrates had proceeded under the immediate directions and orders of the Government [it was denied]. Although his Majesty's ministers felt it to be their duty to support the magistrates, not doubting they had acted conscientiously, yet they were in no way personally responsible for that conduct on the part of the magistrates, which were not directed, and of the intended nature of which they had no previous knowledge . . . this was introduced to inflame the passions of the House [Sir John Copley went over the details again—the drillings, the magistrates' concern, military force in case it was needed.] Mr. Hulton was chosen the chairman, and he appealed to every man who heard him—and who knew that gentleman—whether an individual of higher character, for integrity, firmness, and humanity, existed in his Majesty's dominions; (A laugh). Notwithstanding that sneer, he would confidently repeat his assertion . . . if the magistrates had not proceeded as they did they would have been guilty of a gross dereliction of their duty, which would have rendered them amenable to the laws of their country . . . the Yeomanry had arrived first on the spot; . . . he was satisfied from the evidence at York and of his own stringent inquiry that the moment the yeomanry arrived at the hustings they were assailed with both sticks and stones . . . it was said that the soldiers had been guilty of excesses. If that was so, it was not the result of any order by the magistrates.[2]

[1] Parl. Deb., N.S., Vol. V, pp. 759–60.
[2] Ibid., pp. 766–73.

On the second day of the debate, Horace Twiss, M.P. for one of the corrupt boroughs which the Reform Bill of 1832 abolished, gently pointed out some of the fallacies in Burdett's arguments:

. . . Sir, the reformers undoubtedly fight this question with very considerable advantage. If the House accede to their demand for inquiry then they have the sanction of parliament to colour their assertions; if the inquiry be refused, better still, for then they may tell the crowd that the refusal results from the corruption of parliament. Their views, as to the necessity of inquiry seem to have changed not a little since the time of the transaction itself. Hardly more than a fortnight after the events, a meeting was held in Westminster for the purpose of expressing an opinion upon it; and though certain parties now insist on the necessity of further investigation, this being now the only way of stirring up the public mind again, yet, at that time, when the object was to obtain an immediate summary condemnation, in other words, a prejudication of the conduct of the parties concerned, then the notion of all such ulterior inquiry was treated as nugatory and absurd. On that occasion a speech appears to have been made with great applause and effect upon the audience, in which, after adverting to the objection made by some people, that until more evidence had been obtained these Westminster proceedings, would be premature, the distinguished individual [Sir Francis Burdett] delivering that address vehemently exclaimed 'I say there is evidence enough before us. Are not the facts before us?' The crowd shouted 'They are,' and he proceeded: 'the scandalous, the shameful, the undeniable facts.' . . . that speech, so insisting on the total inutility of further evidence to warrant resolutions reflecting on the integrity and character of the many respectable persons concerned, was uttered by no less an authority than the same hon. baronet who now comes forward to tell us that further and fuller investigation is indispensable to make up our minds on the merits of a question, so long determined without any such light, by his own constituents on his own impassioned exhortation.[1]

Horace Twiss spoke on the ferment in the nation at the time Sir Francis made his speech:

At that time perhaps an inquiry was requisite to calm it. But now, when the irritation has passed away, without danger of revival except from such discussions as these, and when the quiet of the country is an object of such high importance, it surely is not reasonable to argue, that, even granting it to have been fitting for the House to direct investigations in 1819, in order that the ferment might be allayed, it must therefore befit us to direct them in 1821, in order that the ferment might be renewed.[2]

[1] Parl. Deb., N.S., Vol. V, pp. 795–6.
[2] Ibid., p. 796.

John Cam Hobhouse, who followed, had not much time for the legal niceties of Horace Twiss.[1] He quickly got to the heart of the transactions of 16 August. On the opinion of Lord Mansfield (who had been quoted) that soldiers do not lose their rights of citizens when acting to defend themselves when attacked, he agreed:

But they were not attacked. I defy all those around, above, and beneath him to prove that they were attacked. I defy them to show that any single proof can be given of an attack previously to the horrid assault made by the soldiers on the citizens. That resistance—at least some little resistance, too faint indeed and ineffectual, was made after the slaughter began I am ready to admit . . .[2]

That, he confessed, was only to be expected:

But it seems that the gentlemen opposite are still resolved to believe that some attack was made by the people on the military previously to the charge of the yeomanry upon the crowd. I will take this opportunity to observe, that the abettors of this outrage (for so I must call it) have not replied in that manly and candid manner to the appeal of my hon. colleague, which would have done honour to their understandings and to their hearts. On the contrary, though charged with the misstatements made in 1819, though called upon to give up those misstatements, or to show why they should not abandon those refuted errors, they have not been honest enough to retract, nor bold enough to confirm the extraordinary assertions, on which alone the legislative enactments of 1819 were confessedly founded. Something like a struggle is, however, still made to prove the existence of those famous stones and brickbats which figured so notably in the speech of the noble secretary of State for foreign affairs [Lord Castlereagh, in the November, 1819, debate]. Not only the depositions, but Mr. Hulton is adduced to prove this fifty-times refuted fiction . . .

Cam Hobhouse here was showing that all the arguments asserted in the House for the passing of the Six Acts gained the support of members on the strength of the Ministry's now exploded statements of what had happened at Manchester on 16 August; exploded because of the sensational 'revelations' at the York trial.[3] When shorn of all its trimmings, the radical case was that there had been no attack by the people, that

[1] Parl. Deb., N.S., Vol. V, p. 799

[2] Ibid., p. 802.

[3] Such arguments were not confined to this debate. *The Examiner* reported that on Tuesday, 8 May, 'Mr Lennard moved for the repeal of the Seditious Meetings and Libel Acts, in a very sound and argumentative speech. In particular, he placed in a strong light the absurdity and wickedness of continuing Acts passed under the influence of the statements of the Manchester Magistrates, seeing that those statements were afterwards so triumphantly refuted on Mr Hunt's trial at York. . . .' (*The Examiner*, 13 May 1821.)

the aggressors throughout had been the Yeomanry. The Rev. Mr Stanley's privately circulated *Narrative* was in Cam Hobhouse's hands. The 'impartial' narrative of Mr Stanley's had been quoted at a passage which was less impartial than any other. Stanley's opinion on the Yeomanry:

At first, i.e., for a very few paces, their movement was not rapid, and there was some show of an attempt to follow their officer in regular succession, five or six abreast; but, as Mr. Francis Philips in his pamphlet observes, they soon 'increased their speed,' and with a zeal and ardour which might naturally be expected from men acting with delegated power against a foe by whom it is understood they had long been insulted with taunts of cowardice, continued their course, seeming individually to vie with each other which should be first.

Cam Hobhouse did not use the exact quotation, merely a paraphrase: 'they vied with each other in eagerness to show that they were not the cowards they had been represented to be,'[1] The Ministry, in short, argued Cam Hobhouse, would not admit that the Yeomanry had attacked. Indeed they would not. If they did so their whole case would be in danger of collapse. They were probably aware, too, that up to that date, their central fact had not been proved: it had only been asserted by them from the evidence they had, which evidence they were prepared to believe was indisputable. Herein, it is believed by this investigation, lies the reason for their inflexible opposition to a Parliamentary inquiry. They were prepared to defend their position on the law of the realm. They were prepared to let their opponents prove, if they could, that there had been no attack on the Yeomanry. Cam Hobhouse pressed on relentlessly:

The reason, indeed, why complaint alone is to be allowed, but nothing like redress, is not quite to my taste. Forsooth, if we even inquire, we shall (so the member for Dover says), 'paralyze the magistracy.' Sir, if the magistracy only commit vagrants, or affiliate bastards, or sit at quarter sessions in their usual capacity, I would allow them the free exercise of all their faculties; but if they send soldiers to cut the throats of my fellow-countrymen who meet to petition for reform of parliament, I certainly would 'paralyze' them if I could.

★   ★   ★

James Scarlett on the Opposition benches was the most informed of all that anti-Ministerial minority of members. His record, thus far, to all except the Hunts and the Prentices, was impeccable. He referred to

[1] The full quotation had been used by an earlier speaker. Parl. Deb., N.S., Vol. V, pp. 778–9.

his mode of conducting the case against Hunt;[1] he then referred to Hulton:[2]

It had been said that he was well acquainted with the magistrate, Mr. Hulton. He was not well acquainted with him, he knew none of his family; and all he knew of him or his family was to his credit. One of his objects in now addressing the House was to redeem his pledge to Mr. Hulton. Mr. Hulton had been examined; his examination was before the public; it was not so correctly reported as it ought to be; but no intentional misrepresentation could be imputed to any one. The meeting having thus began to assemble, the mode of its assembly, and the increasing numbers of those assembled appeared to inspire the inhabitants of Manchester with considerable alarm. The magistrates, who at that time were assembled at Mr. Buxton's house, did not contemplate anything more than the collecting of a military force in the neighbourhood to watch the meeting, until they received the depositions of thirty or forty respectable gentlemen that the terror of the inhabitants were still further excited. It was not until they had received those depositions that they entertained the design of arresting the leaders of the multitude which was collecting before them. A warrant was then prepared for their arrest, and put into the hands of Nadin, the constable. Mr. Hulton stated that Nadin told him that it would be impossible to execute it without the assistance of a military force. The consequence was, that he ordered a military force to approach the house where the magistrates were sitting. The Manchester Yeomanry were the first troops that came, and they drew up under Mr. Buxton's windows. Mr. Hulton stated, that he never gave them orders to ride into the meeting and attack the multitude. He (Mr. Scarlett) was not able to give any satisfactory information to the House how it happened that the Yeomanry did ride into that meeting. He had, however, been given to understand that they had done so upon the representation of one of the constables. Mr. Hulton declared that he knew nothing of their advance until he saw them engaged with the multitude. They must have advanced with considerable alacrity, inasmuch as they rode over one of their own constables in their course. When they had arrived at the hustings, Mr. Hulton thought, from their appearance that the multitude had obtained an advantage over them . . .[3]

Such a statement from an Opposition member of the House was received with respect. The other facts—Col. L'Estrange's arrival and the order to advance—were examined. Up to this point Scarlett's explanation had exonerated the magistrates from any sinister intentions:

. . . If they had acted under a sense of duty created by an impression of

[1] Parl Deb. N.S., Vol. V, p. 820.
[2] See above, pp. 351–2; 358–9.
[3] Parl. Deb. N.S., Vol. V, pp. 832–3.

alarm, their error was certainly venial. The House ought to judge the conduct of the magistrates, not by the considerations which suggested themselves after the event, but by the considerations which suggested themselves to their minds at the moment. They ought to judge of them by the feelings which must have been foremost on the minds of the magistrates at the instant, and by the apprehensions which they had reason to suppose existed in the minds of the inhabitants of Manchester. A meeting so numerous as that was, must have excited fears in their minds and they might naturally think that the best mode of getting rid of those fears would be by arresting the leaders of the multitude before the multitude had become inflamed by their seditious harangues. If the act were to do over again, he should certainly advise the magistrates, under all the circumstances of the case, not to do it; but it would be too hard to say that they ought to be censured for having done it.[1]

Keeping the central fact still in view of who struck the first blow, Scarlett, with all his sincerity, did not believe that any attack could have come from the people. He had probed the reports of the various eye-witnesses, and had come to the conclusion[2] that not a blow was struck before the arrests were made. He implicitly believed Tyas's report that the moment of aggression was after the arrests—at the moment of Tyas's statement, 'Have at their flags . . . !' He had indeed done what he stated at York that Hulton had done, 'confounded the period' when the attack was made. With that misapprehension fixed in his mind, Scarlett could proceed:

. . . The multitude, however, ought not to have been dispersed at all in the manner it was dispersed. The yeomanry had no right to act at all without the authority of the magistracy. They might think it their duty to ride into the multitude without orders; but in his opinion, it was clearly a great misconception of duty. The learned gentleman then remarked, that in the course of the trial, it had become important to discover, whether any attempt had been made to serve the warrant without the assistance of the military. The learned judge had asked, again and again, whether any application, either personal or by proclamation, was made to the crowd to get out of the way in order that a warrant might be served by the civil power; and the answer which he invariably received was 'No.'[3]

Here, Scarlett was again the victim of his own way of conducting the trial at York. He was referring here to the reading of the Riot Act which his own solitary witness (Hulton) never referred to.

When the constables advanced, they were met, some said by cheers of wel-

[1] Parl. Deb., N.S., Vol. V, p. 834.
[2] See above, p. 221.
[3] Ibid., p. 834.

come; others by cheers of defiance. The cheers perhaps were a mixture of both. Why should they not cheer? Was any gentleman bold enough to say that they had not a right to resist if a parcel of soldiers rode in upon them without a warrant? He must confess that he was not the man bold enough to say so; on the contrary he said that they had a right to resist, if they were rode in upon without the authority of a warrant. Until the moment that Hunt asked for the warrant and Nadin produced it, they had no right to disperse the meeting.

The attack upon the Yeomanry however had already been made at this point. He went on to remark on Lord Sidmouth's letter of thanks. He (Scarlett) was looking at the question 'totally divested of all party feeling' he thought that letter produced universal irritation. He referred to Burdett's letter on which he had been prosecuted; he thought Lord Sidmouth's letter liable to prosecution on the same grounds. It prejudiced the trial then pending. He thought the courts of law could not decide the questions at issue. It was not too late for the House to interfere:

. . . The question then was reduced to this point—was the time too late for the House to interfere? Did the noble lord mean to say that if the constitution had been violated, time should make the people sleep over the injury which they had received? He should indeed think ill of the people of England—he should indeed consider them unworthy of the liberty which they enjoyed— if a short year and a half could make them forget those wrongs which, according to the noble lord [Castlereagh, now Londonderry] made the hearts of those who had only read them bleed to the inmost core.[1]

The Attorney-General (Sir Robert Gifford):

thought the speech of his hon. and learned friend, and the very candid statement he had made on this occasion had not only relieved him from the necessity of addressing many observations to the House, but must have convinced those who sat around him that this motion could not be supported. The hon. baronet [Sir Francis Burdett] in his opening speech, attached great blame upon two parties who were entirely relieved by the speech of his hon. and learned friend, namely his Majesty's ministers and the magistrates. What was the charge against his Majesty's ministers made by the hon. baronet and reiterated by the learned member for Nottingham? Why, that they deliberately authorized the transactions . . . [Mr. Denman] asserted, that he believed the magistrates could not have acted in the way in which they did but for the previous sanction of H.M. Government. What was the next charge? That the magistrates deliberately and wantonly authorized the scene which afterwards took place. What was the testimony of his learned friend [Mr.

[1] Parl. Deb. N.S., Vol. V, p. 837.

Scarlett] fully confirmed as it was by the letter of Mr. Norris and the testimony of Mr. Hulton? that the magistrates never had the intention of dispersing the meeting, or of arresting Mr. Hunt, until after the meeting took place, and those circumstances fell under their notice which rendered it an imperative duty to issue the warrant. Then all the charges which [Sir Francis Burdett] had so lavishly made against ministers, were over-thrown by his learned friend, who had stated, that not only in his conscience did he believe that the magistrates had no intention of dispersing the meeting, but that he believed his Majesty's ministers never authorised or sanctioned the dispersion.[1]

Sir Robert Gifford, on this occasion, did not attempt to put Scarlett right on the point where he had gone wrong. He had certainly done so in the Parliamentary debate in November 1819;[2] he merely made the most of the seemingly tardy admissions that the Government and the magistrates were relieved to a large extent of the odium attached to them. The after-part of the Attorney-General's speech seemed to contain a challenge to the still-disgruntled radicals to have recourse to law where, the Ministry felt sure, they would be finally vindicated:

. . . The question was reduced to this, whether an inquiry was to be instituted at the bar of that House into the conduct of the yeomanry? With respect to that question, it could be investigated and ought to be investigated by the tribunals of the country. Did his learned friend say it could not be discussed by way of action? Had not the greatest constitutional questions been tried by action? . . . They might have brought an issue to try whether the yeomanry were sanctioned, and whether the magistrates could, under such circumstances as presented themselves, order them to advance . . . [on the bills brought before the grand jury] . . . that the grand jury had thrown out those bills. That was, he believed, the first time that the circumstances of a bill being thrown out was offered as a presumption of guilt . . . But what had prevented the parties from preferring bills again, if they were dissatisfied? The natural inference was, that they had no case . . . [the funds raised were used] . . . not for the purpose of bringing an action against the magistrates, or investigating the conduct of the yeomanry, but in defending those persons who were convicted by a jury and whose conviction had at last extracted from the gentlemen opposite that this meeting was illegal.

---

[1] Parl. Deb., N.S., Vol. V, pp. 837–41.

[2] In the November debate, Sir Robert Gifford reminded the hon. member for Peterborough [Scarlett] 'that he must have forgotten that the efforts of the yeomanry were not directed, in the first instance, to disperse the meeting, but to repel an attack that had been made upon them. The fact had been asserted, and had not, and could not be denied; and because the gentlemen on the other side might not have obtained information enough to satisfy them that was no adequate ground for inquiry. . . .' (Parl. Deb. XLI, 1st series, November 1819, pp. 134–5).

Sir Robert Gifford reminded the Opposition of the county meetings having maintained that the 16 August meeting was legal when it was not:

. . . This being the case, were not his Majesty's ministers justified in the course which they had adopted? And, he would ask, what other consequences could follow from an investigation by that House than a prosecution against the yeomanry, which had not been yet instituted, and which, in the absence of all investigation by that House, was still open? If he believed the statements in the petitions presented, there could be no difficulty in instituting these proceedings; seeing that the names of the parties stated to have committed the outrages had been mentioned. If the only question was, the conduct of the yeomanry, that conduct was still open for investigation in the courts of law . . . The speech of his learned friend had exculpated his Majesty's ministers and the magistrates, to whom the hon. baronet [Sir Francis Burdett] had attempted to attach the odium of the transaction. The verdict of guilty against the persons tried at York had justified the conduct of the magistrates, and if the conduct of the yeomanry were culpable, the time which had elapsed did not bar investigation in the courts of law, and parliament would do an injustice to the parties accused, by taking that investigation from the proper tribunals.

The hon. baronet had said that the facts on which the ministerial side of the House relied had been disproved by the evidence at York. He maintained that they had not; but even, supposing that they had, was it fair to characterize the proceedings of the 16th of August as a murder or a massacre? As far as any investigation had been made into the subject, they had been found not to be murder and he would ask, where was that candour on which the honourable gentlemen prided themselves, when they stigmatized with such epithets the actions of men whom they wished to put upon their trial?

Sir Francis Burdett was still not satisfied. The case, he said, remained precisely where it was:

[The gentlemen opposite] and all their adherents seemed determined to shut their eyes to the real and great question, and to endeavour to turn the attention of the House to the minute parts of it. They talked of it as a question between certain persons, who had been aggrieved, and those by whom they had been aggrieved, instead of a question between the people of England and his Majesty's Government. That the people assembled at a public meeting were to have the military let loose upon them, and that it was to be held that no one was amenable for that act, surely afforded the strongest ground for parliamentary inquiry. The House ought to be informed by an inquiry at the bar, whether the troops had committed military execution without the authority of the magistrates, and had of their own head perpetrated the violences which had occurred. They ought to be informed whether ministers stood clear on the subject. Seeing the correspondence that existed between the magistrates and H.M. ministers; seeing that the latter had published the letters of the magistrates but had not ventured to lay before the House their answers; seeing the ungracious answer to the sheriffs of London put into the mouth of his Majesty, who was made to say, that the citizens of London could not know the previous transactions and circumstances at Manchester; seeing all this, it was difficult to believe that what had taken place was not, in a great measure, the result of directions from H.M. Government . . .[1]

The 'minute parts' of the transaction were perhaps more important than Sir Francis thought: 'The attacks of the military upon the people were distinctly proved,' he said, 'indeed, so distinctly, that the learned Judge at York stated to the jury that there appeared no justification for the employment of the military in the execution of the warrant.' The Crown's chickens, James Scarlett's chickens, hatched in the mode of conducting the trial at York, were again coming home to roost. Sir Francis's interpretation of what the judge stated to the jury at York was one of the least of his misapprehensions.[2] He had however as good a conscience as James Scarlett; there were many unanswered questions to which he was genuinely seeking answers:

. . . His reason therefore for pressing this question was, that the public mind was not satisfied; nor would it be satisfied until an inquiry had taken place into these transactions. While he had a seat in the House he would press for this inquiry. If the King's ministers would now say that they would take up the inquiry, and report to the House upon it, then he would rest satisfied; but if that were not done, then he had only to repeat, that the people would never rest satisfied until some satisfaction were had for, or inquiry made into, these calamitous transactions.

The House divided. The 'ayes' for Sir Francis Burdett's motion were 111; the 'noes' 235. The House adjourned at a quarter to three in the morning on Thursday, 17 May 1821. Lord Stanley was in the lobby with Sir Francis.[3] He had not joined in the debate, for obvious reasons. With the now likely course set for bringing the machinery of the law into action against members of the Manchester Yeomanry, he had become almost an interested party. In the November 1819 debate on the transactions at Manchester, he had intervened to speak on behalf of

[1] Parl. Deb., N.S., Vol. V, p. 842.
[2] See above, p. 174.
[3] 'This Whig, Lord Stanley, was also one of the most violent against a parliamentary inquiry into the [Manchester] transaction, when the question was brought before the House of Commons. The Lord deliver us from the tender mercies of the Whigs, I say.' (*Henry Hunt's Memoirs*, III, p. 637). Lord Stanley had also voted *for* inquiry in November 1819!

Capt. Hugh Hornby Birley, commander of the Yeomanry. Hugh Hornby Birley was to be named in the forthcoming suit-at-law as the principal defendant. Sir Robert Wilson's charges of 20 February 1821 in the House of murder by the magistrates were not heard:

. . . The law of Moses, [Sir Robert affirmed] 'a tooth for a tooth, an eye for an eye', had been spoken of, but the hon. baronet [Sir Francis] did not by his proposal require blood for blood, but merely that inquiry should be made where the blame ought to rest . . .[1]

It was a less-assertive Sir Robert Wilson than the same Sir Robert Wilson of 20 February.

★   ★   ★

The Parliamentary debate was fully reported in the *Manchester Observer* in their issues of 19 and 26 May; the editor could yet write, in the following week's issue (2 June):

. . . We find the task (with our feelings on the subject and with a due respect for H.M. Attorney-General and the Constitutional Association) one of difficulty. We have had means and opportunities of knowing more correctly than any other persons, the extent of the sabrings . . . cruel proceedings of the 16th of August . . . Our bosoms have been filled with indignation at the conduct of those tyrannical and cruel men, who could order and execute so dreadful an outrage; and our feelings have been wrought up to the highest pitch of grief, shame and anger, at the disgraceful manner in which all attempts to inquire into this affair, and to punish the aggressors have been evaded.[2]

We, however, looked forward to the re-agitation of the question in the House of Commons with satisfaction, and not without hope:—not hope that the honourable House would institute any inquiry—the manner in which [it] is constituted forbade that; but we expected that the clouds of falsehood which had been raised to prevent the people of England from understanding the merits of the question, would be dissipated; and this expectation has in a great manner been realized.

Bootle Wilbraham, 'the great champion and friend of the Manchester

[1] Parl. Deb., N.S., Vol. V, p. 780.
[2] *The Observer* leader-writer undoubtedly 'had means and opportunities of knowing more correctly than any other persons, the extent of the sabrings . . .' &c. inflicted at Peterloo, and his replies to Bootle Wilbraham's statements made in the House of Commons have some point. That the leader-writer could still insist, after reading what had been said in the House of Commons debate—to which the writer was allegedly replying—that 'cruel men' could 'order and execute so dreadful an outrage', and in so insisting, ignore and make no reply to that which James Scarlett had so painstakingly said, is almost incredible. It is an example, at the very source, that 'the original propagators of the radical version of Peterloo . . . learned nothing, forgot nothing, and admitted nothing.'

magistrates' was castigated mercilessly, and they dismissed his 'thrice-refuted' arguments:

He produced a statement from some curious and hard-swearing antiquary, who had collected the stones from off the field, which had been hurled at the humane and quiescent Yeomanry, and which 'looked as if they had been used'. Perhaps these stones, like the potatoes which on a certain occasion most seditiously and blasphemously threw themselves at our chaste and pious Sovereign 'spoke for themselves'.

That many stones might have been collected from St. Peter's Field immediately after the dispersion of the meeting, *covered with blood*, no one will doubt or deny; but who will say that it was the blood of the Yeomanry . . .

His lordship [Lord Castlereagh] seemed most anxious to clear ministers from all blame on this subject, and left the magistrates and yeomanry and their friends to get out of the scrape as well as they could . . . Now this anxiety of his lordship to exculpate ministers is, of itself, an admission and proof that blame is imputable somewhere, and, therefore, that an inquiry ought to have been instituted before the thanks of the Crown were given to the magistrates and yeomanry, as it must have been known that they had been accused as the authors of the outrage; . . .

The *Observer* leader-writer proceeded with his comments on the *minutiæ*:

. . . But his lordship said, that ministers 'owed it to the magistrates to give an immediate opinion as to whether they had been considered to have acted in a fair point of view or not, without waiting for an inquiry into the *minutiæ* of the transaction.' This mode of acting and of reasoning is certainly most rational and statesmanlike. Did not ministers know that the whole merits of the case might depend on *minutiæ*? Were they so ignorant as not to know that in an affair of the most common assault, the *minutiæ* of how the affair commenced, and who struck the *first blow*, is always inquired into; and that he is held to be the aggressor who commenced the assault? . . . We shall only say, that the peace never was at any time broken *by the people*, but that it was broken *by the yeomanry*, who we can prove sabred and trod upon many persons in their way up to the hustings; and as to 'resistance', we have the authority of Judge Bayley, that the people would have been justified in resisting the wanton and illegal attack of an infuriated and drunken soldiery . . . the yeomanry, who in blind rage, rode over and wounded both their friends and foes;—but for the people, they stood by too tamely—they were taken by surprise, and we defy any one to prove a single act of resistance, until the crowd was nearly dispersed, and the field cleared, when a few brick-bats were hurled at the yeomanry in self-defence . . .

The *Observer* leader-writer was very sure of himself, but in answering Castlereagh he forgot to answer Scarlett:

. . . and yet your lordship asserted that 'exaggerated statements had been made, and that the question had only been brought forward to re-agitate the public mind, on a question which the *thunder* of Parliament had previously decided.' Yes, yes:—the people of England understand your lordship perfectly well, and your lordship also knows that it is not the thunder of your own usurped Joveship, nor of your Parliamentary machines, that the people fear. Your lordship also knows, that without the thunder of certain other machines, to be found in great perfection near the Warren at Woolwich, the people of England would not allow you or your satellites to 'threaten or command'.

The occasion of the Parliamentary debate of 15 and 16 May brought from John Edward Taylor, in his newly-established *Manchester Guardian*, one of the longest leaders perhaps that paper ever printed,[1] a large part of which was taken up in refuting point by point the depositions presented to the House by Bootle Wilbraham in mitigating the casualties. Taylor claimed:

We have gone through the speech of the chosen advocate of the measures of the Manchester magistrates; and we believe that such a tissue of ignorance, error, and misrepresentation as we have exposed has very seldom been witnessed within the walls of the House of Commons. We know that Mr. Wilbraham is not answerable for the truth of the statements he has made; but we do maintain, that had he sought information upon the subject in the spirit of candour, and from a love of truth, he would not have been made the dupe of those gross misrepresentations, which he has been the organ for communicating to the country.

Taylor answered Horace Twiss by pointing out 'six distinct untruths'[2] in the Rev. Mr Hay's letter of 16 August. 'However incredible the assertion,' wrote Taylor, 'it is nevertheless true, that Mr Twiss talks of the "advantage arising to the *rioters*, from the absence of evidence (on the trial at York) as to the conduct of the magistrates and military."' In the eyes of Taylor there were no rioters on St Peter's Field. The Marquis of Londonderry's 'baseless accusations' could not be answered without a 'mixture of pity, disgust, and indignation to which we are not willing to expose ourselves.'

From the period of the Manchester outrage, to the present time, in parliament and elsewhere, and during the last debate, as well as heretofore, we have always been accustomed to hear the magistrates referred to as the persons by whose orders the Yeomanry charged the people; but the tardy message of Mr. Hulton, delivered through the medium of Mr. Scarlett, unsettles all our

---

[1] *Manchester Guardian*, 22 May 1821. 'Taylor devoted nine and a half crowded columns to a report, and criticised the debate in a leader of three columns closely printed in small type.' (Bruton, *Story of Peterloo*, p. 7.)

[2] See above, p. 314.

previous conclusions, dexterously shifts the responsibility from his own
shoulders, and transfers to the Manchester Yeomanry the undivided merit of
the achievement. We have no means of knowing the exact degree of credit
due to this long-delayed magisterial notification; but, if it is true, we ask what
is to become of the evidence upon which the Coroners' juries, in several
inquests, on bodies of persons killed, returned verdicts of 'Died by the pressure of the military, being under the orders of the civil power'? If Mr.
Hulton's account be true, why did he conceal it at York? If false, what will
the Yeomanry say? Their laurels, however, in either case, 'will wear well,
for they have been dearly earned.' We leave the magistrates and Yeomanry
to settle amongst themselves the proportion of their respective claims to the
honours of the day.

Taylor discoursed on the utter futility of bringing actions in the
courts for redress:

It was under the soundest legal advice that this step [applying for criminal
informations against the magistrates] was declined. The application must have
been made upon affidavits: it would have been answered in the same way;
and, as the courts always lean to magistrates, and require the establishment of
improper motives, in order to sanction criminal proceedings against them,
any rule *nisi* which might have been obtained would speedily have been discharged, and the cause of the sufferers further weakened by another un-
successful effort.

The friends of inquiry into the proceedings of the 16th of August were
most anxious to get into court;—they wished to offer oral evidence; they
were desirous to submit their witnesses to the test of the most rigid cross-
examination; but they thought it right to decline a contest in which their
case was sure to be stifled under a heap of unscrupulous affidavits. And if, as
now appears probable, they had been met by oaths that the magistrates did
not authorize the advance of the Yeomanry, how universally would they
have been taunted with ignorance as well as imprudence . . .

John Edward Taylor's faith in the radical case vindicating itself in law
was firm; he was over-confident on what could be proved for that case
by oral evidence under rigorous cross-examination. The trial was a few
months ahead:

Should there be any who think the melancholy transactions of the 16th of
August, 1819, ought to be suffered to 'fall into oblivion' we would bid them
call to mind a recent and self-complacent reference to them at the late birthday dinner, by Mr. Norris, the stipendiary magistrate; and we suggest that
they ought not to be forgotten until they have been investigated. We do not
ask for vengeance, but inquiry. It is due to the sufferings of the living; it is
claimed by the memory of the slain; and above all, it is demanded by the
outraged and insulted majesty of the British Constitution.

Reading between the lines of John Edward Taylor's long and impassioned leader, it would seem that there were many questions he had asked in his *Observations* which he was not asking now. Unlike the *Observer* leader-writer, he had become better informed than he was in 1819; his indignation however, still remained.

The *Manchester Gazette*, now the mouthpiece of Archibald Prentice after the removal of John Edward Taylor, had many questions to ask in its issue of 19 May. Prentice asked for the name of the magistrate who was trampled under foot; he asked to see the bludgeons which had figured in so many accounts; and the stones 'that came in such a miraculous manner into the hands of the people'; 'some other proof other than the *ipse dixit* of that Minister of Jesus, The Rev. Mr E——that the Riot Act was read: the when, the where, the how'; and wanted 'the parties who were the aggressors brought to justice, and punished in the manner that the Constitution and Law of England demanded'. Archibald Prentice, when many of the answers to his questions were given in the forthcoming trial of Redford *v*. Birley failed to notice them, and continued to ask them by his inferences in his *Recollections* of twenty-nine years later.

Henry Hunt, after his comments in prospect, could hardly ignore the debate in retrospect. His letter of 26 May to the Radical Reformers takes up the theme, but only in so far as it affected Henry Hunt:

Well! the Hero's long-talked-of and long-delayed motion upon the Manchester Question has been brought on in the House of Commons at last; and you see, my friends, it has gone off like a 'flash in the pan', as a sportsman would say. Really, my friends, you will soon begin to think me a sort of political prophet. In my address to you published in the Fourteenth Number of my Memoirs, you will recollect, in advising you to send petitions to the Honourable House, I used these remarkable words: 'to try his sincerity once more, I would even send Sir Francis Burdett one or two petitions, *so that they are not very important ones*; for if they are I would not trust them to him.' Only look at the debate in *The Times* upon this question, when he brought on his motion; after some scores of petitions had been presented by the various Members, Sir Francis Burdett rose, and stated 'that he had received a similar petition to those already presented, from John Knight, *but that he had unfortunately not brought it with him into the House*'. Ha! ha!! ha!!! What think you of that, my friends! I have heard of a man who hastened to the battle in such a fright that he forgot the sword with which he meant to defend himself. I have also heard of an absent [*sic*] man who entered a drawing-room full of company having forgotten to put on the usual covering of a pair of breeches: but I never before heard of a Member of Parliament going down to the House to make an important motion, of which he had been babbling nearly a year and a half, and then forgot to bring with him the *only petition* that was instrusted to him, upon which he meant to found his motion. I say Ha! ha!! ha!!! Here is a brave Legislator to run in couples with Lord Fitzwilliam's pocket Member for Peterborough, *Lawyer Scarlett*. They are a precious pair, as the Devil said of his old shoes.

I had a very interesting letter from a Member who was present in the House, and who informs me that with the exception of the time when Sir Robert Wilson presented my second petition, it was most dull and insipid. When that blister was applied, it made some of the gentlemen dance with rage; his words are, 'they quite foamed at the mouth like madmen'! Ha! ha!! ha!!! Mr. Bright, of Bristol, made a furious burst in favour of the discipline of this Bastile; and Mr. Scarlett pledged the *word of a lawyer* that it was all false; he had had a *brief*, faith, from our amiable Gaoler, and therefore any thing that was said against his client, of course, was all false. Mr. Hunt had applied to the Court of King's Bench, and had consented to pay the costs to withdraw his motion, therefore there was no foundation for his charges. But, Mr. Scarlett, you forgot to state the *slight fact* that Sir Charles Bampfylde had removed the cause of the motion, and, therefore, at that time, there was no ground for proceeding with it; but more of this hereafter.

The latter was a reference to the main preoccupation of Hunt's mind at that time, affairs at Ilchester Gaol which later, he claimed, he caused to be razed to the ground.

If, my friends, I should ever, like Sir Francis Burdett, become the object of Mr. Scarlett's idolatry, from that moment I shall be unworthy of your confidence, which I value as I do my life; therefore, rave on, rant on, behind my back, Lawyer Scarlett; if I ever live to meet thee face to face, do not shelter yourself, as you have often attempted before, from my castigation, under the wing of the Court. And, because I could not set this Jay, under borrowed plumes, down, this Lawyer, garbed in the Fitzwilliam livery, I had been guilty of the horrible crime of intimidation, menace, and insult in a Court of Justice. What said Mr. Justice Bayley at York? But more of this hereafter. The clock strikes and the Court is waiting. Now for another occupation. I am, my Friends, yours in haste, H. Hunt.

Henry Hunt returned no more in his Letters to comment on the momentous House of Commons debate of 15 and 16 May 1821; it would have been better for his reputation if he had not 'commented' at all. Bruton, in his *Story of Peterloo* says of him:

. . . His vanity we can forgive, for he rendered yeoman service to the cause of Liberty, but his private life, the details of which we are told with almost brutal candour by himself in his 'Memoirs', will not bear inspection. Of his political record he has no reason to be ashamed.

XXIV

Vindication and Chagrin

On 28 July 1821, there was a celebration of the Coronation of King George IV at Hulton Park. A local paper reported:[1]

Great liberality was evinced on this august occasion by William Hulton, Esqr. His tenant farmers, workpeople, and colliers, amounting to 700 persons, were collected in his beautiful park and treated with a plentiful dinner of roast beef, plum pudding, and as much good old ale as they could drink. After enjoying themselves with every degree of conviviality, and singing 'God Save the King' repeatedly, the whole of the labouring community concluded the joyous day by joining in various rustic games; and the whole feast was terminated by a brilliant display of fireworks.

Twelve miles away from Hulton Park, in Manchester, a radical 'celebration' of the same event was being planned. One of their number handed up to the platform a 'Copy of an amendment, proposed by Mr Saxton, at the Town's Meeting, held at the Police Office, Manchester, convened by the Boroughreeve to consider the means of celebrating the approaching Coronation:'

Resolved: That the nine Wiseacres who acted so inconspicuous a part on the 16th of August, 1819, be tarred and feathered, and that they head the procession, the Rev. Mr. Hay, bearing a black banner, with this inscription: '*Thou shalt do no Murder*', and Mr. Hulton another banner, '*Thou shalt not bear false witness against thy neighbour*'; and that they be followed by the Manchester and Cheshire Yeomanry Cavalry, with jackets turned, mounted with their faces to the horses' tails, and to prevent accidents, the Special Constables be requested to lead their horses during the order of the procession.

Whether Mr Saxton did in fact move such an amendment at a public meeting is not known. The notice appeared in that remarkable publication, Henry Hunt's *Memoirs*, which included 'Letters to Radical Reformers' from Ilchester Gaol (1820–23)[2]. A two-and-a-half years' prison sentence did not still the voice of Hunt. Some of these 'Letters' have been

[1] Quoted in an article, *Bolton Journal*, 24 January, 1880.
[2] Dolby: Strand.

noticed; one letter: 'To the Radical Reformers, male and female, of England, Ireland and Scotland' was headed 'Ilchester Bastile, 10th day, 12th month, 2nd year of the Manchester Massacre, without retribution or inquiry, July 26th, 1821':

The never-to-be-forgotten, never-to-be-forgiven Sixteenth of August, 1819 by what enthusiasm I was received by you when I arrived at Stockport, at Manchester, at Bolton, at Blackburn, at Preston, at Leeds, and in fact every place in the north; I shall be present in imagination with you all on the bloody Sixteenth of August: we shall all be in full communion with each other on that day, although we shall be from two to three hundred miles apart, our hearts and souls will beat in unison and at the very same moment (about twenty minutes past one o'clock) our voices will . . . cry aloud for Justice or vengeance, urged on by the recollection of the dying groans of our slaughtered fellow-countrymen, and heart-rending shrieks and piercing cries of our wounded, bleeding country-women, and their helpless mangled screaming children.

I ask you once more: Can you think of these and be mute? . . . You will visit St. Peter's Field—you will take your children with you to that 'Golgotha' of the present system of terror and misrule . . . take your children with you, that the truth may be handed down to your children's children. Teach them to lisp, with a proper feeling, the irreverend names of Parsons Hay and Ethelston, the name of Hulton, Marriott, Tatton, Norris, Trafford, and the rest of the unworthy nine wiseacres who figured as Magisterial desperadoes on that day. The names of Birley and —— will always be synonymous. I am much mortified that I have never been enabled to publish the names of the whole gang that were confederated against the lives and liberties of the people on that day. Pray let someone send me the Christian names and sirnames of all the nine Wiseacres, age, height, complexion, and places of residence; do. of the officers of the Manchester and Cheshire Yeomanry; do. privates of . . . I will undertake to publish them in my Memoirs for the day of retribution which must and will come . . .

Hunt's 'Letters from Ilchester Gaol' 24 August 1821, showed that Hunt's Manchester followers had heeded his appeal that their 'children's children' be taught, if only in the first generation:

List of Parents' and Children's Names baptized at Christ Church, Hulm[e] by the Revd. J. Scholefield, August 16th, 1821:

Henry Hunt Carlile, s. of William and Mary Wallace.
Henrietta Hunt Carlile dau. of James and Nancy Wheeler.
Henry Hunt, son of John and Sarah Cronshaw.
Henry Hunt, son of Thomas and Elizabeth Stevenson.
Henry Hunt Thomas, son of Benjamin and Ellen Lee.
Henry Hunt, son of Thomas and Mary Bullock.

John Cartwright, son of William and Mary Fildes.
(Parents had a son christened, 20 months ago, Henry Hunt)
Henry Hunt, son of William and Elizabeth Barnes, of Bolton.
Henry Hunt, son of Thomas and Hannah Mores.
Henry Hunt, son of Thomas and Ann Crabtree.

The Revd. Gentlemen preached on parental duties; and paid tribute of praise to their patriotism in calling young Christians after a Man of such great talent and political firmness as Henry Hunt, and trusted his namesakes would emulate his virtues without being subject to the persecutions and misfortunes which had distinguished the life of that noble patriot.[1]

During the autumn of 1821 plans were afoot to bring on the trial, Redford *v.* Birley. In Ilchester Gaol, Henry Hunt, in his letter 'To the Radical Reformers' dated 26 October, gave his opinion:

I have noticed a paragraph published in most of the papers, that the infamous Meagher, the trumpeter of the Manchester Yeomanry, Captain Birley, Withington, Oliver, and Tebutt, three other members of the troop, have been served with King's Bench writs, to answer for an *assault* committed by them on the bloody Sixteenth of August, upon a Mr. Johnson.[2] It is added, that it is not the Mr. Johnson who was tried with Mr. Hunt at York, but some other person, and that a Mr. Hayward, of Tooke's-court, in London, is the attorney. As I know nothing of this Mr. Johnson, or of Mr. Attorney Hayward, nor ever heard of them before, I should very much like to have the particulars inquired into by our friends at Manchester.

It appears to me to be a very extraordinary proceeding at this period, more than two years after the transactions occurred. I own I am become very suspicious as to these matters, I have seen so many tricks played off of late. Suppose it to be all fair and honestly meant, I am very sceptical as to any good that is to arise from this course of proceeding. Murder, murder—black, premeditated murder—was committed on that day, and hundreds were dreadfully maimed with the intent to kill. After the trial at York no one was left in doubt as to the facts. What! are those very men who have had bills of indictment preferred against them before the Grand Jury at Lancaster, for cutting and maiming women with an intent to kill, which bills were thrown out by the Lancashire Squires, who composed that Grand Jury—What! are those men now to have actions brought against them for a common assault,

[1] This same Rev. James Schofield, dissenting minister, had been one of Hunt's witnesses at the York trial. He had, in cross-examination, been accused of being a *Manchester Observer* writer in the post-Peterloo period. He believed he had written before the meeting. Re-examined by Hunt he 'refreshed his memory'—he had written two articles after 16 August. 'The first was a short one, signed "S" and disapproved of the prominent part taken by the clergy in politics, . . .' (*Hunt's Trial,* Pratt edn., p. 143.)
[2] The plaintiff was, of course, Thomas Redford.

to be tried at Lancaster before a special jury, composed of those very same Lancashire Squires? Come, come, my friends, let us look into their affair a little.

A Mr. Hayward is the attorney, it seems; *who*, I should like to know, is to be the *learned friend* that is to have the management of these actions? Ah, there's the rub. If this be all honest, it requires looking after. A pretty mess the learned brother *Brougham* or *Scarlett* would make of this affair.[1] Such a case entrusted to either of them, with a *packed special jury of Lancashire Squires* and *such witnesses* as we know may be produced from *Manchester*, &c. by the defendants, a neat scene will be exhibited at Lancaster Assizes if these actions be brought to trial there; and if it be not all honest, the sooner the plot is exposed the better. . . .

The venue, in spite of Hunt's assertion, was originally laid in the county of Middlesex. A note in the State Trials edition[2] says:

. . . On the application of the defendants it was moved to Lancaster. The defendants (January, 1822) made a joint affidavit in which they said: 'Great prejudice has been created against them, particularly in the county of Middlesex, by means of false and calumnious reports of the circumstances attending that meeting, and of the conduct of the said deponents on that occasion contained in the public newspapers and by false and exaggerated accounts of the same transaction, and inflammatory comments upon their conduct delivered in speeches at public meetings, and such printed accounts have been published and such meetings held and speeches made reflecting upon the conduct and character of the deponents, and calculating to deprive them of the benefit of a fair trial to a greater extent in the county of Middlesex than in any other county.

Henry Hunt made a similar plea when he applied for his trial to be removed from Lancashire into Yorkshire. Perhaps the deponents in the above instance had a better case.

It has been inevitable that Thomas Redford, the plaintiff, has had less

---

[1] 'The Manchester Trial. We wish to correct an erroneous report respecting the counsel in this trial. It was generally understood, and indeed we so stated, that Mr. Brougham was to be the leader for the plaintiff, This however was not the case; and an idea is in consequence very prevalent, that Mr. Brougham declined to hold a brief on the occasion. The fact is, that no brief was offered to him; and however much his assistance might have been desired, the plaintiff had no funds to enable him to make such an offer to Mr. Brougham as would be at all commensurate in the task. The following paragraph on this subject is quoted in the London *Courier*, of Tuesday, and is amply indicative of the avidity with which a despicable faction bluntly assert facts, which it is deemed but necessary to reconcile their own wishes, not to *truth*: "Mr. Scarlett and Mr. Brougham both threw up their briefs in the pending case of the Manchester Radical meeting, but we have not learned from what cause." ' *Maccles-field Courier.—Liverpool Mercury*, 12 April, 1822.

[2] *State Trials*, p. 1085.

than justice done to him by posterity, for readers of the report of the trial, both in the State Trials edition and in the Manchester (Farquharson) edition[1] have been more concerned with what happened generally on St Peter's Field than with what happened to Thomas Redford. The Manchester-printed edition would appear to have had a very extensive circulation, and a remarkably large number of copies have survived. The proceedings of the trial are, to a large extent, a summing-up of the magistrates' and Yeomanry's case, and complete the picture they were trying to put across to the public before this time. That this end was not achieved completely was due to the imbroglio which had gone before. Prentice, as has been seen, ignored the trial by a convenient jump from 1820 to November 1822 (the trial took place in April); Bamford brings his *Passages* to an end on his release from prison in 1821, though he published some reminiscences of later years. Bruton's only substantial reference to it was as: 'the test trial at Lancaster three years after Peterloo when Thomas Redford sued the Manchester Yeomanry for "unlawful cutting and wounding", and the jury found for the defendants in six minutes,—and finally, the periodical discussion of these things in the press—into detail of these matters we do not enter here.' Hunt 'noticed' the trial in the manner already shown, and ten years later claimed it to be a 'mock action'[2]. His comment was:

. . . There was one trial at Lancaster against the Yeomanry, brought by Mr. Redford against Capt. Birley, but he had no hesitation in saying that that was a sham trial; the evidence given by Redford fully showed that such was the case.

This was not allowed to pass in the House of Commons; Sir Robert Peel was scathing:

. . . The House would allow him [Sir Robert] to give a complete contradiction to a statement which had been made by the hon. Member. [Hunt] He had stated that the action brought by Redford against Capt. Birley was a mock action. Was it possible to say anything more unjust towards the counsel employed in the prosecution? Was it probable that two honourable men who were employed by the plaintiff would have been parties to a mock action? The hon. Member said, that the evidence which Redford gave upon the trial was of a nature to confirm his suspicions that the action was a mock one. Now, it happened that Redford, being plaintiff, was not, and could not be examined, and, therefore, the principal ground upon which the hon-Member rested his assertion was taken away. He begged to refer the House to the evidence given by a woman named Mary Dawson. She was asked

[1] C. Wheeler & Son, 1822.
[2] Hansard, Vol. XI, 3rd series, 251, 15 March, 1832.

whether she saw stones thrown: her reply was 'no'. She was asked whether the people made any resistance. She replied, that they did not. She was asked what the soldiery did. She replied that they cut the people as soon as they came on the ground. She was asked whether she saw any persons wounded, and she replied, that she did; and that she took fourteen wounded men into her house, and dressed their wounds. Was this, he would ask the House, the sort of evidence which would have been brought forward, if the object of the plaintiff had been to defeat the ends of justice?

Hunt had, in 1832, to sustain the attitude he had assumed at the time of the trial ten years earlier; his mind had long been made up that Redford *v.* Birley was a 'juggle'. He told his readers in one of the Letters to Radical Reformers dated 8 April 1822:

The infamous Juggle now performing at Lancaster Assizes. The newspapers inform us that the trial . . . has commenced. Mr. Justice Bayley, and the Attorney-General for the County Palatine of Lancaster, *Scarlett*, having declined to become a party to the juggle, the performance is left to the care of Mr. Justice Holroyd, Sergeants Hullock and Cross, Messrs. Littledale and Starkey as Counsel for the defendants; and the profound Messrs. Joshua Evans and *Blackburne* for the plaintiff. *All that I predicted has already come to pass.* The case of Redford is closed; 'good Lord deliver us' from such another.

If Sergeant Hullock had no other object to obtain but a verdict for the defendants, he would have appealed to the Judge, who would, I have no doubt, have directed a *non-suit* at once, without going into any defence, as the plaintiff certainly made out no case at all. However, the witnesses for the defence being *well-drilled* and *well-primed*, and as there was no danger of any detection from the cross-examination of the profound Messrs. Blackburne and Joshua Evans, the defence will be made to serve all the purposes that I anticipated, and as I expected. It is already proved—1st, that the *Riot Act was read*; 2nd, that the *Yeomanry were assailed by the unarmed people*; 3rd, *that the people were locked together arm-in-arm seven or eight deep round the hustings*; 4th, *that Redford himself had been trained and drilled*, &c., &c. Nay, the said Joshua called several of his own witnesses to prove that they had been drilled; and, altogether, he appears to have made a much worse hand of it than I expected. I did expect that the said Joshua would have put on the shew of cross-examination at any rate; but, from the report of the newspapers, they have not kept up common appearances. The juggle is too bare-faced. I shall only insert again what I said upon the subject on the 11th of March, published in the postscript of my letter to the radicals in the 30th number of my *Memoirs* and there I shall leave it for the present.

Hunt, apart from what follows, did 'leave it for the present,' and for a long time afterwards. There were a further four-hundred-and-eighty pages of letters and broadsides from Henry Hunt in his *Memoirs*, but none concern Redford *v.* Birley. It might be thought remarkable, if the date on Hunt's letter is reliable, (8 April, written from Ilchester Gaol), that he should state what had already been 'proved' at the trial. On one point at least—on the reading of the Riot Act, witnesses introduced to 'prove' this did not appear until the 8th of April. What *was*, however, proved by Hunt's letter was his uncanny accuracy in forecasting what would happen at the trial, and forecasting not only on 8 April, but in his letter as early as the 11 March, to which he had referred:

P.S. I see in the *Traveller* newspaper of last night, an account of the fatal action against Messrs. Birley and the Manchester Yeomanry . . . I am still of the opinion that this cannot be an honest *bona-fide* proceeding; because I do not think there can be any person or persons so idiotic, so muddle-headed, so besotted, as to believe that any good can possibly be derived from it; nor can any man be such a contemptible ass as not to anticipate the very worst and most mischievous. Gracious Heaven! I understand a Mr. Joshua Evans is to be pitted against Mr. Scarlett!!! Good Lord deliver us!!! I could weep tears of blood when I think of it. So then at last what the Government have been so long sighing for in vain; what Mr. Scarlett, the Solicitor- and the Attorney-General; what my Lords the Judges, my Lord Castlereagh, and all the Ministers have been begging for in vain, is now to be conceded to them. So then the bloody massacre on the 16th of August at Manchester, where sixteen persons were murdered, and six hundred sabred and badly wounded, is at last to be settled by an action of damages, by a bare calculation of pounds, shillings, and pence, instead of demanding blood for blood.

If I was Castlereagh, if I was one of the Ministers, I would have given a million of money to have obtained such an action, if I could not have got it without. Why, it is worth half this sum to Birley and the authorities. Why if I was Hulton of Hulton, I would have given half, nay all, that I was worth in the world for such an action. Even Scarlett would have given a year's income, penurious as he is. We shall now see Nadin, Parson Hay, &c., and the whole host of swearers come forward; that precious tribe, that very set, who were ready primed and loaded waiting at York with the intention of out-swearing every thing and every body, till they saw the example that I made of *Hulton of Hulton*. We shall now see them all come forward. Hunt is safe in a West Country Bastile, and I should not be at all surprised, if, through the instrumentality of the sagacious Mr. Joshua Evans and Co., they were to prove *The Riot Act being read*—prove the *attack of the unarmed people upon the military*—prove the *sticks, stones, pikes,* &c.

Hunt, as has been seen earlier, was perfectly aware of all that had occurred on St Peter's Field, and this new trial was likely to cast doubts on whether indeed Hulton had perjured himself at York or had not.

Hunt therefore insisted vehemently that the lies were lies all along the line.[1] He continued:

I should not be surprised at all if they were not only to prove all that they attempted and failed in doing at York, but if they should prove all that was asserted in the House of Commons and House of Lords. Gracious God! here will be a mess of it, Mr. Joshua Evans pitted in the court at Lancaster against Mr. Scarlett—a frog against an elephant. Well, well!! We must bear it all; but I never expected to see such a mess of it as this. Why, I abandoned my action against a cowardly ruffian who struck me with a bludgeon upon the head while I was in custody and pinioned by the constables, because I saw all the misery attendant upon a trial at Lancaster, for an assault, after the Grand Jury threw out the bills preferred for a capital felony. Well I would rather have suffered another sentence of two years and six months, than have lived to see *this trial*.

From what I have seen of the evidence produced for the plaintiff, I have not the slightest doubt but there will be a verdict for the defendants, even setting aside the circumstance of its being tried before a Lancashire packed jury; but, supposing that there should be a verdict for the plaintiff, the object of the Government, the Magistrates, and the Yeomanry, will have been completely obtained. I can only say, that amongst the whole number of persons wounded, to the amount of seven or eight hundred, perhaps if the

---

[1] The contemporary radical attitude to the trial of Redford *v.* Birley is instructive. Those whose minds were already made up avoided having to revise their opinions simply by shutting their eyes and their ears—in the Bamford and Prentice manner. Hunt dismissed it as a 'juggle'. Other made-up minds were not, however, so pliable: the writers in *The Examiner*, for instance. They had, in their issue of 28 October, 1821, struck a high moral attitude:

'It is reasonable to infer that our Ministers are conscious of the wicked system by which they govern this country, were it only on account of the profligate disregard of truth and decency which they are continually manifesting in their public assertions. We all remember with what desperate daring they turned the tables on the defenceless multitude at Manchester, and would have made the public believe, forsooth, that the poor people who brought their wives and daughters to the petitioning meeting, were the assailants of the armed police and furious yeomanry. We all remember, likewise, how most of those confident statements of Lord Castlereagh and other Senators were actually *proved* at the great York trial to be, not merely exaggerations of facts that had occurred, but pure inventions either of wilful malice, or of a disgraceful credulity to the fabrications of their own interested slaves . . .' (*The Examiner* 28 October, 1821).

Henry Hunt knew what was being proved in Redford *v.* Birley which was not proved at the great trial at York, and it is not unreasonable to suppose that *The Examiner* writers did as well. Comment had to be made; they made it thus:

'An analysis of the evidence which literally presented nothing which had not been supplied so minutely at the York Trial, would merely tire the reader; more particularly as the proceedings in Court have not been marked by any points of interest worthy of relation on their own account.' *The Examiner*, 14 April, 1822, gave 'a brief summary'.

Government had been allowed to select a case, they could not have found one better adapted to their purpose than that of Redford. Mr. Sergeant Hullock, although he is a heavy, stupid man, yet he appears to be very superior to his profound adversaries, who may, for aught I know, be very honest and honourable men for lawyers; but if they were no party to the juggle, they must be the most simple of mortals.

James Scarlett was not, of course, pitted against Joshua Evans and Mr Blackburne; the 'packed' Lancashire jury was composed of men from north of the Ribble and even from north of the 'Sands'—from the Lonsdale Hundred—which to all intents and purposes was as if from another shire; what had been stated in Parliament was proved, proved because it really had occurred in spite of Hunt's (and others') protestations. To Hunt ever after it was a juggle, a 'mock action'; to the Prentices, Redford *v*. Birley did not exist at all.

At the trial Henry Hunt's great 'false witness' went into the witness-box and, under oath again, gave all his 'false witness' once more. The Rev. Mr Stanley's evidence modified what he had written in his privately-published *Narrative*. The plaintiff's counsel claimed Robert [Hyde] Greg as a witness in his client's favour because he 'saw no resistance whatever offered to the cavalry or anything happen to them, till they began to take away the flags', whereas what Greg actually testified was: 'I cannot say I saw them' [the Yeomanry] 'do anything in advancing to the hustings,' and only when further asked, added: that he 'did not see any resistance offered to them.'

Again, witnesses 'confounded the moment when the attack was made' as did Mr Blackburne, the plaintiff's counsel. He claimed: 'You have not heard any one person, who previous to the attack of the Cavalry upon them has spoken of any one single act of riot on the part of the people, except the Vicar of Rochdale who considered the banners an act of riot.'[1] Mr Blackburne's moment of 'attack' was Bamford's—when the Yeomanry went into the crowd.[2] He probably believed that he had made a point in cross-examining Lieut. O'Donnell of the 15th Hussars:

Q. Do you think the Manchester Yeomanry were not competent to disperse the meeting?
A. They were not numerous enough: not competent to withstand any attack where there was so numerous a meeting.
Q. And therefore if it had been the object of the Magistrates to have dispersed the meeting, it would have been more prudent to have waited for you?

[1] Redford *v*. Birley (Farquharson edn.), p. 535.
[2] Ibid., p. 535.

A. It would have been more effectual.
Q. If their object had been to have dispersed the meeting?
A. If their object had been to disperse the meeting.[1]

The simple truth was, of course, that it was not the magistrates' object to use the Yeomanry to disperse the meeting. Members of the Hussars gave testimony[2] on cutting the horses' bridles and saddle-girths. The Reverends Hay and Ethelston gave their testimony on the reading of the Riot Act. Col. Sylvester, who, it was alleged, had read the Act in the crowd and been knocked down, was not in court:

. . . Mr. Blackburne: Could he not have been called before you to shew whether he had read the riot act or not? Why was he not? No; it was well known that no such thing took place. Colonel Sylvester does not come, but a person comes who sees the proclamation in the room, and sees Colonel Sylvester go out and come back . . .

The learned counsel did not call for Col. Fletcher.

Sergeant Hullock, for the defence, referred to the character and reputation of the defendants:

which have been during two long years, subjected to every species of obloquy and reproach; and also the . . . unwarranted calumnies which factious malignity has been, during the same period, almost unceasingly employed in venting against the integrity and conduct of the magistracy of the counties of Lancaster and Chester.

To which Mr Blackburne replied:

. . . It has been said by my learned Friend, that at length the time has come, when he shall repel, with scorn and indignation, all the calumnies that have been cast upon the Magistracy. I know not of such calumnies; I know not of such imputations; but if such calumnies or if such imputations have been cast upon them, who have been called to rebut any one of them? The Magistrates themselves! . . .

Mr Blackburne claimed the meeting was for 'petitioning'; and he claimed that after the Yeomanry had assisted the constables to make the arrests they ought to have gone back to their stations; it was an echo of James Scarlett's speech in the House of Commons. It was more: it was the most pregnant remark in the whole trial. Had the Yeomanry done, or had they been *allowed* to do, what Mr Blackburne said they ought to have done, the Manchester meeting of 16 August, 1819, would have ranked with that at Smithfield on 21 July in the same year. He

[1] Redford *v.* Birley (Farquharson edn.), p. 520.
[2] Ibid., p. 522.

claimed the linking of arms mattered not. He did not claim, as Hunt had done, that Hulton had perjured himself: Blackburne said:

[on the linking of arms] But every witness you have heard on the part of the defendants, among them Mr. Hulton, saw it before. I do not impute anything to Mr. Hulton. I will now say that in my opinion, Mr. Hulton gave his evidence upon that point, and every other, as fairly as any man I ever heard in a Court of Justice; on which ever side it turns, when I consider the part he took in the transaction, I for one will never be the person to say he did not, when, in my conscience, I believe he did, act to the best of his judgment. How it was he was induced to give this command to the Cavalry, I know not. He might have been misled either by his sight or by his feelings; he might have been perhaps afraid, from the knowledge he had previously formed, from the various informations that had been laid before him, he might have supposed that more injury would have arisen to the military than even did arise to them; and, on that account, he might have imagined that the Yeomanry were in greater danger than they ultimately turned out to be . . . But I say that he is not a more respectable witness than Mr. Stanley.

Mr Blackburne was about the only one from the radical side who was prepared to make such an admission then, before, or thereafter. Archibald Prentice's paper, the *Manchester Gazette*, reported the trial and made a meagre comment: 'The decision seemed to give great satisfaction to the Manchester Magistrates, and some of the Yeomanry, who were present when the verdict was given.'[1] That was an understatement.

Within ten days the motion for a new trial was heard before the judges of the King's Bench. They made long comments on Mr. Justice Holroyd's notes on the trial. Chief Justice Abbot said:

We were addressed by the learned counsel as to the interest the Magistrates were supposed to have had, in upholding the conduct of the military whom they had called in to assist the civil power.[2] Upon that I shall only say, that had the military misconducted themselves, which it appears they did not, they would have been answerable for their conduct.

Mr Justice Bayley:

I am of the opinion, that in this case, no evidence which ought to have been received was rejected; that no evidence was admitted, which ought not to have been admitted . . . I, personally, have had a former opportunity of hearing some evidence upon this subject, and of forming some judgment as to the legal points in the case; but I have no hesitation at all in saying this, what the recollection of the court must bear me out in, that the evidence in this case, goes to points to which in no former case it had gone; and that all

<hr />

[1] *Manchester Gazette*, 20 April, 1822.
[2] Which ought to have removed one of John Edward Taylor's misapprehensions.

PETERLOO: THE CASE REOPENED

the difficulty, and, in a great degree, all the doubt, which could have existed in any former case, was entirely, by the evidence, removed in this . . .

There is abundance of evidence in this case, and I say in this case, for the first time, that without the aid of the military, the warrant could not have been executed. There is the contradictory evidence as to the manner in which the military were treated in their way up to the hustings; and that when they have reached the hustings, the individuals who are there are apprehended; and these individuals being so apprehended, the purpose of the written warrant is answered. But the purposes of the written warrant will be answered, and answered only, provided those persons still remain in custody, and are not rescued; and it may be a matter of prudent discretion, in that case, to consider whether, if there was an appearance of rescue, it would not be in furtherance of the aid of the civil power, for the military to do that which might prevent any such rescue; and whether they might not go on therefore, in order to disperse the mob, and, in dispersing the mob, doing to them no unnecessary degree of injury, and doing no injury to any one who should not resist, and set himself in defiance . . .

. . . the evidence, as to many points, is entirely new and extremely strong; so as to remove, and I hope it will effectually remove from many minds which previously did doubt, those doubts which those minds had entertained.[1] I recollect upon the former trial, there was one particular individual who was called to prove many of those particular points; and he could have been at that time confirmed upon many of those points, as it appears now in evidence he might have been, if the witnesses who were now called had been called in support of the then case. They were not called; and therefore, at that time, he certainly stood with a great body of contradiction and opposition to his testimony . . .

Mr Justice Best:

All they [the Yeomanry defendants] had to do in the first instance, was to advance and take the persons on the hustings into custody; but if they were resisted, that resistance rendered it necessary that they should do all the acts made the subject of complaint against them . . . They were acting under the authority of the Magistrates . . .

[1] One of the greatest 'doubters' amongst the newspapers was the *Liverpool Mercury*. That paper had reported the trial at some length; its leaders on the trial however, had been riddled with doubts. On the motion for a new trial it reported thus:

'Manchester Outrage. In addition to our report of the proceedings in the Court of King's Bench, on Wednesday se'nnight, in the case of Redford v. Birley, we have now to state, that, on the following day, Mr. Justice Holroyd finished reading the evidence of the trial and the report, and reiterated his former opinions, namely that the defendants, Birley, Meagher, and others, were acting in aid of the civil power, to execute a warrant, when an attack was made upon them, and that all subsequent proceedings were done in their own defence. The Chief-Justice and the other Judges concurring, the rule was refused.' *Liverpool Mercury*, 10 May, 1822.

There was no leader and no comment.

. . . We have been told that the conduct of these Magistrates was scandalous; that it was all a trick; and that they might have dispersed the meeting without the military. That is an assertion contradicted by all the evidence and by common sense . . .

Chief Justice Abbot:

It appears to me that the Magistrates acted legally, justifiably, and with a promptitude of spirit that entitles them to the gratitude of the neighbourhood, and the thanks of their country . . .

John Edward Taylor, as has been seen,[1] could, not long after, still refer to 'time-serving lawyers,' and 'all the judges in the kingdom . . .' He made the point, in that same article, about 'facts, undeniable and decisive: The meeting, until the irruption of the Yeomanry, was perfectly peaceable.' It was; and had it not been for his (or Prentice's) report which got to the editor of *The Times* before John Tyas's, it would have been reported as peaceable until the arrests were made, and the writing of history might have been different! From which 'facts, undeniable and decisive' Taylor could draw his false conclusion: 'These are truths, which it is impossible to gainsay—truths, which, if either magistrates or yeomanry can reflect on with complacency, we envy not their feelings or their consciences.' It is regrettable to have to record that Taylor could write thus *after* both the magistrates and the yeomanry believed, and thousands of others believed, that Taylor's 'facts' were not facts any longer. Taylor's 'peaceable, until the irruption of the yeomanry' led him to conclude:

Could we believe that in the capricious wantonness of power, on pretence of executing a warrant of at least doubtful legality (and the one issued on the 16th of August charges no offence against the law) they would expose an unarmed and unoffending multitude to the sabres of a military force, the English language contains no term which would adequately express our reprehension of their conduct. As it is, till the outrages of that day are redressed, whenever, in the meaningless slang of pseudo-loyalty, we are told of the excellence of the British Constitution, and the impartial protection afforded by the laws, we shall point to the ground from which our brethren's blood crieth, as an eloquent and mournful answer to the empty and vainglorious boast.

There were doubtless many who, reading Taylor's vehement words, thought that this was still the old Taylor of 1819; Taylor of the *Observations*, the 'firm', the 'unchangeable' Taylor, as Prentice was to taunt his shade thirty years later. It was not. Taylor in his 1822 quotation,

[1] See above, pp. 403–5.

although still harping on the arrests and on the warrant, says the magistrates were 'wanton' and 'capricious' in 'exposing' the crowd to the military. In 1819 it had been:

I cannot but conclude, that it was *ab initio* intended to dissolve the meeting by force, and that the arrest of Mr. Hunt and his associates was merely the pretext by which the attack was to be justified.

There was a subtle difference.

To Henry Hunt, on the 26 of July 1821, the 'names of Birley and ——— will always be synonymous'. In November, 1822,[1] there was a report of a presentation of a sword to Major Birley by the appreciative members of the Manchester and Salford Yeomanry Cavalry, and to congratulate him on the result of the trial at Lancaster. Henry Hunt's Birley and the Yeomanry's Birley are not quite the same personality. He replied:

In the course of that trial his name had been brought prominently forward, from the circumstances of his having the honour to command the corps. He had watched with anxiety the getting-up of the defence, but had never felt a moment's uneasiness as to the verdict. Still, he would not conceal his dislike of having his name so rudely treated, and his conduct so grossly and shamefully misrepresented. But in this he had not stood alone; and he had not on that account any claim upon the members of the corps. They had shared with him the unmerited censures of the designing and the deceived, for discharging firmly, but with humanity, an unpleasant duty.

It would have been an abandonment of the cause to support which they were embodied, not to assemble when required to do it, in aid of the civil power; and being assembled, not to obey those set over them by law would have been criminal as well as disgraceful. But if they had been reviled for doing their duty, they had at least the satisfaction of knowing that it was by those only who were capable of dealing out an equal measure of injustice to our excellent magistrates, whose services to the country were above all praise. It was impossible that any but the most ignorant or ill-disposed, could feel otherwise than grateful to the magistrates, or entertain the least jealousy of the corps of yeomanry. No unprejudiced persons could really believe them to be unfriendly to the liberties of their country. A desire to support its laws and institutions when assailed by violence gave existence to the corps; it was their bond of union. He trusted they were all firmly attached to those laws, not merely because they were born and had lived under their protection, but from the conviction that they are more friendly to rational liberty in their spirit, and in their actual administration secured a larger share of its blessings, than any other Government ancient or modern ever afforded its subjects . . .

★   ★   ★

[1] *Wheeler's Manchester Chronicle*, 23 November.

On the 23 of March, 1820, Sir Robert Peel (as he later became) had written to Croker: 'Do you not think that the tone of England is more liberal than the policy of the Government?' which is quoted by the D.N.B. writer[1] as 'the earliest sign of his suspicion that toryism of the rigorously unchanging type might prove in his case an inadequate creed.' Peel's views, indubitably, did undergo perceptible change during the 1820s, veering towards reform, and in no case more marked than towards Protestant Ascendancy *versus* Catholic Emancipation in 1828–29. The influences at work on Peel during this period, especially on the necessity of reform, have perhaps been misunderstood. Dr Read, in his final chapter[2] on the political implications of Peterloo, commented on that very letter to Croker:

. . . Peel's thoughts had run on very significantly from a consideration of the Peterloo trials. He had discovered new trends in political opinion. In this development regret for the extremities of Peterloo had clearly exerted its influence, even though the change in opinion would have come about without the massacre.

'Peel's thoughts *had* run on very significantly from a consideration of the Peterloo trials,' but not, it is suggested, on the lines indicated by Dr Read. Robert Peel had, in fact, succeeded Lord Sidmouth at the Home Office on the 17 of January, 1822. The changeover might be thought momentous. It was not quite so momentous as it appeared. On 24 April there was a motion in the House of Commons to remit the sentence on Henry Hunt.[3] Peel as Home Secretary replied:

. . . Was there any man who had read what had occurred in Lancaster[4] within the last fortnight, without being convinced of the magnitude of the [Hunt's] offence? Did any man see, in the full consideration which the subject then received—in the perfect establishment of all that had been stated on the ministerial side of the House—in complete refutation of what had been called the Manchester Massacre—did any man see—in these circumstances, the least reason for supposing, that the [Manchester] meeting was an innocent one? Had the gentlemen read those proceedings? Had they, professing as they did, a respect for the decisions of a jury, considered the verdict which was returned by the jury at Lancaster? Were not the most decisive proofs given of the persons drilling—of the manner in which the parties marched—of their inflammatory emblems—and of expressions which left no doubt as to the almost avowed object of the meeting?

[1] D.N.B., XV, p. 657.
[2] Read, p. 208.
[3] H. of C. Debates, Vol. VII, NS, Col. 36.
[4] In Redford v. Birley trial.

Were they, after such evidence, to be cajoled into a belief that the object of the meeting was peaceable—that it was only assembled to petition parliament for a redress of grievances? Would they suffer themselves to believe this, and allow the constitution to be sapped and undermined and invaded, by those who took advantage of the liberty which that constitution provided, in order to destroy it with greater security? He could never view the sentence pronounced on Mr. Hunt as too severe for the crime he had committed . . . he would never, as a servant of the Crown, advise the Crown to remit any part of the sentence . . .

'. . . the perfect establishment of all that had been stated on the ministerial side of the House, in complete refutation of what had been called the Manchester Massacre'; and, Peel could have added, sometimes on the other side of the House as well. The reply was almost the reply which might have been expected from Peel's predecessor at the Home Office, Lord Sidmouth. It was a reply which certainly did not suggest that in the changeover from Sidmouth to Peel there had been any change of viewpoint or attitude with regard to the transactions at Manchester. 'Peel's thoughts had run on very significantly from a consideration of the Peterloo trials': they were to run on more significantly still during the years when his 'toryism of the rigorously unchanging type' was undergoing some modification in 1828–29. In 1832 Peel was giving his views to the House of Commons again on the Manchester transactions; his 'toryism' on that subject had not, like his former view in 1828–29 on Catholic Emancipation, been modified. To strengthen them he added what he did not know on 24 April 1822: the combined opinions of the Judges given in the Redford *v.* Birley motion for a new trial uttered on 30 April of the same year. In 1832 Peel's views on the Manchester transactions were as uncompromising as ever.[1]

---

[1] The Robert Peel reference occurs in Dr Read's 'Conclusion' (p. 207):

'Peterloo and the Six Acts have often been said to mark a turning-point in national politics, to mark the last throw of repressive Eldonite Toryism. In this context the massacre has sometimes been associated with the contemporary repressive policies of the Holy Alliance on the Continent. [The analogy is false: Peterloo was not desired or precipitated by Lord Liverpool's government; if Manchester magistrates had followed Government's advice there would never have been a massacre.]

'But though the Eldonite Tories did not precipitate the Peterloo Massacre as a deliberate act of policy, it is nonetheless true to say that their association with the outrage helped to weaken their control of the Liverpool ministry. After Peterloo there began a steady alteration in the climate of political opinion which eventually made possible the advent to power of the more liberal Canningite section of the Tory party:

' " Do you not think that the tone of England . . . is more liberal . . . than the policy of the government?" (wrote the young Robert Peel to Croker in March, 1820, while awaiting the verdict of the Hunt trial). "Do not you think that there is a feeling, becoming daily more general and more confirmed . . . in favour of some undefined

That Sir Robert Peel could give countenance to Lord Liverpool's Ministry's part in the Manchester affair, and not only to the Ministry but to the magistrates of Manchester as well, has been inexplicable to many commentators on the period, and has tended to 'taint' his otherwise unassailable public and private character. His reasons have perhaps not been given at the source. In 1822 he was convinced from what had occurred at Lancaster, of 'the perfect establishment of all that had been stated on the ministerial side of the House—in complete refutation of what had been called the Manchester Massacre'. Peel had another good reason to be convinced: he was the sole residuary legatee of Lord Sidmouth's files in the Home Office.[1]

★   ★   ★

change in the mode of governing the country? . . . Will the Government act on the principles on which without being very certain, I suppose they have hitherto professed to act? Or will they carry into execution moderate Whig measures of reform? . . . Can we resist—I mean, not next session or the session after that—but can we resist for seven years Reform in Parliament?" [Quoting *Correspondence and Diaries of . . . John Wilson Croker* (1885) I, p. 170]. Peel's thoughts had run on very significantly from a consideration of the Peterloo trials. He had discovered new trends in political opinion, trends tending towards greater liberalism in public policies. In this development regret for the extremities of Peterloo had clearly exerted its influence, even though the change in opinion would have come about without the massacre.'

[1] The Press in 1822, as in other ages, was often entertaining in its comments on current events; and often wrong. Entertaining (to some) on Sidmouth's retirement: 'Lord Sidmouth, it will be seen, has formally retired from the Home Department, which has been delivered over to Mr. Robert Peel. The title of Manchester being that of a Dukedom, it is reported that, in allusion to his most conspicuous services, the Noble Lord will take a step in the Peerage, as Earl of Peterloo.' *Liverpool Mercury* (quoting the *Traveller*), 18 January, 1822.

Cobbett's Register (quoted by the *Liverpool Mercury*, 8 February, 1822) dashed off its *jeu d'esprit*: 'Peel the Great; Cantate Meum.'

'. . . Bless'd be his head so full of knowledge!
That head just piping hot from College;
College, from whence all learning flows
That College with the Brazen Nose!

'College so fam'd for learned Doctors;
College well fill'd with Priests and Proctors:
College where all good *Fellows* join
To gabble Greek and guzzle Wine!

'Bless'd be young Peel, who gain'd the Prize
At College, where they're all so wise!
Bless'd may he be from head to heel,
Red-headed! Ready, Rhino Peel!'—'Da Capo'.

Entertaining too, but wrong: Peel had been at Christ Church.

In the year 1822 there were many who thought that the long bitter controversy had at last come to an end. The loyalist argument put forward in the earlier months after Peterloo was thought to have prevailed: 'Truth is a very sober-minded quality, and must ultimately prevail. Investigations are to ensue which will draw out complete evidence. By that men must stand or fall.'[1] It seemed to be a fair argument; for a time it was imagined that this was, in fact, what had occurred. They had, however, not reckoned with the grudging reluctance of men going through the unpalatable process of eating their own words and the subsequent indigestion that such an exercise caused. Moreover there were those who scorned to do anything of the sort, their words were to be thrown back into the flabbergasted faces of their erstwhile opponents. From the more-distant corners of Lancashire and Cheshire came echoes of resolutions of congratulation to the magistrates and yeomanry;[2] In Manchester there was mutual congratulation. Hugh Hornby Birley replied to the members of the Manchester Pitt Club:

. . . I cannot but feel convinced that the recent trial will completely establish and justify the conduct of the corps . . . Not that the verdict at Lancaster was necessary to satisfy your minds with reference to our conduct, for we have often received tokens of your approbation. Indeed, many of you were witnesses of our conduct on the day alluded to, and to such, the recent verdict was not necessary; but many persons at a distance were influenced by the calumnies of a venal press which (to use the words of our worthy president) was either wilfully or judicially blind. Such persons, however, must now feel convinced of the injustice of their first impressions . . .[3]

Trafford Trafford Esq. on the same occasion, who had given evidence in Redford v. Birley at Lancaster as one of the Lancashire and Cheshire magistrates:

. . . No man ever persevered in his duty with more firmness than Mr. Hulton . . . a jury of our county has given its verdict, and the Court of King's Bench has also delivered its opinion on our conduct . . . the matter is therefore complete.

It seemed to be. There was a sporadic outburst on the third anniversary of Peterloo at Ashton-under-Lyne:

[Wheeler's Manchester Chronicle 2 November, 1822, reported a belated court appearance]: John Higson had been indicted, with others, for exhibiting a seditious flag. On the 16th August a number of people had, at Charleston, a

1 See above, p. 294.
2 Wheeler's Manchester Chronicle, 18 May, 1822.
3 Wheeler's Manchester Chronicle, 1 June, 1822.

village near Ashton, in order to commemorate the anniversary of the Manchester meeting, gathered together a number of people and exhibited a flag inscribed 'Murder, 16th August'. They had paraded from Charleston to Ashton, and there had hung the flag for several hours from the window of a room used for religious purposes, a room rented and kept by the defendant Higson. They had collected a great crowd by this flag, and afterwards, in the room they sung a seditious song, called 'The Song of the Slaughter' and read a prayer composed by Hunt and a sermon composed by Mr. Cobbett. By exhibiting this flag they had collected many people in the street. The constables and other persons had applied to take the flag away, but they had refused; and their sole object was to keep alive a most wicked spirit amongst the people as to the events of the 16th of August . . . Mr. Ashworth pleaded mitigation &c.

The Rev. Mr Hay at the Quarter Sessions, in view of his being one of the magistrates 'implicated' on 16 August vacated the bench. Radical 'aberrations' such as these were not unexpected.

Henry Hunt's periodical vituperative broadsides from Ilchester Gaol, of which a few specimens have been noticed, ceased with the expiry of his two-and-a-half year's sentence in November 1822:[1] 'At the end of which time,' as Hunt had sagely remarked in his 10 February 1821 letter, he had 'to give security not to attack the system of corruption for five years.' The Manchester Gazette of 16 November 1822, reported Hunt's 'entry into London' speech. It was mildness itself; he alluded to:

certain remarks in the newspapers admitting the harshness of his sentence, but condemning the convening of the Manchester meeting. With the calling of the meeting together, he said, he had no concern; it was legally and constitutionally convened by 700 inhabitants, householders of Manchester and neighbourhood, and he merely attended there by invitation as he might attend any other meeting at the call of his fellow-countrymen . . . The Manchester affair he would never forget, nor ever cease to look to it as an imperative subject for inquiry.

After 1822 most of the members of the 1819 committee of magistrates lapsed into a discreet or a relieved silence, seldom seeming to figure in

1 'The Third Anniversary of the Bloody 16th of August.
' The third anniversary of the blood-thirsty murders committed on St. Peter's Plain, at Manchester, will have passed, before my next Number reaches the public. I have no doubt but every honest Radical in the kingdom will do it justice.
I remain, my excellent Friends,
Your's, most sincerely, H. HUNT.
'P.S. The numerous applications for agency in all parts of the kingdom, for the sale of my Breakfast Powder, shall be attended to as soon as possible; but the demand at present exceeds our power to execute them so promptly as we could wish.
'To the Radical Reformers . . . Ilchester Bastile. 23 July, 1822', p. 30.

the public life of the town where their names had resounded so clamo-
rously and stridently. The Rev. William Robert Hay resigned his
chairmanship of the Salford Hundred Quarter Sessions in 1823, to
devote himself to the cares of his Rochdale living, where a noisy minority
of his parishioners made his life hardly worth living for the rest of his
vicariate which ended by his death in 1839. In the earlier period of
magistrate-baiting he was the regular target for the *Observer* writers.
He was treated to a Christmas card, published 15 January 1820, entitled
'Haymaking at Christmas':

> Well may the men of Rochdale say
> That certain trades alone are thriving;
> Who pay so high a price for Hay?
> Whose *butcher* gets so good a *living*?

The Rev. Charles Wicksteed Ethelston was let off a little more lightly.
He was the victim of a short burst of vituperation; thereafter, by John
Edward Taylor's reference to his magistrates' courtroom utterance; he
was petrified for posterity. His sermons do not appear to have been
collected, it is therefore not possible to refer to the original version of
the homiletic he is alleged to have delivered after Peterloo in the
Collegiate Church, Manchester. The allegation is preserved in a letter
to the editor of the *Observer*, 25 September 1819:

. . . It is scarcely possible to use language sufficiently strong in speaking of
conduct such as yours—truth is no calumny—in what courtly terms must
we speak of that person who could lend himself to trick the people into a
fatal security that there might be a greater number devoted to the sabre; and
a few days afterwards, whilst the blood of the victims was in a manner yet
fresh upon him, to get up in his pulpit and tell his congregation that it is the
will of God . . .

H. G. Bennet, M.P.'s urgent request to Shuttleworth on 18 November 1819, to give him 'an account of the *character* and *situation* of the
Magistrates who signed Hunt's warrant?'[1] was perhaps the inspiration
to one calling himself 'An Old Radical' to go to rather inordinate
lengths to discover the 'character' of the Rev. Mr Ethelston. The result:
an eight-page pamphlet entitled *Manchester Slaughter*[2] which purported
to be a critical review of a slim volume of poetry written by Mr Ethelston sixteen years earlier, in 1803, inspired by the author's reading of

[1] See above, p. 296.
[2] *Manchester Slaughter. Critical Review of the following work 'Suicide with Other
Poems' by the Rev. C. W. Ethelston, M.A., rector of Worthenbury 1803. 8vo, pp. 8
London: Dolby 1819. [By 'An Old Radical'.]*

The Sorrows of Werther, and which appeared under the title, *Suicide, with Other Poems*. A critical review it was, penetrating the reverend gentleman's subconscious, even before the subconscious was known. The original edition of Mr Ethelston's rare volume is seldom met with[1], but the Old Radical transcriber permitted himself a little liberty in the use of capitals. One extract ran:

Where the hired Bravo lurks, and WHETS HIS STEEL

★   ★   ★   ★   ★   ★

The instrument of jealousy and rage,
He perpetuates for HIRE the CRIME OF CAIN.

The analogy was, perhaps, not quite perfect in capitalizing the word 'hire' when referring to the voluntary units of Yeomanry Cavalry. But there was another quotation:

> I knew a man,★ who, in a cursed hour,
> The dicing depradators' club did join.
> Clench'd the detested box, and cast the die
> That plung'd him into beggary and death.

'Was he', a footnote asks at the asterisk, 'a Manchester parson?'

The following lines decide the justice of his [Mr. Ethelston's] exclusive right to become the Epic Poet of Peterloo:

> ——————— *Down they fall*
> *In mangled heaps beneath the crimson blade,*
> And *growl a bitter curse* and *bite the dust:*
> Mown like a prostrate sheaf.

On the Rev. Mr Ethelston's courtroom outburst an appropriate line was found to clinch the tenuous link between 1803 and 1819:

> *May the Redeemer spare thy guilty soul.*

Can this be, asks An Old Radical, the Reverend Magistrate who is reported to have made the following eloquent and elegant address lately to a poor Reformer[2] when he was brought before him at Manchester? Here he openly boasts of the second sight:

Mr. Ethelston: 'I believe you are a downright blackguard reformer. Some of you reformers ought to be hanged, and some of you are sure to be hanged—*the rope is already round your necks*'.

[1] A copy 'in original boards, uncut' is preserved in Chetham's Library.
[2] See above, pp. 300–1.

Only once, so far as can be noticed, did the Rev. Mr Ethelston make any attempt to reply to any of the calumnies which were broadcast; and even then in an attempt to defend his clerical colleague Mr Hay in September 1819:

One of the worst features of the present aspect of society is, an attempt to bring every public character in Church and State into contempt or detestation, who opposes the views of the modern reformists. In this corrupt age, scandal flies and too often blasts like lightning; but, unfortunately, the assassin of your character lurks in secret, shoots his envenomed shafts from an ambush, and wounds you when you are unsuspicious and off your guard. A perfect Proteus, he assumes so many shapes, changes so easily, and varies so adroitly, as to elude the net by which the law endeavours to entangle him. Comparatively speaking, there are but few cases of defamation which by our code of criminal jurisprudence can be brought home to the calumniator. In general, the evil suffered is absolutely irremediable: it being easy to gratify every malignant passion of the heart, and at the same time to escape the grasp of justice . . .[1]

It was futile. There were more men, alas, in September 1819, ready to believe that the Rev. Mr Ethelston and his magisterial colleagues had just gratified 'every malignant passion of the heart, and at the same time' escaped 'the grasp of justice', than there were to believe in Mr Ethelston's protestations.

The Rev. Ethelston died on 23 September 1830, aged 63. Henry Hunt, on his return visit to St Peter's Field on the anniversary day in that year, told his eager auditors how 'Providence' had dealt with some of the actors in the tragedy of Peterloo (actors remote and near): Lord Castlereagh had cut his throat, two of the Yeomanry had committed suicide, the Prince Regent had gone before his Judge, and Parson Ethelston 'was a drivelling idiot'. What mortal illness had afflicted the reverend gentleman is not known, but some years before, he had been thrown from his gig when his horse became a runaway, and had fractured his skull.

[1] *Manchester Gazette*, 25 September, 1819 (quoting a recent issue of *Wheeler's Manchester Chronicle*).

XXV

The Uneasy Peace 1822-8

William Hulton, had he not been a young man in 1822 (he was 35) might have slipped into obscurity like the rest, but he did not. Magisterial duties, after the stormy three-and-a-half years, and in the quieter waters of the post-1822 world would be calm indeed. He resumed his wonted public life. The *Guardian* and the *Gazette* buzzed around his ears from time to time with their waspish remarks. On an occasion of some controversy on the possible creation of new Assize towns in Liverpool and Manchester, the *Guardian* reported, 'Mr William Hulton of Hulton made just a speech as might be expected from him,' and referred to 'Mr Hulton's twaddle.'[1] Perhaps it was; but it was not always so. The loyalist papers, the *Chronicle* and the *Exchange Herald* often came back with editorials in defence of Hulton. In 1823 there was a 'we are informed' paragraph in the *Guardian*[2] on the prospects of a canvass for the Lancashire election, which ended with Taylor's comment: 'Should, however, Mr Hulton's pretensions be obtruded on the County, we trust there is public spirit enough to make the experiment a costly one.' The *Herald*[3] maintained that there had not been the slightest whisper of the prospect of a canvass, and that the *Guardian*'s paragraph had been the mischievous editor's peg on which to cast a slur on a 'gentleman held in the highest respect'. 'Why it was made,' the *Herald* correspondent continued, 'I cannot imagine, except that Mr Hulton, in his magisterial capacity, has been the minister of the laws to some dear Radical friend of the editor.'

On the Manchester William Pitt anniversary in May 1824, Hulton was the principal speaker:

. . . However sceptical men might have been when Mr. Pitt's vast conceptions were first unfolded, no one, who is not irrevocably blind, can now

[1] *Manchester Guardian,* 9 October 1822.
[2] Ibid., 29 April 1823.
[3] *Exchange Herald,* 6 May 1823.

doubt, that to a firm adherence to his principles, England is indebted for its present full enjoyment of national wealth and happiness.[1]

The annual paean of praise to the memory of Pitt was a mere variation on an old theme, which even in 1824 was beginning to irritate minds in opposite schools of thought:

'. . . Why attend Pitt Clubs,' said Hulton, seeming to echo these opponents' criticisms, 'and keep alive that spirit of division which it is so much better to conciliate? If, Gentlemen, by conciliation is meant a display of generous liberality and active benevolence towards my most eager political opponents, I accede cordially to the terms prescribed; but if, in order to conciliate, I am to sacrifice one iota of political principle—there I must make my stand. I have been educated in a school of stern, unbending politics. While I live I shall practise what I have learnt. I only ask for myself that which I am ever ready to grant to all who differ from me—the credit of acting from no unworthy motive . . .

[1] How 'irrevocably blind' were some of William Hulton's contemporaries to the excellencies of William Pitt the Younger, is nowhere better illustrated than in the anti-Pittite view published in the *Liverpool Mercury*, 14 June 1822:
. . . We shall conclude with the following pertinent epitaph, which has been repeatedly published before . . . 'This mausoleum entombs WILLIAM PITT, who died January 23, 1806, aged only forty-seven years. With unprecedented influence, for twenty-three years he was Prime Minister of the British Empire. He possessed great talents, and transcendant eloquence; but his worth may be best estimated by "experience and the evidence of facts". He was the advocate for Reform, which did not succeed; the opposer of the Slave Trade, which increased; the patron of Irish Catholics, who were not emancipated; to England a professed protector, and the avowed enemy to France. During his government, the bulwarks of British freedom were subverted; the ancient nobility degraded; the poor additionally depressed; and the middling classes of society annihilated; popular associations prohibited; and the sources of corruption deepened and enlarged.
Paper was substituted for gold; and real opulence transmuted into imaginary wealth:—he doubled the prices of provisions; tripled the amount of poor-rates and taxes; added three hundred millions to the national debt; and sacrificed two-hundred thousand Britons in "just and necessary wars". He assisted in the subversion of the balance of power; witnessed the destruction of every ally he obtained; and survived the overthrow of Flanders, Holland, Portugal, Switzerland, Spain, Austria, Prussia, Italy, and the Germanic Empire. Let nations glory in such friendship and support! France during his administration, rapidly rose from "the verge and very gulph of bankruptcy" to national wealth; annihilated her public debt; doubled her population; quadrupled her revenue; and obtained the sovereignty of Europe. Let nations deprecate such enmity and hostility! Britons! would you appreciate his character, reflect upon the past—observe the present—and anticipate the future! The committee of Lloyd's Coffee-house, the collectors of taxes, the purchasers of loans, and contractors for the army; the modern nobility, Lord Melville, Mr. Trotter, Mr. Davidson, Mr. Hunt, Mr. Commissioner Bowles, and Napoleon, Emperor of France, enriched, ennobled, protected, and aggrandized by this "Friend of the people!" this "Saviour of Britain!!" this "People's best Hope!!!" this "Heaven-born Minister!!!!" erect this monument, indicative of his unequalled merits, and of their eternal gratitude and inconsolable regret.'

'I may be told that there is something ungracious, something inconsistent with genuine philanthropy, thus to promote a spirit of party . . . [Quoted Burke on parties in Parliament] . . . With the example of Parliament, with the inestimable advantage of a free press, by which men are encouraged not only to think freely, but to think differently, I may also ask from this place, is it possible, that the numerous men of rank, and of cultivated understanding, who reside in this populous district, could tamely acquiesce in one general code of political laws? Least of all, can those gentlemen whose public opinions are opposed to ours blame the distinction which this day's festival is intended to establish. In a treatise on the English constitution, one of their most able leaders, Lord John Russell, declares, that "mock philosophers, sentimental women, and effeminate men, are always making lamentations over political divisions, while men of noble minds know that they are the workshops of national liberty and national prosperity" '.[1]

Hulton believed that his auditors' reception of his remarks meant that they acceded to the proposition 'that party must be sustained'; and 'party' at that moment in time to Hulton meant principally the old Tory party cry of 'Protestant Ascendancy' and 'The British Constitution in Church and State'. They were the watchwords of his youth, they were his beacon-lights still; what is more, they were the beacon-lights of his idols, Wellington[2] and Peel. How bereft he was to be when later those two living examples, Wellington and Peel, 'deserted' and left exposed the bastion in the old Tory citadel which seemed so secure. That was, however, for the future. William Hulton's philosophising on old Tory watchwords, and on the petty political divisions in the still small-town atmosphere of Manchester, would hardly be worth recording were it not for the fact that it led on to his petulant (provoked or provocative) utterance in 1827. Torn out of its context it was later seized on and published throughout the land. The 16th of August 'was the proudest day in his life'! That was the detonator of a new radical explosion, although a delayed-action one, save for a few cracks and bangs in Manchester and district.

Hulton was in correspondence with Robert Peel at the Home Office and with Lord Melbourne, during the labour disturbances of 1826[3] and in the following year he gave evidence before the Government's Select Committee on Emigration. His reports of his visits to the poverty-stricken families in his neighbouring Westhoughton read, as Mr Thompson says who quotes them, 'like an anticipation of the Irish potato famine':

[1] *Wheeler's Manchester Chronicle,* 5 June 1824.
[2] *Wheeler's Manchester Chronicle,* 2 June 1827.
[3] DDHu/48/139–44; 48/167–73. L.C.R.O.

Mrs. Hulton and myself, in visiting the poor, were asked by one person almost starving to go into a house. We found there on one side of the fire a very old man, apparently dying, on the other side a young man about eighteen with a child on his knee, whose mother had just died and been buried. We were going away from that house when the woman said: 'Sir, you have not seen all.' We went upstairs, and under some rags we found another young man, the widower; and turning down the rags, which he was unable to remove himself, we found another man who was dying, and who did die in the course of the day. I have no doubt that the family were actually starving at the time . . .

'The evidence,' continues Mr Thompson, 'came from Westhoughton, where half of the 5,000 inhabitants were "totally destitute of bedding, and nearly so of clothes". Six were described as being in the actual process of starvation.'[1]

Much of Hulton's time in the period 1824–28 was taken up in sponsoring and planning the construction of the first public railway in Lancashire—the Bolton and Leigh Railway,[2] which, the Bill having received the Royal Assent in 1825, opened in 1828. Family tradition of the Hultons[3] says that it was Hulton who sent to Darlington for George Stephenson, who came to live for a time at Hulton Hall 'with the upper servants in the housekeeper's room.' Tradition adds the picturesque, if perhaps incredible, tale that the local schoolmaster gave Stephenson lessons in handwriting. George Stephenson, so one biographer relates, learned to read and write at a night school in his native north-east, but the narrator of the Hulton tradition could produce evidence for his story, namely the possession at Hulton Hall of an old copy-book with the name 'George Stephenson' written on its many pages from top to bottom.

One of the main ideas behind the construction of the Bolton and Leigh Railway was to get William Hulton's coals to a wider market, and to enable the industrialists of Bolton to find a shorter and cheaper route to the port of Liverpool, by avoiding the long detour by canal from Bolton to Liverpool via Manchester. The railway was soon to be linked direct to the Manchester and Liverpool Railway opened in 1830.

Despite such 'distractions' as sponsoring railway bills, selling his coals, and extending his colliery interests, his oratory was in demand at local loyalist gatherings. Not only were there waspish radical newspapers to buzz about his ears in Manchester, there was another much

---

[1] Thompson, p. 286.
[2] (Basnett, Lois) *Hist. Bolton and Leigh Rly.*, L. & Ches. Antiq. Soc. LXII, 1953.
[3] *Bolton Chronicle*, 8 February 1879.

nearer Hulton Park—the *Bolton Chronicle*, later a staid Conservative newspaper, but in the middle 1820s a radical one. A letter to the editor[1] was perhaps the first indication to the world that new radical mines were being laid, and that Hulton himself had provided the detonator. The writer was commenting on the forty-nine 'illiberals' who had met in Bolton to celebrate the memory of Pitt:

. . . They one and all seemed to rejoice that men, women and children, were cut down by the edge of the sword at the Manchester Massacre, and appear to lament that the present Ministers are not likely to allow a recurrence of such wicked deeds . . . Ah! Squire [Hulton] don't you wish the people still to pay you a Tax on your corn in order that you may receive a great rent for your land?

Are you not alarmed lest such men as Sir Francis Burdett (whose name you seem to dread) should shew to the King the letter to the Electors of Westminster, relative to the Manchester Massacre, which places the transactions of that day in a proper light?

Eight years after it was written, six years after Burdett was sentenced, after an almost Jarndyce-like progression through the courts, probably not even the writer, let alone his readers, knew how Burdett's letter terminated.

You seem to congratulate yourself, Mr. Chairman, on the amicable understanding which exists between yourself and your poor neighbours; owing, as you say, to your generous hand. But, Mr. Chairman, would it not be much better for the poor to receive a sufficiency for their labour, instead of eight or nine shillings in the pound being taken from them to maintain respectable placemen, sinecurists . . . The Chairman goes on to tell us 'we should never forget the immense benefit we derive from the Clergy of the Established Church'. If there is any benefit in being without clothes, without a bed to lay down upon, and without food to eat, we certainly do derive benefit from those locusts. In striving to please their Reverences, he tells them that he does not 'intend to keep company with any man, unless he professes his own Creed'. By this is meant one which says 'All dissenters must perish everlastingly'. I beg to tell him, if he will not keep company with the Dissenters in this world, and has no better actions to boast of, than assisting at the Manchester Massacre, as a Dissenter, I pray to Heaven that I may not be in his company in the next world.

The actual text of Hulton's speech is, unfortunately, not available, but his reputation and his record in his native parish of Deane, was quite unassailable.

[1] *Bolton Chronicle,* 9 June 1827.

. . . It is an old saying that 'when drink's in, wit's out', and the twenty-first toast on this occasion verifies the proverb; it runs thus: 'The Chairman of the Magistrates at Manchester, on the memorable 16th of August, 1819, by whose example and exertion our lives and property have been preserved. (Immense cheering).' Mr. Hulton said: 'As allusion had been made several times to the 16th of August, he must be permitted to say, that no man felt more grateful for the deliverance we had experienced on that occasion than he did; he sincerely believed the course adopted at that time was consonant with their benefit, and as a confirmation he had received the thanks of the Monarch upon the throne. The conduct of the Magistrates upon that occasion, of whom he was but one, will go down to posterity; and he should go down to the grave with the conviction, that the 16th of August was the proudest day in his life.'

William Hulton, with a span still ahead of him of thirty-seven years, was to have many convincing proofs that 'the conduct of the magistrates' would surely go down to posterity; but hardly in the way he then imagined. The letter went on:

Now, Messrs. Pittites, you all know well, and so does every Magistrate and Cavalryman who acted on the bloody tragedy, that Manchester was in no more danger on the 16th of August than it was on the 15th or any subsequent day; and that lives were sacrificed, instead of being, as falsely stated, preserved. And I can assure Mr. Hulton that if the Monarch did thank him, he had been wrongly advised, in all probability by that man who afterwards cut his own throat . . . To conclude, I suppose Mr. Hulton, Mr. Fletcher, and Mr. Slade[1] have all heard that the present Ministers have given notice of their intention to reduce the expenditure of the county, consequently no more Secret Service money will be sent to Bolton to reward hired spies for swearing men's lives away . . .

Whatever the truth of Col. Fletcher's activities in the matter of spies had been, Hulton was not implicated; but no distinctions of merit were known to 'Dissenter'.

If ever there was a time when a 'Blue Book' was necessary to keep track of the intricate pattern of the narrative of events after 16 August 1819, it was after 1822 and before 1827. It could, of course, be alleged that the Government was mostly to blame for not going into an inquiry; but rightly or wrongly they believed that a judicial inquiry had been made in two trials, or perhaps even three trials if Burdett's trial and its aftermath were included. Amongst the Hulton papers[2] is a letter from P. N. Norton, headed 10 April 1827, Downing Street, who replaced

[1] Rev. James Slade, vicar of Bolton.
[2] DDHu/48/145.

Hobhouse as under-secretary at the Home Office; he refers to a letter he had written to the *Courier* 'for the purpose of putting down the infamous attacks of *The Times:*' He tells Hulton:

. . . If you think any good is to arise from it, you might get the attack of *The Times* and the letter printed and circulated . . . It unfortunately happens that where the Press sets itself against any principle, unless you fight them with their own weapons they have in the early part of the contest very great advantage, and this in a greater degree where the prejudices and passions of the lower orders are to be called into action.

It is not known what the 'infamous attack of *The Times*' was at that date, but Mr Norton's suggestion was not taken up. Hulton did, in 1831, rush into print on similar lines against Lord Althorp, but with little advantage to himself or his case. It was too late; although had it coincided with the conclusion of the last Manchester Affair debate in the House of Commons in the months following, its effect might have been different. The fact remains, that apart from Francis Philips's *Exposure* of November 1819, there is not a single printed work which makes any attempt to put the record straight from the Government/Magistrates angle. This was to make the establishment of the radical version so much easier.

From the 'inhabitants of the towns of Great and Little Bolton' was sent a petition to Parliament about the same time as 'Dissenter's' comment. It referred to working-class degradation, the causes being a corrupt Parliament, enormous taxation, corn monopoly, a system enriching the aristocracy, clergy &c.; to the appropriation of Church and Crown lands to pay off the National Debt; to religious liberty and the disestablishment of the Church. It also recorded 'their utter detestation of the conduct of those persons who took an active part in butchering the innocent persons who attended the Manchester Meeting on 16 August 1819, and petitioned Parliament for an alleviation of their sufferings.' It 'entreated that the ringleaders concerned in that murderous transaction may be arraigned before a jury of their country,' and prayed for Reform.

Not all the Lancashire reformers in the radical ranks took up the attitude of those in Bolton; in Oldham, in March 1827, there was a large public meeting entirely composed of working classes to petition for Reform. John Knight, one of the arrested radicals of 16 August was amongst the speakers. The *Manchester Chronicle*[1] gave it much space. Charles Walker of Ashton said 'they had grown more sensible than they

[1] 24 March 1827.

were on 16 August' but he recommended his hearers to persevere in their righteous cause, and if their country would unite with them they would speak to the legislature with a voice of thunder. There were other working-class meetings held at this period in Ashton,[1] with Knight and Fitton as the speakers; at Manchester[2] with tirades against the corruption in the House of Commons and on the oppressive nobility; at not one of these did 16 August receive mention. Fear of repercussions inimical to the speakers might have been the reason, but at one meeting in Manchester[3], one speaker broke through the reticence, John Doherty, the cotton spinner, who was later to find minor fame as a working-class reformer. Doherty referred to the bloody butchering in the presence of Parson H—— in St Peter's Field. The chairman, another spinner named Foster, 'intimated that language of rather too strong a character had been used, and hoped no advantage would be taken of poor working men.' Doherty then came forward again

and said he would not retract a syllable of what he had uttered. The language he had used was not strong enough. Could they forget the butcheries of Peterloo?—when a drunken and infuriated set of wretches were turned with naked swords upon their wives and children.

The *Chronicle* reported that these observations were received with loud cheers. The report went on:

At the commencement of the proceedings the chairman very properly recommended the meeting to preserve order and decorum, and to express their sentiments with coolness and candour. From the preceding sketch it will be seen what share of attention the latter part of the recommendation of the chairman received. To crown the business of the night three cheers were given, and afterwards, as an embellishment, three groans for the butcheries of Peterloo.

The paragraph surely suggests that a new pattern was being set, not noticeable, for whatever reason, before. Doherty was addressing working-class meetings in the same strain in August 1827.[4]

During June 1827, the *Manchester Guardian* began a campaign against Pitt and Pitt clubs and claimed that the latter were fast disappearing and their influence waning; they were, but they did not disappear without some death-struggles. A public meeting to address his Majesty on the Corn Laws was held in the Town Hall, Manchester, on

[1] *Wheeler's Manchester Chronicle*, 21 April 1827.
[2] Ibid., 11 August 1827.
[3] Ibid., 24 February 1827.
[4] Ibid., 1 September 1827.

5 July.[1] The meeting was addressed by some of the Pitt Club members who protested against the sentiments of some of the speakers. George William Wood was the main speaker from the opposite camp. He observed:

. . . Certain associations miscalled Pitt Clubs had designated Mr. Canning as an apostate, and he considered it to be his duty to declare that the sentiments uttered in the Pitt Clubs at their recent meetings were not the sentiments of the people of the country. He declaimed against the Cheshire Squires. Mr. Shuttleworth[2] further declaimed: 'We knew of whom the Pitt Associations were formed: amongst others of some country squires, a political parson of the country (a laugh) and the enlightened Squire of Hulton-lane ends. (cheers and hisses).' The anti-Pittites had a large majority.

The *Chronicle*[3] reported also a 'united' Manchester meeting to petition Parliament for representation in the House of Commons. Hugh Hornby Birley was the principal speaker, with Prentice and John Edward Taylor also addressing the meeting. On 28 May, Lord Stanley presented the petition signed by 5,000 persons of 'all denominations and opinions.' Hulton was not one of their number.

How intense was the feeling on Catholic Emancipation in the period 1827–29 can best be realized by studying the press of those years. Hardly an issue passed without copious references to it. To the old Tories Protestant Ascendancy was a sacrosanct doctrine. There were defections. Canning had defected, and on 9 June 1827, a sarcastic paragraph in the *Bolton Chronicle* tilted at Hulton for 'proselytising'; he had been guilty of influencing a prominent townsman to desert Mr Canning:

[Hulton] had produced a correspondence between him and Mr. Peel, which satisfactorily convinced his friend that he ought to desert Mr. Canning and go over to the Pittites. Many urgent arguments might have been used, but the conversion was, under the circumstances, rather sudden and peculiar. New lights do sometimes suddenly spring upon men. Much praise is due to Mr. Hulton and Mr. Peel for resorting to such a *fair and unequivocal* mode of obtaining proselytes.

Hulton's faith in the Protestant champion, Robert Peel, was later to undergo a severe jolt.

There would seem to be little doubt that the rising young Lancashire statesman, Peel, used his influence in 1828 to obtain for Hulton a local honour which Hulton was proud to accept:

---

[1] *Wheeler's Manchester Chronicle*, 7 July 1827.
[2] Probably the John Shuttleworth the erstwhile witness in the Peterloo trials.
[3] *Wheeler's Manchester Chronicle*, 2 June 1827.

Lord Aberdeen to William Hulton [22 May 1828][1]: Sir: I received from Mr. Peel your letter to him on the subject of the office of Constable of Lancaster Castle. As the office is purely honorary, its value must consist in its affording a publick mark of the esteem of those by whom it is conferred; and I presume it will give you pleasure to learn that it was previously my intention to offer it to you as an evidence of the high opinion which I entertain of your general character, and especially of your valuable services as a Magistrate. It is therefore with satisfaction that I am now able to make the offer, with the certainty that it will be agreeable to you to accept it.

The appointment did not give pleasure to John Edward Taylor; there were sarcastic comments in the *Guardian* and counter comments in the loyalist Manchester press. A letter from Hulton fills in the picture:

To the Editor of the *Manchester Chronicle* (June 14th, 1828). Sir: My attention has been called to a paragraph in the *Manchester Guardian* of the 7th of June, in which it is stated that I have been nominated to the office of Constable of Lancaster Castle, the chief duties of which are supposed to consist in 'counting the salary attached to the appointment'. However indifferent I may generally be to any remarks of the Editor of the *Guardian*, yet I am anxious to expose his total want of truth and his wilful attempt to deceive the Public, by representing His Majesty, or the Government, as bestowing, and myself as receiving a *pecuniary* recompense for what he is pleased to term my '*labours in support of the powers that be*'. Those labours had long since been greatly overpaid by the thanks of my gracious Monarch—a reward the highest and most valued which a loyal subject, especially one who glories in the name Tory, can receive.

The *Guardian* states further that the salary of the Constable of Lancaster Castle is £1,200 a year. The office is purely honorary, and its value therefore consists in its affording a public mark of the esteem of those by whom it is conferred. As such, I estimate it to a degree which, doubtless the Editor of the *Guardian* cannot affix to any honour unaccompanied by sordid gain. I hope to render myself not unworthy of the distinction by an unchangeable and faithful devotion to the service of the best of Kings. I remain, Sir, your obedient servant, William Hulton. Hulton Park, June 12th, 1828.

Hulton's lofty tone doubtless pleased his Manchester admirers (and he had many), but his expression of being 'greatly overpaid' for his services was to come hurtling back to his offended ears with compound interest —and from a quarter which probably he least expected. In the meantime the editor of the *Chronicle* rebuked the editor of the *Guardian* for his tirade against William Pitt, against Pitt Clubs in general, and against the Manchester Pitt Club in particular; in addition to his misconceptions

[1] DDHu/48/162; 48/163; 164. L.C.R.O.

of the Constable of Lancaster Castle's office, Taylor had been making some not so shrewd hits against Francis Philips as the writer of some paragraphs in the *Chronicle*. John Edward Taylor was wrong:

. . . Like most of the lucubrations of the *Guardian*, it betrays no deficiencies in modest assurance, nor of that kind of sagacity, which resembling the celebrated Lord Burleigh's nod, is clearly indicative of deep philosophy . . . The *Guardian* was never remarkable for buoyancy[1] whatever claim it may possess to more worthless distinctions. We deem it our duty to exonerate Mr. Philips from the charge of having applied abusive epithets to the *Guardian*, in the use of which, unlike that paper, we are by no means skilful. We see nothing deserving of notice in the *Guardian*'s reiteration, that Mr. Pitt was the most unfortunate Minister that this country ever possessed. The tenour of his observations, if they mean anything, furnishes a direct proof of the correctness of our argument. A bold assertion is an equivocal sort of thing from any one, and the *Guardian* has no doubt discovered long before this that he is not considered either as the best or the wisest of authorities. We insert in another column a letter from Mr Philips, declaring that there is 'not a word of truth in what the *Guardian* says of himself'. If all the personalities and calumnies of that journal were rebutted with the same spirit that has been displayed in the examples set forth by Mr. Hulton and Mr. Philips, it would no longer dare to assail the wise and the good with insolence, under the contemptible pretext, forsooth, of protecting the rights of the people.

It was entertaining, trivial stuff—the thrust and parry of local politics. William Hulton being William Hulton, however, his letter was reprinted by the national press. On 29 June came a boom, from a big gun silent for the past five years:

Hulton of Hulton. To the Editor of the *Morning Herald*. Sir—In your paper of Saturday, there is a letter signed 'W. Hulton' informing your readers that the gentleman of Peterloo celebrity, has been appointed to the office of *Constable*, or head-keeper of Lancaster Castle; and he adds '*that his labours in support of the powers that be* had long since been *greatly overpaid* by the thanks of his gracious Monarch.' Now, Sir, I trust that you will allow me to inform some, and remind others of your numerous readers of what those valuable services 'to the powers that be' consist, and for what those thanks of the King of England were given to the very worthy head-keeper of Lancaster Castle.

Neither Mr. Hulton's name nor services were ever, I believe, heard of till the memorable 16th of August, 1819, when almost a boy, he was appointed by the Magistrates of Manchester their Chairman for the day, in which capacity he gave, partly from fear, and partly from folly, the order for the Manchester

---

[1] A reference to 'attic salt' which would 'float' even 'in a bottle of the Atlantic'.

Yeomanry to charge the unarmed and peaceable multitude of men, women, and children, there assembled to petition for the reform of the Commons House of Parliament, in which charge *fourteen* persons were killed, and *six-hundred and eighteen badly wounded*—for this service did this Gentleman, I believe, receive the thanks of his Monarch. That he was 'greatly overpaid' I think no man in the world will deny; at all events, Sir, I am sure that no one will dispute this who was in the Court at York, who heard and saw him when he 'broke down' under the cross-examination that he received at my hands, on the memorable trial of myself and others, at the Spring Assizes at that City in 1820. I am, Sir, yours H. Hunt. 2, Stamford Street, June 29th.[1]

Henry Hunt had not yet thrown off his five years' habit of reserve in expressing himself; 'partly from fear, and partly from folly' was anything but in the true Hunt vein. It was a reserve out of which he was soon able to shake himself. William Hulton's reaction is not on record; it was probably one of lofty disdain, and the disdain of one conscious of his own rectitude. Moreover, the disdain of one firm in his belief that the view put forward by Hunt was one which had not the slightest possibility of influencing fair-minded men who were differently informed. He brushed it off.

[1] Quoted *Bolton Chronicle*, 12 July 1828.

XXVI

Peel and Hulton

The summer of 1828 saw the opening of the Bolton and Leigh Railway on which Hulton had set so much store; 'several scientific gentlemen from London, Birmingham, Liverpool and Manchester' were entertained at Hulton Hall, and Mrs Hulton 'christened' the Stephenson locomotive 'The Lancashire Witch'. It pulled a weight of forty tons at the rate of seven miles per hour. A crowd of forty thousand people added their plaudits. In October William Hulton was entertaining the future Prime Minister of England.

The Rt Hon. Robert Peel had visited Manchester to attend the Great Musical Festival and to revisit the scenes of his youth; it is not for nothing that the statue of Sir Robert Peel still graces the centre of the Lancashire town of Bury. At a public dinner in Manchester Town Hall,[1] during his visit, the Rt Hon. Robert Peel basked in the light of the almost royal welcome he had received:

. . . This is the place of my birth—the spot where the fortunes of my family were established. I contemplate it with impressions intermediate to those which are suggested by our country and our home. If those feelings which bind us to our native spot, which gives us additional interest in its welfare are founded on prejudice, it is a prejudice to which I never wish to be superior . . . [In replying to the toast; the Ministers of the Crown, he went on] . . . They are deeply sensible of the value of your good opinion. They are the more sensible of it because they know that they shall acquire and retain it, not by pursuing what are called *popular* measures, but by walking directly in that course which their consciences dictate to them as the best.

Gentlemen, in my own capacity of Minister of the Crown, I have had many relations to maintain with this district and with this place. I have co-operated with many of you in times of trouble and alarm. I will not revive the recollections of those scenes, but rather rejoice to witness the general concord which now prevails amongst all classes. I have co-operated with many of you in times of affliction and distress; but I have found that those who were the most strenuous asserters of the law, and the most determined combatants of lawlessness and violence, were the first in the cause of charity.

[1] *Wheeler's Manchester Chronicle,* 11 October 1828.

The hand that was clenched with uncompromising firmness to resist the attacks which were made upon property was open as charity itself when an appeal was made.

When the toast to Protestant Ascendancy was proposed, the *Chronicle* reported, the acclamation was immense. William Hulton's health was drunk with a reference to 'his manly and independent conduct which had endeared him to the county at large, and more especially to this Hundred' (the Hundred of Salford); Hulton replied:

. . . Had my service been such as to call for so marked a compliment, I might have been led to suppose that my health would have been given in the regular routine; but I am not aware that I, more than any other individual in this enlightened assembly, have done anything in public life to call for your approbation . . . Since I must become egogistic I may refer to my life, past, present, and to come. As to the past, you know I have addressed many of you in times of difficulty and prosperity, and I have heard nothing but unanimity proceed from your lips . . . As to the present, I stand before you proud in being placed on the right hand of that Statesman whom I have ever revered with unmixed regard. I stand here a perfect emblem of the union of the commercial and agricultural interests. To-day I stand before you commercially, as a dealer of coals; and to-morrow I shall be assisting as vice-president of one of the first agricultural societies in the kingdom. Amongst the many features for which this town is remarkable this is perhaps the most conspicuous, that, though in no part of the world is exhibited so much mechanical ingenuity, here you will at the same time find the largest Agricultural Society in England.

Now as to the future: I am aware with how much caution an enlightened assemblage like this should receive the opinions of one so humble as myself. But I have before me the brightest example of a man who has conferred upon this country more lustre, with the exception of his own illustrious colleague at the head of the Government, than perhaps any statesman ever did; and I am stimulated also by your example, for by the exertions of all are our unrivalled institutions to be upheld. By that great man's example I pledge myself to abide, as true as shadow is to substance—as echo is to sound. The shadow may be obscured by its humility—the echo may be rendered feeble by distance; but I pledge myself to follow, to the utmost of my ability, that eminent leader, who, I can now boast, is my personal friend.

The Rt Hon. Robert Peel may have been a little embarrassed by the warmness of Hulton's devotion; on the other hand he may not, for the claim to personal friendship was reciprocal. There was to be embarrassment, and before very long, in the very town where the pledge of loyalty was so unstintingly made; but it was to be embarrassment for the disciple, not the leader. Hulton went on :

You may ask, is it not a sacrifice of the independence of the mind to follow implicitly the example of any man? I trust that my past conduct, through evil report and through good report, shows that my independence cannot be abridged. I see in him those qualities by which domestic life is adorned; and I pledge myself to follow him, looking at him as the leader of our political creed, and because I acknowledge him as the most eloquent and also able defender of the religion, liberties, and laws of this country. As the personal friend of the late lamented Duke of York, I look upon him as the uncorrupted Champion of Protestantism; as a man who will not swerve, I am certain, from that Oath of Allegiance which he has taken to George the Fourth, the Defender of the Faith.

Had William Hulton been as familiar with the contemporary undercurrents of opinion, finding full expression in all the press at the time, as he was with his Burnet's *History of the Reformation* and his Foxe's *Book of Martyrs*, he might have realized that those swirling undercurrents were even then removing landmarks which had stood for centuries. But he was not. On this one point Peel was to discover that 'the tone of England' was 'more liberal than the policy of the Government.' as his letter to Croker of 1820 had said. He introduced his bill for Catholic Emancipation into Parliament six months later. But William Hulton was to enjoy his St Luke's Little Summer of October 1828, a little longer.

The Rt Hon. Robert Peel on the Sunday departed for Hulton Park. A distinguished party of Lancashire and Cheshire Tories was there to welcome him. The local press[1] reported:

On Monday morning, the party proceeded to the lawn adjoining the mansion, and the Rt. Hon. Secretary planted an English oak as a memorial of his visit, amidst the cheers of the company and the labourers, the latter pledging the health of Mr. Peel in cups of strong ale. Mr. Peel, attended by the party, then inspected the Bolton and Leigh Railway, and in a waggon fitted up for the occasion they were propelled by the locomotive engine to the top of the inclined plane near the town of [Bolton].

Again, near the scenes of his youth, Mr Peel received a rapturous welcome. He was to attend a 'breakfast' in his honour in the town:

The day was distinguished by general rejoicings. Flags waved from the steeple of the Old Church and from several of the principal factories, and the bells were rung in honour of the event. The time fixed for the breakfast was one o'clock, and long before that hour an immense concourse of persons had assembled in front of the hotel to greet the Rt. Hon. Gentleman on his

[1] *Bolton Chronicle*, 11 October 1828.

arrival. About half-past one o'clock Mr. Peel arrived in his carriage from Hulton Park, accompanied by William Hulton Esq. A royal salute was fired from several pieces of cannon, and the populace rent the air with their joyous acclamations.

Mr Peel, in replying to the toast of his health said he was touched by Bolton's welcome:

I rejoice as a private and as a public man in the marked indications around me of progressive civilization and refinement; and with those gratifying signs of improvement, I rejoice at the equal advancement of the humbler classes, whose appearance as they hailed me when I passed made a deep impression on my mind. I never courted, nor will I ever court, what is called popular applause; but I am not the less sensible of those strong marks of attachment which I have received this day from that class of society to whom I and my family owe the greatest obligations.

The cynics of later days might dismiss such utterances as commonplace platitudes; they were the seeding-ground of the long and loyal attachment the humbler people of Lancashire had for the political causes heralded by Robert Peel.

. . . Another source of gratification [Mr. Peel went on] which my visit to this county has proved is, that I have been able to avail myself of confirming my friendship for a gentleman, by whose exertions this part of the county has derived so much advantage. I need not say that I allude to my friend on my right hand [Mr. Hulton]. I know that I am with the man by whose courage in times of difficulty and danger this district was protected from lawless violence. I am with the man by whose liberality and benevolence in the time of privation and affliction this district was greatly relieved. I am with the man who in the present time of tranquility and prosperity is now cheering and animating his neighbours by his example as a Magistrate and as a private gentlemen . . .

The Boroughreeve of Bolton, in homely phrase, referred to agricultural shows and to 'good stock', which was easily turned to the 'good stock' from which the Rt Hon. Mr Peel sprang; he trusted that 'large stocks may be increased in this county both of the Hultons and the Peels'. Hulton, in replying (it was a toast to his health) observed:

It has often fallen to my lot to address you, sometimes in periods of prosperity, and at other times at periods when it required all the energies of the mind to support the drooping spirits of those around us; but at all times and under all circumstances, I have been encouraged by your affectionate approbation. I have in every situation of life, humble as my situation is, tried to discharge the duties of a good and loyal citizen. But there wanted something further as a proof of that gratitude with which my heart is filled, and I may retire to rest this night pleased with the reflection that I have been the more immediate means of introducing this Rt. Hon. Statesman to your notice.[1] In doing this I have made the best return in my power, and which, I trust, repays the great debt I owe you. I should now, perhaps, sit down; but on this occasion, unwilling as I am to enter into any political discussions which neither the hour nor the time seems fitted for, I must boldly and firmly state, that in looking to the great question which agitates the empire, the world should know that our opinions are unchanged; and that looking to that manly eloquence which has so often defended our religion, we may express our confidence that that eloquence will never be employed but in promoting the welfare and prosperity of our religion, and of the Constitution of our country.

You have appropriately marked the seat appointed for that great Statesman. On one side, behind him, you see 'Church and King', and on the other 'Protestant Ascendancy'. Now, whatever the difference in men's constitutions may be—whatever the difference of heat and warmth may be agreeable to them, I believe that no man would be willing to part with the genial warmth of the sun. For myself, I wish in this northern region to enjoy its full beams; and I am sure that the degree of prosperity which is necessary to keep up our rank among the nations can only be secured by the maintenance of the Protestant faith . . . [On its effects in England; and abroad] . . . while it promotes the arts and sciences, it has reference to that greatest of objects, our dutiful obedience to the laws of God.

I shall now only allude to one great and memorable trait in the life of my Rt. Hon. friend. Gentlemen may talk of trials by jury; but who has improved and rectified the system but Mr. Peel? Gentlemen may talk of the improvement of the law; but who has renovated and ameliorated it? Mr. Peel, Statesman as he is, and defending and maintaining our political relations both at home and abroad as he does, I say of all the statesmen and philosophers who can go down to the grave celebrated for their good works, the greatest is he who improves the laws of his country. He has assured us of his belief that in the defence of our laws, our hearts and our hands are ready to assist him; and so we are, and if we fall, 'For laws, religion, liberty we fall.'

Later on that same day, Hulton was present at the Manchester public dinner given in honour of Mr Peel. A toast was given to 'The Protestant Ascendancy', which, the report added, was received with cheering; many of the gentlemen looked towards Mr Peel when they cheered, as if expecting him to speak on the subject. The Rt Hon. Gentleman, however, remained perfectly quiet. Peel's thoughts were his own. He may, or he may not, have given Hulton some encouragement to hope that on that question on which Hulton felt so strongly, his own views

[1] It was an echo of Hulton's alleged proselytizing from the cause of Canning to that of Peel.

were the same views on which he had seemed so adamant not so long before. On the other hand, the report of his remaining 'perfectly quiet' at the table in Manchester suggests that his opinions were undergoing some modification.

Affairs in Ireland were changing Peel. When the change did come, Hulton was shattered but, as will be seen, not reproachful. Peel's colleagues at Westminster were, some of them, less considerate. Lord Tullamore, in his speech (18 March 1829) on the adjourned debate on the Catholic Relief Bill[1] said:

The Right Hon. Gentleman [Mr. Peel] made a triumphant progress through the northern parts of the country, and heard speeches delivered in support of Protestant principles, and gave no hint as to his intentions. I must look to a Roman Catholic poet for a passage which, like a text of Scripture, may serve as a motto to the mode of his progress:

'Drunk at a Borough; civil at a Ball,
Friendly at Lancashire, faithless at Whitehall.'

I own my confidence in the Rt. Hon. Gentleman was much shaken by the course which he has adopted.

Reproaches were heaped upon Peel in the town of Bolton where he had so recently been received with such acclaim. On 2 March, Hulton, as chairman of the Protestant Committee in Bolton, had to express his sentiments in different terms:[2]

. . . That he felt himself in the most painful situation, to sit at a public meeting and hear a man decried whom he had looked up to as the guide of his political principles, and it was a melancholy feeling that Mr. Peel no longer deserved the valuable and honest applause which in the whole of his public life he had until lately received. No feelings of private friendship, however, should interfere with public duty, and, painful as it was, he should not shrink from expressing his disappointment of the conduct of Mr. Peel, who had sold his political existence. Mr. Hulton then at length censured the conduct of the Duke of Wellington and Mr. Peel in a similar manner . . .

A day or two before, Hulton had asked that his name be withdrawn from the list of members of the Stockport Wellington Club, 'a club bearing the name of an individual who would rob his country of any part of that constitution to which our Protestant church owes her only security.'[3] 'I am told.' Hulton had said in 1817, 'to revise the lessons of my youth'; he was not cast in a waxen mould which could readily

---

[1] Proc. Parliament, Vol. 20 n.s. 1206.
[2] *Bolton Chronicle*, 7 March 1829.
[3] Ibid., 28 February 1829.

be warmed and reshaped; he was cast in a mould of clay. He had always been a high Tory; in 1829 he was a high-and-dry Tory![1]

John Edward Taylor was cock-a-hoop. The *Guardian*'s 'lucubrations,' earlier complained of by the *Chronicle*, were not of the nature to heal wounds, nor even to calm troubled waters; they were inflammable. Their nature may be seen by the reply that Hulton felt forced to issue in self-defence:

To the Protestants of Manchester and the Neighbourhood. Brother Protestants.—I owe it to the only publican in this neighbourhood whose principles are tainted with radicalism and Popery, that I have had an opportunity of reading two paragraphs relating to myself in a Manchester newspaper called *The Guardian*; the first published on the 14th and the second on the 21st of this month. He of the goose-quill thus pompously appeals to me: '*We call upon Mr. Hulton to redeem his pledge, and to erase his name from the anti-Catholic Petitions to which it has just been signed. If he refuses to do this, the public will know what confidence they may place in any solemn pledge he may make hereafter*'. He *calls* upon me 'as a magistrate of the county, and as Constable of Lancaster Castle'. Why is he not content to address me as one of the 'foolish country squires,' (a class to which I am proud to belong) I know not; except, perhaps, that in retrospection he remembers that the power of the magistrate has been exercised for the punishment of political incendiaries; and that his prospective imagination points to him the 'Constable' turning the massive keys of Lancaster Castle on traitors to their King and Country. But I hasten to answer the editorial mandate. I *refuse* to erase my name from the anti-Catholic petitions to which it has been signed. The 'pledge' to which allusion is made, was, I doubt not, correctly stated by the reporters who heard it at the dinner in Manchester to Mr. Peel. Referring to that Statesman, I used the following, amongst other, expressions: 'By that great man's example I pledge myself to abide. You must ask, is it not a sacrifice of the independence of the mind to follow implicitly the example of

[1] Dates are often important. Amongst the private papers of Sir Robert Peel* is a letter dated, Manchester, 17 February 1829, from Colonel Yates, sent to Peel:

'I have been here two or three days, and the public mind begins to be a little more tranquilized on the subject of the new changes. The Boltoners are, however, still very indignant, and it is really the fact that Hulton took on so that the physician bled him and put him to bed. . . .'

To which Peel replied:

'. . . Would I abide by my opinions on the present state of affairs, or would I not? Would I leave others to contend with difficulties which I refused to face? Would I advise the King to swallow a bitter pill, at which I made faces myself? There surely cannot be a doubt as to the course which a man *ought* to take under such circumstances.'

The date of the letter conveying intelligence of Hulton's 'taking on so' was 17 February; he was back on his feet and writing indignantly to the *Guardian* eleven days later.

* Parker, *Sir Robert Peel from his Private Papers*, Vol. II, p. 94 (1899).

any man? I trust I have shown by my past life that my independence cannot be abridged;' but I pledged myself to follow him, '*looking to him as the leader of our political creed; and because I acknowledge him as the most eloquent and able defender of the liberty, laws and religion of his country;—as the personal friend of the late Duke of York, as the uncorrupted and incorruptible champion of Protestantism!*' When the cause ceases, the effect ceases also. Mr. Peel is no longer the champion of Protestantism; and I am no longer his disciple. I appeal to five hundred gentlemen who heard me, I appeal to every man of every party to say on which side *consenting* lies. Further than this self-defending position, *consistency in friendship* forbids me to utter a syllable which would add to the almost unsupportable agony of Mr. Peel's breast.

But I give my renewed, my consistent pledge, that so long as, by the blessing of God, reason is continued to me, so long shall every word and every action of my life, humble though I am, be directed to the maintenance of our pure religion and immutable laws,—so long will I co-operate by all the means I possess in resisting the claims of Associated Papists. If (to use the language of my friend Sir Robert Inglis[1]) a claim be founded in right, I should be ashamed of a government which could be bullied by six clamorous and sturdy millions, into a weak and inconsistent concession'. Let the *Guardian* accuse me of 'breaking my word'. I receive it as a powerful evidence of my veracity. Brother Protestants! all that is valuable in your Constitution; all that was gained for you by the glorious Revolution of 1688 is at stake. Resist, I implore you, the attempted counter-Revolution of 1829. You may, by your immediate, your united, energies, preserve your holy religion; you may rescue your beloved King from his perilous situation; you may bring down from heaven a blessing, and not a curse. I remain, Gentlemen, your faithful friend and servant, William Hulton. Hulton Park, 26th February, 1829.[2]

John Edward Taylor probably knew as well as William Hulton that it was not the latter's veracity which was at stake; he well knew the nature of Hulton's pledge. But Taylor rejoiced at Hulton's discomfiture, and the chance of having a 'go' at the continuing target of his sarcasm from 1819 onwards was too good to miss. Hulton's letter contained also another 'indiscretion' with which to taunt him. The reference to his being proud to belong to that class which Taylor had called' foolish country squires'; as long as the Taylor versus Hulton tilts lasted that was to remain on record. If Hulton's 'manifesto' sounded like a 'call to arms' to his followers, it did not last; his own commercial concerns were to bring, so it was generally alleged, financial anxieties. More than that even; the old sore of 16 August, thinly covered, was

---

[1] Sir Robert Inglis succeeded Peel as M.P. for the University of Oxford after Peel's defection.
[2] *Bolton Chronicle*, 7 March 1829.

shortly to be ripped open; the Taylor tilts were to seem as nothing in comparison.

Hulton, in 1829, as a magistrate, took a prominent part in the agitation for the abolition of the 'truck' system prevalent in the Bolton-Manchester area. At the Bolton Petty Sessions in March 1829, there were many cases reported of the payment of wages in goods. Hulton said:

. . . that the magistrates were determined not to allow any amount of goods had by a workman from his master, to be placed as a set-off against wages. He wished, as there were a number of workpeople present, that they would make it known through the town, that in no *instance* under any *circumstances*, were wages to be paid in goods. The workman must receive the full amount of his wages, and if he owes his master anything for goods, and is not honest enough to pay him out of his wages paid in money, his master's remedy is to sue him for debt, but he must not pay himself out of the man's wages . . .[1]

There were public meetings in Bolton and Wigan on the subject, at which tributes were paid to Hulton for his energy on the bench, by attending the House of Commons to interview Mr Lyttelton and Mr Peel, and in 1830 interviewing Earl Grey and H.M. Ministers on behalf of the Anti-Truck Committees of Bolton and Wigan.[2] As might be expected Hulton's efforts in this agitation did not get much mention in the national press.

In the quiet affairs of the parish of Deane, Hulton's zeal never flagged. Charles James Blomfield (1786–1857), since 1828 the indefatigable Bishop of London, had earlier been Bishop of Chester; there was a firm friendship between Hulton and the bishop. Writing to Hulton in 1829 on the cares occasioned by the continued ill-health of the Vicar of Deane, Blomfield[3] observed that 'if a good squire deserves to have a good parson you are entitled to George Herbert himself, or good Father Gilpin. . . .' Deane, however, possessed neither, and was making do in the absence of the vicar with a rather over-zealous curate, of whom Hulton was rather fond on account of his good works. The curate was a strict sabbatarian and had remonstrated with a local character for burning his brick-kilns on Sunday. The brick-maker was alleged to have been abusive, and the curate requested Squire Hulton to speak to him. The outcome was an appearance in the local magistrates' court[4] of Jacob Boardman, of Rumworth, for exercising his worldly calling on

[1] *Bolton Chronicle*, 7 March 1829.
[2] *Bolton Chronicle*, 21 November 1829; 13 November; 11 December (1830). DDHu/53/71; 48/170; 48/172 L.C.R.O. Collection of Letters.
[3] Blomfield to Hulton &c. DDHu/10/14/1 &c.
[4] *Bolton Chronicle*, 20 June 1829.

the Sabbath-day. Jacob blamed the parson, although he was said to have been rather rude to the squire in calling his attention to the fact that his steam-engines at his collieries worked on Sundays as well (to keep the water-pumps going). Jacob said he was much irritated when he conversed with Mr Hulton from 'what the parson said to me'; he apologized. Normally the incident would never have reached a wider public than that of the local newspapers, but a wider press took it up; it concerned Hulton of Hulton. It was all very playful:

The (London) *Examiner* recalled the American saint who sang: 'Once I stove a cask of beer, because it worked on Sunday,' and continued: We are by no means persuaded of the lawfulness of steam-working on the Sabbath. Indeed, steam-engines perform so many of the offices of man, and have so much the character of animated, intelligent and responsible creatures, that we are decidedly of opinion they should go to church like other folks. Very probably Mr. Hulton's zeal to abate the crying abomination of brick-burning, while his own steam-engines were working at home, is reconcilable by the fact that he considered the steam-engines answerable for their own private conduct, and they are not enumerated amongst those servants whose labour we are commanded not to permit on the day of rest.

A wag on the *Liverpool Mercury* went one better:[1]

Fire and Water. Song.—Tune: The Vicar and Moses.

As fierce as a Sultan
  Said Hulton of Hulton
To a half-famished burner of bricks,
  'If your kiln smokes on Sunday
  As well as on Monday
I'll make you pay dear for such tricks.' Tol-de-rol.

'By my *Cavalry Sword*, man,
  I swear Jacob Boardman,
You *shall* put the fire out, you sinner!'
  'If I put out the fire,'
  Jacob said to the Squire,
'My children would soon want a dinner.' Tol-de-rol.

Hulton swore in great ire
  He should put out the fire,
As he knew he the law was infringing;
  Says Jacob 'Why so, Sir,
  Your honour, you know, Sir,
All Sunday long works your steam engine.' Tol-de-rol.

[1] Quoted by the *Bolton Chronicle*, 4 July.

Then Hulton did rave,
　Call'd Jacob a knave,
And sent for the parish churchwarden,
　Who swore, without bail,
　He should pack off to jail,
If he did not ask Squire Hulton's pardon. Tol-de-rol.

So here ends my song,
　'Tis somewhat too long,
For my muse is still given to wander;
　Whate'er folks may say,
　It is prov'd clear as day,
Sauce for the goose is not sauce for the gander. Tol-de-rol.

William Hulton's letters to the press and the reports of his speeches therein were subjected to a scrutiny which he probably never envisaged. His 'call to Protestants' to defend what had been won in 1688 and the suggestion that the King would adhere to the 1688 settlement was too good to miss. 'A Dissenter', Hulton's erstwhile critic of 1827, was as logical as he was ingenious in following on from Hulton's premises with the following indictment:[1]

. . . It is thus such men as William Hulton Esq. venture to attack even the monarch himself. They dare not openly slander him, but endeavour to render him contemptible by attributing to him their own ignorance of the constitution and their disaffected licentious spirit. They put their own inflammatory language into the mouth of Majesty, and then quote it in support of their cause.

This man, who would fain have us believe that he enjoys the confidence of persons near the Throne, proceeds from libelling the King to vituperate the Ministers. His first complaint of their want of firmness, has by this time, I should imagine, been effectually removed. His *railing* accusations against them, and the threats he utters, his violent and I will say seditious language, excite in my mind feelings of triumph and exultation. Mr. Hulton may have forgotten the year 1819 [!] and some years previous; but there are memories less treacherous. Every man who then stood forward for reform must rejoice to see the situation in which its enemies are now placed, and must especially rejoice to see this particular person brought upon his knees, crestfallen, and most pitifully beseeching the injured people to help him.

We have lately seen some very remarkable changes of opinion and conduct, which one may call conviction and another apostacy; but where shall we look for a more remarkable change, call it what you will, than that which has taken place in the chairman of the Manchester Magistrates? Had it been

[1] *Bolton Chronicle*, 7 March 1829.

predicted by some gifted seer, on the 16th of August, 1819, that this man, in less than ten years, would appear foremost in the ranks of disaffection, would accuse the members of the administration of betraying the rights of the people, and would even employ menacing language to defer them from carrying their measures into execution, who would have given credit to the prophet? Yet, incredible as it must have appeared, it has actually come to pass; that Hulton of Hulton, who acted a most conspicuous part in St. Peter's Square, Manchester, on the 16th of August, 1819, he who was the *nominal*, if not the *real* commander on that day, and who with his colleagues received the thanks of the then existing administration for his services against the people, now calls upon that same people to oppose the existing government, holds up its members to scorn and contempt, and hurls at them his bold defiance.

Impudence and self-ignorance must have successfully conspired to enable such a man to censure others for *changing their principles* and *shifting their ground*. He and some others have good reason to be thankful that the seditious drivelling of persons like themselves, can be indulged with greater impunity under a strong and liberal, than under a weak and bigoted minister. If the temper of the present Premier were like that of certain ministers whose willing agents have been formerly found at Hulton Park and at The Hollins[1] the proprietors of those places would soon find themselves accommodated with a more circumscribed abode. [Hulton is alleged to have said: 'We all know how difficult it is to unclench the fixed fist of infancy; let this Government pause before they dare to throw into a posture of defence, the athletic, the gigantic strength of English men.']

If those Gentlemen will take the trouble to look back a few years they will find that people have been hanged for words not so seditious as those. Fortunately for Mr. Hulton and his friends, English *men* are not disposed to listen to them, otherwise they might chance to attain an elevation to which the most ambitious seldom aspire. The manly strength, the mind, the sterling principle of the country is against them. They perhaps may make something of the infant race. They may possibly succeed in engaging on their side the 'fists of infancy', as it is well known that the extended fingers of a goodly number, armed with a goose-quill, have already fought for them . . . Where can there be found a greater contrast than that between the Hero of Peterloo, Manchester, in 1819, and the Orator of the Bridge Inn, Bolton, in 1829, the staunch supporter of the powers that be, converted into the champion of disaffection, sedition and rebellion! . . . &c.

[1] The residence of Col. Fletcher, of Bolton.

XXVII

Hunt and Prentice return to the Attack

In the year 1830, as if in anticipation of the coming Huntean campaign to re-establish the 'facts' of Peterloo, Archibald Prentice, late writer of the *Manchester Gazette*, and now editor of the *Manchester Times* which he later owned, began his campaign with apparently the same ends in view. Prentice by his insinuations, half-truths, and suppressions was eminently successful: it was the success of 'reasoned' argument, to be embodied in his *Recollections* of 1851. In 1830 he had constantly, by insinuation, put forward the 'truths' of Peterloo. It did not pass unnoticed by his readers, and a correspondent wrote:[1]

In your comments on Mr. H. H. Birley's motion at the Town's Meeting last Thursday, you take occasion to mention that he was the commander of the Yeomanry in 1819. Now, Sir, permit me to put it to you, if you think it fair to lug in a man's former misdeeds upon every occasion when he happens to differ from you?—A Friend of Fair Play.

Prentice answered his correspondent by asking other questions:

Has Mr. Birley ever felt or expressed any contrition for his conduct on the 16th of August, 1819? Has he ever since done one public act to entitle him to especial forbearance? . . .

The *Manchester Times* kept it up. On the occasion of the opening of the Manchester and Liverpool Railway in September, 1830, the Duke of Wellington visited Manchester, and stayed at Heaton Park; he paid visits to local cotton mills, including the famous Sharpe's mill. His next visit, the *Times* report went on:

was to the fortified factory owned by ex-Major Birley, whose deeds of valour on the bloody 16th of August, have immortalized his name. The factory is situated on the banks of the nasty, inky stream, called the river Medlock. What induced the Duke and his retinue to visit this place in preference to factories of far greater importance in the town has puzzled the heads of many of the good people of Manchester, but ultimately they came to

[1] *Manchester Times*, 10 July.

a conclusion that the preference was given to the Major solely because 'he was famed for deeds of arms'. [And in a leader in the same issue (September 18th)]: It is to be regretted that, out of all the factories in Manchester, he should visit one whose owner is stained with the recollections of the 16th of August, 1819, when the Yeomanry under his command cut down the people when peaceably and legally assembled.

Which was about as waspish as it was possible to make it. The return of Henry Hunt to Manchester on 16 August 1830, and the events which were to follow provided Prentice with his real chance of propagating his version of Peterloo which was to be handed down to succeeding generations. 'For some time after his release' (from Ilchester Gaol), says the D.N.B. biographer of Hunt,[1] 'Hunt was comparatively inactive. He contested Somersetshire in 1826, but it was a candidature of protestation only. In August, 1830, he contested Preston, which he had also previously contested in 1820, on Stanley's appointment as chief secretary, and was at the bottom of the poll . . .'. If Henry Hunt needed any solace for his defeat at Preston he received it on the anniversary (to the day) of Monday the 16 of August. Prentice gave the event full measure both before the day and after:

Eleven years ago, in this town, [reported the *Manchester Times*, 14th August, 1830] a meeting, peaceably assembled for the exercise of a constitutional right, was attacked by the military and 11 persons were killed and upwards of 600 wounded. The principal actors in that tragedy were never brought to justice; but, on the contrary, received the thanks of his late Majesty. The person who was to have presided was brought to trial, and having been found guilty of being present at the meeting, was sentenced to an imprisonment of two years and a half, which dreadful sentence was most mercilessly put into execution. How vain was the effort made to extinguish the cry for reform, will be proved on Monday next, when probably 50,000 persons will congregate on the field where that tragedy was enacted, to hear that very person relate the story of his sufferings, and address them probably in the very language he intended to use when he was interrupted by the sabres of the Yeomanry.

Prentice had forgotten, as Hunt was to forget, that there were others who suffered imprisonment as well.

We are not Cobbettites or Huntites. We have no political leader. We acknowledge discipleship to no man. But we are advocates for reform on the broadest basis, and as reformers we are glad to witness a public and unequivocal expression of the opinions which we know to be universally, though somewhat too silently entertained. Mr. Hunt has been a sufferer in

[1] D.N.B., Vol. X, p. 265.

11. Archibald Prentice

the cause of reform; while enduring an imprisonment which would have destroyed the energies of most men, he brought to light the iniquities of his jailer, and caused the jail itself to be razed to the ground; he has since most ably exposed the profligacy of the London Corporation, and has been a firm and consistent reformer. Who is there, therefore, amongst us *now* in these days of universal suffering from misgovernment who will grudge him the triumph prepared for him, or attempt to repress in the slightest degree that cry for reform to which, if the national safety be regarded, government must ultimately listen?[1]

On Monday last, [the issue of August 21st reported] the 11th anniversary of the attack of the military on a peaceable meeting, was celebrated in this town by the public entry, and entertainment at dinner of the gentleman who was to have presided on that fatal day, About 8 o'clock in the morning, a barouche and four horses with postilions, left this town for the purpose of bringing Mr. Hunt from Bolton. On their arrival at the latter town they found in front of the Swan Hotel a great concourse of people assembled, which continued to increase till the number could not be less than six or seven thousand. A little before 11 o'clock Mr. Hunt appeared on the terrace in front of the hotel, and was hailed with loud and continuous shouts of applause. As soon as the acclamations had ceased, he commenced his farewell address, which was delivered with much effect and no little humour, and if we may judge from the repeated plaudits bestowed upon him during the delivery of it, it was gratifying to the assembled multitude. In a very concise and impressive manner he recounted the sufferings he had undergone through attending the Manchester Meeting on the 16th of August, 1819, and drew a contrast between the opinions and the conduct of certain persons at that time and in the present year, 1830. He ironically recounted the exploits of Mr. Hulton of Hulton, whom he designated Miss Polly Hulton. Col. Fletcher, also came in for a portion of Mr. Hunt's biting sarcasm. He adverted to the black-faced spy system, formerly practised in Bolton and its neighbourhood, for the purpose of entrapping the reformers of that day which, he said, was now totally exploded. He lashed the electors of Preston for their veniality in selling their birthright for pots of brewers' poisoned, stinking porter, gin, or brandy, and concluded by a eulogium on the warm-hearted people of Bolton, who, he said, had always treated him in the most honourable manner. Mr. Hunt also informed them that he had been told that the whole of the military and police force had been drawn out for the purpose of doing him honour when he arrived at Manchester, and took his leave of them for the present by expressing his warmest thanks to the whole of the people of Bolton. During the delivery of his address, and at its conclusion, the people rent the air with shouts of applause. Mr. Hunt and his friends then entered the landau, and it now being about 11 o'clock, the horses were put to their mettle, in order to reach Manchester, by the time appointed.

[1] *Manchester Times*, 14 August, 1830.

At Irlams-o' th-Height, another landau, filled with members of the committee and 'gentlemen of the press' met and then followed Mr. Hunt's barouche till they arrived at Pendleton, where they found a great multitude of people assembled, who received them with shouts of 'Hunt for Ever'— 'Hunt and Liberty'. A band of music was also waiting, who placed themselves in advance of Mr. Hunt's barouche, and the people having formed themselves into procession, the band struck up 'See the Conquering Hero Comes', and proceeded on their way towards Manchester. At every step the crowd continued to increase; the windows of the houses were filled with people, and even the tops of the houses were occupied by those of a more adventurous disposition.

By the time the procession had reached Salford, it appeared in the distance as an innumerable moving mass of living beings. The procession moved at a slow but steady pace till it arrived opposite the New Bayley, when the band struck up the national anthem of 'God Save the King' and the people at the same time gave three hearty cheers. The procession, after passing over New Bayley Bridge, turned up Gartside Street, and Quay Street. On the first entrance of the procession into Manchester, four carriages, filled with friends to Mr. Hunt, joined in the procession. Many persons, from timidity, were deterred from adding to the train, for although eleven years have passed since the fatal 16th of August, 1819, they have yet not forgotten the dreadful scenes of that day, and not knowing whether similar measures would again be resorted to, they thought it prudent not to join in the procession till it had passed that part of Salford where it had been industriously circulated that the procession would be opposed at its entrance to the town.

It perhaps may be as well to state here, [Prentice's report gravely went on] that the cause of this expected opposition arose from its being well known that the whole of the military force in the town, amounting to about 600 horse and foot, were ordered to be under arms at an early hour in the morning. The whole of the *posse comitatus* were also ordered to be out upon duty, of course, to be ready to act if their services should be found necessary. Exaggerated statements had also been buzzed about, in the different inns, taverns, and public houses, and many were the opinions as to how the authorities would act on this occasion. The strange and improbable stories circulated, kept women and children in their houses. When the procession arrived in Peter Street, and near to the field of blood, the whole multitude halted. Mr. Hunt requested the men to take off their hats—the band commenced playing the 'Dead March in Saul', and the carriages were slowly drawn, as close as possible to the place where the hustings stood on that never-to-be-forgotten day, when numbers of our townsmen were killed and hundreds wounded, for peaceably assembling to exercise their constitutional right of petitioning parliament for a redress of the manifold grievances which were pressing them to the earth.

The crowd was so dense, that although the plain of 'Peterloo' and its immediate vicinity, will contain upwards of 100,000 people, it was with great difficulty, and a lapse of some time before the carriages could be got through the mass of people which crowded around them to their place of destination. The sight was imposing in the highest degree, the area being nearly filled, and the houses that surrounded the whole of the plain, crowded to excess, and the house-tops and even the chimney-tops, covered with persons anxious to obtain a view of the proceedings of the day. We are sometimes accustomed to the estimation of numbers, and should think that between 30,000 and 40,000 were assembled on the present occasion.

Mr. Hunt, when all was ready, waved his hand and silence was obtained, all being anxious to hear every word uttered by the man who had suffered so much for attending the call of the radical reformers in the year 1819. The following is the substance of Mr. Hunt's address on this memorable day:

Gentlemen: The last time I had the honour to meet you in this field of blood was eleven years ago this day. We met for the purpose of offering up our prayers and petitions to parliament for a repeal of the corn laws, and a reform in the Commons House of Parliament. We were peaceably and legally assembled to perform a constitutional duty when we were attacked by bands of drunken yeomanry, who rushed among the unarmed multitude, of whom 14 were killed and 618 badly wounded. (Cries of shame, shame.) This was the way in which our prayers were answered. You have again honoured me by inviting me to Manchester, not for the purpose of merely paying a compliment to me, but to show to the tyrants of 1819 that the people, the reformers of Manchester, are not to be put down in 1830. (Loud and continued cheering). I am delighted to see you assembled on this occasion, and am extremely gratified at the honour you have done me to see you performing your duty to yourself and to your country this day.

You have met not only for the purpose of paying me a compliment but also to remind those who wish to oppress the people that your cause is the cause of truth, justice, and liberty, and that the bayonets of all the tyrants on earth cannot obliterate this cause from your breasts. (Loud cheers.) Gentlemen, although you have not seen me for eleven years past you have heard of me; but did you ever hear of me neglecting my duty, or being an idler in the cause of reform? (Cries of No, no.) Even when in gaol did you ever hear of me deserting my colours? (No, no, from all parts of the crowd.) The deputy-Boroughreeve, I think, they call him, sent out to me at Pendleton to say that 600 soldiers were awaiting my arrival at Manchester, but I was not to be turned back by such trumpery. (Cheers and laughter). I wish our fellow-citizens the soldiers and their officers were present, and could hear every word I have to say. I never said anything in private that I was ashamed to utter in the face of the whole world. My answer to the statement relative to the soldiers being awaiting me, was this. If the military be there and act as they did eleven years ago, I believe the people will act differently to what they did then. (Great cheering, and cries of 'We would'.) Many of you may be able to recollect that when we assembled here in 1819, the magistrates were assembled in that house, (pointing to the house formerly occupied by Mr. Buxton), and when the drunken yeomanry came galloping down by that corner, they were ordered by Miss Hulton to charge the people. I understand that it is now said that this was a mistake! (Laughter.) It seems that Miss Hulton was at that time troubled with a bowel complaint, and that in her agony she cried out 'Charge!' instead of 'Halt!' (Much laughter). Gentlemen, we were told by a Manchester newspaper, by the *Manchester Times*, of Saturday last, that most probably fifty thousand persons would be assembled here to-day, to hear me recount the tale of my sufferings. Why, Gentlemen, there are one hundred thousand persons on this ground at the present time. (Much cheering). It is a most glorious sight to me, to perceive that the people of Manchester are just and honest to themselves. (Cheers). We have not forgotten what took place eleven years ago, and I hope we shall never forget it, and till we have justice done, never forgive it. (Cheers). They kept it fresh in my memory after you saw me last. While they were taking me into that house, I saw, as I passed, several dead bodies of men and women. (Cries of shame, shame.) One woman had her breast cut off. I heard the shrieks and the groans of the dying and the wounded. (Groans and cries of shame).

I was conducted by two men, Andrews and Nadin, across this field. On a sudden I found that Andrews let me go, and fled, and on turning round to ascertain the cause? I saw two drunken Yeomen coming up. They made a sign to my conductors to retire and leave me to be cut to pieces. But I stuck to Nadin as my shield and buckler. (A laugh). When the Yeomanry came up, instead of his keeping me in custody, I kept him in custody—(laughter)—and I took care to turn him to the front of the battle. (Continued laughter). They reached over his head and cut my hat; and my hand was also slightly cut. They then wheeled round and came again; but I wheeled round also, and still presented Nadin in front. (Laughter).

When I got to the door I found my hat thrust off; I put my head on one side, and instantly there came upon my shoulder a blow from a bludgeon, which would have murdered me if it had come upon my bare head. Who was it that made this attack, do you think? A commanding major-general of the name of Clay.

Hunt's physical dexterity in thus 'using' Nadin as a shield for himself is almost equal to his dexterity in narrative. He had told the court[1] that he had been 'pinioned down, dragged along,' and before that 'seized by the military'; and 'at the moment when his arms were pinioned to his sides, a major-general had struck him from behind . . . His memory of his 'use' of Nadin, as related above, failed to mention that he had earlier said that 'he freely confessed that he owed his life upon that occasion to Nadin'.

[1] See above, p. 357.

When I got into the room I found Miss Hulton, Parsons Hay and Ethelston, and a few others, and shall never forget how Miss Hulton's teeth chattered in her head, and her knees knocked together.

Prentice is not completely candid on this part of Hunt's speech. The radical *Bolton Chronicle* (24 August) gave the passage thus:

. . . I shall never forget the figure that Hulton cut on that occasion; he had witnessed the slaughtered effects of his 'charge'; he had heard the shrieks and groans of the defenceless creatures, and, hardened as he is, his knees smote together, his teeth chattered in his head, and his whole frame shook like an aspen leaf. (Cries of 'That's right, Hunt, give it to them!')

I was taken to the New Bayley, [went on Prentice's report] and placed for eleven days and eleven nights in solitary confinement, and on a charge of high treason. (At this part of Mr. Hunt's speech the band, which had retired to one of the back streets, commenced playing, which rather alarmed a few women and boys at the outskirts of the meeting, who, fearing a renewal of the scenes of 1819, began to retire; but the men, who seemed to have made up their minds for the worst, called out 'Stand firm', and confidence was soon restored. Mr. Hunt then proceeded.) At the end of eleven days I was sent to Lancaster Castle and after being kept there a day and a night was sent back to Manchester. I was afterwards tried at York for attending this meeting, and there I found a whole host of Crown lawyers were arrayed against me. I stood a trial of fourteen days, and they found me guilty of attending this meeting. When we went to Lancaster, bills of indictment were preferred before the grand jury, of which Lord Stanley was foreman, against those who had attacked us, but they were all thrown out; but as soon as bills were preferred against me and others, they found true bills against us, and we were tried at York. I was brought up next spring for judgment as they called it, and was sentenced to two years and six months' imprisonment; three parts of the time was in solitary confinement in a damp and unwholesome dungeon. While I was there you never heard me begging and praying for my liberty, but doing all I could, though I was under the lock and key of the gaoler, to assist my fellow-countrymen in recovering their lost rights . . . (His efforts in Ilchester; gaol razed to the ground.) . . . (The rights of working men &c.)

Mr. Hunt then alluded to the deaths of Lord Castlereagh, Lord Liverpool, Roger Entwistle, and George Torr, three of whom, it will be recollected, destroyed themselves. When I had Polly Hulton in the witness-box at York I twisted her in such a manner that the other magistrates who should have supported her, scampered off in every direction, and left the young lady to her fate. (Loud laughter). Roger Entwistle, a hard-swearing attorney came to the assistance of Miss Hulton and swore . . . but he swore so hard and so falsely that he cut his throat. The deaths of these individuals he attributed to remorse of conscience for the part they had taken relative to the eventful 16th of

August, 1819. He alluded to the thanks of the late King to the perpetrators of these outrages. He also was gone, he said, to give an account of what he had done in the world; but God's will be done. He (Mr. Hunt) was, however, spared, and he trusted he should be spared for some years to come, as he felt —though he was fifty-seven years of age—that he had many a tough years' work in him yet. Mr. Hunt also adverted to the recent transactions in France, which he characterised as of the most glorious description, and drew a contrast between the natural habits of the French working community and the English, much to the disadvantage of the latter, as to their habits of temperance . . .

Henry Hunt was perhaps a little misled by the apparently rapturous reception in St Peter's Field accorded to the vivid recital of his sufferings. In the evening he attended a dinner given in his honour in Salford, and in his speech enlarged on the happenings in the recent revolution in France, and eulogized Tom Paine and all his works. Prentice rose to protest against Paine's theological works, although agreeing with him politically. Hunt referred to Prentice's remarks as a rap on his (Hunt's) knuckles. He returned to a safer topic: the happenings on St Peter's Field 'to-day and eleven years ago'—the 'drunken and infuriated yeomanry'. He had received a 'warning' from the Boroughreeve at Pendleton to-day:

I do not believe [Hunt said] that they (the military) were prepared to play the bloody tragedy which they played before, but if they were prepared to do so, and my life were to be the sacrifice, I am convinced that good would result to my country from the reaction that would take place. God knows that I do not court danger, or possess a superior courage to other men, but when I have once formed a purpose, all the bayonets and cannon on earth would not deter me. (Cheers). Though I believe the minds of the people are in a state of thraldom, I observed that the men only assembled to-day—the women stood aloof; and my honest conviction is that if one drop of blood had been spilled this day, great would have been the retaliation. (Loud cheers). But I think those day are gone by, and from the example set in France, it will be long before the troops are called out again to put them to the sword, as was done on the 16th of August, 1819.

Hunt re-told the scenes of his arrest, and made at that point the attack on Joseph Johnson's double-dealing in the matter of delivering up to the authorities his correspondence.[1] He harked back to the impressive sight on Peterloo 'to-day'. He 'did not despair of yet seeing ample justice done to the authors of the cruelties of 1819. Whether Englishmen were prepared to act as the French had done he knew not.' Hunt

[1] See above, pp. 254–56.

was on fairly safe ground in referring generally to the example of the French. A Manchester reform meeting had been held which had been addressed by many of the middle-class reformers, including Archibald Prentice, J. E. Taylor, Richard Potter, George Hadfield, Mark Philips, and John Shuttleworth; speech after speech had commended the French action and condemned 'Pittism.' One speaker at that meeting had observed that 'something like (the scenes at Paris) had taken place almost in our time at Bunker's Hill.' A voice had shouted: 'Aye, and at Peterloo!' but the point was not taken up. Henry Hunt's view on the French question however, was not quite the same as that of the Manchester reformers': he adverted to the French Sunday—the women at Mass and the men enjoying themselves, which was contrasted with the English outward show of religion; Hunt was back on Paine and his theological works. Prentice was on his feet calling attention to 'the sober-thinking chapel-goers of Manchester—determined reformers'. Hunt refused to answer Prentice's arguments, and to silence him called for a toast to Daniel O'Connell and the Reformers of Ireland. At this point, Prentice's report went on:

John Doherty jumped on the table and addressed Hunt: 'Is this the way, Mr. Hunt, you intend to proceed? Are we to be dragooned into a compliance with your will, and have toasts crammed down our throats whether we will or not? I can only say if this be the way in which you mean to prove your advocacy of the great cause of reform, the sooner you return to London the better!' (Mr. Hunt, however, held out is hand to Mr. Prentice and the meeting broke up).

It was not a very auspicious ending to an otherwise triumphant day. Prentice's leader said:

. . . Manchester had done honour to Hunt for his late labours. They have done justice to a confessedly brave and consistent man, and they have done justice to themselves and to the great cause they support, by refusing to follow even the most popular leader one inch beyond the strict line of propriety.

Hunt's Preston election victory in December, 1830 is a story in itself:

More serious to the Government, (says Butler in *The Passing of the Great Reform Bill* 156] . . . was the actual defeat of Stanley at Preston, by Orator Hunt, whose tumultuous advocacy of the ballot and Radical Reform for once overshadowed the strong Derby interest. Had the result been otherwise, serious rioting was apprehended; Stanley wisely decided not to provoke it by insisting on a scrutiny. Hunt's triumph was a new departure in working-class politics. [And Butler quotes Trevelyan's *John Bright* p. 18, for the delight caused at Rochdale by the victory.]

Delight was apparent not only at Rochdale. Hunt celebrated at Bolton during the campaign; he harangued crowds on reform and other matters:

. . . [Re their opponents at Peterloo] Some had cut their throats; some had gone mad, and some had died in gaol, or drunk themselves to death. Upon some of the magistrates the Finger of God has fallen. There is Ethelston a drivelling idiot.* Hulton is still alive. He has, at a Pitt dinner in this town, some time since, said in returning thanks for his health being drunk, that the 16th of August, 1819, when 14 persons were murdered and 618 wounded; yes, he said, 'that was the proudest day in his life'. (Shame, shame). He (Mr. Hunt) hoped that this Hulton was within hearing, and that he might make him hide his head for shame. The proudest day in his life, indeed! The proudest day of my life, said Mr. Hunt, was the day I had him in the witness-box at York, when after a cross-examination of several hours which I inflicted upon him, I convinced both the Judge and jury that he had perjured himself. Does he, asked Mr. Hunt, still live near this town? If he does it is a disgrace, and, if there had been the same law in the country for poor as there is for rich, the authors of the Manchester Massacre would have been tried and executed years ago.[1]

Later in the day, sixty-four of Mr Hunt's friends sat down to dinner with him. A discussion arose, reported the *Bolton Chronicle*,[2] on the possibility of Mr Hulton being returned for the town of Bolton in case the elective franchise were transferred to the town:

. . . Mr. Hunt and others contended that it would be an eternal disgrace to Bolton [locals admitted it would be disgraceful, but if the £20 assessments remained as the qualification it was likely] . . . The majority of the persons in the room, however, were decidedly of opinion, that sooner than return any man who was connected with the Manchester Massacre, the town would be laid in ashes. Mr. Pearson was asked if he would stand (he believed he would be a candidate for London). Yet, if Mr. Hulton dared to make an attempt to be the representative of Bolton, he would pledge himself that he would come down, and on the hustings throw in his teeth the ghosts of his murdered and sabred countrymen at Peterloo. (Tremendous cheering). Mr. Pearson gave a description of Hunt's cross-examination at York, and concluded by solemnly affirming, that when Mr. Hunt put the question to Hulton whether he could distinguish which row of people were linked in the court, he declared that he could not. Such was the effect upon every

---

[1] *Bolton Chronicle*, 21 December 1830.   *Ethelston had died three months before.

[2] *Bolton Chronicle*, 21 December 1830.

person present that the magistrates came running from the room where they had been sitting, eagerly asking what was the matter.

What, it might be thought, was William Hulton's reaction to this persistent reiteration of these 'exploded facts'? It can only be surmised that he shrugged them off as hardly worth noticing. He certainly made no attempt to answer them. At the Bolton Petty Sessions on January 10 1831, about three weeks after Hunt's visit to Bolton, Hulton was hearing a case of a beer-house licensee serving beer after hours. A witness said he remembered the day well—it was the day Hunt passed through Bolton. 'That circumstance,' said Mr Hulton, 'made a deep impression on you!' No person, the licensee said, had ale that night after ten o'clock . . . 'What! was there not,' asked Mr Hulton, 'a drop of ale extra filled on the joyous occasion of Mr Hunt passing through the town?' Witness; 'No, not a drop . . .'[1]

Hunt's Preston victory was made an occasion for the reaffirmation of his Peterloo 'case'. He rode through Preston at a victory parade on 27 December. Prentice, in the *Manchester Times*[2] gave Hunt's victory lavish space. Charles Pearson, at a celebration dinner that night, named Hunt as 'the same man when the bloody sabre waved o'er his head at Peterloo as they had seen that day reining in his charger when riding through the town of Preston'. Hunt retold his sufferings in Preston; he retold them at Blackburn next day: he trusted there was now some hope of bringing the 'bloody butchers of Manchester to justice. If there had been any law or justice in the country, Hulton of Hulton Park, Parson Hay, and the whole set would have been tried for murder years ago.' His triumphal progress took him to Oldham; and on 8 January 1831, to Manchester where another massive (35,000 strong) demonstration was held on St Peter's Field. The radical version of Peterloo really was in the making:

He now stood on the spot where he had seen the lives of their dear brethren sacrificed by the drunken yeomanry, and he should now make another solemn pledge, that while he had life, and health and strength, he would never cease his exertions, to obtain a full investigation into that tragedy, and bring to justice the perpetrators of the beastly and horrible work. (Tremendous cheering.) Some of the guilty actors in that scene were dead and gone; but he called on the men of Manchester to come forward and aid him in bringing to justice those who remained. The almighty power in the exercise of the supreme law of heaven had already executed justice upon a part of them. It was for us to call for justice on those who remain. (Loud cries of 'We

---

[1] *Bolton Chronicle*, 15 January 1831.
[2] *Manchester Times*, 1 January 1831.

will have it!') He was delighted to observe the change which had taken place in public opinion since that dreadful day. Where were now the proud, haughty, and ignorant magistrates? Where were now the beastly drunken yeomanry? Where were the long lines of hot-headed constables, armed with their bludgeons and ready to break the peace they were sworn to preserve? Thank heaven the time had come when such persons had arrived at the conviction that the people could take care of themselves.

But the change of opinion was nothing, unless it led to justice on the perpetrators of the evil, and if heaven gave him health and strength he would, in his place in Parliament, give such a description of the deeds of the 16th of August, as would make even the unfeeling hearts around him recoil with horror. He would make their coward souls tremble at the sound of the groans of the men, the shrieks of the women, that fell on that terrible day. It should not be his fault if every unfeeling monster of the crew were not brought to condign punishment. (Loud cheers.) In Parliament he should speak to millions instead of thousands, and he would speak to those millions in a language they understood of the wrongs and oppressions they had endured . . . Hunt asked for cheers which might be heard by Parson Hay at Rochdale.

Again there was a public dinner in Hunt's honour. He claimed that becoming an M.P. had worked wonders: John Edward Taylor in the *Guardian* had referred to him as 'that gentleman'. He asked for petitions on Peterloo. He would have, he said, a petition from Mosley Street, one from Market Street, and one from every street in the town, and if these were not sufficient, he would have a petition from every house in the town to inquire into the affairs of the 16 August. He should also move for a 'return of the names of those actors on that occasion who still survived not having cut their throats . . .' He should like to have one or more petitions to present on the first night he took his seat in the House of Commons. A sequel to Hunt's appeal was that meetings were called in some parts of the town to prepare petitions. Henry Hunt on the first day of his Parliamentary career was indeed presenting petitions: his first was one from Somersetshire for the commutation of tithes, &c.; one from Manchester for the repeal of the Corn Laws and for reform; and he gave notice of his intention to question affairs in Ireland. There were one or two more Huntean touches before the Manchester dinner-party broke up:

. . . If Mr. Birley was at home when the procession on that day had passed his house, the roars and groans of the people he was sure would have made his teeth chatter in his head—for these men were like crows, they smelled powder at a great distance. (Applause). He had been informed that a parson magistrate on his last visit to Manchester was riding within the sounds of the shouts of the people, and that those shouts had such an effect upon him, that he went home immediately and had an apoplectic fit in consequence of the horror with which he was seized—and this (said Mr. Hunt) was only a just judgment on that man. As for Miss Hulton and the others whom he had almost forgotten, he must trust to the people of Lancashire to furnish him with a correct list, both of their names and of their worthy deeds. (Cries of you shall have one.)

Up to this time, the early months of 1831, Henry Hunt's almost raving speeches seem to have been received in Manchester with no small amount of tolerance, as aberrations which were temporary. That time was rapidly passing.

Early in the year Hulton was to be the cause of another sensation, although, in this case, none of his own making. A paragraph appeared in the *Bolton Chronicle* (14 March) during the Parliamentary debates on the first Reform Bill:

We are informed by a correspondent that in the event of the new Reform Bill being carried, William Hulton Esq., of Hulton Park, will be invited to stand as one of the additional county members, and that it is probable that he will accept the invitation. [And another paragraph on April 2nd] A requisition has been prepared, and is now receiving the signatures of highly respectable and influential individuals in the Salford Hundred soliciting William Hulton . . . in the event of the Ministerial plan of Reform being carried into effect, to become a candidate for the representation in Parliament of the county of Lancaster.

To many it might have seemed a not unnatural sequence to the widely-signed invitation Hulton had received some years earlier. It produced a sniff from John Edward Taylor in the *Guardian*: 'We should suspect Mr Hulton has just as rational a chance of becoming Khan of Tartary, as member for the county of Lancaster.' And a snort from Archibald Prentice: 'It is not probable that he will be returned. What a beautiful use of reform it would be to send to parliament one of the magistrates who directed the people to be cut down in 1819!'[1] There was, however, another reaction. Henry Hunt, on his way from Preston to Manchester in the first week in April, called at Bolton. He was in dispute with the then editor of the *Bolton Chronicle* on an alleged libellous reporting of his speeches; he addressed the crowds gathered before the Swan Hotel on his opposition to the Reform Bill then being debated. The *Chronicle*[2] reported:

. . . If the Reform Bill take place, [Hunt cried to the crowd], who will put

[1] *Manchester Times,* 2 April, 1831.
[2] *Bolton Chronicle,* 9 April, 1831.

up for the county? (Cries of Hulton, Hulton.) What! Miss Hulton! O! What a disgrace! I understand he is canvassing for the county? . . . (Cries of yes, yes.) What! the man who sat at the head of the magistrates, when a drunken and infuriated yeomanry sabred an unarmed multitude . . . petitioning for Reform? If such a man as that is to be elected to represent this county, it is high time for me to go out of the world! If he dare to show his face, and make such an attempt, I hope that you, the people, will set at him, after the manner of a bull-dog when set on to worry a cat; and that they would drive him completely out of the country. (Loud cheers). If Lancashire sent up this man, all the rest of the country would cry Shame upon it. The ghosts of the men who were murdered, and the blood which was spilt at Peterloo, would rise up in judgment against them; and I hope to have him tried at the bar for his life, for those bloody murders . . .'

Hunt then went on to Manchester, where he addressed (according to the *Manchester Times*) a crowd of 65,000 people on St Peter's Field. It is hardly necessary to give his speech. Manchester's reactions, as voiced in its press leading articles are enough; first *Wheeler's Manchester Chronicle*:

(April 9th) The town has undergone another visitation from Mr. Henry Hunt, the member for Preston. What his real object was in honouring Manchester with his presence it would not be difficult to conjecture; his ostensible design was to rehearse his 'sayings and doings' in the House of Commons, to talk with becoming modesty on his own patriotism, and to reiterate the silly demand for radical nostrums—annual parliaments, universal suffrage, and vote by ballot. We are not aware how much good Mr. Hunt effected by his heterogeneous oration; but we believe that he added to the evils of the Easter fair by keeping thousands of men out of work a whole day when they might have been profitably employed.

We would not unjustly charge even Mr. Hunt with an attempt to create tumult; but we would ask what design could he or his partizans have in exhibiting a black-bordered flag bearing the inscription, 'Murder demands Justice'? Mr. Hunt is a member of the British Senate, and his voice has been raised, though without effect, on the subject of the unhappy affair in August, 1819. Because the House of Commons has refused to listen to demands which would at once be silenced by every man of sense and integrity in the country, did he mean, as a *dernier resort*, to appeal to the tender mercy of the mobocracy of St. Peter's Field? With smooth, oily professions of peace and tranquility upon his lips, he adopted the language of the incendiary and bravo, and presented to the minds of his auditory the revolting picture of the town of Manchester in flames, and half of the inhabitants brutally murdered for the accomplishment of a political object!

The tenour of Mr. Hunt's conduct, in and out of Parliament, proves him to be nothing better than an ignorant and hollow empiric; but his disgusting language on St. Peter's Field on Thursday shows that he is a much worse character. His self-complacency and silly egotism can have no other effect than to excite the smile of derision or contempt; but his profligate demands for conflagration and human butchery ought and will be execrated by every man of right principles in the kingdom.

He may call himself a law-maker if he pleases; but in public opinion he will probably be considered a law-breaker—a breaker of general peace and order—a violator of decency and justice. Is incitement to incendiarism and murder the language of Englishmen? Are the temperate reason and manly courage of the people of this country to give place to infuriate passion and unrestrained, atrocious deeds of blood? If Mr. Hunt will exhibit himself publicly in Manchester—if he will use his mob popularity to collect together multitudes to whose comforts he never was disposed to contribute a farthing, let him restrain his licentiousness of speech, and teach his hearers that which may prove useful and beneficial to them. It can never, however, be forgotten, that he has again thrown down the lighted torch, and that if the people had been as inflammatory as himself, a scene of horror would have been witnessed, at the contemplation of which the heart sickens.

Mr. Hunt's *farrago libelli* on Mr. Hugh Birley in Manchester, and on Mr. Hulton in Bolton, can excite only one feeling in the district. His bitter attempts to persecute them will excite no astonishment when it is remembered that they were justified in the eyes of the law for their conduct on the memorable 16th of August, and that Mr. Hunt was brought to deserved punishment. Mr. Hunt may console himself with the reflection, that his wrath and malignancy are feeble weapons against those gentlemen; for in spite of his speeches they will still be honoured and respected.

The *Chronicle's* leader was a pretty scathing castigation. Hunt's speech at Bolton justified it. In Manchester, too, on St Peter's Field, he had made his usual references to the drunken yeomanry with newly-sharpened sabres murdering the people. Hunt had, he said, told the members of the House of Commons that they had so murdered:

He indulged, [went on *Wheeler's Chronicle* report] in some fierce language against Major Hugh Birley, for his conduct in 1819, and asked whether the great people of Manchester were going to send the nasty butcher of Peterloo among them again? [in the House of Commons]. No, no my good friends, said he, though you are not ten-pounders, you'll take care of that. Rather than submit to that [continued Hunt] if I were a Manchester man, I would lay half Manchester in ashes. He strongly recommended the inhabitants of Wigan to return Mr. Richard Potter at the next election for that borough, and said every Manchester man between 15 and 45 should march over to Wigan with him, and should take care that those who would not vote for him should not vote at all . . .

The *Chronicle* newspaper in 1831 was a supporter of the Ministry's plans for Reform, and backed Benjamin Heywood, the Reform member for Lancashire. The *Guardian* (9 April) was even more scathing:

We have thought proper to give, though it is with disgust and loathing that we have read it, a report of the speech of Mr. Henry Hunt, M.P. for Preston, addressed to an immense mob whom he took the trouble to congregate at St. Peter's Field in this town on Thursday last. Mr. Hunt on this occasion demeaned and expressed himself in a manner, which it would be charitable to consider as arising from drunkenness or madness; we fear, however, that neither of these excuses can be available for him, and that his language, instead of being accounted for only by the supposition that there exists in his char- acter a concentration of malignity and wickedness, such as few persons are cursed by.

In one or two respects, we are not sorry for Mr. Hunt's exhibition of him- self. Our readers now have an opportunity of judging (if any of them have previously doubted), what this man really is. There is no occasion here to do more than to allude to his atrocious statement of the destruction and blood- shed, which, 'were he a Manchester man,' he would produce rather than Mr. Birley should be returned to Parliament for this town.

With respect to his advice to his auditors, that they should, twenty or thirty thousand strong, go over to Wigan at the next election, and exercise 'a constitutional influence!' over the electors, by *nearly pulling their arms off*, if they would not vote for Mr. Richard Potter—advice which must be a *deliberate* incitement for ruffian violence, because it had previously been ten- dered to his Bolton auditors also; it is in beautiful consistency with his loud outcry for the ballot, in order that electors may be enabled to give their suffrages independently. Mr. Potter will surely shrink with disgust from having his claims advocated by such a person as Mr. Hunt, in such a manner as he adopts.

As to Mr. Hunt's story about Sir Charleṣ Wolseley's having been author- ized by the Whigs, when he came out of Ilchester Gaol, to offer that they would subscribe £12,000 for him and put him into Parliament, if he would join their party, we have not the slightest doubt that every word of it is utterly false.

Hunt's attacks on Birley and Hulton, and his scorn for the Whigs, were not the main burden of his speeches or diatribes at that time. He was running a rip-roaring campaign through Lancashire, Yorkshire and Cheshire towns against the Ministry's plans for reform, with a view to convincing his hearers that the Ministry's reform did not go far enough. That explains the *Chronicle's* dismissal as 'nostrums'—annual parliaments, universal suffrage, and vote by ballot, as well as the *Guardian's* dismissal of 'the ballot'. All were then believed to be almost utopian—as indeed they were, belonging to the future. Hunt, as events have turned out, was something of a prophet, but in 1831 a prophet crying in the wilderness.[1] He still maintained most vehemently, in his Preston election literature in the later months of 1831, that the whole of the northern towns were with him. The *Guardian* (16 April) referred to Hunt's opposition to the Reform Bill:

[Hunt] was mistaken about Lancashire men's opinions; he feels his influence decline in proportion as parliamentary reform becomes probable; he therefore hates reform. Under a proper system of representation, there would be no demand for demagogues.

Hunt's visit to Manchester must have caused a considerable amount of embarrassment to Archibald Prentice. In his issue of the *Manchester Times* of 9 April he gave Hunt's visit both to Bolton and to Peterloo lavish space, and he was present at the dinner given to Hunt in Manchester after the meeting on St Peter's Field, and proposed one of the toasts.

But there were two items which gave him deep concern: first, the references to Hulton at Bolton and on St Peter's Field to the possible election of Birley, and to Manchester 'in ashes'; indeed, Prentice decided to suppress them; and in his long report of Hunt's speeches at Bolton and Manchester the complained-of passages are missing; although he did give a milder version of Hunt's suggestions on radicals going over to Wigan to 'assist' Richard Potter. Secondly the discovery that the *Guardian* and the *Chronicle* had written such trenchant leaders, and his suppressions thus made plain to the whole neighbourhood. All three papers appeared on the same day.

Prentice's attitude is important—especially to this narrative—because from this 1831 period he affected to believe that which he transmitted to posterity that John Edward Taylor was moving (as Hammond's *C. P. Scott* puts it) 'from the left to the centre and from the centre to the right'. Taylor's leader of 9 April would doubtless be considered by Prentice, although he does not say so, a hint of this political drift.

There was, however, a further embarrassment to Prentice. This was Henry Hunt's version of radical reform and Hunt's claim that Manchester was with him. In the next issue of the *Manchester Times* Prentice wrote the most naive leader he probably ever wrote. Like the *Guardian*, he claimed that Hunt had misjudged local opinion:

. . . Mr. Hunt's visit was a very hasty one. On Wednesday he arrived in Preston, where he publicly addressed the inhabitants twice, taking his leave

[1] *Manchester Guardian*, 19 May 1832: 'Cuckoo cry of [Huntites] on universal suffrage, annual parliament, and vote by ballot'.

the same evening. On Thursday he addressed the inhabitants of Bolton, and on the same day entered this town and made his speech from his barouche on St. Peter's Field. On Friday morning he left this town for Birmingham. But the visit was not only hasty, but made under circumstances most unfavourable for ascertaining the state of public opinion. The crowds he saw were not met for the purpose of *discussion*; they were not brought together as previous towns' meetings in this place, and at Oldham, Ashton, Bury, and other places had been, purposely to take into consideration the propriety of supporting the Ministers in their intended measures, and consequently all that could be said in favour or against those measures were likely to be, as in fact they were, urged: [Prentice here referred to meetings not of the kind addressed by Hunt which had been held in those towns] they were met solely for the purpose of *hearing Mr. Hunt*; for the purpose of hearing one whose punishment of two years and a half imprisonment for attending a legally convened and peaceable meeting, they considered as most cruel and unjust, whose success at Preston they rejoiced in as a blow at aristocratic nomination, and whose vote in the house against the faction which is opposed to ministers they regard with hearty gratitude.[1]

Here was no opportunity of expressing opinions at variance with his. They had met, not to speak, but to hear him speak; and they applauded the sentiments in favour of a broader reform than that which is contemplated, as men were likely to do who, without any abandonment of those sentiments, were yet willing to believe that the narrower measures were still evidence of honesty of purpose, and that their success would be a great benefit to the community. From that applause must have arisen Hunt's error. He must have concluded that because all that he said of universal suffrage and vote by ballot, was favourably received, the people were opposed to anything that fell short of those points—a palpable *non sequitur* as we think, but such as we will not say, whatever other persons may say, could not be honestly arrived at.

Had Mr. Hunt attended any of the public meetings that were held to discuss the ministerial measures he would not have fallen into this error . . .

Whom Prentice thought he was convincing other than Archibald Prentice is not clear. After such a visit, and such a castigation from the two reform newspapers in Manchester, Hunt was scarcely *persona grata* to moderate opinion in Manchester. To argue that Hunt was 'in error', and in an error 'honestly arrived at, whatever other persons may

---

[1] The political implications of Hunt's Preston victory and of his votes in the House were plain to Reformer Archibald Prentice. Hunt's votes in the House in 1831 were to be less plain to other Reformers:

'It was this general and indiscriminate abuse which Mr. Hunt lavished upon the Whigs, and his accompanying eulogium of the Tories, that gave the first wound to the confidence which his constituents had reposed in him. It was clear to many, and suspected by still more, that Mr. Hunt was fighting the battles of the Tories under radical colours.' Huish, *Life of Henry Hunt* (1836), II, p. 485.

say' suggests that even Prentice thought it would be difficult to convince others. His suggestion that the meeting 'met solely for the purpose of *hearing Mr Hunt*' as though Hunt's Manchester meetings had ever met for any other purpose, is on a par with 'they were not met for the purpose of discussion'; or with, if he had attended other meetings 'he would not have fallen into this error'. Hunt was perhaps disappointing Prentice, but even in his naive leader he managed to 'plug' a point or two in favour of his version of the happenings of the 16 August 1819. The reform agitation of 1831–1832 was in fact a wonderful opportunity to ram home the 'truths' of Peterloo; Prentice and Hunt in their differing ways, never seemed to miss a chance. They had learned nothing; they forgot nothing; and they admitted nothing. Perhaps Hunt had made one admission, but there were to be no more 'partly from fear and partly from folly'[1] admissions by Henry Hunt.

Hunt was again at St Peter's Field, during the last week in April, Parliament had been prorogued, and a general election called. He told his audience at Peterloo that the Preston people had sent up a petition to Parliament approving what he had done. The men of Manchester, he said, with Richard Potter, had sent a petition and raised such a clamour against him that he understood, had he not arrived in the town, it was their intention to have that day burnt him in effigy on Peterloo. The *Manchester Times* (30 April) reported:

. . . He had been told that Birley now professed to be a reformer, and if that were so, well might the reformers of Manchester be suspicious of such allies to their cause. Did the fools think that the burning of a little straw on the same spot would efface the blood shed there about eleven years ago? If they did they were miserably mistaken. (Cheers). He had deserted nothing . . . his opponents now cried 'Stop thief' to prevent their villainy being exposed.

He did not think they would now burn him (Hunt) in effigy. Some of his friends had said they had got an effigy of Richard Potter and Hugh Birley tied back to back, and they would burn them on Peterloo. (Cheers) . . . [He was going to Preston] . . . they would give the best answer . . . but if they should be overpowered—if they should not be able to return him again, the people of England would still be saddled with the Corn Laws . . . they would then have no member who would demand an inquiry into the bloody deeds of the 16th August . . .

Prentice reported that bundles of straw, said to represent Potter and Birley, were burnt in the New Cross area on two occasions later that evening. New Cross was one of the more densely-populated working-class areas of Manchester, the area where the rioting had taken place on

[1] See above, p. 439–40.

the evening of the 16 August, and the area, too, in which Nadin and his constables had alleged they received their 'pelting' with stones before the 16th. Prentice pontificated, in a leader in that same issue, on the vacillations of Hunt: 'We have been thus compelled to decline giving him our active support' [on Hunt's extreme view of reform] 'on account of the harm he had done to the ministers' measures'.

He also referred to William Cobbett who had said in his *Political Register*:

Mr. Prentice, a Manchester editor, is now forced to accuse this fellow [Hunt] of lying; but the same Mr. Prentice could, very coolly, for a year or two, hand about this fellow's lies about me. However, I excuse Mr. Prentice, and hope that it will teach him to be more cautious for the future.

Prentice commented:

Here, in one short sentence are two misstatements. Had we adopted a favourite word in Mr. Cobbett's vocabulary, we might have called them lies. We did not accuse Mr. Hunt of lying, but that he had misrepresented the public opinion of Manchester. Then, as to our handing about the lies of Mr. Hunt against Mr. Cobbett, it is utterly false. We never attached so much consequence to their squabbles as to think it worth while to direct attention to them. It might be gratifying to Mr. Cobbett to call Mr. Hunt a 'fool, a bully, and a coward, and a brazen, unblushing and malignant liar', and to Mr. Hunt to call Mr. Cobbett a 'filthy old beast', but we took no interest in their quarrel, and we paid our readers the compliment of believing that they had no desire to know what sort of names the pot bestowed upon the kettle . . .

The report *The Guardian*[1] put out on the effigy-burning episode was doubtless further evidence for Prentice of John Edward Taylor's recent gravitation to the right.

During the forenoon, in conformity with the advice given by Mr. Hunt, a set of the worst characters in the town assembled in the neighbourhood of New Cross, and having with some difficulty collected a few shabby garments, they proceeded to form them into two effigies, one of which had a large placard in front, with the name of Birley twice printed in conspicuous letters. The other had merely chalked out, nearly illegible on its garments, the name of 'Potter'. These two were fastened back to back, and about 12 o'clock, the rabble commenced a sort of rogues' march through Oldham Street, across Piccadilly, and along Mosley Street. They halted a short time opposite the house of Mr. Birley in that street, holding up the effigies, accompanied with a perfect Babel of groans, yells, and hootings. Several servants were at the windows, who only smiled at the ridiculous mummery; and after staying

[1] *Guardian*, 30 April.

about five minutes, the mob, which at this time amounted to about 500 persons, proceeded towards Peterloo. In their way thither, their numbers were augmented by some scores of the idle and the curious, to whom the dinner-hour gave an opportunity of witnessing the termination of this procedure.

Having reached Peterloo, they obtained some straw and a light, and having set fire to the effigies, capered round them in a delight not much unlike that of cannibals. They then dispersed, with reeky countenances, exulting in having done their duty. A body of police were stationed near Mr. Birley's house, in order to preserve the peace, and prevent any windows being broken; but there was no attempt made, the rabble having satiated their spleen on the effigies.

During the election campaign of the summer of 1831 Manchester seemed to have an irresistible attraction for Henry Hunt; he appeared to be more than mortified at the amount of opposition his particular brand of reform was receiving—and opposition from unexpected quarters. He was back on St Peter's Field on Tuesday, the 3 May, at the invitation of the Manchester Political Union. The *Manchester Times* reported his speech at length, but he had a very small audience of only two or three thousand, partly owing to earlier rain, the crowd occupying only 1600 square yards instead of the 10,000 square yards which had previously been filled:

Hunt alluded to the calumnies heaped upon him by the London press, and particularly noticed the *Morning Chronicle* which had stated that he had been burnt in effigy on that place, the scene of his former glory; that in every place where he went he was hissed and hooted [On account of his opposition to the ministerial plan for reform.] It was false . . . [he referred to] that liar Richard Potter . . . Even the *Voice of the People*[1] had spoken against him. The working people who raised it, should compel its editor to speak the voice of the people, or employ a person who would, or else abandon it altogether. He then alluded to the expressions which he had used when last in Manchester, that if he were a Manchester man, sooner than Birley should be returned as one of their representatives, he would rather see the town in ashes, and some of best blood in the place spilled. This, he said, was merely a figurative expression . . . [He alleged that he got it from the Stanley-Derby interest at Preston who used a similar figure of speech.] . . . Who, he asked, was Mr. [Benjamin] Heywood? Was he a radical reformer? If he was he was a new hatched one, for at Blackburn, the people hissed him . . . In alluding to Lord Stanley's questioning him (Mr. Hunt) concerning the expressions made use of by him at the previous meeting on Peterloo, he indulged himself in making allusions to the personal appearance of Lord

[1] John Doherty, editor.

Stanley, who, he said, was called in the House of Commons 'the pair of tongs' as he was all legs and arms, and had a mouth which reached almost from ear to ear. Hunt also digressed on the Lords as 'reformers' . . . their bastards . . .

Doherty defended himself. The [Reform] Bill gave part only it is true, but he was for a moral revolution not a violent one. Doherty's reporter complained of Hunt trying to shut up the *Voice of the People* . . . but a procession finally moved off up Oldham Street, where there occurred anti-*Voice* demonstrations outside its offices.

Hunt, in June[1] was still bitterly complaining of a conspiracy of the press against him, only the *Poor Man's Guardian*, the *Leeds Patriot*, and the *Midland Reporter* being friendly. Prentice wrote a leader saying that half-a-dozen papers in Lancashire were friends to the working man, and pointed out that they still admired Hunt for his sufferings for attending Peterloo, &c. On 13 June a large working-class demonstration took place on St Peter's Field in favour of reform. The addresses were given by John Doherty, Elijah Dixon, William Brookes, and others; there were no references to the 16 August 1819.

In the 9 July 1831 issue of the *Manchester Times* is traceable, at its source, the 'smear' which Prentice left to posterity on John Edward Taylor, because he had renounced his past; the incident, as it occurs in Prentice's *Recollections* has already been referred to.[2] The relevant passage, it may be reiterated, runs:

. . . Yet, notwithstanding the stain of this 'damned spot' [of Peterloo] ten years had not elapsed [after Taylor's assertions of 1822] ere the editor of the *Guardian* went, hand-in-hand and arm-in-arm with Mr. H. H. Birley, in the attempt to impose a member of Mr. Birley's choice upon newly-enfranchised Manchester! Let no man talk of an unchangeable opinion whose opinion is founded on the present expediency.

Manchester had not, of course, been enfranchised in 1831, but names were being canvassed, and these included George William Wood, who was being strongly backed by John Edward Taylor. Wood was obnoxious to Prentice, as he was the friend of Hugh Hornby Birley; but more particularly because Wood had been strongly in favour of a selective franchise for the Manchester police commissioners. Prentice wrote:[3]

George Wm. Wood is regarded by the great majority of his fellow-townsmen with a dislike little inferior to what they feel for his friend Hugh Hornby

[1] *Manchester Times*, 4 June.
[2] See above, pp. 314–17.
[3] *Manchester Times*, 9 July.

Birley, and, looking to his egregious vanity, with a contempt scarcely less ineffable than that which they entertain for his other friend, John Edward Taylor . . . [Prentice's idea of Wood's canvassing] . . . and should Mr. H. H. Birley, whose name, by some people, is always classed with Mr. Wood's when representatives are talked of, accompany him, how gratefully would he twist his grim visage into a smile, while he too put in his claim:—'Gentlemen I also laboured zealously for your exclusion [in the police franchise] from all management of your own affairs, and, moreover, I cut you down at Peterloo. Pray, favour me with your votes.' . . . We trust however, that the Wood and Birley party will be as much disappointed in their hope of disunion among the reformers as the boroughmongers have been. [Prentice considered that it was the *Guardian's* impudent attempt to scare Mark Philips from the field; Wood being Mark Philips's business partner].

George William Wood, a Dissenter (a Unitarian, as was Taylor) was not a candidate for Manchester in the general election of December, 1832, but was elected one of the two Reform members returned for the Southern Division of Lancashire, and at the head of the poll.

Prentice's disapproval of Taylor's movement to the 'right' is not borne out by the facts which he purports in his *Recollections* to bring as proof. In his paper of 4 August 1832, Prentice is noticing the prospective candidates for Manchester and their friends, and: 'we saw that one of the most prominent amongst them was Hugh Hornby Birley, a man who, with the stain of the 16 August, 1819, upon him, attaches a stain to all on whom he inflicts his friendship . . .' Archibald Prentice did indeed cloud the understanding of generations.

XXVIII

The Bourbon Radical Resurgence

There were no rejoinders to Hunt's vitriolic Bolton speech from Hulton except perhaps a negative one; he did not emerge as a candidate in the forthcoming election after the Reform Bill passed. It is not believed, however, that he withdrew because he was intimidated, but for personal reasons. Prentice's paper reported one piece of news which was actually to Hulton's credit:

Silk Weavers. (Bolton Petty Sessions) There were several complaints from silk weavers in the neighbourhood of Leigh, that the manufacturers were in the habit of making most arbitrary and exhorbitant deductions from their wages. Mr. Hulton declared that something must be done for the poor weavers, as scarcely a day passed but he had persons waiting upon him requiring redress. He had come to the determination to grant summonses to compel the manufacturers to appear at Bolton, in consequence of the magistrates only sitting every fortnight at Leigh. He described Westhoughton as being entirely in a flame, through the conduct of the silk masters, and their agents; for the poor weavers, after labouring hard for weeks, were frequently abated two-thirds of their wages for the most trifling faults.[1]

Even at the time when Hulton's name was being canvassed as the suitable candidate for South Lancashire, and a month before his efforts on behalf of the silk weavers, he had industrial troubles of his own in his coal pits. He was in dispute with the newly-active colliers' union. The dispute was an early instance of a constantly-recurring problem in the history of trade unions between that day and this, the right of trade unionists to insist on full union membership for all men employed, in short, the closed shop. Apparently all Hulton's colliers had become union members, but two there were who had lapsed; the union demanded their dismissal. Hulton refused, and the result was a strike. The details are long and complicated, but Hulton issued two 'manifestoes' to his colliers:

To the Hulton Colliers who have 'Turned Out'. My friends. 'The labourer is

[1] *Manchester Times*, 23 April.

worthy of his hire' (Luke X). Such is the principle upon which I have always endeavoured to found my conduct towards you. If I had unjustly attempted to reduce your wages; if I had ever paid you, or pretended to pay you, in truck; if I had ever given one man an advantage over another, which had not been fairly earned . . . your recent conduct would have been no more than I deserved . . . I have amply rewarded you for your labour . . . relieving your families in sickness or distress . . . educated your children . . . What has been your conduct towards me? . . . wantonly injured me in my purse and wounded my feelings . . . demanded I should dismiss two men . . . [make their] families destitute . . . because they do not belong to the Colliers' Union . . . I never discharged anyone because he *was* a member of your Union. I never dismiss one because he is *not* . . . I am acting justly . . . never be united again as Master and servants.

William Hulton, Hulton Park, March 21st, 1831.[1]

There were counter-charges during the few weeks the dispute dragged on, and finally the men drifted back but there were a few whom Hulton refused to take back.[2] There was a second manifesto[3] in which Hulton answered the counter-charges. It ended: 'We have all suffered from the society improperly called a Union . . . disunited masters and men . . I never turned off a collier because he was a member of that society. I now add I will never engage one who is.' In the years following there was a 'house union' at the Hulton collieries which lasted for many years—until the reasons which called it into being were no longer valid.

William Hulton's candour in the matter of the dispute earned him credit in a quarter where it must have been least expected. The *Bolton Chronicle*,[4] then and later his most determined political opponent locally, came out with a long leader:

. . . We, in fact, had been told and until this moment believed, that Mr. Hulton would discharge any of his colliers who had joined the Union. Mr. Hulton, however, and no one who knows the high sense of honour which has uniformly appertained to that gentleman's character, can for a single instant doubt its truth, made a public declaration, that he never discharged one of his colliers because he *was* a member of the Union; and that he will not dismiss one because he is *not*. The question has altogether presented a new aspect in our view, and we candidly confess that if the conduct of those men who have persecuted others who did not feel themselves called upon to join the Union, appears to us to be at once tyrannical and unjust. . . . We make no compromise in principle—we are not currying favour

1 DDHu/53/72. L.C.R.O.
2 *Bolton Chronicle*, 2 April 1831.
3 DDHu/53/73. L.C.R.O.
4 *Bolton Chronicle*, 26 March 1831; 2 April; 16 April.

with Mr. Hulton or any other gentleman. The political principles of this paper, and those which Mr. Hulton has felt it his duty to adopt, are placed at an immeasurable distance from each other; but though we may differ with him in opinion, we are not such heartless bigots as to be prejudiced against him in a case where his conduct is altogether free from blame, and which defies the most scrupulous censor from exercising his vocation; and we think it right to repeat for the thousandth time, that we shall always be the firm advocates of the rights and privileges of the working classes . . .

There had before been ample evidence that the *Bolton Chronicle* was not 'currying favour' with Mr Hulton; that evidence was shortly to be multiplied ten-fold. The Hulton colliers' turn-out of 1831 seems to belong to another period of history than that of the post-Peterloo and pre-Tolpuddle Martyrs era.

The twelfth anniversary of 16 August 1819, was duly celebrated, organized by the Manchester Political Union. Prentice's paper (20 August) gave it much space, even to reprinting the hand-bill pasted on the walls; the hand-bill read:

Procession. The Radical Reformers of Manchester are respectfully informed that a procession will go from the New Cross, Oldham Road, on Tuesday, the 16th of August, 1831, precisely at twelve o'clock, to St. Peter's Field, to commemorate the fatal 16th of August, 1819; and to mourn for the loss of the brave patriots, who fell on that never-to-be-forgotten day, when they were peacefully assembled to petition the legislature of our country for a reform in parliament, and a repeal of that obnoxious law, called the corn law. Edward Curran, chairman; Wm. Ashmore, secretary.

The perceptive reader of that hand-bill might have sensed a slight change in emphasis in the wording of the notice. It was called a com-memoration—and a Mr Morris, a Unitarian minister, was to deliver an address, an address to which, unhappily, Prentice made no reference except to quote the text, although he spoke for a quarter of an hour.

A little after twelve o'clock, several hundreds[1] of persons assembled opposite the King William the Fourth, New Cross, and having formed themselves in to a procession, were led by Mr. Morris, the Unitarian preacher, dressed in black clothes but wearing a drab hat, on which was fixed a mourning scarf; several others also wore crape on their hats. A band of musicians preceded, playing solemn tunes. There were also carried eight flags[2] on one of which flags was a representation of a yeomanry cavalryman, cutting down a female with a child in her arms, with an inscription, 'Murder Demands Justice'. On

---

[1] The *Guardian* reported 200.

[2] '. . . having collected about a dozen of the hackney flags which adorn every radical procession in this town,' said the *Guardian*.

another flag was, 'Whoso sheddeth man's blood, by man shall his blood be shed'. All the flags were decorated with black crape . . . When arriving at the place where the hustings stood in 1819, when the meeting was dispersed by the military, the procession halted, and Mr Morris gave out a psalm appropriate to the occasion, from Dr Watts's collection, and after the conclusion of the psalm, he desired the company to kneel while he prayed. After the prayer was concluded, he took for his text the first verse of the ninth chapter of Jeremiah: 'Oh that my head were waters, and mine eyes a fountain of tears, that I might weep day and night for the slain of the daughter of my people.' The reverend gentleman commented on his text for about a quarter of an hour, and the procession then re-formed.

The commemoration was over. 'Outside the King William inn, Mr Curran then read the following address from Mr Henry Hunt:

To the brave but persecuted men of Manchester. London, August 14th, 1831. Having heard that you intend on Tuesday next, justly to remind your fellow-townsmen, and to recall to the indignant recollection of the country, the cowardly, cruel, and horrid murders that were perpetrated by a drunken and infuriated band of armed ruffians, upon a peaceable assembly of men, women, and children, on the 16th of August, 1819, legally congregated in your town, professedly and avowedly to petition the parliament for radical reform in the representation of the people in the commons house, and for a repeal of the infamous corn laws so justly denominated by the useful and working classes the starvation acts, I cannot refrain from briefly addressing you, to say that although my body will be immured within the walls of St. Stephen's, my heart and soul will be with you on the blood-stained field of Peterloo.

I cannot trust myself to say what I feel upon this horrid, heart-rending subject, but this I will say, May the men of Manchester never forget the massacre, nor ever forgive the cowardly murderers, or their more cruel abettors, till they have justice! justice!! justice!!! The shrieks of the butchered children, the piercing cries of the slaughtered women, and the dying groans of the murdered men, are still present to my imagination, and they call aloud for justice and retribution . . .

Let me be calm, if it is possible to be calm upon such a subject, and let me ask you my beloved friends and brethren, this plain and simple question. Shall the expiring groans of those martyrs who have suffered military execution and death in the holy struggle for equal political rights—shall the heaving sighs—shall the deep aspirations—shall the curses of those who have filled the cold and damp cells—of those who have been immured in the tyrants' dungeons, for standing up for the rights of every Englishman to exercise the elective franchise—be drowned in the senseless cry for partial suffrage? Shall the legal and just demands of seven millions of the industrious and useful men be abandoned, and their political rights offered up to the shrine of half-a-million of ten-pound householders? Shall seven millions of the working-classes proclaim their own political damnation, and declare that they are content to be virtually represented by half a million of their fellow-men because they live in ten-pound houses? Answer me this question? If Englishmen are content to yield to the selfish views of such canting wretches, and say, Yes!?! my course is plain, I will remain no longer in a country where seven-eights of the people are content to be political slaves. I will pass the remaining years I have to live, and lay my bones amongst those whose opinions are most congenial with my own.

But if the seven millions say that they are not content, and that they will not be satisfied with less than the just rights of the whole people, why then the remainder of my life shall be freely and fearlessly devoted to the service of the people. But they must speak out, and no longer be the easy dupes of the few selfish and venal scribes, but put their shoulders to the political wheel, and rescue the just rights of the people from a more dangerous slough than the slough of despond. I am, Men of Manchester, your sincere friend, H. Hunt.

Whether it was because of Hunt's reference to 'venal scribes', or whether he preferred demonstrations to commemorations, or whether he did not wish to enter into controversy on partial or whole-hog reform, is not known; but Archibald Prentice on the 12th anniversary of Peterloo made no comment nor did he write a leader. Perhaps *Wheeler's Manchester Chronicle*[1] sensed too a different emphasis in the local commemoration:

. . . There might be twelve to fifteen hundred persons upon the [St. Peter's] field, but the great majority consisted of those whom curiosity had brought together, the procession of itself was very unimportant in number. The party and feeling it was intended to represent are happily merging fast into more enlightened views, and broadly national interests; and the rancour which is still called upon by recollections of 'the 16th of August, 1819', will soon, we have no doubt, cease to exist.

Henry Hunt was at Peterloo again on 1 November 1831. In the interim, the House of Lords had rejected the Reform Bill and the dreadful Bristol riots had occurred. It was a more circumspect Henry Hunt. He had always, he said, deprecated violence, and did so now:

It was only Whig mobs that resorted to acts of violence; the reformers knew better how to conduct themselves. The two factions [Tory and Whig] had long domineered over the people, but of the two, he had always said, and would still say, that the Tories were not half so bad as the Whigs (Cheers).[2]

[1] 20 August 1832.
[2] *Manchester Times,* 5 November.

There was not one single reference in Hunt's long speech to the occurrences on that field of twelve years earlier. Up to that date, the omission was unique.

In November 1831, Henry Hunt's political fortunes were probably at a lower ebb than they had ever been. His attitude on reform had not received the support he had hoped for even amongst the radical reformers. Although he kept his seat at Preston, his old allies were not on his side—or rather he was not on theirs. Doherty was against his brand of reform in Manchester with his reform paper *The Voice of the People*, but perhaps the most remarkable anti-Huntite was his old patron and protector of days gone by, Sir Charles Wolseley.

It will be recalled that the *Guardian* had referred contemptuously to Hunt's story that Sir Charles Wolseley was trying to bribe him with £12,000 if he would go over to the Whigs.[1] It was a 'story', as Hunt himself admitted in one of his Preston election leaflets, but the *Manchester Times* told its readers that Sir Charles was anxious to confront Hunt with an indignant rebuttal of the charge, and journeyed to Preston with that intention. Hunt was not there. He referred to Sir Charles's visit in his No. 5 *An Address . . . to Radical Reformers* (November, 1831): 'I have just heard that that old half-cracked, half-idiot baronet— Sir Charles Wolseley has been to Preston'. Hunt was not afraid to meet him; what he had to say would deter him 'from ever showing his old ugly *phiz* in that town again . . . the old turncoat is a bigger fool than ever'. The 'old baronet' was in fact a mere four years Hunt's senior.

If Hunt's fortunes were at a low ebb, so were Hulton's. In the public press of this time, William Hulton was said to be in financial straits; by his own admission he had been injured in his pocket by the turnout; and the taunts and sneers in the press, culminating in Hunt's Bolton attack, *must* have had their effect. In November 1831 came the last straw. A Ministerial spokesman, the Chancellor of the Exchequer, Lord Althorp, had committed the unpardonable offence (to Hulton) of making use, in a House of Commons speech, of the term 'revolting' when referring to the transactions of the 16 August 1819. The offensive passage, as reported in the newspapers, read: 'The loss of lives on that occasion was frightful, all the circumstances were of an extraordinary and revolting nature.'

Hulton asked that his name be removed from the Commission of the Peace. This step prompted Francis Philips (then of Bank Hall, Stockport) to write a rather indignant letter to Lord Althorp, which led to an

[1] See above, p. 468.

exchange of letters between Althorp and Hulton—a correspondence which ended in stalemate.[1] Hulton then sent the letters to the press. The national papers joined in. Hunt was on top of the world once more.

The insinuations of the press, the invective of Hunt, had been ignored by Hulton with disdain. He was aware that Lord Althorp, who in 1819 was member of Parliament for Northamptonshire, had been amongst the Whig critics of the Ministry crying for an inquiry into Peterloo. What seemed unpardonable to Hulton was, that, as a responsible Minister of the Crown, and as Leader of the House of Commons, as Althorp was in 1831, he should have so described an event in which, Hulton said, the magistrates had received 'the thanks of the reigning Monarch, the support of the greatest legal authorities of the day, and the verdicts of two juries.' 'Honour,' Hulton wrote, 'the firmest basis of private life, forbids that I should tamely submit to have the epithet 'revolting' applied to any transactions in which I had participated.' He went on:

Even if the Magistrates' conduct was not acceptable to your lordship, it was gratefully acknowledged at that time (and that time twelve years ago), by nearly all the owners of property in the most crowded Hundred of the Kingdom, then I felt myself called upon as Chairman of the Magistrates upon whom the responsibility in 1819 devolved, publickly to declare that I would not submit to be thus taunted, specially at a crisis when, if I acted according to my deliberate construction of the laws of England, I should repeat the same line of conduct which I pursued in 1819. If I neglected thus to act, I should have to witness a conflagration of the great manufacturing establishments I was bound by my oath to guard, and if I conscientiously performed my duty I should expose myself to a prosecution by His Majesty's Attorney-General. Under such circumstances could I remain on the Bench?[2]

William Hulton wrote, as he spoke, more from his heart than from his head. Had he been writing from his head he might have avoided the pitfall he fell into. Althorp had referred to the 'frightful' loss of life. Hulton did not believe the figures put out by the radicals which he thought were exaggerated; he proceeded to give his own estimates. If he had only recalled that standing on his own library shelves at Hulton Hall was a bound volume of pamphlets[3] dealing with the transactions of 16 August, which contained the separate offprint of George Canning's

---

[1] *Manchester Courier* commented on this incident as early as its 12 November 1831 issue.

[2] The correspondence was printed in most papers, but fully in *Bolton Chronicle*, 24 December 1831; *Manchester Guardian*, 24 December 1831; 31 December 1831. *Manchester Times*, 24 December 1831.

[3] Now in the present writer's possession.

speech in the November, 1819, debate in the House of Commons. George Canning had therein explained the 'common trick' of 'first putting forth a monstrous exaggeration of calamity for the express purpose of inviting contradiction; and then holding up to public indignation the man who reduces the exaggeration to reality[1] . . .' Not that Lord Althorp had done any such thing, for he did not attempt to comment on Hulton's figures; but the nation's press did, mainly on the strength of the more expert 'knowledge' of Archibald Prentice.

Lord Althorp's first letter was urbanity itself, his second not much less so; in his third he had tried to placate Hulton's wounded feelings, but had failed. There appeared to be no point in further pursuing the matter. In his first letter he did not know that he had said anything to cause Hulton pain. When Hulton told him what the terms complained of were, Althorp felt sure that he had not used terms so strong; he was not in the habit of using such strong terms; he did not believe that he 'ever used the words "frightful" and "revolting" in public speaking in his life,' and he certainly had not used any terms which were intended to criticize the magistrates. He admitted that he might have used the words 'most unjustifiable'. Hulton retorted, perhaps petulantly, that if the criticisms were not directed against the magistrates, against 'whom' were the words (even allowing the less superlative terms) used. Althorp was not to be drawn on that, but told Hulton pretty plainly:

. . . You are the best and only judge of what you ought to do [on whether he ought to retire from the Bench or not]. You differ in political opinions from the present administration most decidedly, as I am aware. You have no right to expect that, in coming into office, they should abandon the opinions they have always expressed; and if you do not like to act as a magistrate while the Administration of the country is in the hands of men professing and acting upon those opinions, they cannot be blamed on that account . . .

Hulton replied:

. . . Your lordship 'has no right' [quoting, of course, Althorp's passage above] to assume for a moment that I retired from the Bench because 'I did not like to act as a magistrate while the administration of the country is in the hands of men professing and acting upon political opinions from which I decidedly differ'. I should be as proud to hold my commission under Lord Holland, the present Chancellor of the Duchy of Lancaster, as under the most revered Tory. It was your violent animadversion, made under circumstances to which I have before referred, that drove me from a public station.

[1] See above, p. 220.

Lord Althorp was one of those who were suffering from indigestion brought on by the 'unpalatable exercise of eating their own words'. The following passage occurred in the House of Commons debate, on 15 March 1832:

Lord Althorp: . . . The authors of the [Manchester] calamity had received the thanks of the then Ministry, who, under the circumstance, must be presumed to acquiesce; and he thought that inquiry before the House was not so much needed for the purpose of bringing to justice those who committed, as those who had made themselves participators in the crime.
Sir H. Hardinge: Does the noble Lord mean to accuse the then Ministers of being participators in any crime?
Lord Althorp was obliged to the right hon. Gentleman for the opportunity of correcting himself, as he must admit that he ought not to have used so strong a word as that with which he had just concluded, but he felt that the Ministry of that day were responsible for giving protection to those who were supposed to be guilty of political offences . . .

The *Guardian*[1] gave it Hulton pretty strongly, after having been plainly informed by Lord Althorp that his criticisms were not directed against the magistrates, for asking 'Against *whom*, then?':

The first point that will strike the reader . . . will be the amiable solicitude with which Lord Althorp endeavours to remove unfounded impressions in the mind of Mr. Hulton; and the total want of everything like gentlemanly feeling with which this overture is met. In return for his lordship's kindness Mr. Hulton pens a letter full of the most rancorous feeling of political enmity, and obviously intended for the purpose of offering a deliberate insult to the man who addressed him with the utmost courtesy and kindness. A more unhandsome, ungenerous and ungentlemanly proceeding we never heard of;[2] and it is perhaps, only to be accounted for by supposing that Mr. Hulton really could not comprehend the purpose of his lordship's letter; and as Mr. Hulton is confessedly not overburdened with wisdom, this may be the most probable, as it most certainly is the most charitable supposition.

From the ridiculous importance which has been given to Mr. Hulton's resignation in some quarters, one might have supposed that the administration of the law could hardly have gone on in the country without his assistance, and we imagine Lord Althorp must have been a little imposed upon with respect to the importance and character of the individual with whom he had to deal.

[1] *Manchester Guardian*, 24 December, 1831.
[2] 'In truth,' said the *Manchester Courier*,* 'he [Althorp] cuts a poor figure in this correspondence; and his shuffling, quibbling evasions, contrast ill with the straightforward frankness of his opponent.'
* 12 November, 1831.

That the retirement of Mr. Hulton from any further exercise of the functions of the magistracy will be regretted in his own neighbourhood, we do not at all believe. A man who was not only remarkable for the possession of that quality which is the converse of wisdom, but who was proud of being a 'foolish squire' cannot be any lamentable loss to the commission of the peace; and unless there were some peculiar utility, which we cannot discover, in his crusades against the burning of bricks on Sundays, and some other vagaries with which he was concerned, we imagine the public will think they are well rid of his magisterial services; and if his retirement had been owing to Lord Althorp's observations (with respect to which we have something else to say by and by) the general opinion would be that the county was much obliged to his lordship for having made them.

But we do not believe that the observations of Lord Althorp had anything to do with the retirement of Mr. Hulton. The real cause of that retirement is very well known in Mr. Hulton's own neighbourhood; and though it may have suited that gentleman and some of his friends, to ascribe it to some public cause, it is well known to have been founded on urgent private reasons, and we are very well satisfied that it would equally have taken place if Lord Althorp's speech had never been made.

As we have no intention to revive the expired controversies arising out of the events of the fatal 16th of August . . . [a refutation of some of the statements made by Hulton on the casualties of that day] . . . This paper is full of misstatements . . . Mr. Hulton drawing on the stores of his imagination instead of resorting to any authentic records of fact—a course which will probably cause no great degree of astonishment in the minds of those who recollect the nature of his evidence at York.

That leader by John Edward Taylor was as unworthy of him as anything he ever wrote. If there was one 'expired controversy' it was on Hulton's evidence at York. His evidence at York had been the same as his evidence at Lancaster in Redford *v.* Birley, which had stood the test of the strictest cross-examination, had been commended by the radical counsel at Lancaster, and by Judge Bayley in the subsequent appeal in the strongest terms; and Judge Bayley had heard the evidence at York. Taylor was wrong, too, on the reaction likely to be caused in his own neighbourhood by Hulton's retirement. There was great regret. Hardly worth mentioning is Taylor's slur on Hulton's alleged 'crusades against burning bricks on Sundays', but Taylor again in this instance had fallen for a garbled press story—a press story which, echoed as it was in the national press, became more garbled every time it was copied. Hulton was not even on the bench at the magistrates' court when the case came up. That was the only 'vagary' as a magistrate Taylor could find against Hulton, although he might have found many greatly to Hulton's credit. Taylor well knew from where the 'proud of being a "foolish squire" ' came.

Incredible though it may seem, William Hulton's retirement from the Bench made headlines (so far as headlines were used in that period) in the national press, echoing and 'improving' the comments from Manchester. The *Morning Chronicle*[1] referred to the 'public disgust' the correspondence had excited; it even mentioned Hulton's alleged private reasons which 'conspired to recommend to this individual the prudence of a temporary secession from the splendid orbit of his public duties, no less than the force of political considerations on his patriot mind'. The *Examiner's* Barhamesque versifier was busy:

TO LORD ALTHORP

No, no! my good Lord Althorp! it was scarce correct or clever,
Of washing Tories white, to undertake the wild endeavour;
There's matter for your friends to mourn, your enviers to exult on,
In these extreme urbanities of yours to Squire Hulton.

If really you must find or make perpetual occasions,
To stuff speech or epistle with rhetorical persuasions.
Choose vessels less inflammable wherein to pour a full ton
Of Peter Pindar's oil of fools; but don't choose Squire Hulton.

Exert your parts on fish-fags' hearts, which gin and bitters harden,
Conciliate into chastity the nymphs of Covent Garden.
Soft souls like these aspire to please, but don't draw down insult on
Your harmless head, by meddling with bloodhounds like Squire Hulton.

Reach to the Bench of Bishops' evangelical humility;
Teach Londonderry common sense, the Stock Exchange civility,
Any or all, or great or small, you'll work with more result on
Than when you try to milkify such clods as Squire Hulton.

Hail Hulton! Pride of Peterloo! thy massacres Homeric,
Shall flourish long in speech and song of J.P.s lay and cleric:
A conclave of official fiends thy *hauts faits* shall consult on,
And (last and most) George Quatre's ghost shall whisper:—'Well hit, Hulton!'

The Examiner[1] also wrote:—'It is doubtless thought very hard that a gentleman with a park cannot say what he likes—cannot do as he pleases with his own words—nay, more, with his own facts. If there are any facts which should not be disturbed, surely, they are those which are home-brewed.

[1] Quoted *Manchester Times*, 7 January 1832.

A park wall is, however, no protection against the press; and it has happened that the *Manchester Times* has most unceremoniously demolished Mr. Hulton's statement of the 'Manchester Transactions', and has given some ugly shocks to his authority.

★　　★　　★

It was inevitable that the riots, pillage and burnings at Bristol in October, 1831, during which 'the magistrates lost their heads and Col. Brereton' [the military commander] 'his nerve'[1] would be pointed to as an object lesson. Parallels were drawn and the moral shown that what had occurred in Bristol would have occurred in Manchester in 1819, had the Manchester magistrates not acted as they did. The parallel could be challenged on several grounds, but principally, as Taylor was to point out, that the military garrison at Bristol was meagre, while at Manchester in 1819 it was immense; and there were other valid reasons for rejecting such a parallel. Hulton unwisely made the comparison. Unwisely, because he had a wide enough front to defend in the salient of 16 August, 1819, without widening his perimeter to include the tragic scenes of Bristol. Archibald Prentice was waiting for him, with his Christmas Eve issue of the *Manchester Times*:

There will be a bit of dust in Manchester or elsewhere, and it will be laid in blood, and the new parliament will be chosen in peace and jollity. Such is the answer which is given in a publication expressing the opinions of the Tories, to a question, 'What would follow the substitution of a Peel for a Grey administration?' 'There will be a bit of dust and it will be laid in blood', has been the reckless answer of kindred minds whenever the danger of delaying reform has been urged. The Bristol riots where a supine corporation, self-elected, and having no feelings in common with the citizens, permitted a horde of plunderers uninterruptedly to burn and destroy for three successive days, have been compared to the peaceable assemblage on St. Peter's Field; and when the paralized and worse than useless functionaries of Bristol have been blamed for the want of that promptness which ought to have nipped the servile war in the bud, the reply has been 'Yes, they ought to have acted promptly and energetically as the Manchester magistrates did!' When every word condemning the Bristol magistrates is wrested into a commendation of those who directed the cutting down of an unarmed and peaceable multitude, is it surprising that a hot-headed actor in that woeful tragedy should stand forward and justify the sanguinary doings?

We have given, in another part of our paper, a copy of the correspondence between Lord Althorp and Mr. Hulton, of Hulton. The letters of his lordship are, as the *Globe* well remarks, characterised by the anxiety of a philosophical and amiable minded man to clear himself of the imputation of intentional

[1] Butler, *Passing of the Great Reform Bill*, p. 309.

personal offence, and to heal what he deemed wounded feelings, while the replies of the ex-magistrate to the gentlemanly explanation are distinguished by a vulgar insolence which no doubt he considers manly independence.

But it is upon the gross falseness of his statements, and not upon his rude flippancy of manner, which we intend to comment. The ill-breeding is manifest enough to any one accustomed to the usages of respectable society; but the untruths require grave contradiction.

Mr. Hulton says that 'as to the loss of lives, two people were killed in St. Peter's Field—one, a woman, who having personated the Goddess of Reason, was trampled to death in the crowd; and the other a special constable, who was cut down unintentionally by a private of a dragoon regiment. This was the *frightful* sacrifice of life which saved Manchester from a worse fate than Bristol has since undergone. Two other lives were lost on the night of the 16th of August, when provision shops were assailed by the mob. On the succeeding day, an old pensioner was beaten to death with portions of his own loom, because he had expressed a loyal attachment to the King; and subsequently, a man died whose case formed the celebrated Oldham inquest.'

What followed can be guessed almost without reading it; in perfect fulfilment of George Canning's dictum of twelve years earlier:

We scarcely know in what terms to speak of the falsehood of this statement, and the cold-blooded comment which assumes that by such trifling sacrifice of life, Manchester was saved from a worse fate than Bristol has since undergone. In all our editorial experience, we never saw, in so short a space, so little regard to truth and to the value of human life. What will they who are ignorant of that terrible tragedy think of the man who penned this infamous paragraph, when we say that, independent of its flippant heartlessness, it does not contain one word of truth except the admission that a man died on whom was held the Oldham inquest! It is not true that any woman personated the Goddess of Reason on that occasion. It is not true that the female assumed to have personated the Goddess of Reason was killed. It is not true that a special constable was 'cut down', even 'unintentionally', mistaking him for a reformer. It is not true that 'a private of a dragoon regiment' had any part in the death of a special constable. It is not true that there was any attack on the provision shops.[1] It is not true that 'an old pensioner was beaten to death with portions of his own loom . . .' Every one of these assertions is false, and we have no

---

[1] Which facts were true and which facts were untrue even Prentice did not know in 1831. The *Manchester Observer* was perhaps a less biased witness to the truth of the attack on the provision shops than some other reporters:

'A number of women and children collected around the premises of Mr. Tate, grocer, in Oldham Street, and proceeded to demolish his windows, under what, we are informed, was a mistaken idea of his having been a special constable, and forward in exhibiting the flag of the Female Reformers as a trophy of his prowess. The military were summoned to the spot and, at seven o'clock in the evening, and *not before*, if we may be allowed the induction, the *Riot act* was publicly read: some fatal and serious

doubt Mr. Hulton knew them to be false when he made them; for we cannot imagine there exists a man who took any part in the proceedings of that day who can be so deplorably ignorant of its events as to believe for one single moment in the truth of these statements. We cannot believe in the possibility of such ignorance in Mr. Hulton, and therefore are we driven to the necessity of concluding that he not only has stated falsehoods, but that he perfectly well knew that they were falsehoods when he made them.

Having asserted that Hulton's assessment of the 'who and the how' amongst that day's victims was false, (the evidence on which was the most conflicting and difficult to prove or disprove of all the facts of Peterloo), Prentice could then bolster up his premise with the most extinct of the exploded facts on Peterloo:

We are not the first, who have distrusted Mr. Hulton's evidence. At the trial of Hunt and others at York, the following scene occurred. In his cross-examination by Hunt, he swore: 'I could see distinctly [the men round the hustings with locked arms, using verbatim, almost, the passages on that incident from Hunt's trial, ending with Hunt's question: "Can you, Sir, looking round this court . . ."]' When this question was put, every person near the bench turned round to look upon the court, and a most extraordinary sensation was produced when it was seen that it was quite impossible for any one to say whether the arms of the audience were locked, and it was an instant conclusion that Mr. Hulton's evidence, that he could see at 300 or 400 yards distance, persons in a dense crowd, having their arms locked, was worthless . . .[1]

Like Prentice, 'we cannot imagine there exist[ed] a man who took part' in the recording of 'the proceedings of that day who could be so deplorably ignorant of its events as to believe for one single moment' that the evidence given above had not been completely refuted. He did not even notice that Hulton's 300–400 yards had been proved in both trials to be 100 yards. Prentice goes on:

Mr. Hulton's evidence was to have been supported, by others, but the witnesses after this extraordinary scene *withdrew*. Mr. Hay and the other magistrates

---

accidents were the consequences of this trifling mob; but the town was kept in a state of alarm during the whole of the evening.' *Manchester Observer*, 21 August, 1819.

The same incident, or incidents, has later been summed up by Dr Read:

'On the evening of the 16th a riot broke out at New Cross, the most turbulent part of Manchester. One of the shopkeepers there was supposed by the mob to have been a special constable at Peterloo and to have exhibited a captured Radical flag. For this his shop was attacked. The Riot Act had to be read, and one person was killed by shots from the military.'

Dr Read quotes *The Times*, 24 August, 1819, as his authority.

[1] See above, pp. 172, note 2.

who were to have corroborated his statements absolutely fled. When Hunt, in his defence, was about to pass some personal observations on Mr. Hulton, Mr. Justice Bayley stopped him, by observing that 'Mr. Hulton's was a situation of a very distressing and serious nature'! In summing up, the learned judge recapitulated the voluminous evidence given on the trial, when he came to that of Mr. Hulton, he remarked:

'He thought it probable that that magistrate knowing the great responsibility' &c, the sudden emergency . . . Mr. Hulton agitated and not cool . . . and the need for corroboration of his evidence by other magistrates and from Nadin . . .'

Prentice knew that all the points he was introducing not only received the necessary corroboration in Redford *v*. Birley by the other witnesses, but what is more, in the motion for a new trial were reviewed in a manner favourable to Hulton by the same Judge Bayley who had made the strictures at York. To turn the tables on Mr Prentice in his own words: 'We cannot believe in the possibility of such ignorance in' Mr Prentice, 'and therefore we are driven to the necessity of concluding that not only has he stated' discredited testimonies, 'but that he knew perfectly well that they were falsehoods when he made them'.

But Prentice still proceeds:

Is there a man who considers the judge's reflections on the flurry and agitation of Mr. Hulton, and of the absence of that corroboration which his evidence *ought* to have received from his brother magistrates and Mr. Nadin, who can doubt that though he believed Mr. Hulton to be 'a respectable man,' he had formed precisely the same opinion of the value of his evidence as had been formed by the persons in the Court, who indecorously expressed their conviction of its utter worthlessness by clapping their hands?

Having shewn that we are not the first who have distrusted Mr. Hulton's evidence, when we declare our conviction that it is impossible unless we suppose insanity, that he can be ignorant of the falsehood of his assertion as to the loss of life . . . we proceed to show what was done on that terrible day, by the men who were, or pretended to be, afraid that a legally convened and peaceably assembled meeting, would suddenly take the course recently followed by the Bristol thieves and vagabonds . . . [Following with the radical list of casualties—the wounded and dead] . . . whose death, according to Mr. Hulton, was a cheap price for the preservation of the peace, which he, trembling with groundless and cowardly fear, imagined to be in danger.

But these deaths were not the most afflictive of the events of the day. *560 persons*, many of them women and children, all of them much injured, and nearly one hundred having received dreadful *sabre wounds*, fled from that fatal field, to hide their wounds in their cottages, not daring to apply either for surgical aid, or for parochial relief, lest they should be sent to prison, and thus enduring sufferings almost worse than death. Yet in the face of these terrible and incontrovertible facts, have we Mr. Hulton declaring that 'honour and the firmest basis of private life', forbids him to submit to have the epithet *revolting* applied to the transaction.

Prentice followed with a quotation from the *Morning Chronicle* which was indignant that 'the Tories should seize on so mild a man as Lord Althorp,' making the point that the Tories have been shown too much deference by the Ministry; the *Chronicle* was 'deeply disgusted at seeing the government everywhere in the hands of the Tories, who use their power against the Whigs.'

If there is any blame to be attached, [Prentice concluded] for the re-agitation of this distressing question, it rests on Mr. Philips and Mr. Hulton. We might have let it sleep had not the 'firmness' of the Manchester magistrates been held up as worthy of example and praise.

Archibald Prentice letting the happenings of the 16 August 1819, 'sleep' is the *pièce de resistance* of the whole article. That article has, however, a greater importance in the establishing of the radical (Prentician) version of Peterloo than is perhaps realized. In it were the essentials of the 'terrible and incontrovertible facts', shorn of all the 'murderous' details beloved by Hunt; the 'facts' set against a background of lies, callousness, and the 'cold-blooded comment' of one of the chief actors in it. Prentice's version, copied through the land, sounded reasonable compared with Hunt's. Prentice had cause to preen himself when, in his next issue, he could proudly announce:

Our contradictions of the statements contained in Mr. Hulton's insolent letter to Lord Althorp having been copied into *The Times*, the *Morning Chronicle*, the *Morning Herald*, the *Courier*, and the *Globe*,[1] the whole kingdom is now informed of the real consequences of that attack upon an unarmed and peaceable assemblage, to which the ex-magistrate will not permit the epithet 'revolting' to be applied. Perhaps Mr. Hulton rejoices in the bad fame which is thus revived when it was about to expire; and perhaps he will rejoice in what we are about to say, as an addition to the reputation for which he is covetous. After the terrible tragedy upon St. Peter's Field, he rode down Market Street at the head of a troop of cavalry, and stopping at the front entrance of the Exchange, where raising himself in his stirrups, he waved round his head a fragment of a musical instrument, part of the *spolia opima* of the field, and attempted to excite a cheer. The subscribers to the Exchange, then generally Tories—hating the reformers and not sorry at their dispersion —had yet so much right sentiment, as to see the indecency at making such a

---

[1] They were reprinted by *The Examiner* as well.

manifestation of joy at the cutting down of women and children, legally convened and peaceably assembled, and they turned their backs upon him in silent disgust.

When ought public indignation against the atrocious directors of that tragedy to subside? Never, until they repent of their misdeeds. When those misdeeds are boasted of as virtues, every honest man—every man who desires to prevent the recurrence of such atrocity—ought as a matter of imperative duty, not only to renew his expressions of detestation, but to renew his demands for *justice*.

We repeat that if there is blame to be attached for the re-agitation of this distressing question, it rests on Mr. Philips and Mr. Hulton. WE might have let it sleep, had not the 'firmness' of the Manchester Magistrates been held up as worthy of example and praise. But to let the matter sleep now, when the slaughter of the people is made a matter of proud boast, and when the Tory announcement is that with the possible return of a Tory ascendancy, 'there will be a bit of dust in Manchester and elsewhere, and it will be *laid in blood*', would be cowardly and most culpable forbearance . . .

And thus Archibald Prentice ended, as he had begun, with 'dust in Manchester' to be 'laid in blood' if the Tory party won the next election, with Peterloo as an election cry. It was to be repeated. The national impact of this new Prentician radical offensive was to be noticed in the items the *Manchester Times* quoted from other papers on Prentice's earlier Christmas Eve article:

The *Glasgow Chronicle*: 'how, in reference to the attack upon the unarmed men, women, and children, in St. Peter's Field, could a man of ordinary intellect forget Hulton, any more than he could forget Wellington, in reference to the capitulation of Paris, and the execution of Marshal Ney?'
The *Globe*: 'The Manchester papers accuse Mr. Hulton of not only dealing largely in the rhetorical figure, amplification, but of dealing in that discreditable species of social contraband, designated in Houyhnhnm Land the "thing which is not." For our parts, we deem the whole affair to have been a mere ingenious exhibition to attract attention to the departure of a restless spirit—like "Exit in a flame of fire . . ." '

Hulton's letters acted upon journalists, in that no-holds-barred period of newspaper writing, as if Peterloo had been re-enacted.
From *The Examiner*:

Poor Lord Althorp has been shockingly used by a Lancashire Tory . . . he did but open a friendly communication, as a man might do with a mad bull, asking him what had so transported him; when the savage tossed, tore and gored, and pinned him, and left him speechless . . . A very pleasing letter, such as, coming from a Minister of State, with a great seal to it, notifying the exalted correspondence in the post town—could not have failed to soften the resentment of any magistrate, who had not had a hand in the Manchester transactions. But see the force of habit! Mr Hulton instantly charged upon this peaceable nobleman, in the Peterloo manner, cut him down and trampled him under foot . . .

Mr Hulton has his own taste for fame, but with that we have nothing to do; there may be taste for fame, like that of game most relished by the epicures when it stinks. Those fames, however, which are so very *high*, will not *keep*, and it scarcely surprises us, that so pure a person as Lord Althorp really is, should have his recollections purified from the odour of the Manchester Magistrate . . .

Although Prentice in his new campaign, seemed to exclude vituperation, characteristic of Henry Hunt, proceeding rather with gentler methods, Henry Hunt took great pains to see that he was not left out. He had no newspaper in which to air his views, but at that period he was running his *Addresses from Henry Hunt Esq., to the Radical Reformers of England, Ireland and Scotland, and particularly those of Cheshire, Lancashire, and Yorkshire, on the Measures of the Whig Ministers since they have been in Place and Power.* No. 10 had been about as dull as any printed literature could be, with a résumé of the proposed Reform Bill set out in schedules. The first part of No. 11 was set out similarly, and it would appear that he intended to add to the schedules his comments; he makes one comment, and then proceeds:

I will now proceed to a subject of more vital importance, particularly to the Radical Reformers of Manchester, and of Lancashire and Cheshire, I mean the subject of the bloody tragedy that was perpetrated on the 16th of August, 1819, on the gore drenched field of Peterloo. It appears that Hulton, of Hulton, who was the Chairman of the Manchester magistrates on that lawless day, has lately resigned his seat as a magistrate of that County, under the pretence that Lord Althorp, the Chancellor of the Exchequer, has cast some reflections upon him in a speech that he made in Parliament. [Quotes Althorp's letter and Hulton's reply.] What think you of this, men of Manchester, men of Bolton, men of Lancashire? What think you of this? Well done, Hulton, this beats even your swearing at York.

[Hunt then quotes Hulton's list of casualties.] Only hear Hulton's account of the slaughter; he makes it out to have been a mere trifle. . . . Mark how ably he protects and screens the Manchester Yeomanry! They, kind, gentle, and amiable souls, appear by this Hulton's account to have no hand in any slaughter whatsoever that day. . .

Human nature will blush at this recital. But there is a being in human form who boasts and glories in the transactions of this bloody day, and that being is William Hulton of Hulton, near Bolton, Lancashire. Since I have been in the

House of Commons—the Reform Bill, the eternal Whig Reform Bill, has been the excuse, the ministerial apology for putting off, for delaying all sorts of inquiry. But thank God, Hulton of Hulton has now, by his letter to Lord Althorp brushed away at once all apologies, all excuses, all pretences, for further delay . . . His letter at once demands a full *enquiry* into those bloody deeds. *The enquiry shall forthwith be demanded by me,* and if the Chancellor of the Exchequer, if the Whigs, if the Ministers, have a particle of just feeling left in their bosoms, they will not only grant a Committee of Enquiry into the black deeds, the bloody catalogue of atrocities committed on the 16th of August, 1819, at Manchester, but they will cheerfully aid and assist in promoting that enquiry. We shall see!! [Names the ten magistrates, the Borough-reeve and commanders of the Yeomanry.]

After all, we ought to thank Hulton for ripping up this affair again at this time. Seeing how the House of Commons was composed, I began to despair of having any enquiry into this affair for the present—but thank God, Hulton has grossly insulted Lord Althorp—I believe in the memory of man there never was before such an impudent mass of ignorance and falsehoods thrown in the teeth of a minister of the Crown as there is contained in this precious letter of Hulton to the Chancellor of the Exchequer. But I, for one, thank this impudent, this ignorant, this upstart ex-magistrate, for ripping up the whole affair again; and to show him and the public that I am prepared for the enquiry, and for a full investigation of the whole transaction—I here insert a list of the names and residences of the Manchester Yeomanry on the 16th of August, 1819. These will be useful when the investigation comes on. I will follow it up in my next number, by inserting a list of the names of the maimed and wounded, also the names of the Judges and the Special Jury who tried us at York, and the names of the counsel for the prosecution; also the names of the grand jury at Lancaster, who threw out all the bills preferred against the Yeomanry for cutting and maiming, and who found true bills against myself and all those who were accused of meeting to petition Parliament for a radical reform. I have a list of the witnesses who were examined at York, both for and against the prosecution; I have also a list of those witnesses whom Judge Bayley would not suffer to give evidence against the Yeomanry—in fact, he would not suffer any evidence to be given as to the conduct of the Yeomanry. There has been no inquiry into the conduct yet—no inquiry into the conduct of the magistrates; the inquiry has been all on one side, all ex parte. But let us hope that the time is now come when a full inquiry into this horrid and bloody affair can no longer be withheld, and the truth no longer suppressed.

It hardly needs to be pointed out that there was a fair modicum of truth being suppressed even here; for Henry Hunt in 1831 Redford *v.* Birley did not exist, any more than it did for Prentice. After publishing the list of 1819 members of the Manchester and Salford Yeomanry, Hunt continued:

The above list contains one hundred of as precious fellows as ever graced the pages of history. Let them meet and send a vote of thanks to Hulton for the fresh honour that is conferred upon them; let them offer up their thanks to him for having once more ripped up this affair—the bloody affair of the 10th[1] August, 1819. Hulton was a hero of the day; he received, he says, the thanks of George the Fourth when he was Prince Regent. Let those who boast of and value such thanks, read the life of George IV by Huish: there they may see the character of the man, learn how to estimate the good opinion of such a man.[2] But let us see what those thanks were, and how they were conveyed to Squire Hulton . . . [Quotes the letter.]

So the Prince Regent, the father of his people, expressed his *great satisfaction* at the efficient measures pursued—namely the putting to military execution and death ten men, four women and an infant . . . and cutting and maiming . . . 400 more . . . and his Royal Highness's high approbation of the military heroes in the bloody tragedy. However, let us have a Parliamentary enquiry and then the truth and the whole truth will come out. I will never cease my endeavours to obtain that enquiry. Henry Hunt.

In No. 12 of his 'Addresses . . .' dated 31 December 1831, Henry Hunt writes again. Gone is Hunt's attempt to influence radical reformers on the passage of the Reform Bill; he is back on his old war-horse— the war-horse which had, only a few weeks before, been prostrate and in a state of collapse:

My Excellent Friends. Since I wrote my last address I have seen the Manchester, Bolton, and Preston newspapers, and they one and all have laid it on pretty smartly upon Squire Hulton, of Hulton, near Bolton; they all agree upon this one point that the Squire has given a false account of the murderous slaughter of the 16th of August, 1819; upon which day the Squire played such a conspicuous part. They all agree with me pretty correctly, also as to those which were badly cut, maimed, and wounded [re names already given, now gives names of the wounded.] I believe that our friend Mr. Charles Pearson visited every one on this list . . .

I shall for the present refrain from saying much upon the horrid transactions, the cowardly and bloodthirsty massacre that I was an eyewitness of upon that day; because I shall, if I live, have an opportunity of detailing those deeds, and giving my unqualified opinion of them very soon within the walls of the House of Commons, in the presence and in the hearing of Lord Stanley and many of those who sanctioned and abetted those deeds in the year 1819— within the walls of that House, where there was no man at that time present able to contradict from personal knowledge the inhuman and monstrous

---

[1] A printer's error.
[2] Hunt did not then know that that same writer, Huish, would be the biographer of Henry Hunt; a work which, the D.N.B. writer says, perhaps unjustly, was principally a repetition of Hunt's own memoirs.

misrepresentations that were promulgated there upon the authority of such persons as Hulton of Hulton.

I had the cross-examination of this fellow once in the court at York, but it was an ex parte examination; the Judge would not suffer any questions to be answered as to the conduct either of the Magistrates or that of the Yeomanry; but the result of my cross-examination was this, that Hulton broke down, that his brother-Magistrates, and his twin-brother, Nadin, the high constable of Manchester, when they saw the predicament in which he was, when they saw the pretty Squire in such a pretty pickle, they one and all not only fled in consternation from the Court, but they fled from the city of York in great consternation, fearing that I should call them as witnesses-in-chief to contradict the whole of that which the Hulton Squire was swearing. But this dread of the Squire's colleagues was unnecessary, I caused the Squire before I had finished him off, to do all that was necessary in this way himself. And when he left the witness-box there was not a single person in the court, from the Judge down to the meanest door-keeper that entertained two opinions as to the credibility of the Hulton Squire. As for the testimony of Nadin[1] whilst this cross-examination was going on of the Squire, it had such an effect upon the hardened thief-taker, that the mere anticipation of a similar exhibition upon himself, caused drops of sweat to hunt each other in quick succession down his cadaverous and unblushing cheeks. And yet the Hulton Squire boasts of the share he had in the black catalogue of the bloody deeds which occurred upon that lawless day. [Here Hunt included $6\frac{1}{2}$ pages of the names of the wounded; followed by the names of the Jury at Lancaster and York; and the four Judges.]

Now, my good friends, you will see that I have put upon record the names of the principal actors in the bloody massacre of Peterloo in 1819; the Prince Regent, afterwards George IV being the head of the Government—his father, George III, being confined to Windsor suffering under insanity and blindness —Liverpool, Lord of the Treasury, Castlereagh, Canning, and Sidmouth, the then secretaries of State—*all these* but Sidmouth are called to answer for their deeds before the King of Kings.

As for Hulton, the pretended cause of his resignation is well known to be a sham—it is well known by his brother magistrates that he has been waiting for an excuse for years. A gentleman who is intimate with him writes me this fact; and adds: 'It is a well-authenticated fact that Hulton has not had a single day of prosperity since he gave the murderous order for the Yeomanry to cut down unarmed men, defenceless women, and helpless infants; every speculation that he has entered into since has been blighted, as it were, by the hand of an avenging Providence; he cannot realize a profit even from his *own* coal mines, though his neighbours who have to pay heavy rents have been making princely fortunes out of worse coals. It seems as if that day's BLOOD stuck

[1] There was no 'testimony of Nadin', of course, at York, and he was not in the courtroom.

to him, and as if the Almighty wreaked his dipleasure upon all his worldly concerns.' Another gentleman informs me that this Hulton of Hulton, near Bolton, has at this time one of the Caps of Liberty that was taken on Peterloo, in his dressing-room at Hulton, and that he has seen it there. Was this Cap of Liberty carried by William Dawson, of Saddleworth, who was sabred, cut down, and murdered upon the spot? But let us have patience awhile. I am, my Excellent Friends, your very sincere and faithful servant H. Hunt.[1]

Henry Hunt's renewed vituperation did not perhaps have such a wide circulation as the more insidious propaganda of Prentice. Both, however, had their full impact on the public they were intended to influence; both referred to September 1819, or April 1820 (after Hunt's trial), jumping from one to the other as it suited their argument. Twelve years interval had blurred memories even of those who had followed the tortuous course of the elucidation of the facts. Total recklessness with the assertion of 'facts' was the order of the day, not the least of which was Hulton's giving the 'murderous order for the Yeomanry to cut down unarmed men, defenceless women, and helpless infants'. Hulton, as a result of his correspondence with Lord Althorp, was made the incarnation of all the murder, the atrocity, the lies, the callousness; or, as a modern writer puts it:

. . . the savage repression of the working-class movement . . . charging dragoons and butchered babes, a spectacular hecatomb in which the flower of progressive England was ruthlessly put to the sword.[2]

On 21 January 1832, the *Guardian* published a small item of news of current interest:

The Reformers' Prayer. We have seen a small paper under this title, and apparently printed in this town for halfpenny circulation, in the contents of which it is difficult to say whether blasphemy or sedition most predominates. It is a vile parody, somewhat *a la* Carlile, on portions of the litany of the Church of England, and contains, amongst other 'prayers', the following:

'From all those damnable bishops, lords and peers,—from all those bloody murdering Peterloo butchers—from all those idle drones that live out of the earnings of the people—Good God deliver us'.

To this we may add one of the 'supplications', as it shows that the object of the paper is not to be mistaken.

'That it may please thee to bless the people of these dominions with a full determination to put down all oppression and tyranny, and to gain the day, though death and hell obstruct the way. We beseech thee to hear us good Lord.'

[1] The extract quoted on pp. 29–30 above was also from this series of Hunt's *Addresses*.

[2] Ziegler, *Addington*, p. 196.

In the House of Commons on 2 March 1831, Henry Hunt had intervened in the debate on the Ministerial Plan of Parliamentary Reform:

They had been told, that if the measure before them was not carried, its rejection would lead to revolution and massacre. What sort of massacre? When he attended a meeting at Manchester in the year 1819—a meeting as peaceable and as orderly as that now assembled in the House of Commons, and met, too, for as peaceable and constitutional an object—the attainment of constitutional Reform; when that meeting took place, there was a real massacre. A drunken and infuriated yeomanry (Loud cries of 'No, No,' and 'Question!')—a drunken and infuriated Yeomanry, with swords newly sharpened (Reiterated cries of 'No, No!' and 'Question!') with swords newly sharpened, slaughtered fourteen, and maimed and wounded 648. (Shouts of 'No. No!' and 'Question!') Where is the man who will step forward and say 'No'. I say again (said the hon. Member in a tone of voice louder, and louder still, which was almost drowned by still more vehement cries of 'No!' and 'Order!') that on that day a drunken and infuriated yeomanry murdered 14 and badly cut and maimed 648 of as peaceable and well-disposed persons as any he saw around him . . .[1]

Mr Thompson writes:[2]

In 1819 the action of the loyalists, found many defenders in their own class. Ten years later it was an event to be remembered, even among the gentry, with guilt. As a *massacre* and as 'Peterloo' it went down to the next generation.

The House of Commons in the early months of 1831 was still unreformed and 'corrupt'; it was full of 'gentry'; but they did not appear to display much in the way of 'guilt'! A year later, there were, however, forces at work in the House of Commons and elsewhere who were determined to send the 16 August down to the next generation as a 'massacre', difficult although the task seemed in 1832. The struggle had shifted from the country to the House of Commons. Henry Hunt was lining up his forces.

[1] Parl. Deb., 3rd Series II, p. 1211.
[2] Thompson, p. 683.

XXIX

Hunt's Parliamentary Showdown:
A New Call to the Unconverted

On 17 March[1] Hunt presented a petition from Blackley (Manchester) praying for Reform and for an inquiry into the 'Manchester Massacre'. Hunt said:

It was his intention to bring that subject forward on some future date. Murder, he said, would out, and he knew no reason why that murder should be palliated more than another. Lord Althorp suggested that as the language of the petition was so strong, it ought not to be printed. His own opinions on that occurrence were well known. Petition to lie on the Table.

A little earlier a petition had been sent to Lord Althorp, who was known never to have refused to present petitions when sent to him:

Acting upon that principle, [Lord Althorp said] he had now to present one, in the prayer of which he could not concur. The language was undoubtedly strong, though not stronger than others which the House had received. One of the passages was: 'They had heard with horror and indignation that Mr. Hulton, of Hulton, who was one of the magistrates . . . has in some correspondence which has been printed, spoken of the frightful deeds done at Manchester as meritorious, and even dared to threaten the town with similar occurrences.'

Whether such a petition should be printed was, of course a matter of discretion with the House. It certainly was not his intention to make any motion to that effect himself. The petition was agreed to at a meeting at Cropper Street, Manchester, but it only bore the signature of Mr. Samuel Hewett, the chairman. [It prayed for an inquiry] . . . At this distance of time he believed that further inquiry into that unfortunate circumstance would serve only to rake up and renew old feelings of political animosity, without affording the means of promoting the ends of justice; therefore, although he had moved for inquiry shortly after the circumstances had occurred, he hoped he should not be considered inconsistent if he were opposed to it after a lapse of twelve years.[2]

[1] Parl. Deb., 3rd series, XI, p. 498.
[2] Parl. Deb., 3rd series, X, p. 196.

Other members said that public attention had been excited by the
Hulton-Althorp correspondence, that Hulton had 'dared to avow the
part which he had taken in it'; that the 'feelings of the friends of the
dead should be aroused' was not surprising. Mr Hunt said he 'could
never call what had occurred at Manchester anything less than a cool
deliberate murder. Let there be an inquiry, and let it be shown that the
authorities were not to blame, and he would never open his lips again
on the subject . . . There would never be peace and contentment in
the manufacturing districts until satisfaction was obtained.' Joseph
Hume, the Radical M.P., who was to be Hunt's seconder later, said:

He remembered, as if it were but yesterday, the means which were adopted to
prevent the bringing forward of evidence at the inquests on the occasion in
question. He was satisfied that, in the future history of this country, the
Oldham inquest would always be considered as a most disgraceful transaction.
It appeared to him, also, from the correspondence recently printed in the
newspapers, that Mr. Hulton triumphed in the proceedings of that day—
proceedings which ought to call up none but painful recollections. He hoped
that the noble Lord would alter his mind and allow inquiry . . . Inquiry was
desirable, were it only to impress upon the minds of persons in authority,
that, however long a period might elapse after the commission of an offence,
their conduct would not escape investigation.

The petition was not printed; it lay on the Table. The *Manchester
Guardian*[1] wrote:

There can be no danger of the recurrence of such transactions as those of the
16th of August. The days of Tory domination are gone by. A new state of
things, and in great part, a new generation of men, has arisen amongst us. In
the respectable classes of society there is a much more liberal and kindly
disposition—a much fairer and truer appreciation of each other's motives and
intentions, than was then prevalent; and anything which might tend to shake
these mutual good feelings, would be very greatly to be deprecated. We have
not the least doubt as to the agreement with us of a vast majority of the respectable inhabitants of Manchester, in thinking it highly inexpedient that the time
of the legislature should be wasted in raking up by-gone matters, an accurate
investigation of which the interval of a dozen years has rendered almost
morally impossible, at a time when various important subjects are urgently
requiring an extent and closeness of attention which their very number almost
renders it impossible that they should receive.

One person at least would have found it difficult to see any evidence of
the 'much fairer and truer appreciation of each other's motives and
intentions', but perhaps he was prejudiced.

[1] *Manchester Guardian*, 18 February 1832.

Henry Hunt, on 15 March 1832, was all prepared for what was going to be the final Parliamentary 'show-down' on the transactions of 16 of August. He had earlier complained, in his addresses to Radical Reformers (No. 11), that there was, in 1819, no radical member in the House of Commons at the time when the House was being 'hoaxed' into believing the 'lies' put into Government spokesmen's mouths by men like Hulton. 1832 would be somewhat different. True, there would still be no one there except Hunt, who had first-hand knowledge of what took place on St Peter's Field, but there were still in the House of Commons many old 'allies' who had fought for inquiry before. He would discount, of course, Scarlett (now Sir James Scarlett); he would discount Sir Francis Burdett! But there was John Cam Hobhouse who had chastened Castlereagh in the House and in print; there was Thomas Creevey who had voted consistently with the Whigs when Peterloo came up; there was Alderman Wood, whom Hunt had in 1821 listed (with Creevey) as 'active members' who were prevented by Burdett's motion in the House at that time, from bringing forward their motions for inquiry. There was Denman (now Sir Thomas Denman) who had disbelieved the stones and brickbats story; and there was Alderman Waithman, whose resolution in the Common Council of London had brought the Royal rebuke that he was misinformed. And finally there was Lord Althorp, in whom Hunt had faith enough to ask him to second his motion. Althorp refused. Hunt fell back on Joseph Hume.

The debate is entitled in Hansard[1] 'Affray at Manchester'. Hunt presented petitions from Paisley, Huddersfield, Hull, Halifax, and other places, praying for inquiry. His narration of the events as he then stated them has already been given at length.[2] Hunt's estimate of the numbers attending had dropped from 150,000 to 100,000 'all of whom he could affirm were peaceably disposed.' He added other details:

To give the House one instance of the conduct of the Yeomanry, he must state, that a portion of the crowd, consisting of about thirty to forty persons, men, women, and children, having fled for refuge into a court, from which there was but one egress, two Yeomen stationed themselves at that point, and compelled the poor people to come out, the one holding in his hand a pistol, with which he threatened to blow their brains out if they did not obey, and the other with his drawn sword, cutting at every one of them as they passed out.

One man—an inhabitant of Stockport—had a piece of his skull cut away by a sabre, and here (added the hon. Member, displaying on the palm of his

[1] Vol. XI, 3rd series, p. 251.
[2] See above, pp. 29–30.

hand a fragment of bone about the size of a half-a-crown), here was the piece itself to satisfy hon. Members of the fact.

It could be proved, that the Yeomanry had assailed and wounded helpless females. It could be proved, that one female had been over-turned, and her face being down a hill, part of her person was exposed. Some persons looking from a window called to a Yeoman to render her that assistance which any one, with a sense of decency, would naturally hasten to render on an occasion of the kind. Now, what did this gallant Yeoman do? Would the House believe it? Would Englishmen credit it? This brave, this loyal, soldier, rode up to the prostrate woman and cut her across the thighs with his sabre! He would venture to say, that neither in foreign nor domestic wars, had English soldiers committed acts so disgraceful as those which were perpetrated by the Yeomanry at Peterloo.

Hunt's speech was long, incorporating much which has already been told in this narrative; he hoped he would live to see the day when justice was inflicted on all who committed and abetted the massacre at Manchester.

In vain had that arrogant and insolent party sent Reformer after Reformer to prison—in vain had they gagged the press[1] by acts as alien to the practice as they were novel to the British Constitution—in vain had they passed Bills to prevent public meetings, and to put down the right of petitioning; for, in spite of the menaces of the law, and the terrors of the dungeon, the cause of Reform had proved a giant too powerful for them to cope with . . .

Joseph Hume, who seconded Hunt's motion, recalled Prentice in his approach: he would not, he said, say a word in aggravation of the atrocities of that day, which at the time excited general horror and indignation:

He would content himself with declaring it to be his opinion, that it was no less the duty of the present Government than that of the House to agree to this inquiry . . . He did not pretend to say, that all the long detail of atrocities into which the Hon. Member for Preston had entered was correct; but this he would say, that if one-tenth part of it only were true, there were sufficient grounds and far more than sufficient grounds for inquiry . . . Tens of thousands of men in the north of England were complaining that hitherto justice had not been done.

Mr Lamb had been in favour of inquiry earlier; he was not in favour now; many major and minor actors were beyond the reach of earthly justice; it would be a better course to have preached the Christian doc-

[1] How 'gagged' the press was between 1819 and 1832 could be a matter for dispute.

trine of forgiveness of injuries, instead of exciting them to renew their call for vengeance and for blood. If the day for bringing to justice crime was not passed, the courts were still open for those who felt aggrieved; such investigations would be conducted more satisfactorily in those courts than by a Select Committee of that House. He regretted that Hunt had referred to cold-blooded murders—such were not the terms of a man who sought for impartial inquiry; he cited Redford *v.* Birley.

Sir John Byng said he was not present when the affray took place, but he was on the spot within two hours of its occurrence:

He then being in command of his Majesty's troops stationed in that district, he, of course, had deemed it his duty to inquire into their conduct on the occasion, and, as he was not what could be considered an interested person,[1] he trusted the House would give at least as much credence to his testimony as to that of [another member] whose information could only have been derived from, in all probability, interested sources. That hon. Member had been pleased to charge the military employed by the Magistrates on that occasion with the crime of murder. To say the least of it, that was a harsh term to apply to the conduct of individuals who were compelled to perform a most unpleasant duty. But he had no hesitation in saying its application, in that instance, by the Hon. Member was most ungenerous and unjust. If the inquiry which was proposed was to be confined to his Majesty's troops at Manchester on the 16th of August, 1819, so far from opposing it, he should be one of its most anxious supporters. But, as the motion took a more extended compass, as it would have the effect of raking up circumstances which, for the peace of the country, ought for ever to be buried in oblivion, he could not find it consistent with his duty to support it. He had ever desired that a full inquiry should take place in all cases where his Majesty's troops were engaged, more particularly if such occurrences were attended with loss of life; but it was to be recollected that the present case had formed the subject of three separate judicial inquiries—the proper arena for its consideration—the results of which had been a complete acquittal of the King's troops from all charge of misconduct or unnecessary violence. He could not support the motion.

Sir Robert Peel's opinions in 1822, as Home Secretary and successor to Lord Sidmouth have already been quoted. They were not modified; they were even stronger. In this debate he adverted to a former speaker's charge of the use of spies:

He desired to be understood as having no interest, no bias of partiality or favour, in defending the Manchester Magistrates, for, at the time of the Affray in 1819, he was not in office, and consequently not responsible for any of the events of the period. He understood that, on that occasion, agents,

[1] He was Whig M.P. for Poole.

or spies,[1] if they were to be so called, were employed; but he felt it due towards the individuals who had preceded him in office—Lord Sidmouth and Mr. Hobhouse—to declare his conviction that, in the employment of those spies, no instruction whatever was given which might not be published to the whole world. They were employed, not as was falsely said, to tempt others to the commission of crime, but to enable the Government by timely notice, to protect society from wicked plots against its peace that were then maturing . . .

If any circumstances had impeded an inquiry by the legal tribunals, then the proposal for a parliamentary investigation would have met with his support. But had there been any such impediment? Did the conduct of the parties engaged in the affray escape the notice of judicial tribunals: Was there no decision by a Court of Justice?

Mr. Hunt: There was an unfair one.

Sir Robert Peel supposed the hon. Member alluded to his own case, and he could assure him that it was not his intention to say anything which could hurt his feelings. The hon. Member . . . was not a very disinterested and impartial judge on that point. The fact could not be denied, that the verdict of the jury was against him, and that he was, by Mr. Justice Bayley, sentenced to imprisonment . . .

Peel then referred to the Lancaster trial of Redford v. Birley . . . 'thus was the case twice decided after a solemn investigation. But it underwent a third, and, if possible, a more solemn, inquiry: for . . . a motion for a new trial' [in Redford v. Birley] 'after solemn argument, which lasted two days' [the Judges unanimously] 'expressed their conviction that no blame whatever was attributable to either the magistrates, yeomanry, or military engaged in the affray; so far from it, they stated their opinion that the conduct of those individuals entitled them to the thanks, not only of the people of Manchester, but of the country.'[2]

It was not his own opinion he was propounding [said Peel] he was reading the solemn judgment of the Lord Chief Justice of England judicially delivered. To assent to this motion would be to reverse the judgment of the Lord Chief Justice of England, and other Judges, and to supersede the authority of the Court in which they presided.

Peel then gave the judgment of Judge Bayley, who had had the advantage of hearing the previous trial (Hunt's), and quoted Judge Best and Judge Holroyd. He proceeded:

---

[1] Hunt had alleged in his speech (reported p. 30 of this work) that 'the delay of a week between the two meetings [9 and 16 August] allowed spies to be sent through the country by whose agency the people's passions were excited . . .' This should be compared with Richard Carlile's statement on p. 198.

[2] See above, pp. 417–19.

Such was the decision pronounced upon this transaction by the Judges, after the fullest inquiry, upon evidence given on oath, and while the events in question were fresh in the memory of all the parties concerned. Who could say with truth that this subject had not been inquired into, had not been disposed of finally by the tribunals best qualified to dispose of it justly. For his part, after the opinions of the Judges expressed on the conduct of the parties accused, he would not, for the sake of any popular feeling, be guilty of so shabby and disgraceful an act as to abandon those whose conduct had been pronounced, not only free from blame, but entitled to high commendation; and he should therefore at once, join in meeting the Motion with a direct negative on the plain merits of the question.

If they were to revive those transactions which ought to have been long since buried in oblivion, and subject the individuals accused and honourably acquitted to further examination, they would be doing that which was utterly inconsistent with the first principles of justice. The hand of death had now removed most of the parties who had acted a prominent part on the occasion in question; the long interval of twelve years had put much important testimony out of reach of any human tribunal; full inquiry had been made at the time, and that inquiry had established the innocence of those who were accused. If no time, no acquittal, could protect public officers from new trials, on imperfect evidence, what prudent man would undertake a thankless public duty that exposed him to such persecution?

Henry Hunt repeated his accusation that Redford *v.* Birley was a sham trial, only to receive Peel's crushing rejoinder. Hunt, curiously enough, without much difficulty and with little or no prompting, got to what this investigation has called the heart of the matter:

As to the people being armed at Manchester, he would merely ask, was there a dagger, or a bludgeon, or a sword, found on one of them; and if there had been any such weapons, would they not have been produced? If it could be proved that Lord Sidmouth had hired spies, he would say, that, high as he was, there never was a more fit subject for impeachment. The Rt. hon. Secretary seemed to think that his object in making the Motion was to punish the Yeomanry. He had no such intention. He aimed at higher game, and would be ashamed to prosecute such humble individuals if higher characters could be reached . . .

Hunt said he was sorry Lord Stanley was not in the House to hear what he had to say about the throwing out of bills by the grand jury at Lancaster. Sir James Scarlett, however, was on the benches to hear what Hunt had to say on English justices:

. . . All the counsel against him [Hunt] had been made Judges, with the exception of the hon. Member for Cockermouth [Sir James Scarlett], who, he hoped, had not been neglected, because he [Mr. Hunt] had been rather an overmatch for him. Sergeant Cross, Sergeant Hullock, and Mr. Alderson, had all been made Judges; but how did it happen that Mr. Judge Bayley had never been raised higher? That Judge, he was informed, had declared that he would not subject him to one hour's imprisonment;[1] but his opinion was controlled by the other Judges. The way in which the Judges settled the period of punishment for him was done in the following way, as he had learned from one of the Judge's clerks, and he believed that was the usual mode of proceeding when they differed in opinion, they put down their opinions in writing; Mr. Justice Bayley was against any imprisonment, Mr. Justice Best was for five years, Mr. Justice Holroyd for three, and Mr. Justice Abbot for two; so they added the number up, divided the sum by four, which gave him two years and a-half imprisonment. He must, in conclusion, say, that he liked the decided opposition, to the measure made by one party, than the quibbling of the other side. He hoped the Rt. hon. Member for Tamworth [Peel] would alter his opinion with respect to spies, as he had once before very honourably done on the Catholic question.

Sir Robert Peel returned to Hunt's point that Redford *v.* Birley was a mock trial, and he also replied to Hunt regarding spies:

. . . What he said relative to the employment of spies was this—that the employment of spies for the purposes of fomenting and exciting disturbances, and then bringing the persons who participated in those disturbances to punishment, was an unwarrantable use of improper instruments which ought to subject the persons using them to the heaviest penalty which the Constitution provided for such offence; but he added, that he could not, as an honest man, having some experience of Government, assent to the doctrine that Government were not justified under any circumstances in availing themselves of the assistance of spies . . .

One Member said it was strange that Hunt, who objected so much to the employment of spies, 'should have made use of knowledge avowedly obtained from a servant who had betrayed the secrets of his master.' Another Member denied that Lord Sidmouth had sent spies to Manchester in order to excite the people to outrage; he was incapable of such conduct, nor would he shrink from the defence of any act which he had done in the execution of his duty. Sir James Scarlett had the last word, except for a brief denial by Hunt that he had employed a Judge's clerk to betray the secrets of his master.

Sir James Scarlett said that the hon. Member for Preston had alluded to a triumph which he supposed he had gained over him on a former occasion. He

---

[1] Hunt's reliance on third-party testimony on such a point was disingenuous. Judge Bayley had told him at first hand that on such a point he was misinformed. See above p. 347.

was quite unconscious of the circumstance; but if the idea afforded the hon. Member any pleasure, he might continue to enjoy it. The hon. Member, however, was entirely mistaken in all the facts he had stated respecting the judgment of the Judges. He was astonished that a person of the hon. Gentleman's experience should suppose that the Judges would allow their clerks to know the result of their deliberations. He was sure, that if any Judge in England should be guilty of conduct so absurd and base, Mr. Justice Bayley would not be the man. He would unite with the hon. Member in praising the learning and integrity of that Judge.[1] He conducted the hon. Member's trial in a most impartial manner. The result of the trial was well known. With respect to his share in the proceedings, he would not say a word, because he was always unwilling to allude in that House to transactions in which he had been engaged as counsel.

During the debate the parallel of Manchester with Bristol was referred to; another Member thought the Yeomanry the most unconstitutional force in the country, a fact mentioned here in view of the contrary opinion prevailing on the Opposition benches in 1819. If inquiry was not made now, it was asserted, it would ultimately be granted by a reformed House of Commons. A view which was to be animadverted on with some heat outside the House. The division: Hunt's motion received thirty-one votes; against him 206.[2] Hansard, unfortunately does not give the names of the Members voting against Hunt, only those voting for. All those former 'allies' of Hunt's mentioned earlier either voted against him, or did not vote. The final Parliamentary verdict had been delivered on the Transactions at Manchester. Hunt's 'show-down' was complete.

[1] 'By Heavens, the greatest pleasure I have is to dwell upon the hope that I shall live to *impeach* the four Judges that sentenced me, and particularly the junior Puisne Judge, Sir William Draper Best. Perhaps Mr. Justice Bayley, who tried me, deserves it more than the said William Draper Best, because, he pretends, at least, to be an impartial Judge and a conscientious man. He heard the trial, saw and heard the extraordinary evidence of Hulton and others who appeared against me. He gave me fair play as opposed to Scarlett, but he contrived to get a verdict which no Judge, who wished it, could have missed with a packed and corrupt jury. If I live, and have the opportunity, I will impeach Mr. Justice Bayley; but I should find great difficulty in serving him as, I think, he did me, viz. pass a cruel sentence upon him merely because my brother Judges thought he ought to be punished for some other offence besides that of which he was found guilty. King Alfred always made a point of hanging corrupt Judges as often as he could detect them. . . .' Henry Hunt *To the Radical Reformers* . . . 26 July 1821, p. 14.

[2] In the tiny type of its brief parliamentary report, the division figures were quoted correctly in *The Examiner* of 18 March 1832. In the larger type of its leading article, it drew its conclusion:

'. . . The Ministerial and Tory forces were again allied, and the result was a majority against investigation of 175. The corrupt House has again proved, in another memorable instance, how deservedly it has forfeited the confidence of the country.'

It would, it is suggested, be a mistaken notion to conclude that the result of Hunt's motion in the House of Commons rendered Archibald Prentice speechless for the first time for a long time. That is, however, the inference which could be drawn from the *Manchester Times* leader, dated 24 March 1832:

The Parliamentary debates since our last publication, [the leader begins] have been important enough to induce us to report them at such length as leaves us little room for remark. We have elsewhere given the comments of the leading London papers on Mr. Hunt's motion as corroboratory to all that we have, over and over again, said on the subject of the terrible massacre of a legally convened and peaceably assembled multitude. With *The Times* we agree that 'it was a wanton and unnecessary effusion of human blood'; and with the *Morning Herald* that 'the feelings produced by the affair at Manchester have never been buried', and we have no hesitation in adding that they ought never to be buried till its true character is pronounced by the legislature, and therefore we coincide in the opinion of the *Morning Chronicle* that 'it is not too late to inquire into the circumstances with a view to a solemn parliamentary condemnation of the conduct of the magistracy.'

With the *Examiner* we regret that Lord Althorp should have considered the lapse of time as any reason for the refusal of an inquiry, believing that 'the longer the time, the greater the scandal to justice; unless, indeed the principle is to go forth that crime ceases to be crime, if it can elude retribution for a given period.' And with that able and independent paper 'we cannot help running comparisons between the fiery zeal of the corrupt Commons to give redress to the sinecure parsons, and its vehement anxiety for the respect of the laws in this behalf, with its perfect content that the damning blot should remain on English justice that a great slaughter of unoffending people should have been committed, and none made answerable for the crime.'

Some of the Members of the House of Commons had been at much pains to explain that the opening statement in Prentice's article was not valid any more, that it was not a 'terrible massacre of a legally convened and peaceably assembled multitude'. But perhaps Prentice's next sentence is the most ironic in the article: 'With *The Times* we agree...' meaning —with *The Times* leader-writer *we* agree. There had been another occasion when the 'we' of Prentice's had really been a 'we' and not an 'I'; and on that occasion the 'we' of Prentice's had agreed with the 'we' of *The Times* leader-writer. And the result of that agreement had been the production of the most misleading, and, it is believed, the most far-reaching piece of garbled news ever to issue from a newspaper office. Who wrote that 'historic' article on that fatal evening of 16 August 1819—which of the 'we' who received the credit for it—will perhaps never accurately be known. But it was Prentice who recorded the story in his *Recollections*, and it was Prentice who was 'agreeing' with *The Times* again in March 1832, whilst his erstwhile partner of the 'we' of 1819 was disagreeing. One of the 'we' between 16 August and 21 August 1819, caused the other partner in the 'we' to modify what had been written; from, it may be recapitulated, 'actually hacking their way up to the hustings' to 'instantly charged up to the hustings'. If, in examining the 'we's' literary compositions between 1819 and 1832, the conclusion is come to that one of the two was less prone to 'modifying' what he had written than the other, then the one less prone to modifying is the favourite candidate to have written the original strongly-worded letter to *The Times*. Such, however, can only be mere speculation. On the subject of Peterloo, Prentice is on record with his book—his *Recollections* of 1851. Taylor is on record only (outside Prentice's book) in his *Observations* of December 1819; on record, that is, outside the columns of the *Guardian* which, for the purposes of a study of Peterloo, have seldom been considered, certainly not in depth.

Prentice, in his made-up leader of other papers' opinions, made no attempt to tell his readers that the other papers' opinions he was then printing were precisely the same papers which had glibly echoed what he had said in reply to Hulton. That those 'facts' on Peterloo—exploded facts—put forth by Prentice in reply to Hulton, were imagined correct enough to reprint, is sufficient commentary that the papers which reprinted them were not very correctly informed. They were no more correctly informed after the 'Affray at Manchester' Parliamentary debate. *The Times's* writers of 1832 had probably not the least idea that their predecessors of 1819 had garbled the reporters' copy, any more than *The Times's* history writers had in 1935. They had this to say:

(*The Times*, March 23rd, 1832) Mr. Hunt made his motion last night for an inquiry into the dreadful proceedings which took place at Manchester more than twelve years ago; and the public will see how the question is disposed of. Even now, when passion has, to a degree subsided, and ardent feeling been cooled by time, our reason and reflection preserves us in the same opinion which we originally expressed on that atrocious affair. It was a wanton and unnecessary effusion of human blood. It was what we first called it—a massacre. Of the utility of reviving the inquiry now, we are not equally convinced. The effect of the motion, if granted, would have been to embarrass and disturb ministers in the accomplishment of a vast measure, which, when completed, will render similar events to that which it was proposed to investigate impossible. Let us, then, seek the greater good, and leave the rest to follow in its train.

If it were only meant to give the act which took place on that fatal day, at

Manchester, its proper name, and leave it branded to posterity, that has been done already. The actors are not all within our reach; the chief, who was not present on the field, but without whose assured countenance and support the massacre would never have taken place, is gone to another tribunal. [Castlereagh?][1] Of the inferior personages also, many more have since died; the rest who survive—the meaner instruments—live but to see the obloquy which is justly heaped upon their conduct by the uninfluenced and impartial judgment of their countrymen.

The Times was, probably, more responsible than any other instrument in causing the nation to misjudge what had occurred on St Peter's Field; to their credit, it may be said, that owing to the unfortunate train of circumstances leading up to that 'historic' issue, it was done unwittingly.

Of the other papers featured in Prentice's leader, and which had implicitly believed Prentice's 'facts' not many weeks before, may be mentioned the *Morning Herald*. Their leader thought:

. . . that opinion has undergone a very considerable change within the walls of Parliament since they used to echo with the praises of those valiant persons who had proved their valour upon an unarmed multitude, whose only crime consisted in their numerical display. We hail this change of tone as the harbinger of better feeling and better times. It now appears that the 'Heroes of Peterloo' must henceforth be satisfied with a very different appellation. The most that could be done for them was to appeal to the length of time that had elapsed, and invoke the Christian spirit of forgiveness to interpose between them and the punishment due to their atrocities.

This invocation we cannot disapprove, but great outrages live long in the minds and in the passions of men; and though the transactions at Manchester may possibly be forgiven, they never will be forgotten by those who hate the wanton and wicked effusion of human blood. It is far from our wish to revive any angry feelings, but the fact is, that the feelings produced by the affair at Manchester have never been buried, and the tone of the late discussion in parliament will do more to appease them, by showing that they are held in proper abhorrence, than if the sufferers or their surviving friends were left solely to their own reflections.

[1] '. . . The various suspensions of the Habeas Corpus were the work of that [Lord Castlereagh's] mind, which knew no other mode of checking Reform in England than what had succeeded (for a time) in suppressing rebellion in Ireland,—viz. *force*. The approval of the Manchester Massacre, though the name of Lord Sidmouth was used, evidently required more daring than that poor creature possessed. The whole task of justifying that outrage and denying inquiry, the astounding effrontery of turning the tables on the complaining people, and curbing them by the famous Six Acts, all belonged to' [Lord Castlereagh].
The Examiner's obituary notice of Lord Castlereagh, 18 August 1822.

The 'tone' of some of the thirty-one minority of Members in the House of Commons in the Affray at Manchester debate may have justified such a conclusion; but the 'tone' and the votes of 206 others could be said to lead to a different one. How misinformed was the *Morning Herald*, apart from being misinformed by the earlier Prentice 'facts' is shown by their utter ignorance of what had transpired 'within the walls of parliament' when it was stated that 'they used to echo with the praises of those valiant persons who had proved their valour'. Reference to the debates from 1819 onwards proves the utter invalidity of such an assertion. The feelings at Manchester never were buried; there were many who took good care of that, not the least important person being the individual who went to the trouble of reprinting the articles.

The *Morning Chronicle* was utterly unconvinced: '. . . No transaction in our times has so much contributed to alienate the working population from the higher ranks as the Manchester massacre:

It is, indeed, hardly possible to conceive a more base and cowardly exercise of power than the attack on the 16th of August, 1819 by an armed force, on an immense multitude of men, and women assembled for a lawful object, and conducting themselves in a peaceable manner . . . In no country but England would the strong feelings of kindred have been so subdued [Non-existence of feuds and seeking revenge] as to allow all the actors to escape with impunity. But, though, as was stated by Mr. Hunt, two of the Yeomanry who so wantonly shed the blood of their unoffending fellow-citizens, committed suicide on the 16th of August, and many of them were now to be seen walking about the streets of Manchester, objects of a horrid pity, yet we never heard that the vengeance of the sufferers, the sympathy of friends, and excited feelings of surviving relatives, led to one single retaliation on the guilty Yeomanry . . .

[On the courts being still open for redress]: This is a somewhat stale piece of irony. Against a combination of Tory magistrates, a pretty chance there is of obtaining justice in courts of law, for acts for which redress could not be obtained at the time when the subscriptions of the well-disposed throughout the country secured the aid of legal talents and industry. But though justice cannot now be expected from the tribunals, for the sufferers, it is not too late to inquire into the circumstances with a view to a solemn parliamentary condemnation of the conduct of the magistrates on the 16th of August, 1819, of the conduct of the Ministry who approved of the proceedings, thanked the magistracy, and recommended the Rev. Hay to one of the most valuable church livings at the disposal of the Crown.

Such a condemnation, though far from what offended justice demands, would still serve to fill up the breach between the higher and the working classes. It would serve to restore to the people their ancient confidence, that, whatever were the abuses in our judicial system, human life is still saved from the wanton attacks of power . . . The consciousness of the wrong committed on the 16th of August, 1819, towards the working people, haunts the higher ranks of England; they feel that in screening the actors on that occasion, they have done that for which they deserve to be hated.'

The seeds of the *Morning Chronicle*'s contentions, scattered broadcast over the land of England, brought forth in due time their crop. They were bitter herbs. As the most formidable 1819 critic of the Ministry and the magistrates was to say that same week, a demand for an inquiry of the nature proposed by the *Morning Chronicle*'s article would have prejudged the whole affair from the start. Hunt's lurid fact of the suicides of Yeomanry-men could have been true; they could well have committed suicide, but not for the reasons attributed.

The *Examiner* brought parallels with the Ministry's policy in Ireland: 'It is good to observe how differently the importance is rated of the denial of tithes in Ireland, and the destruction of life in England. The courts are as open to the parsons in Leinster as to the slaughtered at Manchester . . . but, as blood, not benefices, is involved in the question the tendency is thought of no account.'

And yet [*The Examiner* went on] if the people of England should get a notion, that they have no protection against the sabres of a brutal soldiery; and that for lives taken for no illegal act, nothing is to be had but the King's thanks to the butchers,—if this impression should be made, it will go far to produce a feeling in this country which will require the employment of more bayonets and dungeons than it is in the power of any government to supply . . .

Thus Sir John Byng had spoken in vain. The *Examiner* took up the point made by one speaker in the debate that the reformed parliament would certainly institute an inquiry, and if so, then a correct opinion would be formed upon the subject of the transactions at Manchester. It could well be added that, more than a century later, a 'correct opinion' is still needed.

Archibald Prentice did not quote the other local papers on the debate. All had long leaders. The *Manchester Herald*:[1]

. . . That the member for Preston, Mr. Hunt, should revive this subject is not surprising; he tells us he was returned to Parliament for that purpose; but that he should have been supported in his motion or even seconded, after the legal decisions which have taken place, does, we confess, surprise us . . .

What Hunt and Hume, and other radicals, expected from their motion, had it been successful, we cannot imagine. Did they hope to be able to put

[1] *Manchester Herald*, 20 March 1832.

the magistrates upon their trial for doing what the judges of the land have declared entitled them to the thanks of their country? Such a notion is ridiculous; and yet this, or some purpose equally absurd, is the only object to which we can refer such a strange proceeding.

The *Manchester Courier*[1] soon detected the Lord Althorp[2] *faux pas* in referring to 'participators in the crime', which he had quickly retracted; it was too late to be of any benefit to William Hulton.

Wheeler's Manchester Chronicle[3] (not in 1832 the Tory paper Prentice made it out to be):

. . . We never refer to this melancholy transaction without feeling a deep and sincere regret that it is to form part of the history of the country; but after all the consideration we have bestowed upon it we see no reason to depart from the view we took of the affair at the period at which it occurred. We then thought, and still conscientiously believe, that the Magistrates whose painful duty it was to act upon that gloomy day, were desirous of preserving the peace without the least sacrifice, and that their orders were given to the best of their judgment, and with as much discretion as in so trying an emergency, and under such novel circumstances, could be commanded. We are not ready to say that the Magistrates in the present day, would conduct themselves precisely in the same manner as on the 16th of August, because that day's memorable proceedings, with the numerous mob-meetings which have since been held in this district, have taught all classes of the community, high and low, much knowledge on such subjects, of which before they were entirely ignorant.

But while we exonerate the Magistrates from all blame on that day, in what light can we view the conduct of the arch-agitator on that occasion? . . .

Wheeler's Chronicle's views on Hunt in 1819 and 1832 were formed on what they considered to be sound judgment; Hunt, by his words, his actions, and his writings, had been the architect of his own reputation. What he had built he had built, and the *Chronicle* did not find it very comely. They believed that the House of Commons acted wisely in rejecting his motion.

There was, lastly, one literary composition dated 24 March 1832, called into being by Hunt's motion in the House of Commons, which ought to rank high in the canon of writings on the transactions of 16 August 1819. It is entirely unknown. It has been said already that John Edward Taylor ought to have written his masterly critique of Peterloo— his *Observations* of December 1819—at a date a little further removed

---

1 *Manchester Courier*, 20 March 1832.
2 See above, p. 484.
3 *Wheeler's Manchester Chronicle*, 24 March 1832.

from the occurrences which prompted it; and that he deserved better targets to attack than Hay and Philips. Such a one was presented to him in Hunt's motion. The fallacies in it are plain to Taylor; his leader may be viewed as an appendix to his *Observations*, and as the culmination of the development of his opinions as the most important of the contemporary critics of the transactions of 16 August 1819. It is Taylor's final summing-up on his original work, which has been called a 'masterly exposure of a miserable chapter in the history of our national policy'. It marks the end of yet another miserable chapter in that story, the total and final discrediting of Henry Hunt:

(*Manchester Guardian*, March 24th, 1832). Mr. Hunt on Thursday week brought forward his long-talked-of motion for an inquiry into the lamentable transactions which took place at Manchester on the 16th of August, 1819. His speech on the occasion was almost as absurd and violent as could be conceived, and the terms of his motion were as little calculated as possible to conduce to its being complied with. They were 'that a select committee be appointed to inquire into the military execution inflicted on a peaceable and unarmed multitude assembled at Manchester on the 16th of August, 1819, to petition for parliamentary reform'. If the House of Commons had agreed to a motion couched in such terms as these, it would thereby have prejudged the whole affair; and no impartial investigation could have been reasonably expected from a tribunal which had so committed itself.

Our feeling as to the occurrences is well known. We are of opinion that it was the bounden duty of parliament to have investigated them at or near the time of their taking place. We are equally convinced that the proper period for an investigation has now gone by; and we know of no good object that can properly be promoted by the re-agitation of the subject.

Some papers, and some speakers in parliament, we see, are of the opinion that under a reformed House of Commons an investigation of the transactions in question will be so imperatively demanded, that it must be conceded. If we regarded this as at all probable, we should hesitate as to the propriety of reform. But we do not think so. We do not believe there is any general or strong wish that transactions, however indefensible, which occurred more than a dozen years ago, should now be raked up to gratify the revengeful spirit of Mr. Henry Hunt. We have neither seen nor heard of any symptoms of an anxiety for such a profitless occupation of the time of the legislature. There may have been some petitions praying for inquiry. We believe there have. Mr. Hunt has tools and dupes enough to be able to get petitions for any thing. There is no difficulty in such a matter as that. But, we repeat, there is no general, strong or popular wish for a revival of the subject.

It is a matter of notoriety here, that the annual processions of radicals to Peterloo on the mornings of the 16th of August, after having, in a very few years from the occurrence of the affair, fallen into contemptible insignificance, have long ceased altogether.[1] We mention this merely as a proof that in the present, as in almost all similar cases, with the lapse of time, indifference succeeds excitement. The latter may, to a certain extent, be factitiously renewed; but it cannot be kept up. We are glad that the majority against the motion was so great as not to afford much encouragement for any repetition of it.

In giving an abstract of the debate, we have not thought it worth while to repeat Mr. Hunt's statements as to the facts of the meeting and its dispersion. Many of the assertions he made, we believe to have been utterly false. At least, there are many which we have never before heard of; and we know his character quite well enough to feel justified in affirming that his assurances are not worthy of sufficient reliance to entitle them, in a doubtful case, to the smallest portion of credit.

Taylor still refers to the transactions at Manchester as 'indefensible'; he is not utterly convinced, nor perhaps was he during the rest of his life. The greatest doubt in his mind in 1819 had been that it was impossible to believe that an attack had come from the crowd. This doubt probably remained in 1832. But he had come a long way since 1819. How far is best seen by his rejection of the Huntean premise that 'military execution' had been 'inflicted on a peaceable and unarmed multitude'. That had been Taylor's viewpoint in his *Observations*, wherein he said that it had been the intention 'to dissolve the meeting by force, and that the arrest of Hunt and his associates was merely the pretext by which the attack was to be justified'.

In July of 1832, Prentice was to bring forward further 'proof' of the *Guardian*'s drift to the right. He was writing on the conduct of the *Guardian* and its attempts to 'veil its inherent Toryism.':

. . . Having gained all it could from those to whom it owed its origin, it shook them off, and looked for support amongst those against which it had at first waged fierce war [though] it continues its attacks against a few of the weakest . . . It shows up the [Tory] coroner . . . Richard Wright, J.P. was not rich . . . it hit him hard. Folks said: 'It is wrong to say that the *Guardian* truckles to the magistracy. See how boldly it attacks Ralph Wright'. And when Hulton of Hulton assailed Lord Althorp, the *Guardian* hit him in return, and by doing so got credit for some independency from those who were not aware that Hulton had—*become* poor![2]

There was, however, another reaction against Hulton which, no doubt, he felt keenly. This was the reaction of the local paper which

[1] The 1831 'commemoration' (which the *Guardian* reported) must have been considered by Taylor as not coming within the scope of these 'annual processions of radicals'.

[2] *Manchester Times*, 7 July 1832; 4 August 1832.

had not long before been giving tributes to his probity. Prentice's attack was made on Christmas Eve, 1831; the *Bolton Chronicle* sent out its Christmas number on the same date. It referred to the Althorp-Hulton letters:

. . . We would not advert to that correspondence any further than to say that it shews, on the part of Mr. Hulton, the same want of judgment, the same rashness, and wrong-headedness, the same disposition to tyrannize over the thoughts of others, the same insufferable conceit, and the same talent for being wrong and clinging to error, that through the whole of his public career rendered him unfit to perform the functions of a magistrate—an official situation that requires properties exactly the reverse of those possessed by him.

Lord Althorp has acted as became him, and if he committed an error at all, it was in noticing a man who is only known and notorious for that single act in his life, which he now makes his boast; and, as we should suppose, from similar feelings to those which actuated the obscure individual who fired the Temple of Diana. But now that Mr. Hulton has chosen to bring this matter before the public again, we have another duty to perform, and that is, to put Mr. Hulton on his trial before the country for what we consider to be a most illegal and deliberate massacre of the people, when legally and constitutionally met to exercise an undoubted right. Mr. Hulton for many years was excused for this unconstitutional act; he received a kind of reprieve in public opinion; and the verdict of wilful criminality was suspended, on the plea that at that time he was young and inexperienced, and had been made the *cat's paw* of older and more cunning heads. But it appears that if an advance in years invalidates the plea of youth, that inexperience or something worse still sticks to him, for this is the second instance of his having made a public boast of being duly accessory to the commission of an act which must embitter the feeling, and darken with the knowledge of moral guilt, a sensitive mind . . .

Mr Hulton's Bristol analogy was then thrown back into his face: 'Does Mr Hulton suppose that if they [the Peterloo crowd] had been prepared to commit violence and such outrage, they would have suffered any of their body to be heartlessly cut down in cold blood and afterwards have permitted one of the drunken Yeomanry of Manchester to have escaped alive, or even one of the Magistrates, who thus, under the semblance of justice, broke through all law and justice, and gave the word, through the mouth of Mr Hulton, for the Yeomanry to rush upon unarmed men, unprotected women, and children, and, with swords sharpened for the occasion ruthlessly cut them down? Good God! is it possible that any man, after twelve years' reflection, can say that he did this and would do it again, on a deliberate construction of the law?'

It will be seen how ingrained, how embedded, that 'fact'—*The*

Times's original 'dreadful fact' put across to an eagerly waiting nation—had become in twelve years.[1] It was, it has remained, irremovable. The article goes on:

Is there any human being who has ever had the opportunity of bowing a knee to his Maker and petitioning for the endowment of 'grace, wisdom, and understanding', and for 'forgiveness of tresspasses as he forgives trespasses against him', that could deceive himself into a consciousness of having acted right, under the flimsy plea that he was bound by his oath to become the author of such a catastrophe? . . .

The writer went over some of the points which had been referred to scores of times—on what was an illegal meeting. Had people not a right to attend such a meeting?:

Yes; they have quite as much right to meet for that purpose, as Mr. Hulton had to march to a Church and King dinner, and with half his library at his back, place his pygmy powers of reasoning and eloquence against something that the present talented Lord Chancellor had said.

It is not known that Henry Brougham, the then Lord Chancellor, had ever been challenged by William Hulton, so perhaps the writer meant Lord Althorp, the Chancellor of the Exchequer. The leader-writer in the *Bolton Chronicle* had a long tirade on the alleged reading of the Riot Act. If only he had known that Col. Fletcher had been mixed up in this, he would have had more to say; for behind all the to-error-clinging character of Hulton was the sinister influence of Col. Fletcher; the writer had not, apparently, studied the interminable proceedings of the Oldham inquest. William Hulton was told, pretty plainly, what he ought to have done on 16 August:

. . . by such means would have provided a peaceful and honourable remedy against riot and insurrection, instead of a violent, heartless, and inhuman butchery of the people. Mr. Hulton did not do this. He glories that he did not do it; and the responsibility was too great to be turned aside by the practice of the kindlier feelings of our nature! We envy him not in his moments of reflection, for he must have them; nor would we, unimportant as we are, make declarations similar to those he has avowed in his correspondence with Lord Althorp for the brightest jewel in Britain's crown [A disputing of Hulton's casualty figures] . . . But if there had not been one life lost, it does not lessen the revolting nature of the transaction. Mr. Hulton seems to suppose, that to mention these things is to point out for execration such persons as himself. This we deny. The merit of nursing up revenge for injuries, belongs

[1] And even in addition to *The Times* 'dreadful fact' of the yeomanry hacking their way to the hustings was the 'fact' that Hulton had ordered them to do so!

to a different class of persons than those who were so unconstitutionally and illegally attacked at the meeting in question . . .

The *Bolton Chronicle* had in those days a wide circulation in south Lancashire; it reached and influenced a public untouched by Prentice, untouched by Taylor's 1819 *Observations*. Written twelve years after Peterloo to a new rising generation uninformed as to the falsity of the seemingly reasonable premises and the equally false conclusions, it added to the establishment of the radical version of Peterloo in south Lancashire.

An odd news-clipping is preserved amongst the Hulton Papers in the Lancashire County Record Office[1] of unknown origin, but probably from a Manchester paper. It refers to the election in Bolton in 1841:

Bolton, Wednesday. Riot. . . . In consequence of the anti-Corn Law party parading the streets with flags and banners, and attacking the Conservative party, a scene of violence and confusion . . . a considerable number of heads were broken . . . Afterwards the business of nomination was proceeded with . . . From the nomination to the close of the poll on Thursday, the town was one scene of riot and confusion. Mr. Hulton, of Hulton Park, who was quietly walking along the streets in company with Mrs. Hulton and one of the Miss Hultons, was most furiously set upon by a mob of armed ruffians. Some one cried out: 'There goes Old Peterloo,' and immediately a rush was made towards him. The ruffians tried to drag Mrs. Hulton away, saying, they did not wish to hurt her, but she firmly refused to leave the side of her husband, and the unmanly wretches then set upon the party, kicking Mr. Hulton in the most ferocious manner, and maltreating some of the ladies. One fellow was just about to deal a blow upon Miss Hulton's head, which would have felled her to the ground, when one, more manly than the rest, interposed his arm, and received the full weight of the cudgel. The party was at length suc-coured by some respectable persons, who pushed Mr. Hulton and ladies into a shop by main force and thus protected them from further violence . . .

The news item, from a Conservative paper, was a 'party political broad-cast' to show the intimidation carried out in the Bolton election when their party was defeated. 'Many Conservative voters,' the report con-cluded, 'were effectually debarred from recording their votes.' The crop, perhaps, of the dragons' teeth sown 1819–1832.

Henry Hunt, after his 'show-down' in the House of Commons, was utterly discredited in Manchester, except amongst his faithful core of followers—a core which was in number considerable. Hunt was back on St Peter's Field for a meeting on Saturday, 14 July; it was a second

[1] DDHu/53/81.

unique occasion with no reference to 1819, according to the press reports. The *Guardian*'s patience was exhausted:

. . . It were a lamentable waste of our space and our readers' patience to give in detail even one of the numerous harangues to which [Hunt] has given breath in this tour, but there are circumstances connected with his visits to Preston and Peterloo which exhibit so truly the gentlemanly bearing and parliamentary language of the hon. Member that we may perhaps be pardoned noticing them as briefly as compatible with such a subject. [Hunt had been bound over, at Preston, for offering to fight one of the other candidates].

On his second visit to Peterloo on 27 August and on the following day at Rochdale, the *Guardian*'s contempt was even greater. Hunt had vilified Cobbett who, at that time, was candidate at Oldham. At Rochdale, Hunt asked for the cheer for Parson Hay, 'that will make him shake in his chair.' 'After going over a deal more stuff,' the *Guardian* proceeded, 'which had been a hundred times repeated by him [Hunt] within and without the House of Commons, he concluded; and the people went home completely drenched with rain, which had fallen almost incessantly during the afternoon.'

Wheeler's Manchester Chronicle[1] was kindlier disposed and gave him a full report: it was a novel occasion because Hunt had announced that he proposed that his visit to Peterloo would be marked by a torchlight procession:

He [Hunt] said he had received several threatening letters since the announcement that had been given of his intention to visit Manchester by torchlight was published, that if he did presume to do so he would certainly be shot; but he had gone through the town despite these intimations, and there he was before them safe and sound. Having once given his promise to the people, no threats or intimidation had ever yet induced him to deceive them, nor would they ever in future be found sufficient. He recollected when he visited Peterloo [in 1830] after the bloody massacre on that spot on the 16th of August, 1819, he was met on entering the town by the deputy constable with a message from the Boroughreeve, that the ground had been taken up by the military, and that if he persisted in his intention to hold a meeting there, the people would be dispersed.[2] His reply was, that he thought the military were not prepared to act as they had done on a former occasion; but if they were, the people were prepared to act very differently; take that to your master, and—on my friends to Peterloo!

He knew that there were many dark assassins who would like to put him out of the world if they were not afraid of their own safety; but should they

1 *Manchester Chronicle*, 1 September 1832.
2 It was an embellishment on what he had said at Peterloo on 16 August 1830 (qv).

do so, could they suppose that the tar-barrels and torches now flaming before him would quietly burn on Peterloo? No! No!! he found his safety in their fears. He was happy to hear that the people of Manchester had done such honour on Saturday to that excellent friend of the poor, Mr. Sadler. It was true that he was a Tory, but Whig or Tory would be all the same to him if they were friends to the working class . . .

The *Manchester Courier*[1] also gave him space. 'In reviewing the election candidates of the locality, Mr Hunt referred to "Mr Wood" (candidate for South Lancashire who) was approved of by Mr Birley—the "master human-butcher" as Mr Hunt styled him. This statement was received with hootings and other marks of disapprobation . . . Hunt said "He should go to Rochdale to pay a visit to his old friend Parson Hay". (laughter)'.

In September 1832, William Cobbett's parliamentary candidature was somewhat peripatetic; he was seeking also nomination for the borough of Manchester. Peterloo was now an election cry. The *Guardian* reported:

He [Cobbett] resumed his address by appearing on a cart in pretty nearly the same place from which Henry Hunt has so often harangued the same class of people; that class who, when Hunt put the question, all raised their hands in testimony of the opinion that Cobbett was *not* a fit man to represent Manchester. Yet who now, when Cobbett appears before them, are quite as ready to be tickled into lifting their hands to acknowledge him as 'the fittest man in the world'.

After going on at some length into the subject of the 'Manchester massacre' recommending the electors not to vote for any man who would not pledge himself to moving or supporting a motion for the settlement of that matter, and advising the impeachment of Lord Sidmouth, as a far better way of going to work than moving for an inquiry into the affair,—he declared that, if he got into Parliament for Manchester or for any other place, he would not be in the House two months without bringing the matter forward in such a manner as he should upon examination find to be the shortest and clearest, and the most likely to lead to a decision the most just and satisfactory.[2]

Mark Philips, on the other hand, who was elected for Manchester as the Reform candidate, in his election campaign in October,[3] said, in answer to a question, 'he would rather bury in oblivion the circumstances of 16 August 1819, than second any motion for their investigation.'

[1] *Manchester Courier*, 1 September 1832.
[2] *Manchester Guardian*, 15 September 1832.
[3] *Manchester Guardian*, 20 October 1832.

Henry Hunt, by his final appearance on St Peter's Field in the light of torches and tar-barrels departed from the scene of his former triumphs in a blaze of glory. His D.N.B. biographer closes his account with this passage:

. . . The citizens of Preston, however, grew dissatisfied with him. In 1833 he lost his seat,[1] and quitted political life, devoting himself to his business as a blacking manufacturer. On 18th February, 1835, while travelling for orders, he was seized with paralysis, and died at Alresford, Hampshire, and was buried at Parham, in the family vault of his mistress, Mrs. Vince . . .

Henry Hunt, it is to be feared, had been in the 'blacking' business quite a long time.

[1] It was late December 1832, at the Reform election.

XXX

The New Prophets—Old Bourbon Writ Large

The cause of reform in Manchester in 1832 surged forward without the assistance of Henry Hunt, even though some of his followers tried to let it be known that he was still their hope. A great reform meeting, addressed by reformers of all classes was held on St Peter's Field. Henry (*Poor Man's Guardian*) Hetherington was there; so was Robert Philips, of the Park, father of Mark Philips (later M.P.), Robert Hyde Greg, in fact, all the leading Manchester reformers. Charles Walker, of Ashton-under-Lyne was in the chair; Archibald Prentice was one of the speakers. The *Manchester Times* gave it much space, opening its report in the typical Prentice manner (19 May 1832):

The Great Reform Meeting . . . on St. Peter's Field, the scene in 1819 of an attack by the military upon a legally assembled and peaceable meeting . . . banners displayed included one with a representation of the dispersion of the meeting in 1819; another large banner had a full-length portrait of Henry Hunt . . . Charles Walker in the chair called for the use of moderate language, but he firmly resolved to have reform. Nothing was ever got by intemperate language, and it would be a disgrace to the town if on this occasion they could not meet to discuss their grievances, and yet be as unanimous as the reformers at Birmingham and other towns. He entreated them to be temperate; reformers of every description must lay aside all petty jealousies, and unite to overcome the general enemy of reform.

It would appear to be obvious to whom in the crowd and on the platform the chairman's remarks were directed; if Henry Hunt was not present, his spirit was. The meeting proceeded calmly; Robert Philips moved the principal resolution; Robert Hyde Greg made a trenchant denunciation of boroughmongers; but there were no references to 16 August from any other speaker except Prentice: 'if armed men were to be sent among peaceable and legally convened meetings, to cut them down with the sword, he hoped they would be prepared with arms and a determination to use them'. The *Manchester Times* gravely goes on:

The meeting was then about to separate, when Mr. William Brookes moved a vote of thanks to Mr. Hunt, on which Mr. Prentice said the proceeding was irregular, and thought it a little extraordinary that after the unanimity which had been displayed that day, any attempt should be made to throw the apple of discord amongst them. Mr. Brookes then waited for the chair to be vacated, and then called for three cheers for Mr. Hunt, and a number answered the call. Three horrible groans were given for the Duke of Wellington; and then three cheers for Radical Reform and for Mr. Hetherington.

It is evident that Prentice still believed, as he had believed a year earlier, that only Hunt's particular brand of reform was a cause of embarrassment to Manchester audiences. Prentice was as naive in this matter as in writing his leader on that earlier occasion on Hunt's 'error' arrived at honestly, whilst the other Manchester papers were fulminating against Hunt's atrocious methods. Prentice's references to 16 August 1819, were a demonstration of the method he was to adopt of spreading the propaganda about that day, but shorn of all the old vituperation. Henry Hunt would be ignored; after his defeat at Preston in December 1832, Manchester was to see him no more. Archibald Prentice would assume his mantle.

Opportunities for the new prophet after 1832 were few, but they were avidly seized, occasionally with little or no excuse. Such a one was the *Manchester Times* report[1] of the Warrington Clergy Meeting which was held at the Collegiate Church, Manchester, in July 1833. Prentice was, at that time involved in exposing the abuses of the Manchester Grammar School and Chetham's Library. There were caustic comments on the utterances of Canon Wray and other Collegiate Church worthies, and then:

The grand treat of the evening was to come. Hulton of Hulton, a name which we can never mention without a shuddering recollection of the 16th of August, proposed the health of the Earl of Wilton, [of Heaton Park] after a speech in which he dared to mention 'brotherly love and Christian compassion' . . . [There had been an appeal made for clergy widows and orphans.]

Again in November 1833, the Manchester Chamber of Commerce met to honour and make presentations of plate to its first president, Hugh Hornby Birley, who had been connected with the chamber since its inception, and to G. W. Wood, M.P. for South Lancashire, another of its pioneers. Lord Molyneux, the other Reform M.P. for South Lancashire, was the principal guest. The *Manchester Times*[2] gave a long report of the occasion. The presenter had said: '. . . Where is there a man

1 *Manchester Times*, 27 July 1833.
2 *Manchester Times*, 30 November 1833.

to be found in this town who has devoted more valuable time to the promotion of its mercantile interests than Mr Hugh Hornby Birley?[1] . . .' In returning thanks Birley had said:

[on the odium attached to him] He could only say that he was not conscious of having deserved it, and he trusted that he should never be actuated towards the individuals referred to by any other feeling than a hope that they might have a more candid spirit conceded to them, in order that they might learn to judge righteously . . .

The leader comments on this exchange:

. . . Mr. James Wood in his zeal to do the amiable to the object of this special eulogy, lamented that any one should be actuated so much by personal malignity as to attack the fair name of Mr. Birley. Well might that unhappy individual have exclaimed 'Save me from my friends!' with the recollection of the horrors of the 16th of August, 1819, harassing his conscience, well might he shrink from the ill-timed and sycophantic allusion. Mr. Birley owes much to public forbearance. Few, having done so much to excite resentment, have experienced so little in return for this generosity. He ought not to seek occasion to revive those indignant feelings which men seem so little disposed to cherish That indignation is a righteous indignation, and he is a base slanderer who describes it to be the miserable offspring of personal dislike.

It is not necessary to follow Prentice's campaign through the years between 1833 and 1851. With the deaths of Hunt (1835) and Taylor (1844), there were, with the exception of Bamford, whose *Passages* appeared in 1839–44, no other competitors. Some of Prentice's misconceptions, innuendoes and suppressions have already been noticed. His *Recollections* contain others:

[He refers (p. 46) to events in 1812] . . . the assassination of Mr. Perceval in the lobby of the House of Commons. The victim of a madman's revenge fell into the arms of Mr. Francis Philips, of Manchester, a gentleman of whom we shall hear something hereafter as a bitter enemy of reform, and the apologist of the magistracy and of the yeomanry, when a legally convened and peaceably assembled meeting was dispersed with the sword . . .
[The Exchange Riots of 1812; p. 50]. Mr. H. H. Birley (afterwards to be heard of as heading the yeomanry on the 16th of August, 1819) in passing through the square was rather roughly jostled, and obliged to take refuge in a shop . . .
[On an anti-Corn Law meeting in 1815; p. 70] This Mr. Hugh Hornby Birley, Boroughreeve, who convened an anti-corn law meeting, presided over it, and signed its resolutions, subsequently attained the bad pre-eminence of

[1] To this innocuous passage Prentice added 'Hear, Hear, from Mr John Edward Taylor'.

commanding a troop of local yeomanry, which rode furiously, and with newly-sharpened sabres in hand, into the middle of a legally convened and peaceably assembled meeting to petition for the repeal of the corn law, striking indiscriminately unarmed men and defenceless women and children. Why, at an interval of little more than four years, did the petitioners of one period hew down the petitioners of the other? The Birleys and the Greens, the Bradshaws and the Hardmans, of 1815, believed that the enactment of the corn laws would raise wages; and the working men of 1819 asked for its repeal because it had reduced wages . . .

[Even before Prentice begins to describe the events of 1819 (p. 116) he states]: When that tyranny was exercised with still less regard to law and constitutional right,—when a legally convened and peaceably held meeting was exposed to the sabres of a body of yeomanry, eager to obey the impulses of their own heated tempers and their hatred of all reform,—and when magistrates who directed the sanguinary attack received the thanks of royalty—it was seen in the wide and deep expressions of indignation, that the principles of rational reform had made great progress during the time between the Blanket meeting of March, 1817, and the great St. Peter's Field meeting of August, 1819 . . .

[He cites as often as he can the 'reward' given to Rev. W. R. Hay, not even sure of that clerical-magistrate's role at Peterloo; p. 225]: The reverend W. R. Hay, the chairman of the quarter sessions, who had commanded the military attack on a peaceable and defenceless multitude on the 16th of August, and had been rewarded by being presented to the rich living of Rochdale . . .

[On the trial of Hunt, Bamford, &c.—p. 191]: The whole of the high treason, for which, in the first instance these men were to be tried—the whole of the seditious conspiracy for which they were actually tried, thus dwindled down into a conviction for having attended a meeting which was only *at that moment* found to be an illegal one; for, let it be borne in mind, that Mr. Norris, the magistrate acting in the name of the magistracy of the district, writing to Lord Sidmouth at eleven o'clock on the night previous to the meeting, declared his conviction that, as the law stood, he believed nothing could be done on the ground of its illegality, to prevent the meeting being held. If the chairman[1] of the Manchester magistracy, constantly corresponding with Lord Sidmouth, and with all the information that could be obtained from the Crown lawyers, declared his conviction, on Sunday night, at eleven o'clock, that he could not regard the meeting on Monday morning as otherwise than one legally convened and legally held—when he regretted that such was the state of the Law that the magistrates felt they could not prevent that meeting being held—surely it might have been expected, in the sentence pronounced on the prisoners, that their strong belief of the proceedings being in accordance with the law, would be taken into consideration, and the mildest possible punishment inflicted. But Hunt was sentenced to be imprisoned for

[1] Prentice surely knew he was not.

two years and six months, and Johnson, Healey, and Bamford to *one year's* imprisonment; and so rigorously was the sentence carried out, that Johnson was not permitted to go, in custody of an officer, to see his wife on her death-bed!

His strictures on the severity of the imprisonment were apparently forgotten, when he tilted at Bamford in the passage following:

The three prisoners in Lincoln jail, elevated by the severity of their sentence to the rank of martyrs, seem to have had no solace from their compulsory association. Bamford takes some pains to show what a fool Healey was; and he complains that when Mrs. Bamford came to the prison, Mr. Johnson asked her to partake of breakfast with himself and his wife before he told her where her husband was! . . .

Of the selfishness of Hunt, confined in Ilchester jail, Bamford complains also in the bitterest terms, and loses no opportunity of ridiculing his vanity, egotism, and tom-foolery.

Although Prentice, when he wrote his *Recollections,* had the benefit of Bamford's *Passages* he did not take full advantage of Bamford's descriptive narrative of the vital moments. He did not even repeat the original Taylor/Prentice 'dreadful fact' that the yeomanry 'actually hacked their way up to the hustings'.[1] The passage is worth quoting:

. . . when, suddenly, at a quick trot, past the corner of a wall which bounded Brown's cottage, appeared the Manchester Yeomanry, and drew up in front of the house in which the magistrates were met. The crowd received them, as Bamford says, with a shout of good will—as the aggressors said, with a shout of defiance, when as suddenly as they had appeared at the outskirts of the meeting, they drew their swords, waved them round their heads, and dashed into the crowd!

Nadin had said he was afraid to serve the warrant, and this was the way it was to be served. As the yeomanry neared the hustings the inert resistance of those who could not move out of the way increased, and the troops were separated, each man striving to open out his own way, some with pale faces and firmly-closed-eyes, striking with their sabres as if they were insane. At this time two squadrons of the hussars came upon the field. Sir William Jolliffe, who was a lieutenant in the regiment, says . . .[2]

It is a remarkable description from the pen of Archibald Prentice. It might have been thought that he would have been more precise in

[1] 'They instantly dashed at full gallop amongst the crowd, actually hacking their way up to the hustings.' (The Prentice/Taylor letter in *The Times.*) 'All was quiet and orderly, as if the cavalry had been the friends of the multitude, and had marched as such into the midst of them.' (John Tyas's report to *The Times.*)
[2] Prentice *Recollections,* p. 161.

telling what actually happened in the central few moments of the day, but he is studiously vague. It is little wonder that Bruton, writing in 1919, found it difficult to harmonize the conflicting accounts, when two of the prime authorities for the radical version of Peterloo, Bamford and Prentice, writing within a decade of each other, should seem to differ.

Samuel Bamford has been even more responsible than Archibald Prentice for the general acceptance of the radical version of Peterloo.[1] The editor of the 1893 edition of his *Passages* was bold enough to say of the Peterloo meeting, 'Everybody knows how the meeting was broken up, and at what cost of violence and bloodshed'. What he perhaps meant was, that everybody knew how Bamford said it was broken up, which was not quite the same thing. Because, perhaps, of this general knowledge on the part of his readers, the editor omitted, because Bamford had not written it, a considerable part of Bamford's original supporting material, i.e. what *The Times* writer of March 1820, said about the revelations of Hunt's trial. The 1967 editions of the *Passages* give it entire. Its reintroduction showing how Bamford *used* it is more revealing of the true Samuel Bamford than was its omission.

The simple, unaffected style of Samuel Bamford has influenced readers for over a century. It convinced his D.N.B. biographer:

He was brought into great public notoriety on the occasion of that meeting of local clubs the dispersal of which became known as the Peterloo massacre. It was proved that Bamford's contingent to the meeting was peaceful and orderly, and that his speech was of the same tendency. Yet he suffered an imprisonment of twelve months on account of this affair.

The reason for Bamford's imprisonment, like Hunt's, has perhaps been misunderstood, largely through Bamford's own special pleading.

How much Bamford's Chapter XX (Vol. II) has influenced readers in the period between 1844 and the present day is incalculable. Written, as it was, by *The Times* commentator on Hunt's and Bamford's trial, and published in their issue of 30 March 1820, it subsequently became completely untenable because of Redford *v.* Birley, 1822. This trial did not exist for Bamford any more than it did for Prentice. Bamford could yet write twenty years later (with suitable suppressions, as has been seen)[2] his additions to the 1820 exploded facts. He says:

The following remarks in an article of *The Times* newspaper of Tuesday,

1 '. . . Samuel Bamford, the weaver and—when every criticism has been made— the greatest chronicler of early nineteenth-century Radicalism', Thompson, p. 637.
2 See above, pp. 174-5 and 207-8.

March 30th [1820] as to the facts elicited during this important trial and the real nature of the transactions at Manchester, that I need not apologise for their introduction into this work, and especially as but very few of my readers will have seen the remarks, and few still will have recollected their tenor.

The reader of Bamford's Chapter XX will look in vain if he should wish to differentiate between what is Bamford's and what is *The Times* writer's; the quotation marks do not help. But, in fact, only the opening paragraph and the closing paragraph are Bamford's. *The Times* article proceeds:

. . . it is now perfectly clear to all the world, that everything that was stated in the House of Commons [in November, 1819] respecting the riotous character of the Manchester meeting by Lord Castlereagh, the Solicitor-General, and other honourable members, was totally and absolutely false . . .
    . . . Who, we ask, are the real authors of the monstrous untruths above quoted? The dupes, the victims, must now bring these before the public. The too easy, unsuspecting son of guiltlessness, the Solicitor-General, will tell us who seduced his innocent mind into the preposterous belief and assertion that 'the yeomanry were first attacked and unhorsed by the crowd' . . . But the character of the age in which we live is affected by occurrences of this kind. The future student must read the transactions of the present period. If then he take up the parliamentary history, he will find in the speeches of the ministers, readings of riot acts,—magistrates trampled on,—yeomanry assaulted,—hooted, unhorsed,—cart loads of stones,—forests of bludgeons!—not one tittle of which has any existence or place in the state trial [of Hunt] to which he will naturally turn, in order to observe the issue of atrocities so horrible. What will ministers do? Their station in the realm has unfortunately snatched them from obscurity; they must, therefore, either destroy every record of their speeches, or cancel every publication of the late trial, by which all their statements are dissipated and reduced to nothing; or else, [comes the last lamentable clause of the disjunctive] they will stand recorded for ever as having solemnly averred in the house of legislature, that which was found in a court of justice, to be totally untrue.

There at that point came Bamford's 'close quotes', and the seemingly irrefutable indictment of *The Times* leader-writer of March 1820, was handed down to posterity, as evidence of the monstrous injustice of former days. Samuel Bamford added, in his simple homely style:

To this severe, though just exposition, the leading journal might have added, that Lord Stanley was foreman of the grand jury, who, at Lancaster, found true bills of indictment against the reformers, and cut those against the magistrates and yeomanry. Mr. Wilbraham Bootle also was one of the said high functionaries. Their deeds, any more than their words, must not be suffered to escape entirely from our recollection. Posterity must know these things, in order that when they point to the tombs of these noblemen, they may not confound them with those of their family, who had not any such words or deeds to answer for.

Lord Stanley and Edward Bootle Wilbraham (not then Wilbraham Bootle) had, by their statements in the House of Commons, been referred to in *The Times* indictment. Lord Stanley, by the time that Bamford wrote, was suitably disguised as the Earl of Derby; Bamford's double indictment of Wilbraham as a 'false witness' in the House of Commons and a member of the grand jury at Lancaster, had nothing very sinister about it. Wilbraham had indeed been named amongst those forming the grand jury, but he offered to stand down before the bills of indictment were presented:

. . . he had informed the Foreman, Lord Stanley, that having given his opinion as chairman of the Liverpool Sessions on the late Disturbances and Meetings, he thought he ought to withdraw when the Indictments relative thereto were presented; and that he had two relations, a cousin by marriage, and a nephew, magistrates at Manchester . . .[1]

Bamford was not writing history, but he muddied the stream of history. It would not be an exaggeration to claim that such was Bamford's intention from the beginning. On 13 July 1820, he wrote the following (and other) lines from his cell in Lincoln Gaol:

> Give the ruffians time to glory;
> Theirs is but a waning day:
> We have yet another story
> For the page of history.[2]

★   ★   ★

F. A. Bruton set out, in 1919, to 'give as vivid, accurate, and impartial an account of this event as may be possible after the lapse of a hundred years.' He could hardly hope in the forty-six pages of his *Story of Peterloo* to be anything more than superficial. Some of his misconceptions, both trivial and serious, have been enumerated. The famous despatch from Taylor and Prentice; the attribution to Taylor of *Peterloo Massacre*; he says that Taylor's 'vigorous and spirited protests' brought forth Philips's *Exposure*—it was the other way round.[3] In a

[1] *Impartial Narrative*, p. 58.
[2] Published in the *Manchester Observer*, 5 August 1820, 'Written to commemorate the anniversary of the fatal 16th of August.' It was 'Part II' of Bamford's 'Song of the Slaughter'—that part of his 'song' which was truncated in his later editions after 1821.
[3] *Story of Peterloo* (p. 7). Bruton was, of course, under the impression that Philips was answering *Peterloo Massacre*. Taylor's *Observations* answered Philip's *Exposure*.

brief comment on the trials he says 'once more' [in Redford *v.* Birley] 'the Rev. Edward Stanley appeared as a witness.'[1] Stanley appeared as witness only in Redford *v.* Birley. Bruton accepts and states, on the authority of the 19-years'-old Lieut. Jolliffe of the Hussars, that the Manchester Yeomanry 'were placed, most unwisely, as it appeared, under the immediate command of the civil authorities'; and this 'greatly aggravated the disasters of the day.' They were not, as Bruton would have discovered on reference to several other authorities. However accurate Lieut. Jolliffe might have been in describing what he saw, he was hardly the authority to quote on a matter such as that. Bruton, as has been seen,[2] confused the evidence on the newly-sharpened sabres. Jolliffe's misapprehension on the Yeomanry being under the direct command of the civil authorities, led Bruton on to say: 'As we approach the date of Peterloo, the confidence reposed in the volunteer cavalry by the authorities becomes even more apparent . . .'[3]

Bruton's naivety in describing the 9 August meeting and its background has already been noted.[4] On the eve of Peterloo, he writes thus:

. . . No disturbance of any kind took place in Manchester on Sunday, the 15th of August. It was a grand opportunity for a man with *vision*; but the responsible authorities—i.e. the special Committee of the magistrates of Lancashire and Cheshire [which included three clergymen] meeting in Manchester—seem to have been in a panic. They sat till midnight on Sunday without being able to decide what to do. At 11 p.m. one of them wrote to the Home Secretary that although the magistrates, as then advised, did not then think of preventing the meeting, they were alarmed, and were in a state of painful uncertainty.[5]

Bruton described Henry Hunt thus:

Henry Hunt was a country gentleman of Wiltshire, whose personal characteristics made him specially successful as a demagogue, and there is no doubt that he was perfectly sincere. Bamford, whose admiration for him waned in later years, describes him as 'gentlemanly in his manner and attire, six feet and better in height, and extremely well formed'. The white hat which he wore became the symbol of Radicalism. He was shrewd, quick at repartee, and had the copious flow of highly-coloured language which delights a crowd. He was exceptionally clever in handling a great gathering, and was always scrupulously careful to keep within the strict letter of the law. His vanity we can forgive, for he rendered yeoman service to the cause of Liberty, but his private

1 *Story of Peterloo*, p. 8.
2 See above, p. 264.
3 *Story of Peterloo*, p. 14.
4 See above, p. 99.
5 *Story of Peterloo*, p. 18.

life, the details of which are told with almost brutal candour by himself in his *Memoirs*, will not bear inspection. Of his political record he has no reason to be ashamed. He presented the earliest petition to Parliament for Women's Suffrage; he fought the battle of Reform in its darkest days; and he attacked the first Reform Bill, demanding the Ballot, Universal Suffrage, and the repeal of the Corn Laws . . .[1]

Bruton cannot forget the 'importance' of the deduction he had drawn from Jolliffe's misapprehension on the command of the Yeomanry. He describes the dispatch of the messengers for the troops thus:

Hunt had only been speaking for a minute or two, therefore, when riders were dispatched for the troops. It is difficult to understand why a single messenger was not sent to Lieut.-Col. L'Estrange, who was in command of the whole force. By a strange fatality the magistrates, at the same instant that they sent for Colonel L'Estrange, despatched a horseman to Pickford's yard for the troop of Manchester Yeomanry concealed there, which they had chosen to retain under their own control . . . Judging from what followed, Colonel L'Estrange seems to have made a skilful disposition of the forces at his disposal . . .

The ambiguity of that passage cannot fail to be noticed. The colonel 'in command of the whole force' and the Yeomanry under the control of the magistrates; and the colonel making a 'skilful disposition of the forces at his disposal'!

It is probably beyond the wit of any reader to follow Bruton's description of the vital few minutes of the day, or at least to harmonize the different accounts he gives. He divides his narrative into three sections: 'The Charge of the Manchester Yeomanry'; 'The Manchester Yeomanry in Difficulties'; and 'The Fateful Decision. The Hussars Ordered to Charge.' There is a massacre in each of them. In the first, that part of Stanley's narrative with 'swords were up and swords were down', but unsure whether striking or cutting, which Bruton allows Lieut. Jolliffe to decide (who had not then arrived). He includes, too, Bamford's 'chopped limbs and wound-gaping skulls' phrase, and the attenuated 'lame affair *apologia*' of Capt. Birley. In his second part, 'The Manchester Yeomanry in Difficulties', Bruton says, 'We have now arrived at the most dramatic moment in the whole story . . .' He discusses the question of missiles, coming to the conclusion that the crowd had used them, but only in self-defence, quoting Tyas as a witness as one having seen none thrown:

Mr. Tyas, the reporter for *The Times*, says emphatically that when the Yeomanry rode into the crowd 'not a brickbat was thrown at them, not a pistol

[1] *Story of Peterloo*, p. 23.

was fired—during this period all was quiet and orderly, as if the cavalry had been the friends of the multitude and had marched as such into the midst of them.

He follows on with 'Have at their flags' and further evidence of massacre. His mind, however, is made up on from where the attack came:

After the lapse of a century, perhaps we may, while trying to take an impartial view, agree with what Mr. Hobhouse said on this subject in the House of Commons in May, 1821, in supporting Sir Francis Burdett's motion for an inquiry: He 'defied proof that the people began it. When once they were attacked, what could you expect? Were people in the quiet exercise of one of their most undoubted privileges to be unresistingly bayonetted, sabred, trampled underfoot, without raising a hand . . . The Rev. Mr. Stanley, who watched the proceedings from a room above the magistrates, saw no stones or sticks used'.

What the Rev. Mr Stanley saw and what he did not see has been discussed.[1]

The almost incredible method Bruton adopted in considering Birley's evidence is realizable only by comparison. In his *Story of Peterloo*[2] he writes:

Finally, let us hear the officer speak who led the charge in person. At the Royal Birthday festivities on the 29th of April, 1820, Colonel Hugh Birley, in replying to the toast of the Manchester and Salford Yeomanry, made a lengthy speech, in which he complained bitterly of the obloquy and outcry levelled against them, 'which we should have been more or less than men not to feel'. Speaking of the charge into the crowd, he said: 'I observed as I approached the stage a movement in the crowd about the spot from which all accounts agree in stating that the first attack was made upon the Yeomanry. That movement appeared to be intended to throw an obstacle in the way of our advance. Up to that moment the Boroughreeve had walked by my side, but I then quickened my pace in order to prevent an interruption. There was ample space for a front of six men wherever we passed, but I am assured by those who formed the first rank of six that they were obliged to break off into single file before they reached the stage. The mob must therefore have closed in immediately behind the officers who led the squadron.' He goes on to speak of the Yeomanry's dash for the flags, which is mentioned below. He does not attempt to deny that it took place; but there is no object in quoting further from an *apologia* which at the best is a very lame affair.

The passage 'mentioned below' is John Tyas's much-quoted passage, 'Have at their flags . . . from that moment the Manchester Yeomanry

[1] See above, pp. 182, 189, 192, 224.
[2] P. 32.

lost all command of their temper.' which Birley, in fact, was attempting to refute! The relevant parts of Birley's speech are as follows:

. . . To be marked out for abuse by certain persons who live amongst us, affords indeed some evidence of merit, and for their censure no solace was required. Yet even they did not venture to put forth the calumnies which have been so widely circulated, until the example had been set them by the un-principled part of the daily press. That powerful instrument, invaluable as it is when honestly directed, has acquired an ascendancy over the public mind, which, from its liability to abuse, is much to be lamented. The generality of readers adopt, without examination, the opinion of their favourite newspaper. The Editor of *The Times* seems to have felt secure of this when he ventured, in his observations on the dispersion of the meeting of the 16th of August, to assume as a fact what was contradicted by the statement of his own reporter.

Mr. Tyas says the crowd drew back in every direction on our approach. He appears to have fixed his eyes upon the leaders of the column as we went round by the back to the front of the hustings. It was impossible therefore for him, though elevated, by the favour of Mr. Hunt, above *six feet high*, to see what was passing in the rear. I observed, as I approached the stage, a move-ment in the crowd about the spot from which all accounts agree in stating that the first attack was made upon the Yeomanry. That movement appeared to be intended to throw an obstacle in the way of our advance. Up to that moment the Boroughreeve had walked by my side, but I then quickened my pace in order to prevent any interruption. There was ample space for a front of six men wherever we passed, but I am assured by those who formed the very first rank of six, that they were obliged to break off into single file before they reached the stage. The mob must therefore have closed in immediately behind the officers who led the squadron. Mr. Tyas accuses the Yeomanry of cutting, to get at the flags, after Hunt and Johnson had been taken into cus-tody—of losing their command of temper after brickbats had been hurled at them. There is ample evidence to prove that this species of attack had been begun before the hustings were surrounded. The temper of the Yeomanry and of all the troops employed in the dispersion of the meeting is sufficiently marked by the fact, that, notwithstanding the fury with which they were assailed—notwithstanding that a Yeoman was seen struck from his horse senseless, and to all appearance lifeless—not more than one death can fairly be ascribed to a sabre wound.

But passing over these facts, the statement of Mr. Tyas proves that we did not charge into the crowd, riding over friend and foe, and cutting right and left till we had reached the hustings. Such conduct would not have suggested to him the idea of our marching as friends into the midst of the multitude. The calumny was nevertheless circulated, along with several others equally false; and their reiteration gave them currency in various parts of the kingdom, producing an outcry against us which we must have been more or less than men not to feel. We were supported, however, by the consciousness that we had done no more than our duty,—by knowing that we had the approbation of a numerous body of our most respectable fellow-townsmen, who were eyewitnesses of our conduct—of all those amongst whom we live, whose good opinion we value . . .

Had Birley's testimony stood alone, Bruton's dismissal of it as a 'lame affair' would have been more understandable, but when part of it (and the most important part of it) was corroborated by Tyas who stood 'elevated, by favour of Mr Hunt, above six feet high' (a reference to the height of the hustings which was noted by George Swift, said to be responsible for their erection, as having been eight feet), the dismissal of Birley's narrative is remarkable.

On the narrative of Lieut. Jolliffe, Bruton ignored the fact that Prentice had quoted Jolliffe in 1851. Bruton interpolates in Jolliffe's account that 'Sir John Byng was then at Pontefract'. If he was at Pontefract on 16 August, he was in Manchester within two hours of the tragedy. Bruton uses Jolliffe to prove (in his *Story of Peterloo*) that the Yeomanry were more active with their sabres than the Hussars, whereas Jolliffe's testimony is to the contrary. Even in his introduction to Jolliffe's account in *Three Narratives of Peterloo* which gives this testimony, Bruton says:

. . . It seems clear, from the evidence which was given before the Relief Committee, after Peterloo, that there was not the same feeling of resentment against the Hussars as against the local Yeomanry; in fact, it was more than once asserted that troopers of the Hussars actually restrained the Manchester Yeomanry from excessive violence.

'. . . from the evidence which was given before the Relief Committee' would perhaps be more accurately phrased as 'from the allegations made to the Relief Committee' or 'alleged by the radical press'.

Bruton's third eye-witness in his *Three Accounts* was John Benjamin Smith (1794-1879), a narrative which is described by Bruton as:

. . . specially valuable for the account it gives of the circumstances immediately preceding and following the catastrophe, and its estimate of the character of the crowd. In these details it is strikingly corroborative of Bamford's story . . . and of the information given by Mr. John Edward Taylor, who—under the pseudonym of 'An Observer'—edited the contemporary tracts entitled *The Peterloo Massacre*.

That Smith's account was 'corroborative' of Bamford and *Peterloo Massacre* is not surprising in view of the fact that it was written 'towards the close of his life' [1879!] 'at the earnest request of his family'. It is scarcely 'corroborative of Bamford's story' in the vital moments of the day:

[The Yeomanry] halted, and drew up in line. After some hesitation, from what cause I do not know, I heard the order to form three deep, and then the order to march. The trumpeter led the way and galloped towards the hustings, followed by the Yeomanry. Whilst this was passing, my attention was called to another movement coming from the opposite side of the meeting.

It need hardly be said that if Bamford's version of the 'charge' is true, then Mr Smith's attention would have been on the horrific scene which Bamford described no matter what other distraction occurred. It is more corroborative of John Tyas's 'during this period all was quiet and orderly . . .' But Smith continues:

A troop of soldiers, the 15th Hussars, turned round the corner of the house where we stood and galloped forwards towards the crowd. They were succeeded by the Cheshire Yeomanry, and lastly by two pieces of artillery. On the arrival of the soldiers, the special constables, the magistrates, and the soldiers set up loud shouts.

Unless Smith was being unnecessarily ambiguous, the 'arrival of the soldiers' meant the arrival of the Hussars, when shouts were given; the Yeomanry were in the middle of the crowd by then. He continues:

This [the shouts] was responded to by the crowd with waving of hats. After this the soldiers galloped amongst the people creating frightful alarm and disorder. The people ran helter-skelter in every direction. It was a hot, dusty day; clouds of dust arose which obscured the view. When it had subsided a startling scene was presented.

It is to be feared that clouds of something else had obscured Mr J. B. Smith's view between 16 August 1819, and the year of, say, 1870, when the account was written. Bruton perhaps discounted Smith's description of the 'field', and used it because it was 'specially valuable for the account it gives of the circumstances immediately preceding and following the catastrophe.' 'Immediately preceding' the meeting evidence, apart from what Smith said to his aunt, contains nothing that did not appear in the newspapers. For one who sent an account to the *Gazette* of the alleged 'private' meeting of loyalists after Peterloo, Smith was singularly ill-informed on the events in the pre-Peterloo period. He wrote:

. . . On the 25th of January, [Hunt] made a public entry into Manchester from Stockport, accompanied by large crowds with flags and banners. The meeting was enthusiastic but very peaceable. Meetings were held in all the surrounding towns and villages to appoint district delegates to make arrangements for a great meeting to be held in Manchester.[1] This memorable meeting was held on the 16th of August, 1819 . . . The actors in the bloody tragedy of that day were called 'The Heroes of Peterloo,' in contrast with the brave heroes of Waterloo.

Called, mainly, by the radicals, who also called 'the brave heroes of Waterloo' the 'bloody butchers of Waterloo'.[2] The meeting was not called, as Smith says, to 'petition parliament'.

Mr Smith is not much better informed on the events immediately after Peterloo, when, in writing of the protest, which received 4,800 signatures,[3] against the alleged 'private' meeting of the loyalists (which Smith secretly attended), he could say:

By way of counteracting this energetic protest, on the 27th of August[4] Lord Sidmouth communicated to the Manchester Magistrates and to Major Trafford and the military serving under him the thanks of the Prince Regent 'for their prompt, decisive, and efficient measures for the preservation of the public peace on August the 16th.[5]

It was a curious way of 'counteracting' the Manchester protest for Lord Sidmouth to date his letter the 21st of August (and an earlier one, even, of 18 August); the protest had not been sent then!

It is remarkable that Bruton used Smith's 'eye-witness' account at all; it only added to the confusion.

Bruton, in his *Story of Peterloo*, could be said to have left his readers a wide choice between the conflicting accounts which he throws in impartially. He gives the impression that he believes Bamford's account of the incursion of the Manchester and Salford Yeomanry into the crowd, and appears to try to reconcile the other eye-witnesses' versions with it. That he does so is obvious to the reader of his shortened version which he wrote for his *Short History of Manchester and Salford* in 1924, given in full on pp. 24–26 above.

[1] Sandy Brow, Ashton-under-Lyne, Rochdale, it is supposed!

[2] Redford *v.* Birley (Farquharson edn), p. 490.

[3] Bootle Wilbraham, in the House of Commons on 15 May 1821, said that the address to the Prince Regent from the inhabitants of Manchester after Peterloo, supporting the magistrates, was signed by 8,000 persons. *Manchester Observer*, 26 May 1821.

[4] Sidmouth's letter was, of course, dated 21 August.

[5] Bruton might have added that Smith's account was 'strikingly corroborative' of Prentice as well as of Bamford, because the above passage is identical with the paragraph of Prentice's (*Recollections*, p. 166). Both were misapprehensions. Other paragraphs in Smith's narrative are 'lifted' in full from Prentice.

A few minutes later, the Manchester Yeomanry came trotting round what is now the Mount Street corner of the Midland Hotel, and halting for a moment in great disorder, for they had no command of their horses, made a dash for the hustings, striking with their swords as they entered the crowd. Raw and untrained as they were, they were soon so hopelessly entangled and dispersed that the chairman of the Magistrates afterwards described them as 'completely defeated'.

Bruton has shortened his account to such a degree that he has no record of the arrests being made on the hustings. He does, however, say at the close of his account: 'Bamford has left a graphic and, apparently for the most part, a fair account of the whole episode in his *Passages in the Life of a Radical*. Hunt's autobiography and letters are less readable. Besides these, we have descriptions of the event by Bishop Stanley, Lord Hylton, and Mr J. B. Smith, all of whom were present.'

A paragraph in Bruton[1] gives a clue also to another minor propagator of the radical version of Peterloo, where he writes that Mrs Fildes, the female reformer who rode on the box of Hunt's barouche to St Peter's Field, was known to Mrs Linnaeus Banks (1821–1897), the local minor novelist. Mrs Banks's novel *The Manchester Man* (1876) is a story based in the Manchester of the Peterloo period; it is said to be based on fact, and in the illustrated edition of 1896 she has a long appendix purporting to establish her 'facts' which had been contradicted. She remained perfectly convinced that she had not been misinformed about her 'facts'. She claimed a novelist's licence for dating the theatre incident of January 1819 as occurring in August when Hunt came to Manchester; but her description of the scene on St Peter's Field needed no such licence:

[Hunt ascended the platform] The cry 'Soldiers are upon us!' and the 15th Hussars galloped round a corner . . . and threw themselves, men and horse, upon the mass. All had been preconcerted, prearranged . . . From the early morning, magistrates had been sitting in conclave at the Star Inn, and there Hugh Birley, a cotton spinner, was said to have regaled too freely the officers and men of his yeomanry corps, so soon to be let loose on the swinish multitude, as they called them. A cordon of military and yeomanry drawn round St. Peter's Field, like a horde of wolves round a flock of sheep . . . Nadin 'dared not' . . . thus through the blindness, the incapacity, the cowardice, or the self-importance of this one man, soldiery hardened on the battlefield, yeomanry fired with drink, were let loose like barbarians . . . and one of the most atrocious massacres in history was the result.

Some facts Mrs Banks had from her Grandfather Varley; one of

[1] *Story of Peterloo*, p. 24.

them included a variation on the story of the female whose exposed person was brutally maltreated by one of the Yeomanry. Unlike Hunt's version, the unfortunate female was not lying with her head down a hill, but with her dress caught on a nail on the hustings, and thus suspended. Mrs Linnaeus Banks has a small claim to responsibility in establishing the radical version.

★   ★   ★   ★   ★

One scholar whose work on the period is still, even after over fifty years, the great authority: J. R. M. Butler (*Passing of the Great Reform Bill*, 1912) seems to be a little sceptical of the radical version. He deals with Peterloo only briefly before passing on to the momentous events of the 1820s. He has this to say:

. . . But numerous petitions [on Radical Reform] showed the question was attracting serious interest, and when Parliament rose [in the summer of 1819] it was kept alive in the country by crowded meetings. On August 16th was the famous 'massacre' of Peterloo; it arose from the folly of the Manchester Magistrates in sending the Yeomanry to arrest Hunt, at the moment when he was addressing a vast and closely packed assembly on the subject of Reform. Though several lives were lost, the Government did not wait for an inquiry before thanking the parties concerned in effecting the arrests. Their tactlessness raised a storm of indignation. Lord Fitzwilliam protested, and was dismissed from his lord-lieutenancy. Parliament was summoned to pass repressive measures, and met at a crisis of great excitement. This was in many ways an excellent opportunity for the Whigs to come forward and lead a great assault on the hated administration . . .

'Folly' of the magistrates, and 'tactlessness' of the Government does not seem to have been the findings of most writers.

★   ★   ★   ★   ★

Richard Cobden's remarks[1] on the 16 August 1819 written in his pamphlet *Incorporate Your Borough* (1838), have been received as 'informed comment' by posterity. They are worth reproducing in their entirety:

Recollect that the Massacre of the 16th of August, 1819, could not have occurred, if Manchester had then been incorporated according to the provisions of the present municipal reform act;—and why? Because the united magistrates of Lancashire and Cheshire, who then entered the town, to hold their bench at the Star Inn, to take command of the police, and order the soldiers to cut down and trample upon unarmed crowds, would, in such a case, have no

[1] See above, p. 83.

more jurisdiction over Manchester than Constantinople. No!—*Incorporate Your Borough!* and thenceforth, neither Mr. Hulton, of Hulton, nor any Tory squire or parson, will ever come into your town at the head of a dozen magisterial bumpkins, first to let loose a troop of fox hunters, disguised as yeomanry cavalry, to try the metal of their swords upon helpless women and children, and afterwards to return public thanks to the officers and men for their extreme forbearance on the occasion! No; for by one of the provisions of the corporation reform act, no person can be appointed to the office of justice of the peace in any of the boroughs holding quarter sessions, unless he live within the limits prescribed for the residences of the burgesses. In this clause alone, I find sufficient reason, if there were not a hundred others, for applying for an act of incorporation, and thus to place for ever the population of our town and neighbourhood beyond the control of a booby squirearchy, who abhor us not more for our love of political freedom, than for those active and intellectual pursuits which contrast so strongly with that mental stupor in which they exist—I had almost said—vegetate.

To which Cobden added the footnote:

The conduct of the common council of the city of London, at this melancholy and memorable period, proves the advantages derived from a municipal corporation, particularly in times of excitement and danger; and contrasts mournfully with the prostrate and helpless fate of the town of Manchester, for want of such an organization. No sooner was it known that the Prince Regent had been advised to express his approbation of those proceedings, than the common council of London passed resolutions, condemning the conduct of the magistrates and yeomanry as being 'disgraceful to the character of Englishmen'; and they addressed the Prince Regent, remonstrating with his royal highness for having been induced to express his approval of the conduct of the abettors and perpetrators of those atrocities, and praying him to cause the guilty perpetrators thereof to be brought to signal and condign punishment.

Happily, Richard Cobden had a hundred other good reasons to fall back on in his arguments for incorporation. Any one of which must have been far stronger than the one which he advanced with so much emphasis. ★ ★ ★ ★ ★

The cynical reader, if his patience has sustained him thus far in this long and involved narrative, may well ask how such a recital can affect the tragic consequences of that fateful 16th of August.

For a century and a half it has been said to be the Manchester Massacre—it has been likened to the Sicilian Vespers, to the butcheries of St Bartholomew's Eve, and has been said to have acquired an emotive significance to the English mind like the word Buchenwald.

Such equations, it is maintained, can hardly now be sustained. It is true, there have been writers who have attempted to cast doubts on such an interpretation, but they have been overwhelmed by the apparent mass of evidence from the other side. Mr Thompson could say:

It really was a *massacre*. We need not give the hour by hour account once again . . . [Followed by his footnote]: See the accounts in Bamford, Prentice, J. E. Taylor; the contemporary reports by Tyas in *The Times*, by Baines in the *Leeds Mercury*, and by Carlile in Sherwin's *Political Register*; the evidence of witnesses and participants in the *Trial* of Henry Hunt, the *Inquest on John Lees* of Oldham and the action against Colonel Birley; F. A. Bruton, *The Story of Peterloo* (1919) and *Three Accounts of Peterloo* (1921), and (in defence) (Francis Philips), *An Exposure of the Calumnies &c.* (1819).

How good, how bad, those authorities are has been seen. If the radical interpretation of Peterloo is to be re-established, other authorities must be cited.

It may be argued that even though the magistrates are to be acquitted on the charge of 'massacre', they will still be indictable for folly or ineptitude. Such a lesser charge has hitherto scarcely been considered; it will be considered against the background of the newly-discovered evidence. How Peterloo will fit into the general concept of English Regency history, after being wrested from its context and reassessed, is now a matter for the historians.[1]

If the equation of 16 August 1819, with 'massacre' cannot now be sustained, then English history is cleaner for the stain being removed. English public life is cleaner also. The social conscience of England was roused then, in a day almost, to protest against what appeared to be a monstrous outrage. It was not the passage of time which stilled or smothered that frail conscience in spite of assertions to the contrary; It came about because a slow realization came upon men that the transactions at Manchester were not the kind of transactions they had been led to believe had taken place. They realized that the righteous indignation of Henry Hunt was not quite so righteous as he had made it out to be; not so righteous because he knew what had occurred from the start. Others, like John Edward Taylor, did not know, and were only

[1] A passage from W. S. Gilbert's *The Mikado* (Act 2) may seem to have some relevance:
Ko-Ko (*in abject terror*). If your Majesty will accept our assurance, we had no idea—
Mikado: Of course you hadn't. That's the pathetic part of it. Unfortunately the fool of an act says 'compassing the death of the Heir Apparent'. There's not a word about a mistake, or not knowing, or having no notion, There should be, of course, but there isn't. That's the slovenly way in which these acts are drawn. I'll have it altered next session.

reluctantly persuaded, and to the end could hardly bring themselves to believe that such a train of events could have occurred. The Archibald Prentices blindly refused even to consider the plain evidence set before them, and stubbornly refused to throw away the big stick which had been so miraculously placed in their hands, a stick with which to beat the backs of the Tories. The Prentices merely fashioned it anew by planing off the ugly knobs and spikes left thereon by the Henry Hunts; and Prentice prevailed.

★ ★ ★ ★ ★

On 9 October, 1819, the *Manchester Observer* had borrowed some extracts from the *Statesman*. They included a prophecy:

. . . The abominable conduct of the Magistracy of Manchester will accelerate (Reform) 'in no small degree, and fix a stain upon their characters which none of them will have years enough remaining to wipe away . . .'

It was a prophecy to be fulfilled almost to the letter.

Epilogue

If any of the principal actors in the transactions of 16 August 1819, had 'years enough remaining' after that tragic day, William Hulton had—he had forty-five years ahead of him. After that final debate in Parliament in March 1832, he slipped, more or less, into alternately local fame and local notoriety, a destiny which would have been his in any case, had not the tragic chain of circumstances thrust him forward thirteen years previously. His local fame amongst one section of Manchester opinion was diminished by his background; it enhanced his local fame in another. If any echoes of his activities reached the columns of the local press in Manchester, there was soon tagged on to him the *Guardian*'s 'foolish country squire,' or Prentice's *Manchester Times* 'stain of the 16th of August,' or both. It was perhaps inevitable. The affairs of the town of Manchester, however, saw less of William Hulton after 1832, but he became one of the leaders, if not the leader of Right-wing politics in the newly-formed Parliamentary constituency of the Southern division of Lancashire.

John Edward Taylor's private view was: 'he who makes it a boast that, in mature age and on every subject, he retains unmodified the ideas of his youth, is far more likely to have a claim to the title of obstinate, than to the merit of being regarded as consistent';[1] fifteen years previously, Hulton had, he said, been told to revise the lessons of his youth. Had Hulton's life proceeded normally from 1819 onwards, 'stern and unbending' as he claimed to be, he would probably have modified his views. He was 'liberal' enough in his views on trade unionism until the turn-out stiffened him; in the 'truck' agitation, in the victimization of silk weavers, his views, in spite of the reputation the Manchester reform press had given him, were enlightened. More still, his espousal of the views of Robert Peel and his active endorsement of them in the realms of law reform shewed him to be no Eldonite Tory. It was only when Peel seemed to renounce the dearest prejudices in Hulton's mind, founded on what Hulton believed to be unalterable religious principles, that his soul revolted.

Hulton had made, it will be remembered, in 1824, a statement of his

[1] Read, *Press and People*, p. 85.

convictions: 'If by conciliation is meant a display of generous liberality and active benevolence to my most eager opponents, I accede cordially to the terms . . .' It is to be feared, however, that in his political 'education' in the years 1819–1832 his opponents did not give to him what he proposed to give to them: 'the credit of acting from no unworthy motive'; not an action he did or a word he spoke in public in those years but was garbled or wilfully misconstrued by all his political opponents from Hunt to Taylor. It is not surprising that he appeared to consider them all as tarred with the same brush. Had he known what Taylor privately thought: that with the 'coming into office of the moderate Tories, Canning, Peel and Huskisson, the whole conduct of government had changed' he would hardly have believed it. His experience therefore, between 1819 and 1832 had probably confirmed his prejudices rather than modified them.

In the Reform general election in December 1832, the Southern division in Lancashire saw the rout of what *Wheeler's Manchester Chronicle* called 'the blue party'; the results were G. W. Wood (Reform) 5,694; Viscount Molyneux (Reform) 5,575; and Sir Thomas Hesketh 3,082. Hulton was on the hustings and was the principal speaker on the 'blue' side. There was heckling, there was a cry of 'Peterloo'; there was a later castigation of Hulton from the *Guardian* for what that paper called bad taste in his speech; but Sir Thomas Hesketh had said:

. . . No man can witness the present temper and condition of the times and not see that those abuses, whatever they might be, must be radically cured (laughter). But there is a great difference as to the manner in which this must be effected. We, gentlemen, would preserve—or, I will use the term, conserve, all the best blessings (a voice in the crowd 'Pickle them!') of that constitution under which this country has attained that high pinnacle . . .

The word Conservative was coming into use. The Oxford English Dictionary gives its earliest use with a capital C as 1830, and adds 'in early use, a supporter of Sir Robert Peel, 1831'.[1] The *Manchester Herald*, 7 November 1832 (quoting the *Standard*), said:

. . . The name 'Conservative' indeed which is now assumed, and with propriety, as a title of honour by all who oppose revolutionary innovation, was first taken by those who faithfully resisted the first fatal revolutionary step in 1829 . . .

[1] When a Conservative speaker at an Atherton (near Bolton) meeting in 1845 said 'the term "Conservative" was first adopted by Sir Robert Peel', William Ford Hulton, Hulton's son and heir, interjected: 'He was taught it!' *Bolton Chronicle*, 7 June 1845.

One of the first recorded uses of the word seems to have been in an article by John Wilson Croker in the *Quarterly Review*,[1] January 1830:

We are now, as we have always been, decidedly and conscientiously attached to what is called the Tory, and which might with more propriety be called the Conservative party.

whilst Macaulay, in July 1832,[2] wrote that the term 'Conservative' was 'the new cant word'.

It was in south Lancashire, however, that organized Conservative associations were begun, a model which was quickly followed throughout the country. The *Guardian* was animadverting on the south Lancashire proposal in early February 1833, at the inaugural meeting of which William Hulton was named as the principal speaker. A fortnight later the *Guardian* was doing likewise on the formation of a Cheshire Conservative 'club' with branch societies:

This is capital. A parcel of people who have almost made themselves hoarse by declaiming against political unions, are proposing, not only to establish a political union of their own, but to establish one having *branch societies*, and therefore directly in the teeth of the delegations act. Some of them will assuredly be brought to trial for seditious practices, if they do not take care what they are about.[3]

In the Bay Horse Inn, a small hostelry in the still small town of Newton-le-Willows, Lancashire—near where the East Lancashire road (Liverpool to Manchester) passes underneath the M.6 motorway—Conservative associations were born. In 1837, William Hulton was addressing the Bolton Operative Conservative Association:

. . . They knew what could be accomplished from small beginnings by perseverance, and he was anxious to state what great good had resulted from a weak beginning. He had often stated the origin of the South Lancashire Conservative Association, and he would repeat it. When the men of Lancashire were borne down by the unfortunate result of Sir Thomas Hesketh's election, a few despondent individuals sat in the window of a common pothouse in Newton. It occurred to them that it was their duty to call up every friend to the monarchy and the Church to counteract the machinations of the enemies to both; and then, for the first and only time in his life, he ventured to become an anonymous writer. He ventured to call upon the freeholders to meet at Newton on a certain day. Many thought that the old Tory was at the bottom of the conspiracy. He received letter after letter, some encouraging,

---

[1] *Quarterly Review*, p. 276.
[2] *Edinburgh Review*, (July 1832), p. 557.
[3] *Guardian*, 23 February 1833.

and some ridiculing the idea of meeting on an anonymous summons. He believed that the father of their respected Member, Mr. Wilbraham, was the first person to whom he divulged the secret. However, the day of meeting arrived, and from seven they increased to twenty-five—the foundations of the South Lancashire Conservative Association were laid, and from seven desponding persons that association could now boast of three thousand members . . . and from that stem at Newton, Conservative associations had branched out all over her Majesty's dominions . . .[1]

John Edward Taylor's *Guardian* saw the sequel to that original meeting:

. . . We have seen a circular addressed to respectable gentlemen of this town, signed by Thomas White, of Newton, stating that it is in contemplation to form a conservative association for the Southern division of the county of Lancashire. It also intimates that a meeting on the subject was to take place at Newton, on Thursday, the 7th inst.[2]

The week following, the *Guardian* reported again:

On Thursday week a respectable and influential meeting of gentlemen (we use the language of the *Liverpool Standard*) of this division of the county was held at Newton, John Entwistle, of Foxholes, in the chair, for the purpose of forming a county conservative association . . . Mr. Hulton, of Hulton Park, and other gentlemen of the county addressed the meeting at some length; committees were formed for each district of the county . . . and after which, the following declaration was unanimously adopted and signed by all the gentlemen present:

'We, whose names are hereunto subscribed, declare our fixed determination to maintain the tried and ancient principles on which the constitution of our country is founded; and we *hold ourselves pledged to resist all measures by which the necessary connection between the established church and state may be severed or relaxed;*[3] by which the dignity of the monarchy may be impaired, or its existence endangered; by which the privileges of the house of lords as an independent branch of the legislature may be virtually annihilated, or the deliberate powers of the commons house of parliament become fettered or controlled; as we are convinced, that on the united and energetic support of these authorities depend the continuance of social order, the security of property and the interests of religion.'

The constable of Lancaster Castle had better take care, or he may get the key of that fortress turned upon himself. How dare he *pledge himself to resist* measures which the legislature may hold to be indispensable to the public welfare.—Ed. *Manchester Guardian*.

[1] *Bolton Chronicle*, 15 July 1837.
[2] *Manchester Guardian*, 9 February 1833.
[3] The italics were Taylor's.

On 24 August too, the *Guardian* was still fulminating against the South Lancashire Conservative Association—calling it ironically the 'South Lancashire Political Union, which is to all intents and purposes a political union of the most obnoxious and unconstitutional kind'. Again Hulton had been the main speaker at the annual dinner, 'the renowned squire of Hulton, who appears to have exhibited a full share of that folly of which he is so proud . . .':

. . . These people, with a degree of assurance which, in the rest of mankind, would be a little extraordinary, will prate by the hour about the mischievous nature and the unconstitutional designs of other political unions than their own. We believe that political unions of all sorts are mischievous enough; and the tory unions would perhaps be the most mischievous of all, if their power to do evil were not taken away by the contempt which must be engendered by their hypocritical denunciations of others for the very acts which they are ready to commit themselves.

As political parties in opposition are prone to be, the sentiments uttered and particularly by Hulton were considered irresponsible. Hulton, it was alleged, had referred to a 'bought' majority in the House of Commons, which the *Guardian* construed as 'bribed':

. . . Mr. Hulton, it is well known, was a strenuous supporter of that ministry, which, a few years ago, procured the passing of an act of parliament, imposing the penalty of banishment on any man who was found guilty of a libel, tending to bring a house of parliament into contempt. Now, what can tend more to bring a house of parliament into contempt than an assertion that a majority of its members are bribed? Fortunately for Mr. Hulton (if he has uttered the words imputed to him), the act we have named has expired; and the only penalty to which he will have rendered himself liable, are those of fine and imprisonment. Perhaps he may even escape these . . . but he cannot escape that feeling of abhorrence with which wilful and indignant slanderers are always regarded . . .

It all fizzled out, of course, in a spate of words. Perhaps Hulton, for the first time for many years, was enjoying himself. The very idea of 'political unions' which the *Guardian* was charging Conservatives with forming, he had perhaps brought with him from his own experience in earlier days!

Only seldom did William Hulton's utterances reach a wider public than that of south Lancashire; in 1834, however, there was a blast from his erstwhile friend The Thunderer:

. . . Mr. Hulton also favoured the Conservative company with a speech. We suppose that this is the Mr. Hulton who rejoices in describing himself as Mr.

Hulton of Hulton, lest he should be called Mr. Hulton of Peterloo. If so, he is the Mr. Hulton who was one of the magistrates implicated in the bloody business of the 16th of August, 1819. Such a man was peculiarly fitted to carry into effect the designs of Lord Wilton—viz. to convince the people of the kindly feelings that exist towards them on the part of the members of the meeting, and the Tories generally. The loving kindness of Mr. Hulton has been experienced most practically, and certainly it was not the sort which spareth the rod. With a language appropriate to his character, this gentleman said, that since the passing of the reform bill, Conservative principles had spread with 'a stable, *stern*, and *unrelenting* fixedness of purpose'. If his principles have been waxing more *stern* and *unrelenting*, Heaven have mercy on mobs where he directs sabres.[1]

No doubt Archibald Prentice, in the *Manchester Times*, concurred; it was Prenticism unalloyed.

January 23rd, 1835, was to William Hulton—in spite of a former assertion to the contrary—the proudest day of his life. Through the swing of the pendulum or through the success of the organization in which he had been the mainspring, the Southern division of Lancashire returned two Conservative members to Parliament: Lord Francis Egerton and Richard Bootle Wilbraham (the son of the former M.P. for Dover, of Peterloo Parliamentary debates fame). It had been a momentous election: it had produced what may now be thought an anomalous election manifesto emanating from the Weavers' Committee Rooms, Bolton, on January 16th:[2]

To the Electors of South Lancashire. Gentlemen: We, the committee of that unfortunate class of his Majesty's subjects, the Hand-Loom Weavers resident in Bolton and its vicinity . . . have for many years past made application to the legislature to take our deplorable condition into serious consideration, with a view to the protection of our wages . . . but without any material steps being taken on our behalf . . . [tribute to the M.P.s of Bolton] . . . We regret to state that the body generally designated as 'Political Economists' have uniformly turned a deaf ear to our complaints and have recommended the REGULATION of our NUMBERS and EMIGRATION to far distant climes as the only remedies . . . Our only friends in Parliament were the Conservatives and we therefore implore you, for the sake of our starving Wives and Families to Vote for Lord Francis Egerton and the Hon. R. B. Wilbraham, the Conservative candidates for South Lancashire . . . and you will receive the heartfelt gratitude of Thousands of the most impoverished, although eminently Loyal portion of his Majesty's subjects. Signed by Order of the Committee, Thos. Monks, secretary. Weavers' Committee Rooms, Queen Anne, Bolton. January 16th, 1835.

[1] *Bolton Chronicle* (quoting *The Times*) 13 September 1834.
[2] *Bolton Chronicle*, 17 January 1835.

Operative Conservative Associations in Lancashire were in the offing. On the hustings at the close of the poll, Sir Robert Holt Leigh,[1] the Tory doyen of South Lancashire hailed Hulton in glowing terms:

. . . whose soul of fire has carried us on with a degree of ardour and vigour that nothing else than his inspiring genius could have wrought in us. In that gentleman, loyalty is an innate element, a principle which breathes in him, which raises that firm patriotism that, first lighting amongst the drooping spirits of the conservatives, aroused them, gentlemen, with its triumphant voice, to the exertions and to the manly efforts that they have thus success-fully made . . .

There were, the *Guardian* reported, cheers and cries of 'Hulton! Hulton!' Even the *Guardian*, it seemed, hardly begrudged giving a moment of triumph to one who had so often been on the losing side. It reported Hulton:

Gentlemen: It will best become me, if, retiring silently from this proud scene of triumph, I avoid every possible expression of anger or irritation against any of my opponents. My heart and soul has for years been devoted to the cause of my King and my Country. Through times of difficulty and danger I have fought hand in hand with many of those honest hearts I see around me. Through times of persecution, I may say, I have endeavoured to hold up a head of conscious dignity in my heart, and knowing that no power on earth could possibly move me from that strict line of duty which I had chalked out for myself in early life. One only object remained to make me end my days, and pass the remaining part of my life, in happiness and gratitude to that Almighty Being who has so mercifully showered his blessings upon our land. It was to see that day when, in spite of reformers and revolutionists, there should be given to the constituency of this great county an opportunity of openly expressing their sentiments,—knowing that that expression could neither be obtained by money, by favour, nor by ambition. (Cheers) Gentle-men, you have nobly answered to the call lately made upon you. You have sent two men to represent your opinions in parliament who will give back the trust to you uncontaminated by any of the dirty trickery of faction. (Cheers). You have for this the guarantee of the high honour of their ancestors— you have the guarantee of their own immaculate characters,—you have a guarantee that they would be ashamed of themselves if they did not respond to your beating breasts, and lay at the foot of the throne our humble and grateful thanks to his Majesty for his inimitable exercise of his royal prerogative. (Cheers).[2]

It was innocuous enough, even allowing for mixed metaphor; perhaps Hulton could see honest hearts around him, for no doubt his auditors

[1] Of Hindley Hall, near Wigan.
[2] *Manchester Guardian*, 24 January 1835.

were that day wearing them upon their sleeves. From any other speaker the *Guardian* would have passed the speech over; but it was William Hulton:

. . . The proceedings at Newton yesterday, when the Sheriff declared . . . the result of the election . . . It will be seen that the newly elected members spoke of their opponents in a tone of courtesy and conciliation which was creditable to their feelings. We are much disposed in this respect to follow their good examples, and shall therefore abstain from any comment, except upon one point in a speech made, in self-glorification, with which, in the main, we are not disposed to quarrel, said: 'Through times of difficulty and danger I have fought hand in hand with many of those honest hearts I see around me. *Through times of persecution*, I may say, I have endeavoured to hold up a head full of conscious dignity'.

That the worthy squire may have seen times of difficulty is possible enough; but what the dangers are which he has had to encounter, or the persecution he has been fated to endure, we can scarcely venture to guess. Surely Mr. Hulton does not account it a persecution to have his public conduct publicly scrutinized. If so, he should recollect the proverb, 'they who live in glass houses should never throw stones'. We know no man who is more ready to attack others, no one who, in his own judgement is more 'skilful of fence', or fonder of a little gladiatorial display, than Mr. Hulton, and if, in the encounters into which his pugnacious spirit leads him, he now and then gets his head handsomely broken, he of all men ought to take the matter in good part, and utter no complaints about it . . .

John Edward Taylor could be as unfair as he could be incisively critical. He knew 'no man who is more ready to attack others' than William Hulton; he no doubt had in mind the Althorp-Hulton correspondence which Taylor and others like him had construed as an attack. Viewed dispassionately in its context it was nothing of the kind. It is more than remarkable that in the whole of Hulton's recorded utterances on the question which loomed largest in his life, recorded, uttered or written, there is not a single instance to be found of reproaches towards those who bitterly reproached him. He could speak in general terms of 'revolutionists', but with his experience who could blame him? John Edward Taylor had not yet, however, finished with Hulton.

Hulton continued to bask in the light of the South Lancashire victory for some time. He was able to tell his listeners at the Grand Coursing Meeting dinner at Atherton (on the fringe of the Hulton estate) in March 1835,[1] that he had found on a recent visit to London that in the capital there was 'universal exclamation' on the South Lancashire result.

[1] *Bolton Chronicle*, 7 March 1835.

A tit-bit, too, from his old friend James Blomfield (Bishop of London, and Princess Victoria's tutor) that 'she is possessed of all the talents and virtues which can adorn the female character'. He was in the House of Commons when Sir Charles Manners-Sutton, 'that excellent man', was turned out of the Speaker's Chair by the votes of the radicals. His dearest prejudices were unmodified; he could speak of the former administration and 'their miserable majority of seven' which was, Hulton said, created 'not by the votes of Englishmen—forty Irish subjects of His Holiness the Pope voted for the amendment'! He had hopes for the future in Sir Robert Peel's administration; he hoped in vain, for Peel went out the following month (April 1835). Sir Robert Peel's day was yet to come. Among his neighbours, Hulton could preen himself on the one success he had achieved for many a long year:

. . . In 1832, I happened to be one of the seven who issued forth the famed declaration of that loyal body of men. Since that time I have seen 4,500 in our assembly. That declaration has also invaded the strongholds of the political union in Birmingham, where I rejoice to say a Constitutional Association has adopted all our plans and rules. It has also been received with great enthusiasm in Edinburgh . . . [and in replying to the toast to his health] . . . My past life is before you; you may examine it, and you will find it has been devoted to my King and Country . . . You approve of my past conduct . . . I am, gentlemen, one of yourselves—living amongst you as a neighbour, and loving you dearly. My first desire was to devote my services to my country, and I have neither courted the great nor despised the poor. To the former I have rendered no subserviency, and to the latter administered no unjustice. (Cheers). Why is it that you have your trials by jury? Why is it? but that the poorest man may defy the proudest Lord . . .[1]

During the last days of March 1835, a deputation waited upon Hulton to request him to once more resume his place on the Bolton magistrates bench. He asked to be allowed time to consider the matter, and on 3 April he replied:

Mr. Daly, boroughreeve of Bolton . . . When you and other gentlemen did me the honour to deliver to me last Tuesday a memorial from the gentry, merchants, tradesmen, and other residents of the Borough of Bolton to resume . . . [as a magistrate] . . . you kindly permitted me to postpone my reply . . . I demanded the erasure of my name from the Commission of the Peace on the grounds of insulted honour. . . I should not dare to under-take the great responsibilities of protecting property and suppressing crime unless I felt that I could successfully bring to the task all the willing energy of former days—exertions in which I participated and saved from destruction

[1] *Bolton Chronicle*, 7 March 1835.

one emporium of commerce. I have lived to see another sacrificed by supineness, to riot and to flames. Then as to a further essential part of a Magistrate's duty—the mitigation of poverty and sickness. This, I believe, I was enabled to accomplish under the mild, though not faultless code which was once my guide. I should now be bound by enactments which though compulsory by the law of man, are, in my humble conviction, quite contrary to the law of God . . . it will be my endeavour to prevail upon my son to give to the public service the best years of his manhood . . . William Hulton.

The annals of every town in nineteenth-century England are doubtless strewn with letters of similar importance, meriting no further publicity than that which they usually received: mention in the local newspaper. But news was news; the *Guardian* put out a leader. The opening gambit of Taylor's leader was necessary to tell his Manchester readers that on which, otherwise, they would probably have heard nothing:

Perhaps it may not be known to many of our readers that the tories of Bolton, or rather, a section of them,—for it is pretty well known that the *rare* qualities of 'the foolish squire' are not very highly estimated by many, even of his own political party,—that this section of the Bolton tories, with, we understand, Mr. Daly, the boroughreeve of Bolton at their head, thought proper, about three weeks ago, to get up an address, requesting Mr. Hulton to resume his functions as a magistrate in that division of the county. We will pass by that address with the remark, that its concoctors seemed to have jumped to a singular conclusion, in presuming that, because Mr. Hulton's name was not struck out of the Commission when he *demanded* its erasure, at the period of his flippant letters to Lord Althorp, it was because his 'services were too highly appreciated, even by the members of his Majesty's Government at that period, to be dispensed with'! The addressers, writing, of course, prior to the ousting of the late [Sir Robert Peel's] tory Government, conclude thus: 'Recent changes in his Majesty's counsels having taken place, we now anxiously and most earnestly hope and entreat that your invaluable services as a magistrate, equally honourable to yourself and beneficial to the public, may be restored to the community'.

After a 'mature consideration' of three days, Mr. Hulton, on Friday fortnight, (when it was beginning to be no longer doubtful that the Peel ministry could not by any means much longer keep their places,) addressed a letter to Mr. Daly, in which he states that he had demanded the erasure of his name from the Commission of the Peace 'solely on the ground of insulted honour'. Declining to accede to the request made to him, the squire puts forth the following as the motives which forbid his acquiescence therewith: 'The interests of this populous district are so deeply involved in the exertion of the trust, that I should not dare to undertake the great responsibility of protecting property and repressing crime unless I feel that I could successfully bring to the task all the willing energy of former days. Exertions, in which I have participated saved from destruction one emporium of commerce. I have lived to see another sacrificed, by supineness, to riot and flames. Then as to a further essential part of a magistrate's duty, the mitigation of the miseries of poverty and sickness. This I believe I was enabled to accomplish under the mild though not faultless code which was once my guide. I should now be bound by enactments which, though compulsory by the law of men, are in my humble opinion, quite contrary to the law of God. Trusting that the legislature will correct this grievous error,[1] it will be my endeavour to prevail upon my son to give to the public service the best years of his manhood, if life should be spared him.' &c., &c., Alas! for 'the interests of this populous district'. No more shall they flourish by aid of 'the invaluable services as a magistrate' of Mr. Hulton, who declines again to administer justice, because, as he admits with much simplicity, he can 'no longer *successfully* bring to the task all the willing energy of former days', and because he would have occasionally to adjudicate in conformity with the provisions of the poor law amendment act of 'the hated whig government'. But lest the division should be plunged into the deepest despair, Mr. Hulton does hold out a faint hope, that in process of time, his son may sit in his place upon the Bolton Bench.[2]

To return, however, to Mr. Hulton himself: As to his boast that 'exertions in which he participated, saved from destruction one emporium of commerce,' he knows, as well as we do, that it is fatally destitute of truth. If he had had justice done him, those exertions would have been rewarded very differently from what they were; it would not have been left in his power to 'demand' from a Whig ministry in 1832[3] the erasure of his name from the Commission of the Peace on one pretence, when the true reason of his uncomfortableness on the Bolton Bench was well known to be something very different. He would have been *relieved* from the exercise of magisterial functions, without any application on his part, before the close of the year 1820. As, however, this was not done, and, as, if his Bolton addresses may be relied on, Mr. Hulton's name still remains in the Commission, we hope one of the first acts of the new Chancellor of the Duchy of Lancaster, be he whom he may, will be to do him and the public the tardy service of erasing it.

William Hulton, in 1835, probably came to the conclusion that he could not win! Every ace he played was trumped. His fondness for making the parallel of Bristol with Manchester was one of his aces. Others could make even more outlandish parallels and get away with it, but not Hulton. Daniel O'Connell was in Manchester in September 1835; in his speech he referred to a murder in America by the people:

[1] The grievous error, in Hulton's mind, was the separation of man and wife in the then new workhouse proposals of the Poor Law Amendment Act.

[2] His son did; William Ford Hulton (1811–79) qualified as a County Magistrate, 13 April 1835—the day before Taylor's leader appeared.

[3] It was 1831.

. . . There they committed murder; and for such proceedings I am as little the advocate as Sir Robert Peel can be. But what does he do? He attributes that murder to their government. Are there no murders in this country? Did Sir Robert Peel never hear of Peterloo—of what has been called the Manchester Massacre? (Cheers) Why the actors in the hangings in America by what they call Lynch law will be, as they ought to be, punished for their crime; and I warrant the American government will do all it can to punish them; above all, I am sure, it will never applaud or thank or reward any of them. But what did Sir Robert Peel's government do to the authors of the Manchester Massacre? They gave them thanks and rewarded them and honoured them. (Hear). I throw Peterloo in his teeth when he talks of outrages across the Atlantic . . .[1]

With Daniel O'Connell making his doubtful parallels in 1835 and Feargus O'Connor at the Peterloo anniversary in 1836 on St Peter's Field, telling his audience:

. . . that the Peterloo meeting in 1819 had been the great scene of the century in which they lived; the people who were killed at that time were murdered with *malice prepense*, and that the slaughter at the victory of Waterloo was not to be compared to the massacre at Peterloo . . .[2]

The radical version of Peterloo, in 1836, was not in the making, it was made. Even William Hulton gave up the hopeless struggle.

It might be thought remarkable that Hulton did not, at some time in his life, make some *apologia* for his part in the affair of 16 August. He did, in that he began a 'commentary' on the passages on the transactions which appeared in Alison's *History of Europe* (Vol. II p. 403). Alison's work appeared after 1833, so Hulton's notes must belong to that or a later period; because of errors of fact in Hulton's notes, and one error of fact in Alison which Hulton failed to observe, the present writer is inclined to the opinion that Hulton compiled the notes much later than 1833.[3]

Alison had written: 'No serious breach of the peace occurred till the 16th of August, 1819.' Hulton added: About three months[4] preceding this date the Magistrates of the Hundred of Salford had found it necessary to form a standing committee (of which Mr. Hulton was appointed chairman) to whom reports were constantly brought of the training of large bands, especially on Tandle Hills, near Middleton, at late hours of the evening and before sunrise in the morning. Delegates were actively engaged and persons accustomed to

1 *Guardian*, 12 September 1835.
2 *Guardian*, 20 August 1836.
3 The document is preserved DDHu/53/56 L.C.R.O., and the volume and page references to Alison are Hulton's.
4 It was three weeks.

military discipline were appointed to instruct the masses. These facts being sworn to were from time to time laid before Lord Sidmouth, the then Secretary of State for the Home Department, and the advice of the Law Officers of the Crown, especially of Lord Chancellor Eldon was given to the Magistrates.

When a great assemblage took place at Peterloo, near Manchester. (Alison). The mob assembled, Hulton's notes continued, in St. Peter's Square, within the town of Manchester. It was a large open space, only a few houses having been at that time completed. This intended square was afterwards named Peterloo by the Radicals.

Great apprehensions were entertained by the local authorities, and extra-ordinary precautions taken to prevent a breach of the peace. (Alison). The 16th Light Dragoons, went on Hulton,[1] had for some time occupied the Barracks at Manchester. The 31st Regiment were stationed within the town. The additional force called for by the Magistrates were the Cheshire Yeomanry, and two troops of the Manchester Yeomanry under the command of Capt. Birley.

A large body of Special Constables was sworn in and armed with their batons surrounded the hustings where the speakers were to be placed. (Alison).[2] (Hulton proceeded with his commentary): A considerable number of persons including the principal gentlemen of the town were sworn in as special constables, but they were not on the ground as a body. They were desired to protect the 'Factories' which were in great danger of being burned down if the mob succeeded in their plan of operations. A portion of these constables were also employed to watch, on horseback, the approaches to the town, and to bring reports to the Magistrates then assembled at a house from the windows of which was given a complete view of the Square.

The mob arrived by Companies, their leaders giving the word of command. They were preceded by their respective flags with the inscriptions mentioned by Alison. They had also a large Cap of Liberty (now in my possession). It was made of Tin, and painted red, and had the Motto: 'Death or Liberty' in large letters. The female part of the procession wheeled right and left, and the Square was entirely occupied by the men, of whom a semi-circular band linked arm in arm surrounded the hustings which were erected at an extremity of the Square, with two or three high houses at the back.

Hunt arrived in a barouche-and-four, having Carlile and another person in the body of the open carriage and, on the box, a woman representing the Goddess of Reason holding a branch of the Tree of Liberty. On leaving her room in the morning she had boasted that she should return as Mrs. Trafford of Trafford. She was crushed to death in an entry into which she had run for protection.

Depositions having been sworn to, it was thought most advisable to

---

[1] They were the 15th.

[2] The error of constables surrounding the hustings was not noticed by Hulton.

arrest Hunt before the immense crowd became excited by his harangue. Placards breathing vengeance, had been posted for miles around. A quantity of infidel publications were seized in Hunt's carriage. These I now possess. The moment Nadin, the head of the Police, advanced, the mob, amounting to nearly 80,000 began to pelt him and the constables with stones, which were afterwards proved by their form and colour to have been brought from the course of a river. It then became impossible to serve the warrant by the aid of the civil power alone. The military were called to the Square and a general conflict ensued. Hunt and others were captured, Carlile escaped. The greatest injury was inflicted by a Heavy Dragoon who pioneered the Cavalry to the ground. A special constable was killed by a sabre wound. In the evening the Prisoners were sent to Lancaster Castle, but without any disturbance. Two men were shot whilst engaged in a riot at night in another quarter of the town, and a child was also killed in the morning in Mosley Street, the mother in her fright having allowed it to fall from her arms. The town was saved from such pillage and conflagration, as afterwards destroyed a great part of the City of Bristol. The *legality* and *propriety* of the measures adopted, may, perhaps, be best ascertained from the opinion of the Judges on the second Trial. (The document then follows on with copies of the relevant opinions from the printed opinions of the Judges in Redford *v*. Birley, and the paper is signed: W. Hulton.)

It need hardly be emphasized that Hulton, in preparing these comments, had by the time they were made confounded (as Scarlett maintained, though erroneously, he had on the occasion of Hunt's trial), the moment the attack was made. Had this *apologia* been published then (after 1833), or had Hulton written an *apologia* in earlier years, its importance to the narrative of what occurred on St Peter's Field would have been considerable. But it was not. Hulton's memory, as has been seen in an earlier paragraph of the commentary, was at fault when he wrote it; it was equally at fault in the last extract. Hulton may have been refreshing his memory by looking up Nadin's evidence in Redford *v*. Birley. Nadin did indeed testify to a stone being thrown[1] at the period before the Yeomanry moved in, and in the previous column of the report[2] he had said: 'When he had got through the mob, there was a shower of stones came upon us.' Nadin was, however, in this latter quotation, referring to the attack before 16 August at New Cross. On an earlier occasion John Edward Taylor had charged Hulton with trusting to his memory instead of referring to authentic records; Hulton here appears to have referred to authentic records, and referred wrongly. He chose, too, on this occasion to rely on Tyas's estimate of

[1] *State Trials*, 1166.
[2] *State Trials*, 1165.

80,000 as the number of the crowd instead of his own of 50,000–60,000. His memory was completely at fault in saying that the prisoners were sent to Lancaster in the evening of 16 August. Happily (for Hulton and for the resolving of the problems of what occurred on the field that day) the commentary remained secreted in the archives of his family, where it still remains. Hulton's post-1833 opinions on Peterloo are not vital.

In the years which followed Hulton steered himself away from the controversies of 1819. He bought Bamford's *Passages in the Life of a Radical* on its appearance or later, wrote his name in both volumes, and placed it on his shelves without comment. He had still thirteen years' course to run when Prentice's *Recollections* came out in 1851; it possibly seemed pointless to attempt to go through all the refutations again. He appeared on the platforms at meetings protesting against the Government proposals to introduce a secular education system in 1839, with the comment:

. . . The sure results of an education not founded on the Word of God—the real effect of mere intellectual education—is to substitute crimes of fraud for crimes of force.

In his own parish church of Deane he showed his old 1829 prejudices, later translated into a low-Churchmanship of an uncompromising kind, when the Evangelical vicar of Deane (of Hulton's own choosing) had succumbed to a desire to insert a stained-glass window. It was 1845, and the innovators of the Oxford Movement were shaking William Hulton:

. . . In the house of God, Hulton wrote to his vicar, everything ought (according to the apostle's injunction) to be 'done decently and in order', but it does not appear to me that stained glass at a cost of more than £260 is requisite for these qualifications of a Protestant place of worship in a country village.

In spite of Hulton's strictures, the window went in, and is still generally admired. At a local miners' gathering in 1847 echoes of Hulton as a coal-owner were heard when W. Daniels, editor of the *Miners' Advocate* commended him, bidding other coal-owners to 'Go and do thou like-wise . . .' A toast to W. P. Roberts (the honest attorney-general of the Miners' Association) 'May he ever be a terror to evil doers and the pride of those who do well, and may he live long to battle against oppression.' The turn-out of 1831 was not even a memory.

The old heavy rate of mortality amongst the Hultons recurred during William Hulton's lifetime. Of his thirteen children, only three survived him, but amongst those three was his heir, William Ford Hulton (1811–1879), who during the later years of his father's life was Squire Hulton in everything except name. In the smaller world of local affairs in which he moved he essayed to be a pale imitation of his father, but the wider world passed him by unnoticed.[1] By modest and unostentatious mode of living William Ford Hulton is said to have made good the inroads made into the family's fortunes in earlier years.

During the later years of his life William Hulton had lived in retirement at Leamington, being seen only occasionally at Hulton Park. On 2 April 1864, the columns of the *Bolton Chronicle* which had so often in earlier times been filled with the doings of William Hulton, filled up again with different intelligence:

The House of Hulton is again placed in mourning; this time it is for the head, the representative of a family amongst the oldest in the county. Mr. Hulton died on Wednesday at Leamington where, with Mrs. Hulton he had resided for some years. His health had been gradually weakening, and he had been prepared for the change by the friendly medical advice that it might be sudden. Such it really became, as Mr. Hulton was at church on Sunday last, but felt worse in the evening, and on Monday information to that effect was forwarded to Hulton Park. Unfortunately, Mr. William Ford Hulton was prevented from proceeding at once to his parents by the very serious illness of his daughter.

Mr. Hulton was in the 77th year of his age, being High Sheriff of this county in 1810. He held the honourable post of Constable of Lancaster Castle and on her Majesty's first journey to the north (in 1851) he had the honour of presenting the keys in token of the allegiance of her Lancashire people . . .

William Ford Hulton's grief was double. His daughter, aged only 21, died with her newly-born baby in the exhaustions of childbirth seven days after her grandfather. She had been married at Deane church the summer before with almost-royal village celebrations. The changes and chances of this mortal life were vivid in mid-nineteenth century England. William Hulton, as his forbears had been, was brought home to Deane:

. . . From the first dawn of morning [on Tuesday, 5th April] the weather was most wintry, snow falling continuously, with occasional rain. This while adding to the solemnity of the occasion, had the effect of greatly diminishing

---

[1] Perhaps the world ought not to have passed him by unnoticed. He had one not too slight achievement to his credit. Had it not been for William Ford Hulton, England would have been robbed of one of its greatest Prime Ministers—William Ewart Gladstone. These two, when school-friends, were playing on a sandbank at Southport; Gladstone was buried by the sand caving in. Hulton pulled him out, and thereby saved William Ewart Gladstone from an early grave. *Bolton Chronicle*, 7 June 1879 (quoting a previous number of the *Southport Visiter*).

the numbers of those who had desired to show their respect for the deceased by their presence at the interment. Despite the weather, however, hundreds stood, umbrella-canopied, outside the churchyard walls for nearly two hours, braving the pelting, pitiless elements. In the hamlet of Deane the blinds of the houses were drawn; and the stillness which reigned around was not broken but rather made more impressive by the faint tolling of the minute-bell of the ancient parish church . . . Preparations had been made towards draping the pulpit and family-pew with mourning, but an intimation had been received that the deceased by a clause in his will had requested that all such outward tokens might be dispensed with . . . the coffin being borne to the grave on the shoulders of his oldest servants . . . it bore the inscription 'William Hulton, born 23rd October, 1787, died 30th March, 1864' . . .

The place of sepulture, the *Bolton Chronicle* report goes on, is upwards of nine yards deep, having on the east side receptacles of nine tiers, of three in breadth, after the manner of crypts or cells, rising above each other . . .[1]

The vault is sunk, like a colliery-shaft, into the depths of Deane churchyard. The preacher[2] of the memorial sermon on the following Sunday observed that 'Mr Hulton had entered upon life at a period of unparalleled laxity and prostration in the country, and yet he had had the conscientious boldness at once to take a very different line of conduct to that which at that time largely prevailed among the gentry . . .' There was something in what the preacher said. Perhaps William Hulton had done just that!

The current issue of the *Illustrated London News* looked back with perhaps more realism in its obituary notice:

William Hulton Esq., of Hulton Park, J.P. and D.L. and formerly Constable of Lancaster Castle, was the head and representative of one of the most ancient and honourable families in the realm . . . He was High Sheriff of Lancashire in 1809, and he, some nine or ten years after that, while chairman of the Lancashire and Cheshire bench of Magistrates, came much into public notice as having been the Justice who gave the direction to act to the Cheshire Yeomanry at that celebrated and disastrous mêlée known by the somewhat exaggerated but now historic appellation of the 'Manchester Massacre'. Mr. Hulton's conduct was severely criticized at the time by the Reform Party; but it was generally felt and admitted that, whether altogether correctly or not, he acted in what he conscientiously believed to be the strict exercise of his duty. Mr. Hulton as a country gentleman and Magistrate was much respected by all within his own district . . .

The *Illustrated London News* writer, from the almost-apologetic manner in which he stated his facts, might have been looking back over a couple

[1] *Bolton Chronicle*, 9 April 1864.
[2] Rev. Canon Thicknesse, vicar of Deane.

of centuries, instead of over a remarkably well-documented period of a mere forty-five years. Few, however, in 1864 (or afterwards) had the patience or the inclination to wade through the 'documents' of thirteen years or more. Into 'oblivion' they went; or some of them. The London reporters of 1864 were not much better than their forbears of 1819 in getting what 'facts' they did record right. The Cheshire Yeomanry, in spite of the Rev. Mr Stanley's efforts, were given the blame after all. John Edward Taylor's strivings in 1835 to have William Hulton's name struck out of the list of those in the Commission of the Peace were, apparently, not successful.

Hugh Hornby Birley had pre-deceased William Hulton by many years—he died in 1845. He was buried in the family vault of the Birleys under St Peter's Church, St Peter's Square, Manchester. Cromwell-like, (though not for the same reasons) his remains were disturbed when the church was demolished in 1907; Birley and his kinsfolk now rest elsewhere. The published reactions of Archibald Prentice's contemporaries have not been sought to discover what they thought of that writer's passage in his *Recollections* wherein he said that Hay and Ethelston, James Norris, Joseph Nadin, and 'Hugh Hornby Birley, who led the attack on a defenceless multitude' had all 'gone down to their graves, without an assault, without an insult.' Prentice's contemporaries knew, if posterity did not, that the passage in his *Recollections* of 1851 was as untrue as his numerous smears in former issues of the *Manchester Times*, made long before Birley had gone down to his grave, were untrue. To his contemporaries, however, Hugh Hornby Birley—because of his long connections with the town and trade of Manchester, with the Chamber of Commerce, and in spite of Archibald Prentice—lived respected and died lamented. That Prentice in 1851 did not include William Hulton in his more-in-sorrow-than-in-anger roll of the unassaulted and the un-insulted was perhaps not entirely because William Hulton was still above ground. It may have been because William Hulton had been known to stage a come-back. In 1851, it is feared, as surely as in 1864, William Hulton's come-backs were things of the past.

HEEL-PIECE

From Sir Francis Burdett's speech in his motion for inquiry into the Manchester transactions, May 1821. (Parl. Deb. N.S. Vol. V. 738):

'Time has fortunately done that which it never failed to do—it has rent asunder the veil which hypocrisy, and trick, and chicanery, had thrown round this subject.'

Select Bibliography

The literature of Peterloo is magnificently rich; in newspaper reports, speeches, memoirs, autobiographies, pamphlets, poems, the reports of trials, letters official and private, and in memoranda of every conceivable kind, the events of the day were described, argued about and refined to the last legal quibble. There can be few such short episodes in English history so thoroughly and so ably documented; we have the words of the most exalted and the humblest people in the country, people speaking in their own idiom faithfully recorded, people writing under the stress of great emotion with all the resources of experienced rhetoric. There is extant about Peterloo almost every kind of language used with almost every kind of purpose, expecting every kind of response in those who read or heard it. The eyewitness accounts alone have this range. A mere bibliography would stretch to many pages: here it is only possible to hint at the depth of interest that the comparison of these accounts contains. One of the fullest and best of them all is given by Samuel Bamford . . .

So wrote Humphrey House in an essay published posthumously in 1955.[1] In spite of the richness, the lavishness of the literature of Peterloo, and the assertion that 'there can be few such short episodes in English history so ably documented', it is also true to say that no incident in English history has been so completely misunderstood, largely because much of the what-is-thought-to-be contemporary documentation is misinformed. If, as Haslam Mills[2] says, Peterloo was 'the début of the reporter in English public life', and he could well have added and of the newspaper editor, their 'prentice hands made a singularly unfortunate beginning. The immense mass of literature has perhaps been a hindrance to historians rather than a help, for few, if any, have ever waded through it. Some have maintained that there was something unknown. Most, like Humphrey House, have taken at their face value the versions of Samuel Bamford and Archibald Prentice. Modern students are invited to consider Richard Carlile's eyewitness account[3] as a prime original document to illustrate what occurred on St Peter's Field. It is the most perverted and misinformed of them all.

[1] (House) *All in Due Time* (1955).
[2] (Haslam Mills) *The Manchester Guardian, a Century of History* (1921).
[3] (Cole and Filson) *Select Documents—British Working Class Movement*. (Macmillan 1965), p. 163.

The very distrust the earlier radical chroniclers had of each other ought to have suggested some cross-checking; perhaps the most noted example of this distrust was that of Henry Hunt's only biographer, Huish. In describing the greatest event in his subject's life—Peterloo— the radical Huish does not allow, with the exception of a single piece of correspondence, one word of the vivid description of the happenings of that day as related by Hunt himself in his *Memoirs* or elsewhere. Huish's attitude is perhaps unique in biographical literature.

Mr E. P. Thompson's passage, on page 210 of his work,[1] seems to be relevant:

'For, just as an earlier generation of historians who were also social reformers (Thorold Rogers, Arnold Toynbee, the Hammonds) allowed their sympathy with the poor to lead on occasions to a confusion of history with ideology, so we find that the sympathies of some economic historians today for the capitalist entrepreneur have led to a confusion of history and apologetics.'

The 'confusion of history with ideology' and with 'apologetics' has been remarkable in the literature of Peterloo.

Annual Register (1819).
> *The Annual Register's* account of the transactions of the 16th August is compiled almost exclusively from John Tyas's report in *The Times* newspaper of 19th August.

Aston's Exchange Herald.
(Axon, W. E. A.), *The Annals of Manchester.* (Manchester: 1886).
(Baines, Edward), *History of the County Palatine and Duchy of Lancaster.* (Edited James Croston), Vol. 3, (Manchester: 1886).
(Bamford, Samuel), *Miscellaneous Poetry by Samuel Bamford, Weaver of Middleton, in Lancashire, lately imprisoned in the Castle of Lincoln.* (London: 1821).
— Other editions of Bamford's *Poems,* 1843, 1864.
— *Passages in the Life of a Radical,* 2 vols. (Manchester: 1844).
— Edited with introduction by Henry Dunckley, 2 vols. (London: 1893).
— Introduction by W. H. Chaloner. (Cass: 1967).
— Preface by Tim Hilton. (Fitzroy edition: 1967).
(Banks, Mrs. Linnaeus), *The Manchester Man,* 3 vols. (London: 1876).
— Illustrated edition (with historical notes). (1896).
(Basnett, Lois), 'History of the Bolton and Leigh Railway', (Trans. *Lancashire and Cheshire Antiquarian Society,* LXII, 1953).
Bolton Central Library MSS. (Hulton).
Bolton Chronicle, 1829–64.
Bolton Journal 1881–4.

[1] (Thompson, E. P.), *The Making of the English Working Class.*

(Bruton, F. A.), *The Story of Peterloo*. (Manchester: 1919).
— *Three Accounts of Peterloo by Eyewitnesses*. (Manchester: 1921).
— *Short History of Manchester and Salford*. (Manchester: 1924).
(Burdett, Sir Francis), The King v. Burdett (Trial at Leicester, March 23rd, 1820, and proceedings in the Court of King's Bench, June, 1820—February, 1821). Reported in *State Trials*—New Series, Vol. I, 1888, cols. 1–170.
(Butler, J. R. M.), *The Passing of the Great Reform Bill*. (London: 1912).
(Canning, George), *Substance of the Speech of the Rt. Hon. George Canning . . . November 24th, 1819*. (London: 1820).
(Cobden, Richard), *Incorporate Your Borough* (1838). Reprinted by W. E. A. Axon in *Cobden as a Citizen*. (London: 1907).
(Colbey), *Sources of English History*. (London: 1899).
(Cole and Filson), *Select Documents—British Working Class Movements*. (Macmillan: 1965). *The Courier*, 1819–20.
Cowdroy's Manchester Gazette, 1810–18.
(Croston, James), *The County Families of Lancashire and Cheshire*. (Manchester: 1887). (Article on the Hulton family).
Dictionary of National Biography.
Edinburgh Review, 1830.
The Electors' Remembrancer. (London: 1882).
Encyclopedia Britannica. (11th edition).
English MSS., 1197. (John Rylands Library).
  A collection of papers originally amassed by the Rev. W. R. Hay, vicar of Rochdale, chairman of the Salford Quarter Sessions to 1823, and one of the Peterloo magistrates. The collection was later in the possession of J. T. Smith, of Rochdale, then of A. P. Wadsworth, some time editor of the *Manchester Guardian*. Presented to John Rylands Library by Miss Janet Wadsworth in memory of her father, 1957.
(Ethelston, Rev. C. W.), *The Suicide and Other Poems*. (London: 1803).
The Examiner.
(Feiling, Keith), *History of England*. (Macmillan: 1959).
(Hammond, J. L. and B.), *The Skilled Labourer 1760–1832*. (1919).
— *The Town Labourer*. (New edition, 1925).
(Hammond, J. L.), *C. P. Scott*. (1934).
(Hay, Rev. W. R.), Scrapbooks, Commonplace Books, and MSS. at Chetham's Library, Manchester.
  Eighteen scrapbooks containing newspaper cuttings (No. 9 and 10 Peterloo material); one large folio scrapbook containing posters, broadsides, squibs, newspapers, &c., covering the 1819–1820 period. Commonplace books, Vol. 10 containing Peterloo material.
(House, Humphrey), *All in Due Time*. (London: 1955).
  Contains two articles: 'Peterloo I' (reprinted from the *News Chronicle*, 16 August, 1939) and 'Peterloo II' ('not published before'). Humphrey House accepts the radical view.

(Hudson, J. H.), *Peterloo Massacre*. (National Labour Press, 1919).

Hulton Colliery Explosion (*British Medical Journal*, 20th May, 1911, article by W. A. Hatton, M.D.).

Hulton MSS.

Family archives of the Hulton family (DDHu County Record Office, Preston).

(Hunt, Henry), *Addresses from Henry Hunt, Esq. to the Radical Reformers of England, Ireland and Scotland, and particularly those of Cheshire, Lancashire and Yorkshire, on the Measures of the Whig Ministers since they have been in Place and Power*. No. 1–No. 12. (London: 1831).

— (Huish, R.), *Life of Henry Hunt*, 2 vols. (London: 1836).

J. A. Hamilton in his D.N.B. article on Henry Hunt says: 'The principal authority for the life of Henry Hunt is his own *Memoirs* . . . [and . . . Huish's *Life of Hunt* is] 'little more than a repetition of his *Memoirs*'. Such a statement is unfair to Huish, who commented on the *Memoirs*: 'It is also to be regretted that a spirit of egotism pervades the whole work, which is incompatible with the interests of truth' (II, 438). In Vol. I, 415, Huish writes, on the Bristol election, 1812, of Hunt's 'long, egotistical and gasconading account', refers to Hunt's minute description 'which in many instances throws an air of ridicule over the whole proceedings, independently of exciting some few suspicions that fiction has not a little to do in the recital'.

Huish, in view of his doubts as to Hunt's veracity, does not use a single paragraph, (with the exception of the letter to Lord Sidmouth (quoted above, p. 257) written in the New Bayley prison), from Hunt's description of the events of the 16th August. The letter to Sidmouth, says Huish, 'gives a plain and unvarnished account of what took place at Peterloo Massacre' (II, 215). Huish's narrative for Peterloo is culled from press and other reports.

— *Memoirs of Henry Hunt, Esq. written by Himself in His Majesty's Jail at Ilchester*. (London: 1820–21–22).

Issued in monthly and sometimes weekly parts from the time of Hunt's imprisonment. Surviving bound copies of the original edition of Hunt's *Memoirs* provide something of a bibliographical puzzle. The copy in Manchester Public Library contains the following note:

Vol. 3 has no title-page. The title-pages of Vols. 1 and 2 are evidently the same, being without volume number. In this copy the *Memoirs* end imperfectly with Vol. 3 page 608. The British Museum copy ends at the same page. The copies at the John Rylands Library and the London Library run on to page 640, but end incompletely with the words 'Your Petitioner exceedingly . . .' &c. In all probability the *Memoirs* were never finished. L. S. J.

Photostat copies of pages 609–640 were added in 1929.

A photographic reprint of Hunt's *Memoirs* was published in 1967 by Cedric

Chivers Ltd., of Bath 'at the request of the Library Association'. This edition adds the note (at page 641):

All known copies of Vol. III are 'imperfect' and are 'wanting after page 640'. It is possible that these pages were suppressed as they were 'written by himself in H.M.'s Jail at Ilchester'.

Such a statement leaves out of account the known information that an integral part of the *Memoirs*, but not republished in this modern reprint, are Hunt's [*Letters*] *To the Radical Reformers* (1820–1823) which were issued from Ilchester Jail in monthly parts as were the *Memoirs* proper. Hunt continually refers to the *Letters* as his *Memoirs*, and (on December 6th, 1822) as 'the Addenda of my Memoirs'. The *Letters* often survive as two separate volumes, and the only bibliographical clue to their completeness appears to be the dates on the letters; the *Letters* have no consecutive pagination.

It is certain from Hunt's *Letters* dated September 25th, 1822, and July 8th, 1823, that the *Memoirs* were never completed. Hunt apologizes to his subscribers for their non-appearance 'since the 46th number' and explains why he did not complete the work.

— *An Impartial Report of the* . . . (*The King v. Henry Hunt, Joseph Johnson and others*) . . . *for Conspiracy before Mr. Justice Bayley and a Special Jury at York* . . . *16th–27th March, 1820.* (Manchester: Joseph Pratt, 1820).

— In *State Trials.* (Cols. 171–496).

— Dolby edition. (London: 1820).

— An abridged edition. (Leeds: John Barr 1820).

The Trial of Henry Hunt . . . *for an alleged conspiracy* . . . *before Mr. Justice Bayley* . . . *at York* . . . *with the Proceedings on Mr. Hunt's Motion in the Court of King's Bench for a New Trial and the Address of the several Defendants on being brought up to receive judgment.* (Manchester: *Observer* Office 1820).

A more important printed source for an understanding of Hunt's trial than either Dolby's or Pratt's editions, as it contains a long report of the hearings of Hunt's motion for a new trial taken from the reports in the *Manchester Observer* of May 13th and 20th, 1820. The evidence at the York trial is fuller in some instances and briefer in others than the better known printed reports. Presumably it was unknown to the editor of the *State Trials* version.

Illustrated London News, 1864.

An Impartial Narrative of the Late Melancholy Occurrences in Manchester. (Liverpool: 1819).

Generally attributed to the *Liverpool Mercury* journalist, John Smith. (Probably on account of the personal letter to Hunt from Smith printed on p. 18). The *Narrative* is compiled mainly from extracts (sometimes transcribed inaccurately on important points) from newspapers.

(Johnson, Joseph), *A Letter to Henry Hunt, Esq. by Joseph Johnson.* 2nd edition. (Manchester: 1822).

— *A Second Letter to Henry Hunt, Esq. by Joseph Johnson.* (Manchester: 1822). Johnson's replies to the bitter attacks made upon him by Hunt in his *Memoirs.*

Legal Observer. November 1831.

A Letter to Edward Wilbraham Esq., M.P. by an Englishman. (Liverpool: 1819).

Liverpool Mercury.

Manchester Courier.

Manchester Guardian.

Manchester Massacre!! An Authentic Narrative of the Magisterial and Yeomanry Massacre at Manchester; with Remarks on the Illegal Conduct of the Magistrates in Suppressing the Meeting, and their proceedings towards Mr. Hunt; also Anecdotes of the Yeomanry Calvary and Police; Biography of the Magistrates. (London: 1819).

Manchester Mercury, 1768 &c.

Manchester Observer.

There were, during the months of June and July, 1819, two radical *Observer* newspapers being published in Manchester. *Wardle's Manchester Observer.* (No. 1, Vol. I) appeared on 5th June.

Manchester Slaughter. Critical Review of the following work 'Suicide with Other Poems by the Rev. C. W. Ethelston, M.A., rector of Worthenbury, 1803'. (By 'An Old Radical'). (London: 1819).

Manchester Times.

(Marshall, L. S.), *The Development of Public Opinion in Manchester, 1780–1820.* (Syracuse, New York: 1946).

(Mills, Haslam), *The 'Manchester Guardian'—a Century of History.* (Manchester: 1921).

(Molesworth, Rev. W. W.), *History of the Reform Bill.* (London: 1864). Considering its date and place of origin (Molesworth was vicar of St Clement's, Rochdale) a remarkably ill-informed account of Peterloo. It is compiled almost solely from Tyas's account in *The Times* and a little of Stanley's Narrative, shewing only the Manchester Yeomanry being used in the 'cruel and cowardly attack'. Tyas's account knew of no other troops. 'Nothing could be more striking', writes Molesworth, 'than the contrast presented on this occasion between the volunteer force and the troops of the line. The latter acted with mingled coolness and firmness, and inflicted no injury on the crowds'. As Molesworth had already described the event as a solo Manchester Yeomanry affair, this was not surprising.

A Narrative of the Manchester Massacre . . . by the Editor of the 'Black Book'. (London: 1819).

(Oldham Inquest), *The Whole Proceedings before the Coroner's Inquest at Oldham, &c., on the body of John Lees.* Edited by J. A. Dowling. (London: 1820).

Papers Relative to the Internal State of the Country presented to both Houses of Parliament by command of His Royal Highness the Prince Regent, November, 1819. (London: 1819).

(Parker, C. S.), *Sir Robert Peel from his Private Papers*. 3 vols. (London: 1899).

Parliamentary Debates (1819–1832).

The Patriot. (Manchester: 1819–1820).

> Dr Read's statement (p. 91) that *The Patriot* was 'founded in Manchester just before Peterloo' is misleading. A prospectus stated it would appear on August 28th. No. 1 appeared on that date and it lasted until 1st January, 1820.

(Pellew, Hon. George), *The Life and Correspondence of H. Addington, Viscount Sidmouth*. (London: 1847).

Peterloo and Radical Reform, 'Jackdaws' series, No. 17. (Jonathan Cape).

Peterloo, The Answer to. Broadside songsheet, Manchester Public Library collection.

Peterloo Massacre, containing a Faithful Narrative of the Events which preceded, accompanied, and followed the fatal Sixteenth of August, 1819, edited by An Observer. Manchester: *Observer* office, 1819.

> Wrongly attributed, it is believed by F. A. Bruton (1919), to the editorship of John Edward Taylor, founder of the *Manchester Guardian*; an attribution which has been widely copied.

(Philips, Francis), *Exposure of the Calumnies circulated by the Enemies of Social Order, and reiterated by their Abettors against the Magistrates and the Yeomanry Cavalry of Manchester and Salford*. 2nd edition. (London: 1819).

(Prentice, Archibald), *Historical Sketches and Personal Recollections of Manchester, intended to illustrate the Progress of Public Opinion from 1792 to 1832*. 1st edition 1851; 2nd edition 1851.

Quarterly Review, January 1830.

(Raines, Rev. Canon, F. R.), *Vicars of Rochdale*, Chetham Society. New series 11.

— *The Fellows of the Collegiate Church of Manchester*, Chetham Society, New series 23, Part II.

— Raines's MSS. Vol. 36. Chetham's Library.

(Read, Dr Donald), *Peterloo. The 'Massacre' and its Background*. (Manchester: 1958).

> Contains an extensive bibliography of Peterloo and the period.

— *Press and People 1790–1850*. (London: 1961).

Redford v. Birley, Report of the Proceedings on the Trial of . . . at Lancaster . . . 4–9 April, 1822, before Mr. Justice Holroyd and a Special Jury . . . taken from the Shorthand Notes of Mr. Farquharson. (Manchester: 1822).

— Reported in *State Trials*, cols. 1071–1262.

Report on (Manchester Town Hall) Murals. (Town Hall Committee, 18th December, 1878).

A Report of the Manchester Meeting. (Manchester, John Leigh, 1819).

Report of the Metropolitan and Central Committee appointed for the Relief of the Manchester Sufferers. (London: 1820).

The Republican, 1819. (No. 1, Vol. I appeared 27 August 1819).

568

(Ryan, R.), *A Biography of Manchester*. (London: 1937).

Sherwin's Weekly Political Register. 1819.

A Short Historical Account of Peterloo. Liberal Party election pamphlet, no date [1868]: Manchester.

Reports of State Trials. New series, Vol. I. (London: 1888).

(Swift, George), *Narrative* (of Peterloo).
In the form of a letter to his brother, and dated 16th August, 1819, from New Bayley prison, Manchester. It contains information which could only have been written after the 16th. Photo-copy of original in Manchester Public Library.

(Taylor, John Edward), *Notes and Observations, Critical and Explanatory on the Papers Relative to the Internal State of the Country recently presented to Parliament; to which is appended a Reply to Mr. Francis Philips's 'Exposure . . .' by a Member of the Manchester Committee for Relieving the Sufferers of the 16th of August, 1819*. (London: 1820).

The Times.

The Times Literary Supplement.

The History of 'The Times'. The 'Thunderer' in the Making 1785–1841. (London: 1935).

(Thompson, E. P.), *The Making of the English Working Class*. (Gollancz: 1963).

(Trevelyan, G. M.), *English Social History*, Longman.

The Trials of all the Prisoners at the Special Assizes . . . May 23, 1812, at the Castle of Lancaster. (London: [1812]).

Victoria County History Lancashire. Vol. IV, p. 184.; Vol. V, p. 26.

Wheeler's Manchester Chronicle.

(White, R. J.), *Waterloo to Peterloo*. (Mercury Books: 1963).

(Ziegler, Philip), *Addington* (Lord Sidmouth). (Collins: 1965).

Index